PSYC 2301 - General Psychology

Steven Stallings

COLLIN COLLEGE PLANO

PSYCHOLOGY

create.mheducation.com

ISBN-13: 9781308937267

ISBN-10: 1308937261

Contents

CHAPTER 1

What Is Psychology?

Unlocking the Secrets of Heroism

On a train to Paris in the summer of 2015, three young Americans went from vacationing tourists to international heroes in a matter of seconds. Childhood friends—Anthony Sadler (a college student) and Alek Skarlatos and Spencer Stone (both in the U.S. armed forces)—had decided to travel Europe together. The trip, full of great food and sightseeing, turned into an unexpected opportunity for heroism (Southall, 2015). Hearing gunfire and seeing a struggle, the young men immediately jumped into action, subduing and disarming the gunman with the help of another passenger. Miraculously, no one was killed or gravely injured. The men, who received medals from the French government for their bravery, were not even supposed to be on the train that day. Luckily for all aboard, they changed their plans at the last minute.

Reflecting on this incident, many questions pop to mind. How can we understand such courageous behavior? How did the presence of two close friends influence the behavior of each of the men? Why did other riders not intervene? What motivated the gunman to begin with? How does realizing how close the men were to not being on that train influence how we feel about the story of what they did? These are the kinds of questions psychologists might ask about this remarkable heroism.

Although psychologists are interested in extraordinary moments like this one, they are also interested in everyday experiences. The science of psychology is about *all* of human behavior. In fact, ordinary human behavior can become extraordinary when viewed in the right light, with a close lens. Scientists, including psychologists, look at the world with just such a lens. Right now, dedicated scientists are studying things about you that you might have never considered, like how your eyes adjust to a sunny day. There is not a single thing about you that is not fascinating to some psychologist somewhere. Psychologists are passionate about what they study—and what they study is you. ●

PREVIEW

This introductory chapter begins by formally defining psychology and then gives context to that definition by reviewing the history and the intellectual underpinnings of the field. We next examine a number of contemporary approaches to the subject. We explore what psychologists do—including research, teaching, and therapeutic practice—and consider the areas of specialization within psychology. Our introduction to this dynamic field closes with a look at how understanding and applying psychological findings can positively influence human health and wellness.

1. DEFINING PSYCHOLOGY

● **psychology** The scientific study of behavior and mental processes.

● **science** The use of systematic methods to observe the natural world and to draw conclusions.

When you think of the word *psychology,* what first comes to mind? Formally defined, **psychology** is the scientific study of behavior and mental processes. Let's consider the three key terms in this definition: *science, behavior,* and *mental processes.*

As a **science,** psychology uses systematic methods to observe human behavior and draw conclusions. The goals of psychological science are to describe, predict, and explain behavior. In addition, psychologists are often interested in controlling or changing behavior, and they use scientific methods to examine interventions that might help—for example, techniques that might reduce violence or promote happiness.

Researchers might be interested in knowing whether individuals will help a stranger who has fallen down. The investigators could devise a study in which they observe people walking past a person who needs help. Through many observations, the researchers could come to *describe* helping behavior by counting how many times it occurs in particular circumstances. They may also try to *predict* who will help, and when, by examining characteristics of the individuals studied. Are happy people more likely to help? Are women or men more likely to help? After psychologists have analyzed their data, they also will want to *explain* why helping behavior occurred when it did. Finally, these investigators might be interested in changing helping behavior by devising strategies to increase helping.

● **behavior** Everything we do that can be directly observed.

● **mental processes** The thoughts, feelings, and motives that each of us experiences privately but that cannot be observed directly.

Behavior is everything we do that can be directly observed—two people kissing, a baby crying, a college student riding a motorcycle to campus. **Mental processes** are the thoughts, feelings, and motives that each of us experiences privately but that cannot be observed directly. Although we cannot see thoughts and feelings, they are nonetheless real. They include *thinking* about kissing someone, a baby's *feelings* when its mother leaves the room, and a student's *memory* of a motorcycle trip.

The Psychological Frame of Mind

What makes for a good job, a good marriage, or a good life? Although there are a variety of ways to answer the big questions of life, psychologists approach these questions as scientists. This scientific approach means that psychologists test assumptions and rely on objective evidence to answer these puzzles. Psychologists conduct research and rely on that research to provide the bases for their conclusions. They examine the available evidence about some aspect of mind and behavior, evaluate how strongly the data (information) support their hunches, analyze disconfirming evidence, and carefully consider whether they have explored all of the possible factors and explanations. At the core of this scientific approach are four attitudes: critical thinking, skepticism, objectivity, and curiosity.

● **critical thinking** The process of reflecting deeply and actively, asking questions, and evaluating the evidence.

Like all scientists, psychologists are critical thinkers. **Critical thinking** is the process of reflecting deeply and actively, asking questions, and evaluating the evidence (Facione & Gittens, 2016). Thinking critically means asking ourselves *how* we know something. Critical thinkers question and test what some people say are facts. They examine research to see if it soundly supports an idea (Szenes, Tilakaratna, & Maton, 2015). Critical thinking reduces the likelihood that conclusions will be based on unreliable personal beliefs, opinions, and emotions. Thinking critically will be very important as you read *The Science of Psychology.* Some of the things you read will fit with your current beliefs, and some will challenge you to reconsider your assumptions. Actively engaging in critical thinking is vital to making the most of psychology. As you read, think about how what you are learning relates to your life experiences and to your assumptions about others.

In addition, scientists are characterized by *skepticism* (Stanovich, 2013). Skeptical people challenge whether a supposed fact is really true. Being skeptical can mean questioning what "everybody knows." There was a time when "everybody knew" that women were morally inferior to men, that race could influence a person's IQ, and that the earth was flat. Psychologists, like all scientists, look at such assumptions in new and questioning ways and with a skeptical eye. You might use scientific skepticism the next time you encounter an infomercial about the latest diet craze that promises to help you lose weight "without diet or exercise." A skeptic knows that if something sounds too good to be true, it probably is.

Related to critical thinking and skepticism is the distinction between science and pseudoscience. *Pseudo* means "fake," and *pseudoscience* refers to information that is couched in scientific terminology but is not supported by sound scientific research. Astrology is an example of a pseudoscience. Although astrologers may present detailed information about an individual, supposedly based on when that person was born, no scientific evidence supports these assumptions and predictions. One way to tell that an explanation is pseudoscientific rather than scientific is to look at how readily proponents of the explanation will accept evidence to the contrary.

Being open to the evidence means thinking *objectively.* To achieve this goal, scientists apply the empirical method to learn about the world. Using the **empirical method** means gaining knowledge through the observation of events, the collection of data, and logical reasoning. Being objective involves seeing things as they really are, *not as we would like them to be.* Objectivity means waiting to see what the evidence tells us rather than going with our hunches. Does the latest herbal supplement truly help relieve depression? An objective thinker knows that we must have sound evidence before answering that question.

Last, scientists are *curious.* Scientists notice things in the world (a star in the sky, an insect, three heroes on a train) and want to know what it is and why it is that way. Science involves asking questions, even very big questions, such as where did the earth come from, and how does love between two people endure for 50 years? Thinking like a psychologist means opening your mind and imagination to wondering why things are the way they are. Once you begin to think like a psychologist, you might notice that the world looks like a different place. Easy answers and simple assumptions will not do.

As you can probably imagine, psychologists have many different opinions about many different things, and psychology, like any science, is filled with debate and controversy. Throughout this book, we will survey areas of debate in psychology in a feature called Critical Controversy. As the first example, check out this chapter's Critical Controversy concerning whether Facebook use can take a toll on well-being.

Debate and controversy are a natural part of thinking like a psychologist. Psychology has advanced as a field *because* psychologists do not always agree with one another about why the mind and behavior work as they do. Psychologists have reached a more accurate understanding of human behavior *because* psychology fosters controversies and *because* psychologists think deeply and reflectively and examine the evidence on all sides. A good place to try out your critical thinking skills is by revisiting the definition of psychology.

A baby's interactions with its mother and the infant's crying are examples of behavior because they are observable. The feelings underlying the baby's crying are an example of a mental process that is not observable.

(first) © GlowImages/Alamy; (second) © Brand X Pictures/ PunchStock

● **empirical method** Gaining knowledge through the observation of events, the collection of data, and logical reasoning.

Psychology as the Science of All Human Behavior

As you consider the definition of psychology as the science of human behavior, you might be thinking, okay, where's the couch? Where's the mental illness? Psychology certainly does include the study of therapy and psychological disorders. *Clinical psychologists* in particular specialize in studying and treating psychological disorders. By definition, though, psychology is a much more *general* science (Fuchs & Evans, 2013). Surely, psychological disorders are very interesting, and the media often portray psychologists as therapists. Yet the view of psychology as the science of what is wrong with people started long before television was invented. So how did we end up with the idea that psychology is only about mental illness?

When they think about psychology, many people think of Sigmund Freud (1856–1939). Freud believed that most of human behavior is caused by dark, unpleasant, unconscious impulses clamoring for expression. For Freud, even the average person on the street is a mysterious well of unconscious desires. Certainly, Freud has had a lasting impact on psychology and on society; as recently as March 2006, on the occasion of his 150th birthday, Freud was featured on the cover of *Newsweek*. Consider, though, that Freud based his ideas about human nature on the patients whom he saw in his clinical practice—individuals who were struggling with psychological problems. His experiences with these clients, as well as his analysis of himself, colored his outlook on all of humanity. Freud once wrote, "I have found little that is 'good' about human beings on the whole. In my experience most of them are trash" (Freud, [1918] 1963).

Freud's view of human nature has crept into general perceptions of what psychology is all about. Imagine, for example, that you are seated on a plane, having a pleasant conversation with the woman (a stranger) sitting next to you. At some point you ask your seatmate what she does for a living, and she informs you she is a psychologist. You might think to yourself, "Uh oh. What have I already told this person? What secrets does she know about me that I don't know about myself? Has she been analyzing me this whole time?" Would you be surprised to discover that this psychologist studies happiness? Or intelligence? Or the processes related to the experience of vision? The study of psychological disorders is a very important aspect of psychology, but it represents only one part of the science of psychology.

Psychology seeks to understand the truths of human life in *all* its dimensions, including people's best and worst experiences. Psychologists acknowledge that sometimes an individual's best moments emerge amid the most difficult circumstances. Research on the human capacity for forgiveness demonstrates this point (Flanagan & others, 2012). Forgiveness is the act of letting go of our anger and resentment toward someone who has harmed us. Through forgiveness we cease seeking revenge or avoiding the person who did us harm, and we might even wish that person well.

One such example is a tragic event from October 2006. Charles Carl Roberts held 10 young Amish girls hostage in a one-room schoolhouse in Pennsylvania, eventually murdering 5 of them and wounding 5 others before killing himself. The grief-stricken Amish community focused not on hatred and revenge but on forgiveness. In addition to raising money for the victims' families, the Amish insisted on establishing a fund for the murderer's family. As they prepared simple funerals for the dead girls, the community invited the killer's wife to attend. The science of psychology has much to offer to our understanding of not only the perpetrator's violence but also the victims' capacity for forgiveness.

The willingness of the Amish community to forgive this horrible crime is both remarkable and puzzling. Can we scientifically understand the human ability to forgive even what might seem to be unforgivable? Psychologists have taken up the topic of forgiveness in research and clinical practice (Fatfouta, 2015; McCullough, Kurzban, & Tabak, 2013; Peets, Hodges, & Salmivalli, 2013; Sandage & others, 2015). Researchers have explored the relationship between religious commitment and forgiveness (McCullough, Bono, & Root, 2007), the cognitive skills required for forgiveness (Pronk & others, 2010), and the potential dark side of forgiveness, which might emerge, for example, when forgiveness leads an abusive spouse to feel free to continue a harmful behavior (McNulty, 2011). Recent research has even examined how individuals can come to forgive racially motivated offenses (Davis & others, 2015).

CRITICAL CONTROVERSY

Can Facebook Make You Miserable?

Participating in social media is a chance for self-expression and a way to share with family and friends, reignite old friendships, and forge new social connections. Facebook can provide a place for people to seek support after distressing life events such as romantic breakups (Tran & Joormann, 2015) and health crises (Davis, Anthony, & Pauls, 2015). Certainly, maintaining close social relationships and garnering support during difficult times would seem to be very positive things. Does it matter if these experiences occur online instead of in person? Evidence suggests that it just might. For instance, one study showed that the social sharing and support that occurred on Facebook did not translate to feeling supported in "real" life (Li, Chen, & Popiel, 2015). Indeed, one study of young adults showed that time spent on Facebook during a two-week period predicted drops in psychological well-being later (Kross & others, 2013). Yet, clearly people enjoy engaging in social media, and Facebook is wildly popular.

Psychologists have come to understand that well-being depends a great deal on how Facebook is used. Active Facebook use means engaging in exchanges that invite interactions with others—for example, posting a status update or commenting on another post. Passive usage refers to things like scrolling through one's newsfeed or looking at others' pages, without direct exchanges. Passive use involves consuming information but not interacting.

To understand why this distinction is important think about the kinds of things people post online. Research shows that people tend to post extremely positive things about themselves and their lives (Kross & others, 2013; Mehdizadeh, 2010). Passively scrolling through those many positive portrayals of other people's lives can foster feelings of envy, inferiority, shame, and anxiety (Krasnova & others, 2013; Shaw & others, 2015). Not surprisingly, a particularly distressing type of passive Facebook use is scrolling through the profile of one's ex-boyfriend or girlfriend (Tran & Joormann, 2015). Do such experiences lead to declines in well-being?

A team of researchers recently conducted two studies to find out (Verduyn & others, 2015). In the first study, the researchers brought college students into the lab and asked them to log onto Facebook. Half of the students were told to engage actively (and refrain from passive use), and the other half were told to remain passive (and refrain from active use). Later that evening,

participants completed a follow-up questionnaire online, rating how they were feeling emotionally. Those who had engaged in 10 minutes of passive use of Facebook reported lower emotional well-being some 9 hours later. In the second study, researchers found that this decrease in well-being was due to the feelings of envy that ensued following passive Facebook use (Verduyn & others, 2015). Interestingly, other research suggests that responses to Facebook use may depend on gender. For instance, among adolescents, girls are especially likely to benefit from active Facebook use but also to be vulnerable to the emotional toll of passive Facebook usage (Frison & Eggermont, 2015).

© McGraw-Hill Education/John Flournoy, photographer

This research indicates that people's responses to Facebook and other social media are not that different from our reactions to other aspects of life, in that our adjustment depends on how the media are used and by whom. Making the most of social media means using these new ways of connecting to engage actively with others.

WHAT DO YOU THINK?
- How might this research influence the way you and your friends use social media?
- Why do you think people are likely to post about highly positive aspects of their lives?

Some argue that psychology has focused too much on the negative while neglecting qualities that reflect the best of humanity (Seligman & Csikszentmihalyi, 2000). From these criticisms positive psychology has emerged. **Positive psychology** is a branch of psychology that emphasizes human strengths. Research in positive psychology centers on topics such as hope, optimism, happiness, and gratitude (Diener, 2012b; Lopez & others, 2013). One goal of positive psychology is to bring a greater balance to the field by moving beyond focusing on how and why things go wrong in life to understanding how and why

● **positive psychology** A branch of psychology that emphasizes human strengths.

test yourself

1. What makes psychology a science? What are the goals of psychological scientists?
2. What four attitudes are at the core of the scientific approach?
3. Which particular Freudian views of human nature have influenced general perceptions of what psychology is all about?

things go right (Lopez & Gallagher, 2012). Positive psychology is not without its own critics, though. Indeed, some psychologists insist that human weaknesses are the most important topics to study (Lazarus, 2003).

To be a truly general science of human behavior, psychology must address *all* sides of human experience. Surely, controversy—such as that concerning positive psychology—is a part of any science. The healthy debate that characterizes the field of psychology can give rise to new psychological perspectives, and this is a sign of a lively discipline.

2. PSYCHOLOGY IN HISTORICAL PERSPECTIVE

Psychology seeks to answer questions that people have been asking for thousands of years—for example:

- How do we learn?
- What is memory?
- Why does one person grow and flourish while another struggles?

It is a relatively new idea that such questions might be answered through scientific inquiry. From the time human language included the word *why* and became rich enough to enable people to talk about the past, people have created folklore to explain why things are the way they are. Ancient myths attributed most important events to the pleasure or displeasure of the gods. When a volcano erupted, the gods were angry; if two people fell in love, they had been struck by Cupid's arrows. Gradually, myths gave way to *philosophy*—the rational investigation of the underlying principles of being and knowledge—and people began trying to explain events in terms of natural rather than supernatural causes.

Western philosophy came of age in ancient Greece in the fifth and fourth centuries B.C.E. Socrates, Plato, Aristotle, and others debated the nature of thought and behavior, including the possible link between the mind and the body. Later philosophers, especially René Descartes, argued that the mind and body were completely separate, and they focused their attention on the mind. Psychology grew out of this tradition of thinking about the mind and body. The influence of philosophy on contemporary psychology persists today, as researchers who study emotion still talk about Descartes, and scientists who study happiness often refer to Aristotle (Crespo & Mesurado, 2015; Disabato & others, 2015).

In addition to philosophy, psychology also has roots in the natural sciences of biology and physiology. Read on to trace how the modern field of psychology developed.

Wundt's Structuralism and James's Functionalism

Wilhelm Wundt (1832–1920), a German philosopher-physician, integrated philosophy and the natural sciences to create the academic discipline of psychology. Some historians say that modern psychology was born in December 1879 at the University of Leipzig, when Wundt and his students performed an experiment to measure the time lag between the instant a person heard a sound and the moment he or she pressed a telegraph key to signal having heard it. What was so special about this experiment? Wundt's study was about the workings of the brain: He was trying to measure the time it took the human brain and nervous system to translate information into action. At the heart of this experiment was the idea that mental processes could be measured. This notion ushered in the new science of psychology.

Wundt and his collaborators concentrated on discovering the basic elements, or "structures," of mental processes. Their approach was thus called **structuralism** because

William Wundt (1832–1920) Wundt founded the first psychology laboratory (with his coworkers) in 1879 at the University of Leipzig.

©Bettmann/Getty Images

● **structuralism** Wundt's approach to discovering the basic elements, or structures, of mental processes; so called because of its focus on identifying the structures of the human mind.

of its focus on identifying the structures of the human mind, and their method of study was *introspection*. Introspection means looking inside our own minds, by focusing on our own thoughts (literally, "looking inside"). For this type of research, a person in Wundt's lab would be asked to think (introspect) about what was going on mentally as various events took place. For example, the individual might be subjected to a sharp, repetitive clicking sound and then might have to report whatever conscious thoughts and feelings the clicking produced. Introspection relies entirely on the person's conscious reflection. What made this method scientific was the systematic, detailed self-report required of the person in the controlled laboratory setting.

Although Wundt is most often regarded as the founding father of modern psychology, it was psychologist and philosopher William James (1842–1910), perhaps more than anyone else, who gave the field an American stamp. From James's perspective, the key question for psychology is not so much what the mind *is* (that is, its structures) as what it *is for* (its purposes or functions). James's view was eventually named *functionalism*.

In contrast to structuralism, which emphasized the components of the mind, **functionalism** probed the functions and purposes of the mind and behavior in the individual's adaptation to the environment. Whereas structuralists were looking inside the mind and searching for its structures, functionalists focused on human interactions with the outside world and the purpose of thoughts. If structuralism is about the "what" of the mind, functionalism is about the "why." Unlike Wundt, James did not believe in the existence of rigid structures in the mind. Instead, James saw the mind as flexible and fluid, characterized by constant change in response to a continuous flow of information from the world. James called this natural flow of thought a "stream of consciousness."

A core question in functionalism is, why is human thought *adaptive*—that is, why are people better off because they can think than they would be otherwise? When we talk about whether a characteristic is adaptive, we are focusing on how it makes an organism better able to survive. As we will see next, functionalism fit well with the theory of evolution through natural selection proposed by British naturalist Charles Darwin (1809–1882).

William James (1842–1910) James's approach became known as functionalism.
©Bettmann/Getty Images

● **functionalism** James's approach to mental processes, emphasizing the functions and purposes of the mind and behavior in the individual's adaptation to the environment.

Darwin's Natural Selection

In 1859, Darwin published his ideas in *On the Origin of Species* (1979). A centerpiece of his theory was the principle of **natural selection,** an evolutionary process in which organisms that are better adapted to their environment will survive and, importantly, produce more offspring.

Darwin noted that the members of any species are often locked in competition for scarce resources such as food and shelter. Natural selection is the process by which the environment determines who wins that competition. Darwin asserted that organisms with biological features that led to survival and reproduction would be better represented in subsequent generations. Over many generations, organisms with these characteristics would constitute a larger percentage of the population. Eventually, this process could change an entire species.

Importantly, a characteristic cannot be passed from one generation to the next unless it is recorded in the *genes,* those collections of molecules that are responsible for heredity. Genetic characteristics that are associated with survival and reproduction are passed down over generations. According to evolutionary theory, species change through random genetic mutation. That means that, essentially by accident, some members of a species are born with genetic characteristics that make them different from other members. If these changes are adaptive (if they help those members compete for food, survive, and reproduce), they become more common in the species. If environmental conditions were to change, however, other characteristics might become favored by natural selection, moving the process in a different direction.

Evolutionary theory implies that the way we are, at least in part, is the way that is best suited to survival in our environment. The Psychological Inquiry feature lets you critically apply the principles of Darwin's theory of evolution.

● **natural selection** Darwin's principle of an evolutionary process in which organisms that are better adapted to their environment will survive and produce more offspring.

psychological *inquiry*

© Michele Burgess/Corbis

Explore Evolution from Giraffes to Human Beings

Evolution through natural selection and genetic mutation is a slow process. Darwin developed his theory of evolution by observing the tremendous variety of natural phenomena in the world.

Let's take a look at one of these creatures—the giraffe. Giraffes are the tallest mammals on earth, with some reaching a soaring height of 19 feet. Much of that height comes from the giraffe's very long neck. That neck poses a mystery that fascinates scientists: Why does the giraffe have such a long neck? Critically explore some possible reasons below and answer the questions with each.

1. An evolutionary explanation for the giraffe's neck would begin by assuming that, ages ago, some giraffes were genetically predisposed to have longer necks, and others were genetically predisposed to have shorter necks. Take this evolutionary argument one step further: Why do we now see *only* giraffes with long necks?

2. You might reasonably guess that giraffes have long necks in order to reach leaves growing on tall trees—in other words, so that they can eat and survive. However, giraffes often prefer to eat from bushes and relatively low tree branches. Instead, male giraffes use their long necks in fights with other giraffes as they compete over mates. Those that win the fights are more likely to reproduce. Over time, were the winners those with the longer necks or the shorter necks? Explain.

3. The process of evolution sheds light on why members of a particular species share common characteristics. If you were to apply evolutionary theory to human beings, what kinds of characteristics would you focus on and why? Choose one human characteristic and apply the same kinds of questions you considered about the giraffe's long neck. Why are we humans the way we are?

Darwin's theory continues to influence psychologists today because it is strongly supported by observation. We can make such observations every day. Right now, for example, in your kitchen sink, various bacteria are locked in competition for scarce resources in the form of those tempting food particles from your last meal. When you use an antibacterial cleaner, you are playing a role in natural selection, because you are effectively killing off the bacteria that cannot survive the cleaning agents. However, you are also letting the bacteria that are genetically adapted to survive that cleanser to take over the sink. The same principle applies to taking an antibiotic medication at the first sign of a sore throat or an earache. By killing off the bacteria that may be causing the illness, you are creating an environment in which their competitors (so-called antibiotic-resistant bacteria) may flourish. These observations powerfully demonstrate Darwinian selection in action.

If structuralism won the battle to be the birthplace of psychology, functionalism won the war. To this day, psychologists continue to talk about the adaptive nature of human characteristics, although they have branched out to study more aspects of human behavior than Wundt and James would ever have imagined. In a general way, since the days of those pioneers in the field, psychology has defined itself as the science of human behavior. The question of what exactly counts as human behavior, however, has fueled debate throughout the history of the field. For some psychologists, behavior has meant only observable actions; for others, it has included thoughts and feelings; for still others, unconscious processes have been the focal point. Traces of this debate can be seen today in the various contemporary approaches to the science of psychology that we will consider next.

test yourself

1. What is structuralism? How does functionalism contrast with structuralism?
2. What is meant when we say that a particular characteristic of an organism is adaptive?
3. In what ways is Darwin's work relevant to psychology?

3. CONTEMPORARY APPROACHES TO PSYCHOLOGY

In this section we survey seven different approaches that represent the intellectual backdrop of psychological science: biological, behavioral, psychodynamic, humanistic, cognitive, evolutionary, and sociocultural.

The Biological Approach

Some psychologists examine behavior and mental processes through the **biological approach,** which is a focus on the body, especially the brain and nervous system. For example, researchers might investigate the way your heart races when you are afraid or how your hands sweat when you tell a lie. Although a number of physiological systems may be involved in thoughts and feelings, the emergence of neuroscience has perhaps contributed the most to physiological psychology (Everett & others, 2015; Mercado & Henderson, 2013).

Neuroscience is the scientific study of the structure, function, development, genetics, and biochemistry of the nervous system. Neuroscience emphasizes that the brain and nervous system are central to understanding behavior, thought, and emotion. Neuroscientists believe that thoughts and emotions have a physical basis in the brain. Electrical impulses zoom throughout the brain's cells, releasing chemical substances that enable us to think, feel, and behave. Our remarkable human capabilities would not be possible without the brain and nervous system, which constitute the most complex, intricate, and elegant system imaginable.

Although neuroscience is perhaps most often linked with research on human thought, it has spread to many research areas. Today, psychologists from diverse perspectives study topics such as behavioral neuroscience, developmental neuroscience, social neuroscience, and so forth. Although biological approaches might sometimes seem to reduce complex human experience to simple physical structures, developments in neuroscience have allowed psychologists to understand the brain as an amazingly complex organ, perhaps just as complex as the psychological processes linked to its functioning (Le Bihan, 2016).

- **biological approach** An approach to psychology focusing on the body, especially the brain and nervous system.

- **neuroscience** The scientific study of the structure, function, development, genetics, and biochemistry of the nervous system, emphasizing that the brain and nervous system are central to understanding behavior, thought, and emotion.

- **behavioral approach** An approach to psychology focusing on the scientific study of observable behavioral responses and their environmental determinants.

The Behavioral Approach

The **behavioral approach** emphasizes the scientific study of observable behavioral responses and their environmental determinants. It focuses on an organism's visible interactions with the environment—that is, behaviors, not thoughts or feelings. The principles of the behavioral approach have been widely applied to help people change their behavior for the better (Craighead & others, 2013; Roth, Gillis, & DiGennaro Reed, 2014). The psychologists who adopt this approach are called *behaviorists.* Under the intellectual leadership of John B. Watson (1878–1958) and B. F. Skinner (1904–1990), behaviorism dominated psychological research during the first half of the twentieth century.

Skinner (1938) emphasized that psychology should be about what people do—their actions and behaviors—and should not concern itself with things that cannot be seen, such as thoughts, feelings, and goals. He believed that rewards and punishments determine our behavior. For example, a child might behave in a well-mannered fashion because her parents have previously rewarded this behavior. We do the things we

B. F. Skinner was a tinkerer who liked to make new gadgets. Deborah, the younger of his two daughters, was raised in Skinner's enclosed Air-Crib. Some critics accused Skinner of monstrous experimentation with his children; however, the early controlled environment has not had any noticeable harmful effects. Deborah, shown here as a child with her parents, is today a successful artist whose work strongly reflects her unique early childhood experience.
©AP Images

do, behaviorists say, because of the environmental conditions we have experienced and continue to experience.

Contemporary behaviorists still emphasize the importance of observing behavior to gain understanding of an individual, and they use rigorous methods advocated by Watson and Skinner (Miller & Grace, 2013; Rehfeldt, 2011). However, not every behaviorist today accepts the earlier behaviorists' rejection of thought processes, which are often called *cognition*.

The Psychodynamic Approach

● **psychodynamic approach** An approach to psychology focusing on unconscious thought, the conflict between biological drives (such as the drive for sex) and society's demands, and early childhood family experiences.

The **psychodynamic approach** emphasizes unconscious thought, the conflict between biological drives (such as the drive for sex) and society's demands, and early childhood family experiences (Barber & Sharpless, 2015). Practitioners of this approach believe that sexual and aggressive impulses buried deep within the unconscious mind influence the way people think, feel, and behave.

Sigmund Freud, the founding father of the psychodynamic approach, theorized that early relationships with parents shape an individual's personality. Freud's (1924) theory was the basis for the therapeutic technique that he called *psychoanalysis,* which involves an analyst's unlocking a person's unconscious conflicts by talking with the individual about his or her childhood memories, as well as the individual's dreams, thoughts, and feelings. Certainly, Freud's views have been controversial, but they remain a part of contemporary psychology. Today's psychodynamic theories tend to place less emphasis on sexual drives and more on cultural and social experiences as determinants of behavior.

Sigmund Freud (1856–1939)
Freud was the founding father of the psychodynamic approach.

© Time & Life Pictures/Getty Images

The Humanistic Approach

● **humanistic approach** An approach to psychology focusing on a person's positive qualities, the capacity for positive growth, and the freedom to choose one's destiny.

The **humanistic approach** emphasizes a person's positive qualities, the capacity for positive growth, and the freedom to choose one's destiny. Humanistic psychologists stress that people have the ability to control their lives and are not simply controlled by the environment (Maslow, 1971; Rogers, 1961). They theorize that rather than being driven by unconscious impulses (as the psychodynamic approach dictates) or by external rewards (as the behavioral approach emphasizes), people can choose to live by higher human values such as *altruism*—unselfish concern for other people's well-being—and free will. Many aspects of this optimistic approach appear in research on motivation, emotion, health, and personality psychology (Church & others, 2013; Friederichs & others, 2015; Rahman & others, 2015).

The Cognitive Approach

● **cognitive approach** An approach to psychology focusing on the mental processes involved in knowing: how we direct our attention, perceive, remember, think, and solve problems.

According to cognitive psychologists, the human brain houses a "mind" whose mental processes allow us to remember, make decisions, plan, set goals, and be creative (Eysenck & Keane, 2015). The **cognitive approach,** then, emphasizes the mental processes involved in knowing: how we direct our attention, perceive, remember, think, and solve problems. Many scientists who adopt this approach focus on *information processing,* the ways that the human mind interprets incoming information, weighs it, stores it, and applies it to decision making. Cognitive psychologists seek answers to questions such as how we solve math problems, why we remember some things for only a short time but others for a lifetime, and how we use our imagination to plan for the future.

Cognitive psychologists view the mind as an active and aware problem-solving system (Pezzuti & others, 2014). This view contrasts with the behavioral view, which portrays behavior as governed by external environmental forces. In the cognitive view, an individual's mental processes are in control of behavior through memories, perceptions, images, and thinking.

The Evolutionary Approach

Although arguably all of psychology emerges out of evolutionary theory, some psychologists emphasize an **evolutionary approach** that uses evolutionary ideas such as adaptation, reproduction, and natural selection as the basis for explaining specific human behaviors. Evolutionary inquiries sometimes involve examining the behavior of nonhuman primates to look for clues for the origins of human behavior (Santos & Rosati, 2015). David Buss (2015) argues that just as evolution molds our physical features, such as body shape, it also influences our decision making, level of aggressiveness, fears, and mating patterns. Thus, evolutionary psychologists argue, the way we adapt is traceable to problems early humans faced in adapting to their environment (Zeigler-Hill, Welling, & Shackelford, 2015).

Evolutionary psychologists believe their approach provides an umbrella that unifies the diverse fields of psychology (Bjorklund & Ellis, 2014). Not all psychologists agree with this conclusion, however. For example, some critics stress that the evolutionary approach inaccurately explains why men and women have different social roles and does not adequately account for cultural diversity and experiences (Cohen & Bernard, 2013; Eagly & Wood, 2013). Yet, even psychologists who disagree with applying the evolutionary approach to psychological characteristics still agree with the general principles of evolutionary theory.

The Sociocultural Approach

The **sociocultural approach** examines the ways in which social and cultural environments influence behavior. Socioculturalists argue that understanding a person's behavior requires knowing about the cultural context in which the behavior occurs (Gauvain, 2013; Matsumoto & Juang, 2017). Researchers who focus on sociocultural influences might compare people from different cultures to see whether they are similar or different in important ways (Gelfand, Chiu, & Hong, 2014).

The sociocultural view focuses not only on comparisons of behavior across countries but also on the behavior of individuals from different ethnic and cultural groups within a country (Balsam & others, 2015; Leong & others, 2013; Yates & Marcelo, 2014). Rising cultural diversity in the United States in recent years has prompted increasing interest in the behavior of ethnic minority groups, especially the factors that have restricted or enhanced their ability to adapt and cope with living in a predominantly non-Latino White society (Buckingham & Brodsky, 2015). Further, as the nations of the world grow increasingly economically interdependent, it becomes especially important to understand cultural influences on human interaction. For example, psychologists are interested in studying how psychological characteristics may help or hinder negotiations among individuals from different cultures (Caruso, 2015).

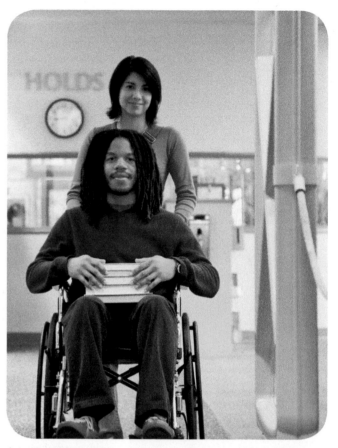

According to humanistic psychologists, warm, supportive behavior toward others helps us to realize our capacity for self-understanding.
©Anderson Ross/Blend Images

● **evolutionary approach** An approach to psychology focusing on evolutionary ideas such as adaptation, reproduction, and natural selection as the basis for explaining specific human behaviors.

● **sociocultural approach** An approach to psychology focusing on the ways in which social and cultural environments influence behavior.

Summing Up the Seven Contemporary Approaches

These seven psychological approaches provide different views of the same behavior, and all of them may offer valuable insights that the other perspectives miss. Think about the simple experience of seeing a cute puppy. Looking at that puppy involves physical processes in the eyes, nervous system, and brain—the focus of the biological approach to psychology. The moment you spot that puppy, though, you might smile without thinking and reach down to pet the little guy. That reaction might be a response based on your

test yourself

1. What are two differences between the cognitive and psychodynamic approaches to psychology?
2. How are the biological and evolutionary perspectives on psychology similar and how are they different?
3. What specific ideas did B. F. Skinner's behaviorist approach emphasize?

past learning with your own dog (behavioral perspective), or on unconscious memories of a childhood dog (psychodynamic perspective), or on conscious memories that you especially like this dog breed (cognitive perspective), or even on evolutionary processes that promoted cuteness to help offspring survive (evolutionary approach). You might find yourself striking up a conversation with the puppy's owner, based on your shared love of dogs (humanistic perspective). Further, sociocultural factors might play a role in your decision about whether to ask the owner if you could touch the puppy, whether you share those warm feelings about the puppy with others, and even whether (as in some cultures) you might view that puppy as food.

4. WHAT PSYCHOLOGISTS DO

People who think of themselves as psychologists work in a wide range of settings and engage in many different activities. Figure 1 shows the various settings in which psychologists practice their profession. In this section we look at what psychologists do, and then we zoom in on the areas of specialization.

Careers in Psychology

Individuals with undergraduate training in psychology might use their expertise in occupations ranging from human resources and business consulting to doing casework for individuals struggling with psychological disorders. Those with graduate training in psychology might work as therapists and counselors, researchers and teachers in universities, or as business consultants or marketing researchers.

Individuals who are primarily engaged in helping others are often called *practitioners* of psychology. They spend most of their time in clinical practice, seeing clients and offering them guidance as they work through problems. However, even psychologists who are primarily concerned with clinical practice pay attention to scientific research. For these individuals, rigorous research guides their therapeutic practice and their efforts to make improvements in the lives of their patients. Increasingly, psychologists who primarily provide therapy engage in *evidence-based practice*—that is, they use therapeutic tools whose effectiveness is supported by empirical research (Holt & others, 2015).

An important distinction that is often not well understood is the difference between a clinical psychologist and a psychiatrist. A clinical psychologist typically has a doctoral degree in psychology, which requires approximately four to five years of graduate work and one year of internship in a mental health facility. In contrast, a psychiatrist is a physician with a medical degree who subsequently specializes in abnormal behavior and psychotherapy. Another difference between a clinical psychologist and a psychiatrist is that a psychiatrist can prescribe drugs, whereas a clinical psychologist generally cannot. Despite these differences, clinical psychologists and psychiatrists are alike in sharing an interest in improving the lives of people with mental health problems.

Many psychologists who are employed at universities divide their time between teaching and doing research. Research in psychology creates the knowledge that is presented in this book and that you will be learning about in your introductory psychology course.

Human behavior is a vast, complex topic. Most psychologists specialize in a particular area of study, as we consider next.

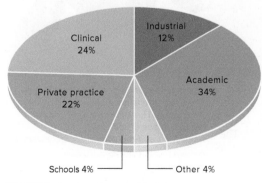

FIGURE 1 Settings in Which Psychologists Work More psychologists work in academic environments (34 percent), such as colleges and universities, than in any other setting. However, clinical (24 percent) and private practice (22 percent) settings—both of them contexts in which many psychologists in the mental health professions work—together make up almost half of the total settings.

Areas of Specialization

Psychology has many areas of specialization. Currently, there are 56 divisions in the American Psychological Association, each focusing on a specific subfield of psychology. Division 1, the Society for General Psychology, seeks to provide a coherent integration of the vast science of psychology. Division 2, the Society for the Teaching of Psychology, is dedicated to devising the best ways to help students learn about this fascinating science. The other main specializations in the field of psychology include the following.

Physiological Psychology and Behavioral Neuroscience

Researchers who study *physiological psychology* are interested in the physical processes that underlie mental operations such as thinking and memory. Physiological psychologists may use animal models (that is, they may employ animals, such as rats, to study processes that are difficult or impossible to study in the same way in humans) to examine such topics as the development of the nervous system. The field of *behavioral neuroscience* also focuses on biological processes, especially the brain's role in behavior (Conboy & others, 2015). In the chapter "Biological Foundations of Behavior" we will examine the many ways that physiological processes relate to psychological experience.

Richard J. Davidson of the University of Wisconsin, Madison, shown with the Dalai Lama, is a leading researcher in behavioral neuroscience.

© University of Wisconsin, Madison. Photo by Jeff Miller.

Sensation and Perception

Researchers who study *sensation and perception* focus on the physical systems and psychological processes that allow us to experience the world—to listen to a favorite song (Rinaldi & others, 2016) and to see the beauty of a sunset (Cohen, Rhee, & Alvarez, 2016). These complex processes are the subject of the chapter "Sensation and Perception".

Learning

Learning is the intricate process by which behavior changes in response to changing circumstances. Many researchers study the basic principles of learning using animals such as rats and pigeons (Gibson, Leber, & Mehlman, 2015). Learning has been addressed from the behavioral and cognitive perspectives (Craighead & others, 2013). This topic is covered in the chapter "Learning".

Cognitive Psychology

Cognitive psychology (explored in the chapter "Memory" and the chapter "Thinking, Intelligence, and Language") is the broad name given to the field of psychology that examines attention, consciousness, information processing, and memory. Cognitive psychologists are also interested in skills and abilities such as problem solving, decision making, expertise, and intelligence, topics covered in the chapter "Thinking, Intelligence, and Language" (Flensborg-Madsen & Mortensen, 2015; Sternberg & others, 2014). Researchers in cognitive psychology and sensation perception are sometimes called *experimental psychologists.*

Developmental Psychology

Developmental psychology is concerned with how people become who they are, from conception to death. In particular, developmental psychologists concentrate on the biological and environmental factors that contribute to human development. Developmentalists study child development (Overton, Molenaar, & Lerner, 2015) but also adult development and aging (Stawski, Smith, & MacDonald, 2015). Their inquiries range across the biological, cognitive, and social domains of life. The chapter "Human Development" reviews the key findings in this fascinating area.

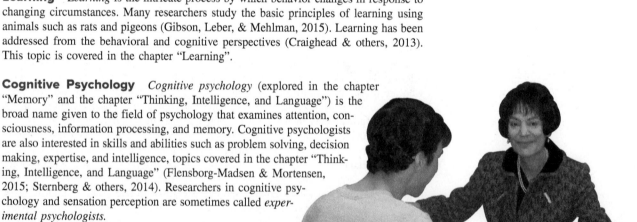

The research of Carol S. Dweck of Stanford University spans developmental and social psychology. Her influential work looks at how our ideas of self play a role in motivation, self-regulation, and achievement.

Courtesy of Carol S. Dweck, Stanford University

Motivation and Emotion

Researchers from a variety of specializations are interested in *motivation and emotion,* two important aspects of experience. Scientists who study motivation address research questions such as how individuals persist to attain a difficult goal and how rewards affect the experience of motivation. Emotion researchers delve into topics including the physiological and brain processes that underlie emotional experience, the role of emotional expression in health, and the possibility that emotions are universal. These fascinating questions are examined in the chapter "Motivation and Emotion".

Psychology of Women and Gender Those researchers studying the *psychology of women* consider the psychological, social, and cultural influences on women's development and behavior. This field stresses the integration of information about women with current psychological knowledge and beliefs and applies that information to society and its institutions (Capdevila & Lazard, 2015; Hyde & Else-Quest, 2013). Psychologists are also interested in understanding the broad topic of *gender* and the way in which our biological sex influences our ideas about ourselves as men and women. We consider these important topics in the chapter "Gender, Sex, and Sexuality".

Personality Psychology *Personality psychology* considers personality, consisting of the relatively enduring characteristics of individuals. Personality psychologists study topics such as traits, goals, motives, genetics, personality development, and well-being. Researchers in personality psychology are interested in those aspects of your psychological makeup that make you uniquely you. The field of personality is explored fully in the chapter "Personality".

Social Psychology *Social psychology* deals with people's interactions with one another, relationships, social perceptions, social cognition, and attitudes. Social psychologists are interested in the influence of groups on our thinking and behavior and in the ways that the groups to which we belong influence our attitudes. The research questions that concern social psychologists include understanding and working to reduce racial prejudice, determining whether two heads really are better than one, and exploring how the presence of others influences performance. The chapter "Social Psychology" reviews the major research findings of social psychology.

Social psychologists explore the powerful influence of groups (such as, clockwise, Chinese Americans, members of motorcycle clubs, gay Americans, inner-city youths, and military families) on individuals' attitudes, thinking, and behavior.

Industrial and Organizational Psychology *Industrial and organizational psychology (I-O psychology)* centers on the workplace—both the workers and the organizations that employ them. I-O psychology is often divided into *industrial psychology* and *organizational psychology*. Among the main concerns of industrial psychology are personnel matters and human resource management. Thus, industrial psychology is increasingly referred to as *personnel psychology. Organizational psychology* examines the social influences in organizations, as well as organizational leadership. The chapter "Industrial and Organizational Psychology" investigates the key concerns and findings of I-O psychology.

Clinical and Counseling Psychology *Clinical and counseling psychology* is the most widely practiced specialization in psychology. Clinical and counseling psychologists diagnose and treat people with psychological problems. Counseling psychologists sometimes work with people to help solve practical problems in life (Baker & Joyce, 2013). For example, counseling psychologists may work with students, advising them about personal problems and career planning. Clinical psychologists are interested in **psychopathology**— the scientific study of psychological disorders and the development of diagnostic categories and treatments for those disorders. The chapters "Psychological Disorders" and "Therapies" explore the intriguing world of psychological disorders and therapies.

● **psychopathology** The scientific study of psychological disorders and the development of diagnostic categories and treatments for those disorders.

Health Psychology *Health psychology* is a multidimensional approach to human health that emphasizes psychological factors, lifestyle, and the nature of the healthcare delivery system. Many health psychologists study the roles of stress and coping in people's lives. Health psychologists may work in physical or mental health areas. Some are members of multidisciplinary teams that conduct research or provide clinical services. Health psychology is examined in the chapter "Health Psychology".

This list of specialties cannot convey the extraordinarily rich knowledge you will gain as a student in introductory psychology. To whet your appetite for what is to come, check out the Psychological Inquiry feature and try answering some of the questions that fascinate psychologists.

The specialties that we have discussed so far are the main areas of psychology that we cover in this book. However, they do not represent an exhaustive list of the interests of the field. Other specializations in psychology include the following.

Community Psychology *Community psychology* concentrates on improving the quality of relationships among individuals, their community, and society at large. Community psychologists are practitioner scientists who provide accessible care for people with psychological problems. Community-based mental health centers are one means of delivering services such as outreach programs to people in need, especially those who traditionally have been underserved by mental health professionals (Dalton & others, 2013).

Community psychologists strive to create communities that are more supportive of their residents by pinpointing needs, providing services, and teaching people how to access resources that are already available (Shinn, 2015). Community psychologists are also concerned with prevention. That is, they try to prevent mental health problems by identifying high-risk groups and then intervene with appropriate services and resources in the community.

School and Educational Psychology *School and educational psychology* centrally concerns children's learning and adjustment in school. School psychologists in elementary and

Feeling lost, lonely, desperate?

When it seems like there's no hope, there is help.

If you feel trapped...If you feel you have no one to turn to...If you've been feeling down for a while and you're not exactly sure why...

It's important to talk to someone. You can talk to someone right now by calling the Lifeline. Help is available at any time of the day or night—and it's completely free and confidential. We're here to listen and to help you find your way back to a happier, healthier life.

If you or someone you know is thinking about suicide, call the National Suicide Prevention Lifeline:

1-800-273-TALK (8255)

With help comes hope.

SUICIDE PREVENTION LIFELINE 1-800-273-TALK www.suicidepreventionlifeline.org

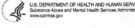
U.S. DEPARTMENT OF HEALTH AND HUMAN SERVICES
Substance Abuse and Mental Health Services Administration
www.samhsa.gov

Community psychologists provide accessible care to local populations, often through efforts such as the suicide-prevention program advertised in this poster.
U.S. Department of Health and Human Services

psychological *inquiry*

Questions That Psychology Specialists Ask

This table identifies the chapter topics we will investigate in this book (column 1). For each topic, a question is posed that the chapter will answer (column 2). What do you think the research will show about each of these questions? In the space provided in the note pad, jot down your guesses. Be bold—there are no right answers (yet)!

Chapter Topic	Question
Psychology's Scientific Method	How is deception used in psychological research?
Biological Foundations of Behavior	How does behavior change the brain?
Sensation and Perception	Is there evidence for the existence of ESP?
States of Consciousness	What do dreams mean?
Learning	How do pop quizzes influence studying?
Memory	Are you likely to remember what you've learned in intro psychology this year 50 years from now?
Thinking, Intelligence, and Language	If you know you are fighting a losing battle, does it make sense to quit or keep trying?
Human Development	What kind of parenting is associated with children who are responsible and kind?
Motivation and Emotion	Does pursuing happiness make people happier?
Gender, Sex, and Sexuality	Where does sexual orientation come from?
Personality	Are personality characteristics genetically determined?
Social Psychology	How can we best combat racial prejudice?
Industrial and Organizational Psychology	What kind of leadership leads to success?
Psychological Disorders	What role do genes play in psychological disorders?
Therapies	Does psychotherapy work?
Health Psychology	What is the role of religion and spirituality in influencing healthy choices?

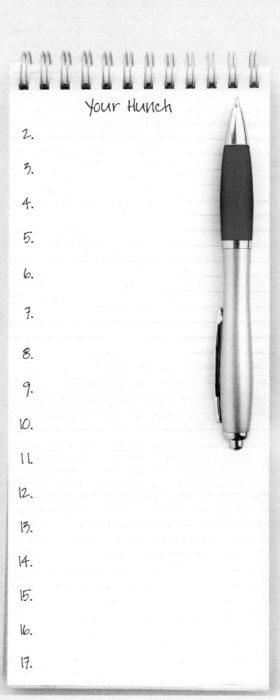

Your Hunch

2.
3.
4.
5.
6.
7.
8.
9.
10.
11.
12.
13.
14.
15.
16.
17.

INTERSECTION

Personality, Developmental, and Cross-Cultural Psychology: Why Do We Grow Up, Psychologically?

Early adulthood can be a time of great change. Consider all the choices that are made and all the events that occur: leaving home, going to college, graduating, starting a career, finding a life partner, perhaps starting a family. These many events, experiences, and life changes, often clustered in a person's 20s and 30s, have important ramifications throughout the rest of life.

Another type of change that occurs during this same time period is personality change. Specifically, between the ages of 18 and 40, people are likely to become more conscientious (responsible, reliable, and hardworking), more agreeable (kind and compassionate), and more emotionally stable (less worrying and prone to distress). That's right: Research shows that over time, people tend to become more mature (Specht & others, 2014). This pattern of personality trait change has been termed the *maturity principle* because it appears that, on average, people are growing up, psychologically (Roberts, Wood, & Caspi, 2008).

It would seem to be great news that young slackers can grow up to be conscientious members of society. But what drives these changes? And why do many people show this pattern of personality change? Answering these questions requires scientific evidence from a diverse array of sources, including personality psychology, life-span development, and cross-cultural psychology (Bleidorn, 2015).

Like all psychological characteristics, becoming mature in early adulthood is likely the product of both genetics and the environment (Bleidorn, Kandler, & Caspi, 2014). Which matters more to personality development is a topic of debate.

A first approach, suggested by the leading trait theorists, is that these changes are largely controlled by biological or genetic processes (McCrae & Costa, 2008). These scholars believe that, regardless of experience, growing up psychologically is just what people do. Support for this idea comes from the fact that many studies show that genes have a substantial influence on personality characteristics throughout life (Bleidorn, 2015).

An alternative perspective suggests that these trait changes are a response to the roles people occupy in young adulthood (Roberts, Wood, & Smith, 2005). When a person becomes a spouse, an employee, or a parent, social expectations for their behavior change drastically. From this perspective, we grow up psychologically because life demands it. Support for this idea comes from the fact that social environments become more stable and exert more influence on personality beginning in young adulthood, just when maturation is taking place (Bleidorn, Kandler, & Caspi, 2014).

(first) © unclepodger/iStock/Getty Images; (second) © Naborahfatima/iStock/Getty Images

Which perspective is correct? A fascinating way to resolve this issue is to examine personality maturation *across different cultures*. The strong genetic argument would predict little to no cultural variation in changes in personality traits over time. If maturation is driven by an unfolding biological process, it should not be affected by cultural differences. In contrast, if social roles trigger maturation, we might expect greater cultural variability in the timing of trait changes.

A study of over 880,000 young adults from 62 different countries (Bleidorn & others, 2013) showed that, across cultures, age was associated with higher levels of conscientiousness, agreeableness, and emotionally stability. This means that regardless of country, young adults tended to show maturation, providing strong support for the genetic argument. However, and interestingly, experience *did* matter to the timing of these changes. Strikingly, the most important experience precipitating personality changes was employment. And in nations where young adults take on the role of full-time employee sooner (for example, Pakistan and Malaysia), changes in personality happened faster. In nations such as the United States and the Netherlands, where young adults delay full-time employment, the trait of conscientiousness, in particular, changed more gradually.

So, why do we grow up, psychologically? This research suggests that maturation can be thought of as an unfolding of biological process that occurs in and is affected by social demands. Many of us may have the capacity to become more responsible, considerate, and emotionally stable, but we may need the roles we occupy to push us toward that better, more mature self.

How have you grown up, psychologically?

---

secondary school systems test children, make recommendations about educational placement, and collaborate on educational planning teams. Educational psychologists work at colleges and universities, teach classes, and do research on teaching and learning.

Environmental Psychology   *Environmental psychology* is the study of the interactions between people and their physical environment. Environmental psychologists explore the effects of physical settings in most major areas of psychology, including perception, cognition, learning, development, abnormal behavior, and social relations. Topics that an environmental psychologist might study range from how different building and room arrangements influence behavior to what strategies might be used to reduce human behavior that harms the environment (Steg, 2015).

Forensic Psychology   *Forensic psychology* is the field of psychology that applies psychological concepts to the legal system (Najdowski & others, 2015). Social and cognitive psychologists increasingly conduct research on topics related to psychology and law. Forensic psychologists are hired by legal teams to provide input about many aspects of trials, such as jury selection. Those forensic psychologists with clinical training may also testify as experts in trials, such as when they are asked to evaluate whether a person is likely to be a danger to society.

Sport Psychology   *Sport psychology* applies psychology's principles to improving sport performance and enjoying sport participation (Rotella, 2010). Sport psychology is a relatively new field, but it is rapidly gaining acceptance. It is now common to hear about elite athletes working with a sport psychologist to improve their game.

Cross-Cultural Psychology   Cross-cultural psychology is the study of culture's role in understanding behavior, thought, and emotion (Bullock, 2013). Cross-cultural psychologists compare the nature of psychological processes in different cultures with a particular focus on whether psychological phenomena are universal or culture specific. Comparing different cultures can provide a way to answer some of the most fascinating questions that psychologists in other areas puzzle over.

Keep in mind that psychology is a collaborative science in which psychologists work together to examine a wide range of research questions. It is common for scholars from different specialties within psychology to join forces to study some aspect of human behavior. The Intersection feature reviews research that represents collaboration among scientists from different specialties to investigate the same question. See how looking at psychology through the lens of culture can influence our conclusions by checking out this chapter's Intersection.

test yourself

1. What are some career options for a person with an undergraduate degree in psychology? What careers might someone with a graduate degree in psychology pursue?
2. What are the important distinctions between a clinical psychologist and a psychiatrist?
3. Name five areas of specialization in psychology and describe the primary concerns of each.

5. THE SCIENCE OF PSYCHOLOGY AND HEALTH AND WELLNESS

We have reviewed a variety of ways that psychologists approach human behavior, and psychologists have learned much about behavior that is relevant to you and your life. By tying research in psychology to your physical health and psychological wellness, in *The Science of Psychology* we seek to answer the question, what does psychology have to say about *you?* At the close of each chapter, we will consider how the topics covered matter to your mind and your physical body. This link between the mind and the body has fascinated philosophers for centuries. Psychology occupies the very spot where the mind and body meet.

How the Mind Impacts the Body

When you think about psychology, your first thought might be about the mind and the complex feelings—such as love, gratitude, hate, and anger—that emanate from it. Psychologists have come to recognize more and more the degree to which that mind is intricately connected to the body. As you will see when we examine neuroscience in the chapter "Biological Foundations of Behavior", observations of the brain at work reveal that when mental processes change, so do physical processes.

Health psychologists talk about health behavior as just a subset of behaviors that are relevant to physical health. These behaviors might include eating well, exercising, not smoking, performing testicular and breast self-exams, brushing teeth, and getting enough sleep. But think about it: Is there ever really a time when your behavior is *not* relevant to your body and therefore to your health? Is there ever a time when you are doing something—thinking, feeling, walking, running, singing—when your physical body is not present? As long as your body is there—with your heart, lungs, blood, and brain activated—your health is affected. In short, *everything* we do, see, think, and feel is potentially important to our health and well-being.

It might be instructive to think concretely about the ways the mind and body relate to each other, even as they are united in the physical reality of a person. Let's say you buy an activity tracker like a Fitbit to become more active and to transform your body into a toned, muscled, calorie-burning machine. Commitment, goal setting, and self-discipline will be among the many mental processes necessary to change your body. In this example, the mind works on the body by producing behaviors that change its shape and size.

©Leonard Zhukovsky/Shutterstock

How the Body Impacts the Mind

Similarly, the body can influence the mind in dramatic ways. Consider your fuzzy morning thinking after a late night on the town and how much easier it is to solve life's problems when you have had a good night's sleep. Also recall your outlook on the first day of true recovery from a nagging cold: Everything just seems better, and your mood and your work improve. Clearly, physical states such as illness and health influence the way we think.

The relationship between body and mind is illustrated in a major question that psychologists regularly encounter: What is the impact of nature (genetic heritage) versus nurture (social experience) on a person's psychological characteristics? The influence of genetics on a variety of psychological features and the ways that genetic endowments can themselves be altered by social experience will be addressed in many of the main topics in this book, from development (in the chapter "Human Development") to personality (in the chapter "Personality") to psychological disorders (in the chapter "Psychological Disorders"). You will see that your physical and mental selves are intertwined in ways you may have never considered.

Throughout *The Science of Psychology*, we investigate the ways that all of the various approaches to psychology matter to your life. Psychology is crucially about *you*—essential to your understanding of your life, your goals, and the ways that you can use the insights of thousands of scientists to make your life healthier and happier. In taking introductory psychology, you have an amazing opportunity. You will learn a great deal about human beings, especially one particular human being: you. Whether the psychological research presented is about emotions and motivation or the structures of the nervous system, it is still essentially about the mystery that is you.

test yourself

1. What has psychology increasingly come to recognize about the relationship between the mind and the body?
2. What are some mental processes that might be involved in efforts to change your physical body, as through diet or exercise?
3. What is some real-life evidence of the body's impact on the mind? Give examples that are different from those in the text.

SUMMARY

1. DEFINING PSYCHOLOGY

Psychology is the scientific study of human behavior and mental processes. Psychologists approach human behavior as scientists who think critically and are curious, skeptical, and objective. Behavior includes everything organisms do that can be observed. Mental processes are thoughts, feelings, and motives.

As a truly general science, psychology addresses all sides of human experience—positive and negative, strengths and weaknesses. Psychology is characterized by controversy and debate, and new psychological perspectives sometimes arise when some scientists question the views of others.

2. PSYCHOLOGY IN HISTORICAL PERSPECTIVE

Psychology emerged as a science from the fields of philosophy and physiology. Two founders of the science of psychology are Wilhelm Wundt and William James. Wundt's structuralism emphasized the conscious mind and its structures. James's functionalism focused on the functions of the mind in human adaptation to the environment. The functionalist emphasis on the mind's adaptive character fit well with the new understandings that came from Charles Darwin's theory of evolution.

3. CONTEMPORARY APPROACHES TO PSYCHOLOGY

Different approaches to psychology include biological, behavioral, psychodynamic, humanistic, cognitive, evolutionary, and sociocultural views. All of these consider important questions about human behavior from different but complementary perspectives.

The biological approach focuses on the body, especially the brain and nervous system. Technological advances in brain imaging have allowed researchers to examine the brain in all its complexity. The behavioral approach emphasizes the scientific study of observable behavioral responses and their environmental determinants. John B. Watson and B. F. Skinner were important early behaviorists. The psychodynamic approach emphasizes unconscious thought, the conflict between biological instincts and society's demands, and early childhood family experiences. Sigmund Freud was the founding father of the psychodynamic approach. The humanistic approach emphasizes a person's capacity for positive growth, freedom to choose one's destiny, and positive qualities. The cognitive approach emphasizes the mental processes involved in knowing. Cognitive psychologists study attention, thinking, problem solving, remembering, and learning. The evolutionary approach stresses the importance of adaptation, reproduction, and "survival of the fittest." The sociocultural approach focuses on the social and cultural determinants of behavior and encourages us to attend to the ways that our behavior and mental processes are embedded in a social context.

4. WHAT PSYCHOLOGISTS DO

Psychologists work in a wide range of settings and engage in many different activities. Individuals with undergraduate training in psychology hold occupations ranging from human resources and business consulting to doing casework for individuals struggling with psychological disorders. Those with graduate training in psychology might work as therapists and counselors, researchers and teachers in universities, or as business consultants or marketing researchers.

A clinical psychologist typically has a doctoral degree in psychology, whereas a psychiatrist is a medical doctor who specializes in treating people with abnormal behavior. A psychiatrist treats patients with psychotherapy and can prescribe drugs; a clinical psychologist generally cannot prescribe medication.

Main areas of specialization in psychology include physiological psychology and behavioral neuroscience, developmental psychology, sensation and perception, cognitive psychology, learning, motivation and emotion, personality psychology, social psychology, industrial and organizational psychology, clinical and counseling psychology, and health psychology. Other specialties include community psychology, school and educational psychology, environmental psychology, the psychology of women, forensic psychology, sport psychology, and cross-cultural psychology.

5. THE SCIENCE OF PSYCHOLOGY AND HEALTH AND WELLNESS

Psychologists recognize that the mind and the body are intricately related. The mind can influence the body. The way we think has implications for our nervous system and brain. Our motives and goals can influence our bodies as we strive to be physically fit and eat well. In turn, the body can have an impact on the mind. We think differently when our bodies are rested versus tired, healthy versus unhealthy.

Plan to make the most of your experience in taking introductory psychology by applying your learning to your life. Psychology is, after all, the scientific study of you—your behavior, thoughts, goals, and well-being.

key *terms*

behavior	empirical method	natural selection	psychopathology
behavioral approach	evolutionary approach	neuroscience	science
biological approach	functionalism	positive psychology	sociocultural approach
cognitive approach	humanistic approach	psychodynamic approach	structuralism
critical thinking	mental processes	psychology	

apply your *knowledge*

1. Ask 10 friends and family members to tell you the first thing that comes to mind when they think of psychology or a psychologist. After hearing their answers, share with them the broad definition of psychology given in this chapter. How do they react?

2. Visit the website of a major book retailer (such as Amazon) and enter "psychology" as a search term. Read the descriptions of five to seven of the most popular psychology books listed. How well do the themes covered in these books represent your perceptions of what psychology is? How well do they represent the approaches to psychology discussed in the text? Are any perspectives over- or underrepresented? If so, why do you think that is?

3. In the directory for your school (or for another institution), look up the psychology faculty. Select several faculty members and see what the areas of specialization are for each person (be careful: their specialty areas may not be the same as the classes they teach).

How do you think their areas of academic training might affect the way they teach their classes?

4. Human beings evolved long ago in a very different environment than we occupy today. The survivors were those who were most able to endure extremely difficult circumstances, struggling to find food, avoid predators, and create social groups. What do you think were the most adaptive traits for these early humans? Are those traits still adaptive? To what specific environments are humans adapting today?

5. Adopt Wilhelm Wundt's approach to understanding the human mind and behavior. Invite three friends to listen to a piece of music, and then ask them to reflect on the experience. Examine what each of them say about various aspects of the music. What does this exercise tell you about the subjectivity of introspection? In what ways do you think the method is worthwhile and in what ways is it limited?

CHAPTER 2

Psychology's Scientific Method

Can One Hour Change a Life?

Do I belong here? Do I have what it takes to succeed?

Coming to college can be exciting, but it can also be stressful. First-generation college students (those who are the first ones in their families to go to college) can experience a mix of emotions—from excitement, hope, and pride to homesickness, guilt, and worry (Covarrubias & Fryberg, 2015; Garriott & others, 2015). Many universities have instituted orientation procedures to ease the transition for such students.

At one school, new students listened for an hour as seniors shared stories about coming to college and learning how to be successful. In this "difference-education" program, the stories highlighted students' diverse backgrounds and how these experiences influenced their college life, both as weaknesses and as strengths. Sounds inspiring, but can something as minor as an hour in an orientation program really have an impact on how students adjust to college over the long haul?

A recent study examined this very question. Two years after this orientation experience, the researchers recruited students who had taken part in the difference-education experience as well as students who had participated in an orientation program about the transition to college but that did not highlight diverse backgrounds (Stephens & others, 2015). The students came to the lab and were asked to complete a series of stressful tasks, including giving a speech about themselves and completing standardized tests. Their bodily responses to the stressful tasks were measured, and the results of the study were striking: Even two years later, participants who had received the difference-education orientation were more likely to talk about their own diverse backgrounds as strengths in their speeches. In addition, first-generation students who had received difference education were more physiologically balanced during the stressful tasks. These results speak to the enduring power of a simple experience to help students recognize that they do have what it takes to succeed in college.

This is an example of scientific inquiry. Leaders, policymakers, and concerned people everywhere might come up with an idea to fix a problem. But finding out if the solution works requires scientific observation. ●

PREVIEW

Being a psychologist means being a scientist who studies psychology. In this chapter, we review the scientific method. You will read about the ways that psychologists have applied this general method to a variety of important topics and about the steps that are involved in recognizing research questions, developing methods to test them, and using statistical techniques to understand the results. Later in the chapter we consider some of the ethical issues that are involved in scientific inquiry. Psychology shares a great deal with other sciences, but as you will see, topics that psychologists study sometimes require special methodological and ethical consideration. To close the chapter, we examine the role of psychological research in health and wellness.

Science is defined not by what it studies but by how it investigates. Photosynthesis, butterflies, and happiness all can be studied in a scientific manner.

(first) Creatas PunchStock; (second) © George Doyle & Ciaran Griffin/Stockbyte/Getty Images

● **theory** A broad idea or set of closely related ideas that attempts to explain observations and to make predictions about future observations.

1. PSYCHOLOGY'S SCIENTIFIC METHOD

Science is defined not by *what* it investigates but by *how* it investigates. Whether you want to study photosynthesis, butterflies, Saturn's moons, or happiness, the *way* you study your question of interest determines whether your approach is scientific. The scientific method is how psychologists gain knowledge about mind and behavior.

It is the use of the scientific method that makes psychology a science (Fuchs & Evans, 2013; Rosnow & Rosenthal, 2013). Indeed, most of the studies published in psychological research journals follow the scientific method, which comprises these five steps (Figure 1):

1. Observing some phenomenon
2. Formulating hypotheses and predictions
3. Testing through empirical research
4. Drawing conclusions
5. Evaluating the theory

Step 1. Observing Some Phenomenon

The first step in conducting a scientific inquiry involves observing some phenomenon in the world. The curious, critically thinking psychologist—much like a detective—sees something in the world and wants to know why or how it is the way it is (Smith & Davis, 2013). Examples of moments that might inspire a scientific inquiry include:

- Current events, such as public protests of various policies.
- Social issues, like the low number of women in engineering professions.
- Personal experiences, such as an argument with one's spouse or an interaction with a child.

As scientists consider answers to such questions, they often develop theories. A **theory** is a broad idea or set of closely related ideas that attempts to explain observations. Theories tell us about the relations between variables on a conceptual level. They seek to explain why certain things have happened and can be used to make predictions about future observations.

It can sometimes be difficult to really grasp what a theory is or why theories are important. Theories are a testable set of propositions that describe something important about the world and allow scientists to make predictions. Psychologists have proposed theories that describe human behavior and that lead to specific predictions about that behavior. For instance, some psychologists theorize that the most important human need is the need to belong to a social group (Baumeister & Leary, 2000). From this theory we might come up with a variety of predictions. For example, we might expect that people will be highly motivated to fit in and feel especially distressed when they are not

1
Observing Some Phenomenon

We feel good when we give someone a gift. However, do we genuinely feel better giving something away than we might feel if we could keep it? Elizabeth Dunn, Lara Aknin, and Michael Norton (2008) decided to test this question.

2
Formulating Hypotheses and Predictions

These researchers hypothesized that spending money on other people would lead to greater happiness than spending money on oneself.

3
Testing Through Empirical Research

In an experiment designed to examine this prediction, the researchers randomly assigned undergraduate participants to receive money ($5 or $20) that the students had to spend on either themselves or someone else by 5 P.M. that day. Those who spent the money on *someone else* reported greater happiness that night.

4
Drawing Conclusions

The experiment supported the hypothesis that spending money on others can be a strong predictor of happiness. Money might not buy happiness, the researchers concluded, but spending money in a particular way, that is, on other people, may enhance happiness.

5
Evaluating the Theory

The experimental results were published in the prestigious journal *Science*. Now that the findings are public, other researchers might investigate related topics and questions inspired by this work, and their experiments might shed further light on the original conclusions.

FIGURE 1   **Steps in the Scientific Method: Is It Better to Give Than to Receive?** This figure shows how the steps in the scientific method were applied in a research experiment examining how spending money on ourselves or others can influence happiness.
(first photo) © Stockdisc/PunchStock; (third photo) © Masterfile

accepted by others (Leary & others, 2015). This theory might also lead to the prediction that being rejected by others would be a very distressing experience (Hartgerink & others, 2015). Theories make sense of some aspect of human behavior and allow us to extrapolate into different circumstances and domains to think about what we should expect. Those expectations are hypotheses and predictions.

Step 2. Formulating Hypotheses and Predictions

The second step in the scientific method is stating a hypothesis. A **hypothesis** is an educated guess that derives logically from a theory. It is an expectation that can be tested. A theory can generate many hypotheses. If more and more hypotheses related to a theory turn out to be true, the theory gains in credibility. So, a researcher who believes that social belonging is the most important aspect of human functioning might predict that people who belong to social groups will be happier than those who do not. Another hypothesis from the theory that belongingness is important to human functioning might be that individuals who have been socially excluded should feel less happy than those who have been socially included. These general hypotheses can be tested in different studies. A **prediction** is a specific expectation for the outcome of a study.

● **hypothesis** An educated guess that derives logically from a theory; a prediction that can be tested.

● **prediction** A statement about the specific expectation for the outcome of a study.

Step 3. Testing Through Empirical Research

The next step in the scientific method is to test the hypothesis by conducting empirical research. The **empirical method,** as discussed in the "What Is Psychology?" chapter, means gaining knowledge by observing objective evidence. In empirical research, we learn about the world by conducting systematic inquiries, collecting data, and analyzing the information. At this point, it is time to design a study that will test predictions that are based on the theory. To do so, a researcher first needs a concrete way to measure the variables of interest. Empirical researchers gain knowledge from observation of

● **empirical method** Gaining knowledge through the observation of events, the collection of data, and logical reasoning.

objective evidence, not simply by relying on belief or theory. The person who designed the difference-education intervention described in the opening of this chapter probably believed that it would help students. But a scientist requires empirical research to determine whether it was helpful or not.

The phenomena that scientists study are called *variables*, a word related to the verb *to vary*. A **variable** is anything that can change. All the different things psychologists study are variables, including experiences like happiness, gratitude, aggression, belongingness, conformity, and so forth. An **operational definition** provides an objective description of how a variable is going to be measured and observed in a particular study. Operational definitions eliminate the fuzziness that might creep into thinking about a problem. Imagine, for instance, that everyone in your psychology class is asked to observe a group of children and to keep track of kind behaviors. Do you think that all your classmates will define "kind behaviors" in the same way? Establishing an operational definition ensures that everyone agrees on what a variable means.

To measure personal happiness, for example, prominent psychologist Ed Diener and his students (1985) devised a self-report questionnaire that measures how satisfied a person is with his or her life, called the Satisfaction with Life Scale. (You will get a chance to complete the questionnaire later in this chapter.) Scores on this questionnaire are then used as measures of happiness. Research using this scale and others like it has shown that certain specific factors—marriage, religious faith, purpose in life, and good health—are strongly related to being happy (Diener, 1999, 2012b).

Importantly, there is not just one operational definition for any variable. Although Diener and his colleagues used a questionnaire, researchers have used diverse operational definitions for this variable—in this case, happiness. For instance, in a study of the relationship between happiness and important life outcomes, researchers used the facial expressions displayed by women in their college yearbook pictures as a measure of happiness. The women in the pictures had graduated 30 years prior. The researchers coded the photographs for the appearance of *Duchenne smiling* (Harker & Keltner, 2001). This type of smiling is genuine smiling—the kind that creates little wrinkles around the outer corner of the eyes—and it has been shown to be a sign of true happiness. (If you want to see whether someone in a photograph is smiling genuinely, cover the bottom of the person's face. Can you still tell that he or she is smiling? A genuine smile is evident in the eyes, not just the mouth.) In addition to coding those photos, the researchers followed up on the women's life experiences since graduating and found that happiness, as displayed in yearbook pictures, predicted positive life outcomes, such as successful marriages and satisfying lives, some 30 years later (Harker & Keltner, 2001).

So, in Diener's research, happiness was operationally defined as a score on a questionnaire; however, in this second study, happiness was operationally defined as Duchenne smiling. These definitions are just two among the many ways that psychologists have operationalized happiness. Another way to operationally define happiness is to *make* people happy, for example, by giving them an unexpected treat like candy or cookies or having them watch an amusing video.

Devising effective operational definitions for the variables in a study is a crucial step in designing psychological research (Kirk, 2013). To study anything, we must have a way to see it or measure it. Clearly, to establish an operational definition for any variable, we first have to agree on what we are trying to measure. If we think of happiness as something that people know about themselves, then a questionnaire score might be a good operational definition of the variable. If we think that people might not be aware of how happy they are (or aren't), then a facial expression might be a better operational definition. In other words, our definition of a variable must be set out clearly before we operationally define it. You might try your hand at operationally defining the following variables: generosity, love, maturity, exhaustion, and physical attractiveness. What are some things that *you* find interesting? How might you operationally define these variables?

● **variable** Anything that can change.

● **operational definition** A definition that provides an objective description of how a variable is going to be measured and observed in a particular study.

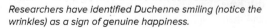

Researchers have identified Duchenne smiling (notice the wrinkles) as a sign of genuine happiness.

© Mirko Iannace/AGE Fotostock/Getty Images

Because operational definitions allow for the measurement of variables, researchers have a lot of numbers to deal with once they have conducted a study. A key aspect of the process of testing hypotheses is data analysis. *Data* are all the information (all those numbers) researchers collect in a study—say, the questionnaire scores or the behaviors observed. Data analysis means "crunching" those numbers mathematically to see if they support predictions. We will cover some of the basics of data analysis later in this chapter.

Let's consider an example that demonstrates the first three steps in the scientific method. One theory of well-being is *self-determination theory* (Deci & Ryan, 2000, 2012a; Ryan & Deci, 2009). According to this theory, people are likely to feel fulfilled when their lives meet three important needs: relatedness (warm relations with others), autonomy (independence), and competence (mastering new skills).

One hypothesis that follows logically from this theory is that people who value money, material possessions, prestige, and physical appearance (that is, *extrinsic rewards*) over the needs of relatedness, autonomy, and competence (*intrinsic rewards*) should be less fulfilled, less happy, and less well adjusted. In a series of studies entitled "The Dark Side of the American Dream," researchers Timothy Kasser and Richard Ryan asked participants to complete self-report measures of values and of psychological and physical functioning (Dittmar & others, 2014; Kasser & Ryan, 1996; Kasser & others, 2004). Thus, the operational definitions of values and psychological functioning were questionnaire scores. The researchers found that individuals who value material rewards over more intrinsic rewards do indeed tend to suffer as predicted.

Step 4. Drawing Conclusions

Based on the results of the data analyses, scientists then draw conclusions from their research. Do the data support the predictions or not? What do the findings tell us about the theory that guided the study? Psychologists write articles presenting those findings. The articles are submitted for publication in scientific journals. Once submitted, they undergo rigorous review by other scientists who evaluate the work for its scientific merit. If the paper and the research it reports are judged to be of sufficiently high quality, the paper is published for all to see and read.

Step 5. Evaluating the Theory

The final step in the scientific method is one that never really ends. Once a paper is published, the community of scientists continues to evaluate it in light of other research. When many studies have been conducted on the same topic, scholars go back and consider the theory that started it all. Do the studies really support the theory? It is important to keep in mind that usually a theory is revised only after a number of studies produce similar results.

A key step after a study has been published is *replication*. Replicating a study means repeating it and getting the same results. Scientific conclusions rely on showing that the results remain the same, regardless of the specific scientist who conducts the study or the specific group of people who were studied. *Direct replication* means doing the study precisely as it was conducted in its original form. *Conceptual replication* means doing the study with different methods or different types of samples. For instance, a researcher might want to know if a particular strategy to enhance social skills works not only for college students but for older adults or for individuals with autism. If a research finding is shown again and again—that is, if it is *replicated*—across different researchers and different specific methods, it is considered *reliable*. It is a result on which we can depend.

One special type of study involves a meta-analysis. **Meta-analysis** is a statistical procedure that summarizes a large body of evidence from the research literature on a particular topic. For a meta-analysis, a researcher tries to find all of the studies that have been done on the topic of interest. The researcher then compares all the studies and their findings. A meta-analysis allows researchers to conclude whether a result is consistent

● **meta-analysis** A statistical procedure that summarizes a large body of evidence from the research literature on a particular topic, allowing the researcher to assess the strength of the relationship between the variables.

30 📎 CHAPTER 2 **Psychology's Scientific Method**

in the literature and to estimate the magnitude of the relationship between variables (Cooper, 2016).

Meta-analytic results are more powerful than the results of any single study because they combine many findings in the literature. For example, consider the question, How does procrastination affect academic performance? Instructors and students have certainly debated this question. It seems that for every student who performs poorly on a test after procrastinating, there is another one who aces it based on last-minute cramming. Further, some individuals who are very academically successful appear to have achieved a great deal in life despite (not because of) their procrastination. A recent meta-analysis summarized the results of 33 studies of academic performance involving a total of nearly 40,000 participants (Kim & Seo, 2015). The results showed that, indeed, procrastination is negatively related to academic performance.

The research community maintains an active conversation about what scientists know, and this dialogue constantly questions conclusions (Stanovich, 2013). From published studies, a scholar may come up with a new idea that will eventually change the thinking on a particular topic. Steps 3, 4, and 5 in the scientific method are part of an ongoing process. That is, researchers go back and do more research, revise their theories, hone their methods, and draw and evaluate their new conclusions.

test yourself

1. What are the five steps in the scientific method?
2. What is an operational definition, and what is its value in a study?
3. What is a meta-analysis? Why do researchers use this procedure?

2. TYPES OF PSYCHOLOGICAL RESEARCH

Psychologists commonly use three types of research. *Descriptive research* involves finding out about the basic dimensions of some variable (for example, what the average level of happiness is for men in the United States). *Correlational research* is interested in discovering relationships between variables (for instance, whether being married predicts greater happiness for men). *Experimental research* concerns establishing causal relationships between variables (such as, whether women perceive men as more attractive if the men are smiling). In this section, we examine each of these types of research.

Descriptive Research

Just as its name suggests, **descriptive research** is about describing some phenomenon—determining its basic dimensions and defining what this thing is, how often it occurs, and so on. Descriptive research can help identify problems, such as the spread of a disease or the frequency of negative outcomes, such as violent crime. By itself, descriptive research cannot prove what causes some phenomenon, but it can reveal important information about people's behaviors and attitudes. Descriptive research methods include observation, surveys and interviews, and case studies.

OBSERVATION

Imagine that you are going to conduct a study on how children who are playing together resolve conflicts that arise. The data that are of interest to you concern conflict resolution. As a first step, you might go to a playground and simply observe what the children do—how often you see conflict resolution occur and how it unfolds. You would likely keep careful notes of what you observe.

This type of scientific observation requires an important set of skills (Graziano & Raulin, 2013). Unless you are a trained observer and practice your skills regularly, you might not know what to look for, you might not remember what you saw, you might not realize that what you are looking for is changing from one moment to the next, and you might not document and communicate your observations effectively. Furthermore, you might not realize the value of having one or more others do the observations as well, so that you develop a sense of the accuracy of your observations. In short, for observations to be effective, they must be systematic. You must know whom you are observing, when and where you will observe, and how you

● **descriptive research** Research that determines the basic dimensions of a phenomenon—defining what it is, how often it occurs, and so on.

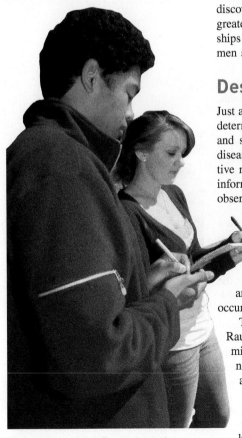

© McGraw-Hill Education/John Flournoy, photographer

will make the observations. Also, you need to know in advance in what form you will document them: in writing, by sound recording, or by video.

SURVEYS AND INTERVIEWS

Sometimes the best and quickest way to get information about people is to ask them for it. One technique is to interview people directly. A related method that is especially useful when you need information from many people is the *survey,* or questionnaire. A survey presents a standard set of questions, or *items,* to obtain people's self-reported attitudes or beliefs about a particular topic.

Although surveys can be a straightforward way to measure psychological variables, constructing them requires care (Leedy & Ormrod, 2013). For example, surveys can measure only what people think about themselves. Thus, if we are interested in studying a variable that we believe is unconscious, such as a psychodynamic drive, we cannot use a survey. Furthermore, people do not always know the truth about themselves. If you were answering a survey that asked, "Are you a generous person?" how might your answer compare to that of a friend who is asked to make that same rating about you? One particular problem with surveys and interviews is the tendency of participants to answer questions in a way that will make them look good rather than in a way that communicates what they truly think or feel (Reynolds & Suzuki, 2013).

Another challenge in survey construction is that when a questionnaire is used to define variables operationally, it is crucial that the items clearly measure the specific topic of interest and not some other characteristic. Therefore, the language used in a survey must be clear and understandable if the responses are to reflect the participants' actual feelings.

Surveys and interviews can examine a wide range of topics, from religious beliefs to sexual habits to attitudes about gun control (Rosnow & Rosenthal, 2013). Some survey and interview questions are unstructured and open-ended, such as "How fulfilling would you say your marriage is?" Such questions allow for unique responses from each person surveyed. Other survey and interview questions are more structured and ask about specific things. For example, a structured question might ask, "How many times have you talked with your partner about a personal problem in the past month: 0, 1–2, 3–5, 6–10, 11–30, every day?"

Questionnaires often use rating scales as a way for participants to indicate their agreement with a statement. Such scales, sometimes called *Likert scales* (after their inventor, Rensis Likert) usually involve the subject selecting a number that indicates the person's level of agreement with a statement. For example, in response to the item, "I am outgoing and sociable," the respondent might be asked to select a number from 1 (indicating not at all) to 7 (indicating very much). Later in this chapter, you will be completing a questionnaire that uses such a scale.

● **case study or case history** An in-depth look at a single individual.

CASE STUDIES

A **case study or case history** is an in-depth look at a single individual. Case studies are performed mainly by clinical psychologists when, for either practical or ethical reasons, the unique aspects of an individual's life cannot be duplicated and tested with other individuals. A case study provides information about one person's goals, hopes, fantasies, fears, traumatic experiences, family relationships, health, and anything else that helps the psychologist understand the person's mind and behavior. Case studies can also involve in-depth explorations of particular families or social groups.

An example of a case study is the analysis of India's spiritual leader Mahatma Gandhi (1869–1948) by psychodynamic theorist Erik Erikson (1969). Erikson studied Gandhi's life in great depth to discover how his positive spiritual identity developed, especially during his youth. In piecing together Gandhi's identity development, Erikson described the contributions of culture, history, family, and various other factors that might affect the way people form an identity.

A case history provides a dramatic, detailed portrayal of a person's life, but we must be cautious about applying what we learn from one person's life to others. The subject of a case study is unique, with a genetic makeup and personal history that no one else

Mahatma Gandhi was India's spiritual leader in the mid-twentieth century. Erik Erikson conducted an extensive case study of Gandhi's life to determine what factors contributed to his identity development.

©Bettmann/Getty Images

shares. Case studies can be very valuable as the first step of the scientific method, in that they often provide vivid observations that can then be tested in a variety of ways through psychological research. However, and importantly, an in-depth study of a single case may not be generalizable to the wider population. This means that a case study may tell us a great deal about the individual person being studied but not very much about people in general.

THE VALUE OF DESCRIPTIVE RESEARCH

Descriptive research allows researchers to get a sense of a subject of interest, but it cannot answer questions about how and why things are the way they are. Nevertheless, descriptive research does explore intriguing topics, such as the experience of happiness in different cultures. Before reading about and considering the value of that research, complete the measure below. Specifically, using the 7-point scale, indicate your agreement with each item that follows the scale.

1	2	3	4	5	6	7
Strongly Disagree	Disagree	Slightly Disagree	Neither Agree nor Disagree	Slightly Agree	Agree	Strongly Agree

1. In most ways my life is close to my ideal.
2. The conditions of my life are excellent.
3. I am satisfied with my life.
4. So far I have gotten the important things I want in life.
5. If I could live my life over, I would change almost nothing.

You have just completed the Satisfaction with Life Scale (or SWLS; Diener & others, 1985), one operational definition of happiness. To find out your score, add up your ratings and divide by 5. This average rating could be considered your level of general happiness. Many different kinds of studies from many different countries have used this scale and others like it to measure happiness levels. Based on such research, Ed and Carol Diener (1996) concluded that most people are pretty happy because they score above the midpoint, 4, on the scale you just completed. However, research on happiness in various cultures has generally centered on relatively developed countries. What about developing societies that are not as prosperous?

One study examined levels of happiness in groups of people who have not generally been included in psychological studies (Biswas-Diener, Vittersø, & Diener, 2005). The research assessed three groups: the Inughuits (Inuits) of Greenland, the Maasai of southern Kenya, and the American Old Order Amish. All three groups completed measures that were essentially the same as the one you just did.

The Inughuits live at 79 degrees latitude (very far north), in the harshest climate inhabited by a traditional human society. Rocks, glaciers, and the sea dominate the landscape. Farming is impossible. The Inughuits have some modern conveniences, but they generally adhere to a traditional hunting culture. It is not uncommon to find an Inughuit hunter carving a seal or caribou on the kitchen floor while children watch TV in the next room. Most of us might feel a little blue in the winter months when gloomy weather seems to stretch on, day after day. For the Inughuits, however, the sun never rises at all throughout the winter months, and in the summer, it never sets. How happy could an individual be in such a difficult setting? Pretty happy, it turns out, as the Inughuits averaged a 5.0 on the Satisfaction with Life Scale.

The Maasai are an indigenous (native) African nomadic group who live in villages of about 20 people, with little exposure to the West. Maasai are fierce warriors, and their culture has many traditional ceremonies built around a boy's passage from childhood to manhood. Boys are circumcised between the ages of 15 and 22, and they are forbidden from moving or making a sound during the procedure. Girls are also circumcised as they enter puberty, in a controversial ritual that involves the removal of the clitoris and that makes childbirth extremely difficult. The Maasai practice child marriage and polygamy. Maasai women have very little power and are generally expected to do most of the work.

How happy could an individual be in this context? Maasai men and women who completed the measure orally in their native tongue, Maa, averaged a 5.4 on the Satisfaction with Life Scale (Biswas-Diener, Vittersø, & Diener, 2005).

Finally, the Old Order Amish of the midwestern and northeastern United States belong to a strict religious sect that explicitly rejects modern aspects of life. The Amish separate themselves from mainstream society and travel by horse and buggy. The women wear bonnets, and the men sport beards, dark clothes, and dark brimmed hats. The Amish farm without modern machinery and dedicate their lives to simplicity—without washing machines, cars, computers, TVs, iPads, and smartphones. Still, the Amish are relatively happy, averaging 4.4 on the 7-point happiness scale (Biswas-Diener, Vittersø, & Diener, 2005).

Like a host of other studies in developed nations, these results indicate that most individuals are pretty happy. Such descriptive findings provide researchers who study well-being with a valuable foundation for further exploring the processes that lead to these feelings of happiness in different cultural settings. If researchers wanted to extend these findings to investigate predictors of happiness in different cultures, they would then turn to a correlational design.

Correlational Research

We have seen that descriptive research tells us about the basic dimensions of a variable. In contrast, **correlational research** tells us about the relation between two variables. The purpose of correlational research is to examine whether and how two variables *change together*. That is, correlational research looks at a *co*-relation. For instance, if one of the variables increases, what happens to the other one? When two variables change together, we can predict one from the other, and we say that the variables are correlated.

Correlational research is so named because of the statistical technique *correlation* that is typically used to analyze these types of data. The key feature of a correlational study is that the factors of interest are measured or observed to see how they are related (Morling, 2015). If we want to know whether shy people are happy, we might give the same people two questionnaires—one that measures shyness and another that assesses happiness. For each person we would have two scores, and we would then see whether shyness and happiness relate to each other in a systematic way.

The degree of relation between two variables is expressed as a numerical value called a *correlational coefficient,* which is most commonly represented by the letter *r*. The correlation coefficient is a statistic that tells us two things about the relationship between two variables—its strength and its direction. The value of a correlation always falls between −1.00 and +1.00. The number or magnitude of the correlation tells us about the *strength* of the relationship. The closer the number is to ±1.00, the stronger the relationship. The sign (+ or −) tells us about the *direction* of the relation between the variables. A positive sign means that as one variable increases, the other also increases. A negative sign means that as one variable increases, the other decreases. A zero correlation means that there is no systematic relation between the variables.

Examples of scatter plots (a type of graph that plots scores on the two variables) showing positive and negative correlations appear in Figure 2. Note that every dot in this figure represents both scores for one person.

● **correlational research** Research that examines the relationship between variables with the purpose of determining whether and how two variables change together.

CORRELATION IS NOT CAUSATION

Look at the terms in bold type in the following newspaper headlines:

Researchers **Link** Coffee Consumption to Cancer of Pancreas

Brain Size Is **Associated** with Gender

Psychologists Discover **Relationship** Between Religious Faith and Good Health

Reading these headlines, one might conclude that coffee causes pancreatic cancer, gender causes differences in brain size, and religious faith causes good health. The boldface words are synonymous only with correlation, however, not with causality.

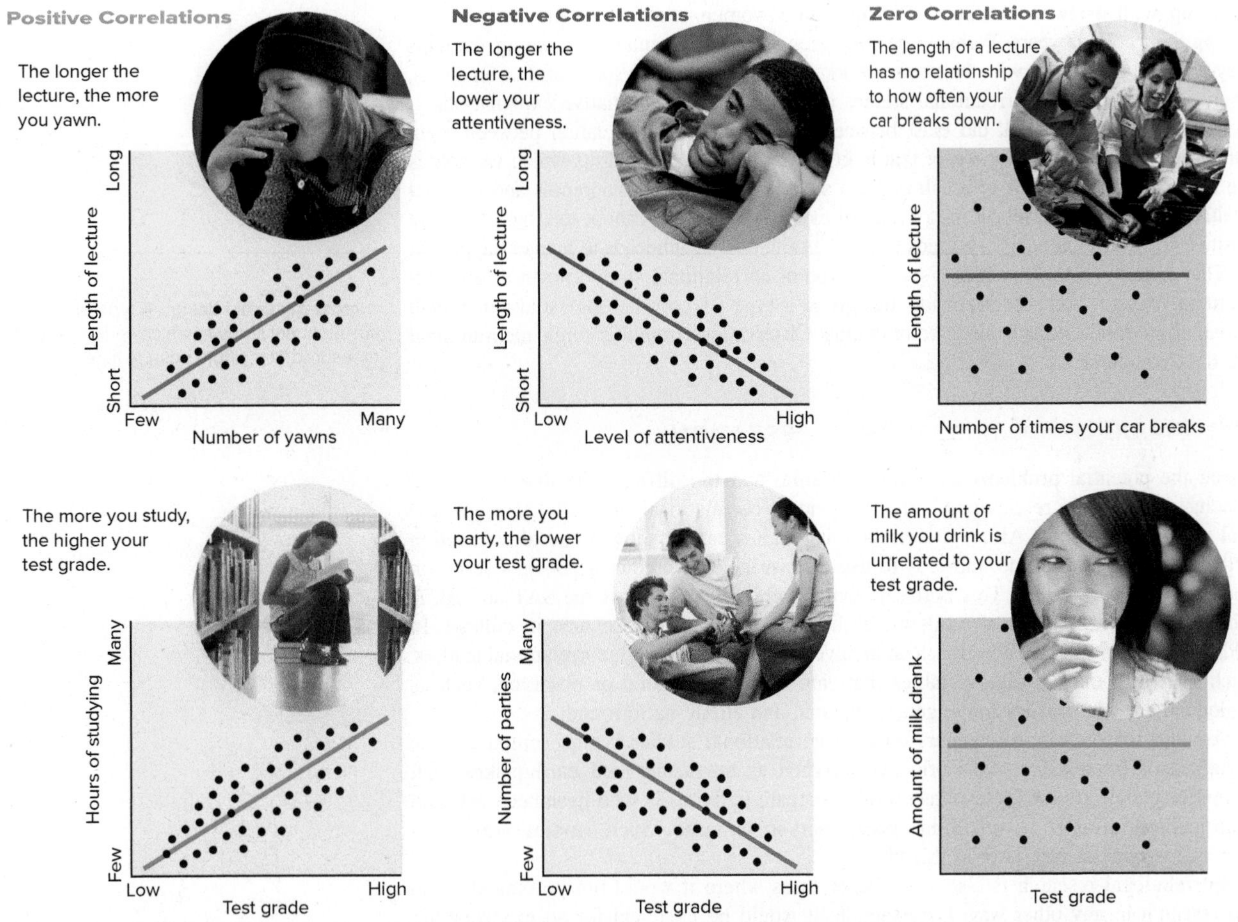

Positive Correlations

The longer the lecture, the more you yawn.

The more you study, the higher your test grade.

Negative Correlations

The longer the lecture, the lower your attentiveness.

The more you party, the lower your test grade.

Zero Correlations

The length of a lecture has no relationship to how often your car breaks down.

The amount of milk you drink is unrelated to your test grade.

FIGURE 2 Scatter Plots Showing Positive, Negative, and Zero Correlations A positive correlation is a relationship in which two factors vary in the same direction, as shown in the two scatter plots on the left. A negative correlation is a relationship in which two factors vary in opposite directions, as shown in the two scatter plots in the middle. A zero correlation is illustrated by the scatter plots on the right.
(first photo) © Doug Menuez/Getty Images; (second photo) © BananaStock/JupiterImages; (third photo) © ColorBlind Images/Getty Images; (fourth photo) © Veer; (fifth photo) © Stockbyte/PunchStock; (sixth photo) © JGI/Blend Images LLC

● **third variable problem** The circumstance in which a variable that has not been measured accounts for the relationship between two other variables. Third variables are also known as confounds.

Correlation does not equal causation. Remember, correlation means only that two variables change together. Being able to predict one event based on the occurrence of another event does not necessarily tell us anything about the cause of either event. At times some other variable that has not been measured accounts for the relationship between two others. Researchers refer to this circumstance as the **third variable problem.**

To understand the third variable problem, consider the following example. A researcher measures two variables: the number of ice cream cones sold in a town and the number of violent crimes that occur in that town throughout the year. The researcher finds that ice cream cone sales and violent crimes are positively correlated, to the magnitude of +.50. This high positive correlation would indicate that as ice cream sales increase, so do violent crimes. Would it be reasonable for the local paper to run the headline "Ice Cream Consumption Leads to Violence"? Should concerned citizens gather outside the local Frosty Freeze to stop the madness? Probably not. Perhaps you have already thought of the third variable that might explain this correlation—heat. Indeed, when it is hot outside, people are more likely both to purchase ice cream and to act aggressively (Anderson & Bushman, 2002). Such a third variable is also called a *confound.*

Consider that interesting study on smiling in college yearbook pictures and happy marriages. What are some third variables that might explain that association? If we think about the reasons women might not be smiling in those yearbook pictures, we might come up with a few possibilities. Perhaps those women experienced parental divorce during their college years. Perhaps they experienced a recent romantic breakup. Perhaps they were having trouble with their coursework, leading them to less successful occupations. Even very compelling correlational studies might be open to alternative explanations.

Further, if a causal link did exist between two variables, a correlation between them cannot tell us about the *direction* of that link. A correlation cannot tell us which variable is the cause and which is the effect. Imagine a study that shows that happiness and physical health are positively correlated in a group of elderly people. We cannot tell, based on that positive correlation, if happiness leads to better health or if health leads to greater happiness.

This example also illustrates a specific type of correlational study known as a cross-sectional design. A **cross-sectional design** is a type of correlational study in which variables are measured at a single point in time. Observations from this single measurement are then compared.

● **cross-sectional design** A type of correlational study in which variables are measured at a single point in time.

THE VALUE OF CORRELATIONAL RESEARCH

Given the potential problems with third variables and the difficulty in drawing causal conclusions, why do researchers bother to conduct correlational studies? There are several very good reasons. Although correlational studies cannot show a causal connection between variables, they do allow us to use one variable to predict a person's score on another (Caldwell, 2013). This is the reasoning behind tests such as the SAT and ACT, which provide a measure of academic ability that predicts performance in college. In addition, some important questions can be investigated only through correlational studies. Such questions may involve variables that can only be measured or observed, such as biological sex, personality traits, genetic factors, and ethnic background.

Another reason why researchers conduct correlational studies is that sometimes the variables of interest are real-world events, such as hurricanes and earthquakes, that influence people's lives. Researchers might compare individuals who have been exposed to a natural disaster to a similar group not so exposed. Such studies are called *quasi-experimental* (see later in this chapter).

Correlational research is also valuable in cases where it would not be ethical to do the research in any other way. For example, it would be unethical for an experimenter to direct expectant mothers to smoke varying numbers of cigarettes in order to see how cigarette smoke affects birth weight or infant development.

Although we have focused mainly on relations between just two variables, researchers often measure many variables in their studies. In this way, they can assess whether a connection between two variables is explained by a third variable (or a fourth or fifth variable). An interesting question that researchers have examined in this fashion is, do happy people live longer? In one study, 2,000 Mexican Americans ages 65 and older were interviewed twice over the course of two years (Ostir & others, 2000). In the first assessment, participants completed measures of happiness but also reported about potential third variables such as diet, physical health, smoking, marital status, and distress. Two years later, the researchers contacted the participants again to see who was still alive. Even with these many potential third variables taken into account, happiness predicted who was still living two years later.

Correlational studies also are useful when researchers are interested in studying everyday experience. For example, correlational researchers often use daily reports that track experiences,

Correlational research is useful for studying the impact on people's lives of events such as Hurricane Sandy in 2012.

© Angel Chevrestt/ZumaPress/Alamy

psychological *inquiry*

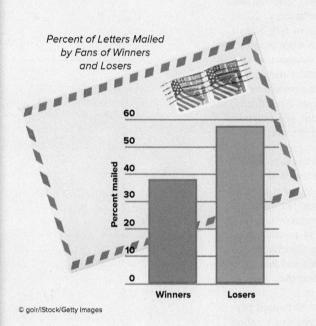

Percent of Letters Mailed by Fans of Winners and Losers

Percent mailed

60
50
40
30
20
10
0

Winners   Losers

© goir/IStock/Getty Images

Miserable but Helpful?

Many studies have shown that happy individuals are more helpful than people in a negative mood. Social psychologist R. F. Soames Job (1987) was interested in examining how mood relates to helping. In a clever study, he used naturally occurring mood and an unusual measure of helpfulness.

The study took place outside a major rugby match pitting Canterbury-Bankstown against St. George, in Sydney, Australia. Rugby is enormously popular in Sydney, and more than 40,000 people attended the match.

While the game was going on, the researchers placed 100 stamped letters on the windshields of cars parked around the sporting grounds. The letters were addressed to the same person, and a handwritten note on each letter said, "Found near your car." The researchers identified which cars belonged to supporters of each team by the different colored streamers, team stickers, and posters. Fifty letters were placed on the cars of supporters of each team. The researchers then waited to see which type of fan was most likely to put the letter in the mailbox—a fan of the winning team or of the losing team.

The figure shows the results. Try your hand at the questions below.

1. What were the variables of interest in this study?

2. How did the study operationally define these variables?

3. Why is this a correlational study?

4. Job concluded that these data support the notion that negative mood relates to helping. Is this conclusion justified, in your opinion? Why or why not?

5. Identify at least one third variable that might explain the results of this study.

---

known as the *experience sampling method (ESM),* to assess people in their natural settings. ESM studies involve having people report on their experiences in a diary a few times a day or to complete measures of their mood and behavior whenever they are beeped by an electronic organizer or by a smartphone (Ebner-Priemer & Trull, 2012). A similar method, *event-contingent responding,* asks participants to complete a report each time they engage in a particular behavior, such as drinking alcohol or having sex after a romantic breakup (Barber & Cooper, 2014). Such methods allow researchers to get close to real life as it happens.

Although the correlation coefficient is often used to express the relation between two variables, it is important to keep in mind that what makes a study correlational is not the statistic researchers use to analyze the data. Rather, a study is correlational when it relies on measuring variables to see how they are related. To get a sense of this distinction and learn about some clever ways in which psychologists have operationalized variables, check out the Psychological Inquiry above.

LONGITUDINAL DESIGNS

● **longitudinal design** A special kind of systematic observation, used by correlational researchers, that involves obtaining measures of the variables of interest in multiple waves over time.

One way that correlational researchers can deal with the issue of causation is to employ a special kind of systematic observation called a **longitudinal design.** Longitudinal research involves obtaining measures of the variables of interest in multiple waves over time (Windle, 2012). (Note that longitudinal designs differ from cross-sectional designs in that cross-sectional designs measure the variables only once.) Longitudinal research can suggest potential causal relationships because if one variable is thought to cause changes in another, it should at least come before that variable in time.

One intriguing longitudinal study is the Nun Study, conducted by David Snowdon and his colleagues (Grossi & others, 2007; Mortimer, Snowdon, & Markesbery, 2009; Snowdon, 2003). The study began in 1986 and has followed a sample of 678 School Sisters of Notre Dame (SSND) ever since. Ranging in age from 75 to 103 when the study began, the nuns complete a variety of psychological and physical measures annually. This sample is unique in many respects. However, certain characteristics render the participants an excellent group for correlational research. For one thing, many potential extraneous third variables are relatively identical for all the women in the group. Specifically, their biological sex, living conditions, diet, activity levels, marital status, and religious participation are essentially held constant, so there is little chance that differences would arise in these variables that might explain the study's results.

Researchers assessed the link between happiness and longevity using this rich dataset. All of the nuns had been asked to write a spiritual autobiography when they entered the convent (for some, up to 80 years prior). In one study, these documents were used as indicators of happiness earlier in life by counting the number of positive emotions expressed in the autobiographies (note that here we have yet another operational definition of happiness) (Danner, Snowdon, & Friesen, 2001). Higher levels of positive emotion expressed in autobiographies written at an average age of 22 were associated with a 2.5-fold difference in risk of mortality when the nuns were in their 80s and 90s. That is, women who included positive emotion in their autobiographies when they were in their early 20s were 2.5 times more likely to survive some 60 years later.

Recently, researchers replicated this finding using autobiographies of 88 famous psychologists. They found that when the psychologists used more active positive emotion words (such as *lively* and *excited*) to describe their life, they lived longer (Pressman & Cohen, 2012).

Longitudinal designs provide ways by which correlational researchers may attempt to demonstrate causal relations among variables (Pulkkinen & Kokko, 2012). Still, it is important to be aware that even in longitudinal studies, causal relationships are not completely clear. An excellent longitudinal study still cannot prove causation. For example, the nuns who wrote happier autobiographies may have had happier childhood experiences that might be influencing their longevity, or a particular genetic factor might explain both their happiness and their survival.

As you read about correlational research studies throughout this book, do so critically and with a modicum of skepticism; consider that even the brightest scientist may not have thought of all of the potential third variables that could have explained the results. It is easy to assume causality when two events or characteristics are merely correlated. Remember those innocent ice cream cones, and critically evaluate conclusions that may be drawn from simple observation.

Experimental Research

To determine whether a causal relationship exists between variables, researchers must use experimental methods (Morling, 2015). An **experiment** is a carefully regulated procedure in which the researcher manipulates one or more variables that are believed to influence some other variable. Researchers cannot demonstrate causation without experimental research. Imagine, for example, that a researcher notices that people who listen to classical music seem to be of above average intelligence. A correlational study on this question would not tell us if listening to classical music *causes* increases in intelligence. In order to demonstrate causation, the researcher would manipulate whether or not people listen to classical music. He or she might create two groups: one that listens to classical music and one that does not. To test for differences in intelligence, the researcher would then measure intelligence.

● **experiment** A carefully regulated procedure in which the researcher manipulates one or more variables that is believed to influence some other variable.

● **random assignment** The assignment of participants to experimental groups by chance, to reduce the likelihood that a study's results will be due to preexisting differences between groups.

If that manipulation led to differences between the two groups on intelligence, we could say that the manipulated variable *caused* those differences: The experiment has demonstrated cause and effect. This notion that experiments can demonstrate causation is based on the idea that if participants are *randomly assigned* to groups, the only systematic difference between them must be the manipulated variable. **Random assignment** means that researchers assign participants to groups *by chance*. Random assignment is an essential aspect of experimental research, and it is because psychologists use random assignment that they can assume that there are no preexisting differences between groups (Morling, 2015).

The logic of random assignment is this: If participants in an experiment are assigned to each group only by chance, the potential differences between the groups will cancel out over the long run. So, for instance, in the example of classical music and intelligence, we might wonder if it is possible that the groups differed on intelligence to begin with. Because participants were randomly assigned, we assume that intelligence is spread across the groups evenly.

Random assignment does not always work. One way to improve its effectiveness is to start with a relatively large pool of people. Let's say that you decided to do that study—examining whether listening to classical music (as compared to no music) prior to taking an intelligence test leads to higher scores on the test. Although you wisely use random assignment, you begin with just 10 people. Unbeknownst to you, there are two geniuses (people with extraordinarily high IQs) in that small pool of participants. Each person has a 50–50 chance of ending up in either group, so there is a 25 percent chance that both geniuses will both end up in the classical music group and a 25 percent change they will both end up in the control group. In other words, there is a 50 percent chance that your groups will differ systematically in intelligence before you even start the study.

In contrast, if your study had begun with, say, 100 people, intelligence scores would likely be more evenly distributed throughout the overall pool. When these individuals are randomly assigned to groups, differences in intelligence would be much more likely to cancel out across the two groups. That is why it is important that random assignment is allowed to work its magic on a larger pool of people.

To get a sense of what experimental studies, as compared to correlational studies, can reveal, consider the following example. Psychologists have long assumed that experiencing one's life as meaningful is an important aspect of psychological well-being (Frankl, [1946] 2006; Steger, 2012). Because surveys that measure well-being and meaning in life correlate positively (that is, the more meaningful your life, the happier you are), the assumption has been that experiencing meaning in life causes greater happiness. However, because the studies involved in exploring this relationship have been correlational, the cause is unclear. Meaning in life may lead people to be happier, but the reverse might also be true: Happiness might make people feel that their lives are more meaningful.

To address this issue, Laura King and her colleagues (Hicks & others, 2012; King & others, 2006) conducted a series of laboratory experiments. In one study, the researchers put some participants in a positive mood by having them listen to happy music. Other participants listened to neutral music. Participants who listened to happy music rated their lives as more meaningful than did individuals who listened to neutral music (King & others, 2006). Note that participants were randomly assigned to one of two conditions, happy music or neutral music, and then rated their meaning in life using a questionnaire. In this case happiness was operationally defined by the type of music participants heard, and meaning in life was operationally defined by ratings on a questionnaire. Because participants were randomly assigned to conditions, we can assume that the only systematic difference between the two groups was the

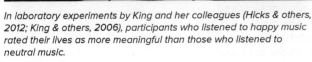

In laboratory experiments by King and her colleagues (Hicks & others, 2012; King & others, 2006), participants who listened to happy music rated their lives as more meaningful than those who listened to neutral music.

© Fuse/Getty Images

type of music they heard. As a result, we can say that the happy music caused people to rate their lives as more meaningful.

INDEPENDENT AND DEPENDENT VARIABLES

Experiments have two types of variables: independent and dependent. An **independent variable** is a manipulated experimental factor. The independent variable is the variable that the experimenter changes to see what its effects are; it is a potential cause. In the example of listening to classical music and intelligence, the independent variable is whether or not participants listened to music. In the study of positive mood and meaning in life, the independent variable is mood (positive versus neutral), operationally defined by the type of music participants heard.

A **dependent variable** in an experiment is the variable that may change as a result of manipulations in the independent variable. It represents the outcome (effect) in an experiment. As researchers manipulate the independent variable, they measure the dependent variable to test for any effect of the manipulated variable. In the example of listening to classical music and intelligence, the dependent variable is intelligence. In the study by King and others of positive mood and meaning in life (2006), meaning in life is the dependent variable.

Any experiment may include several independent variables, or factors that are manipulated, to determine their effect on the outcome. Similarly, many experiments include more than one dependent variable as well, to examine the effects of manipulations on a number of outcomes.

Independent and dependent variables are two of the most important concepts in psychological research. Despite their similar names, they are very different. Remember that the independent variable is the *cause,* and the dependent variable is the *effect.* The independent variable is the one that is manipulated, and the dependent variable is the outcome.

Independent and dependent variables can be operationalized in many ways. Sometimes the independent variable involves an individual's social context. Social psychologists often manipulate the social context with the help of a confederate. A **confederate** is a person who is given a role to play in a study so that the social context can be manipulated.

Let's consider one more example to review the process of experimental research step-by-step. Have you ever noticed how sometimes when a friend tells you about an upsetting event in his or her life you start to feel the same emotions your friend is feeling, as if that event had happened to you? A team of social psychologists led by David Cwir was interested in studying this phenomenon (Cwir & others, 2011). They hypothesized that being socially connected to someone *causes* us to experience that person's experience as if it were our own. To test this hypothesis in an experiment, they needed to manipulate social connection and then measure how a person might be affected by someone else's experience.

Here's what they did. First, a few weeks before the experiment, all of the participants completed a survey gauging their favorite music, TV shows, movies, actors, books, and so forth. When participants came to the lab for the experiment, they were told that the study was about the effects of physical exercise on cardiovascular function, and their heart rate and blood pressure were measured. Next, each participant was introduced to a confederate (who the participant thought was just another subject in the study). The experimenter told the participant and the confederate to chat to get to know each other.

What the participants did not know is that the confederate had been given a script to follow during this chat. Participants were, in fact, randomly assigned to interact either with a confederate who mentioned interests very similar to their own, as noted on the earlier measure, or with a confederate who did not mention those interests.

Next, the participant and confederate completed different activities. The confederate was instructed to run in place, vigorously, for 3 minutes while the participant sat and watched. Finally, the researchers measured participants' heart rate and blood pressure (a second time). The results showed that the group that had interacted with a confederate to whom they felt connected had greater change in heart rate and blood pressure (from the initial measure) after watching that confederate run in place, compared to the group that watched a confederate to whom they did not have a sense of connection (Cwir & others, 2011).

● **independent variable** A manipulated experimental factor; the variable that the experimenter changes to see what its effects are.

● **dependent variable** The outcome; the variable that may change in an experiment in response to changes in the independent variable.

● **confederate** A person who is given a role to play in an experiment so that the social context can be manipulated.

Let's review the concepts covered so far in the context of this clever experiment. The researchers had hypothesized that being socially connected to someone would lead to greater responsiveness to that other person's experience. The independent variable (the cause) in this study is social connection. The operational definition of that variable is interacting with someone who shared the participants' interests (or not). The dependent variable (the effect) is the responsiveness of participants to the other person's experience. The operational definition of this variable is participants' heart rate and blood pressure. Participants were randomly assigned to groups, so that the researchers could be sure that the groups did not differ systematically from each (in this case, on variables such as heart rate or blood pressure, or on psychological characteristics like empathy). The confederate is the individual who acted like just another participant but was actually part of the manipulation of the independent variable.

This study involved two groups: one that experienced social connection with the confederate and one that did not. Why did the researchers need *both* of these groups? They were only interested in how social connection influences shared feelings, so why did they have a group that did not feel a social connection? Notice that if they did not have that second group, they would have nothing with which to compare their results—no way to determine whether social connection mattered. This is the basic logic behind the concepts of experimental and control groups, our next topic.

EXPERIMENTAL AND CONTROL GROUPS

Experiments involve comparing different groups that have been exposed to differing versions of the independent variable. These groups have names. An **experimental group** consists of the participants in an experiment who are exposed to *the change* that the independent variable represents. A **control group** in an experiment is as much like the experimental group as possible and is treated in every way like the experimental group *except for that change*. The control group provides a comparison against which the researcher can test the effects of the independent variable.

We now have reviewed three examples of experimental and control groups:

- In our imaginary study of music and intelligence, the experimental group is the group that listened to classical music; the no-music group is the control group.
- In the study of happiness and meaning in life, participants who listened to happy music are the experimental group; those who heard neutral music are the control group.
- In the study of social connection and shared experiences, participants who interacted with a confederate who shared their interests are the experimental group; those who interacted with a confederate who did not share their interests are the control group.

Many questions can be addressed both through experimental and correlational research. To see how experimental and correlational research can illuminate the relations between variables, check out the Intersection.

QUASI-EXPERIMENTAL DESIGNS

Another approach to experimental research is to use a *quasi-experimental design*. As the prefix *quasi-* ("as if") suggests, this type of design is similar to an experiment, but it is not quite the same thing. The key difference is that a quasi-experimental design does not randomly assign participants to conditions because such assignment is either impossible or unethical (West, Cham, & Liu, 2014).

Quasi-experimental designs might be used to study groups that already exist—say, soldiers who have seen combat versus those who have not, children whose school was destroyed by a tornado versus those in a neighboring town where the school was not affected, or adults who are single, divorced, or remarried. In a quasi-experimental design, researchers examine participants in varying groups, but their group assignment is not determined randomly.

- **experimental group** The participants in an experiment who receive the drug or other treatment under study; those who are exposed to the change that the independent variable represents.

- **control group** The participants in an experiment who are as much like the experimental group as possible and who are treated in every way like the experimental group except for a manipulated factor, the independent variable.

INTERSECTION

Motivation and Social Psychology: Can a Sense of Purpose Buffer Distress in the Face of Diversity?

Today's world is one of enormous diversity. Although that diversity adds richness to our existence, it can also be a challenge. Some individuals may find interacting with those who differ from them to be confusing or distressing. Are there ways to buffer these experiences?

Two studies examined the possibility that having a strong sense of purpose might allow people to avoid these feelings of distress (Burrow & Hill, 2013). These studies are notable not only because they include correlational and experimental designs, but also because they show how clever psychologists can be in choosing research settings and operational definitions. Both studies involved the emotional experiences of passengers on an urban trains. In each study, the ethnic composition of the passengers was recorded by a research assistant on the train. In addition, participants in the studies rated their emotional feelings throughout the ride. In the first study, prior to getting on the train, participants completed a

© David Grossman/Alamy Stock Photo

questionnaire measuring their sense of purpose in life. As suspected, greater ethnic diversity on the train was related to passengers feeling more negative, but this was not the case for those with a high sense of purpose. Among those who believed their lives were purposeful, ethnic diversity did not lead to greater stress (Burrow & Hill, 2013).

Notice, though, that the first study was correlational. This means that although the results support the idea that purpose may buffer against stress, the findings do not demonstrate a causal connection.

Do you have a strong sense of purpose?

To address this issue, in the second study the researchers manipulated a sense of purpose. To do this, they randomly assigned participants to one of two groups prior to them getting on the train. The experimental group was told to write about the topic, "What does it mean to have a sense of purpose in life?" The control group was instructed to write about the last movie they saw. Remember that random assignment means that the two groups are equivalent prior to the manipulation. Then the participants boarded the train and reported on their emotions just as in the first study. The results of the second study demonstrated that the control group showed increasing negative mood as the train passengers became more diverse. In contrast, for those in the purpose group, negative mood remained low throughout the journey.

This research shows how correlational and experimental research can be brought together to address important research questions. Note that each type of method has its own strengths and weaknesses. Without the correlational study, we might question whether a naturally occurring sense of purpose could have the same effect as the experimental manipulation. Without the experiment, we would not be able to state that sense of purpose causes decreased distress.

For example, researchers interested in the influence of using online learning tools on performance in introductory psychology classes might compare students from two different sections of a class—one that uses online tools and one that does not. Because students typically choose which section of a course they take, the experimenter cannot randomly assign them to sections. Assessing differences between the groups might provide information about the merits of online learning tools. However, there might be confounding factors (whether students are morning people or not, for example) that could account for differences between the groups. Although quasi-experimental designs are common, it is important to keep in mind that they do not allow for the strong causal conclusions that can be drawn from true experiments that employ random assignment (West, Cham, & Liu, 2014).

SOME CAUTIONS ABOUT EXPERIMENTAL RESEARCH

Earlier we noted that psychologists are interested in drawing conclusions not just from a single study but from a whole body of research on a given topic. We discussed the idea that if a finding is replicated (that is, repeated again and again), it is considered *reliable;* we would expect that this finding will stand the test of time. However, even a reliable finding may not be *valid*.

Validity refers to the soundness of the conclusions that a researcher draws from an experiment. In experimental designs, there are two broad types of validity that matter. The first is **external validity,** which refers to the degree to which an experimental design actually reflects the real-world issues it is supposed to address. Often, operationalizing variables in the lab involves creating analogues to real-world experiences. External validity is concerned with how well those analogues represent the real-world contexts they are meant to represent. In other words, the researcher assesses external validity to see whether the experimental methods and the results *generalize*—whether they apply—to the real world.

● **external validity** The degree to which an experimental design actually reflects the real-world issues it is supposed to address.

Imagine, for example, that a researcher is interested in the influence of stress (the independent variable) on creative problem solving (the dependent variable). The researcher randomly assigns individuals to be blasted with loud noises at random times during the session (the high-stress or experimental group) or to complete the task in relative quiet (the control group). As the task, the researcher gives all participants a chance to be creative by asking them to list every use they can think of for a cardboard box. Counting up the number of uses that people list, the researcher discovers that those in the high-stress group generated fewer uses of the box. This finding might seem to indicate that stress reduces creativity. In considering the external validity of this study, however, we might appropriately ask some questions: How similar are the blasts of loud, random noises to the stresses people experience every day? Is listing uses for a cardboard box really an indicator of creativity? Even if a large number of laboratory studies demonstrated this effect, we would still need to consider whether this result generalizes to the real world. We are asking, in other words, if these operational definitions do a good job of reflecting the real-world processes they are supposed to represent.

● **internal validity** The degree to which changes in the dependent variable are due to the manipulation of the independent variable.

The second type of validity is **internal validity,** which refers to the degree to which changes in the dependent variable are genuinely due to the manipulation of the independent variable. In the case of internal validity, we want to know whether the experimental methods are free from biases and logical errors that may render the results suspect.

Although experimental research is a powerful tool, it requires safeguards. Expectations and biases can, and sometimes do, tarnish results, as we now consider.

Experimenter Bias Experimenters may subtly (and often unknowingly) influence their research participants. **Experimenter bias** occurs when the experimenter's expectations influence the outcome of the research. No one designs an experiment without wanting meaningful results. Consequently, experimenters can sometimes subtly communicate to participants what they want the participants to do. A **demand characteristic** is any aspect of a study that communicates to participants how the experimenter wants them to behave. The influence of experimenter expectations can be very difficult to avoid.

● **experimenter bias** The influence of the experimenter's expectations on the outcome of the research.

● **demand characteristic** Any aspect of a study that communicates to the participants how the experimenter wants them to behave.

In a classic study, Robert Rosenthal (1966) turned college students into experimenters. He randomly assigned the participants rats from the same litter. Half of the students were told that their rats were "maze bright," whereas the other half were told that their rats were "maze dull." The students then conducted experiments to test their rats' ability to navigate mazes. The results were stunning. The so-called maze-bright rats were more successful than the maze-dull rats at running the mazes. The only explanation for the results is that the college students' expectations, conveyed in their behaviors, affected the rats' performance.

Often the participants in psychological studies are not rats but people. Imagine that you are an experimenter, and you know that a participant is going to be exposed to disgusting pictures in a study. Is it possible that you might treat the person differently than you would if you were about to show him photos of cute kittens? The reason experimenter bias is important is that it introduces systematic differences between the experimental group and the control groups; this means that we cannot know if those who looked at disgusting pictures were more, say, upset because of the pictures or because of different treatment by the experimenter.

Like third variables in correlational research, these systematic biases are called *confounds*. In experimental research, confounds are factors that "ride along" with the experimental manipulation, systematically and undesirably influencing the dependent variable. Experimenter bias, demand characteristics, and confounds may all lead to biased results.

Research Participant Bias and the Placebo Effect   Like experimenters, research participants may have expectations about what they are supposed to do and how they should behave, and these expectations may affect the results of experiments (Gravetter & Forzano, 2012). **Research participant bias** occurs when the behavior of research participants during the experiment is influenced by how they think they are supposed to behave or by their expectations about what is happening to them.

One example of the power of participant expectations is the placebo effect. The **placebo effect** occurs when participants' expectations, rather than the experimental treatment, produce a particular outcome. Participants in a drug study might be assigned to an experimental group that receives a pill containing an actual painkiller or to a control group that receives a placebo pill. A **placebo** is a harmless substance that has no physiological effect. This placebo is given to participants in a control group so that they are treated identically to the experimental group except for the active agent—in this case, the painkiller. Giving individuals in the control group a placebo pill allows researchers to determine whether changes in the experimental group are due to the active drug agent and not simply to participants' expectations.

Another way to ensure that neither the experimenter's nor the participants' expectations affect the outcome is to design a **double-blind experiment.** In this design, neither the experimenter administering the treatment nor the participants are aware of which participants are in the experimental group and which are in the control group until the results are calculated. This setup ensures that the experimenter cannot, for example, make subtle gestures signaling who is receiving a drug and who is not. A double-blind study allows researchers to distinguish the specific effects of the independent variable from the possible effects of expectations—both the experimenter's and the participants—about the study.

● **research participant bias** In an experiment, the influence of participants' expectations, and of their thoughts on how they should behave, on their behavior.

● **placebo effect** A phenomenon in which the expectation of the participants, rather than actual treatment, produces an outcome.

● **placebo** In a drug study, a harmless substance that has no physiological effect, given to participants in a control group so that they are treated identically to the experimental group except for the active agent.

● **double-blind experiment** An experimental design in which neither the experimenter nor the participants are aware of which participants are in the experimental group and which are in the control group until the results are calculated.

Advertisements for prescription drugs usually describe not only the side effects on people taking the actual drug but also the effects experienced by individuals receiving a placebo.

Image courtesy of The Advertising Archives

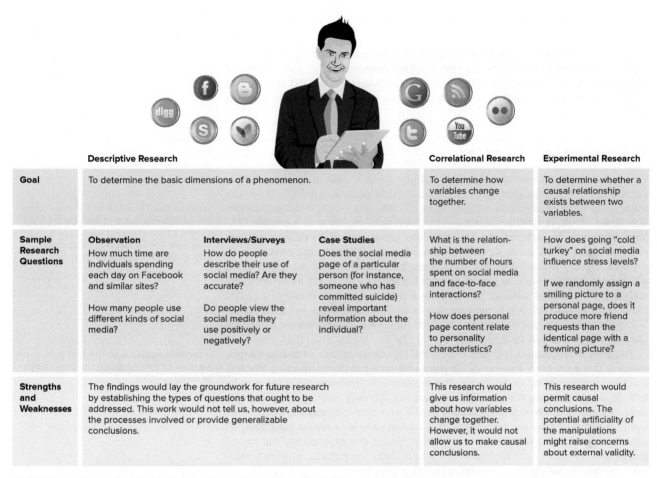

	Descriptive Research			Correlational Research	Experimental Research
Goal	To determine the basic dimensions of a phenomenon.			To determine how variables change together.	To determine whether a causal relationship exists between two variables.
Sample Research Questions	**Observation** How much time are individuals spending each day on Facebook and similar sites? How many people use different kinds of social media?	**Interviews/Surveys** How do people describe their use of social media? Are they accurate? Do people view the social media they use positively or negatively?	**Case Studies** Does the social media page of a particular person (for instance, someone who has committed suicide) reveal important information about the individual?	What is the relationship between the number of hours spent on social media and face-to-face interactions? How does personal page content relate to personality characteristics?	How does going "cold turkey" on social media influence stress levels? If we randomly assign a smiling picture to a personal page, does it produce more friend requests than the identical page with a frowning picture?
Strengths and Weaknesses	The findings would lay the groundwork for future research by establishing the types of questions that ought to be addressed. This work would not tell us, however, about the processes involved or provide generalizable conclusions.			This research would give us information about how variables change together. However, it would not allow us to make causal conclusions.	This research would permit causal conclusions. The potential artificiality of the manipulations might raise concerns about external validity.

FIGURE 3 **Psychology's Research Methods Applied to Studying Social Media** Psychologists can apply different methods of study to the same phenomenon. The popularity of social media has opened up a host of new research questions for psychologists.

Applications of the Three Types of Research

All three types of research—descriptive, correlational, and experimental—can be used to address the same topic (Figure 3). For instance, various researchers have used different research methods to explore the role of intensely positive experiences in human functioning, as follows.

Abraham Maslow believed that people who were the healthiest and the happiest were capable of having intense moments of awe; he used the descriptive case study approach (1971) to examine the role of "peak experiences" in the lives of such individuals, who seemed to enjoy the best of life. In contrast, Dan McAdams (2001) used correlational research to probe individuals' descriptions of their most powerful positive experiences. He found that individuals who were motivated toward warm interpersonal experiences tended to mention such experiences as the best memories of their lives. Finally, experimental researchers have also investigated this topic by randomly assigning individuals to write about their most intensely positive experiences for a few minutes each day for two or three days. Those who wrote about emotional and happy topics experienced enhanced positive mood as well as fewer physical illnesses two months later, as compared to individuals in control groups who wrote about topics that were not emotional (Burton & King, 2004, 2009). So, researchers coming from many different methodological perspectives can address the same topic, leading to different but valuable contributions to knowledge.

test yourself

1. Define descriptive, correlational, and experimental research.
2. Explain why correlation is not the same as causation.
3. What is the difference between an experimental group and a control group?

3. RESEARCH SAMPLES AND SETTINGS

Regardless of whether a study is correlational or experimental, among the important decisions to be made about collecting data is whom to choose as the participants and where to conduct the research. Will the participants be people or animals? Will they be children, adults, or both? Where will the research take place—in a lab or in a natural setting?

The Research Sample

When psychologists conduct a study, they usually want to be able to draw conclusions that will apply to a larger group of people than the participants they actually study. The entire group about which the investigator wants to draw conclusions is the **population.** The subset of the population chosen by the investigator for study is a **sample.** The researcher might be interested only in a particular group, such as all children who are gifted and talented, all young women who embark on science and math careers, or all gay men. The key is that the sample studied must be representative of the population to which the investigator wants to generalize his or her results. That is, the researcher might study only 100 gifted adolescents, but he or she wants to apply these results to all gifted and talented adolescents. A representative sample for the United States would reflect the U.S. population's age, socioeconomic status, ethnic origins, marital status, geographic location, religion, and so forth.

● **population** The entire group about which the investigator wants to draw conclusions.

● **sample** The subset of the population chosen by the investigator for study.

To mirror the population as closely as possible, the researcher uses a **random sample,** a sample that gives every member of the population an equal chance of being selected. Random sampling improves the chances that the sample is representative of the population. In actual practice, however, random sampling typically only *approximates* this ideal—for example, by randomly sampling people who have telephones or people who live in a particular town or state. Note that a random sample is *not* the same thing as random assignment. Random assignment is about making sure experimental and control groups are equivalent, and a random sample is about selecting participants from a population so that the sample is representative of that population.

● **random sample** A sample that gives every member of the population an equal chance of being selected.

In selecting a sample, researchers must strive to minimize bias, including gender bias (Hyde & Else-Quest, 2013). Because psychology is the scientific study of human behavior, it should pertain to *all* humans, and so the participants in psychological studies ought to be representative of humanity as a whole. Early research in the field often included just the male experience—not only because the researchers themselves were

The research sample might include a particular group, such as all gay men or all women runners.

typically male but also because the participants too were usually male (Matlin, 2012). For a long time, the human experience studied by psychologists was primarily the male experience.

There is also a growing realization that psychological research needs to include more people from diverse ethnic groups (Leong & others, 2013). Because a great deal of psychological research involves college student participants, individuals from groups that have not had as many educational opportunities have not been strongly represented in that research. Given the fact that individuals from diverse ethnic groups have been excluded from psychological research for so long, we might reasonably conclude that people's real lives are more varied than past research data have indicated.

These issues are important because scientists want to be able to predict human behavior broadly speaking, not just the behavior of male, non-Latino White college students. Imagine if policymakers planned their initiatives for a wide range of Americans based on research derived from only a small group of individuals from a particular background. What might the results be?

The Research Setting

All three types of research you studied in the preceding section can take place in different physical settings. The setting of the research does not determine the type of research it is. Common settings include the research laboratory and natural settings.

Because psychology researchers often want to control as many aspects of the situation as possible, they conduct much of their research in a laboratory—a controlled setting with many of the complex factors of the real world, including potential confounding factors, removed. Although laboratory research provides a great deal of control, doing research in the laboratory has drawbacks. First, it is almost impossible to conduct research in the lab without the participants knowing they are being studied. Second, the laboratory setting is not the real world and therefore can cause the participants to behave unnaturally. A third drawback of laboratory research is that individuals who are willing to go to a university laboratory may not be representative of groups from diverse cultural backgrounds. Those who are unfamiliar with university settings and with the idea of "helping science" may be intimidated by the setting. Fourth, some aspects of the mind and behavior are difficult if not impossible to examine in the laboratory.

Natural settings and laboratories are common locales for psychological studies. (first) *Jane Goodall, who specializes in animal behavior, has carried out extensive research on chimpanzees in natural settings. Her work has contributed a great deal to our understanding of these intelligent primates.* (second) *Barbara L. Fredrickson (on the right in the photo, pointing to the monitor) is a psychologist at the University of North Carolina, Chapel Hill, whose work investigates topics such as positive emotions and human flourishing. Here she conducts a laboratory study.*

Research can also take place in a natural setting. **Naturalistic observation** is viewing behavior in a real-world setting. Psychologists conduct naturalistic observation at sporting events, child-care centers, work settings, shopping malls, and other places that people frequent. If you wanted to study the level of civility on your campus for a research project, most likely you would include naturalistic observation of how people treat one another in gathering places such as the cafeteria and the library reading room. In another example of a natural setting, researchers who use survey methods are increasingly relying on web-based assessments that allow participants to complete the measures using the Internet.

The type of research a psychologist conducts, the operational definitions of the variables of interest, and the choice of sample and setting are decisions that ideally are guided by the research question itself. However, sometimes these decisions represent a compromise between the psychologist's key objective (for example, to study a representative sample of Americans) and the available resources (for instance, a sample of 100 college students). For a closer look at the process of conducting an experiment in a real-world setting, check out the Psychological Inquiry.

- **naturalistic observation** The observation of behavior in a real-world setting.

test yourself

1. What is a population in a research study? What is a sample?
2. What is the difference between a random sample and random assignment?
3. What are two common physical settings for research?

4. ANALYZING AND INTERPRETING DATA

Once psychologists collect data, whether in a lab or a natural setting, it is time to analyze and interpret those data. For this task they use *statistics,* mathematical methods for reporting data (Privitera, 2016). There are two basic categories of statistics: descriptive statistics, which are used to describe and summarize data, and inferential statistics, which are used to draw conclusions about those data.

Psychology students are sometimes surprised to learn that a statistics course is often a requirement for the major. In this section, as we look at how psychologists analyze and interpret research data, you will get a sense of the importance of math in the science of psychology.

Descriptive Statistics

Most psychological studies generate considerable numerical data. Simply listing all of the scores (or other measures) generated by a study—for each individual in the study—is not very meaningful. **Descriptive statistics** are the mathematical procedures researchers have developed to describe and summarize sets of data in a meaningful way. Descriptive statistics reveal the "big picture"—the overall characteristics of the data and the variation among them.

- **descriptive statistics** Mathematical procedures that are used to describe and summarize sets of data in a meaningful way.

MEASURES OF CENTRAL TENDENCY

A *measure of central tendency* is a single number that indicates the overall characteristics of a set of data. The three measures of central tendency are the mean, the median, and the mode.

Most quantitative techniques in psychological science begin with the mean. The **mean** is what people often call the average. The mean is calculated by adding all the scores in a set of scores and then dividing by the number of scores. As a good indicator of the central tendency for a group of scores, the mean is the measure that is used most often. When your instructors provide students with their exam grades, they might mention the test mean, because this average gives the class a general idea of how the group performed.

- **mean** A measure of central tendency that is the average for a sample.

psychological *inquiry*

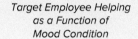

Target Employee Helping
as a Function of
Mood Condition

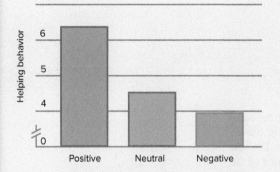

Adapted from Forgas, Dunn, & Granland, 2008.

©Ted S. Warren/AP Images

Experimentation in a Natural Setting

A team of social psychologists was interested in studying how mood influences helping behavior in the real world (Forgas, Dunn, & Granland, 2008). They hypothesized that, especially among the less experienced members of a sales staff, mood would guide behavior, so that happy salespeople would be most helpful to customers and unhappy salespeople less so. The researchers conducted an experiment in a Target department store, as follows.

First, the experimenters trained two confederates. The first confederate was in charge of manipulating the employees' mood across three conditions:

■ In the *positive mood condition,* the confederate said, "I just wanted to let someone know that I am so impressed with the service at this store! The store looks great, and the staff is so nice. I was able to get what I wanted and will be coming back to this store again."

■ In the *negative mood condition,* the confederate said, "I just wanted to let someone know that I am so disappointed with the service at this store. The store looks terrible, and the staff is rude. I couldn't get anything I wanted and won't be coming back here again."

■ In the *neutral mood condition,* the confederate simply observed, "Interesting, I have been coming here quite regularly, and this store seems always the same, nothing much changes."

Employees were chosen randomly by the confederate and were randomly assigned to the conditions.

Then, after the first confederate interacted with the employees, the second confederate, who was blind to the mood procedure (meaning unaware of the mood condition for each participant), approached the employees individually and asked, "Excuse me, could you tell me where I could find the book *The White Bear*?" This second confederate surreptitiously recorded (1) the number of helpful responses, (2) the number of actual attempts to help, and (3) the time spent helping. These three values were averaged to create an overall helpfulness score. (If the salesperson saw the confederate jotting things down, the confederate pretended to be checking a shopping list.) The researchers were also interested in how workers' experience level influenced the results.

The figure shows the results for the less-experienced sales staff. As you can see, those in a positive mood were most helpful. The researchers concluded that mood caused these differences. Now, answer these questions to see how much you remember about experimental design.

1. Despite the natural setting, this was an experiment. Why?

2. What was the independent variable and what was its operational definition?

3. What was the dependent variable and what was its operational definition?

4. Why is it important that the second confederate was "blind" to the mood condition?

5. Why were the employees assigned to mood condition randomly?

6. The store management was aware of the study, but the employees were not. Do you think the experiment was ethical? Why or why not?

The mean is not so helpful, however, when a group of scores contains a few extreme scores, especially if the number of cases in the group is small. Consider the annual earnings for the two groups of five people shown in the table below.

Group 1		Group 2	
	$19,000		$19,000
	19,000		19,000
	23,000		23,000
	24,000		24,000
	25,000		45,000,000
Mean	$22,000	Mean	$9,017,000
Median	$23,000	Median	$23,000
Mode	$19,000	Mode	$19,000

Group 1 lists the earnings of five ordinary people. Group 2 is composed of the earnings of four ordinary people plus the approximate earnings of movie director Steven Spielberg. Now look at the means that have been calculated for the two groups. The vast difference between them is due to the one extreme score. In such a situation, one of the other two measures of central tendency, the median or the mode, would give a more accurate picture of the data overall.

The **median** is the score that falls exactly in the middle of the distribution of scores after they have been arranged (or ranked) from highest to lowest. When you have an odd number of scores (say, five or seven), the median is the score with the same number of scores above it as below it. In the table above, each group has a median income of $23,000. Notice that, unlike the mean, the median is unaffected by extreme scores. The medians are the same for both groups ($23,000), but their means are extremely different ($22,000 versus $9,017,000). Of course, if there is an even number of scores, there is no "middle" score. This problem is dealt with by averaging the scores that share the middle location.

● **median** A measure of central tendency that is the middle score in a sample.

The **mode** is the score that occurs most often in a dataset. In our earnings example, the mode is $19,000, which occurs twice in each group. All of the other annual incomes occur only once. The mode is the least used measure of central tendency. Yet the mode can be particularly useful, for example, in cases in which information is desired about preference or popularity. Consider a teacher who wants to know which child is the most popular or the least popular in her classroom. She might create a questionnaire and ask students which of their classmates they like the most or the least. The most frequently nominated child would be the mode in these instances.

● **mode** A measure of central tendency that is the most common score in a sample.

Although the mode and the median of a dataset can provide useful information, the most commonly used measure of central tendency in psychological research is the mean. As you will see, the mean is also a key component of calculating other important descriptive statistics—measures of dispersion.

MEASURES OF DISPERSION

In addition to revealing the central characteristics of a sample, descriptive statistics can also give us *measures of dispersion,* which describe how much the scores in a sample differ from one another. That is, these measures give us a sense of the spread of scores, or how much variability exists in the data. Like measures of central tendency, measures of dispersion involve a single number that characterizes a dataset. But although measures of central tendency involve numbers that tell us about the scores in that dataset, measures of dispersion tell us about the differences among those scores. Let's look at some common ways that researchers measure dispersion.

© Cyberstock/Alamy

● **range** A measure of dispersion that is the difference between the highest and lowest scores.

● **standard deviation** A measure of dispersion that indicates how much the scores in a sample differ from the mean in the sample.

To begin, suppose that four students rate their positive mood on a scale from 1 (not at all positive) to 7 (extremely positive), as follows:

Positive Mood

Sarah	7
Sun Mee	6
Josh	2
Rodney	5

(You might note that the mean for these data is 20/4, or 5.) One common measure of dispersion is the **range,** which is the distance between the highest and the lowest scores. In the example above, the range in positive mood is 5 (that is, the highest score, 7, minus the lowest score, 2). Generally speaking, the range is a rather simplistic estimate of the variability within a group of scores. Because the range takes into account only the lowest and highest scores, it can produce a misleading picture of how different the scores in the dataset actually are. Note that for positive mood, most people in the example have fairly similar scores, but using the range alone gives the impression that scores are widely dispersed.

A more informative measure of dispersion, and the one most commonly used in psychological research, is the standard deviation. The **standard deviation** measures how much scores vary, on average, around the mean of the sample. There is a little hitch, however. One of the mathematical properties of the mean is that if you add up each person's difference from the mean, the sum will always be 0. So, we cannot calculate the average difference (or deviation) from the mean and get a meaningful answer.

To get around this problem, we take each person's difference from the mean and multiply it by itself (or square it). This removes the negative numbers, and the sum of these differences will no longer equal 0. We add these squared deviations together and then divide by the number of cases (minus 1). Finally, we take the square root of that number (to get rid of the squaring we did earlier). Essentially, then, the standard deviation is the square root of the average squared deviation from the mean. The smaller the standard deviation, the less variability in the dataset. A small standard deviation indicates that, on average, scores are close to the mean.

The following table presents the information needed to calculate the standard deviation for the positive mood ratings given above.

Participant	Rating	A Difference from the mean (5)	B *Squared* difference from the mean (5)	C
Sarah	7	2	4	
Sun Mee	6	1	1	
Josh	2	−3	9	
Rodney	5	0	0	
MEAN = $\frac{(7 + 6 + 2 + 5)}{4}$ = **5.0**		Sum of this column = 0	Sum of these differences = 4 + 1 + 9 + 0 = 14	

Column A presents the ratings by each participant. Column B shows the differences of these scores from the mean (5). Notice that if we add up column B, the answer is 0. Column C shows the squared deviations from the mean for each participant. Adding up those squared differences, we get 14. Next, we divide 14 by the number of participants minus 1, in this case 14 divided by 3, which is 4.67, and then we take the square root of that number, which is 2.16. This is the standard deviation of our sample, which, compared to the range of 5, tells us that the group is actually fairly closely arranged around the mean.

The mean and standard deviation together yield a lot of information about a sample. Indeed, given the raw scores, the means, and the standard deviations of two variables, we can calculate the correlation coefficient in no time. The correlation coefficient is not a descriptive statistic but rather an inferential statistic, our next topic.

Inferential Statistics

Imagine that, inspired by the research of LeeAnne Harker and Dacher Keltner on college yearbooks (see earlier in this chapter), you conduct a study on the relationship between expressions of positive emotion and interpersonal success. In your project, you video job candidates being interviewed, code the videos for Duchenne smiling by the candidates, and document which of the job seekers were called back for a second interview. Let's say you calculate that the mean number of smiles for candidates who were not called back is 3.5, and the mean number of smiles for candidates who were called back is 6.5. So, those who were called back generated, on average, 3 more smiles than those who were not called back. Does that difference matter? It seems pretty big, but is it big enough? Could we have obtained the same difference simply by chance?

To draw conclusions about differences we observe in studies, we want to know that the difference is likely to be one that can be replicated or found consistently in a variety of studies. Inferential statistics are the tools that help us to state whether a difference is unlikely to be the result of chance. More specifically, **inferential statistics** are the mathematical methods used to indicate whether the data sufficiently support a research hypothesis (Privitera, 2016). A psychologist conducting a study would certainly calculate the means and standard deviations to describe the sample, but in order to *test predictions* about that sample, the researcher needs inferential statistics.

The logic behind inferential statistics is relatively simple. Inferential statistics yield a statement of probability about the differences observed between two or more groups; this probability statement gives the odds that the observed differences were due simply to chance. In psychological research the standard is that if the odds are 5 out of 100 (or .05) or less that the differences are due to chance, the results are considered *statistically significant*. In statistical language, this is referred to as the .05 level of statistical significance, or the .05 *confidence level*. Put another way, statistical significance means that the differences observed between two groups are large enough that it is highly unlikely that those differences are merely due to chance. The .05 level of statistical significance is considered the minimum level of probability that scientists will accept for concluding that the differences observed are real, thereby supporting a hypothesis.

Recall that although we study a sample, we typically wish to generalize our findings to a population. Inferential statistics are the bridge between a sample and a population, because they tell us the likelihood that the results we found with a sample reflect differences in the larger population. It makes sense that the larger our sample is, the more likely it is to represent that population. Thus, significance tests are based in part on the number of cases in a sample. The higher the number of cases, the easier it is to get statistical significance. As a result, with a very large sample, even very small differences may be significant.

However, statistical significance is not the same thing as real-world significance. Even if a difference is found to be statistically significant, its real-world value remains to be evaluated by critically thinking scientists.

● **inferential statistics** Mathematical methods that are used to indicate whether the data sufficiently support a research hypothesis.

test yourself

1. What is meant by a measure of central tendency? Name three measures of central tendency.
2. What do measures of dispersion describe?
3. What does standard deviation measure?

5. CONDUCTING ETHICAL RESEARCH

Ethics is a crucial consideration for all science. This fact came to the fore in the aftermath of World War II, for example, when it became apparent that Nazi doctors had forced concentration camp prisoners to participate in experiments. These atrocities spurred scientists to develop a code of appropriate behavior—a set of principles about the treatment that participants in research have a right to expect. In general, ethical principles of

Being part of a research study can potentially lead to unintended consequences for the participants.
©Sam Edwards/Glow Images

research focus on balancing the rights of the participants with the rights of scientists to ask important research questions (Nestor & Schutt, 2015).

The issue of ethics in psychological research may affect you personally if at some point you participate in a study. In that event, you need to know your rights as a participant and the researchers' responsibilities in ensuring that these rights are safeguarded. Experiences in research can have unforeseen effects on people's lives.

Consider, for instance, that many researchers who are interested in close relationships might ask romantic couples to keep diaries tracking the quality of their interactions (Sherry & others, 2014). Might just paying close attention to this variable influence it?

Other researchers have couples come into the lab and discuss a topic that is a source of conflict in that relationship (Campbell & others, 2013). Such procedures are important to measuring how couples handle conflicts. But, could such interactions influence the couple long after the study is over? Researchers have a responsibility to anticipate the personal problems their study might cause and, at least, to inform the participants of the possible fallout.

Ethics comes into play in every psychological study. Even smart, conscientious students sometimes think that members of their church, athletes in the Special Olympics, or residents of the local nursing home present great samples for psychological research. Without proper permission, though, the most well-meaning and considerate researchers still violate the rights of the participants.

Ethics Guidelines

A number of guidelines have been developed to ensure that research is conducted ethically. At the base of all of these guidelines is the notion that people participating in psychological research should be no worse off coming out of the study than they were going in.

Today colleges and universities have a review board, typically called the *institutional review board (IRB)*, that evaluates the ethical nature of research conducted at their institutions. Proposed research plans must pass the scrutiny of a research ethics committee before the study can be initiated. In addition, the American Psychological Association (APA) has developed ethics guidelines for its members. The code of ethics instructs psychologists to protect their participants from mental and physical harm. The participants' best interests need to be kept foremost in the researcher's mind (Nestor & Schutt, 2015). The APA's guidelines address four important issues:

- *Informed consent:* All participants must know what their participation will involve and what risks might develop. For example, participants in a study on dating should be told beforehand that a questionnaire might stimulate thoughts about issues in their relationships that they have not considered. Participants also should be informed that in some instances a discussion of the issues might improve their relationships but that in others it might worsen the relationships and even end them. Even after informed consent is given, participants must retain the right to withdraw from the study at any time and for any reason.

- *Confidentiality:* Researchers are responsible for keeping all of the data they gather on individuals completely confidential and, when possible, completely anonymous. Confidential data are not the same as anonymous. When data are confidential, it is possible to link a participant's identity to his or her data.

- *Debriefing:* After the study has been completed, the researchers should inform the participants of its purpose and the methods they used. In most cases, the experimenters also can inform participants in a general manner beforehand about the purpose of the research without leading the participants to behave in a way that they think that the experimenters are expecting. When preliminary information about the study is likely to affect the results, participants can at least be debriefed after the study's completion.

■ *Deception:* This is an ethical issue that psychologists debate extensively. In some circumstances, telling the participants beforehand what the research study is about substantially alters the participants' behavior and invalidates the researcher's data. Recall the study of social connectedness and cardiovascular function described earlier. The participants were not told that the person they interacted with was a confederate following a script. Had the psychologist informed the participants beforehand that this was the case, the whole study would have been ruined. Thus, the researcher deceived participants about the purpose of the study (recall they were told it was about cardiovascular function and physical activity) as well as about the nature of their relationship with the interaction partner. In all cases of deception, the psychologist must ensure that the deception will not harm the participants and that the participants will be told the true nature of the study (will be debriefed) as soon as possible after the study is completed.

Note that when a study uses deception, the principle of informed consent is violated. This is why participants in studies involving deception should have the option of withdrawing consent after they find out what the study is actually about. To read more about the use of deception in psychological research, see the Critical Controversy.

The federal government also takes a role in ensuring that research involving human participants is conducted ethically. The Office for Human Research Protections is devoted to ensuring the well-being of participants in research studies. Over the years, the office has dealt with many challenging and controversial issues—among them, informed consent rules for research on mental disorders, regulations governing research on pregnant women and fetuses, and ethical issues regarding AIDS vaccine research.

Ethical Treatment of Research Animals

For generations, psychologists have used animals in some research. Animal studies have provided a better understanding of and solutions for many human problems (Dewsbury, 2013). Neal Miller (1985), who has made important discoveries about the effects of biofeedback on health, listed the following areas in which animal research has benefited humans:

©sidsnapper/Getty Images

■ Psychotherapy techniques and behavioral medicine for a variety of issues

■ Rehabilitation for neuromuscular disorders

■ Alleviation of the effects of stress and pain

■ Drug treatments for anxiety and severe mental illness

■ Methods for avoiding drug addiction and relapse

■ Treatments for premature infants to help them gain weight

■ Methods for alleviating memory deficits in elderly people

About 5 percent of APA members use nonhuman animals in their research. Rats and mice account for 90 percent of all psychological research with animals. It is true that researchers sometimes use procedures with animals that would be unethical with humans, but these scientists are guided by standards for housing, feeding, and maintaining the psychological and physical well-being of their animal subjects. Researchers are required to weigh potential benefits of the research against possible harm to the animal and to avoid inflicting unnecessary pain. In short, researchers must follow stringent ethical guidelines, whether animals or humans are the subjects in their studies.

test yourself

1. What two things do the ethical principles used in research seek to balance?
2. With respect to the participants in a study, what do the various ethical guidelines covering research all fundamentally seek to protect?
3. What four key issues do the APA's ethics guidelines address?

CRITICAL CONTROVERSY

Is It Ethical to Use Deception in Research?

Imagine that you are participating in an experiment. The experimenter tells you that the study concerns visual perception. You will be shown a series of slides that show dots on the right or left of a line. Your job is to push one of two buttons indicating whether you see more dots on the right or the left side of the line. The experimenter says that you will receive 5 cents for each time you say there are more dots on the left and 50 cents for each time you say there are more dots on the right side. As the task continues, there are some trials when it is obvious there are more dots on the left. But responding honestly to the trials will cost you 45 cents. What would you do?

After you complete the visual perception task, the experimenter tells you that this study was actually not about visual perception at all. Instead, it was about *lying*. This experiment, which was in fact conducted in real life by Maryam Kouchaki and Isaac Smith (2014), tested the prediction that people will be more likely to lie in the afternoon (when they are tired from a long day) compared to the morning (when they are fully rested). The researchers found that people were more likely to lie in the afternoon than the morning.

Certainly, this interesting study has implications for understanding ethical behaviors. Many real-world situations involve unethical behaviors that occur because people have less energy to devote to self-control. The role of something as simple as time of day on moral behavior is an important question for scientists to probe.

Yet consider the irony implicit in a study like this. A study about *lying*, an unethical behavior, employed *deception*. A study on lying involved lying to participants. Is that really okay?

Deception in psychological research can range from deception by omission to active deception. *Deception by omission* means not telling participants what a study is really about. *Active deception* means misleading participants about what is going on in a study. Active deception might include, for example, giving participants false feedback about their performance on a task or leading them to believe that a confederate is just another participant in the study.

The use of deception in research has been criticized on a variety of grounds (Hertwig & Ortmann, 2008; Kimmel, 2012). First, religions and cultures around the world regard lying as morally wrong. We do make exceptions, of course, in situations that call for "little white lies." Are psychological studies also an exception to this rule?

Second, using deception in psychological research is criticized because of its influence on availability of naive participants. Once individuals have been deceived in a study, they may be less likely to believe researchers in later studies, even when no deception is involved, threatening the validity of future studies (Hertwig & Ortmann, 2008). Such a possibility has led to a general prohibition against deception in experiments in economics (Ariely & Norton, 2007).

U.S. Mint

Finally, deception in psychological research may erode public trust in the science of psychology itself (Kimmel, 2012). If people believe psychological researchers regularly engage in unethical behavior, why should they believe anything these scholars have to say?

As you continue your journey through introductory psychology, you will encounter many studies that use deception. The deception can be as substantial as leading people to believe they are administering harmful electrical shocks to another person (in classic and controversial research by Stanley Milgram, which we will review in the chapter "Social Psychology"). Researchers who employ deception in their studies must be able to justify lying to participants, because doing so is vital to the scientific merit of their work (Benham, 2008).

Although it might seem like fun to fool people, psychological researchers regard deception as a serious issue and employ it only when no other option would allow them to ask the questions they seek to answer.

WHAT DO YOU THINK?
- How do you feel about the use of deception in psychological research?
- If you participated in a study and later found out it involved deception, would that experience change your perspective about participating in future studies? Why or why not?

6. THINKING CRITICALLY ABOUT PSYCHOLOGICAL RESEARCH

Not all psychological information presented for public consumption comes from professionals with excellent credentials and reputations at colleges or universities or in applied mental health settings (Norcross & others, 2013; Stanovich, 2013). Because journalists, television reporters, online bloggers, and other media personnel are not usually trained in psychological research, they often have trouble sorting through the widely varying material they find and making sound decisions about the best information to present to the public. In addition, the media often focus on sensationalistic and dramatic psychological findings to capture public attention.

Even when the media present the results of excellent research, they sometimes have trouble accurately informing people about the findings and their implications for people's lives. *The Science of Psychology* is dedicated to carefully introducing, defining, and elaborating on key concepts and issues, research, and clinical findings. The media, however, do not have the luxury of so much time and space to detail and specify the limitations and qualifications of research. In the end, *you* have to take responsibility for evaluating media reports on psychological research. To put it another way, you have to consume psychological information critically and wisely. Five guidelines follow.

Avoid Overgeneralizing Based on Little Information

Media reports of psychological information often leave out details about the nature of the sample used in a given study. Without information about sample characteristics—such as the number of participants, their sex, or their ethnic representation—it is wise to take research results with a grain of salt. For example, research that demonstrated the classic "fight or flight" response to stress has had great impact on how we understand the body's response to threatening situations. Yet the original work on this topic included only male participants (Taylor, 2011a). The implications of the lack of women in these studies will be explored in the chapter "Biological Foundations of Behavior".

Distinguish Between Group Results and Individual Needs

Just as we cannot generalize from a small group to all people, we also cannot apply conclusions from a group to an individual. When you learn about psychological research through the media, you might be disposed to apply the results to your life. It is important to keep in mind that statistics about a group do not necessarily represent each individual in the group equally well. Imagine, for example, taking a test in a class and being told that the class average was 75 percent, but you got 98 percent. It is unlikely that you would want the instructor to apply the group average to your score.

Sometimes consumers of psychological research can get the wrong idea about whether their own experience is "normal" if it does not match group statistics. New parents face this issue all the time. They read about developmental milestones that supposedly characterize an entire age group of children; one such milestone might be that most 2-year-olds are conversing with their parents. However, this group information does not necessarily characterize *all* children who are developing normally. Albert Einstein did not start talking until he was the ripe old age of 3.

© JGI/Jamie Grill/Blend Images/Getty Images

Look for Answers Beyond a Single Study

The media might identify an interesting piece of research and claim that its conclusions are phenomenal and have far-reaching implications. Although such pivotal studies do occur, they are rare. It is safer to assume that no single study will provide conclusive answers to an important question, especially answers that apply to all people. In fact, in most psychological domains that prompt many investigations, conflicting results are common. Answers to questions in research usually emerge after many scientists have conducted similar investigations that yield similar conclusions. Remember that you should not take one research study as the absolute, final answer to a problem, no matter how compelling the findings.

Avoid Attributing Causes Where None Have Been Found

Drawing causal conclusions from correlational studies is one of the most common mistakes the media make. For example, the results of the Nun Study described earlier suggest that happy people live longer. However, we cannot state that happiness *caused* them to live longer. When a true experiment has not been conducted—that is, when participants have not been randomly assigned to treatments or experiences—two variables might have only a non-causal relation to each other. Remember from the discussion of correlation earlier in the chapter that causal interpretations cannot be made when two or more factors are simply correlated. We cannot say that one causes the other. When you hear about correlational studies, be skeptical of words indicating causation until you know more about the particular research.

Consider the Source of Psychological Information

Studies conducted by psychologists are not automatically accepted by the rest of the research community. The researchers usually must submit their findings to an academic journal for review by their colleagues, who make a decision about whether to publish the paper, depending on its scientific merit. Although the quality of research and findings is not uniform among all psychology journals, in most cases journals submit the findings to far greater scrutiny than do the popular media.

Within the media, though, you can usually draw a distinction. The reports of psychological research in respected newspapers such as the *New York Times* and the *Washington Post,* as well as in credible magazines such as *Time* and the *Atlantic Monthly,* are far more trustworthy than reports in tabloids such as the *National Enquirer* and *Star* or online bloggers without scientific credentials. Yet, whatever the source—serious publication, tabloid, blog, or even academic journal—you are responsible for reading the details behind the reported findings and for analyzing the study's credibility.

7. THE SCIENTIFIC METHOD AND HEALTH AND WELLNESS

Throughout this book we examine a host of ways that psychological research has implications for health and wellness. In this chapter's concluding section, we focus on a research topic in which the scientific method has played a particularly important role in the conclusions drawn—the power of expressive writing to enhance health and wellness.

James Pennebaker has conducted a number of studies that converge on the same conclusion: that writing about one's deepest thoughts and feelings concerning one's most

test yourself

1. For what reasons are media reports on psychological studies often problematic?

2. Why is it wise to look beyond the conclusions of just one research study?

3. How does the submission of research findings to a respectable academic journal aid both researchers and the public?

traumatic life event leads to a number of health and well-being benefits (Pennebaker & Chung, 2007). This research began with a correlational study comparing two groups of individuals—those who had lost a spouse to suicide and those who had lost a spouse to an accident (Pennebaker & O'Heeron, 1984). The results of the study showed that survivors of spouse suicide were more likely to have gotten sick in the months after the death, compared to those whose spouses had died of an accident. Importantly, the difference was explained by the fact that individuals whose spouses had committed suicide were much less likely to talk about their loss, compared to the other participants.

These correlational findings led Pennebaker to wonder whether it might be possible to manipulate expressing one's thoughts and feelings about a traumatic event *experimentally* and thereby to receive the benefits of socially sharing the trauma. So, in subsequent studies, participants were randomly assigned to write about one of two topics—either the individual's most traumatic life event or a relatively uninteresting topic (for example, the person's plans for the day). Assignment of the specific topic was meant to control for the act of writing itself so that the control group was as much like the experimental group as possible (Baddeley & Pennebaker, 2009; Pennebaker & Graybeal, 2001).

The research of James Pennebaker of the University of Texas, Austin, explores the connections among traumatic life experience, expressive writing, physical and mental health, and work performance.

Courtesy of James W. Pennebaker, University of Texas. Photo by Marsha Miller.

The participants wrote about the same topic for three or four consecutive days for about 20 minutes each day. Weeks or months after writing, participants in the trauma writing group had better physical health than those in the control group. Since the first traumatic writing study, a host of researchers have replicated these effects, showing that writing about trauma is associated with superior immune function, better response to a vaccine, higher psychological well-being, better adjustment to starting college, and more quickly finding employment after being laid off from work (Lepore & Smyth, 2002; Pennebaker, 1997a, 1997b, 2004). Thus, we might conclude that documenting one's deepest thoughts and feelings about traumatic life events is necessary to attain the health benefits of writing.

Note, however, that the participants in the trauma group were not just writing about a trauma. They were also documenting an important personal experience. Thinking about these results in terms of the internal validity of the conclusions, we might ask if focusing on a trauma is the key ingredient in producing health benefits. Might there be other, less negative aspects of life that are equally meaningful and that might promote good health when they are the subject of personal writing? Indeed, subsequent research has shown that health benefits can emerge from writing about a variety of topics, including how one has grown from a negative experience (King & Miner, 2000; Low, Stanton, & Danoff-Burg, 2006), one's life dreams (King, 2001), and one's most intensely positive experiences (Burton & King, 2004, 2009). In one study, participants who wrote about either a traumatic life event or an extremely positive event for just 2 minutes a day over two days reported fewer illnesses a month later (Burton & King, 2008).

The body of evidence for the effects of expressive writing on health is substantial and has been subjected to two meta-analyses, the procedure described earlier in this chapter. These meta-analyses indicate that individuals who write over a period of days that are spaced apart tend to benefit most from writing and that feeling distressed while writing is not necessary to enjoy these benefits (Frattaroli, 2006; Smyth, 1998).

If you would like to explore the benefits of writing in your own life, use the simple guidelines below:

■ Find a quiet place to write.

■ Pick just one topic to explore through writing.

© Brand X Pictures

test yourself

1. Briefly describe Pennebaker's initial correlational study comparing two groups of individuals who had lost a spouse.
2. What did Pennebaker's subsequent experimental research show?
3. What does the accumulated body of evidence indicate about the effects of expressive writing on health?

■ Dedicate yourself to a few minutes of writing each day, perhaps writing once a week for a few weeks.

■ While writing, do not worry about punctuation, grammar, or spelling—just let yourself go and write about all of the thoughts, emotions, and feelings associated with the experience you are documenting.

■ If you feel that writing about something negative is not for you, try writing about your most positive life experiences, the people you care about, or all the things for which you feel grateful.

The long and growing literature on the effects of expressive writing on health demonstrates how research methods influence the conclusions that scientists reach and how the process of scientific research builds from one study to the next. This literature also demonstrates how psychological research is relevant to the daily life of everyone with a story to write—and how an individual can benefit from writing that story.

SUMMARY

1. PSYCHOLOGY'S SCIENTIFIC METHOD

Psychologists use the scientific method to address research questions. This method involves starting with a theory and then making observations, formulating hypotheses, testing these through empirical research, drawing conclusions, and evaluating the theory. The science of psychology is an ongoing conversation among scholars.

2. TYPES OF PSYCHOLOGICAL RESEARCH

Three types of research commonly used in psychology are descriptive research (finding out about the basic dimensions of some variable), correlational research (finding out if and how two variables change together), and experimental research (determining the causal relationship between variables). Descriptive research includes observation, surveys, interviews, and case studies. Correlational research often includes surveys and interviews as well as observation. Experimental research often occurs in a lab but can also be done in a natural setting.

In an experiment, the independent variable is manipulated to see if it produces changes in the dependent variable. An experiment involves comparing two groups: the experimental group (the one that receives the treatment or manipulation of the independent variable) and the control group (the comparison group or baseline that is equal to the experimental group in every way except for the independent variable). Experimental research relies on random assignment to ensure that the groups are roughly equivalent before the manipulation of the independent variable. Quasi-experimental designs are similar to experiments, but they do not involve random assignment of participants to groups.

3. RESEARCH SAMPLES AND SETTINGS

Two important decisions that must be made for psychological research are whom to study and where to study them. A sample is the group that participates in a study; a population is the group to which the researcher wishes to generalize the results. A random sample is the best way of ensuring that the sample reflects the population.

Research settings include both the laboratory and real-world, naturalistic contexts. The laboratory allows a great deal of control, but naturalistic settings may give a truer sense of natural behavior.

4. ANALYZING AND INTERPRETING DATA

Descriptive statistics are used to describe and summarize samples of data in a meaningful way. Two types of descriptive statistics are

measures of central tendency and measures of variability. Measures of central tendency are the mean (or the mathematical average), the median (the middle score), and the mode (the most common score). Measures of variability include the range (the difference between the highest and lowest scores) and the standard deviation (the square root of the average squared deviation from the mean).

Inferential statistics are used to draw conclusions about data. Inferential statistics aim to uncover statistical significance, which means that the differences observed between groups (or the correlation between variables) are unlikely to be the result of chance.

5. CONDUCTING ETHICAL RESEARCH

For all kinds of research, ethical treatment of participants is crucial. Participants should leave a psychological study no worse off than they were when they entered. Some guiding principles for ethical research in psychology include informed consent, confidentiality, debriefing (participants should be fully informed about the purpose of a study once it is over), and explaining the use of deception in a study. Researchers must follow stringent ethical guidelines, whether animals or humans are the subjects in their studies.

6. THINKING CRITICALLY ABOUT PSYCHOLOGICAL RESEARCH

In your everyday life and in introductory psychology, you will be exposed to psychological research findings. In approaching psychological research in the media, you should adopt the attitude of a scientist and critically evaluate the research presented. This means being careful to avoid overgeneralizing based on little information, realizing that group results may not apply to every individual, looking for answers beyond a single study, and avoiding attributing causation when none has been found. Finally, it is important to consider the source when you encounter research in the popular media.

7. THE SCIENTIFIC METHOD AND HEALTH AND WELLNESS

A great deal of psychological research has relevance to health and wellness. An example is research by James Pennebaker on the effects of expressive writing on health and well-being. This research has shown that individuals who are randomly assigned to write about a traumatic life event for a few minutes a day over three or four days show a host of health and well-being benefits compared to those in a control condition. Subsequent research has shown that these health benefits can be obtained by writing about positive life experiences and even just writing for a couple of minutes.

This research demonstrates how a research question can begin as a correlational study and then move to the laboratory to demonstrate causation. When many studies have been done on a topic, a meta-analysis can provide a sense of the overall importance of the results. This example also shows how psychological research can have important implications for everyday life.

key *terms*

case study or case history	empirical method	mean	random assignment
confederate	experiment	median	random sample
control group	experimental group	meta-analysis	range
correlational research	experimenter bias	mode	research participant bias
cross-sectional design	external validity	naturalistic observation	sample
demand characteristic	hypothesis	operational definition	standard deviation
dependent variable	independent variable	placebo	theory
descriptive research	inferential statistics	placebo effect	third variable problem
descriptive statistics	internal validity	population	variable
double-blind experiment	longitudinal design		

apply your *knowledge*

1. It's time to get out those old photos from the prom, wedding, or family reunion and see just how happy people were (or weren't). Look at some pictures from your own life and see who was genuinely smiling and who was faking it. Just cover the mouths with your finger—you can see who is happy from their eyes.

2. Is an old diary of yours hanging around somewhere? Pull it out and take a look at what you wrote. Count up your positive emotion words or negative emotion words. Are there themes in your diary from years ago that are still relevant to your life today? Does looking at your own diary change the way you might think about the results of the Nun Study? Explain.

3. What are some positive and negative correlations that you have observed in your own experience? What are some third variables that might explain these relationships? Do you think these relationships may be causal? How would you design an experiment to test that possibility?

4. In the next few days, look through several newspapers and magazines for reports about psychological research. Also notice what you find on the Internet and on television about psychology. Apply the guidelines for being a wise consumer of information about psychology to these media reports.

5. The opening of this chapter presented research on a difference-education program for college students. Design a replication of this work using a different population of participants. How might you study this phenomenon among middle-aged adults, elderly individuals, or children?

6. Pick a topic of interest to you and define the variables. Then list as many ways to operationalize the variables as you can. Come up with at least one behavioral measure of the variable. Would your topic be best studied using a correlational or an experimental method? How would you conduct the study?

CHAPTER 3

CHAPTER OUTLINE

Biological Foundations of Behavior

Finding the Secrets of Wisdom, in the Brain

As a graduate student in 2010, Tamar Gefen worked on a project involving adults who were in their 80s. These individuals, called SuperAgers, were special because their memory abilities were equal to or better than those of adults in their 50s. Administering tests and interviewing these folks was a delight, and Tamar found their resilience inspiring: "It takes wisdom to a whole new level" (quoted by Zimmer, 2015). Fast forward five years, and a number of the SuperAgers in the study have died. As part of the original project, they donated their remarkable brains to science. And now Tamar has the opportunity to study what made these individuals remarkable in a completely different way—by examining their brains for clues (Gefen & others, 2015).

What she and her colleagues have found has opened up a whole new mystery. The brains of the SuperAgers have an unusually large number of cells called von Economo neurons, which are densely packed in a band of the brain called the anterior cingulate cortex. Found in whales, apes, cows, and humans, von Economo neurons are stick-shaped, and they are quite a bit larger than other neurons. Their function is not well understood. Could these neurons reveal the secret of healthy cognitive aging? The researchers hope that it just might (Gefen & others, 2015).

The secrets of wisdom—the secrets of all of human behavior, thoughts, and feelings—lie in the incredible organ that is reading these words right now. Imagine: This intricate 3-pound structure that you are reading about is the engine that is doing the work of reading itself. The brain is at once the object of study and the reason we are able to study it. ●

PREVIEW

In this chapter, our focus is the biological foundations of human behavior. We review the essentials of what we know about the nervous system and its command center—the brain. We then look at how genetic processes influence who we are as individuals and how we behave. Finally, we explore the role of the brain and nervous system in the experience of stress and consider ways to unlock the brain's unique resources to better meet life's challenges and maintain health and well-being.

1. THE NERVOUS SYSTEM

● **nervous system** The body's electrochemical communication circuitry.

The **nervous system** is the body's electrochemical communication circuitry. The field that studies the nervous system is called *neuroscience*. The human nervous system is made up of billions of communicating nerve cells, and it is likely the most intricately organized aggregate of matter on the planet. A single cubic centimeter (about the size of a snack cube of cheese) of the human brain consists of well over 50 million nerve cells, each of which communicates with many other nerve cells in information-processing networks that make the most elaborate computer seem primitive.

Characteristics of the Nervous System

The brain and nervous system guide our interactions with the world around us, move the body through the world, and direct our adaptation to the environment. Several extraordinary characteristics allow the nervous system to command our behavior: complexity, integration, adaptability, and electrochemical transmission.

COMPLEXITY

The human brain and nervous system are enormously complex. This complexity is demonstrated in the orchestration of the billions of nerve cells in the brain—to allow you to talk, write, sing, dance, and think. This capacity is simply awe-inspiring. As you read *The Science of Psychology,* your brain is carrying out a multitude of functions, including seeing, reading, learning, and (we hope) breathing. Extensive assemblies of nerve cells participate in each of these activities, all at once.

INTEGRATION

The brain does an amazing job of pulling information together. Think of everything going on around you right now, as well as a number of processes happening in your body—like breathing, the digestion of your last meal, the healing of a cut. Somehow, you need to make sense of all of these various stimuli. Similarly, the shapes on this page are not simply splashes of ink but letters, and those letters compose words that make sense. It is your brain that draws your experiences together into a coherent whole. Sounds, sights, touches, tastes, and smells—the brain integrates all of these sensory inputs so that you can function in the world.

The nervous system has different levels and many different parts. Brain activity is integrated across these levels through countless interconnections of brain cells and extensive pathways that link different parts of the brain and body. Each

As we dance, write, play sports, talk, think, and connect with the world in countless other ways, the brain and the nervous system guide our every interaction, movement, and adaptation.

(first) © DreamPictures/Blend Images/Getty Images; (second) © Digital Vision/Getty Images

nerve cell communicates, on average, with 10,000 others, making an astronomical number of connections. The complexity of connections in the brain is one of its most notable features (Park & Friston, 2013). The evidence for these connections is observable, for example, when a loved one takes your hand. How does your brain know, and tell you, what has happened? Bundles of interconnected nerve cells relay information about the sensation in your hand through the nervous system in a very orderly fashion, all the way to the areas of the brain involved in recognizing that someone you love is holding your hand. Then the brain might send a reply and prompt your hand to give your loved one a little squeeze.

ADAPTABILITY

Think about all the different places human beings live or could live some day. People inhabit deserts where the average daily temperature is well over 100 degrees and frozen tundra where the temperature can be 100 below 0. People live in bustling cities and small rural communities. They hunt and farm and work online. Yet, in all these different places, people possess the same amazing engine, the brain, that helps them solve the problems of survival. If we send people to live on Mars, that same organ will be required to figure out how to exist there. Human beings need a brain that is ready to meet these varied challenges.

To survive, we must adapt to new conditions. The brain and nervous system together serve as our agent for adapting to the world. Although nerve cells reside in certain brain regions, they are not unchanging structures. They have a hereditary, biological foundation, but they are constantly adapting to changes in the body and the environment (Zich & others, 2015).

The term **plasticity** refers to the brain's special physical capacity for change. Although injuries to the brain can often produce devastating effects, sometimes the brain heals in ways that are extraordinary. For example, Jason Padgett, a young man who worked as a clerk at a futon store, was brutally attacked by muggers one night and suffered a concussion. During the months of recovery, Jason noticed a dramatic change in himself. A college dropout who had never been particularly interested in math, he suddenly began seeing the world as made up of intricate, mathematic patterns. And he discovered he had a special talent for creating artwork based on the arithmetic laws he saw everywhere in his world. During his recovery, Jason's brain seems to have unlocked capacities he had never known before (Karlinsky & Frost, 2012).

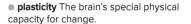
● **plasticity** The brain's special physical capacity for change.

Less dramatic examples of plasticity occur in all of us. Because of the brain's plasticity, it can change in response to experience. For example, you might believe that thinking is a mental process, not a physical one. Yet thinking *is* a physical event, because every thought you have is reflected in physical activity in the brain.

Moreover, the brain can be changed by experience. London cab drivers who have developed a familiarity with the city show increases in the size of the area of the brain thought to be responsible for reading maps (Maguire & others, 2000). Think about that: When you change the way you think, you are *literally* changing the brain's physical processes and even its shape. Our daily experiences contribute to the wiring or rewiring of the brain, just as do the experiences of those London cab drivers (Petrosini, Cutuli, & De Bartolo, 2013).

ELECTROCHEMICAL TRANSMISSION

The brain and the nervous system function essentially as an information-processing system powered by electrical impulses and chemical messengers. When an impulse travels down a nerve cell, or *neuron,* it does so electrically. When that impulse gets to the end of the line, it communicates with the next neuron using chemicals, as we will consider in detail later in this chapter.

©Katie Collins/AP Images

Pathways in the Nervous System

As we interact with and adapt to the world, the brain and the nervous system receive and transmit sensory input (like sounds, smells, and flavors), integrate the information taken in from the environment, and direct the body's motor activities. Information flows into the brain through input from our senses, and the brain makes sense of that information, pulling it together and giving it meaning. In turn, information moves out of the brain to the rest of the body, directing all of the physical things we do.

The nervous system has specialized pathways that are adapted for different functions. These pathways are made up of afferent nerves, efferent nerves, and neural networks (discussed later in the chapter). **Afferent nerves** or **sensory nerves** carry information *to* the brain and spinal cord. These sensory pathways communicate information about the external environment (for example, the sight of a sunrise) and internal conditions (for example, fatigue or hunger) from sensory receptors to the brain and spinal cord. **Efferent nerves or motor nerves** carry information *out of* the brain and spinal cord—that is, they carry the nervous system's output. These motor pathways communicate information from the brain and spinal cord to other areas of the body, including muscles and glands, instructing them, in a sense, to get busy. Notice that the fact that we have separate afferent and efferent nerves tells us something interesting about neurons: Each neuron is a one-way street in the nervous system.

These terms can be complicated. Remember that sensory nerves are afferent nerves. They bring the brain and spinal cord information about the world. Motor nerves are efferent nerves that send information out from the brain and spinal cord. It might help to remember the functions of afferent and efferent nerves by noting that *a*fferent nerves *a*rrive at the brain and spinal cord, and *e*fferent nerves *e*xit these components of the nervous system.

Divisions of the Nervous System

This truly elegant system is highly ordered and organized for effective function. Figure 1 shows the two primary divisions of the human nervous system: the central nervous system and the peripheral nervous system.

The **central nervous system (CNS)** is made up of the brain and spinal cord. More than 99 percent of all nerve cells in our body are located in the CNS. The **peripheral nervous system (PNS)** is the network of nerves that connects the brain and spinal cord to other parts of the body. The functions of the peripheral nervous system are to bring information to and from the brain and spinal cord and to carry out the commands of the CNS to execute various muscular and glandular activities.

The peripheral nervous system has two major divisions: the somatic nervous system and the autonomic nervous system. The **somatic nervous system** consists of sensory nerves, whose function is to convey information from the skin and muscles to the CNS about conditions such as pain and temperature, and motor nerves, whose function is to tell the muscles what to do. The function of the **autonomic nervous system** is to take messages to and from the body's internal organs, monitoring such processes as breathing, heart rate, and digestion.

The autonomic nervous system also is divided into two parts. The first part, the **sympathetic nervous system,** arouses the body to mobilize it for action, while the second, the **parasympathetic nervous system,** calms the body. The sympathetic nervous system is involved in the "fight or flight" response, the body's reaction to a threat (an incident that you can either stay and fight or flee). When you feel your heart pounding and your hands sweating under stress, those experiences reveal the sympathetic nervous system in action. If you need to run away from a dangerous situation, the sympathetic nervous system sends blood out to your extremities to prepare you for taking off. The parasympathetic nervous system is responsible for the ways you calm down once you have escaped the danger. While the sympathetic nervous system is associated with "fight or flight," the parasympathetic nervous system might be thought of as the system that "rests and digests."

afferent nerves or sensory nerves Nerves that carry information about the external environment *to* the brain and spinal cord via sensory receptors.

efferent nerves or motor nerves Nerves that carry information *out of* the brain and spinal cord to other areas of the body.

central nervous system (CNS) The brain and spinal cord.

peripheral nervous system (PNS) The network of nerves that connects the brain and spinal cord to other parts of the body.

somatic nervous system The body system consisting of the sensory nerves, whose function is to convey information from the skin and muscles to the CNS about conditions such as pain and temperature, and the motor nerves, whose function is to tell muscles what to do.

autonomic nervous system The body system that takes messages to and from the body's internal organs, monitoring such processes as breathing, heart rate, and digestion.

sympathetic nervous system The part of the autonomic nervous system that arouses the body to mobilize it for action and thus is involved in the experience of stress.

parasympathetic nervous system The part of the autonomic nervous system that calms the body.

Human Nervous System

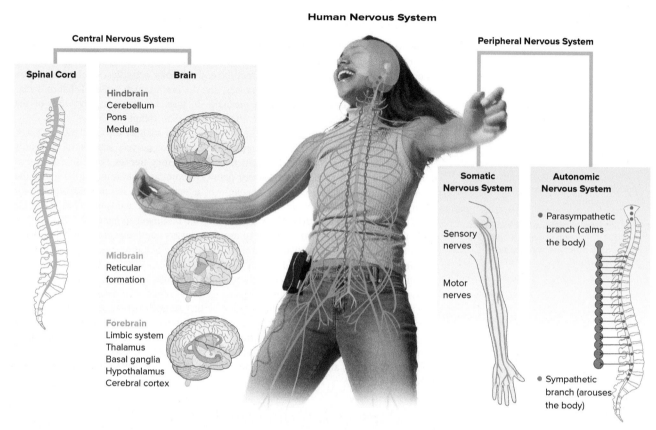

Central Nervous System

Spinal Cord

Brain

Hindbrain
Cerebellum
Pons
Medulla

Midbrain
Reticular
formation

Forebrain
Limbic system
Thalamus
Basal ganglia
Hypothalamus
Cerebral cortex

Peripheral Nervous System

Somatic Nervous System

Sensory nerves

Motor nerves

Autonomic Nervous System

● Parasympathetic branch (calms the body)

● Sympathetic branch (arouses the body)

FIGURE 1 **Major Divisions of the Human Nervous System** The nervous system has two main divisions. One is the *central nervous system* (*left*), which comprises the brain and the spinal cord. The nervous system's other main division is the *peripheral nervous system* (*right*), which itself has two parts—the *somatic nervous system,* which controls sensory and motor neurons, and the *autonomic nervous system,* which monitors processes such as breathing, heart rate, and digestion. These complex systems work together to help us successfully navigate the world. (photo) © RubberBall Productions

In an emergency, the sympathetic nervous system also triggers the body's release of powerful hormones (Owen, Mangelsdorf, & Kliewer, 2015). These stress hormones allow you to focus attention on what needs to be done *now.* For example, in an emergency, people sometimes report feeling strangely calm and doing what has to be done, whether calling 911 or applying pressure to a serious wound. Such experiences reveal the benefits of stress hormones in times of acute emergency (Dougall & others, 2013). We will revisit the relationship between the experience of stress and the nervous system at the close of this chapter.

2. NEURONS

Within each division of the nervous system, much is happening at the cellular level. Nerve cells, chemicals, and electrical impulses work together to transmit information at speeds of up to 330 miles per hour. As a result, information can travel from your brain to your hands (or vice versa) in a matter of milliseconds. Just how fast is 330 miles per hour? Consider that the NASCAR speed record was set in 1987 by Bill Elliott, who completed a lap driving at 212.8 miles per hour.

There are two types of cells in the nervous system: neurons and glial cells. **Neurons** are the nerve cells that handle information processing; we will generally concentrate on neurons in this chapter. The human brain contains about 100 billion neurons. The average neuron is a complex structure with as many as 10,000 physical connections with other cells.

test yourself

1. Name and explain four characteristics that allow the nervous system to direct human behavior.
2. What is the difference between afferent and efferent nerves?
3. What are the two main parts of the autonomic nervous system, and what is the function of each?

● **neurons** One of two types of cells in the nervous system; neurons are the type of nerve cell that handles the information-processing function.

66   CHAPTER 3   Biological Foundations of Behavior

● **mirror neurons** Nerve cells in the brain that are activated (in human and nonhuman primates) both when an action is performed and when the organism observes the action being performed by another.

Researchers have been particularly interested in a special type of neuron called **mirror neurons.** Mirror neurons are activated (in human and nonhuman primates) both when we perform an action and when we watch someone else perform that same activity (Ferrari & Rizzolatti, 2015; Oztop, Kawato, & Arbib, 2013). You might be wondering why that is such a big deal. Remember, neurons are specialized: Motor neurons do not respond to sensory information, and sensory neurons do not respond to motor information. Yet, mirror neurons appear to respond to both kinds of information—doing and seeing (Gallese & others, 2011; Oztop, Kawato, & Arbib, 2013). This responsiveness to two different kinds of input is one characteristic that makes mirror neurons so fascinating.

The discovery of mirror neurons has led to provocative predictions about the function of these neurons in imitation, social cognition (that is, thinking about oneself and others), empathy, and understanding behavior (Vanderwert, Fox, & Ferrari, 2013). Some scientists have argued that "broken mirror neurons" play an important role in autism, a disorder of neural development characterized by impairment in communication and social interaction (Lauvin & others, 2012; Ramachandran & Oberman, 2006). Indeed, some scholars hail mirror neurons as a promising new direction in understanding the origins of human sociability (Ramachandran, 2000). Others charge that such claims far overstep the evidence (Gernsbacher & Pripas-Kapit, 2012; Hickok, 2009).

● **glial cells or glia** The second of two types of cells in the nervous system; glial cells provide support, nutritional benefits, and other functions and keep neurons running smoothly.

Glial cells or **glia** are the other type of cell that provides support, nutritional benefits, and other functions in the nervous system (Trevisiol & Nave, 2015). Glial cells keep neurons running smoothly. These cells are not specialized to process information in the way that neurons are, and there are many more of them in the nervous system than there are neurons. In fact, for every neuron there are about 10 glial cells. You might think of the glial cells as the pit crew in the raceway of the nervous system.

Neuroscientists know much less about the function of glial cells than neurons, but dramatic new discoveries have shed light on ways in which glial cells might be involved in behavior (Edgar & Sibille, 2012; Gundersen, Storm-Mathisen, & Bergersen, 2015). Until recently, it was thought that glia do not have synapses or release neurotransmitters, both of which, as we will see, are crucial for neural transmission. However, research now suggests that some glial cells are not just passive bystanders to neural transmission but may detect neural impulses and send signals to other glial cells (Fields, Woo, & Basser, 2015). Glial cells have been recognized in a host of important human experiences, including memory (Hassanpoor, Fallah, & Raza, 2012); neurogenerative diseases such as Alzheimer disease (Melo & others, 2011); pain (Hanani, 2015); and psychological disorders (Noda, 2015). Still, by far the majority of information processing in the brain is done by neurons, not glial cells.

Specialized Cell Structure

Not all neurons are alike, as they are specialized to handle different functions. However, all neurons do have some common characteristics. Most neurons are created very early in life, but their shape, size, and connections can change throughout the life span. The way neurons function reflects the major characteristic of the nervous system described at the beginning of the chapter: plasticity. That is, neurons can and do change.

● **cell body** The part of the neuron that contains the nucleus, which directs the manufacture of substances that the neuron needs for growth and maintenance.

● **dendrites** Treelike fibers projecting from a neuron, which receive information and orient it toward the neuron's cell body.

● **axon** The part of the neuron that carries information away from the cell body toward other cells.

Every neuron has a cell body, dendrites, and an axon (Figure 2). The **cell body** contains the *nucleus,* which directs the manufacture of substances that the neuron needs for growth and maintenance. **Dendrites,** treelike fibers projecting from a neuron, receive information and orient it toward the neuron's cell body. Most nerve cells have numerous dendrites, which increase their surface area, allowing each neuron to receive input from many other neurons. The **axon** is the part of the neuron that carries information away from the cell body toward other cells. (Remember that *axon* and *away* both start with the letter *a*). Although extremely thin (1/10,000th of an inch—a human hair by comparison is 1/1000th of an inch), axons can be very long, with many branches. In fact, some extend more than 3 feet—all the way from the top of the brain to the base of the spinal cord. Finally, covering all surfaces of the neurons, including the dendrites and axons, is a very thin cellular membrane that allows substances to move in and out of the cell. We will examine this membrane and its functions in more detail later.

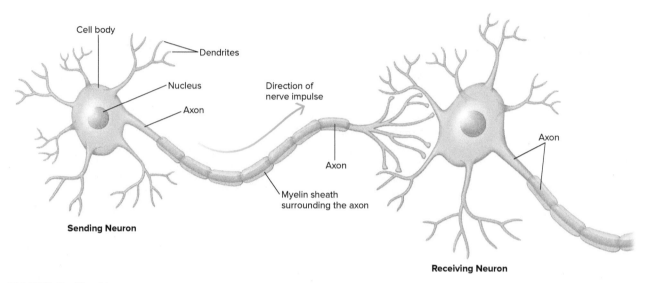

FIGURE 2 **The Neuron** The drawing shows the parts of a neuron and the connection between one neuron and another. Note the cell body, the branching of dendrites, and the axon with a myelin sheath.

A **myelin sheath,** a layer of cells containing fat, encases and insulates most axons. By insulating the axons, myelin sheaths speed up transmission of nerve impulses (Whalley, 2015). The myelin sheath developed as the nervous system evolved. As brain size increased, it became necessary for information to travel over longer distances in the nervous system. Axons without myelin sheaths are not very good conductors of electricity. However, with the insulation of myelin sheaths, axons transmit electrical impulses and convey information rapidly (Miller & others, 2012). We can compare the myelin sheath's development to the evolution of interstate highways as cities grew: Highways keep fast-moving, long-distance traffic from getting snarled by slow, local traffic.

● **myelin sheath** A layer of fat cells that encases and insulates most axons.

Numerous disorders are associated with problems in either the creation or the maintenance of myelin. One of them is multiple sclerosis (MS), a degenerative disease of the nervous system in which myelin tissue hardens, disrupting neuronal communication. In MS, scar tissue replaces the myelin sheath. Symptoms of the disease include blurry and double vision, tingling sensations throughout the body, and general weakness.

The Neural Impulse

To transmit information to other neurons, a neuron sends brief electrical impulses (let's call them "blips") through its axon. As you reach to turn this page, hundreds of such impulses will stream down the axons in your arm to tell your muscles when to flex and how quickly. By changing the rate of the signals, or blips, the neuron can vary its message. Those impulses traveling down the axon are electrical. How does a neuron—a living cell—generate electricity? To answer this question, we need to take a moment to examine the axon and the cellular membrane that surrounds it.

The axon is a tube encased in a membrane. There are fluids both inside and outside the axon. Floating in those fluids are electrically charged particles called *ions*. Some of these ions, notably sodium and potassium, carry positive charges. Negatively charged ions of chlorine and other elements also are present. The membrane surrounding the axon prevents negative and positive ions from randomly flowing into or out of the cell. That membrane has thousands of tiny gates in it. These gates are generally closed, but they can open. We call the membrane *semipermeable* because fluids and ions can sometimes flow into and out of it. In fact, the neuron creates electrical signals by moving positive and negative ions back and forth through its outer membrane.

Jack Osbourne, son of musician Ozzy Osbourne, announced he has multiple sclerosis (MS) in 2012.

© Paul Archuleta/FilmMagic/Getty Images

FIGURE 3 **The Resting Potential**
An oscilloscope measures the difference in electrical potential between two electrodes. When one electrode is placed inside an axon at rest and one is placed outside, the electrical potential inside the cell is −70 millivolts (mV) relative to the outside. This potential difference is due to the separation of positive (+) and negative (−) charges along the membrane.

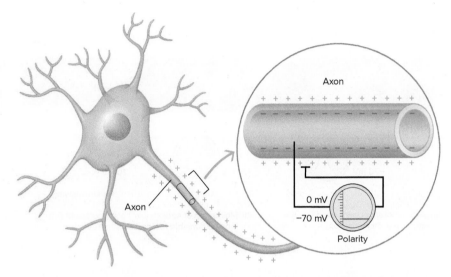

● **resting potential** The stable, negative charge of an inactive neuron.

● **action potential** The brief wave of positive electrical charge that sweeps down the axon.

● **all-or-nothing principle** The principle that once the electrical impulse reaches a certain level of intensity (its threshold), it fires and moves all the way down the axon without losing any intensity.

Normally, when the neuron is resting—that is, not transmitting information—the tiny gates in the membrane, called *ion channels*, are closed, and a slight negative charge is present along the inside of the cell membrane. On the outside of the cell membrane, the charge is positive. Because of the difference in charge, the membrane of the resting neuron is said to be *polarized*, with most negatively charged ions on the inside of the cell and most positively charged ions on the outside. This polarization creates a voltage between the inside and outside of the axon wall (Figure 3). That voltage, called the neuron's **resting potential,** is between −60 and −75 millivolts. A millivolt (mV) is 1/1000th of a volt.

How does the movement of ions occur across the membrane? Those ion channels open and close to let the ions pass into and out of the cell. For ions, it is true that opposites attract. The negatively charged ions on the inside of the membrane and the positively charged ions on the outside of the membrane will rush to each other if given the chance. Impulses that travel down the neuron do so by opening and closing ion channels, allowing the ions to flow in and out.

A neuron becomes activated when an incoming impulse—a reaction to, say, a pinprick or the sight of someone's face—raises the neuron's voltage, and the sodium gates at the base of the axon open briefly. This action allows positively charged sodium ions to flow into the neuron, creating a more positively charged neuron and *depolarizing* the membrane by decreasing the charge difference between the fluids inside and outside of the neuron. Then potassium channels open, and positively charged potassium ions move out through the neuron's semipermeable membrane. This outflow returns the neuron to a negative charge. Then the same process occurs as the next group of channels flips open briefly.

So it goes all the way down the axon, like a long row of cabinet doors opening and closing in sequence. It is hard to imagine, but this system of opening and closing tiny doors is responsible for the beautiful fluid movements of a ballet dancer and the flying fingers of a pianist playing a concerto.

The term **action potential** describes the brief wave of positive electrical charge that sweeps down the axon (Figure 4). An action potential lasts only about 1/1000th of a second, because the sodium channels can stay open for only a very brief time. They quickly close again and become reset for the next action potential. When a neuron sends an action potential, it is commonly said to be "firing."

The action potential abides by the **all-or-nothing principle,** meaning that once the electrical impulse reaches a certain level of intensity, called its *threshold,* it fires and moves all the way down the axon without losing any of its intensity. The impulse traveling down an axon is comparable to the burning fuse of a firecracker. Whether you use

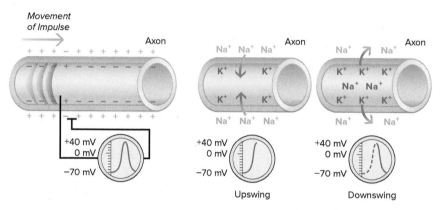

Movement of Impulse

(a) Action potential generated by an impulse within a neuron

(b) Movement of sodium (Na⁺) and potassium (K⁺) ions responsible for the action potential

FIGURE 4   The Action Potential An action potential is a brief wave of positive electrical charge that sweeps down the axon as the sodium channels in the axon membrane open and close. (*a*) The action potential causes a change in electrical potential as it moves along the axon. (*b*) The movements of sodium ions (Na^+) and potassium ions (K^+) into and out of the axon cause the electrical changes.

a match or a blowtorch to light the fuse, once the fuse has been lit, the spark travels quickly and with the same intensity down the fuse. So, the intensity of the impulse is communicated not by the size of the electrical charge but by the rate of the blips coming down the axon.

Synapses and Neurotransmitters

The movement of an impulse down an axon may be compared to a crowd doing "the wave" in a stadium. With the wave, there is a problem, however—the aisles. How does the wave get across the aisle? A similar problem arises for neurons, because they do not touch one another directly, and electricity cannot cross the space between them. Yet somehow neurons manage to communicate.

Here is where the chemical part of electro*chemical* transmission comes in. Neurons communicate with one another through chemicals that carry messages across the space. This connection between one neuron and another is one of the most intriguing and highly researched areas of contemporary neuroscience (Herman & Rosenmund, 2015). Figure 5 gives an overview of how this connection between neurons takes place.

SYNAPTIC TRANSMISSION

Synapses are tiny spaces (the aisle in our stadium analogy) between neurons, and the space between neurons that the synapses create is referred to as the *synaptic gap*. Most synapses lie between the axon of one neuron and the dendrites or cell body of another neuron (Chapeton & others, 2012). Before an impulse can cross the synaptic gap, it must be converted into a chemical signal.

Each axon branches out into numerous fibers that end in structures called *terminal buttons*. Stored in very tiny synaptic vesicles (*sacs*) within the terminal buttons are chemicals called **neurotransmitters.** As their name suggests, neurotransmitters transmit, or carry, information across the synaptic gap to the next neuron. When a nerve impulse reaches the terminal button, it triggers the release of neurotransmitter molecules from the synaptic vesicles. The neurotransmitter molecules flood the synaptic gap. Their movements are random, but some of them bump into receptor sites in the next neuron.

The neurotransmitters are like pieces of a puzzle, and the receptor sites on the next neuron are differently shaped spaces. If the shape of a receptor site corresponds to the shape of a neurotransmitter molecule, the neurotransmitter fits into the space opening the receptor site, so that the neuron receives the signals coming from the previous neuron. You might think of the receptor site as a keyhole in a lock and the neurotransmitter as the key that fits that lock. After delivering its message, some of the neurotransmitter is used up in the production of energy, and some of it is reabsorbed by the axon that

● **synapses** Tiny spaces between neurons; the gaps between neurons are referred to as synaptic gaps.

● **neurotransmitters** Chemical substances that are stored in very tiny sacs within the terminal buttons and involved in transmitting information across a synaptic gap to the next neuron.

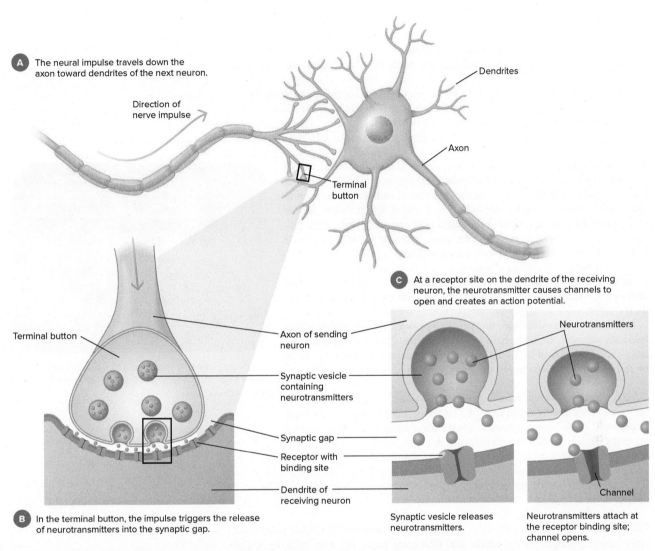

A The neural impulse travels down the axon toward dendrites of the next neuron.

Direction of nerve impulse

Dendrites

Axon

Terminal button

C At a receptor site on the dendrite of the receiving neuron, the neurotransmitter causes channels to open and creates an action potential.

Terminal button

Axon of sending neuron

Synaptic vesicle containing neurotransmitters

Synaptic gap

Receptor with binding site

Dendrite of receiving neuron

Neurotransmitters

Channel

B In the terminal button, the impulse triggers the release of neurotransmitters into the synaptic gap.

Synaptic vesicle releases neurotransmitters.

Neurotransmitters attach at the receptor binding site; channel opens.

FIGURE 5 How Synapses and Neurotransmitters Work (*A*) The axon of the presynaptic (sending) neuron meets dendrites of the postsynaptic (receiving) neuron. (*B*) This is an enlargement of one synapse, showing the synaptic gap between the two neurons, the terminal buttons, and the synaptic vesicles containing a neurotransmitter. (*C*) This is an enlargement of the receptor site. Note how the neurotransmitter opens the channel on the receptor site, triggering the neuron to fire.

released it to await the next neural impulse. This reabsorption is called *reuptake*. Essentially, a message in the brain is delivered across the synapse by a neurotransmitter, which pours out of the terminal button just as the message approaches the synapse.

NEUROCHEMICAL MESSENGERS

There are many different neurotransmitters. Each plays a specific role and functions in a specific pathway. Whereas some neurotransmitters stimulate or excite neurons to fire, others can inhibit neurons from firing. Some neurotransmitters are both excitatory *and* inhibitory.

Most neurons secrete only one type of neurotransmitter, but often many different neurons are simultaneously secreting different neurotransmitters into the synaptic gaps of a single neuron. At any given time, a neuron is receiving a mixture of messages from the neurotransmitters. At the neuron's receptor sites, the chemical molecules bind to the membrane and either excite the neuron, bringing it closer to the threshold at which it will fire, or inhibit the neuron from firing. Usually the binding of an excitatory neurotransmitter from one neuron will not be enough to trigger an action potential in the receiving neuron. Triggering an action potential often requires a number of neurons sending excitatory messages simultaneously, or fewer neurons sending rapid-fire excitatory messages.

Scientists do not know exactly how many neurotransmitters exist, and more are discovered every year. In organisms ranging from snails to whales, neuroscientists have found the same neurotransmitter molecules that our own brains use. To get a better sense of what neurotransmitters do, let's consider eight that have major effects on behavior.

Acetylcholine   *Acetylcholine (ACh)* usually stimulates the firing of neurons and is involved in muscle action, learning, and memory (Zhen & Samuel, 2015). ACh is found throughout the central and peripheral nervous systems. The venom from the bite of the black widow spider causes ACh to gush out of the synapses between the spinal cord and skeletal muscles, producing violent muscle spasms and weakness. The role of ACh in muscle function also comes to light in the working of Botox, a brand-name product made from botulin. A bacterial poison, botulin destroys ACh, so that when someone gets an injection of Botox, the person's facial muscles—which are activated by ACh—are prevented from moving, with the result that wrinkles do not form.

Individuals with Alzheimer disease, a degenerative brain disorder that gradually destroys memory, have an acetylcholine deficiency (Hachisu & others, 2015). Some of the drugs that alleviate Alzheimer symptoms do so by compensating for the loss of the brain's supply of acetylcholine.

The neurotransmitter-like venom of the black widow spider does its harm by disturbing neurotransmission.
Centers for Disease Control

GABA   *GABA (gamma aminobutyric acid)* is found throughout the central nervous system. It is believed to be the neurotransmitter present in as many as one-third of the brain's synapses. GABA plays a key function in the brain by inhibiting many neurons from firing (Purkayastha & others, 2015); indeed, GABA is the brain's brake pedal, helping to regulate neuron firing and control the precision of the signal being carried from one neuron to the next. Low levels of GABA are linked with anxiety (Li & others, 2015). Valium and other antianxiety drugs increase the inhibiting effects of GABA.

Glutamate   *Glutamate* is the most prevalent neurotransmitter. If GABA is the brain's brake pedal, glutamate is the accelerator. Glutamate has a key role in exciting many neurons to fire and is especially involved in learning and memory (Purkayastha & others, 2015). Too much glutamate can overstimulate the brain and trigger migraine headaches or even seizures. Glutamate is also thought to be a factor in anxiety, depression, schizophrenia, Alzheimer disease, and Parkinson disease (Volk & others, 2015). Because of the widespread expression of glutamate in the brain, glutamate receptors have increasingly become the targets of drug treatment for a number of neurological and psychological disorders (Bishop & others, 2015).

Norepinephrine   Stress stimulates the release of another of the body's neurotransmitters—*norepinephrine* (Sun, Hunt, & Sah, 2015). When we respond to stress, multiple things must happen at once, and so it is not surprising that norepinephrine (also called *noradrenaline*) has a number of effects on the body. If you think of all the things your body does when you are experiencing extreme fear, for instance, you might be able to guess some of the ways norepinephrine affects your body. It *inhibits* the firing of neurons in the central nervous system, but it simultaneously *excites* the heart muscle, intestines, and urogenital tract.

This neurotransmitter also helps to control alertness. Too much norepinephrine triggers agitation or jumpiness. For example, amphetamines and cocaine cause hyperactive, manic states of behavior by rapidly increasing norepinephrine levels in the brain (Shorter, Domingo, & Kosten, 2015). However, too little norepinephrine is associated with depression.

Recall from the beginning of the chapter that one of the most important characteristics of the brain and nervous system is integration. In the case of neurotransmitters, they may work in teams of two or more. For example, norepinephrine works with acetylcholine to regulate states of sleep and wakefulness.

Dopamine   *Dopamine* helps to control voluntary movement and affects sleep, mood, attention, learning, and the ability to recognize opportunities for rewarding experiences in the environment (Meyer, 2012). Stimulant drugs such as cocaine and amphetamines produce excitement, alertness, elevated mood, decreased fatigue, and sometimes increased motor activity mainly by activating dopamine receptors (Cheng & others, 2015). Dopamine is related to the personality trait of extraversion (being outgoing and gregarious) (Wacker & Smillie, 2015), as we will see in the chapter "Personality". Problems in regulating dopamine are associated with a variety of psychological disorders, especially schizophrenia (Whitton, Treadway, & Pizzagalli, 2015), a severe disorder we examine in the chapter "Psychological Disorders".

Low levels of dopamine are associated with Parkinson disease, a degenerative neurological disorder in which a person develops jerky physical movements and a tremor and has difficulty with speech and walking (Fallon & others, 2015). This disease affects about a million people in the United States (D. H. Park & others, 2009); actor Michael J. Fox has been diagnosed with this disease. Parkinson impairs coordinated movement to the point that just walking across a room can be a major ordeal.

Serotonin   *Serotonin* is involved in the regulation of sleep, mood, attention, and learning. In regulating states of sleep and wakefulness, it teams with acetylcholine and norepinephrine. Serotonin's role in mood regulation has been an important focus of research. One prominent theory maintains that lowered levels of serotonin are associated with depression (Karg & Sen, 2012). Medications used to treat depression often act upon serotonin, slowing down its reuptake into terminal buttons and thereby increasing brain levels of serotonin (Little, Zhang, & Cook, 2006). There are 15 known types of serotonin receptors in the brain (Hoyer, Hannon, & Martin, 2002), and each type of antidepressant drug has its effects on different receptors. It is important to bear in mind that the hypothesized role of serotonin in depression is not without its critics (Healy, 2015). Figure 6 shows the brain pathways for serotonin.

Endorphins   *Endorphins* are natural opiates—substances that depress nervous system activity and eliminate pain—that mainly stimulate the firing of neurons. As opiates, endorphins shield the body from pain and elevate feelings of pleasure. A long-distance runner, a woman giving birth, and a person in shock after a car wreck all have elevated levels of endorphins (Bali, Randhawa, & Jaggi, 2015).

As early as the fourth century B.C.E., the Greeks used wild poppies to induce euphoria. More than 2,000 years later, the magical formula behind opium's addictive action was finally discovered. In the early 1970s, scientists found that opium plugs into a sophisticated system of natural opiates that lie deep within the brain's pathways (Pert, 1999; Pert & Snyder, 1973). Morphine (the most important narcotic of opium) mimics the action of endorphins by stimulating receptors in the brain involved with pleasure and pain (Navratilova & others, 2015).

Oxytocin   *Oxytocin* is a hormone and neurotransmitter that plays an important role in the experience of love and social bonding. A powerful surge of oxytocin is released in mothers who have just given birth, and oxytocin is related to the onset of lactation (milk production) and breastfeeding (Vrachnis & others, 2011). Oxytocin, however, is involved in more than a mother's ability to provide nourishment for her baby. It is also a factor in the experience of parents who find themselves "in love at first sight" with their newborn (Young, 2009).

Oxytocin is released as part of sexual orgasm and is thought to play a role in the human tendency to feel pleasure during orgasm and to form emotional bonds with romantic

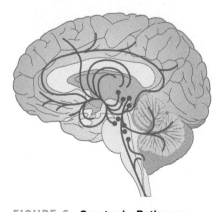

FIGURE 6   Serotonin Pathways
Each of the neurotransmitters in the brain has specific pathways in which it functions. Shown here are the pathways for serotonin.

CRITICAL CONTROVERSY

Does Oxytocin Make People More Trusting?

Unsurprisingly, oxytocin has been one of the most studied chemicals in all of the behavioral sciences. Imagine: a neurotransmitter that appears to be a kind of natural love potion. Some have called it "liquid trust"! Even better, oxytocin can be administered to people in a simple nasal spray.

Some of the earliest experiments involving administering oxytocin produced fascinating results. For instance, a team of investigators led by Moïra Mikolajczak set out to examine whether oxytocin would lead people to be more trusting of another with personal information (Mikolajczak & others, 2010). Participants were randomly assigned to receive a nasal spray containing oxytocin or a placebo. The dependent variable, trust, was operationalized using "the envelope task." For this task, participants completed a questionnaire containing a series of highly personal, intimate questions (for example, preferences for various sexual practices). Participants were then asked to put the questionnaire in an envelope and give it to the experimenter (who assured the participants that he or she would not look at the responses). Participants were told that they could seal the envelope and were offered tape for the seal. The key dependent measure was whether (and how) participants sealed the envelope.

Results were dramatic: Over 80 percent of those in the placebo group sealed the envelope with tape, compared to less than 7 percent in the oxytocin group. In addition, 60 percent of those in the oxytocin group did not seal the envelope at all (Mikolajczak & others, 2010). Maybe oxytocin really is liquid trust! Or is it?

Years later, the same team of researchers tried to reproduce their findings, and they couldn't (Lane & others, 2015). In fact, in two studies they found that oxytocin did not affect how individuals

treated the envelope at all: Those who received oxytocin were just as protective of their personal information as those in the placebo group. What could explain the difference?

Comparing the earlier study to the newer ones, a key difference emerged: The original study was only "single blind." This means that, although participants did not know what they received in the nasal spray, the experimenter interacting with them did. Mikolajczak and colleagues reasoned that the experimenter treated participants in subtly different ways, leading the oxytocin group to behave differently (Lane & others, 2015).

Replication is the foundation of good science. It is important for experimenters to verify their own work, again and again. This example shows us that even the most clever research design requires rigorous standards.

© BrianAJackson/iStock/Getty Images

WHAT DO YOU THINK?
- If you thought that someone you were interacting with had been given "liquid trust," how might you behave?
- Can you think of a different way to test the hypothesis that oxytocin is liquid trust?

partners (Magon & Kalra, 2011). One study found that a higher level of oxytocin was present in new lovers and persisted at a higher level six months later compared to non-attached single young adults (Schneiderman & others, 2012). In this study, higher oxytocin levels were associated with positive affect, affectionate touch, and preoccupation with one's partner and the relationship.

Provocative research also has linked oxytocin to the way that some individuals respond to stress (Neumann & Landgraf, 2012). According to Shelley Taylor (2011a, 2011b), women under stress do not experience the classic "fight or flight" response—rather, the influx of oxytocin they experience suggests that women may seek bonds with others when under stress. Taylor refers to this response as "tend and befriend" and believes that it more accurately represents the stress response of women.

You would probably not be surprised to hear that oxytocin has fascinated not only scientists but the public as well. It sounds like a kind of natural love potion. Recently, some research on the effects of oxytocin on interpersonal trust has been called into question. To read about that work, see the Critical Controversy.

DRUGS AND NEUROTRANSMITTERS

Recall that neurotransmitters fit into the receptor sites like keys in keyholes. Other substances, such as drugs, can sometimes fit into those receptor sites as well, producing a variety of effects. Many animal venoms, such as that of the black widow spider mentioned above, act by disturbing neurotransmission. Similarly, most drugs that influence behavior do so mainly by interfering with the work of neurotransmitters.

Drugs can mimic or increase the effects of a neurotransmitter, or they can block those effects. For example, the drug morphine mimics the actions of endorphins by stimulating receptors in the brain and spinal cord associated with pleasure and pain, producing feelings of pleasure. Other drugs can block a neurotransmitter's action by preventing it from getting into the receptor site. Drugs used to treat schizophrenia, for example, interfere with the activity of dopamine.

Neural Networks

So far, we have focused mainly on how a single neuron functions and on how a nerve impulse travels from one neuron to another. Now let's look at how large numbers of neurons work together to integrate incoming information and coordinate outgoing information.

● **neural networks** Networks of nerve cells that integrate sensory input and motor output.

Most information processing occurs when information moves through **neural networks**— interconnected pathways of nerve cells that integrate sensory input and motor output. For example, as you read your class notes, the input from your eyes is transmitted to your brain and then passed through many neural networks, which translate the characters on the page into neural codes for letters, words, associations, and meanings. Some of the information is stored in the neural networks, and, if you read aloud, some is passed on as messages to your lips and tongue.

Neural networks can take years to develop and make up most of the brain. Working in networks allows neurons to amplify the brain's computing power (Park & Friston, 2013; Wolf, Grein, & Queisser, 2013). Figure 7 shows a simplified drawing of a neural network and gives you an idea of how the activity of one neuron is linked with that of many others.

Some neurons have short axons and communicate with other nearby neurons. Other neurons have long axons and communicate with circuits of neurons some distance away. These neural networks are not static. They can be altered through changes in the strength of synaptic connections.

Any piece of information, such as a name, might be embedded in hundreds or even thousands of connections between neurons (Yuste, 2015). In this way, human activities such as being attentive, memorizing, and thinking are distributed over a wide range of connected neurons. Differences in these neural networks are responsible for the differences observed in those London cab drivers discussed earlier in this chapter.

test yourself

1. What are neurons, and what are their three parts?
2. What is meant by the neuron's action potential? How does the all-or-nothing principle apply to it?
3. What do neurotransmitters do? Name four specific neurotransmitters and describe the role each plays.

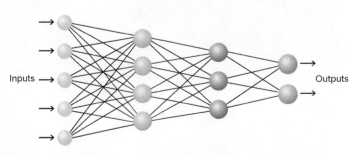

FIGURE 7   An Example of a Neural Network *Inputs* (information from the environment and from sensory receptors, such as the details of a person's face) become embedded in extensive connections between neurons in the brain. This embedding process leads to *outputs* such as remembering the person's face.

3. STRUCTURES OF THE BRAIN AND THEIR FUNCTIONS

The extensive and intricate networks of neurons in the living brain are invisible to the naked eye. Fortunately, technology is available to help neuroscientists form pictures of the structure and organization of neurons and of the larger systems they make up without harming the organism being studied. This section explores the techniques that scientists use in brain research, and we consider what these tools reveal about the brain's structures and functions. We pay special attention to the cerebral cortex, the region of the brain that is most relevant to the topics in this book.

How Researchers Study the Brain and Nervous System

Early knowledge of the human brain came mostly from studies of individuals who had suffered brain damage from injury or disease or who had brain surgery to relieve another condition. Modern discoveries have relied largely on technology that enables researchers to "look inside" the brain while it is at work. Increasingly researchers have begun to combine multiple techniques in one study to fully capture the brain and its activity (Jorge, van der Zwaag, & Figueiredo, 2014). Let's examine some of these innovative techniques.

BRAIN LESIONING

Brain lesioning is an abnormal disruption in the tissue of the brain resulting from injury or disease. In a lab setting, neuroscientists produce lesions in laboratory animals to determine the effects on the animal's behavior (Albasser & others, 2015; Nelson & others, 2015). They create the lesions by surgically removing brain tissue, destroying tissue with a laser, or eliminating tissue by injecting it with a drug. Examining the person or animal that has the lesion gives the researchers a sense of the function of the part of the brain that has been damaged.

Do you know anyone who has experienced a stroke or brain-damaging head injury? These events create lesioned areas in the brain. Identifying the areas affected by a stroke or brain injury and then observing the aspects of a person's life that are affected by the injury can allow researchers to identify the kinds of functions associated with specific brain areas (de Guise & others, 2015; Farinelli & others, 2015).

ELECTRICAL RECORDING

An *electroencephalograph (EEG)* records the brain's electrical activity. Electrodes placed on the scalp detect brain-wave activity, which is recorded on a chart known as an *electroencephalogram* (Figure 8). This device can assess brain damage, seizure disorder, and other problems (Gradisnik & others, 2015; Muraja-Murro & others, 2015).

EEGs have been used in research examining the brain and happiness. Paul Ekman, Richard Davidson, and Wallace Friesen (1990) measured EEG activity during emotional experiences provoked by watching film clips. Individuals in this study watched amusing clips (such as a puppy playing with flowers and monkeys taking a bath) as well as clips likely to provoke fear or disgust (a leg amputation and a third-degree burn victim). How does the brain respond to such stimuli? The researchers found that while watching the amusing clips, people tended to exhibit more left than right prefrontal activity, as shown in EEGs. In contrast, when the participants viewed the unpleasant or fear-provoking films, the right prefrontal area was generally more active than the left.

Do these differences generalize to overall differences in feelings of happiness? They just might. Heather Urry and her colleagues (2004) found that individuals who have relatively more left than right prefrontal activity (what is called *prefrontal asymmetry*) tend to rate themselves higher on a number of measures of well-being, including self-acceptance, positive relations with others, purpose in life, and life satisfaction.

Not every recording of brain activity is made with surface electrodes that are attached to the scalp. In *single-unit recording,* which provides information about a single neuron's electrical activity, a thin probe is inserted in or near an individual neuron. The probe transmits the neuron's electrical activity to an amplifier so that researchers can "see" the activity (Teleńczuk & others, 2015).

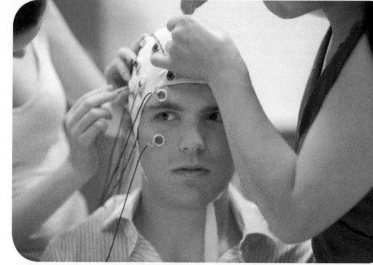

FIGURE 8 **An EEG Recording** The electroencephalograph (EEG) is widely used in sleep research. The device has led to some major breakthroughs in understanding sleep by showing how the brain's electrical activity changes during sleep. © annedde/E+/Getty Images

BRAIN IMAGING

For years, medical practitioners have used X rays to reveal damage inside the body, both in the brain and in other locations. A single X ray of the brain is hard to interpret, however, because it shows a two-dimensional image of the three-dimensional interior of the brain. An improved imaging technique called *computerized axial tomography (CAT scan or CT scan)* produces a three-dimensional image obtained from X rays of the head that are assembled into a composite image by a computer. The CT scan provides valuable information about the location and extent of damage involving stroke, language disorder, or loss of memory (Muschelli & others, 2015).

Another imaging method, *positron-emission tomography (PET scan),* is based on metabolic changes in the brain related to activity. PET measures the amount of glucose in various areas of the brain and sends this information to a computer for analysis. Neurons use glucose for energy, so glucose levels vary with the levels of activity throughout the brain. Tracing the amounts of glucose generates a picture of the brain's activity levels. PET scans have been used in a wide variety of studies (Ossenkoppele & others, 2015; Spadoni & others, 2015). PET scans can be used to examine the amount of neurotransmitters waiting to be released into the synaptic gap in neurons in the brain (Jabbi & others, 2013).

In addition to CT and PET scans, another technique psychologists use to image the brain is *magnetic resonance imaging (MRI).* MRI involves creating a magnetic field around a person's body and using radio waves to construct images of the person's tissues and biochemical activities. The magnetic field used to create an MRI image is over 50,000 times more powerful than the earth's magnetic field (Parry & Matthews, 2002). MRI takes advantage of the fact that the human brain contains a great deal of water (like the rest of the body, the brain is 70 percent water). Within each water molecule there are hydrogen atoms (remember, water is H_2O). These hydrogen atoms can be thought of as tiny magnets. When these magnetlike hydrogen atoms encounter a very strong magnetic field, they align themselves with it. Neurons have more water in them than do other brain tissues, and that contrast is what provides the nuanced brain images that MRI is able to produce (Parry & Matthews, 2002).

MRI generates very clear pictures of the brain's interior, does not require injecting the brain with a substance, and (unlike X rays) does not pose a problem of radiation overexposure. In fact, there are no known side effects of MRI. Getting an MRI scan involves lying still in a large metal tunnel, similar to a barrel. MRI scans provide an excellent picture of the architecture of the brain and allow researchers to see if and how experience affects brain structure.

Katrin Amunts and colleagues (1997; Gärtner & others, 2013) have used MRI to document the link between the number of years a person has practiced musical skills (playing the piano or violin, for example) and the size of the brain region that is responsible for controlling hand movements, demonstrating again that behavior can influence the very structure of the brain. The structure of the brains of those who have practiced a musical instrument differ from those who have not. Note that these brain changes reflect, as well, the development of neural networks.

Although MRI scans can reveal considerable information about brain *structure,* they cannot portray brain *function.* Other techniques, however, can serve as a window to the brain in action. One such method, *functional magnetic resonance imaging,* or *fMRI,* allows scientists literally to see what is happening in the brain while it is working (Le Bihan, 2016) (Figure 9). The use of fMRI in psychological studies has increased dramatically in the twenty-first century. The field of

INTERSECTION

Environmental Psychology and Neuroscience: How Does Spending Time in Nature Affect the Brain?

One way that human beings make themselves miserable is by ruminating on negative events. Rumination, or brooding, involves prolonged, self-focused, negative thinking. Rumination can involve replaying the same problem or personal mistake over and over.

The remedy for rumination is pretty obvious: Think about something else. But, in order for those other thoughts to truly combat rumination, they must be compelling. Might nature provide an excellent distraction from negative thoughts? In a recent study, Gregory Bratman and his colleagues (2015) sought to explore this very question.

Might nature provide an excellent distraction from negative thoughts?

The researchers randomly assigned participants to take a 90-minute walk either in an urban setting or in a natural environment. The dependent variables examined the effects of nature in two ways. First, participants rated how much their thoughts involved rumination, before and after the walk. Second, fMRI was used to measure brain activation in a brain region called the subgenual prefrontal cortex. This area of the brain is active during negative emotional states, such as sadness and stress. The results showed that after the nature walk, participants showed declines in rumination and in activation in the subgenual prefrontal cortex. Among those who walked in the urban setting, no differences were found (Bratman & others, 2015).

These results fit with other studies demonstrating the benefits of time in nature to well-being (Brown, Barton, & Gladwell, 2013). For instance, research shows that those who have window views including nature are associated with better memory, attention (Taylor, Kuo, & Sullivan, 2002), and feelings of happiness (Kaplan, 2001). Such studies are especially important in today's world. More than half of modern humans live in urban environments, and estimates are that by 2050 over 70 percent of people will live in urban settings (Bratman & others, 2015).

Our brains are marvelously adaptable, but we might want to bear in mind the environments within which our brains evolved. Taking your brain back to nature may be just the remedy for whatever is on your mind.

cognitive neuroscience, which involves linking cognitive processes and their underlying neural bases, has especially benefited from progress in fMRI (Amso & Scerif, 2015; Eres & others, 2015).

Like the PET scan, fMRI rests on the idea that mental activity is associated with changes in the brain. Although PET relies on the use of glucose as fuel for thinking, fMRI exploits changes in blood oxygen that occur in association with brain activity. When part of the brain is working, oxygenated blood rushes into the area. This oxygen, however, is more than is needed. In a sense, fMRI is based on the fact that thinking is like running sprints. When you run the 100-yard dash, blood rushes to the muscles in your legs, carrying oxygen. Right after you stop, you might feel a tightness in your legs, because the oxygen has not all been used. Similarly, if an area of the brain is hard at work—for example, solving a math problem—the increased activity leads to a surplus of oxygenated blood. This "extra" oxygen allows the brain activity to be imaged.

Getting an fMRI involves reclining in the same large metal barrel as does an MRI, but in the case of fMRI the person is actively doing something during the procedure. The individual may be listening to audio signals sent by the researcher through headphones or watching visual images on a screen that is mounted overhead. During these procedures, pictures of the brain are taken, both while the brain is at rest and while it is engaging in an activity such as listening to music, looking at a picture, or making a decision. By comparing the at-rest picture to the activity picture, fMRI tells us what specific brain activity is associated with the mental experience being studied.

Note that saying that fMRI tells us about the brain activity *associated* with a mental experience is a *correlational* statement. As we saw in the chapter "Psychology's Scientific Method", correlations point to the *association* between variables, not to the potential causal link between them. For example, although identifying a picture as a cat may relate to activation in a particular brain area, we do not know if recognizing the cat *caused* the brain activity (Dien, 2009). Still, fMRI is used in experiments in very interesting ways—bolstering what people might say about themselves with evidence directly from the brain. To read about a fascinating study that tracked the effects of time spent in a natural environment on the brain, see the Intersection.

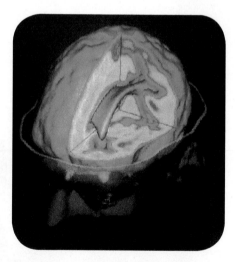

FIGURE 9 Functional Magnetic Resonance Imaging (fMRI) Through fMRI, scientists can literally see what areas of the brain are active during a task by monitoring oxygenated blood levels.

© Peter Arnold, Inc./Stegerphoto/Getty Images

Functional MRI is used not only to establish links between brain areas and behaviors but also to understand the links among different brain areas. *Functional connectivity* refers to the correlation between different brain areas or the degree to which their operation is dependent on each other. Studies of functional connectivity are important because they can tell us about how the brain operates, as a whole, in accomplishing the many complex tasks that it does (Rohr & others, 2015).

An additional method for studying brain functioning, and one that *does* allow for causal inferences, is *transcranial magnetic stimulation (TMS)* (Parkin, Ekhtiari, & Walsh, 2015). First introduced in 1985 (Barker, Jalinous, & Freeston, 1985), TMS is often combined with brain-imaging techniques to establish causal links between brain activity and behavior, to examine neuronal functioning following brain-injuring events such as accidents and strokes, and even to treat some neurological and psychological disorders.

In the TMS procedure, magnetic coils are placed over the person's head and directed at a particular brain area. TMS uses a rapidly changing magnetic field to induce brief electrical current pulses in the brain, and these pulses trigger action potentials in neurons (Parkin, Ekhtiari, & Walsh, 2015). Immediately following this burst of action potentials, activity in the targeted brain area is inhibited, causing what is known as a *virtual lesion*. Completely painless, this technique, when used with brain imaging, allows scientists to examine the role of various brain regions. If a brain region is *associated* with a behavior, as demonstrated using fMRI or PET, then the temporary disruption of processing in that area should disrupt that behavior as well.

So, for instance, in a recent study researchers were interested in identifying the precise areas in a part of the brain called the inferior parietal lobule (or IPL, located on the left side of the brain) that are used to identify word meanings and word sounds as we read (Sliwinska, James, & Devlin, 2015). Participants were asked to provide word meanings or read a word out loud while different areas of the IPL were disrupted using TMS. The results showed that disrupting processing in one area was consistently related to slower response to word meanings, while disruption in another area was associated with slower responses in identifying word sounds. Using TMS, the researchers were able to conclude that these areas play a *causal* role in word perception. TMS is not only used in research but also in treatment (Li & others, 2013).

How the Brain Is Organized

As a human embryo develops inside its mother's womb, the nervous system begins forming as a long, hollow tube on the embryo's back. At three weeks or so after conception, cells making up the tube differentiate into a mass of neurons, most of which then develop into three major regions of the brain: the hindbrain, which is adjacent to the top part of the spinal cord; the midbrain, which rises above the hindbrain; and the forebrain, which is the uppermost region of the brain (Figure 10).

HINDBRAIN

The **hindbrain,** located at the skull's rear, is the lowest portion of the brain. The three main parts of the hindbrain are the medulla, cerebellum, and pons. Figure 11 locates these brain structures.

The *medulla* begins where the spinal cord enters the skull. The medulla controls many vital functions, such as breathing and heart rate. It also regulates our reflexes. The *pons* is a bridge in the hindbrain that connects the cerebellum and the brain stem. It contains several clusters of fibers involved in sleep and arousal (Mijangos-Moreno & others, 2015).

Taken together, the medulla, pons, and much of the hindbrain (as well as the midbrain, discussed below) are called the **brain stem,** which gets its name because it looks like a stem. Embedded deep within the brain, the brain stem connects with the spinal cord at its lower end and then extends upward to encase the reticular formation in the midbrain.

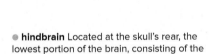

● **hindbrain** Located at the skull's rear, the lowest portion of the brain, consisting of the medulla, cerebellum, and pons.

● **brain stem** The stemlike brain area that includes much of the hindbrain (excluding the cerebellum) and the midbrain; it connects with the spinal cord at its lower end and then extends upward to encase the reticular formation in the midbrain.

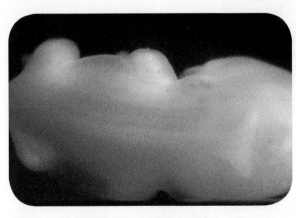

FIGURE 10 Embryological Development of the Nervous System The photograph shows the primitive tubular appearance of the nervous system at six weeks in the human embryo. © Petit Format/Science Source

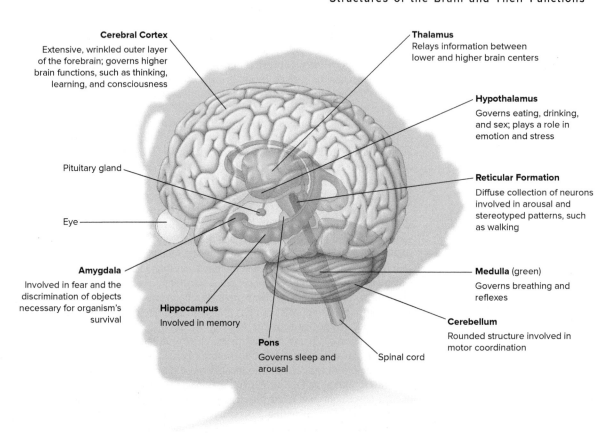

FIGURE 11   Structure and Regions in the Human Brain To get a feel for where these structures are in your own brain, use the eye (*pictured on the left of the figure*) as a landmark. Note that structures such as the thalamus, hypothalamus, amygdala, pituitary gland, pons, and reticular formation reside deep within the brain.

The most ancient part of the brain, the brain stem evolved more than 500 million years ago, when organisms needed to breathe out of water (Hagadorn & Seilacher, 2009). Clumps of cells in the brain stem determine alertness and regulate basic survival functions such as breathing, heartbeat, and blood pressure (Chivers, Constantinescu, & Tench, 2015; Lee & others, 2015). Interestingly, just as musical training can influence other areas of the brain, it relates to differences in the brain stem as well (Weiss & Bidelman, 2015).

The *cerebellum* extends from the rear of the hindbrain. It consists of two rounded structures thought to play important roles in motor coordination (Bosch & others, 2015; Hardwick & others, 2013). The cerebellum coordinates leg and arm movements; for example, when we walk, play golf, and practice the piano, the cerebellum is hard at work. When a wide receiver makes an amazing catch, scraping his toes in bounds, or an outfielder grasps a tricky pop fly, the cerebellum of each deserves credit. If another portion of the brain commands us to send a quick text message to a friend, it is the cerebellum that integrates the muscular activities required to do so. Damage to the cerebellum impairs the performance of coordinated movements. When this damage occurs, people's movements become awkward and jerky. Extensive damage to the cerebellum makes it impossible to stand up.

MIDBRAIN

The **midbrain,** located between the hindbrain and forebrain, is an area in which many nerve-fiber systems ascend and descend to connect the higher and lower portions of the brain (Watabe-Uchita & others, 2012). In particular, the midbrain relays information between the brain and the eyes and ears. The ability to attend to an object visually, for example, is linked to one bundle of neurons in the midbrain.

● **midbrain** Located between the hindbrain and forebrain, an area in which many nerve-fiber systems ascend and descend to connect the higher and lower portions of the brain; in particular, the midbrain relays information between the brain and the eyes and ears.

Parkinson disease damages a section near the bottom of the midbrain called the *substantia nigra* (Lenfeldt & others, 2015), causing deterioration in body movement, rigidity, and tremors. The substantia nigra contains a large number of dopamine-producing neurons. This part of the midbrain feeds dopamine into the *striatum,* the central input station for the basal ganglia, to which we will turn our attention in a moment. The midbrain is rich in dopamine receptors, and as such this area of the brain is especially involved in reward experiences, pleasure, and also addiction (Goertz & others, 2015; Morales & others, 2015).

Another important system in the midbrain is the reticular formation (see Figure 11). The **reticular formation** is a diffuse collection of neurons involved in stereotyped patterns of behavior such as walking, sleeping, and turning to attend to a sudden noise (Jones & Benca, 2013; Nofzinger & others, 2015).

FOREBRAIN

You try to understand what all of these terms and parts of the brain mean. You talk with friends and plan a party for this weekend. You remember that it has been six months since you went to the dentist. You are confident you will do well on the next exam in this course. All of these experiences and millions more would not be possible without the **forebrain**—the brain's largest division and its most forward part (Nord & others, 2015).

But before we explore the structures and function of the forebrain, let's stop for a moment and examine how the brain evolved. The brains of the earliest vertebrates were smaller and simpler than those of later animals. Genetic changes during the evolutionary process were responsible for the development of more complex brains with additional parts and interconnections (Broglio & others, 2015; Luzzati, 2015).

The Psychological Inquiry compares the brain of a rat, a cat, a chimpanzee, and a human. In both the chimpanzee's brain and (especially) the human's brain, the hindbrain and midbrain structures are covered by a forebrain structure called the *cerebral cortex.* The human hindbrain and midbrain are similar to those of other animals, so it is the relative size of the forebrain that mainly differentiates the human brain from the brain of animals such as rats, cats, and chimps. The human forebrain's most important structures are the limbic system, thalamus, basal ganglia, hypothalamus, and cerebral cortex.

Limbic System   The **limbic system,** a loosely connected network of structures under the cerebral cortex, is important in both memory and emotion. Its two principal structures are the amygdala and the hippocampus (see Figure 11).

The **amygdala** is an almond-shaped structure located inside the brain toward the base. In fact, there is an amygdala (the plural is *amygdalae*) on each side of the brain. The amygdala is involved in the discrimination of objects that are necessary for the organism's survival, such as appropriate food, mates, and social rivals. Neurons in the amygdala often fire selectively at the sight of such stimuli, and lesions in the amygdala can cause animals to engage in incorrect behavior such as attempting to eat, fight with, or even mate with an object like a chair.

In both humans and animals, the amygdala is active in response to unpredictable stimuli (Herry & others, 2007). In humans, damage to the amygdala can result in an inability to recognize facial expressions of distress (Adolphs, 2009). The amygdala also is involved in emotional awareness and expression through its many connections with a variety of brain areas (Whalen & others, 2013). One study showed that individuals who are particularly good at regulating their emotions had greater functional connectivity between the amygdalae and the area of the brain that is just behind your forehead (Rohr & others, 2015). This area, called the *prefrontal cortex,* is associated with planning, self-control, and decision making. Interestingly, the size of both the left and right amygdalae is linked to the size of a person's social network (Von Der Heide, Vyas, & Olson, 2014). Throughout this book you will encounter the amygdalae whenever we turn to discussions of intense emotions.

The **hippocampus** has a special role in memory (Czerniawski & others, 2015; Schapiro & others, 2016). Individuals who suffer extensive hippocampal damage cannot retain any

● **reticular formation** A system in the midbrain comprising a diffuse collection of neurons involved in stereotyped patterns of behavior such as walking, sleeping, and turning to attend to a sudden noise.

● **forebrain** The brain's largest division and its most forward part.

● **limbic system** A loosely connected network of structures under the cerebral cortex, important in both memory and emotion. Its two principal structures are the amygdala and the hippocampus.

● **amygdala** An almond-shaped structure within the base of the temporal lobe that is involved in the discrimination of objects that are necessary for the organism's survival, such as appropriate food, mates, and social rivals. There is one amygdala in each hemisphere of the brain.

● **hippocampus** The structure in the limbic system that has a special role in the storage of memories.

psychological *inquiry*

The Brain in Different Species

The below illustration compares the brain of a rat, a cat, a chimpanzee, and a human. In examining the figure, keep in mind that each species is adapted to differing environmental challenges.

1. In what ways is each brain well suited to the challenges faced by its particular species?

2. What structures are similar across all the species? Why do you think certain brain structures are common for these various species? What challenges do all of these species face that would account for the common features of their brains?

3. Note how much larger the cerebral cortex becomes as we go from the brain of a rat to the brain of a human. Why don't rats have a large cerebral cortex?

4. We often think of the human brain as an amazing accomplishment of nature. How might life be different for a rat or a cat with a human brain?

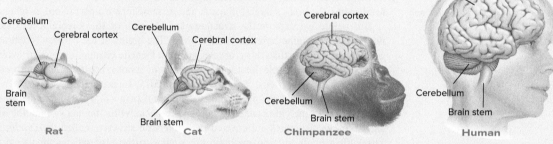

(first photo) © Photodisc/Getty Images; (second photo) © Stockdisc/Stockbyte/Getty Images; (fourth photo) © McGraw-Hill Education/JW Ramsey, photographer

new conscious memories after the damage. It is fairly certain, though, that memories are not stored "in" the limbic system. Instead, the limbic system seems to determine what parts of the information passing through the cortex should be "printed" into durable, lasting neural traces in the cortex. The hippocampus seems to help us recall things by waking up the areas of the brain that were used when we originally encountered the information (Rugg, Johnson, & Uncapher, 2015).

Thalamus   The **thalamus** is a forebrain structure that sits at the top of the brain stem in the central core of the brain (see Figure 11). It serves as a very important relay station, functioning much like a server in a computer network. That is, an important function of the thalamus is to sort information and send it to the appropriate places in the forebrain for further integration and interpretation (Makinson & Huguenard, 2015). For example, one area of the thalamus receives information from the cerebellum and projects it to the motor area of the cerebral cortex. Indeed, most neural input to the cerebral cortex goes through the thalamus. Whereas one area of the thalamus works to orient information from the sense receptors (hearing, seeing, and so on), another region seems to be involved in sleep and wakefulness, having ties with the reticular formation.

● **thalamus** The forebrain structure that sits at the top of the brain stem in the brain's central core and serves as an important relay station.

Basal Ganglia   Above the thalamus and under the cerebral cortex lie large clusters, or *ganglia,* of neurons called **basal ganglia.** The basal ganglia work with the cerebellum and the cerebral cortex to control and coordinate voluntary movements (Nambu, 2015). Basal ganglia enable people to engage in habitual activities such as riding a bicycle and vacuuming a carpet. Individuals with damage to basal ganglia suffer from either unwanted movement, such as constant writhing or jerking of limbs, or too little movement, as in the slow and deliberate movements of people with Parkinson disease (Rolinski & others, 2015).

● **basal ganglia** Large neuron clusters located above the thalamus and under the cerebral cortex that work with the cerebellum and the cerebral cortex to control and coordinate voluntary movements.

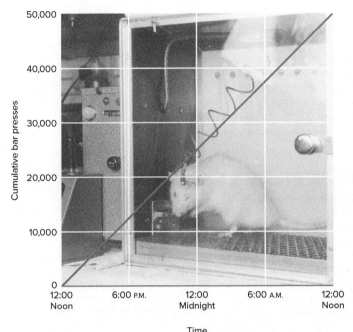

FIGURE 12   Results of the Experiment on the Role of the Hypothalamus in Pleasure The graphed results for one rat show that it pressed the bar more than 2,000 times an hour for a period of 24 hours to receive stimulation to its hypothalamus (Olds, 1958). A rat is shown here pressing a similar bar. © Science Source

● **hypothalamus** A small forebrain structure, located just below the thalamus, that monitors three pleasurable activities—eating, drinking, and sex—as well as emotion, stress, and reward.

Hypothalamus   The **hypothalamus,** a small forebrain structure just below the thalamus, monitors three rewarding activities—eating, drinking, and sex—as well as emotion, stress, and reward (see Figure 11 for the location of the hypothalamus). As we will see later, the hypothalamus also helps direct the endocrine system.

Perhaps the best way to describe the function of the hypothalamus is as a regulator of the body's internal state. It is sensitive to changes in the blood and neural input, and it responds by influencing the secretion of hormones and neural outputs. For example, if the temperature of circulating blood near the hypothalamus is increased by just one or two degrees, certain cells in the hypothalamus start increasing their rate of firing. As a result, a chain of events is set in motion. Increased circulation through the skin and sweat glands occurs immediately to release this heat from the body. The cooled blood circulating to the hypothalamus slows down the activity of some of the neurons there, stopping the process when the temperature is just right—37.1 degrees Celsius (98.6 degrees Fahrenheit). These temperature-sensitive neurons function like a finely tuned thermostat to maintain a balanced state in the body.

The functions of the hypothalamus go far beyond a thermostat, however (Alvarez-Bolado, Grinevich, & Puelles, 2015). The hypothalamus also is involved in emotional states and stress, playing an important role as an integrative location for handling stress. Much of this integration is accomplished through the hypothalamus's action on the pituitary gland—an important endocrine gland located just below it.

If certain areas of the hypothalamus are electrically stimulated, a feeling of pleasure results. In a classic experiment, James Olds and Peter Milner (1954) implanted an electrode in the hypothalamus of a rat's brain. When the rat ran to a corner of an enclosed area, a mild electric current was delivered to its hypothalamus. The researchers thought the electric current would cause the rat to avoid the corner. Much to their surprise, the rat kept returning to the corner. Olds and Milner believed they had discovered a pleasure center in the hypothalamus. Olds (1958) conducted further experiments and found that rats would press bars until they dropped over from exhaustion just to continue to receive a mild electric shock to their hypothalamus. One rat pressed a bar more than 2,000 times an hour for a period of 24 hours to receive the stimulation to its hypothalamus (Figure 12).

Today researchers agree that the hypothalamus is involved in pleasurable feelings, but they have found that other brain areas, such as the limbic system and two other structures—the nucleus accumbens and the ventral tegmental area, to be discussed in the chapter "States of Consciousness"—are also important in the link between the brain and pleasure (Castro, Cole, & Berridge, 2015).

Certainly, the Olds studies have implications for drug addiction (Barson & others, 2015). We will explore the effects of drugs on the reward centers of the brain in the chapter "States of Consciousness".

The Cerebral Cortex

● **cerebral cortex** Part of the forebrain, the outer layer of the brain, responsible for the most complex mental functions, such as thinking and planning.

● **neocortex** The outermost part of the cerebral cortex, making up 80 percent of the cortex in the human brain.

The **cerebral cortex** is part of the forebrain and is the most recently developed part of the brain in the evolutionary scheme. The word *cortex* means "bark" (as in tree bark) in Latin, and the cerebral cortex is in fact the outer layer of the brain. It is in the cerebral cortex that the most complex mental functions, such as thinking and planning, take place.

The **neocortex** (or "new bark") is the outermost part of the cerebral cortex. In humans, this area makes up 80 percent of the cortex (compared with just 30 to 40 percent in most other mammals). The size of the neocortex in mammals is strongly related to the size of the social group in which the organisms live. Some scientists theorize that this part of the human brain, which is responsible for high-level thinking, evolved so that human beings could make sense of one another (Dunbar, 2014).

The neural tissue that makes up the cerebral cortex covers the lower portions of the brain like a sheet that is laid over the brain's surface. In humans, the cerebral cortex is greatly convoluted, with a lot of grooves and bulges, and these considerably enlarge its surface area (compared to a brain with a smooth surface). The cerebral cortex is highly connected with other parts of the brain (Bota, Sporns, & Swanson, 2015). Millions of axons connect the neurons of the cerebral cortex with those located elsewhere in the brain.

LOBES

The wrinkled surface of the cerebral cortex is divided into two halves called *hemispheres* (Figure 13). Each hemisphere is subdivided into four regions, or *lobes*—occipital, temporal, frontal, and parietal (Figure 14).

The **occipital lobes,** located at the back of the head, respond to visual stimuli. Connections among various areas of the occipital lobes allow for the processing of information about aspects of visual stimuli such as their color, shape, and motion (Krigolson, Cheng, & Binsted, 2015). A person can have perfectly functioning eyes, but the eyes only detect and transport information. That information must be interpreted in the occipital lobes in order for the viewer to "see it." A stroke or a wound in an occipital lobe can cause blindness or, at a minimum, can wipe out a portion of the person's visual field.

The **temporal lobes,** the part of the cerebral cortex just above the ears, are involved in hearing, language processing, and memory. The temporal lobes have a number of connections to the limbic system. For this reason, people with damage to the temporal lobes cannot file experiences into long-term memory (Voets & others, 2015).

The **frontal lobes** are the portions of the cerebral cortex behind the forehead that are involved in personality, intelligence, and the control of voluntary muscles. A fascinating case study illustrates how damage to the frontal lobes can significantly alter personality. Phineas T. Gage, a 25-year-old foreman who worked for the Rutland and Burlington Railroad, was the victim of a terrible accident in 1848. Phineas and several coworkers were using blasting powder to construct a roadbed. The crew drilled holes in the rock and gravel, poured in the blasting powder, and then tamped down the powder with an

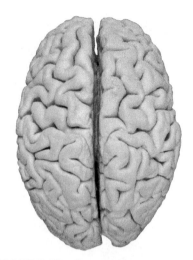

FIGURE 13 The Hemispheres of the Human Brain The two halves (hemispheres) of the human brain can be seen clearly in this photograph.
©McGraw-Hill Education/Christine Eckel, photographer

● **occipital lobes** Structures located at the back of the head that respond to visual stimuli.

● **temporal lobes** Structures in the cerebral cortex that are located just above the ears and are involved in hearing, language processing, and memory.

● **frontal lobes** The portions of the cerebral cortex behind the forehead that are involved in personality, intelligence, and the control of voluntary muscles.

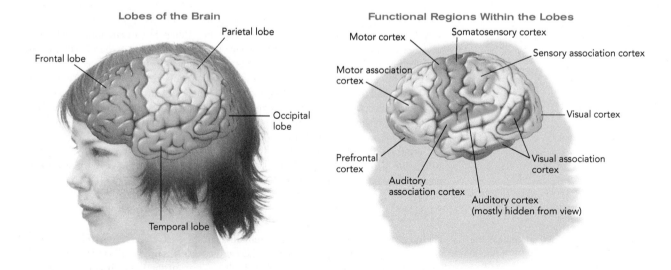

Lobes of the Brain

Frontal lobe
Parietal lobe
Occipital lobe
Temporal lobe

Functional Regions Within the Lobes

Motor cortex
Somatosensory cortex
Motor association cortex
Sensory association cortex
Prefrontal cortex
Visual cortex
Auditory association cortex
Visual association cortex
Auditory cortex (mostly hidden from view)

FIGURE 14 The Lobes and Association Areas of the Cerebral Cortex The cerebral cortex (*left*) is roughly divided into four lobes: occipital, temporal, frontal, and parietal. The cerebral cortex (*right*) also consists of the motor cortex and somatosensory cortex. Further, the cerebral cortex includes association areas, such as the visual association cortex, auditory association cortex, and sensory association cortex. (photo) © ER Productions/Getty Images

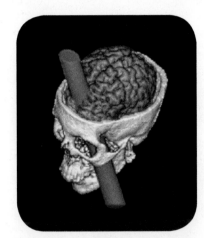

A computerized reconstruction of Phineas T. Gage's accident, based on measurements taken of his skull.

© Patrick Landmann/Science Source

● **parietal lobes** Structures at the top and toward the rear of the head that are involved in registering spatial location, attention, and motor control.

● **somatosensory cortex** A region in the cerebral cortex that processes information about body sensations, located at the front of the parietal lobes.

● **motor cortex** A region in the cerebral cortex that processes information about voluntary movement, located just behind the frontal lobes.

iron rod. While Phineas was still tamping it down, the powder exploded, driving the iron rod up through the left side of his face and out through the top of his head. Although the wound healed in a matter of weeks, Phineas had become a different person. Previously he had been mild-mannered, hardworking, and emotionally calm, well liked by all who knew him. Afterward, he was stubborn, hot-tempered, aggressive, and unreliable. Damage to the frontal lobe area of his brain had dramatically altered Phineas's personality.

The frontal lobes of humans are especially large when compared with those of other animals. For example, in rats the frontal cortex barely exists; in cats, it occupies just 3.5 percent of the cerebral cortex; in chimpanzees, 17 percent; and in humans, approximately 30 percent.

An important part of the frontal lobes is the *prefrontal cortex,* which is at the front of the motor cortex (see Figure 14). The prefrontal cortex is involved in higher cognitive functions such as planning, reasoning, and self-control (Berridge & Arnsten, 2015; Domenech, & Koechlin, 2015).

The **parietal lobes,** located at the top and toward the rear of the head, are involved in registering spatial location, attention, and motor control (Bonino & others, 2015). Thus, the parietal lobes are at work when you are judging how far you have to throw a ball to get it to someone else, when you shift your attention from one activity to another (look away from the TV to a noise outside), and when you turn the pages of a book. Parietal lobes are also involved in our perception of numerical information (Eger & others, 2015). The brilliant physicist Albert Einstein said that his reasoning often was best when he imagined objects in space. It turns out that his parietal lobes were 15 percent larger than average (Witelson, Kigar, & Harvey, 1999).

A word of caution is in order about going too far in localizing function within a particular lobe. Although this discussion has attributed specific functions to a specific lobe (such as vision in the occipital lobe), considerable integration and connection occur between any two or more lobes and between lobes and other parts of the brain.

SOMATOSENSORY CORTEX AND MOTOR CORTEX

Two other important regions of the cerebral cortex are the somatosensory cortex and the motor cortex (see Figure 14). The **somatosensory cortex** processes information about body sensations. It is located at the front of the parietal lobes. The **motor cortex,** at the rear of the frontal lobes, processes information about voluntary movement.

The map in Figure 15 shows which parts of the somatosensory and motor cortexes are associated with various parts of the body. It is based on research done by Wilder Penfield (1947), a neurosurgeon at the Montreal Neurological Institute. He worked with patients who had severe epilepsy, and he often performed surgery to remove portions of the epileptic patients' brains. However, he was concerned that removing a portion of the brain might impair some of the individuals' functions. Penfield's solution was to map the cortex during surgery by stimulating different cortical areas and observing the responses of the patients, who were given a local anesthetic so that they would remain awake during the operation. He found that when he stimulated certain somatosensory and motor areas of the brain, patients reported feeling different sensations or different parts of a patient's body moved.

Penfield's approach is still used today when neurosurgeons perform certain procedures—for example, the removal of a brain tumor. Keeping the patient awake allows the neurosurgeon to ask questions about what the individual is seeing, hearing, and feeling and to be sure that the parts of the brain that are being affected are not essential for consciousness, speech, and other important functions. The extreme precision of brain surgery ensures that life-saving operations do as little harm as possible to the delicate human brain.

For both somatosensory and motor areas, there is a point-to-point relation between a part of the body and a location on the cerebral cortex. In Figure 15, the face and hands are given proportionately more space than other body parts because the face and hands are capable of finer perceptions and movements than are other body areas and therefore need more cerebral cortex representation.

The point-to-point mapping of somatosensory fields onto the cortex's surface is the basis of our orderly and accurate perception of the world (Hsiao & Gomez-Ramirez, 2013).

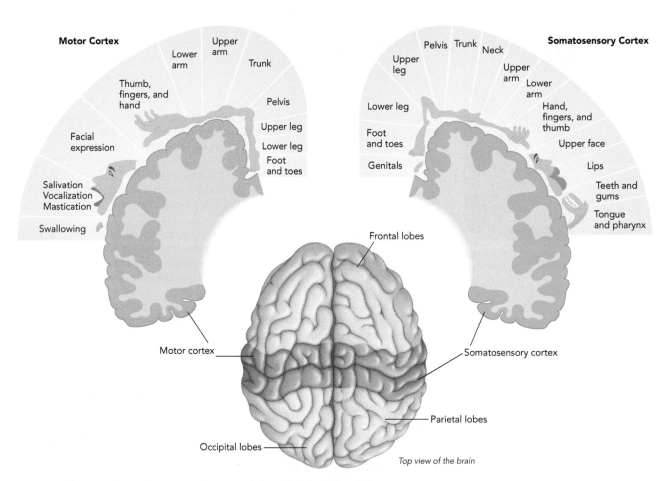

FIGURE 15   Disproportionate Representation of Body Parts in the Motor and Somatosensory Areas of the Cortex
The amount of cortex allotted to a body part is not proportionate to the body part's size. Instead, the brain has more space for body parts that require precision and control. Thus, the thumb, fingers, and hand require more brain tissue than does the arm.

When something touches your lip, for example, your brain knows what body part has been touched because the nerve pathways from your lip are the only pathways that project to the lip region of the somatosensory cortex.

ASSOCIATION CORTEX

Association cortex or **association area** refers to the regions of the cerebral cortex that integrate sensory and motor information. (The term *association cortex* applies to cortical material that is not somatosensory or motor cortex—but it is not filler space.) There are association areas throughout the brain, and each sensory system has its own association area in the cerebral cortex. Intellectual functions, such as thinking and problem solving, occur in the association cortex. Embedded in the brain's lobes, association cortex makes up 75 percent of the cerebral cortex (see Figure 14).

Interestingly, damage to a specific part of association cortex often does not result in a specific loss of function. With the exception of language areas, which are localized, loss of function seems to depend more on the extent of damage to association cortex than on the specific site of the damage. By observing brain-damaged individuals and using a mapping technique, scientists have found that association cortex is involved in linguistic and perceptual functioning.

The largest portion of association cortex is located in the frontal lobes, directly behind the forehead. Damage to this area does not lead to somatosensory or motor loss but rather

● **association cortex or association area**
The region of the cerebral cortex that is the site of the highest intellectual functions, such as thinking and problem solving.

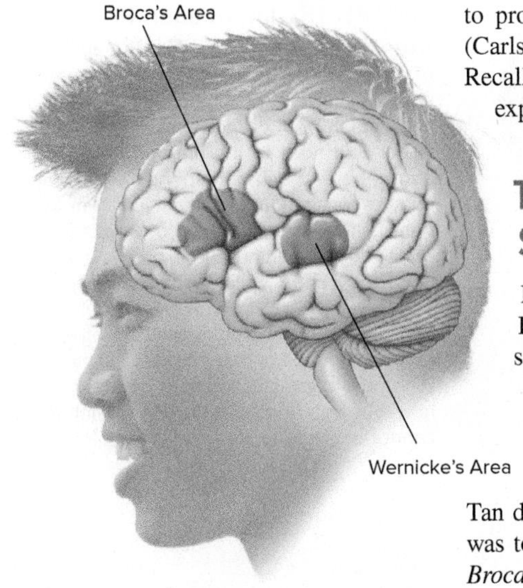

to problems in planning and problem solving, or what are called *executive functions* (Carlson, Zelazo, & Faja, 2013). Personality also may be linked to the frontal lobes. Recall the misfortune of Phineas Gage, whose personality radically changed after he experienced frontal lobe damage.

The Cerebral Hemispheres and Split-Brain Research

Recall that the cerebral cortex is divided into two halves—left and right (see Figure 13). Do these hemispheres have different functions? A discovery by French surgeon Paul Broca provided early evidence that they do.

In 1861 Broca saw a patient who had received an injury to the left side of his brain about 30 years earlier. The patient became known as Tan because *tan* was the only word he could speak. Tan suffered from *expressive aphasia* (also called *Broca's aphasia*), a language disorder that involves the inability to produce language. Tan died several days after Broca evaluated him, and an autopsy revealed that the injury was to a precise area of the left hemisphere. Today we refer to this area of the brain as *Broca's area,* and we know that it plays an important role in the production of speech.

Another area of the brain's left hemisphere that has an important role in language is *Wernicke's area.* This area is named for Carl Wernicke, a German neurologist, who noticed in 1874 that individuals with injuries in the left hemisphere had difficulties in understanding language. Damage to this region causes problems in comprehending language; although an individual with an injury to Wernicke's area can produce words, he or she may not be able to understand what others are saying. Figure 16 shows the locations of Broca's area and Wernicke's area. It is easy to confuse Broca's area (associated with speech production) and Wernicke's area (associated with language comprehension). You might remember that Broca's famous patient was called Tan because that was the only word he could produce, so Broca's area is about speech production.

Today there continues to be considerable interest in the degree to which the brain's left hemisphere or right hemisphere is involved in various aspects of thinking, feeling, and behavior (Falasca & others, 2015; Ruiz & Hupé, 2015; Takamiya & others, 2015). For many years, scientists speculated that the **corpus callosum,** the large bundle of axons that connects the brain's two hemispheres, has something to do with relaying information between the two sides (Figure 17).

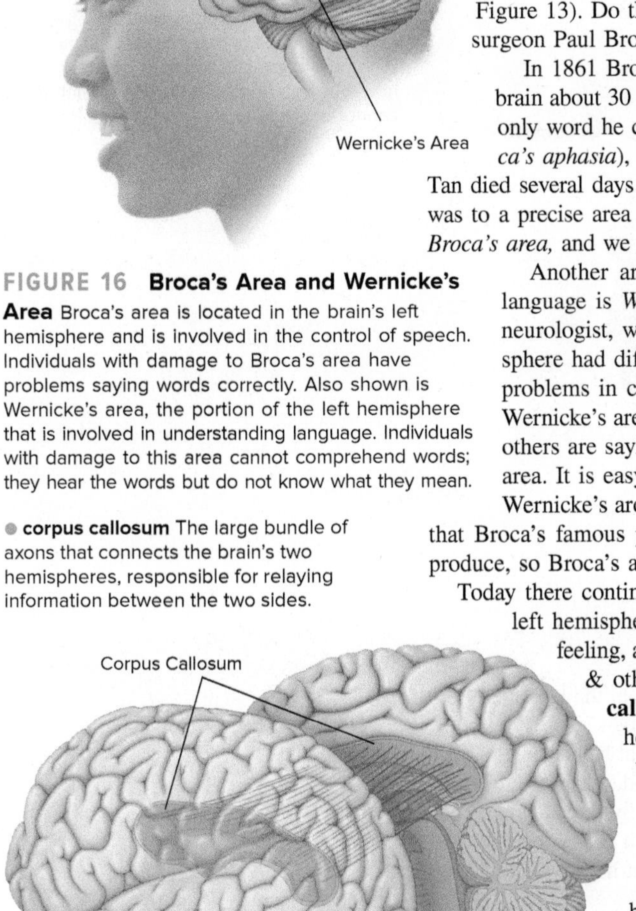

Roger Sperry (1974) confirmed this in an experiment in which he cut the corpus callosum in cats. He also severed certain nerves leading from the eyes to the brain. After the operation, Sperry trained the cats to solve a series of visual problems with one eye blindfolded. After a cat learned the task—say, with only its left eye uncovered—its other eye was blindfolded, and the animal was tested again. The "split-brain" cat behaved as if it had never learned the task. In these cats, memory was stored only in the left hemisphere, which could no longer directly communicate with the right hemisphere.

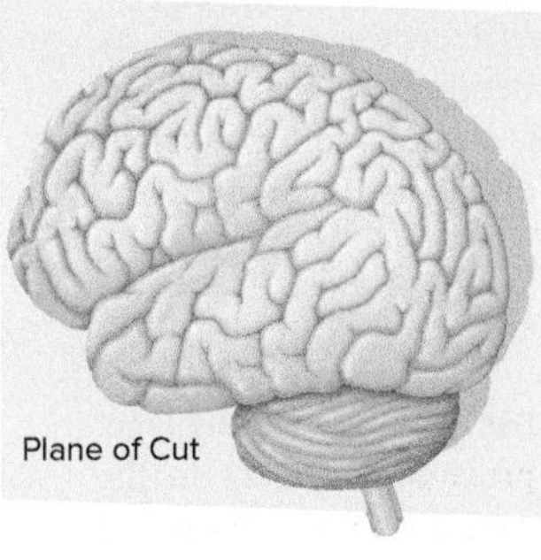

Further evidence of the corpus callosum's function has come from studies of patients with severe, even life-threatening, forms of epilepsy. Epilepsy is caused by electrical "brainstorms" that can flash uncontrollably across the corpus callosum. In one famous case, neurosurgeons severed the corpus callosum of an epileptic patient now known as W. J. in a final attempt to alleviate his unbearable seizures. Sperry (1968) examined W. J. and found that the corpus callosum functions the same in humans as in animals—cutting the corpus callosum seemed to leave the patient with "two separate minds" that learned and operated independently.

FIGURE 16 Broca's Area and Wernicke's Area Broca's area is located in the brain's left hemisphere and is involved in the control of speech. Individuals with damage to Broca's area have problems saying words correctly. Also shown is Wernicke's area, the portion of the left hemisphere that is involved in understanding language. Individuals with damage to this area cannot comprehend words; they hear the words but do not know what they mean.

● **corpus callosum** The large bundle of axons that connects the brain's two hemispheres, responsible for relaying information between the two sides.

FIGURE 17 The Corpus Callosum The corpus callosum is a thick bundle of fibers (essentially axons) that connects the brain cells in one hemisphere to those in the other. In healthy brains, the two sides engage in a continuous flow of information via this neural bridge.

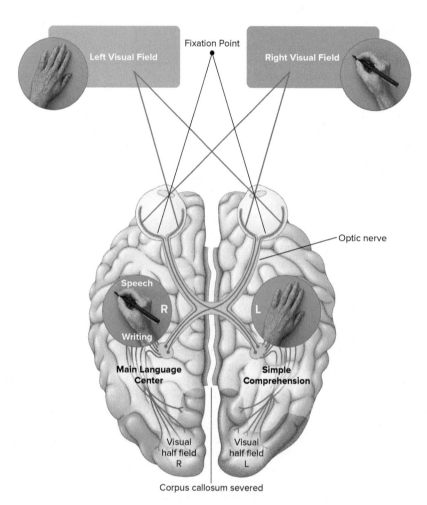

FIGURE 18 **Information Pathways from the Eyes to the Brain** Each of our eyes receives sensory input from both our left and our right field of vision. Information from the left half of our visual field goes to the brain's right hemisphere (which is responsible for simple comprehension), and information from the right half of our visual field goes to the brain's left hemisphere (the brain's main language center, which controls speech and writing). The input received in either hemisphere passes quickly to the other hemisphere across the corpus callosum. When the corpus callosum is severed, however, this transmission of information cannot occur.

As it turns out, the right hemisphere receives information only from the left side of the body, and the left hemisphere receives information only from the right side of the body. When you hold an object in your left hand, for example, only the right hemisphere of your brain detects the object. When you hold an object in your right hand, only the left hemisphere of the brain detects it (Figure 18). In individuals with a normally functioning corpus callosum, both hemispheres receive this information eventually, as it travels between the hemispheres through the corpus callosum. In fact, although we might have two minds, we usually use them in tandem.

You can appreciate how well the corpus callosum rapidly integrates your experience by considering how hard it is to do two things at once (Stirling, 2002). Maybe as a child you tried to pat your head and rub your stomach at the same time. Even with two separate hands controlled by two separate hemispheres, such dual activity is hard.

In people with intact brains, hemispheric specialization of function occurs in some areas. Researchers have uncovered evidence for hemispheric differences in function by sending different information to each ear. Remember, the left hemisphere gets its information (first) from the right ear, and the right hemisphere hears what is going on (first) in the left ear. Such research has shown that the brain tends to divide its functioning into one hemisphere or the other, as we now consider.

LEFT HEMISPHERE FUNCTION

The most extensive research on the brain's two hemispheres has focused on language. Although it is a common misconception that *all* language processing occurs in the brain's left hemisphere, *much* language processing and production does come from this hemisphere (Prat, 2013; Wu & others, 2015). For example, when we are reading, the left hemisphere recognizes words and numbers and comprehends syntax (rules for forming phrases and sentences) and grammar (Skeide, Brauer, & Friederici, 2015), but the right hemisphere does not. The left hemisphere is also keenly involved when we sing the words of a song. In addition, although not generally associated with spatial perception, the left hemisphere can direct us in solving some basic spatial puzzles, such as identifying whether an object is inside or outside a box.

RIGHT HEMISPHERE FUNCTION

The right hemisphere is not as verbally oriented as the left hemisphere, but it does play a role in language. The reason we know that the right hemisphere is the source of some human verbal abilities is that people with split brains can draw (with their left hand) pictures of things that are communicated to them in words that are spoken to them (in their left ear). Also, researchers have found increasing evidence that following damage to the left hemisphere, especially early in development, the right hemisphere can take over some language functions (de Bode & others, 2015; Staudt, 2010). Moreover, the right hemisphere is adept at picking up the meaning of stories and the intonations of voices, and it excels at catching on to song melodies (Bidelman & Chung, 2015; Qi & others, 2015). Furthermore, a recent study revealed that the right hemisphere is involved in conversation processing (Holtgraves, 2012).

The real strength of the right hemisphere, however, appears to lie in the processing of nonverbal information such as spatial perception, visual recognition, and emotion (Kensinger & Choi, 2009). With respect to interpreting spatial information, the right hemisphere is involved in our ability to tell if something is on top of something else, how far apart two objects are, and whether two objects moving in space might crash.

The right hemisphere is the one mainly at work when we process information about people's faces (Caspers & others, 2015; Kanwisher, 2006). How do we know? One way we know is that researchers have asked people to watch images on a computer screen and to press a button with either their right or left hand if they recognize a face. Even right-handed people are faster to recognize faces with their left hand because the information goes directly from the part of the brain that recognizes faces (the right hemisphere) to the left hand (Gillihan & Farah, 2005).

Research by Nancy Kanwisher and her colleagues has provided evidence for the role of a specialized area in the brain for processing faces (Kanwisher & Yovel, 2010; McKone, Crookes, & Kanwisher, 2010; Pitcher & others, 2012). This area, located in the fusiform gyrus in the right temporal lobe, is called the *fusiform face area (FFA)*. The FFA is a dime-size spot just behind your right ear. Using fMRI, researchers have shown that the FFA is especially active when a person is viewing a face—a human face, a cat's face, or a cartoon face—but not cars, butterflies, or other objects (Tong & others, 2000).

The right hemisphere may be more involved than the left hemisphere, too, in processing information about emotions—both when we express emotions ourselves and when we interpret others' emotions (Carmona, Holland, & Harrison, 2009). People are more likely to remember emotion words if they hear them in the left ear. As well, much of our sense of humor resides in the right hemisphere (Bartolo & others, 2006; Coulson & Wu, 2005). If you want to be sure that someone laughs at your joke, tell it to the person's left ear!

RIGHT-BRAINED VERSUS LEFT-BRAINED

People commonly use the terms *left-brained* (meaning logical and rational) and *right-brained* (meaning creative or artistic) as a way of categorizing different brain functioning in themselves and others. Such generalizations have little scientific basis, however—and that is a good thing. We have both hemispheres for a reason: We use them both. For most complex human activities, there is interplay between the brain's two hemispheres (Hinkley & others, 2012).

test yourself

1. Describe three techniques that allow researchers to examine the brain while it is working.
2. What specific part of the brain is responsible for directing our most complex mental functions, such as thinking and planning, and where is it located?
3. In what ways are the brain's left and right hemispheres specialized in terms of their functioning?

Integration of Function in the Brain

How do all of the regions of the brain cooperate to produce the wondrous complexity of thought and behavior that characterizes humans? Neuroscience still does not have answers to questions such as how the brain solves a murder mystery or composes an essay. Even so, we can get a sense of integrative brain function by using a real-world scenario, such as the act of escaping from a burning building.

Imagine that you are sitting at your computer, writing an e-mail, when a fire breaks out behind you. The sound of crackling flames is relayed from your ear through the thalamus, to the auditory cortex, and on to the auditory association cortex. At each stage, the stimulus is processed to extract information, and at some stage, probably at the association cortex level, the sounds are finally matched with something like a neural memory representing sounds of fires you have heard previously.

The association "fire" sets new machinery in motion. Your attention (guided in part by the reticular formation) shifts to the auditory signal being held in your association cortex and on to your auditory association cortex, and simultaneously (again guided by reticular systems) your head turns toward the noise.

Now your visual association cortex reports in: "Objects matching flames are present." In other regions of the association cortex, the visual and auditory reports are synthesized ("We have things that look and sound like fire"), and neural associations representing potential actions ("flee") are activated. However, firing the neurons that code the plan to flee will not get you out of the chair. For that task, the basal ganglia must become engaged, and from there the commands will arise to set the brain stem, motor cortex, and cerebellum to the work of transporting you out of the room. All of this happens in mere seconds.

So, which part of your brain did you use to escape? Virtually all systems had a role. By the way, you would probably remember this event because your limbic circuitry would likely have started memory formation when the association "fire" was triggered. The next time the sounds of crackling flames reach your auditory association cortex, the associations triggered would include this most recent escape. In sum, considerable integration of function takes place in the brain. All of the parts of the nervous system work together as a team to keep you safe and sound.

4. THE ENDOCRINE SYSTEM

The nervous system works closely with another bodily system—the endocrine system. The **endocrine system** consists of a set of glands that regulate the activities of certain organs by releasing their chemical products into the bloodstream. **Glands** are organs or tissues in the body that produce chemicals that control many bodily functions. The endocrine glands consist of the pituitary gland, the thyroid and parathyroid glands, the adrenal glands, the pancreas, the ovaries in females, and the testes in males (Figure 19). The chemical messengers produced by these glands are called **hormones.** The bloodstream carries hormones to all parts of the body, and the membrane of every cell has receptors for one or more hormones. Let's take a closer look at the function of some of the main endocrine glands.

The **pituitary gland,** a pea-sized gland just beneath the hypo-thalamus, controls growth and regulates other glands (Figure 20). The anterior (front) part of the pituitary is known as the *master gland,* because almost all of its hormones direct the activity of target glands elsewhere in the body. In turn, the anterior pituitary gland is controlled by the hypothalamus.

● **endocrine system** The body system consisting of a set of glands that regulate the activities of certain organs by releasing their chemical products into the bloodstream.

● **glands** Organs or tissues in the body that create chemicals that control many bodily functions.

● **hormones** Chemical messengers that are produced by the endocrine glands and carried by the bloodstream to all parts of the body.

● **pituitary gland** A pea-sized gland just beneath the hypothalamus that controls growth and regulates other glands.

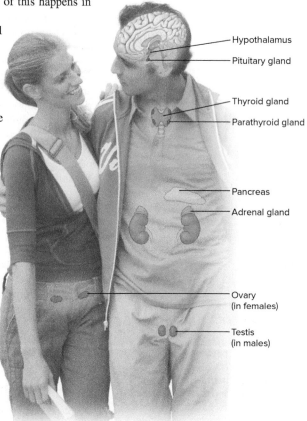

Hypothalamus
Pituitary gland
Thyroid gland
Parathyroid gland
Pancreas
Adrenal gland
Ovary (in females)
Testis (in males)

FIGURE 19   The Major Endocrine Glands The pituitary gland releases hormones that regulate the hormone secretions of the other glands. The pituitary gland is regulated by the hypothalamus. (photo) © PhotoAlto/PunchStock

90 CHAPTER 3 Biological Foundations of Behavior

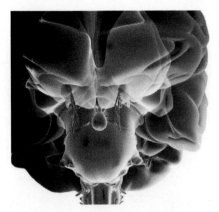

FIGURE 20 The Pituitary Gland
The pituitary gland, which hangs by a short stalk from the hypothalamus, regulates the hormone production of many of the body's endocrine glands. Here it is enlarged 30 times. © MedicalRF.com

● **adrenal glands** Glands at the top of each kidney that are responsible for regulating mood, energy level, and the ability to cope with stress.

● **pancreas** A dual-purpose gland under the stomach that performs both digestive and endocrine functions.

● **ovaries** Sex-related endocrine glands that produce hormones involved in female sexual development and reproduction.

● **testes** Sex-related endocrine glands in the scrotum that produce hormones involved in male sexual development and reproduction.

test yourself

1. What is the endocrine system's function, and what role do hormones play in it?
2. What two adrenal gland secretions prepare the body to react quickly to emergencies, and what specifically do they do?
3. Through what brain structure are the nervous and the endocrine systems connected, and what do the two systems work together to control?

The **adrenal glands,** located at the top of each kidney, regulate mood, energy level, and the ability to cope with stress. Each adrenal gland secretes epinephrine (also called *adrenaline*) and norepinephrine (also called *noradrenaline*). Unlike most hormones, epinephrine and norepinephrine act quickly. Epinephrine helps a person get ready for an emergency by acting on smooth muscles, the heart, stomach, intestines, and sweat glands. In addition, epinephrine stimulates the reticular formation, which in turn arouses the sympathetic nervous system, and this system subsequently excites the adrenal glands to produce more epinephrine.

Norepinephrine also alerts the individual to emergency situations by interacting with the pituitary and the liver. You may remember that norepinephrine functions as a neurotransmitter when it is released by neurons. In the adrenal glands, norepinephrine is released as a hormone. In both instances, norepinephrine conveys information—in the first case, to neurons; in the second case, to glands (Nicolaides, Charmandari, & Chrousos, 2015). The activation of the adrenal glands has an important role to play in stress and physical health, as we will see at the end of this chapter (Lovallo, 2015).

The **pancreas,** located under the stomach, is a dual-purpose gland that performs both digestive and endocrine functions. The part of the pancreas that serves endocrine functions produces a number of hormones, including insulin. This part of the pancreas, the *islets of Langerhans,* busily turns out hormones like a little factory. Insulin is an essential hormone that controls glucose (blood sugar) levels in the body and is related to metabolism, body weight, and obesity.

The **ovaries,** located in the pelvis on either sides of the uterus in females, and **testes,** located in the scrotum in males, are the sex-related endocrine glands that produce hormones involved in sexual development and reproduction. These glands and the hormones they produce play important roles in developing sexual characteristics, as we will discover in the chapter "Gender, Sex, and Sexuality". They are also involved in other characteristics and behaviors, as we will see throughout this book.

Neuroscientists have discovered that the nervous system and endocrine system are intricately interconnected. They know that the brain's hypothalamus connects the nervous system and the endocrine system and that the two systems work together to control the body's activities. Recall from earlier in the chapter that the autonomic nervous system regulates processes such as respiration, heart rate, and digestion. The autonomic nervous system acts on the endocrine glands to produce a number of important physiological reactions to strong emotions, such as rage and fear.

The endocrine system differs significantly from the nervous system in a variety of ways. For one thing, as you saw in Figure 19, the parts of the endocrine system are not all connected in the way that the parts of the nervous system are. For another, the endocrine system works more slowly than the nervous system, because hormones are transported in our blood through the circulatory system. Our hearts do a mind-boggling job of pumping blood throughout the body, but blood moves far more slowly than the neural impulses do in the nervous system's superhighway.

5. BRAIN DAMAGE, PLASTICITY, AND REPAIR

Recall from the discussion of the brain's important characteristics earlier in this chapter that plasticity is an example of the brain's remarkable adaptability. Neuroscientists have studied plasticity, especially following brain damage, and have charted the brain's ability to repair itself (Chen & others, 2015; Schneider & others, 2014; Sun, 2016). Brain damage can produce horrific effects, including paralysis, sensory loss, memory loss, and personality deterioration. When such damage occurs, can the brain recover some or all of its functions? Recovery from brain damage varies considerably, depending on the age of the individual and the extent of the damage (Kolb & Teskey, 2012).

The Brain's Plasticity and Capacity for Repair

The human brain shows the most plasticity in young children, before the functions of the cortical regions become entirely fixed (Spencer-Smith & Anderson, 2011). For example, if the speech areas in an infant's left hemisphere are damaged, the right hemisphere assumes much of this language function. However, after age 5, damage to the left hemisphere can permanently disrupt language ability. We examine the brain's plasticity further in the chapter "Sensation and Perception" and the chapter "Human Development".

A key factor in recovery is whether some or all of the neurons in an affected area are just damaged versus whether they are destroyed (Huang & Chang, 2009). If the neurons have not been destroyed, brain function often becomes restored over time. There are three ways in which repair of the damaged brain might take place:

- *Collateral sprouting,* the process by which axons of some healthy neurons adjacent to damaged cells grow new branches.
- *Substitution of function,* the process by which the damaged region's function is taken over by another area or areas of the brain.
- *Neurogenesis,* the process by which new neurons are generated.

Researchers have found that neurogenesis occurs in mammals such as mice. In mice, exercise increases neurogenesis whereas social isolation decreases it (Clemenson, Deng, & Gage, 2015; Gil-Mohapel & others, 2011; Leasure & Decker, 2009). It is now accepted that neurogenesis can occur in humans (Göritz & Frisén, 2012; Inta & Gass, 2015; Sun, 2016). However, to date, the presence of new neurons has been documented only in the hippocampus, which is involved in memory, and the olfactory bulb, which is involved in the sense of smell (Anacker, Denny, & Hen, 2015; Xu & others, 2013). And researchers are exploring how the grafting of neural stem cells to various regions of the brain, such as the hypothalamus, might increase neurogenesis (Dadwal & others, 2015; Decimo & others, 2012). If researchers can discover how new neurons are generated, possibly the information can be used to fight degenerative diseases of the brain such as Alzheimer disease and Parkinson disease.

Brain Tissue Implants

The brain naturally recovers some, but not all, functions that are lost following damage. Recent research has generated excitement about *brain grafts*—implants of healthy tissue into damaged brains (Hattiangady & Shetty, 2012). Brain grafts have greater potential success when the brain tissue used is from the fetal stage—an early stage in prenatal development (Thomas & others, 2009). The reason for this advantage is that the fetal neurons are still growing and have a much higher probability of making connections with other neurons than does mature brain tissue. In a number of studies, researchers have damaged part of an adult rat's brain, waited until the animal recovered as much as possible by itself, and assessed its behavioral deficits. They then took the corresponding area of a fetal rat's brain and transplanted it into the damaged brain of the adult rat. In these studies, the rats that received the brain transplants demonstrated considerable behavioral recovery (Reyes, Tajiri, & Borlongan, 2015; Shetty, Rao, & Hattiangady, 2008).

Might such grafts be successful in humans suffering from brain damage? The research results are promising, but finding donors is a problem (Glaw & others, 2009). Although using brain tissue from aborted fetuses is a possibility, there are ethical concerns about that practice.

Perhaps one of the most heated debates in recent years has concerned the use of human embryonic stem cells in research and treatment. The human body contains more than 220 different types of cells, but **stem cells** are unique because they are primitive cells that have the capacity to develop into most types of human cells.

Stem cells were first harvested from embryos by researchers at the University of Wisconsin, Madison, and Johns Hopkins University in 1998. Because of their amazing

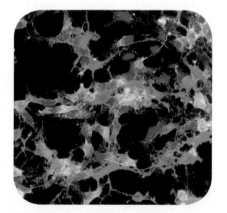

This fluorescent micrograph shows glial stem cells. Like other stem cells, these have the capacity to develop into a wide range of other cells.

©Riccardo Cassiani-Ingoni/Science Source

● **stem cells** Unique primitive cells that have the capacity to develop into most types of human cells.

plasticity, stem cells might potentially replace damaged cells in the human body, including cells involved in spinal cord injury and brain damage (Rosser & Bachoud-Lévi, 2012; Yoo, Kim, & Hwang, 2013).

Typically, researchers have harvested the stem cells from frozen embryos left over from *in vitro fertilization* procedures. In these procedures, a number of eggs, or *ova*, are collected from a woman's ovaries in order to be fertilized in a lab. In successful in vitro fertilization, the ova are brought together with sperm, producing human embryos. Because the procedure is difficult and delicate, doctors typically fertilize a large number of eggs in the hope that some will survive when implanted in the woman's uterus. In the typical procedure, there are leftover embryos. These embryos are in the *blastocyst* stage, which occurs five days after conception. At this stage the embryo has not yet attached to the uterus and has no brain, no central nervous system, and no mouth—it is an undifferentiated ball of cells.

Some supporters of stem cell technology emphasize that using these cells for research and treatment might relieve a great deal of human suffering. Opponents of abortion disapprove of the use of stem cells in research or treatment on the grounds that the embryos die when the stem cells are removed. (In fact, leftover embryos are likely to be destroyed in any case.) In 2009, President Barack Obama removed restrictions on stem cell research.

test yourself

1. Describe three ways in which a damaged brain may repair itself.
2. What specific discovery have researchers made about neurogenesis in human beings? For what kinds of disease might knowledge about the process lead to promising treatment?
3. What are brain grafts, and why does the use of fetal tissue in grafts often lead to successful results?

• **chromosomes** In the human cell, threadlike structures that come in 23 pairs, one member of each pair originating from each parent, and that contain the remarkable substance DNA.

• **deoxyribonucleic acid (DNA)** A complex molecule in the cell's chromosomes that carries genetic information.

• **genes** The units of hereditary information, consisting of short segments of chromosomes composed of DNA.

A positive result from the Human Genome Project. Shortly after Andrew Gobea was born, his cells were genetically altered to prevent his immune system from failing.

© Mark J. Terrill/AP Images

6. GENETICS AND BEHAVIOR

In addition to the brain and nervous system, other aspects of our physiology also have consequences for psychological processes. Genes, the focal point of this section, are an essential contributor to these processes (Bishop, 2015; Pluess, 2015). As noted in the "What Is Psychology?" chapter, the influence of nature (our internal genetic endowment) and nurture (our external experience) on psychological characteristics has long fascinated psychologists. We begin by examining some basic facts about the central internal agent of our human differences: our genes.

Chromosomes, Genes, and DNA

Within the human body are literally trillions of cells. The nucleus of each human cell contains 46 **chromosomes,** threadlike structures that come in 23 pairs, with one member of each pair originating from each biological parent. Chromosomes contain the remarkable substance **deoxyribonucleic acid (DNA),** a complex molecule that carries genetic information. **Genes,** the units of hereditary information, are short chromosome segments composed of DNA. The relationship among cells, chromosomes, genes, and DNA is illustrated in Figure 21.

Genes hold the code for creating proteins out of amino acids forming the bases for everything our bodies do. Specifically, genes direct and regulate the production of these proteins. Although every cell in our body contains a full complement of our genes, different genes are active in each cell. Many genes encode proteins that are unique to a particular cell and give the cell its identity. Will it be a neuron or a bone cell? The activation of our genes holds the key to this question. Some genes are involved in the development of the embryo and then are turned off for the rest of life. Genes do not operate independently but work with one another and in collaboration with hormones and the environment to direct the body's function (Goossens & others, 2015; Moore, 2013).

An international research program called the Human Genome Project (*genome* refers to an organism's complete genetic material, as discussed below) is dedicated to documenting the human genome. Human beings have approximately 20,500 genes (National Human Genome Research Institute, 2015). When these 20,500 genes from one parent combine at conception with the same number of genes from the other parent, the number of possibilities is staggering. Although scientists are still a long way from unraveling all the mysteries about the way genes work, some aspects of this process are well

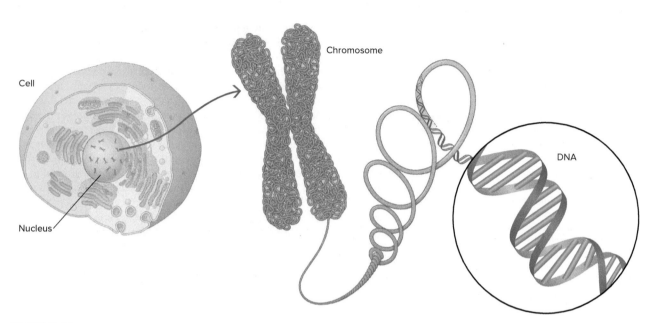

FIGURE 21 Cells, Chromosomes, Genes, and DNA (*Left*) The body houses trillions of cells, which are the basic structural units of life. Each cell contains a central structure, the nucleus. (*Middle*) Chromosomes and genes are located in the nucleus of the cell. Chromosomes are made up of threadlike structures composed mainly of DNA molecules. Note that inside the chromosome are the genes. (*Right*) A gene is a segment of DNA that contains the hereditary code. The structure of DNA resembles a spiral ladder.

understood, starting with the fact that multiple genes interact to give rise to observable characteristics.

The Study of Genetics

Historically speaking, genetics is a relatively young science. Its origins go back to the mid-nineteenth century, when an Austrian monk, Gregor Mendel, studied heredity in generations of pea plants. By crossbreeding plants with different characteristics and noting the characteristics of the offspring, Mendel discovered predictable patterns of heredity and thereby laid the foundation for modern genetics.

Mendel noticed that some genes seem to be more likely than others to show up in the physical characteristics of an organism. In some gene pairs, one gene is dominant over the other. If one gene of a pair is dominant and one is recessive, the **dominant-recessive genes principle** applies, meaning that the dominant gene overrides the recessive gene—that is, it prevents the recessive gene from expressing its instructions. The recessive gene exerts its influence only if *both* genes of a pair are recessive. If you inherit a recessive gene from only one biological parent, you may never know you carry the gene.

In the world of dominant-recessive genes, brown eyes, farsightedness, and dimples rule over blue eyes, nearsightedness, and freckles. If, however, you inherit a recessive gene for a trait from *both* of your biological parents, you will show the trait. That is why two brown-haired parents can have a child with red hair: Each parent would have dominant genes for brown hair and recessive genes for red hair. Because dominant genes override recessive genes, the parents have brown hair. However, the child can inherit recessive genes for red hair from each biological parent. With no dominant genes to override them, the recessive genes would make the child's hair red.

Yet the relationship between genes and characteristics is complex. Even simple traits such as eye color and hair color are likely the product of *multiple* genes. Moreover, many different genes probably influence complex human characteristics such as personality and intelligence. Scientists use the term *polygenic inheritance* to describe the influences of multiple genes on behavior.

● **dominant-recessive genes principle** The principle that, if one gene of a pair is dominant and one is recessive, the dominant gene overrides the recessive gene. A recessive gene exerts its influence only if both genes of a pair are recessive.

Present-day researchers continue to apply Mendel's methods, as well as the latest technology, in their quest to expand our knowledge of genetics. We next survey four ways in which scientists investigate our genetic heritage: molecular genetics, selective breeding, genome-wide association method, and behavior genetics.

MOLECULAR GENETICS

The field of *molecular genetics* involves the manipulation of genes using technology to determine their effect on behavior. There is currently a great deal of enthusiasm about the use of molecular genetics to discover the specific locations on genes that determine an individual's susceptibility to many diseases and other aspects of health and well-being (Bartels & Baselmans, 2015; Kendler & others, 2012; Li & others, 2015; Polfus, Gibbs, & Boerwinkle, 2015).

SELECTIVE BREEDING

Selective breeding is a genetic method in which organisms are chosen for reproduction based on how much of a particular trait they display. Mendel developed this technique in his studies of pea plants. A more recent example involving behavior is the classic selective breeding study conducted by Robert Tryon (1940). He chose to study maze-running ability in rats. After he trained a large number of rats to run a complex maze, he then mated the rats that were the best at maze running ("maze bright") with each other and the ones that were the worst ("maze dull") with each other. He continued this process with 21 generations of rats. As Figure 22 shows, after several generations, the maze-bright rats significantly outperformed the maze-dull rats.

Selective breeding studies demonstrate that genes are an important influence on behavior, but that does not mean experience is unimportant. For example, in another study, maze-bright and maze-dull rats were reared in one of two environments: (1) an impoverished environment that consisted of a barren wire-mesh group cage or (2) an enriched environment that contained tunnels, ramps, visual displays, and other stimulating objects (Cooper & Zubeck, 1958). When they reached maturity, only the maze-dull rats that had been reared in an impoverished environment made more maze-learning errors than the maze-bright rats.

It is unethical to conduct selective breeding studies with human beings. (*Eugenics* refers to the application of selective breeding to humans; Adolf Hitler notoriously espoused this practice in Nazi Germany.) In humans, researchers generally examine the influence of genetics on psychological characteristics by using behavior genetics.

GENOME-WIDE ASSOCIATION METHOD

Completion of the Human Genome Project has led to use of the *genome-wide association method* to identify genetic variations linked to a particular disease, such as cancer, cardiovascular disease, or Alzheimer disease (National Human Genome Research Institute, 2015). To conduct a genome-wide association study, researchers obtain DNA from individuals who have the disease under study and from those who do not. Then, each participant's complete set of DNA, or genome, is purified from the blood or cells and scanned on machines to determine markers of genetic variation. If the genetic variations occur more frequently in people who have the disease, the variations point to the region in the human genome where the disease-causing problem exists. Genome-wide association studies have been conducted for a variety of diseases and

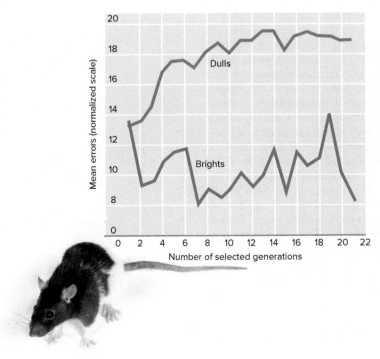

FIGURE 22   Results of Tryon's Selective Breeding Experiment with Maze-Bright and Maze-Dull Rats These results demonstrate genetic influences on behavior. © PunchStock/BananaStock

disorders, including Alzheimer disease (Raj & others, 2012) and depression (Major Depressive Disorder Working Group, 2013).

Genes that are close to one another in our DNA are more likely to be inherited together. This link between genes is used in what is called *linkage analysis.* This analysis may help identify the location of certain genes by referring to other genes whose position is already known, which is a strategy often used to search for genes associated with a disease (Ott, Wang, & Leal, 2015). Gene linkage studies are now being conducted on a wide variety of disorders and health issues.

A key challenge in genome-wide association studies, as well as genetic linkage studies, is replication. Recall that replicating a research finding means repeating it. If a genetic characteristic is associated with a particular disorder, disease, or characteristic in one sample of participants, this association should emerge as well in another sample. Unfortunately, many early findings using genome-wide analyses did not replicate; that is, genes that were associated with a particular characteristic in one sample did not show the same association in later studies. As a result, scientists who use these tools have become increasingly cautious about drawing conclusions (Jannot, Ehret, & Perneger, 2015).

BEHAVIOR GENETICS

Behavior genetics is the study of the degree and nature of heredity's influence on behavior. Behavior genetics is less invasive than the other types of genetic investigation. Using methods such as the *twin study,* behavior geneticists examine the extent to which individuals are shaped by their heredity and their environmental experiences (Ilies & Dimotakis, 2015; Knopik & others, 2015; South, 2015).

In the most common type of twin study, researchers compare the behavioral similarity of identical twins with the behavioral similarity of fraternal twins (Bell & Saffery, 2012). *Identical twins* develop from a single fertilized egg that splits into two genetically identical embryos, each of which becomes a person. *Fraternal twins* develop from separate eggs and separate sperm, and so they are genetically no more similar than non-twin siblings. They may even be of different sexes.

By comparing groups of identical and fraternal twins, behavior geneticists capitalize on the fact that identical twins are more similar genetically than are fraternal twins. In one study, 428 identical and fraternal twin pairs in Italy were compared with respect to their levels of self-esteem, life satisfaction, and optimism for the future (Caprara & others, 2009). The identical twins were much more similar than the fraternal twins on these measures. Furthermore, the researchers found that these various aspects of the person's well-being were similarly affected by genes but differently influenced by the environment. That means that there appeared to be a genetic tendency to have a positive attitude toward different aspects of one's life. In contrast, the environment explained how a person might have high self-esteem but lower life satisfaction (Caprara & others, 2009).

In another type of twin study, researchers evaluate identical twins who were reared in separate environments. If their behavior is similar, the assumption is that heredity has played an important role in shaping their behavior. This strategy is the basis for the Minnesota Study of Twins Reared Apart, directed by Thomas Bouchard and his colleagues (1996). The researchers bring identical twins who have been reared apart to Minneapolis from all over the world to study their behavior. They ask thousands of questions about their family, childhood, interests, and values. Researchers obtain detailed medical histories with information about diet, smoking, and exercise habits. However, drawing strong conclusions about genetics from twins reared apart has been criticized for various reasons. First, some of the separated twins in the Minnesota study had been together several months prior to their adoption and some had been reunited prior to testing (in certain cases, for a number of years). In addition, adoption agencies often put identical twins in similar homes. Finally, even strangers (of the exact same age) are likely to have some coincidental similarities (Joseph, 2006).

You have probably heard of instances of twins who were separated at birth and who, upon being reunited later in life, found themselves strikingly similar to each other. To think critically about such cases, consider the Psychological Inquiry.

psychological *inquiry*

© Kenneth Sponsler/Getty Images

Identical Twins

We've all heard stories about identical twins who were separated at birth. When these twins meet up in adulthood, people often find the similarities between them to be uncanny. Are these similarities evidence of the extraordinary power of genes? Let's take a closer look.

1. Imagine that you did not see this photo of twins and were simply asked how similar two people of the same gender, ethnicity, and age might be. In what ways might such people be alike?

2. How might such individuals, even growing up in very different environments, evoke similar responses from others?

3. Do you think that people of this same gender, age, and ethnicity might enjoy similar hobbies? Have similar jobs?

4. What does this Psychological Inquiry tell you about the power of vivid and unusual cases in the conclusions we reach?

Our height depends significantly on the genes we inherit. However, even if we have genes that call for the stature of a basketball center, we may not reach that "genetically programmed" height if we lack good nutrition, adequate shelter, and medical care.

© Leon Bennett/Getty Images

● **genotype** An individual's genetic heritage; one's actual genetic material.

● **phenotype** An individual's observable characteristics.

Genes and the Environment

So far, we have focused a lot on genes, and you are probably getting the picture that genes are a powerful force in an organism. The role of genetics in some characteristics may seem obvious; for instance, how tall you are depends to a large degree on how tall your parents are. However, imagine a person growing up in an environment with poor nutrition, inadequate shelter, little or no medical care, and a mother who had received no prenatal care. This individual may have genes that call for the height of an NBA or a WNBA center, but without environmental support for this genetic capacity, he or she may never reach that genetically programmed height.

The relationship between an individual's genes and the actual person we see before us is not a perfect one-to-one correspondence. Even for a characteristic such as height, genes do not fully determine where a person will stand on this variable. We need to account for the role of nurture, or environmental factors, in the characteristics we see in the fully grown person.

If the environment matters for an apparently simple characteristic such as height, imagine the role it might play in a complex psychological characteristic such as being outgoing or intelligent. For such a trait, genes are, again, not directly reflected in the characteristics of the person. Indeed, genes cannot tell us exactly what a person will be like. Genes are simply related to some of the characteristics we see in a person.

To account for this gap between genes and actual observable characteristics, scientists distinguish between a genotype and a phenotype. A **genotype** is an individual's genetic heritage, the actual genetic material present in every cell in the person's body. A **phenotype** is the individual's observable characteristics. The relationship between a genotype and phenotype is not always obvious. Recall that some genetic characteristics are dominant and others are recessive. Seeing that a person has brown eyes (his or her phenotype) tells us nothing about whether the person might also have a gene for blue eyes (his or her genotype) hiding out as well. The phenotype is influenced both by the genotype and by environmental factors.

The word *phenotype* applies to both physical *and* psychological characteristics. Consider a trait such as extraversion—the tendency to be outgoing and sociable. Even if we knew the exact genetic recipe for extraversion, we still could not perfectly predict a person's level of (phenotypic) extraversion from his or her genes, because at least some of this trait comes from the person's experience. We will revisit the concepts of genotype and phenotype throughout this book—for example, when we look at intelligence, when we explore human development, and when we examine personality.

Whether a gene is "turned on"—that is, directing cells to assemble proteins—is a matter of collaboration between hereditary and environmental factors. *Genetic expression,* a term that refers to gene activity that affects the body's cells, is influenced by the genes' environment (Gottlieb, 2007). For example, hormones that circulate in the blood make their way into the cell, where they can turn genes on and off. This flow of hormones can be affected by external environmental conditions, such as the amount of light, the length of the day, nutrition, and behavior. Another factor that can influence DNA synthesis is stress, a powerful factor in health and wellness as we consider next.

7. PSYCHOLOGY'S BIOLOGICAL FOUNDATIONS AND HEALTH AND WELLNESS

So far, we have explored the structure and function of various aspects of the nervous system. The components of the nervous system play an essential role in our health and wellness.

Stress is the response of individuals to **stressors,** which are the circumstances and events that threaten them and tax their coping abilities. Recall that the sympathetic nervous system jumps into action when we encounter a threat in the environment. When we experience stress, our body readies itself to handle the assault.

You certainly know what stress feels like. Imagine, for example, that you show up for class one morning, and it looks as if everyone else knows that there is a test that day. You hear others talking about how much they have studied, and you nervously ask yourself: "Test? What test?" You might start to sweat, and your heart might thump fast and hard in your chest. Sure enough, the instructor shows up with a stack of exams. You are about to be tested on material you have not even thought about, much less studied.

As we have seen, stress begins with a "fight or flight" response sparked by the sympathetic nervous system. This reaction quickly mobilizes the body's physiological resources to prepare us to deal with threats to survival. An unexpected exam is not literally a threat to your survival, but the human stress response is such that it can occur in reaction to *anything* that threatens personally important motives (Sapolsky, 2004).

Acute stress is the stress that occurs in response to an immediate perceived threat. When the stressful situation ends, so does acute stress. Acute stress is adaptive, because it allows us to do the things we need to do in an emergency. Once the danger passes, the parasympathetic nervous system can calm us down and focus on body maintenance. However, we are not in a live-or-die situation most of the time when we experience stress. Indeed, we can even "stress ourselves out" just by thinking.

Chronic stress—stress that goes on continuously—may lead to persistent autonomic nervous system arousal (Morey & others, 2015). While the sympathetic nervous system is working to meet the demands of whatever is stressing us out, the parasympathetic nervous system is not getting a chance to do its job of maintenance and repair, of digesting food, and of keeping our organs in good working order. Furthermore, in chronic stress, the stress hormones adrenaline and norepinephrine, produced by the endocrine system, are constantly circulated in the body, eventually causing a breakdown of the immune system (Sapolsky, 2004). In other words, over time, chronic autonomic nervous system activity can bring about an immune system collapse, leaving the person vulnerable to disease (Tell & others, 2015).

Chronic stress is clearly best avoided. The brain, a structure that is itself powerfully affected by chronic stress, can be our ally in helping us avoid such continuous stress. Consider that when we face a challenging situation, we can exploit the brain's abilities and interpret the experience in a way that is not so stressful. For example, maybe we

test yourself

1. What is the relationship among chromosomes, genes, and DNA?
2. According to the dominant-recessive genes principle, how could two brown-haired parents have a blonde-haired child?
3. What term refers to our genetic makeup, and what term refers to the observable physical expression of that genetic makeup?

● **stress** The responses of individuals to environmental stressors.

● **stressors** Circumstances and events that threaten individuals and tax their coping abilities and that cause physiological changes to ready the body to handle the assault of stress.

can approach an upcoming audition for a play not so much as a stressor but as an opportunity to shine. Changing the way people think about their life challenges and experiences can help them live less stressfully and maintain good health (McGregor & others, 2015; Sannes & others, 2015).

At the beginning of this chapter, we considered how changing the way we think leads to physical changes in the brain and its operations. In light of this remarkable capacity, it is reasonable to conclude that we can use our brain's powers to change how we look at life experiences—and maybe even to deploy the brain as a defense against stress.

The biological foundations of psychology are in evidence across the entire nervous system, including the brain, the intricately working neurotransmitters, the endocrine system, and our genes. These physical realities of our body work in concert to produce our behavior, thoughts, and feelings. The activities you perform every day are all signs of the success of this physical system. Your mastery of the material in this chapter is only one reflection of the extraordinary capabilities of this biological achievement.

test yourself

1. Explain what stress and stressors are.
2. What part of the nervous system sets off the "fight or flight" reaction, and how does this reaction affect the body?
3. What is the difference between acute stress and chronic stress?

SUMMARY

1. THE NERVOUS SYSTEM

The nervous system is the body's electrochemical communication circuitry. Four important characteristics of the brain and nervous system are complexity, integration, adaptability, and electrochemical transmission. The brain's special ability to adapt and change is called plasticity.

Decision making in the nervous system occurs in specialized pathways of nerve cells. Three of these pathways involve sensory input, motor output, and neural networks.

The nervous system is divided into two main parts: central (CNS) and peripheral (PNS). The CNS consists of the brain and spinal cord. The PNS has two major divisions: somatic and autonomic. The autonomic nervous system consists of two main divisions: sympathetic and parasympathetic. The sympathetic nervous system drives our body's response to threatening circumstances, while the parasympathetic nervous system is involved in maintaining the body, digesting food, and healing wounds.

2. NEURONS

Neurons are cells that specialize in processing information. They make up the communication network of the nervous system. The three main parts of the neuron are the cell body, dendrite (receiving part), and axon (sending part). A myelin sheath encases and insulates most axons and speeds up transmission of neural impulses.

Impulses are sent from a neuron along its axon in the form of brief electrical impulses. Resting potential is the stable, slightly negative charge of an inactive neuron. The brief wave of electrical charge that sweeps down the axon, called the action potential, is an all-or-nothing response. The synapse is the space between neurons. At the synapse, neurotransmitters are released from the sending neuron, and some of these attach to receptor sites on the receiving neuron, where they stimulate another electrical impulse. Neurotransmitters include acetylcholine, GABA, glutamate, norepinephrine, dopamine, serotonin, endorphins, and oxytocin. Neural networks are clusters of neurons that are interconnected and that develop through experience.

3. STRUCTURES OF THE BRAIN AND THEIR FUNCTIONS

The main techniques used to study the brain are brain lesioning, electrical recording, and brain imaging. These methods have revealed a great deal about the three major divisions of the brain—the hindbrain, midbrain, and forebrain.

The cerebral cortex makes up most of the outer layer of the brain, and it is here that higher mental functions such as thinking and planning take place. The wrinkled surface of the cerebral cortex is divided into hemispheres, each with four lobes: occipital, temporal, frontal, and parietal. There is considerable integration and connection among the brain's lobes.

The brain has two hemispheres. Two areas in the left hemisphere that involve specific language functions are Broca's area (speech) and Wernicke's area (language comprehension). The corpus callosum is a large bundle of fibers that connects the two hemispheres. Research suggests that the left brain is more dominant in processing verbal information (such as language) and the right brain in processing nonverbal information (such as spatial perception, visual recognition, faces, and emotion). Nonetheless, in a person whose corpus callosum is intact, both hemispheres of the cerebral cortex are involved in most complex human functioning.

4. THE ENDOCRINE SYSTEM

The endocrine glands release hormones directly into the bloodstream for distribution throughout the body. The pituitary gland is the master endocrine gland. The adrenal glands play important roles in moods, energy level, and ability to cope with stress. Other parts of the endocrine system include the pancreas, which produces insulin, and the ovaries and testes, which produce sex hormones.

5. BRAIN DAMAGE, PLASTICITY, AND REPAIR

The human brain has considerable plasticity, although this ability to adapt and change is greater in young children than later in development. Three ways in which a damaged brain might repair itself are collateral sprouting, substitution of function, and neurogenesis. Brain grafts are implants of healthy tissue into damaged brains. Brain grafts are more successful when fetal tissue is used. Stem cell research is a controversial area of science that may allow for novel treatments for damaged nervous systems.

6. GENETICS AND BEHAVIOR

Chromosomes are threadlike structures that occur in 23 pairs, with one member of each pair coming from each parent. Chromosomes contain the genetic substance deoxyribonucleic acid (DNA). Genes, the units of hereditary information, are short segments of chromosomes composed of DNA. According to the dominant-recessive genes principle, if one gene of a pair is dominant and one is recessive, the dominant gene overrides the recessive gene.

Two important concepts in the study of genetics are the genotype and phenotype. The genotype is an individual's actual genetic material. The phenotype is the observable characteristics of the person.

Different ways of studying heredity's influence are molecular genetics, selective breeding, genome-wide association method, and behavior genetics. Two methods used by behavior geneticists are twin studies and adoption studies.

Both genes and environment play a role in determining the phenotype of an individual. Even for characteristics in which genes play a large role (such as height and eye color), the environment also is a factor.

7. PSYCHOLOGY'S BIOLOGICAL FOUNDATIONS AND HEALTH AND WELLNESS

Stress is the body's response to changes in the environment. Stressors are the agents of those changes—that is, the circumstances and events that threaten the organism. The body's stress response is largely a function of sympathetic nervous system activation that prepares us for action in the face of a threat. The stress response involves slowing down maintenance processes (such as immune function and digestion) in favor of rapid action.

Acute stress is an adaptive response, but chronic stress can have negative consequences for our health. Although stress may be inevitable, our reaction to a stressful event is largely a function of how we think about it.

key *terms*

action potential	corpus callosum	hormones	peripheral nervous system
adrenal glands	dendrites	hypothalamus	(PNS)
afferent nerves or sensory	deoxyribonucleic acid	limbic system	phenotype
nerves	(DNA)	midbrain	pituitary gland
all-or-nothing principle	dominant-recessive genes	motor cortex	plasticity
amygdala	principle	myelin sheath	resting potential
association cortex or association	efferent nerves or motor	neocortex	reticular formation
area	nerves	nervous system	somatic nervous system
autonomic nervous system	endocrine system	neural networks	somatosensory cortex
axon	forebrain	neurons	stem cells
basal ganglia	frontal lobes	neurotransmitters	stress
brain stem	genes	occipital lobes	stressors
cell body	genotype	ovaries	sympathetic nervous system
central nervous system	glands	pancreas	synapses
(CNS)	glial cells or glia	parasympathetic nervous	temporal lobes
cerebral cortex	hindbrain	system	testes
chromosomes	hippocampus	parietal lobes	thalamus

apply your *knowledge*

1. Consider the four characteristics of the nervous system discussed in this chapter. Suppose you had to do without one of them. Which would you choose, and what would be the consequences of your decision for your behavior?

2. Do an Internet search for "nutrition" and "the brain." Examine the claims made by one or more of the websites. In light of what you have learned about the nervous system in this chapter, how could nutrition affect brain function? Based on your scientific knowledge, how believable are the claims on the site? Explain.

3. Imagine that you could make one part of your brain twice as big as it is now. Which part would it be, and how do you think your behavior would change as a result? What if you had to make another part of your brain half its current size? Which part would you choose to shrink, and what would the effects be?

4. Search the Internet for information about a worry gene. How would you evaluate research on such a gene, given what you have read so far in this book? What (if anything) would the existence of such a gene mean for your well-being?

5. Do you know anyone who has experienced a brain-damaging event, such as a stroke or head injury? If you feel comfortable doing so, ask the person about the experience and the life changes it may have caused. Based on your interview, which areas of the individual's brain might have been affected?

CHAPTER 9

© Michael H/DigitalVision/Getty Images

Human Development

A Little Boy with a Very Quick Temper

Once there was a little boy who had a very quick temper. Prone to tantrums, he would rage so much that his face would turn purple. He once threw a chair at a teacher (who promptly quit her job). His playmates became targets as well. He threw a ball at this sister's head and once clobbered another child with a toy. Although his academic performance, particularly in math, was always good, the boy did not attend regular school for long. At age 15, he graduated by taking courses and exams in a business department at a high school. What might the future hold for such a youth? The answer to that question may surprise you: That quick-tempered little boy turned out to be Albert Einstein, perhaps the most famous genius in the world. Looking at a raging child, it may be hard to imagine that this angry little person might one day change the way we look at the universe.

Like Einstein, we were all once children. What were you like as a child, and how are you the same and different now? How did you move from the child you were to the adult who is reading these words right now? And what might the future hold for you? These fascinating questions are given scientific answers by developmental psychologists. ●

288 CHAPTER 9 Human Development

PREVIEW

Developmental psychologists are interested in all the ways a person grows and changes throughout the time travel that is life, from its beginning to its inevitable end. We begin this chapter by examining the meaning of development and exploring key questions in the field. We then trace the processes of physical, cognitive, and socioemotional development throughout the life span: prenatally (before birth), during childhood, and in adolescence and adulthood. We round off our tour of the human life span with a look at development and wellness.

1. EXPLORING HUMAN DEVELOPMENT

● **development** The pattern of continuity and change in human capabilities that occurs throughout life, involving both growth and decline.

Development refers to the pattern of continuity and change in human capabilities that occurs throughout the course of life. Most development involves growth, although it also is concerned with decline (for example, physical abilities may decline with age). Developmental psychology is interested in how people change—physically and psychologically—as they age. These changes occur on three different levels:

■ *Physical processes* involve changes in an individual's biological nature. Genes inherited from parents; the hormonal changes of puberty and menopause; and changes throughout life in the brain, height and weight, and motor skills—all of these reflect the developmental role of biological processes. Such biological growth processes are called *maturation*.

■ *Cognitive processes* involve changes in an individual's thought, intelligence, and language. Observing a colorful mobile as it swings above a crib, constructing a sentence about the future, imagining oneself as a movie star, memorizing a new telephone number—these activities reflect the role of cognitive processes in development.

■ *Socioemotional processes* involve changes in an individual's relationships with other people, in emotions, and in personality. An infant's smile in response to her mother's touch, a girl's development of assertiveness, an adolescent's joy at the senior prom, a young man's aggressiveness in sport, and an older couple's affection for each other all reflect the role of socioemotional processes.

Human development is complex because it is the product of several processes. A child's growth in height and weight, a phone user's tapping out a friend's number from memory, and a young couple's joy on the occasion of their prom reflect physical, cognitive, and socioemotional processes, respectively.

(first) ©Katrina Wittkamp/Lifesize/Getty Images; (second) ©ESB Professional/Shutterstock; (third) ©Hill Street Studios/Blend Images

These physical, cognitive, and socioemotional processes are intricately interwoven. As you read this chapter, remember that you are studying the development of an integrated human being, in whom body, mind, and emotion are interdependent.

Researchers in developmental psychology are interested in the ways that these three processes—physical, cognitive, and socioemotional—change over the human life span. Their work centrally investigates how a person's *age* relates to different aspects of his or her physical, cognitive, and socioemotional characteristics. Because age is a variable that cannot be experimentally manipulated, studies on the relationship between age and other characteristics are by definition correlational in nature. This aspect of developmental research carries important implications for research design, as we now consider.

Research Methods in Developmental Psychology

Human development is about the changes that occur with age. To know what age-related differences mean, however, we must consider the kind of research presented.

In *cross-sectional studies,* a number of people of different ages are assessed at one point in time, and differences are noted. By examining how the ages of these individuals relate to the characteristics measured, researchers can find out whether younger individuals differ from older ones. Age differences, however, are not the same as developmental change.

One problem in cross-sectional studies is cohort effects. A cohort is a generational group, people born in the same time period. *Cohort effects* are differences between individuals that stem not from their ages but from the historical and social time period in which they were born and developed (Wadsworth & Kuh, 2016). For instance, individuals who were born in the 1940s might be less likely to have attended college than those born in the 1990s. Differences observed between these groups might be due not to their age but rather to these differing experiences.

In contrast to a cross-sectional study, a *longitudinal study,* as described in the chapter "Psychology's Scientific Method", assesses the same participants multiple times over a lengthy period. A longitudinal study can find out not only whether age groups differ but also whether the same individuals change with respect to a particular characteristic as they age (Reznick, 2013).

To appreciate the difference between a cross-sectional and a longitudinal design, consider a cross-sectional study of approximately 28,000 individuals ages 18 to 88 indicating that happiness increases with age (Yang, 2008). About 33 percent of the participants were very happy at 88 years of age, compared to only about 24 percent of those in their late teens and early 20s. From this work we *might* conclude that people become happier as they age, but this conclusion is limited by the cross-sectional nature of the design used. We cannot know if the happy 88-year-olds were less happy when they were in their 20s. It may be that these individuals were very happy even in their 20s. Perhaps the explanation is that relatively more happy people survive into their senior years.

Clearly, many conclusions about developmental changes in psychological characteristics require longitudinal designs (Lindenberger & others, 2011; Reinikainen, Karvanen, & Tolonen, 2016). Using these and other methods, human development researchers have grappled with three big questions that are relevant to all of psychology, as we consider next.

How Do Nature and Nurture Influence Development?

Developmental psychologists seek to understand how nature and nurture influence development. **Nature** refers to an individual's biological inheritance, especially his or her genes; **nurture** refers to the individual's environmental and social experiences.

In the chapter "Biological Foundations of Behavior", we considered the concept of a *genotype* (the individual's genetic heritage—his or her actual genetic material). We also examined the idea of a *phenotype* (the person's observable characteristics). The phenotype shows the contributions of both nature (genetic heritage) and nurture (environment). The genotype may be expressed in various ways, depending on both the environment and characteristics of the genotype itself. Recall, for example, that a recessive gene, though part of the genotype, will not show up in the phenotype at all if it is paired with a dominant gene.

● **nature** An individual's biological inheritance, especially his or her genes.

● **nurture** An individual's environmental and social experiences.

290 CHAPTER 9 Human Development

Researchers often rely on twins to measure the influence of nature or genetics on development. Keep in mind that even among twins, the nurture, or experience, matters.

©Digital Vision/Punchstock

Environmental factors can help or harm the developing person. Some experiences can have profoundly negative effects. For example, persistent poverty in childhood is associated with long term issues in emotional, cognitive, and social development (Dickerson & Popli, 2016; Raver, Blair, & Garrett-Peters, 2015; Yoshikawa, Aber, & Beardslee, 2012). It is for this reason that many scientists and policy makers view targeting poverty as a key in preventing developmental problems. It is important to bear in mind that poorer parents often hold many of the same beliefs, values, hopes and dreams for their children that wealthier parents do; however they simply lack the resources to provide the opportunities and material goods provided by wealthier parents (Duncan, Magnuson, & Votruba-Drzal, 2014).

Experience not only affects development directly. It can also influence the ways that genetic characteristics are expressed. An illustration of the role of environmental influences in genetic expression is a condition called *phenylketonuria (PKU)*. Caused by two recessive genes, PKU results in an inability to metabolize the amino acid phenylalanine (a major component of the artificial sweetener aspartame, used in many soft drinks and other products). Decades ago, it was thought that the genotype for PKU led to a specific phenotype: irreversible brain damage, developmental disabilities, and seizures. However, we now know that as long as those with the PKU genotype stick to a diet that is very low in phenylalanine, these phenotypic characteristics can be avoided (Brown & Lichter-Konecki, 2016; Cliff & others, 2016). Thus, environmental precautions can change the phenotype associated with this genotype.

PKU demonstrates that a person's observable and measurable characteristics (phenotype) might not reflect his or her genetic heritage (genotype) very precisely because of experience. Instead, for each genotype, a *range* of phenotypes may be expressed, depending on environmental factors. An individual can inherit the genetic potential to grow very tall, but good nutrition, an environmental factor, is important for achieving that potential. The person whom we see before us emerges through the interplay of genetic and environmental experiences. Development is the product of nature, nurture, and the complex interaction of the two (Lester, Conradt, & Marsit, 2016).

One of the factors that must be taken into account in the development process is the developer himself or herself, as we consider next.

What Is the Developer's Role in Development?

Nature and nurture have at least one thing in common. Because we cannot pick our genes or our parents, each of us would seem to be stuck with the genes and environment we got at birth. However, importantly, the developing human being also has a role to play in development (Turkheimer, 2011). Although you might think of nature and nurture as the raw ingredients of yourself as a person, the fact is that you take those ingredients and make them into the person you are.

Indeed, some psychologists believe that we can develop beyond what our genetic inheritance and our environment give us. They argue that a key aspect of development involves seeking optimal experiences in life (Armor, Massey, & Sackett, 2008; Opendak & Gould, 2015). They cite examples of individuals who go beyond what life has given them to achieve extraordinary things. These individuals build and shape their own lives, authoring a unique developmental path, and sometimes transforming apparent weaknesses into real strengths.

Microsoft founder Bill Gates and his wife Melinda have quested after—and carved out—meaningful life experiences as they have progressed through their development.

©STRDEL/AFP/Getty Images

In our efforts to experience our lives in optimal ways, we develop *life themes* that involve activities, social relationships, and life goals (Köber, Schmiedek, & Habermas, 2015; McAdams & Guo, 2015; Rathunde, 2010). Some individuals are especially successful at constructing optimal life experiences. For example, Martin Luther King, Jr., Mother Teresa, Nelson Mandela, Bill and Melinda Gates, and Oprah Winfrey looked for and found meaningful life themes as they developed. Their lives were not restricted to biological survival or to settling for their particular life situations. Many of them, in fact, faced hardships early in life and yet managed to contribute to the world in meaningful ways. A developmental question that naturally flows from this discussion is whether early or later life experiences are more important to a person's development over the life span.

Are Early or Later Life Experiences More Important in Development?

A key question in developmental psychology centers on the extent to which childhood experiences (nurture) determine aspects of later life. If early experiences provide the foundation for later development, does that mean that childhood experiences are likely to influence (and limit or damage) us for the rest of our lives?

Developmental psychologists debate whether early experiences or later experiences are more important (Dixon & others, 2013; Kagan, 2013). Some believe that unless infants receive warm, nurturing caregiving in their first year or so of life, they will not develop to their full potential (Cassidy & others, 2011; Numan & Young, 2016). Other psychologists emphasize the power of later experience, arguing that important development occurs later on in life as well (Antonucci, Birditt, & Ajrouch, 2013).

Life-span developmentalists, who study both children and adults, stress that researchers have given too little attention to adult development and aging. They argue that although early experiences contribute powerfully to development, they are not necessarily more influential than later experiences (Hershfield & others, 2013; Park & McDonough, 2013). These experts say that both early and later experiences make significant contributions to development, and thus no one is doomed to be a prisoner of his or her childhood.

A key concept in understanding the role of negative early experiences in later development is resilience. **Resilience** is a person's ability to recover from or adapt to difficult times. Resilience means that even in the face of adversity, a person shows signs of positive functioning (Johnson & Wood, 2016). Resilience can refer to factors that compensate for difficulties, buffering the individual from the effects of these, or to the fact that moderate difficulties may themselves help to promote development (Ager, 2013).

Despite undergoing hardship time and time again, resilient children grow up to be capable adults. Researchers have found that resilient children have one or more advantages—such as strong intellectual functioning or a close, supportive relationship with a parent or other adult—that help them to overcome their disadvantages (Masten, 2015). Although often studied as an aspect of childhood and adolescence, resilience can also characterize development in adulthood and old age (Cosco & others, 2016; Gooding & others, 2012; Jeste & others, 2013).

Having a supportive relationship with a parent or a competent adult outside the home can contribute to childhood resilience.
© Ty Allison/Photographer's Choice/Getty Images

● **resilience** A person's ability to recover from or adapt to difficult times.

test yourself

1. What three broad processes of change do developmental psychologists study?
2. Why are longitudinal studies commonly used to investigate developmental questions? What are the limitations of cross-sectional studies with respect to studying such questions?
3. In what ways can the developing individual play a role in his or her own development?

2. CHILD DEVELOPMENT

In this section we focus on the three fundamental developmental processes—physical, cognitive, and socioemotional—of childhood. To understand childhood in all its dimensions, we must begin before it even starts, with prenatal development.

Prenatal Development

Prenatal development is a time of astonishing change, beginning with conception. *Conception* occurs when a single sperm cell from the male merges with the female's ovum (egg) to produce a *zygote,* a single cell with 23 chromosomes from the mother and 23 from the father.

THE COURSE OF PRENATAL DEVELOPMENT

Development from zygote to fetus is divided into three periods:

- *Germinal period—weeks 1 and 2:* The germinal period begins with conception. After 1 week and many cell divisions, the zygote is made up of 100 to 150 cells. By the end of 2 weeks, the mass of cells has attached to the uterine wall.
- *Embryonic period—weeks 3 through 8:* The rate of cell differentiation intensifies, support systems for the cells develop, and the beginnings of organs appear (Figure 1a). In the third week, the neural tube, which eventually becomes the spinal cord, starts to take shape. Within the first 28 days after conception, the neural tube is

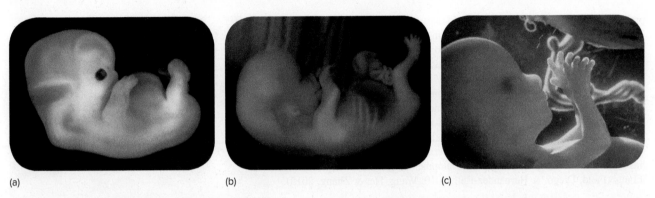

(a)　　　　　　　　　　　　(b)　　　　　　　　　　　　(c)

FIGURE 1　From Embryo to Fetus (*a*) At about 4 weeks, an embryo is about 0.2 inch (less than 1 centimeter) long. The head, eyes, and ears begin to show; the head and neck are half the length of the body; the shoulders will be located where the whitish arm buds are attached. (*b*) At 8 weeks, the developing individual is about 1.6 inches (4 centimeters) long and has reached the end of its embryonic phase. It has become a fetus. Everything that will be found in the fully developed human being has now begun to form. The fetal stage is a period of growth and perfection of detail. The heart has been beating for a month, and the muscles have just begun their first exercises. (*c*) At 4½ months, the fetus is just over 7 inches (about 18 centimeters) long. When the thumb comes close to the mouth, the head may turn, and the lips and tongue begin their sucking motions—a reflex for survival. (a) ©Dr. G. Moscoso/Science Source; (b) ©Anatomical Travelogue/Science Source; (c) ©Nestle/Petit Format/ Science Source

formed and closes, encased inside the embryo. By the end of the embryonic period, the heart begins to beat, the arms and legs become more differentiated, the face starts to form, and the intestinal tract appears (Figure 1b).

■ *Fetal period—months 2 through 9:* At 2 months, the fetus is the size of a kidney bean and has started to move around. At 4 months, the fetus is 5 inches long and weighs about 5 ounces (Figure 1c). At 6 months, the fetus has grown to a pound and a half. The last 3 months of pregnancy are the time when organ functioning increases, and the fetus puts on considerable weight and size, adding baby fat.

Although it floats in a well-protected womb, the fetus is not immune to the larger environment surrounding the mother. Sometimes, normal development is disrupted by environmental insults.

THREATS TO THE FETUS

A *teratogen* is any agent that causes a birth defect. Teratogens include chemical substances ingested by the mother (such as nicotine if the mother smokes and alcohol if she drinks) and certain illnesses (such as rubella, or German measles). Substances that are ingested by the mother can lead to serious birth defects (Roozen & others, 2016; Stancil & others, 2016).

For example, *fetal alcohol spectrum disorders (FASD)* are a cluster of abnormalities and problems that appear in the offspring of mothers who drink alcohol heavily during pregnancy (Charness, Riley, & Sowell, 2016; Roozen & others, 2016). These abnormalities include a small head, defects in the limbs and heart, and below-average intelligence (Popova & others, 2016). Heavy drinking is linked to FASD, but even moderate drinking can lead to serious problems (Charness, Riley, & Sowell, 2016). The best advice for a woman who is pregnant or thinking of becoming pregnant is to avoid alcohol.

The effects of chemical teratogens depend on the timing of exposure. The body part or organ system that is developing when the fetus encounters the teratogen is most vulnerable (Ingber & Pohl, 2016). Genetic characteristics may buffer or worsen the effects of a teratogen. Perhaps most importantly, the environment the child encounters *after birth* can influence the ultimate effects of prenatal insults.

Sexually transmitted infections (STIs) also threaten the fetus. Some STIs, such as gonorrhea, can be transferred to the baby during delivery. Others, including syphilis and the human immunodeficiency virus (HIV), the virus that causes AIDS, can also infect the fetus while it is in the womb. Besides transmission of infections to the fetus and newborns, STI exposure enhances the risk of stillbirth, as well as a number of other problems, such as eye infections and blindness (in the case of gonorrhea). Many STIs also increase the risk of preterm birth.

A *preterm infant,* one who is born prior to 37 weeks after conception, may also be at risk for developmental difficulties. Whether a preterm infant will have developmental problems is a complex issue, however. Preterm infants who grow up in poverty are more likely to have problems than are those who live in better socioeconomic conditions (Winchester & others, 2016).

Adults who were born preterm tend to report poorer health and well-being (Winstanley & others, 2015). Postnatal experience plays a crucial role in determining the ultimate effects of preterm birth. For example, research has shown that massage can improve developmental outcomes for premature infants (Field, Diego, & Hernandez-Reif, 2010; Wang, He, & Zhang, 2013).

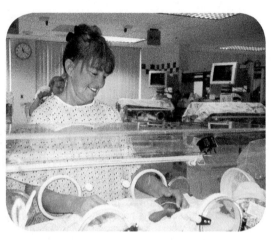

Tiffany Field is shown massaging a newborn infant. Field's research has demonstrated the power of massage in improving the developmental outcome of at-risk infants. Under her direction, the Touch Research Institute in Miami, Florida, investigates the role of touch in a number of domains of health and well-being.

Courtesy of Dr. Tiffany Fields/Touch Research Institutes

Physical Development in Infancy and Childhood

Human infants are the world's most helpless newborns. One reason for their helplessness is that they are born not quite finished. Our enormous brain sets humans apart from other animals. Getting that big brain out of the relatively small birth canal is a challenge that nature has met by sending human babies out of the womb before the brain has fully developed. The first months and years of life allow the developing human (and the environment) to put the finishing touches on that important organ.

REFLEXES

Newborns come into the world equipped with several genetically wired reflexes that are crucial for survival. Babies are born with the ability to suck and swallow. If they are dropped in water, they will naturally hold their breath, contract their throats to keep water out, and move their arms and legs to stay afloat at least briefly. Some reflexes persist throughout life—coughing, blinking, and yawning, for example. Others, such as automatically grasping something that touches the fingers, disappear in the months following birth, as higher brain functions mature and infants develop voluntary control over many behaviors. Figure 2 shows some examples of reflexes.

Rooting	Gripping	Toe Curling	Moro or Startle	Galant
What provokes the response? Stroking of the infant's cheek	*What provokes the response?* Something that is placed in the infant's hand	*What provokes the response?* Stroking of the inner or outer sole of the infant's foot	*What provokes the response?* Sudden noise or movement	*What provokes the response?* Stroking of the infant's lower back, next to the spinal cord
What the infant does Head turns in the direction of the touch, and the infant opens his or her mouth for feeding.	*What the infant does* The infant grasps the item and can hold on very well—almost enough to support his or her own weight.	*What the infant does* If the inner sole is stroked, the infant curls his or her toes. If the outer sole is stroked, the toes spread out.	*What the infant does* The infant throws his or her head back and arms and legs out (and then cries).	*What the infant does* The infant curves toward the side that was stroked—and looks like a fencer when doing so.

FIGURE 2   **Some Infant Reflexes** Infants are born with a number of reflexes to get them through life, and they are incredibly cute when they perform them. These reflexes disappear as infants mature.

294 CHAPTER 9 Human Development

MOTOR AND PERCEPTUAL SKILLS

Relative to the rest of the body, a newborn's head is gigantic, and it flops around uncontrollably. Within 12 months, the infant becomes capable of sitting upright, standing, stooping, climbing, and often walking. During the second year, growth decelerates, but rapid gains occur in activities such as running and climbing. Researchers used to think that motor milestones—such as sitting up, crawling, and walking—unfolded as part of a genetic plan. However, psychologists now recognize that experience, not simply genetics, plays a role in motor development (Gerson, Bekkering, & Hunnius, 2015; Serdarevic & others, 2016).

One of the most remarkable motor skills attained by infants is the ability to reach for things. Reaching may seem to be a small thing to you, but, for an infant, the act of extending one's own arm to grasp an object in the world is an enormously complex act, filled with implications (Williams, Corbetta, & Cobb, 2015). When a baby sees a stuffed bunny and reaches for it, he or she has mastered a skill that transforms the infant's relationship to the world: The infant's focus shifts from people to objects, including toys, food, grandma's earrings, and all the things that he or she can now get his or her hands on (Corbetta & Snapp-Childs, 2009).

Emerging between 3 and 5 months of age, the ability to reach for an object involves a wide array of processes (Corbetta, Williams, & Haynes, 2016; Williams, Corbetta, & Cobb, 2015):

- *Sensory capacities:* being able to see or hear the object
- *Motivation:* wanting to grasp the object
- *Attention:* being able to focus on a particular thing, among all the other interesting things in the baby's world
- *Bodily control:* having the ability to control posture, manage head movement, and calibrate the movement of one's arms
- *Learning:* getting positive reinforcement from the experience of getting the object of their desire

Developmental psychologists have long studied the ways that infants acquire this important skill. Many of these studies have focused on the role of experience in the acquisition of reaching. In one study, 3-month-old infants participated in play sessions wearing "sticky mittens"—mittens with Velcro-covered palms that allow the infants to more easily "pick up" objects (toys in this study) (Needham, Barrett, & Peterman, 2002) (Figure 3). The rationale for the use of these mittens is that they might give infants the chance to simulate real reaching and grasping and enjoy the reinforcement of getting what they want. This reinforcement should, in turn, boost their abilities to engage with the world.

In this research, parents were instructed to incorporate the mittens into their playtime for at least 10 minutes every day for two weeks. In a later testing session, infants who participated in sessions with the mittens grasped and manipulated objects earlier in their development than a control group of infants who did not have the mitten experience. After their sticky mitten training, the experienced infants looked at objects longer, swatted at them, and were more likely to put the objects in their mouth.

As you consider that adorable infant in Figure 3, let's review a few aspects of the original sticky mitten study. The independent variable was whether or not infants experienced the sticky mitten sessions. The dependent variables were their behaviors toward objects in the testing session. Now, can we be sure that it was the sticky mittens and the way they simulated grasping ability that accounts for the results? The infants

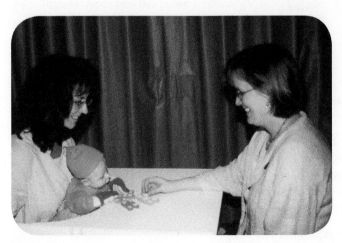

FIGURE 3 **Infants' Use of "Sticky Mittens" to Explore Objects** Amy Needham and her colleagues (2002) found that infants who were trained with "sticky mittens" were more likely to explore objects later. *Courtesy of Amy Needham, Duke University*

CRITICAL CONTROVERSY

Do "Sticky Mittens" Foster Reaching in Infants?

The "sticky mittens" study was landmark in demonstrating that experience with simulated grasping could give infants a head start on the way to independent reaching. But were those sticky mittens indeed the active ingredient in those results? Was it sticky mittens, parental attention, or something else that led those babies to become more interested in exploring objects? A recent study sought to answer these questions (Williams, Corbetta, & Guan, 2015).

In the study, 3-month-old infants were randomly assigned to one of three groups. One group wore sticky mittens, another wore the same mittens but without the Velcro (non-sticky

© Ruth Jenkinson/Getty Images

mittens). For both of these groups, the finger tips and thumbs of the mittens were left open so the babies could have the sensation of feeling objects. A third group served as a control group. This group had no mittens and were only tested on the first and last day of the study.

Two experimenters visited the mitten groups at home 14 consecutive days. After placing the mittens on the baby's hands, an experimenter would place a toy on a table in front of the infant, allowing the child to interact with it. The experimenter did not talk to the baby but simply watched. If a toy stuck to the sticky mittens, babies were allowed to hold them for about 10 seconds, and then the toy was replaced with another one on the table. Note that these procedures removed the possible confound of parental attention.

On day 16, in videotaped sessions, the babies came into the lab, were placed in an infant seat behind a table, and were shown various toys by an experimenter. Arm and hand movements were monitored electronically.

Results showed that *both mitten groups* progressed toward independent reaching more than controls (Williams, Corbetta, & Guan, 2015). In addition, infants with the non-sticky mittens spent more time looking at the toys during the testing session. The researchers concluded that it was repeated exposure to different objects that led babies in the original sticky mitten study to improve (Corbetta, Williams, & Haynes, 2016; Williams, Corbetta, & Guan, 2015).

Research on infant reaching continues, and sticky mittens might yet show some advantages for infants (Needham, Wiesen, & Libertus, 2015). Nevertheless, they may be less important than attention and playtime with parents and repeated exposure to interesting objects.

WHAT DO YOU THINK?

- If you were a parent and read about research showing that infants could get a head start using some unusual device, would you buy it? Why or why not?

- What recent developmental accomplishment in your life do you think others take for granted?

---

in the control group were simply tested at the end of the 2-week period. Their parents were given no instructions and may not have spent 10 minutes each day playing with their babies at all. In addition, they did not spend 10 minutes each day focused on a particular object.

These differences might constitute *confounds,* aspects of the experiment that could explain the results. Might the infants in the mitten group have shown changes in their behavior simply because they received extra parental attention and encouragement? To read about research addressing these and other issues in infant research methods, see the Critical Controversy.

Infants are active developers, and their motor and perceptual skills develop together and mutually promote each other. Babies are continually coordinating their movements with information they perceive through their senses to learn how to maintain their balance, reach for objects in space, and move across various surfaces and terrains (Adolph & Berger, 2013; Adolph & Robinson, 2013). Moving from place to place in the environment teaches babies how objects and people look from different perspectives and whether surfaces will support their weight (Gibson, 2001). Actively participating in behaviors strongly influences infant development, but infants can also gain motor skills in more passive ways, by watching and modeling adult behavior (Somogyi & others, 2015).

Psychologists face a daunting challenge in studying infant perception. Infants cannot talk, so how can scientists tell what they can see, hear, or feel? Researchers who study infants have no choice but to become very clever methodologists, relying on what infants can *do* to understand what infants think (Cristia & others, 2016; S. P. Johnson, 2012, 2013).

● **preferential looking** A research technique that involves giving an infant a choice of what object to look at.

One thing infants can do is look. The **preferential looking** technique involves giving an infant a choice of what object to look at. If an infant shows a reliable preference for one stimulus (say, a picture of a face) over another (a scrambled picture of a face) when these are repeatedly presented in differing locations, we can infer that the infant can tell the two images apart. Using this technique, researchers have found that as early as *7 days old,* infants are already engaged in organized perception of faces and are able to put together sights and sounds. If presented with two faces with mouths moving, infants will watch the face whose mouth matches the sounds they are hearing (K. Lee & others, 2013b; Lewkowicz & Hansen-Tift, 2012). At 3 months, infants prefer real faces to scrambled faces and prefer their mother's face to a stranger's (Slater, Field, & Hernandez-Reif, 2007). By 6 months, babies can detect human faces more quickly than they can detect animal faces, just as adults do (Jakobsen, Umstead, & Simpson, 2016).

How do researchers know where infants are looking? In some studies, researchers simply watch and record where babies are focused. An important technological advance in this domain is the use of sophisticated eye-tracking equipment. Figure 4 shows an infant wearing eye-tracking headgear in recent research on visually guided motor behavior and social interaction.

Eye tracking also is being used to study development in many other areas, including attention, memory, and face processing (Hessels & others, 2015; Waxman & others, 2016; Xiao & others, 2015) as well as to detect subtle differences that might reveal risks for disorders, such as autism spectrum disorder (Thorup & others, 2016). Such techniques have provided a great deal of information about infants' remarkable abilities, but they are also limited. Research using brain imaging suggests that infants may know more than even these clever strategies reveal (Cannon & others, 2016; Wilcox & Biondi, 2015).

THE BRAIN

As an infant plays, crawls, shakes a rattle, smiles, and frowns, the baby's brain is changing dramatically. At birth and in early infancy, the brain's 100 billion neurons have only minimal connections. The infant brain literally is ready and waiting for the experiences that will create these connections (Bale, 2015; Markant & Thomas, 2013). During the first 2 years of life, the dendrites of the neurons branch out, and the neurons become far more interconnected (Figure 5). Myelination, the process of encasing axons with fat cells (the myelin sheath described in the chapter "Biological Foundations of Behavior"), begins prenatally and continues after birth well into adolescence and young adulthood (Dubois & others, 2015; Fuhrmann, Knoll, & Blakemore, 2015; Qiu, Mori, & Miller, 2015).

During childhood, *synaptic connections* increase dramatically (Schnack & others, 2015; R. E. Watson & others, 2006). Recall from the chapter "Biological Foundations of Behavior" that a *synapse* is a gap between neurons that is bridged by chemical neurotransmitters. Nearly twice as many synapses are available as will ever be used (Huttenlocher, 1999). The connections that are made become stronger and will survive; the unused ones will be replaced by other neural pathways or disappear (Krogsrud & others,

FIGURE 4   What Are You Looking At? Eye-tracking technology allows infant perception researchers to identify exactly what infants are looking at. © Chen Yu

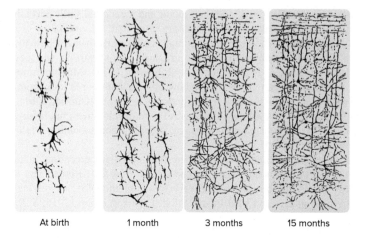

FIGURE 5   Dendritic Spreading
Note the increase among neurons over the course of the first fifteen months of life.

At birth   1 month   3 months   15 months

2016; Luna & others, 2015). In the language of neuroscience, these unused connections are "pruned." Figure 6 illustrates the steep growth and later pruning of synapses during infancy in specific areas of the brain.

Brain-imaging studies demonstrate that children's brains also undergo remarkable anatomical changes (Vértes & Bullmore, 2015). Repeated brain scans of the same children up to the age of 4 years show that the amount of brain material in some areas can nearly double within as little as a year, followed by a drastic loss of tissue as unneeded cells are purged, and the brain continues to reorganize itself. From 3 to 6 years of age, the most rapid growth takes place in the frontal lobe areas, which are involved in planning and organizing new actions and in maintaining attention to tasks (Gogtay & Thompson, 2010). These brain changes are not simply the result of nature; new experiences in the world also promote brain development (Cicchetti, 2016; Gerson, Bekkering, & Hunnius, 2015; Lamb, 2013). Thus, as in other areas of development, nature and nurture operate together in the development of the child's brain.

As the brain develops, thinking matures. This cognitive development is the topic we consider next.

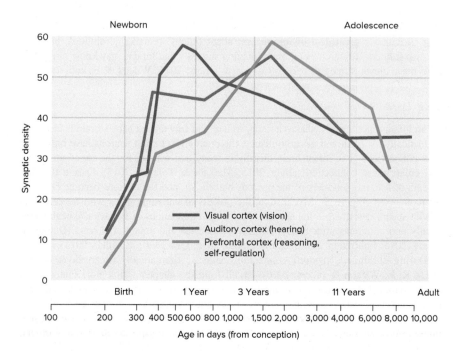

FIGURE 6   Synaptic Density in the Human Brain from Infancy to Adulthood The graph shows the dramatic increase and then pruning in synaptic density in three regions of the brain: visual cortex, auditory cortex, and prefrontal cortex. Synaptic density is believed to be an important indication of the extent of connectivity between neurons.

Jean Piaget (1896–1980) Piaget, the famous Swiss developmental psychologist, changed the way we think about the development of children's minds.

©Patrick Grehan/Corbis Historical/Getty Images

● **assimilation** An individual's incorporation of new information into existing knowledge.

● **accommodation** An individual's adjustment of his or her schemas to new information.

● **sensorimotor stage** Piaget's first stage of cognitive development, lasting from birth to about 2 years of age, during which infants construct an understanding of the world by coordinating sensory experiences with motor (physical) actions.

● **object permanence** Piaget's term for the crucial accomplishment of understanding that objects and events continue to exist even when they cannot directly be seen, heard, or touched.

Cognitive Development in Infancy and Childhood

Cognitive development refers to how thought, intelligence, and language processes change as people mature. *Cognition* refers to the way individuals think and also to their cognitive skills and abilities. In this section we review one of the most important theories in psychology (Barrouillet, 2015)—that proposed by Jean Piaget (1896–1980), the famous Swiss developmental psychologist. In addition, we consider alternatives to Piaget's view and more recent information-processing approaches to cognitive development.

PIAGET'S THEORY OF COGNITIVE DEVELOPMENT

Piaget believed that children *actively construct* their cognitive world as they go through a series of stages. In Piaget's view, children use schemas to make sense of their experience.

Recall from the chapter "Memory" that a *schema* is a mental concept or framework that organizes and provides a structure for interpreting information. Schemas are expressed as various behaviors and skills that the child can exercise in relation to objects or situations. For example, sucking is a simple early schema. More complex schemas that occur later in childhood include licking, blowing, and crawling. In adulthood, schemas represent more complex expectations and beliefs about the world.

Piaget (1952) described two processes responsible for how schemas develop:

■ **Assimilation** occurs when individuals incorporate new information into existing knowledge. This means that faced with a new experience, the person applies old ways of doing things. An infant who sucks on whatever new thing he encounters, an adolescent who applies skills learned playing video games to driving a car, and an adult who uses strategies that worked in the past with previous romantic partners to resolve a conflict with a spouse are all using assimilation. In assimilation, a person's schemas do not change; the person simply uses existing schemas in a new way.

■ **Accommodation** occurs when individuals adjust their schemas to new information. Rather than using one's old ways of doing things, a new experience promotes new ways of dealing with experience. Existing schemas can be changed, and new schemas can be developed. An infant who has been sticking everything in her mouth might begin to accommodate the sucking schema by being more selective with it. An adolescent who has typically gone with the flow of social pressure might develop a new way of dealing with such pressure by standing up for his beliefs. For an adult, accommodation may mean rethinking old strategies for problem solving when a new challenge, such as the loss of a job, presents itself. In contrast to assimilation, then, accommodation means that schemas change. Brand-new ways of interacting with the world can emerge as a function of new and different experiences.

According to Piaget, we go through four stages in understanding the world (Figure 7). Each stage involves a qualitatively different way of making sense of the world than the one before it.

Sensorimotor Stage Piaget's first stage, the **sensorimotor stage,** lasts from birth to about 2 years of age. You can remember this stage as the first one because as the label implies, it is based on the very limited capacities that an infant has: sensation and movement. In this stage, infants construct an understanding of the world by coordinating sensory experiences (such as seeing and hearing) with motor (physical) actions—hence the term *sensorimotor*. As newborns they have little more than reflexive patterns with which to work. By the end of this stage, 2-year-olds show complex sensorimotor patterns and are beginning to use symbols or words in their thinking.

Perhaps the biggest event of the sensorimotor stage is object permanence. **Object permanence** is Piaget's term for the crucial accomplishment of understanding that

Sensorimotor Stage	**Preoperational Stage**	**Concrete Operational Stage**	**Formal Operational Stage**
The infant constructs an understanding of the world by coordinating sensory experiences with physical actions. An infant progresses from reflexive, instinctual action at birth to the beginning of symbolic thought toward the end of the stage.	The child begins to represent the world with words and images. These words and images reflect increased symbolic thinking and go beyond the connection of sensory information and physical action.	The child can now reason logically about concrete events and classify objects into different sets.	The adolescent reasons in more abstract, idealistic, and logical ways.
Birth to 2 Years of Age	**2 to 7 Years of Age**	**7 to 11 Years of Age**	**11 Years of Age Through Adulthood**

FIGURE 7   **Piaget's Four Stages of Cognitive Development** Jean Piaget described how human beings, through development, become ever more sophisticated thinkers about the world. To remember the stages, try this mnemonic: "**S**mart **P**eople **C**an't **F**orget."

(first photo) © Stockbyte/Getty Images; (second photo) © BananaStock/PunchStock; (third photo) © image100/Corbis; (fourth photo) © Image Source/Corbis

objects and events continue to exist even when they cannot directly be seen, heard, or touched. Piaget believed that "out of sight" literally means "out of mind" for very young infants. Object permanence is an enormous developmental milestone. Once the infant knows that objects still exist even if she cannot see them, the infant can think about future events. Piaget studied object permanence by showing an infant an interesting toy and then covering the toy with a blanket. Piaget reasoned that if the baby understood that the toy still existed, the infant would try to uncover it.

Piaget's object permanence task has been criticized for not giving infants a chance to show their stuff. To get a sense of the limitations of Piaget's task, check out the Psychological Inquiry.

To understand the next two stages of cognitive development, it is vital to understand cognitive activities that Piaget called operations. **Operations** are mental representations that are reversible. For example, imagine that you need to pack a sweater into a carry-on bag for an airplane flight. You do not want to check the bag, but the sweater is very bulky. You painstakingly roll the sweater into the tiniest possible cylinder and cram it into the bag. If you compare "before" and "after" photos of the sweater, you might take great pride. But what you would also know, and what shows that you can perform "operations," is that when you get to your destination, that sweater, after a quick shaking out, is going to go back to its original size. You know that the change you have made to the sweater is superficial and temporary. Nothing central has changed about that sweater because you managed to transform its size. Not understanding that simple fact is what separates preoperational thought from more mature thinking.

● **operations** Piaget's term for mental representations of changes in objects that can be reversed.

Preoperational Stage   Piaget's second stage of cognitive development, the **preoperational stage,** lasts from approximately 2 to 7 years of age. Preoperational children have difficulty understanding that reversing an action may restore the original conditions from which the action began.

● **preoperational stage** Piaget's second stage of cognitive development, lasting from about 2 to 7 years of age, during which thought is more symbolic than sensorimotor thought.

psychological *inquiry*

Thinking Critically About Object Permanence

Let's revisit the classic object permanence task developed by Piaget to consider how the aspects of this task might have led Piaget to underestimate infants' abilities. Remember that from Piaget's perspective, "proving" object permanence meant that the child must search for the hidden toy, reach out, and retrieve it.

Let's assume that the child does believe that the toy exists even if he or she cannot see it. What skills must the child possess in order to enact the behaviors that Piaget thought would indicate object permanence? Answer the following questions to sharpen your understanding of this measure of object permanence.

1. Look at the two photos. Assuming that the child does understand that the toy still exists behind the board, what behavior must the baby exhibit to indicate that understanding?

2. What motor and perceptual skills are required for the child to enact those behaviors?

3. What motivational states (or goals) are required for the child to enact them?

4. If the baby does not reach out for the toy even though he knows it still exists, what might the failure mean?

5. Why do you think it took over 50 years for psychologists to question the appropriateness of Piaget's methods?

(first) ©D. Goodman/Science Source; (second) ©D. Goodman/Science Source

A well-known test of whether a child can think "operationally" is to present a child with two identical beakers, A and B, filled with liquid to the same height (Figure 8). Next to them is a third beaker: C. Beaker C is tall and thin, whereas beakers A and B are short and wide. The liquid is poured from B into C, and the child is asked whether the amounts in A and C are the same. The 4-year-old child invariably says that the amount of liquid in the tall, thin beaker (C) is greater than that in the short, wide beaker (A). The 8-year-old child consistently says the amounts are the same. The 4-year-old child, a preoperational thinker, cannot mentally reverse the pouring action; that is, she cannot imagine the liquid going back from container C to container B. Piaget said that such a child has not grasped the concept of *conservation,* a belief in the permanence of certain attributes of objects despite superficial changes.

To sharpen your sense of preoperational thought, consider the following example. Babysitting for two thirsty 4-year-olds, you might give them each the same amount of apple juice poured into two different cups: one tall and thin and the other short and wide. Try as you might to explain to them that the amounts are the same, they will fight over the tall, thin cup because *it looks like more.* Now, in the same situation, older children—who are operational thinkers—would not bat an eye, because they understand that the amounts are equal.

Preoperational thought is more symbolic than sensorimotor thought. In preschool years, children begin to represent their world with words, images, and drawings. The type of symbolic thinking that children are able to accomplish during this stage is limited.

(a)

(b)

FIGURE 8 **Piaget's Conservation Task** The beaker test determines whether a child can think operationally—that is, can mentally reverse action and understand conservation of the substance. (*a*) Two identical beakers are presented to the child, each containing the same amount of liquid. As the child watches, the experimenter pours the liquid from B into C, which is taller and thinner than A and B. (*b*) The experimenter then asks the child whether beakers A and C have the same amount of liquid. The preoperational child says no. When asked to point to the beaker that has more liquid, the child points to the tall, thin one. (photo) ©Maya Barnes Johansen/The Image Works

Children's thought in the preoperational stage is egocentric because preoperational children cannot put themselves in someone else's shoes. Preoperational thinking is also intuitive, meaning that preoperational children make judgments based on gut feelings rather than logic. In reaching a basic level of operational understanding, children progress to the third of Piaget's cognitive stages.

Concrete Operational Stage   Piaget's **concrete operational stage,** from 7 to 11 years of age, involves using operations and replacing intuitive reasoning with logical reasoning in concrete situations. Children in the concrete operational stage can successfully complete the beaker task described above. They are able to imagine the operation of reversing the pouring of the liquid back into the wide beaker. Many of the concrete operations identified by Piaget are related to the properties of objects. For instance, when playing with Play-doh, the child in the concrete operational stage realizes that changing its shape does not change the amount of Play-doh.

● **concrete operational stage** Piaget's third stage of cognitive development, lasting from about 7 to 11 years of age, during which the individual uses operations and replaces intuitive reasoning with logical reasoning in concrete situations.

One important skill at this stage of reasoning is the ability to classify things into different sets or subsets and to consider their interrelations. Children in the concrete operational stage might enjoy playing games that involve sorting objects into types and identifying objects that do not fit with a group. (You might remember the childhood song that goes, "One of these things is not like the others," which aimed to coax you into concrete operations.)

Concrete operational thought involves logical reasoning in concrete but not hypothetical contexts. According to Piaget, this kind of abstract, logical reasoning occurs in the fourth, and final, cognitive stage.

Formal Operational Stage   Individuals enter the **formal operational stage** of cognitive development at 11 to 15 years of age. This stage continues through the adult years. Formal operational thought is more abstract and logical than concrete operational thought. Most important, formal operational thinking includes thinking about things that are not concrete, making predictions, and using logic to come up with hypotheses about the future.

● **formal operational stage** Piaget's fourth stage of cognitive development, which begins at 11 to 15 years of age and continues through the adult years; it features thinking about things that are not concrete, making predictions, and using logic to come up with hypotheses about the future.

Unlike elementary schoolchildren, adolescents can conceive of hypothetical, purely abstract possibilities. This type of thinking is called *idealistic* because it involves comparing how things are to how they might be. Adolescents also think more logically. They begin to think more as a scientist thinks, devising plans to solve problems and systematically testing solutions. Piaget called this type of problem solving *hypothetical-deductive reasoning.* The term denotes adolescents' ability to develop hypotheses, or best hunches, about ways to solve a problem such as an algebraic equation. It also denotes their ability to systematically deduce, or come to a conclusion about, the best path for solving the problem. In contrast, before adolescence, children are more likely to solve problems by trial and error.

In summary, over the course of Piaget's four developmental stages, a person progresses from sensorimotor cognition to abstract, idealistic, and logical thought. Let's consider the current thinking about Piaget's theories of cognitive development.

EVALUATING PIAGET'S THEORY

Piaget opened up a new way of looking at how the human mind develops (P. H. Miller, 2011). We owe him for a long list of masterful concepts that have enduring power and fascination. We also owe Piaget for the currently accepted vision of children as active, constructive thinkers who play a role in their own development.

Nevertheless, just as other psychological theories have been criticized and amended, so have Piaget's. First, Piaget may have *overestimated* the cognitive acumen of adolescents and adults. Formal operational thought does not emerge as consistently and universally in early adolescence as Piaget envisioned (Kuhn, 2009). Many adolescents and adults do not reason as logically as Piaget proposed. Second, Piaget likely *underestimated* the cognitive capacities of very young children. As methods have improved for assessing infants and children, researchers have found that many cognitive abilities emerge earlier than Piaget envisioned (Baillargeon, Scott, & Bian, 2016; de Hevia & Spelke, 2010; Meltzoff, 2011; Quinn, 2011).

THE NATIVIST APPROACH TO INFANT COGNITION

A number of scientists who study cognitive development in infancy have asserted that infants know a great deal more about the world than Piaget concluded. According to this *nativist* approach, infants possess primitive expectancies about events and objects in the world that are less dependent upon experience than Piaget imagined. Research has shown, for instance, that infants as young as 3 months of age know that objects continue to exist even when hidden, and even these very young infants have expectations about objects in the world that seem quite a bit more sophisticated than Piaget imagined (Baillargeon, 2014; Baillargeon & others, 2012; Luo, Kaufman, & Baillargeon, 2009).

In one study, researchers presented 3-month-old infants a puppet show featuring Minnie Mouse (Luo & Baillargeon, 2005). In the center of the stage was a flat cardboard cutout of a castle. Minnie entered stage right and proceeded toward the castle, disappearing behind it. When Minnie went behind the castle wall from one side, the infants looked for her to appear in the doorway and to come out on the other side, suggesting that even though Minnie was out of sight, she was not out of mind. Not only did these 3-month-olds realize that Minnie still existed, but they also *had expectations* about where she was heading.

Such findings have led many developmental psychologists to assert that we must expand our appreciation for the perceptual and cognitive tools that are available to infants with very little experience (Baillargeon, Scott, & Bian, 2016; Spelke, Bernier, & Snedeker, 2013). In a sense, babies possess a very simple sense of physics, an architecture that appears to be present as early as scientists have been able to measure it (Hespos & van Marle, 2012; Kinzler, Dupoux, & Spelke, 2013). Nativist thinkers recognize later experience as important but see it as building on this architecture (Spelke & Kinzler, 2007).

The *nativist* approach contrasts with the *empiricist* approach (Witherington, 2015). The empiricist approach emphasizes the role of experience in the world as the central driver of cognitive and perceptual development (Newcombe, 2002). The empiricist perspective points out that even if very young infants show an understanding of object permanence, that capacity might still originate in (very early) experience (Spencer & others, 2009). Of course, those very young infants would still have learned object permanence much earlier than Piaget asserted.

VYGOTSKY'S SOCIOCULTURAL COGNITIVE THEORY

Piaget did not think that culture and education play important roles in children's cognitive development. For Piaget, the child's active interaction with the physical world was all that was needed to go through these stages. The Russian psychologist Lev Vygotsky

(1962) took a different approach, recognizing that cognitive development is very much an interpersonal process that happens in a cultural context (Ioa & others, 2015; Wang, 2015).

Vygotsky thought of children as apprentice thinkers who develop as they interact in dialogue with more knowledgeable others, such as parents and teachers (Daniels, 2011). Vygotsky theorized that these expert thinkers spur cognitive development by interacting with a child in a way that is just above the level of sophistication the child has mastered. In effect, these interactions provide *scaffolding* that allows the child's cognitive abilities to be built higher and higher.

Teachers and parents, then, provide a framework for thinking that is always just at a level the child can strive to attain. Furthermore, in Vygotsky's view, the goal of cognitive development is to learn the skills that will allow the individual to be competent in his or her particular culture. Expert thinkers are not simply guiding a child into a level of cognitive sophistication but also, along the way, sharing with the child important aspects of culture, such as language and customs. For Vygotsky, a child is not simply learning to think about the world—he or she is learning to think about *his or her own world*.

© Image Source/Alamy

INFORMATION-PROCESSING THEORY

The *information-processing theory* of development focuses on how individuals encode information, manipulate it, monitor it, and create strategies for handling it (Alloway & others, 2015; Barrouillet, 2015; Cowan & others, 2015). In contrast to Piaget's emphasis on broad stages of cognitive development, information-processing theory focuses on specific cognitive processes, such as memory, as we have reviewed in previous chapters.

For instance, rather than focusing on whether infants and children can master particular cognitive skills, contemporary researchers study topics such as the emergence of autobiographical memory as children come to mentally represent the events that make up their life stories (Bauer, 2015; Fivush, 2011; Wang & others, 2015). *Working memory,* that mental workspace that is used for problem solving (see the chapter "Memory"), is linked to many aspects of children's development (de Wilde, Koot, & van Lier, 2016; Saarinen & others, 2015). Children who have better working memory are more advanced in reading comprehension, math skills, and problem solving than their counterparts with less effective working memory (Kroesbergen, van't Noordende, & Kolkman, 2014; Nevo & Breznitz, 2013). One study found that working memory in *preschool* predicted high school dropout rates. Students with low working memory were at higher risk of dropping out of high school, even accounting for socioeconomic status and IQ (Fitzpatrick & others, 2015).

A particularly important aspect of cognitive development in childhood is executive function. Recall that **executive function** refers to higher-order, complex cognitive processes, including thinking, planning, and problem solving. Executive function involves managing one's thoughts to engage in goal-directed behavior and to exercise self-control.

In preschoolers, executive function involves cognitive skills such as holding back on one's automatic impulses, being cognitively flexible, setting goals, and forgoing an immediate pleasure or reward for a more desirable one later (Bell & Cuevas, 2013; Carlson & White, 2011; Vuontela & others, 2013; Woltering & others, 2016; Zelazo & Muller, 2011). To be successful in school, one must be able to sit still, wait in line, raise one's hand, and so forth. These simple tasks require self-control and the capacity to inhibit one's automatic responses (Diamond & Lee, 2011). It is not surprising then that executive function during the preschool years is linked to school readiness, perhaps even more strongly than general IQ (Blair & Raver, 2015). Executive function also predicts the development of social cognitive abilities, including theory of mind: the understanding that other people experience private knowledge and mental states (Marcovitch & others, 2015).

A large longitudinal study showed that aspects of executive function assessed in early childhood predict less risk taking, decreased dropout rates, and less drug use in adolescence, as well as better physical and psychological health, better earnings, and less criminal behavior in adulthood (some 30 years later) (Moffitt & others, 2011). Clearly, then, executive function is important. Can it be fostered by experience?

● **executive function** Higher-order, complex cognitive processes, including thinking, planning, and problem solving.

Parents and teachers play important roles in the development of executive function. Parents who model executive function and self-control can serve as scaffolds for these skills (Herbers & others, 2011). A variety of activities increase children's executive function, such as training to improve working memory (Kirk & others, 2015), aerobic exercise (Diamond, 2015), and mindfulness training (Poehlmann-Tynan & others, 2016).

Sometimes very specific cognitive activities, ones that require children to stretch the way they think, can influence executive function. For example, in one study, 5-year-olds who were instructed to complete an executive function measure as if they were someone else (for example, Batman) performed better than children without these special instructions (White & Carlson, 2016).

Socioemotional Development in Infancy and Childhood

When we observe the newborns behind the window of a hospital nursery, one thing is clear: Humans differ from one another in terms of their emotional demeanor from the very beginning of life. Some are easygoing, and some are prone to distress. Furthermore, in the earliest days of life, infants encounter a social network that will play an important role as they develop their sense of self and the world. To begin our exploration of the socioemotional aspects of development, we focus first on these raw ingredients of emotional and social characteristics that are present early in life—infant temperament and attachment.

TEMPERAMENT

● **temperament** An individual's behavioral style and characteristic ways of responding.

Temperament refers to an individual's behavioral style and characteristic way of responding. There are a number of ways to think about infant temperament. For example, psychiatrists Alexander Chess and Stella Thomas (1977, 1996) identified three basic types of temperament in children:

■ *The easy child* generally is in a positive mood, quickly establishes regular routines in infancy, and easily adapts to new experiences.

■ *The difficult child* tends to react negatively and to cry frequently, engages in irregular daily routines, and is slow to accept new experiences.

■ *The slow-to-warm-up child* has a low activity level, is somewhat negative, is inflexible, and is very cautious in the face of new experiences.

Other researchers suggest that infant temperament also includes other dimensions, such as *effortful control* or *self-regulation* (controlling arousal and not being easily agitated), *inhibition* (being shy and showing distress in an unfamiliar situation), and *positive* and *negative affectivity* (tending to be happy and even tempered or frustrated and sad) (Kagan, 2013; Rothbart & Gartstein, 2008). A recent study showed that mothers' memories of their children's temperament at age 4 months predicted school readiness during preschool; specifically, children with positive emotionality and high levels of self-regulation exhibited a higher level of school readiness (Gartstein, Putnam, & Kliewer, 2016).

The emotional characteristics that a child brings into the world are thought to serve as a foundation for later personality (Casalin & others, 2012; Soto & Tackett, 2015). Similarly, the child's earliest social bonds might set the stage for later social relationships.

ATTACHMENT

Just as infants require nutrition and shelter, they need warm social interaction to survive and develop. A classic study by Harry Harlow (1958) demonstrates the essential importance of warm contact. Harlow separated infant monkeys from their mothers at birth and placed them in cages with two artificial "mothers." One of the mothers was a physically cold wire mother; the other was a warm, fuzzy cloth mother (the "contact comfort" mother). Each mother could be outfitted with a feeding mechanism. Half of the infant monkeys were fed by the wire mother, half by the cloth mother. The infant monkeys

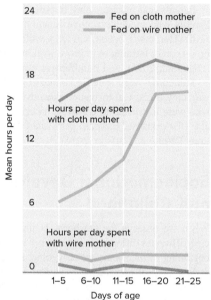

24

Fed on cloth mother
Fed on wire mother

18

Hours per day spent
with cloth mother

12

6

Hours per day spent
with wire mother

0

1–5 6–10 11–15 16–20 21–25
Days of age

Mean hours per day

FIGURE 9 Contact Time with Wire and Cloth Surrogate Mothers
Regardless of whether the infant monkeys were fed by a wire or a cloth mother, they overwhelmingly preferred to spend contact time with the cloth mother.
(photo) © Science Source

nestled close to the cloth mother and spent little time on the wire one, even if it was the wire mother that gave them milk (Figure 9). When afraid, the infant monkeys ran to the comfy mom.

Harlow's work is important because it demonstrates that contact comfort, not feeding, is crucial to an infant's attachment to its caregiver. This work set the stage for our modern understanding of the vital role of warm physical contact between caregivers and infants.

Infant attachment is the close emotional bond between an infant and its caregiver. British psychiatrist John Bowlby (1969, 1989) theorized that the infant and the mother instinctively form an attachment. For Bowlby, the newborn comes into the world equipped to stimulate the caregiver to respond; it cries, clings, smiles, and coos. Bowlby thought that this early relationship with our primary caregiver was internalized so that it served as our schema for our sense of self and the social world. Many developmental psychologists concur that such attachment during the first year provides an important foundation for later development (Bretherton, 2012; Sroufe, Coffino, & Carlson, 2010).

Mary Ainsworth devised the *strange situation test* to measure children's attachment (Ainsworth, 1979; Ainsworth & others, 2015). In this procedure, caregivers leave infants alone with a stranger and then return. Children's responses to this situation are used to classify them into one of three attachment styles. **Secure attachment** means infants use the caregiver, usually the mother, as a secure base from which to explore the environment. In the strange situation, the secure infant is upset when the mother leaves, but calms down and appears happy to see her when she returns (Behrens, Parker, & Haltigan, 2011). The securely attached infant moves freely away from the mother but also keeps tabs on her by periodically glancing at her.

In contrast, there are two types of **insecure attachment:** *avoidant* and *anxious/ambivalent*. In the strange situation, the avoidant infant might not even notice the mother has gone. The anxious/ambivalent infant responds with intense distress, only to rage at the mother when she returns.

Although attachment theory has been very influential it has also been criticized, for three main issues:

- It does not adequately account for cultural variations (van IJzendoorn & Bakermans-Kranenburg, 2010). For example, in some cultures infants show strong attachments to many people, not just to their primary caregiver (Rothbaum & others, 2000, 2007).

● **infant attachment** The close emotional bond between an infant and its caregiver.

● **secure attachment** The ways that infants use their caregiver, usually their mother, as a secure base from which to explore the environment.

● **insecure attachment** Infants do not use the caregiver as a secure base from which to explore; instead, they experience their relationship with the caregiver as unstable and unreliable. The two types of insecure attachment are avoidant and anxious/ambivalent (also called preoccupied).

Trust Versus Mistrust	**Autonomy Versus Shame and Doubt**	**Initiative Versus Guilt**	**Industry Versus Inferiority**
Developmental period: Infancy (birth to 1½ years)	**Developmental period:** Toddlerhood (1½ to 3 years)	**Developmental period:** Early childhood (preschool years, ages 3–5)	**Developmental period:** Middle and late childhood (elementary school years, 6 years–puberty)
Characteristics: A sense of trust requires a feeling of physical comfort and minimal amount of fear about the future. Infants' basic needs are met by responsive, sensitive caregivers.	**Characteristics:** After gaining trust in their caregivers, infants start to discover that they have a will of their own. They assert their sense of autonomy, or independence. They realize their will. If infants are restrained too much or punished too harshly, they are likely to develop a sense of shame and doubt.	**Characteristics:** As preschool children encounter a widening social world, they are challenged more and need to develop more purposeful behavior to cope with these challenges. Children are now asked to assume more responsibility. Uncomfortable guilt feelings may arise, though, if the children are irresponsible and are made to feel too anxious.	**Characteristics:** At no other time are children more enthusiastic than at the end of early childhood's period of expansive imagination. As children move into the elementary school years, they direct their energy toward mastering knowledge and intellectual skills. The danger at this stage involves feeling incompetent and unproductive.

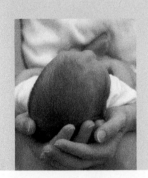   

FIGURE 10 **Erikson's Eight Stages of Psychosocial Development** Erikson changed the way psychologists think about development by tracing the process of growth over the entire life span. (first photo) © Tarinoel/iStock/Getty Images; (second photo) © Stock 4B; (third photo) © Ariel Skelley/Getty Images; (fourth photo) © Ariel Skelley/Getty Images; (fifth photo) © Digital Vision; (sixth photo) © Blue Moon Stock/Alamy; (seventh photo) © McGraw-Hill Education/Ken Karp, photographer; (eighth photo) © Ryan McVay/Getty Images

© Thomas Barwick/Getty Images

- It fails to take infant temperament into account. Some babies are simply more difficult than others and their personalities may color the attachment relationship.

- Finally, it fails to acknowledge that caregivers and infants likely share genetic characteristics. The attachment relationship might be a product of these shared genes (Pappa & others, 2015).

Despite such criticisms, there is ample evidence that secure attachment is important to development (R. A. Thompson, 2013a, 2013b, 2013c). Moreover, even across cultures, maternal sensitivity to infants and mothers' willingness to serve as a secure base predict infant attachment over time (Posada & others, 2015).

From Bowlby's perspective, an infant's experiences lay the groundwork for expectations about what human relationships will be like, setting the stage for future relationships, including our romantic relationships as adults.

Given these raw ingredients of temperament and attachment, how does a human being develop in the socioemotional domain? Erik Erikson, who devised a theory of what he called *psychosocial development,* addressed this question. Like Piaget's theory of cognitive development, Erikson's theory has guided thinking about how human beings' social and emotional capacities develop throughout the life span.

ERIKSON'S THEORY OF SOCIOEMOTIONAL DEVELOPMENT

Erik Erikson (1902–1994) proposed eight psychosocial stages of development from infancy through old age. In Erikson's (1968) view, the first four stages take place in childhood; the last four, in adolescence and adulthood (Figure 10).

Identity Versus Identity Confusion	**Intimacy Versus Isolation**	**Generativity Versus Stagnation**	**Integrity Versus Despair**
Developmental period: Adolescence (10–20 years) **Characteristics :** Individuals are faced with finding out who they are, what they are all about, and where they are going in life. An important dimension is the exploration of alternative solutions to roles. Career exploration is important.	**Developmental period:** Early adulthood (20s, 30s) **Characteristics :** Individuals face the developmental task of forming intimate relationships with others. Erikson described intimacy as finding oneself yet losing oneself in another person.	**Developmental period:** Middle adulthood (40s, 50s) **Characteristics :** A chief concern is to assist the younger generation in developing and leading useful lives.	**Developmental period:** Late adulthood (60s–) **Characteristics :** Individuals look back and evaluate what they have done with their lives. The retrospective glances can be either positive (integrity) or negative (despair).

Erikson's theory is important because he viewed socioemotional development as a *lifelong* process, marked by important developmental milestones in young and middle adulthood and into old age. Each of Erikson's stages represents a developmental task that the individual must master at a particular place in the life span.

Erikson's developmental tasks are represented by two possible outcomes—one, greater strength and competence; the other, greater weakness and vulnerability. Which outcome occurs depends on whether the person's needs at each stage are well met or frustrated. Using Erikson's stages as a guide, let's consider the various ways that human beings develop in terms of their capacities for interpersonal relationships and emotional well-being in infancy and childhood.

SOCIOEMOTIONAL DEVELOPMENT IN INFANCY AND CHILDHOOD: FROM TRUST TO INDUSTRY

We examine Erikson's adolescence and adult stages later in this chapter. His four childhood stages are:

- *Trust versus mistrust:* Trust is built in infancy (birth to 18 months) when a baby's basic needs—such as comfort, food, and warmth—are met by responsive, sensitive caregivers. At this stage, the helpless infant depends on caregivers to establish a sense that the world is a predictable and friendly place. Once trust is established, toddlers begin to see themselves as independent agents in the world.

- *Autonomy versus shame and doubt:* During toddlerhood (18 months through 3 years), children can develop either a positive sense of independence and autonomy or negative feelings of shame and doubt. In seeking autonomy, they are likely to develop a strong sense of independence. A toddler who is experiencing toilet training is learning the beginnings of self-control. The toddler's growing independence is evident in the child's insistence that no matter how difficult the task,

Erik Erikson (1902–1994) Erikson generated one of the most important developmental theories of the twentieth century.

©Ted Streshinsky Photographic Archive/Getty Images

"I can do it myself!" Similarly common is the toddler's assertion of autonomy with a simple two-letter word: "No!"

- *Initiative versus guilt:* In early childhood (3 to 5 years), preschoolers experience what it is like to forge their own interests and friendships and to take on responsibilities. If you have ever spent time with a 3-year-old, you know how often the child wants to help with whatever an adult is doing. When they experience a sense of taking on responsibility, preschoolers develop initiative. Otherwise, according to Erikson, they may feel guilty or anxious.

- *Industry versus inferiority:* Children in middle and late childhood (6 years to puberty) can achieve industry by mastering knowledge and intellectual skills. When they do not, they can feel inferior. At the end of early childhood, children are ready to turn their energy to learning academic skills. If they do not, they can develop a sense of being incompetent and unproductive. During the beginnings of elementary school, children learn the value of what Erikson called *industry,* gaining competence in academic skills and acquiring the ability to engage in self-discipline and hard work.

From Erikson's perspective, then, children should grow toward greater levels of autonomy and self-confidence as they progress from infancy to school age and beyond. At each stage, Erikson said, parents can facilitate the child's growth, or they can thwart it by being overly protective or neglectful.

EVALUATING ERIKSON'S THEORY

Like Piaget's theory, Erikson's conclusions have had their critics (Kroger, 2007). Erikson mainly practiced case study research, which some reject as the sole research foundation for his approach. Critics also argue that Erikson's attempt to capture each developmental stage with a single concept leaves out other important developmental tasks. For example, as we will see, Erikson said that the main task for young adults is to resolve a conflict between intimacy and isolation, yet another important developmental task at this life stage revolves around careers and work.

PARENTING AND CHILDHOOD SOCIOEMOTIONAL DEVELOPMENT

Various researchers have tried to identify styles of parenting associated with positive developmental outcomes. Diana Baumrind (1991, 1993, 2012) described four basic styles of interaction between parents and their children:

- **Authoritarian parenting** is a strict punitive style. The authoritarian parent firmly limits and controls the child with little verbal exchange. In a difference of opinion about how to do something, for example, the authoritarian parent might say, "You do it my way or else." Children of authoritarian parents sometimes lack social skills, show poor initiative, and compare themselves with others.

  Importantly, culture influences the effects of authoritarian parenting. In one study (Rudy & Grusec, 2006), collectivist mothers (in this case Iranian, Indian, Egyptian, and Pakistani) described themselves as more authoritarian but did not express negative attitudes about their children, and the children did not show these more negative outcomes. For Latino families, some psychologists have suggested that authoritarian parenting may express culturally valued childrearing goals such as family, respect, and education and that this parenting style must be understood in the context of these cultural ideals (Halgunseth, Ispa, & Rudy, 2006).

- **Authoritative parenting** encourages the child to be independent but still places limits and controls on behavior. This parenting style is more collaborative. Extensive verbal give-and-take is allowed, and parents are warm and nurturing toward the child. An authoritative father might put his arm around the child in a comforting way and say, "You know you should not have done that; let's talk about how you can handle the situation better next time." Children whose parents are authoritative tend to be socially competent, self-reliant, and socially responsible.

• **authoritarian parenting** A restrictive, punitive style in which the parent exhorts the child to follow the parent's directions.

• **authoritative parenting** A parenting style that encourages the child to be independent but that still places limits and controls on behavior.

- **Neglectful parenting** is distinguished by a lack of parental involvement in the child's life. Children of neglectful parents might develop a sense that other aspects of their parents' lives are more important than they are. Children whose parents are neglectful tend to be less competent socially, to handle independence poorly, and (especially) to show poor self-control.

- **Permissive parenting** involves placing few limits on the child's behavior. A permissive parent lets the child do what he or she wants. Some parents deliberately rear their children this way because they believe that the combination of warm involvement and few limits will produce a creative, confident child. However, children with very permissive parents typically rate poorly in social competence. They often fail to learn respect for others, expect to get their own way, and have difficulty controlling their behavior. Recall that socioemotional development involves becoming increasingly adept at controlling and regulating one's emotions and behaviors (Vazsonyi & Huang, 2010). Children may require structure from their caregivers in order to acquire these skills.

● **neglectful parenting** A parenting style characterized by a lack of parental involvement in the child's life.

● **permissive parenting** A parenting style characterized by the placement of few limits on the child's behavior.

Moral Development in Childhood

Another aspect of social development that psychologists study is how an individual becomes a person of character—someone who behaves morally. This aspect of development features yet another classic theory in developmental psychology, that of Lawrence Kohlberg (1927–1987). Moral development involves changes over time in thoughts, feelings, and behaviors regarding the principles and values that guide what people should do.

KOHLBERG'S THEORY

Kohlberg (1958) began his study of moral thinking by creating a series of stories and asking children, adolescents, and adults questions about the stories. One of the stories goes something like this. A man, Heinz, whose wife is dying of cancer, knows about a drug that might save her life. He approaches the pharmacist who has the drug, but the pharmacist refuses to give it to him without being paid a very high price. Heinz is unable to scrape together the money and eventually decides to steal the drug.

After reading the story, each person interviewed was asked a series of questions about the moral dilemma. Should Heinz have stolen the drug? Kohlberg was less interested in the answer to this question than he was to the next one: Why? Based on the reasons people gave for their answers, Kohlberg (1986) evaluated their level of moral development. Kohlberg's stages of moral development consist of three general levels:

1. *Preconventional:* The individual's moral reasoning is based primarily on the consequences of behavior and punishments and rewards from the external world. Moral reasoning is guided by not wanting Heinz to go to jail or concern for the druggists' profits.

2. *Conventional:* The individual abides by standards learned from parents or society's laws. At this level the person might reason that Heinz should act in accord with expectations or his role as a good husband or reason that Heinz should follow the law no matter what.

3. *Postconventional:* The individual recognizes alternative moral courses, explores the options, and then develops an increasingly personal moral code. At this level, the person might reason that saving Heinz's wife is more important than a law.

Kohlberg believed that moral development advances because of the maturation of thought, the availability of opportunities for role taking, and the chance to discuss moral issues with a person who reasons at a stage just above one's own.

Kohlberg studied with Piaget, and Kohlberg's approach to moral reasoning emphasized the individual's capacity to reason in a sophisticated way, as did Piaget's theory. As we will see, subsequent theories of moral development have focused on its social and emotional components. For Kohlberg, a sense of justice was at the heart of moral reasoning, which he believed laid the foundation for moral behavior.

Lawrence Kohlberg (1927–1987) Kohlberg created a provocative theory of moral development. In his view, "Moral development consists of a sequence of qualitative changes in the way an individual thinks."

© Lee Lockwood/Time & Life Pictures/Getty Images

Carol Gilligan (b. 1936) Gilligan argues that Kohlberg's approach does not give adequate attention to relationships. In Gilligan's view, "Many girls seem to fear, most of all, being alone—without friends, family, and relationships."

© Paul Hawthorne/Getty Images

EVALUATING KOHLBERG'S THEORY

Kohlberg's ideas have stimulated considerable research about how people think about moral issues (Lapsley & Yaeger, 2013; Narvaez, 2013; Nucci, 2013; L. J. Walker, 2013). At the same time, his theory has numerous critics.

One criticism is that moral *reasoning* does not necessarily mean moral *behavior.* When people are asked about their moral reasoning, what they say might fit into Kohlberg's advanced stages, but their actual behavior might involve cheating, lying, and stealing. The cheaters, liars, and thieves might know what is right but still do what is wrong.

Another criticism is that Kohlberg's view does not adequately reflect concern for other people and social bonds (Hardy & Carlo, 2011). Kohlberg's theory is called a *justice perspective* because it focuses on the rights of the individual as the key to sound moral reasoning. In contrast, the *care perspective,* which lies at the heart of Carol Gilligan's (1982) approach to moral development, views people in terms of their connectedness with others and emphasizes interpersonal communication, relationships, and concern for others. From Gilligan's perspective, this weakness in Kohlberg's approach explains why, using his measures, women generally score lower than men on moral development.

Similarly, culture can influence whether a person approaches a moral dilemma from the perspective of justice or care (Gibbs, 2010; J. Miller, 2013; Tappan, 2013; Wainryb, 2013). In Western cultures, where people generally tend toward an individualistic sense of self and are therefore inclined to take a justice perspective, individuals might score higher in Kohlberg's scheme than their counterparts in collectivistic Asian cultures, where people have a sense of the self as part of a larger group.

One final criticism of Kohlberg centers on his overestimation of the role of logical reasoning in moral judgments. Contemporary research suggests that Kohlberg missed the very large role of emotion and intuition in moral decision making (Greene & Haidt, 2002).

CURRENT RESEARCH ON MORAL DEVELOPMENT

A great deal of contemporary research on moral reasoning concerns not simply to the two sides of morality identified by Kohlberg (justice) and Gilligan (care) but multiple principles or *moral foundations* that people take into account as they reason about moral issues. From this perspective, there are at least five foundations that people consider as they render moral judgments (Graham & others, 2012):

- *Care:* People consider kindness and compassion toward others as well as avoiding harm to others.
- *Fairness:* People think about just outcomes and having outcomes be fair for all involved.
- *Loyalty:* People consider their allegiances to groups and being true to the groups to which they belong.
- *Authority:* People consider what their leaders believe and seek to obey them.
- *Purity:* People base moral judgments on whether they find a behavior to be noble or, in contrast, disgusting or animalistic.

● **prosocial behavior** Behavior that is intended to benefit other people.

Researchers interested in moral development have increasingly studied **prosocial behavior,** behavior that is intended to benefit other people (Carlo & others, 2016; Ferreira & others, 2016). For example, researchers are probing how, when, and why children engage in everyday acts of kindness toward others (Carlo & others, 2011) or tell lies (Williams & others, 2016). Studies have found that supportive parenting and parental monitoring relate to increased helping and comforting of others (Dodge, Coie, & Lynam, 2006). Furthermore, research suggests that the capacities to empathize with others and engage in prosocial behavior are linked with the ability to engage in self-control more generally (Eisenberg, Spinrad, & Morris, 2013).

Other recent research has focused on when a child first shows signs of possessing a conscience (Carlo & others, 2016). Having a conscience means hearing that voice in our head that tells us that something is morally good or bad. Deborah Laible and Ross Thompson (2000, 2002, 2007) have examined the conversations between mothers and toddlers at times when the child did something well or got into trouble. They have found that by 3 years of age, children begin to show signs of early conscience development. Parent–child interactions that are clear, elaborate, and rich with emotional content and that include shared positive emotion foster this development. Childhood characteristics are important because longitudinal research shows that kind, moral children are more likely to be kind, moral adults (Eisenberg, Fabes, & Spinrad, 2006; Narvaez, Wang, & Cheng, 2016).

3. ADOLESCENCE

Adolescence is the developmental period of transition from childhood to adulthood, beginning around ages 10 to 12 and ending at 18 to 21. Adolescents are not all the same. Variations in ethnicity, culture, history, gender, socioeconomic status, and lifestyle characterize their life trajectories. In this section we examine the changes that occur in adolescence in the domains of physical, cognitive, and socioemotional development.

Physical Development in Adolescence

Dramatic physical changes characterize adolescence, especially early adolescence. Among the major physical changes of adolescence are those involving puberty and the brain.

PUBERTAL CHANGE

The signature physical change in adolescence is **puberty,** a period of rapid skeletal and sexual maturation that occurs mainly in early adolescence. We will look at these developments more specifically in the chapter "Gender, Sex, and Sexuality".

Hormonal changes lie at the core of pubertal development. The concentrations of certain hormones increase dramatically during puberty (Crone, Duijvenvoorde, & Peper, 2016; Susman & Dorn, 2013). *Testosterone*—an **androgen,** which is the class of sex hormones that predominate in males—is associated in boys with the development of genitals, an increase in height, and voice change. *Estradiol*—an **estrogen,** the class of sex hormones that predominate in females—is associated in girls with breast, uterine, and skeletal development. Developmental psychologists believe that hormonal changes account for at least some of the emotional ups and downs of adolescence, but hormones are not alone responsible for adolescent behavior (Hendrick, Cance, & Maslowsky, 2016; Negriff, Susman, & Trickett, 2011).

Remember that physical and socioemotional development are intertwined. Nowhere is this link more apparent than in the timing of puberty. Boys and girls who mature earlier than their peers often experience different trajectories, with early-blooming boys having more positive and fewer negative outcomes than early-blooming girls. Boys who mature earlier than their peers are more popular with their peers and have higher self-esteem (Graber, Brooks-Gunn, & Warren, 2006). These boys are more successful and less likely to drink alcohol, smoke cigarettes, or engage in delinquent behaviors than late-maturing boys (Taga, Markey, & Friedman, 2006; van der Geest, Blokland, & Bijleveld, 2009).

In contrast, girls who are early bloomers are less likely to engage in academic pursuits and are less popular; also, they are more likely to become sexually active and to engage in unsafe sex (Blumenthal & others, 2011; Sontag-Padilla & others, 2012). Among early-blooming girls, these outcomes are at least partially due to early use of substances such as drugs and alcohol (Hendrick, Cance, & Maslowsky, 2016).

THE ADOLESCENT BRAIN

Brain-imaging studies show important changes in the brain during adolescence (Blakemore & Mills, 2014; Fuhrmann, Knoll, & Blakemore, 2015). These changes focus on the earlier

test yourself

1. What are teratogens? Give several examples of them.
2. According to Piaget, what two processes are responsible for how people use and adapt their schemas, and what is involved in each process? What are some key aspects of Vygotsky's theory and information-processing theory?
3. What are Erikson's four childhood stages of development, and with what is each centrally concerned?

● **puberty** A period of rapid skeletal and sexual maturation that occurs mainly in early adolescence.

● **androgens** The class of sex hormones that predominate in males, produced by the testes in males and by the adrenal glands in both males and females.

● **estrogens** The class of sex hormones that predominate in females, produced mainly by the ovaries.

312 CHAPTER 9 Human Development

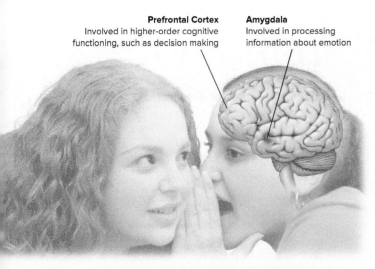

Prefrontal Cortex
Involved in higher-order cognitive functioning, such as decision making

Amygdala
Involved in processing information about emotion

FIGURE 11 Developmental Changes in the Adolescent's Brain The amygdalae, which are responsible for processing information about emotion, mature earlier than the prefrontal cortex, which is responsible for making decisions and other higher-order cognitive functions. (photo) © BrandX Pictures/PunchStock

development of the amygdala, which involves emotion, and the later development of the prefrontal cortex, which is concerned with reasoning and decision making (Figure 11).

These changes in the brain may help to explain why adolescents often display very strong emotions but cannot yet control these passions. It is as if the adolescent brain does not have the brakes to slow down emotions. Because of the relatively slow development of the prefrontal cortex, which continues to mature into early adulthood, adolescents may lack the cognitive skills to control their impulses effectively. This developmental disjunction may account for increased risk taking and other problems in adolescence (Steinberg, 2012, 2013).

Biological changes in the brain are linked with experiences (Dishion, 2016; Whittle & others, 2016). For instance, one study of adolescents found that resisting peer pressure was correlated with prefrontal cortex thickening and more brain connections (Paus & others, 2008). This correlational study cannot tell us if the brain changes promoted peer-pressure resistance or if this resistance promoted changes in the brain, but it does highlight the nature–nurture question that permeates the study of development.

Cognitive Development in Adolescence

As they advance into Piaget's formal operational thinking, adolescents undergo other significant cognitive changes. One characteristic of adolescent thinking, especially in early adolescence, is egocentrism. Although children are also considered egocentric, *adolescent egocentrism* has a different focus; it involves the belief that others are as preoccupied with the adolescent as he or she is. Egocentric adolescents perceive others as observing them more than actually is the case—think of the eighth-grade boy who thinks that everyone has noticed the small pimple on his face. In addition, adolescents show a belief that they are invincible (that is, incapable of being harmed). Adolescents display a particularly problematic pattern in their perception of risks; unlike adults, they underestimate risks associated with various behaviors even as they prefer riskier experiences (Modecki, 2016).

Socioemotional Development in Adolescence

Among the key aspects of adolescent development are identity exploration and the roles that parents and peers play in adolescent development.

IDENTITY

Recall from Figure 10 that Erikson (1968) viewed the key challenge of adolescence (his fifth stage) as *identity versus identity confusion*. Erikson's approach to the formation of identity during adolescence is one of his most important contributions (Kroger, 2012). In seeking an identity, adolescents face the challenges of finding out who they are, what they are all about, and where they are going in life. Adolescents are confronted with many new roles and adult statuses—from jobs and careers to friendships and romantic relationships. If they do not adequately explore their identity during this stage, they end up confused about who they are. Erikson argued that parents should allow adolescents to explore many different roles and many paths within a particular role.

Adolescents who spend this time in their lives exploring alternatives can reach some resolution of the identity crisis and emerge with a new sense of self. Those who do not successfully resolve the crisis suffer what Erikson calls *identity confusion,* which is expressed in one of two ways: The individual either withdraws, becoming isolated from peers and family, or the person loses himself or herself in the crowd.

psychological *inquiry*

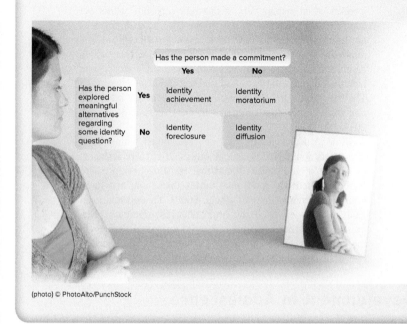

(photo) © PhotoAlto/PunchStock

Exploring Identity Exploration

This figure summarizes Marcia's conceptualization of identity development. Notice that the different quadrants of the square represent the crossings of the two factors of commitment and exploration and that every possible combination of the two is represented. Then answer the following questions.

1. Imagine a young woman who comes from a family in which no one ever attended college. What sorts of experiences might influence her journey to identity? How might her background influence her identity exploration?

2. Find yourself in this figure. That is, in which quadrant is your own identity located? Do you feel that you fully explored your potential identities? Why or why not?

3. Which path to identity do you believe is most common in young people today? Why?

4. Finding one's path in life is a common theme in popular books, TV, and film. Can you identify a book or movie that depicts the combination of exploration and resolution? Why do you think this theme is so popular?

Marcia's Theory on Identity Status   Building on Erikson's ideas, James Marcia proposed the concept of *identity status* to describe a person's position in the development of an identity (Kroger, Martinussen, & Marcia, 2010; Marcia, 1980, 2002). In Marcia's view, two dimensions of identity, exploration and commitment, are important. *Exploration* refers to a person's investigating various options for a career and for personal values. *Commitment* involves making a decision about which identity path to follow and making a personal investment in attaining that identity. Various combinations of exploration and commitment give rise to one of four identity statuses.

Marcia's approach focuses on identity as an active construction, an outcome of a process of thinking about and trying on different identities (Klimstra & others, 2009, 2010). To master Marcia's approach, check out the Psychological Inquiry.

Ethnic Identity   Developing an identity in adolescence can be especially challenging for individuals from ethnic minority groups (Schwartz & others, 2012, 2013). As they mature cognitively, many adolescents become acutely aware of how the majority culture views their ethnic group. In addition, an increasing number of minority adolescents face the challenge of *biculturalism* or *multiculturalism*—identifying in some ways with their ethnic minority group and in other ways with the majority culture (Hong & others, 2016).

Research has shown that for ethnic minority youth, feeling both a positive attachment to their minority group and an attachment to the larger culture is related to more positive academic and emotional outcomes (Serrano-Villar & Calzada, 2016). Although it might seem that being a member of an ethnic minority would make life more stressful, studies have indicated that having a strong ethnic identity can buffer adolescents from the effects of discrimination.

In addition to ethnic identity, adolescence can be a time when other aspects of one's identity come to the fore, such as sexual orientation and gender role. We discuss these issues in depth in the chapter "Gender, Sex, and Sexuality".

The managerial role of parenting involves effective monitoring of the adolescent's friends, social activities, and academic efforts.

© Andersen Ross/Blend Images/Getty Images

PARENT AND PEER INFLUENCES

Parents and peers play important roles in adolescent development, including helping adolescents explore and answer the central questions of identity: "Who am I, and who do I hope to become?" (Bornstein, Jager, & Steinberg, 2013).

Parenting   As in childhood, the preferred parenting style for most adolescents is authoritative, being associated with positive outcomes (Baumrind, 2012). To help adolescents reach their full potential, a key parental role is to be an effective manager—one who locates information, makes contacts, helps to structure offsprings' choices, and provides guidance. By assuming this managerial role, parents help adolescents to avoid pitfalls and to work their way through the decisions they face (Simpkins & others, 2009).

Although adolescence is a time of establishing independence, a crucial aspect of the managerial role of parenting is effective monitoring (Romo & others, 2016). Monitoring includes supervising the adolescent's choice of social settings, activities, and friends, as well as his or her academic efforts. However, it is important for parents to be flexible and match their involvement with their son or daughter's life. This kind of flexible approach has been termed *vigilant care* (Omer, Satran, & Driter, 2016). This idea captures the ways that parents must allow adolescents to explore while keeping an eye out for warning signs of problems.

How competent the adolescent will become often depends on access to legitimate opportunities for growth, such as a quality education, community and societal support for achievement and involvement, and good jobs. Especially important in adolescent development is long-term, deeply caring support from adults (Lerner & others, 2013). Successfully parenting adolescents means allowing adolescents to explore their own identity and handle increasing levels of autonomy in a positive manner, while also remaining an involved parent.

Peer Relations   During adolescence, individuals spend more time with peers than they did in childhood. These peer influences can be positive or negative (Criss & others, 2016). A significant aspect of positive peer relations is having one or more close friends. Adolescents can learn to be skilled and sensitive partners in intimate relationships by forging close friendships with selected peers (Tucker & others, 2012). However, some peers and friends can negatively impact adolescents' development. Researchers have found that hanging out with delinquent peers in adolescence can be a strong predictor of substance abuse, delinquent behavior, and depression (Laursen & others, 2012).

test yourself

1. What characteristics of the adolescent brain help to explain why adolescents often display strong emotions that they cannot control?
2. According to Erikson, what challenges do adolescents face in trying to establish an identity, and what happens if they do not successfully resolve this crisis?
3. In what ways do parents and peers contribute to adolescent development?

4. EMERGING ADULTHOOD, ADULT DEVELOPMENT, AND AGING

Development continues throughout adulthood. Developmental psychologists identify three approximate periods in adult development: early adulthood (20s and 30s), middle adulthood (40s and 50s), and late adulthood (60s until death). Each phase features distinctive physical, cognitive, and socioemotional changes.

Erikson believed that once the issues of identity are resolved, the young adult turns to the important domain of intimate relationships. However, more recently, scholars have noted that during the life stage after adolescence, many young people are putting off the commitments to marriage, family, and career that are traditionally associated with adult life. Jeffrey Arnett introduced the concept of *emerging adulthood* to describe this transitional period, which is partly an extended adolescence and partly a "trying on" of adult roles (Arnett, 2004, 2007, 2010, 2012). If you are a traditional-age college student, you are at this point in the life span. We begin our survey of postadolescent development by briefly examining this transitional life stage.

Emerging Adulthood

Emerging adulthood is the transitional period from adolescence to adulthood (Arnett, 2004, 2006, 2007, 2012). The age range for emerging adulthood is approximately 18 to 25 years of age. Experimentation and exploration characterize the emerging adult. At this point in their development, many individuals are still exploring which career path they want to follow, what they want their identity to be, and what kinds of close relationships they will have.

Jeffrey Arnett (2006) identified five main features of emerging adulthood:

- *Identity exploration, especially in love and work:* Emerging adulthood is the time of significant changes in identity for many individuals.
- *Instability:* Residential changes peak during emerging adulthood, a time during which there also is often instability in love, work, and education.
- *Self-focus:* Emerging adults "are self-focused in the sense that they have little in the way of social obligations, [and] little in the way of duties and commitments to others, which leaves them with a great deal of autonomy in running their own lives" (Arnett, 2006, p. 10).
- *Feeling "in between":* Many emerging adults consider themselves neither adolescents nor full-fledged adults.
- *Age of possibilities, a time when individuals have an opportunity to transform their life:* Arnett (2006) described two ways in which emerging adulthood is the age of possibilities: (1) Many emerging adults are optimistic about their future; and (2) for emerging adults who have experienced difficult times while growing up, emerging adulthood presents an opportunity to guide their lives in a positive direction.

● **emerging adulthood** The transitional period from adolescence to adulthood, spanning approximately 18 to 25 years of age.

Physical Development in Adulthood

Like other developmental periods, our bodies change during adulthood. Most of the changes that occur following adolescence involve declines in physical and perceptual abilities, as we now consider.

PHYSICAL CHANGES IN EARLY ADULTHOOD

Most adults reach their peak physical development during their 20s and are the healthiest then. Early adulthood, however, is also the time when many physical skills begin to decline. The decline in strength and speed often is noticeable in the 30s. Perceptual abilities also decline. Hearing loss is very common with age. It may be difficult to believe but sensory changes occur even as early as the late teens: Starting at about age 18, hearing begins a gradual decline, though it is so slow that most people do not notice it until the age of 50 or so.

PHYSICAL CHANGES IN MIDDLE AND LATE ADULTHOOD

By the 40s or 50s, the skin has begun to wrinkle and sag because of the loss of fat and collagen in underlying tissues. Small, localized areas of pigmentation in the skin produce age spots, especially in areas exposed to sunlight such as the hands and face (Haluza, Simic, & Moshammer, 2016). Hair becomes thinner and grayer due to a lower replacement rate and a decline in melanin production. Individuals lose height in middle age, and many gain weight (Winett & others, 2014). Once individuals hit their 40s, age-related vision changes usually become apparent, especially difficulty in seeing things up close and after dark.

For women, entering middle age means that menopause will soon occur. Usually in the late 40s or early 50s, a woman's menstrual periods cease completely. With menopause comes a dramatic decline in the ovaries' production of estrogen. Estrogen decline can produce uncomfortable symptoms such as *hot flashes* (sudden, brief flushing of the skin and a feeling of elevated body temperature), nausea, fatigue, and rapid heartbeat. Menopause does not produce serious psychological or physical problems for most women (Roberts & Hickey, 2016).

For both men and women, a variety of bodily systems are likely to show the effects of wear and tear as the body becomes less and less able to repair damage and regenerate itself (Parr, Coffey, & Hawley, 2013). Physical strength declines, motor speed slows, and bones may become more brittle (especially for women). Nearly every bodily system may change with age.

Significantly, however, even as age is associated with some inevitable decline, important aspects of successful aging are within the person's control (Bertrand, Graham, & Lachman, 2013; I. C. Siegler & others, 2013a, 2013b). For instance, a healthy diet and regular exercise can help to slow the effects of age (Vissers & others, 2013). Regular physical activity can have wide-reaching benefits not only for physical health but for cognitive functioning as well (Morikawa & others, 2013).

One way older adults navigate the physical changes associated with age is through a process of changing their goals and developing new ways to engage in desired activities. Psychologists refer to this process as *selective optimization with compensation*, which means that older adults match their goals with their current abilities and compensate for declines by finding other ways to do the things they enjoy (Freund, Nikitin, & Riediger, 2013; Hutchinson & Nimrod, 2012). A 75-year-old who can no longer drive because of cataracts might become an expert on her city's train and bus system, for example.

On the island of Okinawa (part of Japan), individuals live longer than anywhere else in the world, and Okinawa has the world's highest prevalence of *centenarians*—individuals who live to 100 years or beyond. Examination of Okinawans' lives provides insights into their longevity. Specific factors are diet (they eat nutritious foods such as grains, fish, and vegetables); lifestyle (they are easygoing and experience low stress); community (Okinawans look out for one another and do not isolate or ignore older adults); activity (they lead active lifestyles, and many older adults continue to work); and spirituality (they find a sense of purpose in spiritual matters) (Willcox & others, 2008). Just as physical changes are interwoven with socioemotional processes in childhood and adolescence, they are similarly intertwined as human beings enter the later stages of life.

BIOLOGICAL THEORIES OF AGING

Of the many proposed biological theories of aging, three especially merit attention: cellular-clock theory, free-radical theory, and hormonal stress theory.

Cellular-Clock Theory   Leonard Hayflick's (1977) *cellular-clock theory* is that cells can divide a maximum of about 100 times and that, as we age, our cells become less capable of dividing. Hayflick found that cells extracted from adults in their 50s to 70s had divided fewer than 100 times. The total number of cell divisions was roughly related to the individual's age. Based on the way cells divide, Hayflick places the human life span's upper limit at about 120 years.

Scientists have been examining why cells lose their ability to divide (Broer & others, 2013). The answer may lie at the tips of chromosomes. Each time a cell divides, the *telomeres* protecting the ends of chromosomes shorten. After about 100 replications, the telomeres are dramatically reduced, and the cell no longer can reproduce (Prescott & others, 2011).

It is not surprising then that scientists are interested in discovering ways to maintain high levels of the telomere-extending enzyme—telomerase. Some have examined how genetic manipulation of telomerase activators might influence levels of telomerase (C. Harrison, 2012). Meditation, described in the chapter "States of Consciousness", might also help to enhance telomerase activity. One study found that individuals who participated in a three-month meditation retreat showed greater telomerase activity relative to a control group (Jacobs & others, 2011).

Free-Radical Theory   A second biological theory of aging is the *free-radical theory*. This theory states that people age because unstable oxygen molecules known as *free radicals* are produced inside their cells. These molecules damage DNA and other cellular structures (Bachschmid & others, 2013). The damage done by free radicals may lead to a range of disorders, including cancer and arthritis (Valko & others, 2016).

Keep in mind, however, that although free radicals sound like the enemy of a healthy body, these cells are themselves important to the body's survival. Immune cells will attack invading bacteria with free radicals to annihilate them. You have probably seen fruit juices and other foods labeled as rich in antioxidants. The notion that foods high in antioxidants are good for health and longevity rests on the free-radical theory of cellular aging, though the actual benefits of antioxidant supplements have not been borne out by research (Moyer, 2013).

Hormonal Stress Theory A third theory of aging, *hormonal stress theory,* argues that aging in the body's hormonal system can lower resistance to stress and increase the likelihood of disease. As individuals age, the hormones stimulated by stress stay in the bloodstream longer than is the case for younger people (Finch, 2011). These prolonged, elevated levels of stress hormones are linked to increased risks for many diseases, including cardiovascular disease, cancer, and diabetes (Gems & Partridge, 2013). Research on the hormonal stress theory of aging has focused on the role of chronic stress in reducing immune system functioning (Naumova & others, 2013).

AGING AND THE BRAIN

Just as the aging body has a greater capacity for renewal than previously thought, so does the aging brain. For decades, scientists believed that no new brain cells are generated past early childhood. However, researchers have discovered that adults *can* grow new brain cells throughout life (Buchman & others, 2016; Curtis, Kam, & Faull, 2011; Kazanis, 2013), although the evidence is limited to the hippocampus and the olfactory bulb (H. Xu & others, 2013). Researchers currently are studying factors that might inhibit and promote neurogenesis, including various drugs, stress, and exercise (Buchman & others, 2016). Research with rats suggests that sustained aerobic exercise (like long-distance running) leads to higher levels of neurogenesis (Nokia & others, 2016). They also are examining how grafting neural stem cells to various brain regions, such as the hippocampus, might increase neurogenesis (Doeppner & others, 2016; Srivastava & others, 2016).

FIGURE 12 **The Brains of the Mankato Nuns** Nun Study participant Sister Nicolette Welter remained an active, contributing member of her community until her death at age 102. (*inset*) A neuroscientist holds a brain donated by one of the Mankato Nun Study participants. (Sister Nicolette Welker) ©Scott Takushi/KRT/Newscom; (brain) © Steve Liss/Time Life Pictures/Getty Images

Research from the Nun Study (described in the chapter "Psychology's Scientific Method") provides evidence for the role of experience in maintaining the brain. Recall that this study involves nearly 700 nuns in a convent in Mankato, Minnesota (Snowdon, 2003, 2007) (Figure 12). Although earlier we surveyed the aspects of the study related to happiness, this research has also investigated brain functioning. By examining the nuns' donated brains as well as those of others, neuroscientists have documented the aging brain's remarkable ability to grow and change. Even the oldest Mankato nuns lead intellectually challenging lives, and neuroscientists believe that stimulating mental activities increase dendritic branching. Keeping the brain actively engaged in challenging activities can help to slow the effects of age.

Even in late adulthood, the brain has the ability to repair and change itself to compensate for and adapt to age-related changes (Dunnett, 2013; Greenberg & Jin, 2013). Changes in lateralization provide one type of adaptation in aging adults. *Lateralization* is the specialization of function in one hemisphere of the brain or the other. Using neuroimaging techniques, researchers have found that brain activity in the prefrontal cortex is lateralized less in older adults than in younger adults when they are engaging in mental tasks (Brambilla & others, 2015; Cabeza, 2002; Raw & others, 2012). This means that for many tasks, younger adults can complete the task using just one hemisphere, while older adults will use both. The decrease in lateralization in older adults might play a compensatory role in the aging brain (Brambilla & others, 2015). That is, using both hemispheres may help to maintain the mental abilities of older adults.

Cognitive Development in Adulthood

Recall that for Piaget, each stage of cognitive development entails a way of thinking that is *qualitatively different* from the stage before. From Piaget's perspective, meaningful cognitive development ceases after the individual reaches the formal operational stage. Subsequent research has examined not qualitative differences in thinking over time, but the ebb and flow of cognitive abilities as a function of age. What kind of cognitive changes occur in adults?

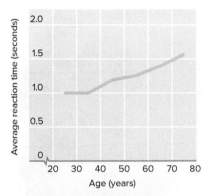

FIGURE 13   The Relationship Between Age and Reaction Time In one study, the average reaction time slowed for individuals in their 40s, and this decline accelerated for those in their 60s and 70s (Salthouse, 1994). The task used to assess reaction time required individuals to match numbers with symbols on a computer screen.

● **wisdom** Expert knowledge about the practical aspects of life.

COGNITION IN EARLY ADULTHOOD

Just as physical abilities peak in early adulthood, might intellectual skills also peak during this time in life (Kitchener, King, & DeLuca, 2006)? Some experts on cognitive development argue that the typical idealism of Piaget's formal operational stage is replaced in young adulthood by more realistic, pragmatic thinking (Labouvie-Vief, 1986). Gisela Labouvie-Vief (2006) proposed that the increasing complexity of cultures in the past century has generated a greater need for reflective, more complex thinking that takes into account the changing nature of knowledge and the kinds of challenges contemporary thinkers face. She emphasizes that key aspects of cognitive development for young adults include deciding on a particular worldview, recognizing that the worldview is subjective, and understanding that diverse worldviews should be acknowledged. In her perspective, only some individuals attain the highest level of thinking.

COGNITION IN MIDDLE ADULTHOOD

What happens to cognitive skills in middle adulthood? Although some cross-sectional studies indicate that middle adulthood is a time of cognitive decline, longitudinal evidence presents a different picture. K. Warner Schaie is conducting an extensive longitudinal study (started in 1956) by repeatedly measuring a host of different intellectual abilities in adults (Schaie, 1994, 2007, 2010, 2012). The highest level of functioning for four of the six intellectual abilities occurred in middle adulthood (Schaie, 2006, 2010, 2012). Only two of the six abilities declined in middle age. Based on the longitudinal data he has collected so far, Schaie concludes that *middle* (not early) adulthood is the period when many people reach their peak for a range of intellectual skills.

COGNITION IN LATE ADULTHOOD

Many contemporary psychologists conclude that some dimensions of intelligence decline in late adulthood, whereas others are maintained or may even increase (Dixon & others, 2013). One of the most consistent findings is that when the speed of processing information is involved, older adults do not perform as well as their younger counterparts (Figure 13). This decline in speed of processing is apparent in middle-aged adults and becomes more pronounced in older adults (Salthouse, 2012).

Older adults also tend to not do as well as younger adults in most, but not all, aspects of memory (Jack & others, 2016). In the area of memory involving knowledge of the world (for instance, the capital of Peru), older adults usually take longer than younger adults to remember the information, but they often are able to retrieve it (Singh-Manoux & others, 2012). Decline occurs for working memory as well (Sung, 2016).

Some aspects of cognition might improve with age. One such area is **wisdom,** expert knowledge about the practical aspects of life (Ferrari & Westrate, 2013; Staudinger & Gluck, 2011). Wisdom may increase with age because of the buildup of life experiences, but individual variations characterize people throughout their lives (Grossman & others, 2010). Thus, not every older person has wisdom, and some young people are wise beyond their years.

Some factors can lessen the decline in cognitive ability among older adults. Training these adults to use specific strategies can enhance their memory, and there is increasing evidence that physical fitness sharpens the thinking skills of older adults (Mortimer & others, 2012). When older adults continue to increase their engagement in cognitive and physical activities, they are better able to maintain their cognitive functioning in late adulthood (C. L. Brown & others, 2012; Lindwall & others, 2012; Mitchell & others, 2012). Still, many experts conclude that older adults are less able to adapt than younger adults and thus are limited in how much they can improve their cognitive skills (Finch, 2009; Salthouse, 2012).

Socioemotional Development in Adulthood

In the physical and the cognitive domains, the developmental story is generally one of rapid growth during childhood, with continuing gains in adolescence, followed by steady decline with age. Does a similar pattern hold for socioemotional development? Let's consider the changes that characterize adult socioemotional development, first returning to Erikson's stage theory of life-span development and then looking at what current research has to say.

SOCIOEMOTIONAL DEVELOPMENT IN EARLY ADULTHOOD

According to Erikson (1968), during early adulthood people face a developmental dilemma involving *intimacy versus isolation* (see Figure 10). At this stage, individuals either form intimate relationships with others or become socially isolated. If the young adult develops healthy friendships and an intimate relationship with a partner, intimacy will likely be achieved. One key way that a young adult achieves intimacy is through a long-term relationship with a romantic partner, often in the form of marriage.

Just as the notion of emerging adulthood would indicate, men and women have been waiting longer to marry in the last few decades. In 2011, the average age for a first marriage in the United States climbed to 28.7 years for men and 26.5 years for women, higher than at any other point in history (Cohn, 2011). In 1980, the average age for a first marriage in the United States was 24 years for men and 21 years for women. This trend may be good news, because a woman's age at her first marriage is related to the ultimate survival of the marriage. Approximately 6 in 10 marriages in which the wife is younger than 18 end in divorce within 15 years, compared with 4 in 10 marriages in which the woman is 20 or older (Center for Family and Demographic Research, 2002).

What makes a marriage successful? John Gottman has been studying married couples' lives since the early 1970s (Gottman, 2006). He interviews couples, films them interacting with each other, and even takes measures of their heart rate and blood pressure during their interactions (Gottman, Swanson, & Swanson, 2002; Madhyastha, Hamaker, & Gottman, 2011). He also checks back with the couples every year to see how their marriages are faring. Gottman and his colleagues continue to follow married couples, as well as same-sex partners, to try to understand what makes relationships thrive. Gottman (2006) has identified four principles at work in successful marriages:

© Image Club

- *Nurturing fondness and admiration:* Partners sing each other's praises. When couples put a positive spin on their talk with and about each other, marriages tend to work.

- *Turning toward each other as friends:* Partners see each other as friends and turn toward each other for support in times of stress and difficulty.

- *Giving up some power:* Bad marriages often involve one partner who is a powermonger. Abuse of power is more common in husbands, but some wives have the problem as well.

- *Solving conflicts together:* Couples work to solve problems, regulate their emotion during times of conflict, and compromise to accommodate each other.

SOCIOEMOTIONAL DEVELOPMENT IN MIDDLE ADULTHOOD

According to Erikson, following the resolution of the intimacy versus isolation dilemma, the adult turns to concerns about *generativity versus stagnation* (see Figure 10). *Generativity* means making a contribution to the next generation. The feeling that one has made a lasting and memorable contribution to the world is related to higher levels of psychological well-being (Busch & Hofer, 2012; Cox & others, 2010; Momtaz & others, 2016). Although Erikson did not think that parenting alone was a guarantee of generativity, he did believe that parenting could be a way to experience this important developmental accomplishment.

SOCIOEMOTIONAL DEVELOPMENT AND AGING

From Erikson's perspective, the person who has entered the later years of life is engaged in looking back—evaluating his or her life and seeking meaning. Erikson called this stage of life *integrity versus despair* (see Figure 10). Through this process of life review and reminiscence, the older adult comes to a sense of meaning or despair, Erikson theorized. The

© Javier Pierini/Taxi/Getty Images

individual is also occupied with coming to terms with his or her own death, according to Erikson. If the individual has a well-established sense of integrity, experiencing life as a meaningful and coherent whole, he or she faces the later years with a strong sense of meaning and low fear of death. In the absence of integrity, the older adult is filled with despair and fear.

RESEARCH ON ADULT SOCIOEMOTIONAL DEVELOPMENT

Research on socioemotional development and aging reveals that Erikson was correct in his view that meaning is a central concern for older adults. However, he may have overlooked that this meaning derives not only from the past but also from the present. Let's conclude our look at socioemotional development in adulthood by considering recent research findings about how adults' lives change socially and emotionally over time.

In terms of social relationships, older adults may become more selective about their social networks (Carstensen, 2006, 2008, 2011; Carstensen & others, 2011). At the same time, older adults report greater happiness than their younger counterparts (Carstensen & others, 2011; Mroczek & Spiro, 2005; Ram & others, 2008; Stanley & Isaacowitz, 2012; Wrzus & others, 2012) and that satisfaction with life increases with age. One study showed that happiness increased for individuals in their 80s (Stone & others, 2010).

Laura Carstensen developed *socioemotional selectivity theory* to address the narrowing of social contacts and the increase in positive emotion that occur with age (Carstensen, 2006, 2011). The theory states that older adults tend to be selective in their social interactions in order to maximize positive, meaningful experiences. Although younger adults may gain a sense of meaning in life from long-term goals, older adults gain a sense of meaning by focusing on satisfying relationships and activities in the *present*. Unlike younger adults, who may be preoccupied with the future, older adults embrace the present moment with increasing vitality (Hicks & others, 2012; Kotter-Grühn & Smith, 2011; Lachman & others, 2008).

Socioemotional selectivity theory posits that it is not old age itself that spurs people to maximize positive meaning in the present but, rather, limited time. Young adults who are asked to imagine having limited time (for instance, because they are about to go on a long trip) show the same pattern of maximizing time they spend with a narrow set of important friends and family members (Carstensen, 2011).

With age, engagement in one's *present life* can be a vital source of meaning. The more active and involved older people are, the more satisfied they are and the more likely they are to stay healthy (Hendricks & Hatch, 2006). Older people who go to church, attend meetings, take trips, and exercise are happier than those who sit at home (George, 2006).

The capacity to regulate emotions, maximizing positive experiences, appears to be a central feature of aging (Sullivan, Mikels, & Carstensen, 2010). Researchers have found that across diverse samples—Norwegians, Catholic nuns, African Americans, Chinese Americans, and non-Latino White Americans—older adults report better control of their emotions than younger adults (Charles & Carstensen, 2010).

The benefits of emotion regulation may have far-reaching consequences. In one study, adults who had expressed positive attitudes about aging some 20 years previously, lived, on average, 7½ years longer than those with more negative attitudes about aging (Levy & others, 2002). An important factor in the link between attitudes and longevity was a person's belief that life was full, hopeful, and worthwhile.

Emotion regulation is also a key issue in one of the most important roles in adulthood—parenting. To read about the influence of emotion regulation in the experience of parenting, see the Intersection.

5. HUMAN DEVELOPMENT AND HEALTH AND WELLNESS

Compared to childhood, development in adulthood is more likely to be a conscious process and therefore a truer mark of an individual's accomplishment (King & Hicks, 2007). In this concluding section we consider the active developer as the individual meets the challenges of adulthood, and we seek to understand how adults "grow" themselves.

test yourself

1. What are the five main features of emerging adulthood?
2. What is brain lateralization, and how might a decrease in lateralization in older adults play a role in the aging brain?
3. What do longitudinal studies indicate about intellectual abilities in middle adulthood?

INTERSECTION

Developmental Psychology and Emotion: How Does the Emotional Work of Parenting Influence Well-Being?

One of the more contentious topics of research is the association between parenting and happiness. Research supports the notion that parenting can be a rich and rewarding experience, but it can also be emotionally complicated (Nelson, Kushlev, & Lyubomirsky, 2014). Parents are often found to be happier than childless individuals but not always. What is it about parenting that might take a toll on happiness?

One possibility is the demands that parenting places on emotion regulation. Think about it: Being a parent often means not showing your true feelings. By necessity, parents must sometimes seem more interested than they really are in, say, the book they are reading for the 157th time this week to their 3-year-old. Similarly, a parent who is tired and frustrated with an obstinate child must often hold back expressing that feeling and channel the anger in other directions.

© manley099/Vetta/Getty Images

Does faking emotions take a toll on happiness?

These are obviously part of caring for someone you love who happens to be small, helpless, and often stubborn. Still, could this kind of emotion regulation take a toll on parents' happiness? Recent research suggests it might.

In these studies, parents were found to feel lower levels of authenticity, well-being, and relationship quality when they suppressed negative emotion or amplified positive emotion in interactions with their children (Le & Impett, 2016). These relationships were independent of parents' perceptions of children's mood—meaning that even when the kids were being very good, parental well-being was lowered when parents felt they had to fake emotions.

Of course, no one would advise parents to openly express their feelings when such expressions are likely to hurt a child's feelings. Yet, helping parents feel more authentic in their emotional expression with their children might help them avoid lowered well-being. After all, they are managing their emotions because they genuinely love their child.

To parents raising young children, these results likely ring true. Yet the results also have implications for other relationships. Although it may be necessary to hide one's deepest feelings in interactions with children, the studies tell us that, in close relationships, hiding who we really are may take a toll.

Coping and Adult Development

One way that adults develop is through coping with life's difficulties. Psychologist Carolyn Aldwin and her colleagues have suggested that stress and coping play a role in development (Aldwin, 2007; Aldwin, Levenson, & Kelly, 2009; Aldwin, Spiro, & Park, 2006; Aldwin, Yancura, & Boeninger, 2007; Boeninger & others, 2009). To understand how, consider that Piaget's ideas of assimilation and accommodation in childhood cognitive development may be applied to adult development as well (Block, 1982).

Recall that in assimilation existing cognitive structures are used to make sense out of the current environment. Assimilation allows the person to enjoy a feeling of meaning because experiences fit into his or her preexisting schemas (King & Hicks, 2007). However, life does not always conform to our expectations. When experience conflicts with existing schemas, it is necessary to modify current ways of thinking.

Accommodation is the process whereby existing schemas are modified or new structures are developed. Accommodation helps us to change so that we can make sense of life's previously incomprehensible events. When we encounter a negative life circumstance, such as an illness or a loss, we have the opportunity to change—to develop and to mature (Bauer, Schwab, & McAdams, 2011; Gunty & others, 2011; Pasupathi, Fivush, & Hernandez-Martinez, 2016). Indeed, research suggests that individuals who are faced with difficulties in life are more likely to come to a rich, complex view of themselves and the world (King & Hicks, 2007; Wrosch, Amir, & Miller, 2011).

Volunteering our time and talents and working with younger people can contribute to our well-being and life satisfaction as we age.

© Emely/cultura/Corbis

test yourself

1. How does Piaget's idea of assimilation apply to adult development?
2. How does accommodation, in Piaget's sense of the term, help adults to cope with life's difficulties?
3. What is involved when an individual pursues a life theme?

Life Themes and Life-Span Development

A life theme involves a person's efforts to cultivate meaningful optimal experiences (Massimini & Delle Fave, 2000; Rathunde & Csikszentmihalyi, 2006). Consider someone who has spent much of his or her adult life pursuing wealth and career success and who turns to selfless pursuits in middle age. To contribute to the well-being of the next generation, the individual devotes more energy and resources to helping others—for example, by volunteering or working with young people. This reorientation can ease the individual into a positive and meaningful old age.

These motivations are demonstrated by numerous individuals who use their successes for the betterment of the world. Actor George Clooney, for example, has dedicated himself to a variety of humanitarian causes. Clooney cofounded the organization Not On Our Watch to end the genocide in Sudan as well as to stop atrocities elsewhere. However, one need not be middle-aged to attend to the motivations to make the world a better place. For instance, Facebook founder Mark Zuckerberg donated $100 million to public schools in Newark, New Jersey.

As children, our psychological development occurs in concert with physical development. As we become strong and skilled enough to walk, the horizons of our world open up to new discoveries. In adulthood, we get many of our developmental cues from ourselves—where do we go, once we have managed the many tasks we faced in childhood and adolescence? Development, then, is a lifelong process—as we encounter opportunities to grow, to change, and to make a mark in the world in which we live. Every morning when we wake up, we step out of the amazing time machine of human life into a whole new world of possibilities.

SUMMARY

1. EXPLORING HUMAN DEVELOPMENT

Development is the pattern of change in human capabilities that begins at birth and continues throughout the life span. Research on human development can be cross-sectional, which demonstrates age differences, or longitudinal, which demonstrates age-related change. To make strong conclusions about development, longitudinal data are necessary.

Both nature (biological inheritance) and nurture (environmental experience) extensively influence development. However, people are not at the mercy of either their genes or their environment when they actively construct optimal experiences. Resilience refers to the capacity of individuals to thrive during difficulties at every stage of development.

2. CHILD DEVELOPMENT

Prenatal development progresses through the germinal, embryonic, and fetal periods. Particular drugs, such as alcohol and nicotine, as well as certain illnesses, can adversely affect the fetus. These environmental threats are called teratogens. Preterm birth is another potential problem, especially if the infant is very small or grows up in an adverse environment.

The infant's physical development is dramatic in the first year, and a number of motor milestones are reached in infancy. Extensive changes in the brain, including denser connections between synapses, take place in infancy and childhood.

With regard to cognitive development, in Piaget's view, children use schemas to actively construct their world, either assimilating new information into existing schemas or adjusting schemas to accommodate that information. Piaget identified four stages of cognitive development: the sensorimotor stage, the preoperational stage, the concrete operational

stage, and the formal operational stage. Two other theoretical views of children's cognitive development are Vygotsky's sociocultural cognitive theory and information-processing theory. Key aspects of information-processing theory are focusing on detailed aspects of cognitive processes, especially attention, memory, and executive function.

Socioemotional development in childhood includes consideration of Erikson's psychosocial stages as well as moral development. Erikson presented a major, eight-stage psychosocial view of life-span development; its first four stages occur in childhood. In each stage, the individual seeks to resolve a particular socioemotional conflict. Kohlberg proposed a cognitive theory of moral development with three levels (preconventional, conventional, and postconventional). More recent research has focused on the development of prosocial behavior and the influence of socioemotional factors in putting moral reasoning into action.

3. ADOLESCENCE

Puberty is a period of rapid skeletal and sexual maturation that occurs mainly in early adolescence. Its onset occurs about two years earlier in girls than in boys. Hormonal changes trigger pubertal development.

According to Piaget, cognitive development in adolescence is characterized by the appearance of formal operational thought, the final stage in his theory. This stage involves abstract, idealistic, and logical thought.

One of the most important aspects of socioemotional development in adolescence is identity. Erikson's fifth stage of psychosocial development is identity versus identity confusion. Marcia proposed four statuses of identity based on crisis and commitment. A special concern is the development of ethnic identity. Despite great differences among adolescents, the majority develop competently.

4. EMERGING ADULTHOOD, ADULT DEVELOPMENT, AND AGING

Psychologists refer to the period between adolescence and adulthood as emerging adulthood. This period is characterized by the exploration of identity through work and relationships, instability, and self-focus.

Most adults reach their peak physical performance during their 20s and are healthiest then. Physical skills begin to decline during the 30s. The cellular-clock, free-radical, and hormonal stress theories are three important biological explanations for aging. Even in late adulthood, the brain has remarkable repair capacity and plasticity.

Piaget argued that no new cognitive changes occur in adulthood. However, some psychologists have proposed that the idealistic thinking of adolescents is replaced by the more realistic, pragmatic thinking of young adults. Longitudinal research on intelligence shows that many cognitive skills peak in middle age. Overall, older adults do not do as well on memory and other cognitive tasks and are slower to process information than younger adults. However, older adults may have greater wisdom than younger adults.

Erikson's three stages of socioemotional development in adulthood are intimacy versus isolation (early adulthood), generativity versus stagnation (middle adulthood), and integrity versus despair (late adulthood). A special concern, beginning when individuals are in their 50s, is the challenge of understanding life's meaning. Researchers have found that remaining active increases the likelihood that older adults will be happy and healthy. They also have found that older adults often reduce their general social affiliations and instead are motivated to spend more time with close friends and family members. Older adults also experience more positive emotion, are happier, and are more satisfied with their lives than younger adults.

Until recently, the positive dimensions of aging were largely ignored. Developmentalists now recognize that many adults can sustain or even improve their functioning as they age. Researchers today widely view adult development as a self-motivated process limited only by the individual's imagination.

5. HUMAN DEVELOPMENT AND HEALTH AND WELLNESS

Though often associated with childhood, psychological development can continue throughout life. Psychologists have suggested that coping with life's difficulties is one way in which adults may develop. For adults, taking an active approach to "growing" oneself may be an important motivator in development.

Piaget's concepts of assimilation and accommodation have been applied to the process of developing through difficult times. An individual may experience meaning in life by applying his or her current understanding of the world (assimilation). In contrast, the individual may find that some experiences require a revision of that understanding (accommodation). In adulthood, people have the opportunity to pursue new goals that represent important life themes, such as leaving a legacy for the future.

key *terms*

accommodation	emerging adulthood	neglectful parenting	prosocial behavior
androgens	estrogens	nurture	puberty
assimilation	executive function	object permanence	resilience
authoritarian parenting	formal operational stage	operations	secure attachment
authoritative parenting	infant attachment	permissive parenting	sensorimotor stage
concrete operational stage	insecure attachment	preferential looking	temperament
development	nature	preoperational stage	wisdom

apply your *knowledge*

1. Consider the style of parenting with which you were raised. It might help to think of specific situations or moments when your parents put limits on your behavior (or did not). If you have one or more siblings, ask for their opinion, too. Do you agree with one another about your parents' style? Now give these definitions to your parents and ask which, if any, describes them. Sometimes there are as many different views of a family as there are members of that family.

2. A major part of any child's life is playing—and when kids are playing, they are often playing with toys. Using the information on perceptual and cognitive development reviewed in this chapter, design a toy that you think is a perfect fit for a child aged 2 months, 2 years, and 10 years. With respect to the child's development, what features of the toy are especially good for the child of each age group?

3. Go online and Google "parenting discussion boards." Click on one or two of the many sites that come up, and see what parents are talking about. What issues seem to concern them most? Do these parents appear to have a sense of the issues addressed by developmental psychologists? Does the advice that parents share with one another seem to be based on the science of psychology?

4. Set aside 15 minutes to write a brief essay as follows. Think about your life in the future, when you are 70 or 80 years old. Imagine that everything has gone as well as it possibly could, and you have achieved your life dreams. What is your life like at this stage? What things about you are the same as they are for you now as a student of psychology? What things have changed? What is your best possible older adult self? How have aspects of your life today contributed to this happily-older-after?

5. You might have heard the statement that "40 is the new 30" or "50 is the new 40." What trend do these statements reflect? What might explain this trend? What might it mean for our understanding of adult development?

CHAPTER 5

States of Consciousness

When the Mind Is a Buried Treasure

The daily life of Erik Ramsey would seem to be the stuff of nightmares. In 1999, at age 16, he was horribly injured in a car accident. A blood clot in his brain stem caused a stroke, leaving Erik with a rare and permanent condition called *locked-in syndrome* (Foer, 2008). Erik cannot move or speak. He can feel an itch on his face but cannot reach up and scratch it. Erik uses his eye movements (the only muscles over which he has control) to communicate, answering yes (by looking up) or no (by looking down). For all the limitations in his life, Erik has one important thing left: his mind.

Researchers are working tirelessly to develop computer–brain interfaces that might allow Erik and others like him, to communicate using the ability to think (Chorost, 2011). The interfaces use the brain's electrical signals to communicate through a speech synthesizer, to transform thoughts into words. The interfaces can involve wearing an EEG cap that detects brain activity or having electrodes implanted in the brain (Piore, 2015). Computer–brain interfaces are not simply the stuff of science fiction. They serve the important purpose of liberating locked-in patients from their silent prison.

When Erik became too ill to continue participating in research, one of his doctors, neuroscientist Phil Kennedy, took the extraordinary step of having implants placed in his own brain (Piore, 2015). This drastic and controversial step allowed Kennedy to refine his methods, using a patient with the ability to speak. (The electrodes have since been removed.) Why would anyone take such a risk? Why would a scientist risk his brain to move this research forward? He and other scientists working on this problem are devoted to this task because a conscious mind, locked in a body however limited, is still a person very much worth reaching. Such is the power of consciousness. ●

PREVIEW

In this chapter, we review various states of consciousness, as well as the world of sleep and dreams. We also survey two channels of altered states of consciousness—psychoactive drugs and hypnosis. Finally, we consider the effects of achieving a meditative state of consciousness on health and well-being.

1. THE NATURE OF CONSCIOUSNESS

Consciousness is a crucial part of human experience (Overgaard & Mogenson, 2016; Rochat, 2015). Our conscious awareness represents that private inner mind where we think, feel, plan, wish, pray, imagine, and quietly relive experiences. Consider that if we did not have private thoughts and feelings, we could not tell a lie.

In 1890, psychology pioneer William James described the mind as a **stream of consciousness,** a continuous flow of changing sensations, images, thoughts, and feelings (James, 1950). The content of our awareness changes from moment to moment. Information moves rapidly in and out of consciousness. Our minds can race from one topic to the next—from the person approaching us to our physical state today to the café where we will have lunch to our strategy for the test tomorrow.

In his description of the stream of consciousness, James included aspects of our awareness that he described as on the "fringe" of the stream of consciousness. This fringe includes all of the thoughts and feelings that we have *about* our thoughts. We are aware not only of those things that take center stage in our mental life, those shiny fish in the stream of consciousness, but also of all the thoughts and feelings that surround those fish.

Today, psychologists use the term *metacognition* to describe the processes by which we think about thinking (Schwarz, 2015). This term includes our awareness of the fringe elements of the conscious stream. When we read a text, for instance, the difficulty or ease with which we comprehend what is written can influence how we feel about what we read. When written text is easy to read, we are more likely to think that what we are reading is true and accurate (Petrova, Schwarz, & Song, 2012; Schwarz, Song, & Xu, 2009).

The metacognitive experience of ease can impact our thought processes in surprising ways (Lick & Johnson, 2015; Smith & Oyserman, 2015). Consider the two items below, taken from a questionnaire that measures the experience of meaning in life (Steger & others, 2006). The top one is printed in a difficult-to-read font, the bottom one in a clear, easy-to-read font:

I HAVE found *a really significant meaning in* my life.
I have found a really significant meaning in my life.

A recent study found that participants rated their meaning in life to be lower when the scale used the difficult-to-read font (Trent, Lavelock, & King, 2013).

Other research has shown that when youth experienced metacognitive difficulty in thinking about their life goals, they were less likely to believe they could reach those goals (Oyserman, Elmore, & Smith, 2012). The logic behind such results is that while thinking about his or her life goals, the person might reason, "If it is this hard for me to even imagine myself pursuing these goals, they must not be very possible."

During much of the twentieth century, psychologists focused less on the study of mental processes and more on the study of observable behavior. More recently, the study of consciousness has regained widespread respectability in psychology (Aly & Yonelinas, 2012; Ball & Busch, 2015; Elliot, Baird, & Giesbrecht, 2016). Scientists from many different fields are interested in consciousness (Gallagher, 2015; Lutz & others, 2015; Shkurko, 2013; Tsuchiya & others, 2015).

● **stream of consciousness** Term used by William James to describe the mind as a continuous flow of changing sensations, images, thoughts, and feelings.

Defining Consciousness

We define consciousness in terms of its two parts: awareness and arousal. **Consciousness** is an individual's awareness of external events and internal sensations under a condition of arousal. *Awareness* includes awareness of the self and thoughts about one's experiences. Consider that on an autumn afternoon, when you see a beautiful tree, vibrant with color, you do not simply perceive the colors; you are also *aware* that you are seeing them.

The second part of consciousness is *arousal,* the physiological state of being engaged with the environment. Thus, a sleeping person is not conscious in the same way that he or she would be while awake.

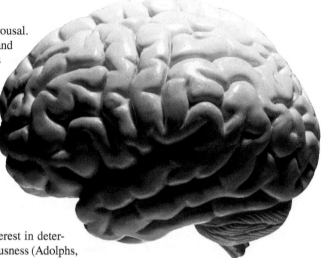

© Creatas/PunchStock

Consciousness and the Brain

There has been a dramatic increase in theoretical and research interest in determining more specifically how the brain functions to produce consciousness (Adolphs, 2015; Block, 2015; Linden, 2015; Qin & others, 2015; Salti & others, 2015). Scientists have sought to identify what it is that happens in the brain when we feel that we are conscious of our experience (Bisenius & others, 2015; Solovey & others, 2015). This task can be quite important. For instance, it is very difficult to tell if a person with locked-in syndrome is conscious or unconscious from a brain scan (Barttfeld & others, 2015).

We know that the two aspects of consciousness, awareness and arousal, are associated with different parts of the brain. First, let's consider brain areas and processes associated with *awareness*—the subjective state of being conscious of what is going on. Areas of the prefrontal cortex appear to be especially involved in the ways that awareness goes beyond the input of sensory information. For instance, these areas of the brain are active when we taste complex flavors, such as umami, and track the subjective pleasure that accompanies rewarding experiences (Kringelbach, 2005). However, scientists still do not know many of the details that link consciousness with brain states (Tsuchiya & others, 2015).

Some neuroscientists have suggested that rather than being located in a particular area of the brain, the experience of conscious awareness is the outcome of a broad brain process. These scientists assert that the feeling of awareness occurs in a *global brain workspace* that involves a variety of brain areas working in parallel (Barttfeld & others, 2015; Dehaene & Changeux, 2011; Faugeras & others, 2012). This wide-reaching brain workspace is an assembly of neurons that are thought to work in cooperation to produce the subjective sense of consciousness. From this perspective, multiple areas in the brain are working together to create the feeling of awareness.

The second part of consciousness, *arousal,* is a physiological state determined by the **reticular activating system,** a network of structures including the brain stem, medulla, and thalamus. Arousal refers to the ways that awareness is regulated: If we are in danger, we might need to be on "high alert," but if we are in a safe environment with no immediate demands, we can relax, and our arousal may be quite low.

You might think of consciousness as the mind—that part of yourself that contains your private thoughts and feelings. It might seem obvious that other people have private thoughts and feelings as well, but the human ability to recognize the subjective experience of another is a true developmental accomplishment, requiring the ability to think about others in a particular way (Bradford, Jentzsch, & Gomez, 2015). **Theory of mind** refers to individuals' understanding that they and others think, feel, perceive, and have private experiences (Sodian & Kristen-Antonow, 2015; Wellman, 2011). Although previous research suggested that theory of mind was likely to emerge around the age of 4, more recently studies have shown that if the tasks used to measure theory of mind are simplified, even younger children demonstrate a capacity to understand that other people have their own perspective on things (Rubio-Fernández & Geurts, 2013).

● **consciousness** An individual's awareness of external events and internal sensations under a condition of arousal, including awareness of the self and thoughts about one's experiences.

● **reticular activating system** A network of structures including the brain stem, medulla, and thalamus that are involved in the experience of arousal and engagement with the environment.

● **theory of mind** Individuals' understanding that they and others think, feel, perceive, and have private experiences.

Theory of mind is essential to many valuable social capacities, such as empathy and sympathy (Reniers & others, 2012; Sebastian & others, 2012). Simon Baron-Cohen (1995, 2008, 2011) is an expert on *autism spectrum disorder,* a disorder that affects communication, social interaction, and behavior. He has proposed that the emergence of theory of mind is so central to human functioning that evolution would not leave it up to chance. Baron-Cohen suggests that we are born with a brain mechanism that is ready to develop a theory of mind; he hypothesizes that autistic individuals lack a well-developed theory of mind, a condition that would explain their unique social deficits. In studies, children and adolescents with autism spectrum disorder show lower activation in areas of the brain that are usually active when typically developing individuals think about social information (Cheng & others, 2015; Kana & others, 2015).

Levels of Awareness

The flow of sensations, images, thoughts, and feelings that William James spoke of can occur at different levels of awareness. Although we might think of consciousness as either present or not, there are in fact shades of awareness, just as there are shades of perception in signal detection theory, as discussed in the chapter "Sensation and Perception". Here we consider five levels of awareness: higher-level consciousness, lower-level consciousness, altered states of consciousness, subconscious awareness, and no awareness (Figure 1).

HIGHER-LEVEL CONSCIOUSNESS

● **controlled processes** The most alert states of human consciousness, during which individuals actively focus their efforts toward a goal.

In **controlled processes,** the most alert states of human consciousness, individuals actively focus their efforts toward a goal (Ulrich & others, 2015). For example, watch a classmate as he struggles to master the unfamiliar buttons on his new smartphone. He does not hear you humming or notice the intriguing shadow on the wall. His state of focused awareness illustrates the idea of controlled processes. Controlled processes require selective attention (see the chapter "Sensation and Perception"): the ability to concentrate on a specific aspect of experience while ignoring others. Controlled processes are slower than automatic processes and are more likely to involve the prefrontal

FIGURE 1 Levels of Awareness
Each level of awareness has its time and place in human life.

Level of Awareness	Description	Examples
Higher-Level Consciousness	Involves controlled processing, in which individuals actively focus their efforts on attaining a goal; the most alert state of consciousness	Doing a math or science problem; preparing for a debate; taking an at-bat in a baseball game
Lower-Level Consciousness	Includes automatic processing that requires little attention, as well as daydreaming	Punching in a number on a cell phone; typing on a keyboard when one is an expert; gazing at a sunset
Altered States of Consciousness	Can be produced by drugs, trauma, fatigue, possibly hypnosis, and sensory deprivation	Feeling the effects of having taken alcohol or psychedelic drugs; undergoing hypnosis to quit smoking or lose weight
Subconscious Awareness	Can occur when people are awake, as well as when they are sleeping and dreaming	Sleeping and dreaming
No Awareness	Freud's belief that some unconscious thoughts are too laden with anxiety and other negative emotions for consciousness to admit them	Having unconscious thoughts; being knocked out by a blow or anesthetized

cortex (Jeon & Friederici, 2015; Logue & Gould, 2014). Often, after we have practiced an activity a great deal, we no longer have to think about it while doing it. It becomes automatic and faster.

A key aspect of controlled processing is executive function. **Executive function** refers to higher-order, complex cognitive processes, including thinking, planning, and problem solving. These cognitive processes are linked to the functioning of the brain's prefrontal cortex (Braun & others, 2015; Carlson, Zelazo, & Faja, 2013). Executive function is the person's capacity to harness consciousness, to focus in on specific thoughts while ignoring others. This aspect of executive function is called *cognitive control;* it is the ability to maintain attention by reducing interfering thoughts and being cognitively flexible (Zelazo, 2015).

From managing finances (Drever & others, 2015) to emotional and social well-being (Dawson & others, 2015; Schmeichel & Tang, 2015), it is hard to imagine a domain of life in which executive function is not valuable.

LOWER-LEVEL CONSCIOUSNESS

Beneath the level of controlled processes are other levels of conscious awareness. Lower levels of awareness include automatic processes and daydreaming.

Automatic Processes   A few weeks after acquiring his smartphone, your classmate sends a text message in the middle of a conversation with you. He does not have to concentrate on the keys and hardly seems aware of the device as he continues to talk to you while finishing his lunch. Using his phone has reached the point of automatic processing.

Automatic processes are states of consciousness that require little attention and do not interfere with other ongoing activities. Automatic processes require less conscious effort than controlled processes. When we are awake, our automatic behaviors occur at a lower level of awareness than controlled processes, but they are still conscious behaviors. Your classmate pushed the right buttons, so at some level he apparently was aware of what he was doing. This kind of automatic behavior suggests that we can be aware of stimuli on some level without paying attention to them.

Daydreaming   Another state of consciousness that involves a low level of conscious effort is *daydreaming,* which lies between active consciousness and dreaming while asleep. It is a little like dreaming while we are awake (Berntsen, Rubin, & Salgado, 2015; Domhoff, 2011). Daydreams usually begin spontaneously when we are doing something that requires less than our full attention.

Mind wandering is probably the most obvious type of daydreaming (Smallwood & Schooler, 2015). We regularly take brief side trips into our own private kingdoms of imagery and memory while reading, listening, or working. When we daydream, we drift into a world of fantasy. We perhaps imagine ourselves on a date, at a party, on television, in a faraway place, or at another time in our life. Sometimes our daydreams are about everyday events, such as paying the rent, going to the dentist, and meeting with somebody at school or work.

The semiautomatic flow of daydreaming can be useful. As you daydream while ironing a shirt or walking to the store, you may make plans, solve a problem, or come up with a creative idea. Daydreams can remind us of important things ahead. Daydreaming keeps our minds active while helping us to cope, create, and fantasize (Neupert & others, 2015). When our mind wanders, it often wanders to the future (Smallwood & Schooler, 2015).

ALTERED STATES OF CONSCIOUSNESS

Altered states of consciousness or *awareness* are mental states that are noticeably different from normal awareness. Altered states of consciousness can range from losing one's sense of self-consciousness to hallucinating. Such states can be produced by trauma, fever, fatigue, sensory deprivation, meditation, hypnosis, and psychological disorders. Drug use can also induce altered states of consciousness, as we will consider later in this chapter.

● **executive function** Higher-order, complex cognitive processes, including thinking, planning, and problem solving.

● **automatic processes** States of consciousness that require little attention and do not interfere with other ongoing activities.

SUBCONSCIOUS AWARENESS

In the chapter "Biological Foundations of Behavior", we saw that a great deal of brain activity occurs without that activity impinging on awareness. Right now you are unaware of many things your brain is doing to keep your body functioning or even the many stimuli in the environment to which your brain is responding. Your brain is processing information without you even noticing it. Psychologists are increasingly interested in the subconscious processing of information, which can take place while we are awake or asleep (Gainotti, 2012; Straube, Mothes-Lasch, & Miltner, 2011).

Waking Subconscious Awareness   When we are awake, processes are going on just below the surface of our awareness (Almeida & others, 2013; Mealor & Dienes, 2013). For example, while we are grappling with a problem, the solution may pop into our head. Such insights can occur when a subconscious connection between ideas is so strong that it rises into awareness.

Incubation refers to the subconscious processing that leads to a solution after a break from conscious thought about the problem. The phenomenon of incubation is interesting because it suggests that even as you have stopped actively thinking about a problem, on some level your brain is still working on finding a solution. Interestingly, successful incubation requires that we first expend effort thinking carefully about the problem (Sio & Ormerod, 2015). This suggests that although subconscious processing can ultimately lead to a solution, it first requires that the appropriate information be thoughtfully considered. What we do while we are incubating can influence the creativity of our problem solving. A recent study showed that people who took a break and enjoyed humorous videos produced more creative solutions to problems, compared to those who worked continuously or who were shown sad videos instead (Hao & others, 2015).

Recall the discussion in the chapter "Sensation and Perception" about the parallel processing of visual information. Subconscious information processing also can occur simultaneously in a distributed manner along many parallel tracks. For example, when you look at a dog running down the street, you are consciously aware of the event but not of your subconscious processing of the object's identity (a dog), its color (black), and its movement (fast). In contrast, conscious processing occurs in sequence and is slower than much subconscious processing. Note that the various levels of awareness often work together. You rely on controlled processing when memorizing material for class, but later the answers on a test just pop into your head as a result of automatic or subconscious processing.

Subconscious Awareness During Sleep and Dreams   When we sleep and dream, our level of awareness is lower than when we daydream, but sleep and dreams are not the *absence* of consciousness (Hobson & Friston, 2012; Windt & Noreika, 2011); rather, they are *low levels* of consciousness.

Researchers have found that when people are asleep, they remain aware of external stimuli to some degree. In sleep laboratories, when people are clearly asleep (as determined by physiological monitoring devices), they are able to respond to faint tones by pressing a handheld button (Ogilvie & Wilkinson, 1988). In one study, the presentation of pure auditory tones to sleeping individuals activated auditory processing regions of the brain, whereas participants' names activated language areas, the amygdalae, and the prefrontal cortex (Stickgold, 2001). We return to the topics of sleep and dreams in the next section.

NO AWARENESS

The term *unconscious* generally applies to someone who has been knocked out by a blow or anesthetized, or who has fallen into a deep, prolonged unconscious state (Laureys & Schiff, 2012; Lobo & Schraag, 2011). However, Sigmund Freud (1924) used the term *unconscious* in a very different way. **Unconscious thought,** said Freud, is a reservoir of unacceptable wishes, feelings, and thoughts that are beyond conscious awareness. In other words, Freud's interpretation viewed the unconscious as a storehouse for vile, animalistic

● **unconscious thought** According to Freud, a reservoir of unacceptable wishes, feelings, and thoughts that are beyond conscious awareness.

CRITICAL CONTROVERSY

Is Human Kindness Automatic?

Prosociality means engaging in behaviors aimed at improving the well-being of another. Prosociality is sometimes considered a defining aspect of humanity because, unlike other animals, people extend kindness and trust not only to kin but to strangers (Zaki & Mitchell, 2013). If you doubt the level of trust among humans is that high, consider how easy it is to pay for something with a credit card: You believe that whomever is taking that information will not reuse it or share it. Accounting for the extreme prosociality of human beings is an important goal for the science of human behavior. Let's consider this issue using controlled and automatic processes. Must we reflect carefully to be kind? Or can kindness be automatic?

Some research suggests that prosocial behavior does not require reflection. For example, studies show that when people go with their first instinct, are under time pressure, or are too distracted to think things through, they behave more generously (Rand, Greene, & Nowak, 2012; Schulz & others, 2014). In fact, some studies suggest that reflection leads to more selfishness (Rand, Greene, & Nowak, 2012). These studies at least suggest that automatic behavior can be generous and prosocial.

In addition, research links prosocial behavior to reward areas of the brain (Pfaff, 2014; Zaki & Mitchell, 2013), areas that are not generally associated with conscious reflection (Jeon & Friederici, 2015). We share these brain areas with other animals, suggesting that the capacity for kindness unites us with other creatures (de Waal, 2015).

Still, research using EEG, measuring electrical activity in the brains of preschoolers (Cowell & Decety, 2015) and adults (Carlson, Aknin, & Liotti, 2015), paints a more complex picture. For example, in young children, awareness of the difference between helping and harming another appears to be largely automatic, but actually doing a kind act (for example, sharing some stickers with a stranger) relies as well on controlled processes. Thinking may be

© David Sacks/Digital Vision/Getty Images

needed to put our kind impulses into action (Paulus, 2015). Other research has shown that when people are tired, and presumably more like to rely on "auto pilot," they behave more (not less) selfishly (Achtziger, Alós-Ferrer, & Wagner, 2015).

What's the bottom line? First, it seems that both automatic and controlled processes can play a role in prosocial behavior. The question is when and how they do so. Second, remember that activities that at first require careful thought can become more automatic if we do them repeatedly. People who make kindness a habit are more likely to show automatic generosity toward others (Rand, Greene, & Nowak, 2012).

WHAT DO YOU THINK?
- When did you last behave prosocially? Did you think it through carefully or act automatically?
- Do you think people are, by nature, mostly selfish or selfless? Why?

---

impulses. He believed that some aspects of our experience remain unconscious for good reason, as if we are better off not knowing about them. For example, from Freud's perspective, the human mind is full of disturbing impulses such as a desire to have sex with our parents. For Freud, the conscious mind was needed to keep the wild beast of the unconscious in check. If we all went with our first impulses, the world would be a very frightening place, indeed.

Freud's view is an extreme version of an assumption that many people share: that the human capacity for kindness emerges from socialization and our abilities to reflect on our actions. We might think that children, for instance, must be taught to be kind. Is this assumption true? Are our first instincts likely to be selfish or selfless? Answering these questions means considering one of the biggest questions of existence: Is human nature essentially good or bad? Recent research has led some to wonder if, in fact, the unconscious is quite a bit nicer than Freud ever imagined. To read about this provocative work, see the Critical Controversy.

Although Freud's interpretation remains controversial, psychologists now widely accept that unconscious processes do exist (Emmanouil, Burton, & Ro, 2013). Recently,

test yourself

1. Describe the global brain workspace approach to consciousness and our experience of consciousness.
2. What are controlled processes and automatic processes? In what level or levels of consciousness is each involved?
3. What is daydreaming, according to the text discussion?

● **sleep** A natural state of rest for the body and mind that involves the reversible loss of consciousness.

● **biological rhythms** Periodic physiological fluctuations in the body, such as the rise and fall of hormones and accelerated and decelerated cycles of brain activity, that can influence behavior.

● **circadian rhythms** Daily behavioral or physiological cycles that involve the sleep/wake cycle, body temperature, blood pressure, and blood sugar level.

● **suprachiasmatic nucleus (SCN)** A small brain structure that uses input from the retina to synchronize its own rhythm with the daily cycle of light and dark; the body's way of monitoring the change from day to night.

researchers have found that many mental processes (thoughts, emotions, and perceptions) can occur outside of awareness. These unconscious processes can have a substantial impact on behavior. In the chapter "Sensation and Perception", for example, we saw how stimuli presented outside of awareness can influence thoughts and behaviors; in the chapter "Learning", we will see that many forms of learning operate without the need for awareness.

2. SLEEP AND DREAMS

By this point in your life, you have had quite a bit of experience with sleep. You already know that sleep involves a decrease in body movement and (typically) having one's eyes closed. What is sleep, more exactly? We can define **sleep** as a natural state of rest for the body and mind that involves the reversible loss of consciousness. Surely, sleep must be important, because it comprises a third of our life, taking up more time than anything else we do. But *why* is sleep so important? Before tackling this question, let's first consider how sleep is linked to our internal biological rhythms.

Biological Rhythms and Sleep

Biological rhythms are periodic physiological fluctuations in the body. We are unaware of most biological rhythms, such as the rise and fall of hormones and accelerated and decelerated cycles of brain activity, but they can influence our behavior. These rhythms are controlled by biological clocks, which include annual or seasonal cycles, like those involving the migration of birds and the hibernation of bears, as well as 24-hour cycles like the sleep/wake cycle and temperature changes in the human body. Let's further explore the body's 24-hour cycles.

CIRCADIAN RHYTHMS

Circadian rhythms are daily behavioral or physiological cycles. Daily circadian rhythms involve the sleep/wake cycle, body temperature, blood pressure, and blood-sugar level (Crowley & Eastman, 2015; Thun & others, 2015). For example, body temperature fluctuates about 3 degrees Fahrenheit in a 24-hour day, peaking in the afternoon and dropping to its lowest point between 2 A.M. and 5 A.M.

Researchers have discovered that the body monitors the change from day to night by means of the **suprachiasmatic nucleus (SCN),** a small brain structure that uses input from the retina to synchronize its own rhythm with the daily cycle of light and dark (Adamantidis, 2015; Gabel & others, 2015). The SCN sends information to the hypothalamus and pineal gland to regulate daily rhythms such as temperature, hunger, and the release of hormones such as melatonin (Gandhi & others, 2015). The SCN also communicates with the reticular formation to regulate daily rhythms of sleep and wakefulness (Figure 2). Although a number of biological clocks seem to be involved in regulating circadian rhythms, the SCN is critical (Adamantidis, 2015).

Our capacity to sleep, then, is embedded in the world we live in, a world that has daylight and nighttime (Dijk & Skeldon, 2015). The SCN is guided by the information it receives from the retina to tell us it is time to go to sleep. Many individuals who are totally blind experience lifelong sleeping problems because their retinas cannot detect light. These people may suffer from a condition called non–24-hour sleep/wake disorder because their circadian rhythms often do not follow a 24-hour cycle (Lockley & others, 2015).

DESYNCHRONIZING THE BIOLOGICAL CLOCK

Biological clocks can become *desynchronized,* or thrown off their regular schedules. If you fly from Los Angeles to New York and then go to bed at 11 P.M. eastern time, you may have trouble falling asleep because your body is still on west coast time. Even if

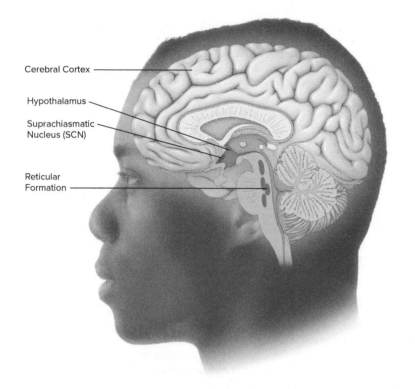

Cerebral Cortex

Hypothalamus

Suprachiasmatic
Nucleus (SCN)

Reticular
Formation

FIGURE 2   Suprachiasmatic Nucleus The suprachiasmatic nucleus (SCN) plays an important role in keeping our biological clock running on time. The SCN is located in the hypothalamus. It receives information from the retina about light, which is the external stimulus that synchronizes the SCN. Output from the SCN is distributed to the rest of the hypothalamus and to the reticular formation.

you sleep for 8 hours that night, you may have a hard time waking up at 7 A.M. eastern time, because your body thinks it is 4 A.M. If you stay in New York for several days, your body will adjust to this new schedule.

The jet lag you experience when you fly from Los Angeles to New York occurs because your body time is out of phase, or synchronization, with clock time (Mazuski & Herzog, 2015). Jet lag is the result of two or more body rhythms being out of sync. You usually go to bed when your body temperature begins to drop, but in your new location, you might be trying to go to sleep when it is rising. In the morning, your adrenal glands release large doses of the hormone cortisol to help you wake up. In your new geographic time zone, the glands may be releasing this chemical just as you are getting ready for bed at night.

Circadian rhythms may also become desynchronized when shift workers change their work hours. A number of near accidents in air travel have been associated with pilots who have not yet become synchronized to their new shifts and are not working as efficiently as usual (Powell, Spencer, & Petrie, 2011). Shift-work problems most often affect night-shift workers who never fully adjust to sleeping in the daytime after they get off work. Not only might these individuals struggle to stay awake at work, but they may face a heightened risk of illness, gastrointestinal disorders, obesity, and impaired immune system functioning (Guerrero-Vargas & others, 2015; Loprinzi, 2015; Sabath, Báez-Ruiz, & Buijs, 2015; Van Dycke & others, 2015).

RESETTING THE BIOLOGICAL CLOCK

If your biological clock for sleeping and waking becomes desynchronized, how can you reset it? With regard to jet lag, if you take a transoceanic flight and arrive at your destination during the day, it is a good idea to spend as much time as possible outside in the daylight. Bright light during the day, especially in the morning, increases wakefulness, whereas bright light at night delays sleep. In a few days, jet lag typically resolves. Another common treatment for jet lag

Changing to a night-shift job can desynchronize one's biological clock and affect circadian rhythms and performance.

© Tim Pannell/Corbis

is taking melatonin supplements (Simmons, McGrane, & Wedmore, 2015). Melatonin, a hormone that increases at night in humans, can help reduce jet lag by advancing the circadian clock.

Jet lag is not simply a drag for vacationers. Airline pilots, flight crews, members of the military, and international athletes must be able to quickly adapt to new time zones. Recent research has shown that very intense light, administered through the ear canals, can speed recovery from jet lag (Jurvelin, Jokelainen, & Takala, 2015).

Why Do We Need Sleep?

All animals require sleep. Furthermore, the human body regulates sleep, as it does eating and drinking, and this fact suggests that sleep may be just as essential for survival. Yet why we need sleep remains a bit of a mystery (Krueger & others, 2016; Rattenborg & Martinez-Gonzalez, 2015).

THEORIES ON THE NEED FOR SLEEP

A variety of theories have been proposed for the need for sleep. First, from an evolutionary perspective, sleep may have developed because animals needed to protect themselves at night. The idea is that it makes sense for animals to be inactive when it is dark, because nocturnal inactivity helps them to avoid both becoming other animals' prey and injuring themselves due to poor visibility.

A second possibility is that sleep is a way to conserve energy (Schmidt, 2014). Spending a large chunk of any day sleeping allows animals to conserve their calories, especially when food is scarce (Siegel, 2005). For some animals, moreover, the search for food and water is easier and safer when the sun is up. When it is dark, it is adaptive for these animals to save their energy. Animals that are likely to serve as someone else's food sleep the least of all. Figure 3 illustrates the average amount of sleep per day of various animals.

A third explanation for the need for sleep is that sleep is restorative (Holst & Landolt, 2015; Jerath & others, 2014). Scientists have proposed that sleep restores, replenishes, and rebuilds the brain and body, which the day's waking activities can wear out (Mistl-berger, 2015). This idea fits with the feeling of being tired before we go to sleep and restored when we wake up.

In support of the theory of a restorative function of sleep, many of the body's cells show increased production and reduced breakdown of proteins during deep sleep (Vazquez & others, 2008). Protein molecules are the building blocks needed for cell growth and for repair of damage from factors such as stress. Sleep deprivation can affect the body much like stress itself (Lavie, 2015).

A final explanation for the need for sleep centers on the role of sleep in brain plasticity. Recall from the chapter "Biological Foundations of Behavior" that the plasticity of the brain refers to its capacity to change in response to experience. Sleep has been recognized as playing an important role in the ways that experiences influence the brain, especially in how sleep affects synaptic connections (Frank, 2015).

If sleep affects connections in the brain, we might expect it to play a role in consolidating memories, and research supports that conclusion (Ravassard & others, 2015). During sleep, memories are pulled together, resulting in the retention of specific information, skills, learned associations, and emotional experiences (Blumberg, 2015; Moroni & others, 2014; Pace-Schott, Germain, & Milad, 2015; Perogamvros, & Schwartz, 2015).

Why does sleep improve memory? One possible explanation is that during sleep the cerebral cortex is free to conduct activities that strengthen memory associations, so that memories formed during recent waking hours can be integrated into long-term memory storage. Lost sleep often results in lost memories. So, if you are thinking about studying all night for your next test, you might want to think again. Sleep can enhance your memory.

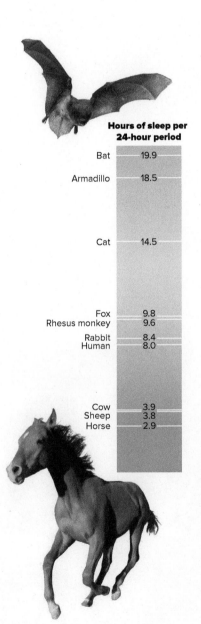

	Hours of sleep per 24-hour period
Bat	19.9
Armadillo	18.5
Cat	14.5
Fox	9.8
Rhesus monkey	9.6
Rabbit	8.4
Human	8.0
Cow	3.9
Sheep	3.8
Horse	2.9

FIGURE 3 From Bats to Horses: The Wide Range of Sleep in Animals We might feel envious of bats, which sleep nearly 20 hours a day, and more than a little in awe of horses, still running on just under 3 hours of rest.
(first photo) © Frank Greenaway/Getty Images; (second photo) © DLILLC/Corbis

THE EFFECTS OF CHRONIC SLEEP DEPRIVATION

Most people think of 8 hours of sleep as a good night's rest. However, the basic amount of sleep each person needs may vary from person to person and as a function of age and activities (Hirshkowitz & others, 2015). For example, the optimal amount of sleep for infants is between 14 and 17 hours in a 24-hour period. For an adult, the optimal night's sleep is between 7 and 9 hours.

Lack of sleep is stressful (Lavie, 2015) and has an impact on the brain, as well as on the rest of the body (Fernandez-Mendoza & others, 2015; Virtanin & others, 2015). The sleep-deprived brain cannot operate at the same level of complexity as the well-rested brain. Sleep deprivation decreases brain activity in the thalamus and the prefrontal cortex (Almklov & others, 2015; Libedinsky & others, 2011). The thalamus is crucial to receiving and responding to sensory information, and the prefrontal cortex is the brain area associated with thinking and planning. The tired brain must compensate by using different pathways or alternative neural networks when thinking (Koenis & others, 2013).

Given these effects on the brain, it is not surprising that when deprived of sleep, people have trouble paying attention to tasks and solving problems (Jackson & others, 2011). Sleep deprivation can reduce our ability to make sound decisions, including about moral issues (Barnes, Gunia, & Wagner, 2015) and healthy food choices (Kruger & others, 2014).

The profound effects of sleep deprivation are vividly evident in a very rare disorder known as *fatal familial insomnia (FFI)*. This disorder, caused by a genetic mutation, involves a progressive inability to sleep (Peng & others, 2015). Over time, the person sleeps less and less, becomes agitated, engages in strange motor movements, and is confused. The individual may hallucinate and enact dreams. FFI has no known cure, and it leads to death, typically about 18 months after symptoms appear. The disorder can be difficult to diagnose and may be mistaken for other neurological disorders, such as dementia, or for psychological disorders that include hallucinations. Although few people suffer from FFI, this unusual condition demonstrates the vital restorative power of sleep. In addition, FFI highlights the role of the thalamus in sleep, because in cases of FFI the thalamus shows enormous damage.

Why do Americans get too little sleep? Pressures at work and school, family responsibilities, and social obligations often lead to long hours of wakefulness and irregular sleep/wake schedules. Not having enough hours to do all that we want or need to do in a day, we cheat on our sleep. As a result we may suffer from a "sleep debt," an accumulated level of exhaustion. Even a small sleep debt can take a toll on well-being. A large-scale study of over 27,000 high school students found that even 1 less hour of sleep predicted higher incidence of hopelessness, suicidal thoughts, and substance abuse (Winsler & others, 2015).

Stages of Wakefulness and Sleep

Have you ever awakened from sleep and been totally disoriented? Or momentarily woken up in the middle of a dream and then gone right back into the dream as if it were a movie running just below the surface of your consciousness? These two experiences reflect two distinct stages in the sleep cycle.

Stages of sleep correspond to massive electrophysiological changes that occur throughout the brain as the fast, irregular, and low-amplitude electrical activity of wakefulness is replaced by the slow, regular, high-amplitude waves of deep sleep. Using the electroencephalograph (EEG) to monitor the brain's electrical activity, as well as electromyography (EMG) to monitor the action of motor neurons, scientists have identified four stages of sleep (Müller & others, 2015).

The following stages (of wakefulness and sleep) are defined by both the brain's activity and muscle tone. The stages are named by letters and numbers that represent what is going on at that stage, including whether

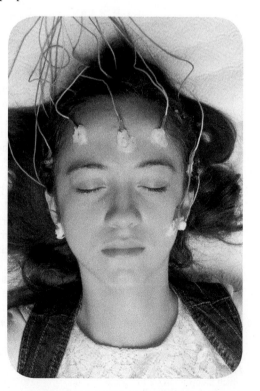

An individual being monitored by an EEG in a sleep experiment.

©minemero/Getty Images

the person is awake or asleep and whether he or she is experiencing rapid eye movement (REM). Non-REM sleep is characterized by a lack of rapid eye movement and little dreaming, as described below.

Stage W   The "W" here stands for "wake." During this stage, when a person is awake, EEG patterns exhibit two types of waves: beta and alpha. *Beta waves* reflect concentration and alertness. These waves are the highest in frequency and lowest in amplitude—that is, they go up and down a great deal but do not have very high peaks or very low ebbs. They also are more *desynchronous* than other waves, meaning that they do not form a very consistent pattern. Inconsistent patterning makes sense given the extensive variation in sensory input and activities we experience when we are awake.

When we are relaxed but still awake, our brain waves slow down, increase in amplitude, and become more *synchronous,* or regular. These waves, associated with relaxation or drowsiness, are called *alpha waves*.

Stage N1 (Non-REM1) Sleep   When people are just falling asleep, they enter the first stage of non-REM sleep. The "N" stands for "non-REM," meaning that rapid eye movements do not occur during these stages. Stage N1 is characterized by drowsy sleep. In this stage, the person may experience sudden muscle movements called *myoclonic jerks*. If you watch someone in your class fighting to stay awake, you might notice his or her head jerking upward. This reaction demonstrates that this first stage of sleep often involves the feeling of falling.

EEGs of individuals in stage N1 sleep are characterized by *theta waves,* which are even slower in frequency and greater in amplitude than alpha waves. The difference between being relaxed and being in stage N1 sleep is gradual. Figure 4 shows the EEG pattern of stage N1 sleep, along with the EEG patterns for the other stages of wakefulness and sleep.

FIGURE 4   Characteristics and Formats of EEG Recordings During Stages of Wakefulness and Sleep
Even while you are sleeping, your brain is busy. No wonder you sometimes wake up feeling tired.

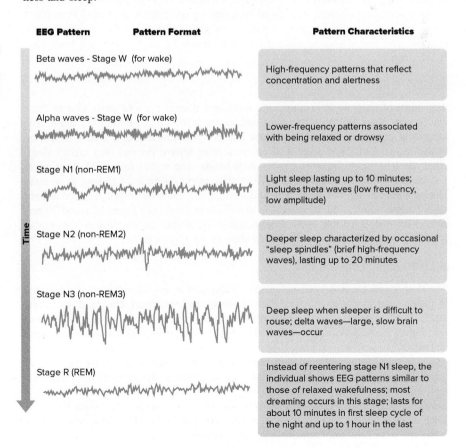

EEG Pattern	Pattern Format	Pattern Characteristics
Beta waves - Stage W (for wake)		High-frequency patterns that reflect concentration and alertness
Alpha waves - Stage W (for wake)		Lower-frequency patterns associated with being relaxed or drowsy
Stage N1 (non-REM1)		Light sleep lasting up to 10 minutes; includes theta waves (low frequency, low amplitude)
Stage N2 (non-REM2)		Deeper sleep characterized by occasional "sleep spindles" (brief high-frequency waves), lasting up to 20 minutes
Stage N3 (non-REM3)		Deep sleep when sleeper is difficult to rouse; delta waves—large, slow brain waves—occur
Stage R (REM)		Instead of reentering stage N1 sleep, the individual shows EEG patterns similar to those of relaxed wakefulness; most dreaming occurs in this stage; lasts for about 10 minutes in first sleep cycle of the night and up to 1 hour in the last

Time

Stage N2 (Non-REM2) Sleep   In stage N2 sleep, muscle activity decreases, and the person is no longer consciously aware of the environment. Theta waves continue but are interspersed with a defining characteristic of stage N2 sleep: *sleep spindles*. These involve a sudden increase in high-frequency wave bursts (Lechinger & others, 2015). Stages N1 and N2 are both relatively light stages of sleep, and if people awaken during one of these stages, they often report not having been asleep at all.

Stage N3 (Non-REM3) Sleep   Stage N3 sleep is characterized by *delta waves,* the slowest and highest-amplitude brain waves during sleep. Delta sleep is our deepest sleep, the time when our brain waves are least like our brain waves while we are awake. Delta sleep is also called *slow-wave sleep*. This is also the stage when bedwetting (in children), sleepwalking, and sleep talking occur. When awakened during this stage, people usually are confused and disoriented.

Stage R (REM) Sleep   After going through stages N1 to N3, sleepers drift up through the sleep stages toward wakefulness. Instead of reentering stage N1, however, they enter stage R, a different form of sleep called REM (rapid eye movement) sleep (Llewellyn & Hobson, 2015). **REM sleep** is an active stage of sleep during which the most vivid dreaming occurs (Frainge & others, 2015; Landmann & others, 2015). The EEG pattern for REM sleep shows fast waves similar to those of relaxed wakefulness, and the sleeper's eyeballs move up and down and from left to right (Figure 5).

A person who is awakened during REM sleep is more likely to report having dreamed than when awakened at any other stage. Even people who claim they rarely dream frequently report dreaming when they are awakened during REM sleep. The longer the period of REM sleep, the more likely the person will report dreaming. Dreams also occur during slow-wave or non-REM sleep, but the frequency of dreams in these stages is relatively low (Llewellyn & Hobson, 2015), and we are less likely to remember these dreams. Reports of dreaming by individuals awakened from REM sleep are typically longer, more vivid, more physically active, more emotionally charged, and less related to waking life than reports by those awakened from non-REM sleep.

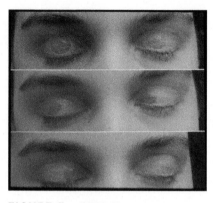

FIGURE 5   REM Sleep During REM sleep, your eyes move rapidly. ©Allan Hobson/ Science Source

● **REM sleep** An active stage of sleep during which dreaming occurs.

SLEEP CYCLING THROUGH THE NIGHT

The stages of sleep we have considered make up a normal cycle of sleep. One of these cycles lasts about 90 to 100 minutes and recurs several times during the night. The amount of deep sleep (stage N3) is much greater in the first half of a night's sleep than in the second half. Most stage R sleep takes place toward the end of a night's sleep, when the REM stage becomes progressively longer. The night's first REM stage might last for only 10 minutes, but the final REM stage might continue for as long as an hour. During a normal night of sleep, individuals will spend about 60 percent of sleep in light sleep (stages N1 and N2), 20 percent in slow-wave or deep sleep (stage N3), and 20 percent in REM sleep (Webb, 2000). So, you can think of your night's sleep as starting out with deep sleep and ending with the big show of the night's REM.

SLEEP AND THE BRAIN

The sleep stages are associated with distinct patterns of neurotransmitter activity initiated in the reticular formation, the core of the brain stem (Sorooshyari, Huerta, & de Lecea, 2015). In all vertebrates, the reticular formation plays a crucial role in sleep and arousal (see Figure 2). As previously noted, damage to the reticular formation can result in coma and death.

Three important neurotransmitters involved in sleep are serotonin, norepinephrine, and acetylcholine (Markov & Goldman, 2014). As sleep begins, the levels of neurotransmitters sent to the forebrain from the reticular formation start dropping, and they continue to fall until they reach their lowest levels during the deepest sleep stage—stage N3. REM sleep (stage R) is initiated by a rise in acetylcholine, which activates the cerebral cortex while the rest of the brain remains relatively inactive.

psychological *inquiry*

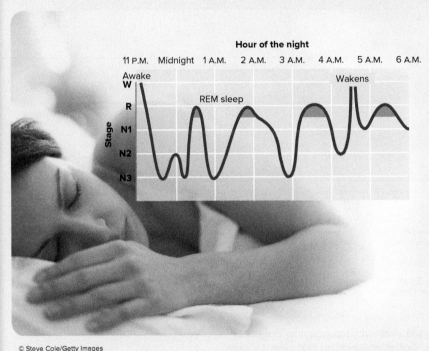

© Steve Cole/Getty Images

Hour of the night

Taking a Ride on the Sleep Cycles

This graph depicts a night's sleep. During nightly sleep, we go through several cycles. Depth of sleep decreases, and REM sleep (shown in light blue) increases as the night progresses. Look carefully at the graph and answer the following questions.

1. How many sleep cycles are presented?
2. What time does the sleeper wake up?
3. If you woke the sleeper up at 2 A.M., would the sleeper be likely to remember a dream? Explain.
4. How much time is this sleeper spending in slow-wave sleep?
5. Trace the rise and fall of the neurotransmitters acetylcholine, serotonin, and norepinephrine in the sleep cycle depicted.
6. Has this sleeper, whose night's sleep is illustrated here, achieved a good night's rest? Why or why not?

Recall that acetylcholine is the neurotransmitter that typically gets our bodies moving. REM sleep ends when there is a rise in serotonin and norepinephrine, which increase the level of forebrain activity nearly to the awakened state (Frainge & others, 2015). You are most likely to wake up just after a REM period. If you do not wake up then, the level of the neurotransmitters falls again, and you enter another sleep cycle. To review the sleep cycles, complete the Psychological Inquiry exercise.

Sleep Throughout the Life Span

Getting sufficient sleep is important at every stage of human life. Figure 6 shows how total sleep time and time spent in each type of sleep varies over the life span.

Sleep may benefit physical growth and brain development in infants and children. For example, deep sleep coincides with the release of growth hormones in children. Children are more likely to sleep well when they avoid caffeine, experience a regular bedtime routine, go to bed and wake up at regular hours, and do not have a television or electronic devices in their bedroom (Buxton & others, 2015).

As children age, their sleep patterns change. Many adolescents stay up later at night and sleep longer in the morning than they did when they were younger, and these shifting sleep patterns may influence their psychological well-being (Tu, Erath, & El-Sheikh, 2015) and academic work (Asarnow, McGlinchey, & Harvey, 2014; Titova & others, 2015). Left to their own devices, adolescents will sleep over 9 hours a night (Crowley & Carskadon, 2010; Tarokh & Carskadon, 2010). This need for sleep may be linked to the important brain development that occurs during adolescence (Campbell & others, 2012).

Yet, many adolescents get quite a bit less than 9 hours of sleep a night, especially during the week. This shortfall creates a sleep debt that adolescents often attempt to

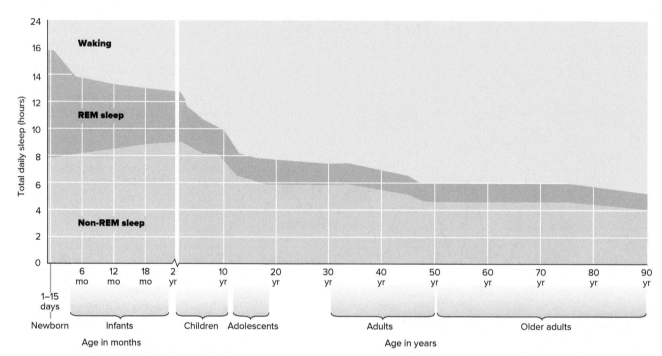

FIGURE 6   **Sleep Across the Human Life Span** With age, humans require less sleep. Source: Roffwarg, H. P., Muzio, J. N., & Dement, W. C. (1966, 29 April). Ontogenetic development of human dream–sleep cycle *Science, 152* (3722), 604–619.

make up on the weekend. Having one's weekday and weekend sleep schedules drastically at odds is sometimes referred to as *social jet lag*. Social jet lag means that even without traveling, a person's sleep clock can be desynchronized. Social jet lag is associated with poorer academic performance for adolescents (Díaz-Morales & Escribano, 2015).

It is important to bear in mind that adolescent sleep changes are not simply about academic work or social pressures. Rather, adolescents' biological clocks undergo a shift as they get older, delaying their period of wakefulness by about an hour. A delay in the nightly release of the sleep-inducing hormone melatonin seems to underlie this shift. Melatonin is secreted at about 9:30 P.M. in younger adolescents and approximately an hour later in older adolescents (Eckerberg & others, 2012). Based on research on the adolescent sleep cycle, numerous school districts have begun to delay the start time for high school students. Although experimental evidence is limited, a recent review suggested that later start times lead to more sleep, less sleepiness at school, and less tardiness (Minges & Redeker, 2016).

Do sleep patterns change in emerging adulthood (18–25 years of age)? Research indicates that they do (Galambos, Howard, & Maggs, 2011). In one study, the weekday bedtimes and rise times of first-year college students were approximately 1 hour and 15 minutes later than those of seniors in high school (Lund & others, 2010). However, the first-year college students had later bedtimes and rise times than third- and fourth-year college students, indicating that between 20 and 22 years of age, a reverse in the timing of bedtimes and rise times occurs. An important correlate of poorer sleep in young adults is media use in the 2 hours before bed (Orzech & others, 2016).

Sleep patterns also change as people age through the middle-adult (40s and 50s) and late-adult (60s and older) years (Luik & others, 2015; Scullin & Bliwise, 2015). Many adults in these age spans go to bed earlier at night and wake up earlier in the morning than they did in their younger years. As well, beginning in their 40s, individuals report that they are less likely to sleep through the entire night than when

© Rubberball/Alamy

they were younger. Middle-aged adults also spend less time in deep sleep than they did before their middle years.

One study found that changes in sleep duration across five years in middle age were linked to cognitive abilities such as problem solving and memory (Ferrie & others, 2011). In this study, a decrease from 6, 7, or 8 hours of sleep and an increase from 7 or 8 hours were related to lower scores on most cognitive assessments. Many older adults complain of having difficulty sleeping (Lemola & Richter, 2013). Poor sleep is related to lower level of cognitive functioning (Seelye & others, 2015).

Sleep and Disease

Sleep plays a role in a large number of diseases and disorders (Wright & others, 2015). Lack of sleep relates to disease risk (Carroll & others, 2015), poorer health, and earlier death (Hall & others, 2015). Importantly, although lack of sleep is often associated with health problems, sleeping too much may also be a sign of problems (Grossi & others, 2015; Hale & others, 2013).

Neurons that control sleep interact closely with the immune system (Hahn, Günter, & Autenrieth, 2015; Imeri & Opp, 2009). As anyone who has had the flu knows, infectious diseases make us sleepy. The probable reason is that chemicals called *cytokines,* produced by the body's cells while we are fighting an infection, are powerfully sleep-inducing (Besedovsky, Lange, & Born, 2012). Sleep may help the body conserve energy and other resources it needs to overcome infection (Irwin & others, 2006). Essentially, lack of sleep is stressful and affects the body just as stressful experiences do (McEwen & Karatsoreos, 2015).

Sleep problems afflict most people who have psychological disorders, including those with depression (Ashworth & others, 2015). Individuals with depression often awaken in the early hours of the morning and cannot get back to sleep, and they typically spend less time in delta-wave or deep sleep than do individuals who are not depressed.

Sleep problems are common in many medical disorders, such as Alzheimer disease, stroke, and cancer (Cumming & others, 2015; McClam & others, 2015; Savard & others, 2015). In some cases, however, these problems may arise not from the disease itself but from the drugs used to treat the disease.

Sleep Disorders

Many individuals suffer from undiagnosed and untreated sleep disorders that leave them feeling unmotivated and exhausted throughout the day. The major sleep disorders include insomnia, sleepwalking and sleep talking, nightmares and night terrors, narcolepsy, and sleep apnea.

INSOMNIA

A common sleep problem is *insomnia,* the inability to sleep. Insomnia can involve a problem in falling asleep, waking up during the night, or waking up too early (Gehrman, Findley, & Perlis, 2012). In the United States, in 2006 one in five adults was estimated to have insomnia (Pearson, Johnson, & Nahin, 2006). In the last decade, that number has tripled (Pandey & Phillips, 2015). Insomnia is more common among women, older adults, and those with diabetes (Ford & others, 2015; National Sleep Foundation, 2007).

For short-term insomnia, most physicians prescribe sleeping pills. However, most sleeping pills stop working after several weeks of taking them nightly, and their long-term use can interfere with good sleep. Mild insomnia often can be reduced by simply practicing good sleep habits, such as always going to bed at the same time, even on weekends, and sleeping in a dark, quiet place. In more serious cases, researchers are experimenting with light therapy, melatonin supplements, and other ways to alter circadian cycles (Tang & others, 2015). Behavioral changes (such as avoiding naps and caffeine and setting an alarm in the morning) can help insomniacs increase their sleep time and awaken less frequently in the night.

SLEEPWALKING AND SLEEP TALKING

Somnambulism is the formal term for sleepwalking, which occurs during the deepest stages of sleep (Petit & others, 2015). For many years, experts believed that somnambulists were acting out their dreams. However, somnambulism takes place during stages N2 and N3, usually early in the night, when a person is unlikely to be dreaming (Zadra & Pilon, 2012).

The specific causes of sleepwalking have not been identified, but it is more likely to occur when individuals are sleep deprived or when they have been drinking alcohol. There is nothing abnormal about sleepwalking, and despite superstition, it is safe to awaken sleepwalkers. In fact, they probably should be awakened, as they may harm themselves wandering around in the dark.

Another quirky night behavior is sleep talking, or *somniloquy*. If you interrogate sleep talkers, can you find out what they did, for instance, last Thursday night? Probably not. Although sleep talkers will converse with you and make fairly coherent statements, they are soundly asleep. Thus, even if a sleep talker mumbles a response to your question, do not count on its accuracy.

You may have heard of cases of other strange behaviors occurring while people sleep, especially if they have taken medicine to help them sleep. Sleep eating and, and, and even sleep driving, have been reported as unusual side effects of some sleep aids (Paulke, Wunder, Toennes, 2015; Popat & Winslade, 2015). For example, some Ambien users began to notice odd things upon waking up from a much-needed good night's sleep, such as candy wrappers strewn around the room, crumbs in the bed, and food missing from the refrigerator. Ambien users can also notice unusual weight gain (Mitchell, 2014).

The phenomena of sleep eating and sleep driving illustrate that even when we feel fast asleep, we may be "half-awake." In such a state we might put together unusual late-night snacks, such as salt sandwiches and raw bacon, or find our car keys and set off on a trip. For individuals who are battling persistent insomnia, a drug that provides a good night's rest may be worth the risk of these side effects. Furthermore, no one should abruptly stop taking any medication without consulting a physician.

NIGHTMARES AND NIGHT TERRORS

A *nightmare* is a frightening dream that awakens a dreamer from REM sleep (Germain, 2012). The nightmare's content invariably involves danger—the dreamer is chased, robbed, or thrown off a cliff. Nightmares are common (Schredl, 2010); most of us have had them, especially as young children. Reported frequency of nightmares or worsening nightmares are often associated with an increase in life stressors such as the loss of a job, the death of a loved one, or conflicts with others.

A *night terror* features sudden arousal from sleep and intense fear (Petit & others, 2015). Night terrors are accompanied by a number of physiological reactions, such as rapid heart rate and breathing, loud screams, heavy perspiration, and movement (Zadra & Pilon, 2012). Night terrors, which peak at 5 to 7 years of age, are less common than nightmares, and unlike nightmares, they occur during slow-wave stage N3 (non-REM) sleep.

NARCOLEPSY

The disorder *narcolepsy* involves the sudden, overpowering urge to sleep. This urge is so uncontrollable that the person may fall asleep while talking or standing up. Narcoleptics immediately enter REM sleep rather than progressing through the first four sleep stages (Ratcliffe & Kallappa, 2015). Individuals with narcolepsy are often very tired during the day. Narcolepsy can be triggered by extreme emotional reactions, such as surprise, laughter, excitement, or anger. The disorder appears to involve problems with particular neurons in the hypothalamus and may have an autoimmune component (Arango, Kivity, & Shoenfeld, 2015).

SLEEP APNEA

Sleep apnea is a sleep disorder in which individuals stop breathing because the windpipe fails to open or because brain processes involved in respiration fail to work properly.

People with sleep apnea experience numerous brief awakenings during the night so that they can breathe better, although they usually are not aware of their awakened state. During the day, these people may feel sleepy because they were deprived of sleep at night. A common sign of sleep apnea is loud snoring, punctuated by silence (the apnea).

Sleep apnea affects approximately 4 percent of U.S. adults (Jaradat & Rahhal, 2015). The disorder is most common among infants and adults over the age of 65. Sleep apnea also occurs more frequently among obese individuals (Koren & others, 2015), men, and individuals with large necks and recessed chins (Sinnapah & others, 2015). Untreated sleep apnea can cause high blood pressure, stroke, and sexual dysfunction (Parati, Lombardi, & Narkiewicz, 2007; Vitulano & others, 2013). In addition, the daytime sleepiness caused by sleep apnea can result in accidents, lost productivity, and relationship problems. Sleep apnea is commonly treated by weight-loss programs, side sleeping, propping the head on a pillow, or wearing a device (called a CPAP, for *continuous positive airway pressure*) that sends pressurized air through a mask to prevent the airway from collapsing.

Sleep apnea may also be a factor in *sudden infant death syndrome (SIDS)*, the unexpected sleep-related death of an infant less than 1 year old. SIDS is typically confirmed with an autopsy that reveals no specific cause of death. It is common for infants to have short pauses in their breathing during sleep, but for some infants frequent sleep apnea may be a sign of problems in regulating arousal (Kato & others, 2003; Lipford & others, 2015). There is evidence that infants who die of SIDS in fact experience multiple episodes of sleep apnea in the days before the fatal event (Cohen & de Chazal, 2015). One possible explanation for SIDS is an abnormality in the brain stem areas responsible for arousal (Lavezzi, Ottaviani, & Matturri, 2015). Such an abnormality may lead to sleep apnea, which in turn might worsen the brain stem damage, ultimately leading to death.

Dreams

Have you ever dreamed that you left your long-term romantic partner for a former lover? If so, did you tell your partner about that dream? Not likely. However, you probably wondered about the dream's meaning, and if so you would not be alone. The meaning of dreams has eternally fascinated human beings. As early as 5000 B.C.E., Babylonians recorded and interpreted their dreams on clay tablets. Egyptians built temples in honor of Serapis, the god of dreams. Dreams are described at length in more than 70 passages in the Bible. Psychologists have also examined this intriguing topic.

FREUD'S PSYCHODYNAMIC APPROACH

Sigmund Freud put great stock in dreams as a key to our unconscious minds. He believed that dreams (even nightmares) symbolize unconscious wishes and that analysis of dream symbols could uncover our hidden desires. Freud distinguished between a dream's manifest content and its latent content. **Manifest content** is the dream's surface content, which contains dream symbols that disguise the dream's true meaning; **latent content** is the dream's hidden content, its unconscious—and true—meaning. For example, if a person had a dream about riding on a train and talking with a friend, the train ride would be the dream's manifest content. The manifest content is simply the dream itself. The latent content is the dream's deeper true meaning.

Freud thought that this manifest content expresses a wish in disguised form. To get to the latent or true meaning of the dream, the person would have to analyze the dream images. In our example, the dreamer would be asked to think of all the things that come to mind when the person thinks of a train, the friend, and so forth. By following these associations to the objects in the manifest content, the latent content of the dream could be brought to light.

More recently, psychologists have considered dreams not as expressions of unconscious wishes but as mental events that come from various sources. Research has revealed a great deal about the nature of dreams (De Koninck, 2012). A common misconception is that dreams are typically bizarre or strange, but many studies of thousands of dreams,

● **manifest content** According to Freud, the surface content of a dream, containing dream symbols that disguise the dream's true meaning.

● **latent content** According to Freud, a dream's hidden content; its unconscious and true meaning.

© Thinkstock/PunchStock

collected from individuals in sleep labs and sleeping at home, have shown that dreams generally are not especially strange. Instead, research shows that dreams are often very similar to waking life (Domhoff, 2007; Schredl, 2009; Schwartz, 2010).

So, *why* do many of us believe that our dreams are very peculiar? The probable reason is that we are likely to remember our most vividly bizarre dreams and to forget those dreams that are more mundane. Thus, we never realize how commonplace most dreams are. Although some aspects of dreams *are* unusual, dreams often are no more bizarre than a typical fairy tale, TV show episode, or movie plot. However, dreams do generally contain more negative emotion than everyday life; and certainly some unlikely characters, including dead people, sometimes show up in dreams.

There is also no evidence that dreams provide opportunities for problem solving or advice about how to handle life's difficulties. We may dream about a problem we are facing, but we typically find the solution while we are awake and thinking about the problem, not during the dream itself (Domhoff, 2007). There is also no evidence that people who remember their dreams are better adjusted psychologically than those who do not (Blagrove & Akehurst, 2000).

So, if the typical dream involves doing ordinary things, what *are* dreams? Two examples of theories that attempt to explain dreams are cognitive theory and activation-synthesis theory (Zink & Pietrowsky, 2015).

COGNITIVE THEORY OF DREAMING

The **cognitive theory of dreaming** proposes that we can understand dreaming by applying the same cognitive concepts we use in studying the waking mind. The theory rests on the idea that dreams are essentially subconscious cognitive processing, arguing that there is continuity between waking thought and dreams (Domhoff & Fox, 2015; Lee & Kuiken, 2015). Dreaming involves information processing and memory. Indeed, thinking during dreams appears to be very similar to thinking in waking life (De Gennaro & others, 2012; Domhoff, 2011; Kahan & Sullivan, 2012).

● **cognitive theory of dreaming** Theory proposing that dreaming can be understood by applying the same cognitive concepts used to study the waking mind.

In the cognitive theory of dreaming, there is little or no search for the hidden, symbolic content of dreams that Freud sought. Instead, dreams are viewed as dramatizations of general life concerns that are similar to relaxed daydreams. Even very unusual aspects of dreams—such as odd activities, strange images, and sudden scene shifts—can be understood as metaphorically related to a person's preoccupations while awake (Domhoff, 2011; Zadra & Domhoff, 2011). The cognitive theory also ties the brain activity that occurs during dreams to the activity that occurs during waking life. The term *default network* refers to a collection of neurons that are active during mind wandering and daydreaming, essentially whenever we are not focused on a task. Research suggests that dreaming during sleep may also emerge from the activity of this network (Domhoff, 2011; Domhoff & Fox, 2015).

The cognitive theory of dreaming strongly argues that dreams should be viewed as a kind of mental simulation that is very similar in content to our everyday waking thoughts. The purpose of dreams is to process information, solve problems, and think creatively about the issues we face in our daily lives. This perspective on dreams contrasts with activation-synthesis theory of dreaming.

ACTIVATION-SYNTHESIS THEORY OF DREAMING

According to **activation-synthesis theory of dreaming**, dreaming occurs when the cerebral cortex synthesizes neural signals generated from activity in the lower part of the brain (Zink & Pietrowsky, 2015). Dreams result from the brain's attempts to find logic in random brain activity that occurs during sleep (Hobson, 1999; Hobson & Friston, 2012; Hobson & Voss, 2011).

● **activation-synthesis theory of dreaming** Theory that dreaming occurs when the cerebral cortex synthesizes neural signals generated from activity in the lower part of the brain and that dreams result from the brain's attempts to find logic in random brain activity that occurs during sleep.

When we are awake and alert, our conscious experience tends to be driven by *external* stimuli—all those things we see, hear, and respond to. During sleep, according to activation-synthesis theory, conscious experience is driven predominantly by internally generated stimuli that have no apparent behavioral consequence. A key source of such internal stimulation is spontaneous neural activity in the brain stem (Hobson, 2000). Of course, some of the neural activity that produces dreams comes from external sensory experiences. If a fire truck with sirens blaring drives past your house, you might find yourself dreaming about an emergency. Many of us have had the experience of incorporating the sound of our phone alarm (or alarm clock) going off in an early morning dream.

Supporters of activation-synthesis theory have suggested that neural networks in other areas of the forebrain play a significant role in dreaming (Hobson, Pace-Schott, & Stickgold, 2000). Specifically, they believe that the same regions of the forebrain that are involved in certain waking behaviors also function in particular aspects of dreaming (Lu & others, 2006). As levels of neurotransmitters rise and fall during the stages of sleep, some neural networks are activated and others shut down.

Random neural firing in various areas of the brain leads to dreams that are the brain's attempts to make sense of the activity. So, firing in the primary motor and sensory areas of the forebrain might be reflected in a dream of running and feeling wind on your face. From the activation-synthesis perspective, our nervous system is cycling through various activities, and our consciousness is simply along for the ride (Hobson, 2004). Dreams are merely a flashy sideshow, not the main event (Hooper & Teresi, 1993). Indeed, one activation-synthesis theorist has referred to dreams as so much "cognitive trash" (Hobson, 2002, p. 23).

Research continues to evaluate whether dreams should be considered as interpretations of random activity or whether they should be regarded as strongly related to waking life. One big reason for the mystery associated with dreams is that dreams, like other content of our mind, are private. Although we can share our dreams with others by talking about them or creating art that seeks to capture them, they are in some ways only truly available to the dreamer.

3. PSYCHOACTIVE DRUGS

One way that people seek to alter their own consciousness is through the use of psychoactive drugs. In fact, illicit drug use is a global problem. According to the United Nations Office on Drugs and Crime (UNODC), more than 246 million people between the ages of 15 and 64 worldwide use drugs each year (UNODC, 2015). Among those, approximately 27 million individuals are characterized as problem drug users—individuals whose drug habit interferes with their ability to engage in work and social relationships (UNODC, 2015).

Drug consumption among youth is a special concern because of its links to problems such as unsafe sex, sexually transmitted infections, unplanned pregnancy, depression, and school-related difficulties (UNODC, 2015). The use of drugs among U.S. secondary school students declined in the 1980s but began to increase in the early 1990s (Johnston & others, 2016). Then in the late 1990s and early 2000s, the proportion of secondary school students reporting the use of any illicit drug again declined (Johnston & others, 2016).

Drug use by U.S. high school seniors since 1975 and by U.S. eighth- and tenth-graders since 1991 has been tracked in a national survey called Monitoring the Future (Johnston & others, 2016). This survey is the focus of the Psychological Inquiry feature. Let's take a look at these trends.

Uses of Psychoactive Drugs

Psychoactive drugs act on the nervous system to alter consciousness, modify perception, and change mood. Some people use psychoactive drugs as a way to deal with life's difficulties. Drinking, smoking, and taking drugs reduce tension, relieve boredom and fatigue, and help people to escape from the harsh realities of life. Some people use drugs because they are curious about their effects.

The use of psychoactive drugs, whether it is to cope with problems or just for fun, can carry a high price tag. These include losing track of one's responsibilities, problems in the workplace and in relationships, drug dependence, and increased risk for serious,

---

test yourself

1. Describe how the human body monitors the change from day to night.
2. What happens during each of the five stages of sleep?
3. According to researchers, what functions does sleep play in infants and children? What functions does it play in adolescents?

● **psychoactive drugs** Drugs that act on the nervous system to alter consciousness, modify perception, and change mood.

psychological *inquiry*

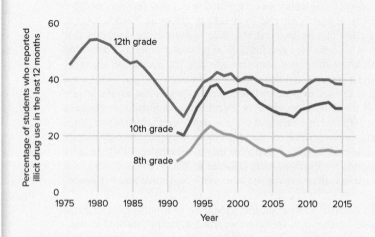

Drug Use by U.S. Teenagers

This graph shows the percentage of U.S. eighth-, tenth-, and twelfth-grade students who reported having taken an illicit drug in the last 12 months from 1991 to 2015 (for eighth- and tenth-graders) and from 1975 to 2015 (for twelfth-graders) (Johnston & others, 2016). The vertical axis shows the percentage of children and adolescents who report using illegal substances. The horizontal axis identifies the year of data collection. The most notable declines in adolescent drug use in the twenty-first century have occurred for marijuana, LSD, Ecstasy, steroids, and cigarettes. As you examine the data, answer these questions.

1. Do some research to find out about the social and cultural climate in each of the decades represented. Who was president at the time, and what historical events occurred? How does adolescent drug use reflect those times?

2. Data were not collected from eighth- and tenth-graders until 1991. Why do you think these two age groups were added?

3. After the mid-1990s, all age groups showed a similar decline in drug use. Why might this pattern have occurred in all three groups?

4. What are the implications of using self-reports from children and adolescents to track their drug use? Do you think each age group is similarly likely to report honestly, to overreport, or to underreport their drug use? Explain.

---

sometimes fatal diseases (UNODC, 2015). For example, drinking alcohol may initially help people relax and forget about their worries. If, however, they turn more and more to alcohol to escape reality, they may develop a dependence that can destroy their relationships, career, and health.

Continued use of psychoactive drugs leads to **tolerance,** the need to take increasing amounts of a drug to get the same effect (Mars & others, 2015). For example, the first time someone takes 5 milligrams of the tranquilizer Valium, the person feels very relaxed. However, after taking the pill every day for six months, the individual may need to consume twice as much to achieve the same calming effect.

Continuing drug use can also result in **physical dependence,** the physiological need for a drug that causes unpleasant withdrawal symptoms such as physical pain and a craving for the drug when it is discontinued. **Psychological dependence** is the strong desire to repeat the use of a drug for emotional reasons, such as a feeling of well-being and reduction of stress. Experts on drug abuse use the term **addiction** to describe either a physical or a psychological dependence, or both, on the drug (Everitt & Robbins, 2016).

How does the brain become addicted? Psychoactive drugs increase dopamine levels in the brain's reward pathways (Karoly, YorkWilliams, & Hutchison, 2015). This reward pathway is located in the *ventral tegmental area (VTA)* and *nucleus accumbens (NAcc)* (Figure 7). Only the limbic and prefrontal areas of the brain are directly activated by dopamine, which comes from the VTA (Beier & others, 2015). Although different drugs have different mechanisms of action, each drug increases the activity of the reward pathway by increasing dopamine transmission. As we will see throughout this book, the neurotransmitter dopamine plays a vital role in the experience of rewards.

tolerance The need to take increasing amounts of a drug to get the same effect.

physical dependence The physiological need for a drug that causes unpleasant withdrawal symptoms such as physical pain and a craving for the drug when it is discontinued.

psychological dependence The strong desire to repeat the use of a drug for emotional reasons, such as a feeling of well-being and reduction of stress.

addiction Either a physical or a psychological dependence, or both, on a drug.

depressants Psychoactive drugs that slow down mental and physical activity.

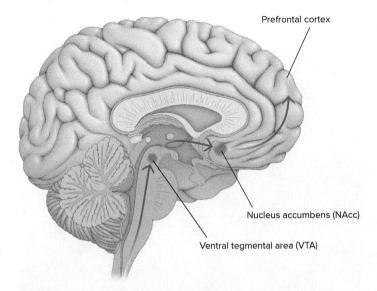

Prefrontal cortex

Nucleus accumbens (NAcc)

Ventral tegmental area (VTA)

FIGURE 7   The Brain's Reward Pathway for Psychoactive Drugs The ventral tegmental area (VTA) and nucleus accumbens (NAcc) are important locations in the reward pathway for psychoactive drugs (Russo & others, 2010). Information travels from the VTA to the NAcc and then up to the prefrontal cortex. The VTA is located in the midbrain just above the pons, and the NAcc is located in the forebrain just beneath the prefrontal cortex.

Respond yes or no to the following items:

Yes	No	
☐	☐	I have gotten into problems because of using drugs.
☐	☐	Using alcohol or other drugs has made my college life unhappy at times.
☐	☐	Drinking alcohol or taking other drugs has been a factor in my losing a job.
☐	☐	Drinking alcohol or taking other drugs has interfered with my studying for exams.
☐	☐	Drinking alcohol or taking other drugs has jeopardized my academic performance.
☐	☐	My ambition is not as strong since I've been drinking a lot or taking drugs.
☐	☐	Drinking or taking other drugs has caused me to have difficulty sleeping.
☐	☐	I have felt remorse after drinking or taking drugs.
☐	☐	I crave a drink or other drugs at a definite time of the day.
☐	☐	I want a drink or other drug in the morning.
☐	☐	I have had a complete or partial loss of memory as a result of drinking or using other drugs.
☐	☐	Drinking or using other drugs is affecting my reputation.
☐	☐	I have been in the hospital or another institution because of my drinking or taking drugs.

College students who responded yes to items similar to these on the Rutgers Collegiate Abuse Screening Test were more likely to be substance abusers than those who answered no. If you responded yes to just 1 of the 13 items on this screening test, consider going to your college health or counseling center for further screening.

FIGURE 8   Do You Abuse Drugs? Take this short quiz to see if your use of drugs and alcohol might be a cause for concern.

Types of Psychoactive Drugs

Three main categories of psychoactive drugs are depressants, stimulants, and hallucinogens. All have the potential to cause health or behavior problems or both. To evaluate whether you abuse drugs, see Figure 8.

DEPRESSANTS

Depressants are psychoactive drugs that slow down mental and physical activity. Among the most widely used depressants are alcohol, barbiturates, tranquilizers, and opiates.

Alcohol   Alcohol is a powerful drug. It acts on the body primarily as a depressant and slows down the brain's activities. This effect might seem surprising, as people who tend to be inhibited may begin to talk, dance, and socialize after a few drinks. However, people "loosen up" after a few drinks because the brain areas involved in inhibition and judgment slow down. As people drink more, their inhibitions decrease even further, and their judgment becomes increasingly impaired. Activities that require intellectual functioning and motor skills, such as driving, become harder to perform. Eventually the drinker falls asleep. With extreme intoxication, the person may lapse into a coma and die. Figure 9 illustrates alcohol's main effects on the body.

The effects of alcohol vary from person to person. Factors in this variation are body weight, the amount of alcohol consumed, individual differences in the way the body metabolizes alcohol, and the presence or absence of tolerance. Men and women differ in terms of the intoxicating effects of alcohol. Because of differences in body fat as well as stomach enzymes, women are likely to be more strongly affected by alcohol than men.

How does alcohol influence the brain? Like other psychoactive drugs, alcohol goes to the VTA and the NAcc (Karoly, YorkWilliams, & Hutchison, 2015). Alcohol also increases the concentration of the neurotransmitter gamma aminobutyric acid (GABA), which is widely distributed in many brain areas, including the cerebral cortex, cerebellum, hippocampus, amygdala, and nucleus accumbens (Kim & others, 2015).

Recall that GABA is the brain's break peddle, and the increase in GABA has a calming effect. In addition, increases in dopamine in reward areas are associated with the experience of pleasure and a decrease in anxiety (Trantham-Davidson & Chandler, 2015). Alcohol consumption also may affect the areas of the frontal cortex involved in judgment and impulse control (Koob, 2015). It is further believed that the basal ganglia, which are involved in compulsive behaviors, may lead to a greater demand for alcohol, regardless of reason and consequences (Brink, 2001).

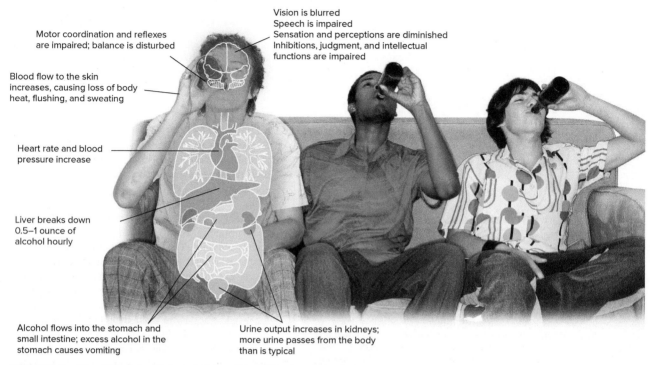

Motor coordination and reflexes are impaired; balance is disturbed

Vision is blurred
Speech is impaired
Sensation and perceptions are diminished
Inhibitions, judgment, and intellectual functions are impaired

Blood flow to the skin increases, causing loss of body heat, flushing, and sweating

Heart rate and blood pressure increase

Liver breaks down 0.5–1 ounce of alcohol hourly

Alcohol flows into the stomach and small intestine; excess alcohol in the stomach causes vomiting

Urine output increases in kidneys; more urine passes from the body than is typical

FIGURE 9   The Physiological and Behavioral Effects of Alcohol Alcohol has a powerful impact throughout the body. It affects everything from the operation of the nervous, circulatory, and digestive systems to sensation, perception, motor coordination, and intellectual functioning. (photo) © George Doyle/Stockbyte/Getty Images

After caffeine, alcohol is the most widely used drug in the United States. According to the Centers for Disease Control and Prevention (CDC), as many as two-thirds of U.S. adults drink beer, wine, or liquor at least occasionally, and approximately one in six adults reported drinking more than eight drinks at one sitting four times a month (CDC, 2015a). The common use of alcohol is related to other serious problems, including death and injury from driving while drinking. In the United States, on average, one person dies every 51 minutes in traffic accidents involving an alcohol impaired driver (CDC, 2015b).

Research has also found a link between alcohol and violence and aggression (Gallagher & Parrott, 2010; Noel & others, 2009). More than 60 percent of homicides involve alcohol use by the offender or the victim, and 65 percent of aggressive sexual acts against women are associated with alcohol consumption by the offender. Studies have linked substance use to dating violence in adolescents and college students (Reyes & others, 2015; Testa & others, 2015). Some individuals may be especially susceptible to the effects of alcohol on aggressive behavior (Miczek & others, 2015).

Alcohol use by U.S. secondary school and college students has long been a concern. However, the percentage of U.S. high school seniors who reported consuming alcohol in the last 30 days dropped from 73 percent in 1980 to 39 percent in 2013 (Johnston & others, 2016). Binge drinking (defined as having five or more drinks in a row in the last week) also declined among high school seniors, from 41 percent in 1980 to 26 percent in 2013.

Binge drinking often increases during the first two years of college, peaking at age 21 to 22 years of age (Johnston & others, 2016). Binge drinking can take a serious toll on students, personally and academically (Dunne & Katz, 2015). In a national survey of drinking patterns on college campuses, almost half of the binge drinkers reported problems such as missed classes, injuries, trouble with the police,

© Ingram Publishing/Alamy

© Cardinal/Corbis

and unprotected sex (Wechsler & others, 2000, 2002). Binge-drinking college students were 11 times more likely to fall behind in school, 10 times more likely to drive after drinking, and 2 times more likely to have unprotected sex as college students who did not binge drink.

However, many emerging adults decrease their alcohol use as they assume adult responsibilities—such as a permanent job, marriage or cohabitation, and parenthood—and as they mature psychologically (Lee, Ellingson, & Sher, 2015). Intensity of binge drinking in college can predict later problem drinking (Reich & others, 2015).

Alcoholism is a disorder that involves long-term, repeated, uncontrolled, compulsive, and excessive use of alcoholic beverages and that impairs the drinker's health and social relationships. Approximately 18 million people in the United States are alcoholics (MedlinePlus, 2015). Those who have their first drink of alcohol at younger ages are at risk for heavy drinking and alcohol problems (Liang & Chikritzhs, 2015; Xuan & others, 2015).

One in nine individuals who drink continues down the path to alcoholism. A key risk factor is family history. Family studies consistently find a high frequency of alcoholism in the close biological relatives of alcoholics (Buscemi & Turchi, 2011; Sorocco & others, 2015). A possible explanation is that the brains of people genetically predisposed to alcoholism may be unable to produce adequate dopamine, the neurotransmitter that can make us feel pleasure (Groenman & others, 2015; Landgren & others, 2011). For these individuals, alcohol may increase dopamine concentration and resulting pleasure to the point where it leads to addiction (Meyer, Meshul, & Phillips, 2009).

Like other psychological characteristics, though, alcoholism is not all about nature: Nurture matters too. Indeed, research shows that experience plays a role in alcoholism (Kendler, Gardner, & Dick, 2011). Many alcoholics do not have close relatives who are alcoholics (Duncan & others, 2006), a finding that points to environmental influences (Sorocco & others, 2015).

What does it take to stop alcoholism? About one-third of alcoholics recover whether they are in a treatment program or not. This finding came from a long-term study of 700 individuals (Vaillant, 2003). George Vaillant followed these individuals for over 60 years, and he formulated the so-called one-third rule for alcoholism: By age 65, one-third are dead or in terrible shape; one-third are still trying to beat their addiction; and one-third are abstinent or drinking only socially. In his extensive research, Vaillant found that recovery from alcoholism was predicted by (1) having a strong negative

● **alcoholism** A disorder that involves long-term, repeated, uncontrolled, compulsive, and excessive use of alcoholic beverages and that impairs the drinker's health and social relationships.

experience with drinking, such as a serious medical emergency; (2) finding a substitute dependency, such as meditation, exercise, or overeating (which has its own adverse health effects); (3) developing new, positive relationships; and (4) joining a support group such as Alcoholics Anonymous.

Barbiturates   **Barbiturates,** such as Nembutal and Seconal, are depressant drugs that decrease central nervous system activity. Physicians once widely prescribed barbiturates as sleep aids. In heavy dosages, they can lead to impaired memory, poor decision making, and difficulty breathing. When combined with alcohol (for example, sleeping pills taken after a night of binge drinking), barbiturates can be lethal. Heavy doses of barbiturates by themselves can cause death. For this reason, barbiturates are the drug most often used in suicide attempts. Abrupt withdrawal can produce seizures. Because of the addictive potential and relative ease of toxic overdose, barbiturates have largely been replaced by tranquilizers in the treatment of insomnia.

Tranquilizers   **Tranquilizers,** such as Valium and Xanax, are depressant drugs that reduce anxiety and induce relaxation. In small doses tranquilizers can bring on a feeling of calm; higher doses can lead to drowsiness and confusion. Tolerance for tranquilizers can develop within a few weeks of usage, and these drugs are addictive. Widely prescribed in the United States to calm anxious individuals, tranquilizers can produce withdrawal symptoms when use is stopped. Prescription tranquilizers were part of the lethal cocktail of drugs that ended the life of Whitney Houston in 2012.

Opiates   Narcotics, or **opiates,** consist of opium and its derivatives; they depress the central nervous system's activity. These drugs are used as powerful painkillers. The most common opiate drugs—morphine and heroin—affect synapses in the brain that use endorphins as their neurotransmitter. When these drugs leave the brain, the affected synapses become understimulated. For several hours after taking an opiate, the person feels euphoric and pain-free and has an increased appetite for food and sex. Opiates are highly addictive, and users experience craving and painful withdrawal when the drug becomes unavailable. The powerful effects of opiates lie behind addictions to prescription pain medications as well as heroin addiction.

In recent years, as heroin has become less expensive, the number of people addicted to the drug has surged. Deaths from heroin overdose nearly quadrupled from 1993 to 2013 (Fisher, 2015), and overdoses of heroin combined with cocaine have led to the tragic and untimely deaths of actors Philip Seymour Hoffman, John Belushi, and River Phoenix. The website http://www.justthinktwice.com/ documents many of the lives ruined by or lost to opiates and other addictive drugs.

Opiate addiction can also raise the risk of exposure to HIV, the virus that causes AIDS, as well as exposure to hepatitis. Most heroin addicts inject the drug intravenously. When drug users share needles without sterilizing them, one infected person can transmit viruses to others.

STIMULANTS

Stimulants are psychoactive drugs that increase the central nervous system's activity. The most widely used stimulants are caffeine, nicotine, amphetamines, and cocaine.

Caffeine   Often overlooked as a drug, caffeine is the world's most widely used psychoactive drug. Caffeine is a stimulant and a natural component of the plants that are the sources of coffee, tea, and cola drinks. Caffeine also is present in chocolate, in many nonprescription medications, and in energy drinks such as Red Bull. People often perceive the stimulating effects of caffeine as beneficial for boosting energy and alertness, but some experience unpleasant side effects.

Caffeinism refers to an overindulgence in caffeine. It is characterized by mood changes, anxiety, and sleep disruption. Caffeinism often develops in people who drink

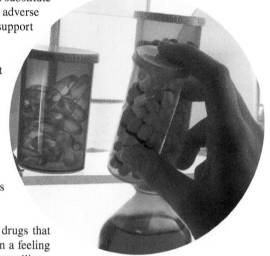
© Ingram Publishing/SuperStock

● **barbiturates** Depressant drugs, such as Nembutal and Seconal, that decrease central nervous system activity.

● **tranquilizers** Depressant drugs, such as Valium and Xanax, that reduce anxiety and induce relaxation.

● **opiates** Opium and its derivatives; narcotic drugs that depress the central nervous system's activity and eliminate pain.

● **stimulants** Psychoactive drugs—including caffeine, nicotine, amphetamines, and cocaine—that increase the central nervous system's activity.

FIGURE 10   The Physiological and Behavioral Effects of Nicotine
Smoking has many physiological and behavioral effects. Highly addictive, nicotine delivers pleasant feelings that encourage more smoking, but tobacco consumption poses very serious health risks in the individual. (photo) © Anton Dotsenko/123RF

Attention and alertness improve

At high levels, muscles become more relaxed; anxiety and anger may be reduced; pleasant feelings induce the individual to smoke more

Circulation to extremities decreases

Heart rate and blood pressure increase

In a pregnant woman, nicotine freely passes through the placenta wall into amniotic fluid

Smoker loses appetite for carbohydrates

five or more cups of coffee (at least 500 milligrams) each day. Common symptoms are insomnia, irritability, headaches, ringing ears, dry mouth, increased blood pressure, and digestive problems (Krankl & Gitlin, 2015).

Caffeine affects the brain's pleasure centers, so it is not surprising that it is difficult to kick the caffeine habit. When individuals who regularly consume caffeinated beverages remove caffeine from their diet, they typically experience headaches, lethargy, apathy, and concentration difficulties. These symptoms of withdrawal are usually mild and subside after several days.

Nicotine   Nicotine is the main psychoactive ingredient in all forms of smoking and smokeless tobacco. Even with all the publicity given to the enormous health risks posed by tobacco, we sometimes overlook the highly addictive nature of nicotine. Nicotine stimulates the brain's reward centers by raising dopamine levels (Beckmann & others, 2015). Behavioral effects of nicotine include improved attention and alertness, reduced anger and anxiety, and pain relief. Figure 10 shows the main effects of nicotine on the body.

Tolerance develops for nicotine both in the long run and on a daily basis, so that cigarettes smoked later in the day have less effect than those smoked earlier. Withdrawal from nicotine often quickly produces strong, unpleasant symptoms such as irritability, craving, inability to focus, sleep disturbance, and increased appetite. Withdrawal symptoms can persist for months or longer.

Tobacco poses a much larger threat to public health than illegal drugs. According to the CDC, tobacco is involved in one in every five deaths in the United States (CDC, 2015c). That is more than the total number killed by AIDS, alcohol, motor vehicles, homicide, illegal drugs, and suicide combined. According to the World

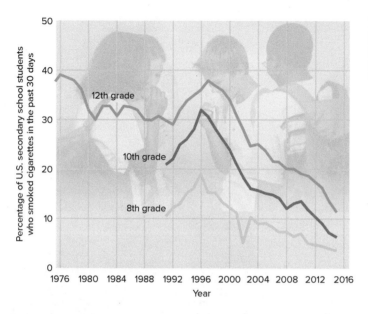

FIGURE 11 **Trends in Cigarette Smoking by U.S. Secondary School Students** Cigarette smoking by U.S. high school students is on the decline. (photo) © Digital Vision/PunchStock

Health Organization (2015), there are 1 billion smokers, globally, and smoking will kill at least half of them.

Cigarette smoking is decreasing among both adolescents and college students. In the national Monitoring the Future survey, the percentage of U.S. adolescents who are current cigarette smokers has declined especially in the last year, with all age groups showing a significant drop from 2014 to 2015 (Johnston & others, 2016) (Figure 11).

The drop in cigarette use by U.S. youth may have several sources, including higher cigarette prices, less tobacco advertising reaching adolescents, more antismoking advertisements, and more negative publicity about the tobacco industry than previously. Increasingly, adolescents report perceiving cigarette smoking as dangerous, disapprove of it, are less accepting of being around smokers, and prefer to date nonsmokers (Johnston & others, 2016). With respect to college students and young adults, smoking has shown a smaller decline than adolescent and adult smoking (Johnston & others, 2016).

In sum, cigarette smoking appears to be generally on the decline. Most smokers recognize the serious health risks of smoking and wish they could quit. The chapter "Health Psychology" explores the difficulty of giving up smoking and strategies for quitting.

Amphetamines   Amphetamines, or uppers, are stimulant drugs that people use to boost energy, stay awake, or lose weight. Often prescribed in the form of diet pills, these drugs increase the release of dopamine, which enhances the user's activity level and pleasurable feelings. Prescription drugs for attention deficit disorder, such as Ritalin, are also stimulants.

Perhaps the most insidious illicit drug for contemporary society is crystal methamphetamine, or crystal meth. Smoked, injected, or swallowed, crystal meth (also called "crank" or "tina") is a synthetic stimulant that causes a powerful feeling of euphoria, particularly the first time it is ingested. Meth is made using household products such as battery acid, cold medicine, drain cleaner, and kitty litter, and its effects have been devastating, notably in rural areas of the United States.

Crystal meth releases enormous amounts of dopamine in the brain, producing intense feelings of pleasure. The drug is highly addictive. The extreme high of crystal meth leads to a severe "come down" experience that is associated with strong cravings. Crystal meth also damages dopamine receptors, so that the crystal meth addict is chasing a high that the person's brain can no longer produce. A person's very first experience with crystal meth can lead to ruinous consequences making it a drug not worth trying, even once.

168 🐚 CHAPTER 5 **States of Consciousness**

FIGURE 12 **Cocaine and Neurotransmitters** Cocaine concentrates in areas of the brain that are rich in dopamine synapses such as the VTA and the nucleus accumbens (NAcc). (*top*) What happens in normal reuptake. The transmitting neuron releases dopamine, which stimulates the receiving neuron by binding to its receptor sites. After binding occurs, dopamine is carried back into the transmitting neuron for later release. (*bottom*) What happens when cocaine is present in the synapse. Cocaine binds to the uptake pumps and prevents them from removing dopamine from the synapse. The result is that more dopamine collects in the synapse, and more dopamine receptors are activated.

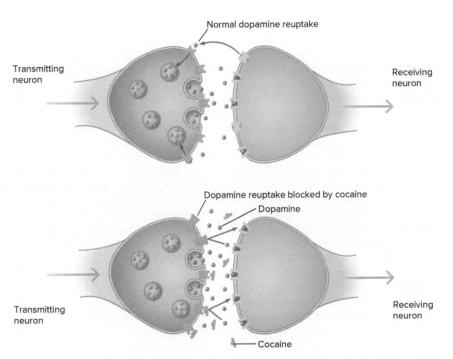

Cocaine　Cocaine is an illegal drug that comes from the coca plant, native to Bolivia and Peru. Cocaine is either snorted or injected in the form of crystals or powder. Used this way, cocaine floods the bloodstream rapidly, producing a rush of euphoric feelings that lasts for about 15 to 30 minutes. Because the rush depletes the brain's supply of the neurotransmitters dopamine, serotonin, and norepinephrine, an agitated, depressed mood usually follows as the drug's effects decline. Figure 12 shows how cocaine affects dopamine levels in the brain.

Crack is a potent form of cocaine, consisting of chips of pure cocaine that are usually smoked. Scientists believe that crack is one of the most addictive substances known. Treatment of cocaine and crack addiction is difficult (DeVito & others, 2015; Rovaris & others, 2015).

MDMA (Ecstasy)　MDMA—called Ecstasy, X, or XTC—is an illegal synthetic drug with both stimulant and hallucinogenic properties (Degenhardt, Bruno, & Topp, 2010). People have called Ecstasy an "empathogen" because under its influence, users tend to feel warm bonds with others. Not surprisingly, then, MDMA is associated with increased sexual risk taking (May & Parrott, 2015). MDMA produces its effects by releasing serotonin, dopamine, and norepinephrine. MDMA impairs memory and cognitive processing. Even new users of Ecstasy show cognitive deficits (Wagner & others, 2015).

HALLUCINOGENS

● **hallucinogens** Psychoactive drugs that modify a person's perceptual experiences and produce visual images that are not real.

Hallucinogens are psychoactive drugs that modify a person's perceptual experiences and produce visual images that are not real. Hallucinogens are also called *psychedelic* (from the Greek meaning "mind-revealing") drugs. Marijuana has a mild hallucinogenic effect; LSD, a stronger one.

Marijuana　Marijuana is the dried leaves and flowers of the hemp plant *Cannabis sativa,* which originated in Central Asia but is now grown in most parts of the world. The plant's dried resin is known as hashish. The active ingredient in marijuana is THC (delta-9-tetrahydrocannabinol). Unlike other psychoactive drugs, THC does not affect a specific neurotransmitter. Rather, marijuana disrupts the membranes of neurons and affects the functioning of a variety of neurotransmitters and hormones (Naguib & Foss, 2015).

The physical effects of marijuana include increased pulse rate and blood pressure, reddening of the eyes, coughing, and dry mouth. Like tobacco cigarettes and any other drugs ingested through smoking, marijuana smoke can damage the lungs (Mannino, 2015). Psychological effects of marijuana include a mixture of excitatory, depressive, and mildly hallucinatory characteristics that make it difficult to classify the drug. Marijuana can trigger spontaneous unrelated ideas; distorted perceptions of time and place; increased sensitivity to sounds, tastes, smells, and colors; and erratic verbal behavior. The drug can also impair attention and memory. Long-term marijuana use can lead to addiction and difficulties in quitting.

Marijuana is the illegal drug most widely used by high school students. In the Monitoring the Future survey, about 35 percent of U.S. high school seniors said they had tried marijuana in their lifetime, and 21 percent reported that they had used marijuana in the last 30 days (Johnston & others, 2016). One concern about adolescents' use of marijuana is that the drug might be a gateway to the use of other more serious illicit substances. Although there is a correlational link between using marijuana and using other illicit drugs, evidence for the notion that using marijuana leads to using other drugs is mixed (Kandel & Kandel, 2015; Tarter & others, 2006).

Marijuana is used in the treatment of a variety of illnesses including AIDS, cancer, and chronic pain (Thompson, 2015). In the United States, 23 states and the District of Columbia currently allow the medicinal use of marijuana. Alaska, Oregon, Colorado, and Washington have legalized the possession and recreational use of marijuana. However, federal law continues to treat marijuana as an illegal substance.

LSD   LSD (lysergic acid diethylamide) is a hallucinogen that even in low doses produces striking perceptual changes. Objects change shape and glow; colors become kaleidoscopic, and astonishing images unfold. LSD-induced images are sometimes pleasurable and sometimes grotesque. LSD can also influence a user's sense of time so that brief glances at objects are experienced as deep, penetrating, and lengthy examinations, and minutes turn into hours or even days. A bad LSD trip can trigger extreme anxiety, paranoia, and suicidal or homicidal impulses.

LSD's effects on the body can include dizziness, nausea, and tremors. LSD acts primarily on the neurotransmitter serotonin in the brain, although it also can affect dopamine (González-Maeso & Sealfon, 2009). Emotional and cognitive effects may include rapid mood swings and impaired attention and memory. The use of LSD peaked in the 1960s and 1970s, and its consumption has been decreasing in the twenty-first century (Johnston & others, 2016).

Figure 13 summarizes the effects of a variety of other psychoactive drugs.

4. HYPNOSIS

Shelley Thomas, 53 years old, arrived at a London hospital for a 30-minute pelvic surgery. Before the operation, with her hypnotherapist guiding her, Shelley counted backward from 100 and entered a hypnotic trance. Her surgery was performed with no anesthesia (Song, 2006); rather, Shelley relied on hypnosis to harness her mind's powers to overcome pain.

You are probably aware of hypnosis as a procedure. You may have seen a hypnotist on TV or in a nightclub, putting a person into a trance and then perhaps making the individual act like a chicken or pretend to be a contestant on *The Voice* or enact some similarly strange behavior. When we observe someone in such a trance, we might be convinced that hypnosis involves a powerful manipulation of another person's consciousness. What is hypnosis, really? What is going on inside the mind of the person who has been hypnotized? The answer to this question is itself the source of some debate (Elkins & others, 2015; Lynn & others, 2015).

Some psychologists think of hypnosis as an altered state of consciousness (Pekala, 2015). Others believe that it is simply a product of everyday social cognitive processes, such as focused attention, expectations, and a relationship between two people (Lynn

test yourself

1. What are psychoactive drugs, and for what reasons do people use them?
2. Describe what stimulants and depressants are, and give three examples of each.
3. What are hallucinogens? What are two common examples of hallucinogens?

170 CHAPTER 5 States of Consciousness

Drug Classification	Medical Uses	Short-Term Effects	Overdose Effects	Health Risks	Risk of Physical/ Psychological Dependence
Depressants					
Alcohol	Pain relief	Relaxation, depressed brain activity, slowed behavior, reduced inhibitions	Disorientation, loss of consciousness, even death at high blood-alcohol levels	Accidents, brain damage, liver disease, heart disease, ulcers, birth defects	Physical and psychological: moderate
Barbiturates	Sleeping pill	Relaxation, sleep	Breathing difficulty, coma, possible death	Accidents, coma, possible death	Physical and psychological: moderate to high
Tranquilizers	Anxiety reduction	Relaxation, slowed behavior	Breathing difficulty, coma, possible death	Accidents, coma, possible death	Physical: low to moderate Psychological: moderate to high
Opiates (narcotics)	Pain relief	Euphoric feelings, drowsiness, nausea	Convulsions, coma, possible death	Accidents, infectious diseases such as AIDS	Physical: high Psychological: moderate to high
Stimulants					
Amphetamines	Weight control	Increased alertness, excitability; decreased fatigue, irritability	Extreme irritability, feelings of persecu-tion, convulsions	Insomnia, hypertension, malnutrition, possible death	Physical: possible Psychological: moderate to high
Cocaine	Local anesthetic	Increased alertness, excitability, euphoric feelings; decreased fatigue, irritability	Extreme irritability, feelings of persecu-tion, convulsions, cardiac arrest, possible death	Insomnia, hypertension, malnutrition, possible death	Physical: possible Psychological: moderate (oral) to very high (injected or smoked)
MDMA (Ecstasy)	None	Mild amphetamine and hallucinogenic effects; high body temperature and dehydration; sense of well-being and social connectedness	Brain damage, especially memory and thinking	Cardiovascular problems; death	Physical: possible Psychological: moderate
Caffeine	None	Alertness and sense of well-being followed by fatigue	Nervousness, anxiety, disturbed sleep	Possible cardiovascular problems	Physical and psychological: moderate
Nicotine	None	Stimulation, stress reduction, followed by fatigue, anger	Nervousness, disturbed sleep	Cancer and cardio-vascular disease	Physical and psychological: high
Hallucinogens					
LSD	None	Strong hallucinations, distorted time perception	Severe mental disturbance, loss of contact with reality	Accidents	Physical: none Psychological: low
Marijuana*	Treatment for glaucoma, cancer, and chronic pain, as well as stimulating appetite and well-being for individuals with conditions such as AIDS	Euphoric feelings, relaxation, mild hallucinations, time distortion, attention and memory impairment	Fatigue, disoriented behavior	Accidents, respiratory disease	Physical: very low Psychological: moderate

FIGURE 13 Categories of Psychoactive Drugs: Depressants, Stimulants, and Hallucinogens Note that these various drugs have different effects and negative consequences. *Classifying marijuana is difficult, because of its diverse effects.

& others, 2015). In fact, both views are reasonable, and we may define **hypnosis** as an altered state of consciousness or as a psychological state of altered attention and expectation in which the individual is unusually receptive to suggestions. People have used basic hypnotic techniques since the beginning of recorded history, in association with religious ceremonies, magic, and the supernatural.

Today, psychology and medicine recognize hypnosis as a legitimate process, although researchers still have much to learn about how it works. In addition, there is continuing debate about whether hypnosis truly is an altered state of consciousness (Elkins & others, 2015).

● **hypnosis** An altered state of consciousness or a psychological state of altered attention and expectation in which the individual is unusually receptive to suggestions.

The Nature of Hypnosis

When Shelley Thomas was in a hypnotic trance, what exactly was happening in her brain? Patterns of brain activity during the hypnotic state suggest that hypnosis produces a state of consciousness similar to other states of consciousness. For example, individuals in a typical hypnotic state display a predominance of alpha and beta waves, characteristic of people in a relaxed waking state, when monitored by an EEG. In a very deep state of hypnosis the brain can show a predominance of theta waves (Cavallaro & others, 2010; Williams & Gruzelier, 2001). The pattern of brain activation associated with the hypnotic state is not unlike that found when people engage in mental imagery (Faymonville, Boly, & Laureys, 2006). In sum, a hypnotic state is not like being asleep. It is more similar to being relaxed and awake. How does the hypnotist lead people into this state of relaxation and imagery?

THE FOUR STEPS IN HYPNOSIS

Hypnosis involves four steps. The hypnotist

1. Minimizes distractions and makes the person to be hypnotized comfortable.
2. Tells the person to concentrate on something specific, such as an imagined scene or the ticking of a watch.
3. Informs the person what to expect in the hypnotic state, such as relaxation or a pleasant floating sensation.
4. Suggests certain events or feelings he or she knows will occur or observes occurring, such as "Your eyes are getting tired." When the suggested effects occur, the person interprets them as being caused by the hypnotist's suggestion and accepts them as an indication that something is happening. This increase in the person's expectations that the hypnotist will make things happen in the future makes the person even more suggestible.

INDIVIDUAL VARIATIONS IN HYPNOSIS

Some people are more easily hypnotized than others, and some are more strongly influenced by hypnotic suggestions. *Hypnotizability* refers to the extent to which a person's responses *are changed* by being hypnotized (Cojan, Piguet, & Vuilleumier, 2015; Frischholz & others, 2015a). If you have the capacity to immerse yourself deeply in an imaginative activity—listening to a favorite piece of music or reading a novel, for example—you might be a likely candidate for hypnosis (Frischholz & others, 2015b).

Explaining Hypnosis

How does hypnosis have its effects? Contemporary theorists disagree as to whether hypnosis is a divided state of consciousness or simply a learned social behavior (Lynn & others, 2015).

A DIVIDED STATE OF CONSCIOUSNESS

Ernest Hilgard (1977, 1992), in his **divided consciousness view of hypnosis,** proposed that hypnosis involves a special divided state of consciousness, a splitting of consciousness into separate components. One component follows the hypnotist's commands, while another component acts as a "hidden observer."

● **divided consciousness view of hypnosis** Hilgard's view that hypnosis involves a splitting of consciousness into two separate components: one that follows the hypnotist's commands and the other that acts as a "hidden observer."

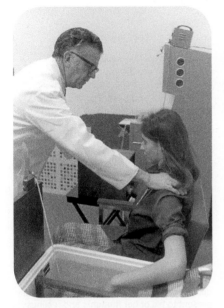

FIGURE 14 Hilgard's Divided Consciousness Experiment Ernest Hilgard tests a participant in the study in which he had individuals place one hand in ice-cold water. © Stanford News Service

● **social cognitive behavior view of hypnosis** The perspective that hypnosis is a normal state in which the hypnotized person behaves the way the individual believes that a hypnotized person should behave.

Hilgard placed one hand of hypnotized individuals in a bucket of ice-cold water and told them that they would not feel pain but that a part of their mind—a hidden part that would be aware of what was going on—could signal any true pain by pressing a key with the hand that was not submerged (Figure 14). The individuals under hypnosis reported afterward that they had not experienced any pain; yet while their hand had been submerged in the ice-cold water, they had pressed the key with their non-submerged hand, and they had pressed it more frequently the longer their hand was in the cold water. Thus, in Hilgard's view, in hypnosis consciousness has a hidden part that stays in contact with reality and feels pain while another part of consciousness feels no pain.

Critics of Hilgard's view suggest that the hidden observer simply demonstrates that the hypnotized person is not in an altered state of consciousness at all. From this perspective, the hidden observer is simply the person himself or herself, having been given permission to admit to the pain that he or she was always feeling (Green & others, 2005). This argument is part of the social cognitive behavior view of hypnosis.

SOCIAL COGNITIVE BEHAVIOR

Some psychologists are skeptical that hypnosis is an altered state of consciousness (Lynn, Laurence, & Kirsch, 2015). In the **social cognitive behavior view of hypnosis,** hypnosis is a normal state in which the hypnotized person behaves the way the individual believes that a hypnotized person should behave. The social cognitive perspective frames the important questions about hypnosis around cognitive factors—the attitudes, expectations, and beliefs of good hypnotic participants—and around the powerful social context in which hypnosis occurs. Individuals being hypnotized surrender their responsibility to the hypnotist and follow the hypnotist's suggestions; and they have expectations about what hypnosis is supposed to be like.

Experts have continued to debate whether hypnosis is indeed an altered state of consciousness or simply a reaction to a special social situation (Kihlstrom, 2005). Although there may be no consensus about what hypnosis is, scientists use hypnosis to explore the brain and its functions, and health professionals have begun to apply this powerful technique to a number of problems.

Uses of Hypnosis

As psychologists' interest in studying consciousness has grown, hypnosis has emerged as a useful tool (Tomé-Pires & Miró, 2012). Some researchers employ hypnosis in a way similar to transcranial magnetic stimulation (described in the chapter "Biological Foundations of Behavior"), to experimentally dampen brain processes (Cox & Bryant, 2008). Combining hypnosis with brain imaging allows researchers to understand both the effects of hypnosis itself and the brain's functioning (Oakley & Halligan, 2011).

Beyond its role in basic research, hypnosis has been applied to a variety of problems. In the United States, practitioners of hypnosis use the technique to treat alcoholism, somnambulism, depression, suicidal tendencies, post-traumatic stress disorder, overeating, diabetes, smoking, and various types of pain (Abdeshahi & others, 2013; Madden & others, 2012; Tahiri & others, 2012). Whether hypnosis actually works for these diverse problems remains debatable (Brown, 2007). Individuals in these treatment programs rarely achieve dramatic results unless they are already motivated to change. Hypnosis is most effective when combined with psychotherapy (Rossi, 2009). Psychotherapy, a major focus in the chapter "Therapies", is a form of nonmedical treatment in which a professional seeks to help someone overcome life difficulties.

A long history of research and practice has clearly demonstrated that hypnosis can reduce the experience of pain (Elkins, Johnson, & Fisher, 2012). Brain-imaging studies show that hypnosis appears to have widespread effects on the brain's pain network (Del Casale & others, 2015). A fascinating study examined the pain perceptions of hypnotized individuals, with the goal of changing their pain threshold. In that study, the brains of participants were monitored while they received painful electrical shocks (rated 8 or higher on a 1 to 10 pain scale) (Schulz-Stübner & others, 2004). Those who were hypnotized to find the shocks less painful did rate them as lower in pain (giving them a 3 or less). The brain-scanning results were most interesting: The subcortical brain areas (the brain stem and midbrain) of the hypnotized patients responded the same as those of the patients who were not hypnotized, suggesting that these brain structures recognized the painful stimulation. However, the sensory cortex was not activated in the hypnotized patients, indicating that although they sensed pain on some level, they were never conscious of it. In essence, the "ouch" signal never made it to awareness.

In summary, although the nature of hypnosis remains a mystery, evidence is increasing that hypnosis can play a role in a variety of health contexts, and it can influence the brain in fascinating ways. For psychologists, part of the ambiguity about the definition of hypnosis comes from the fact that it has been studied in specific social contexts, involving a hypnotist. It is also possible, however, to experience altered states of consciousness without these special circumstances, as we next consider.

5. CONSCIOUSNESS AND HEALTH AND WELLNESS: MEDITATION

The altered consciousness of hypnosis can also be achieved through meditation. **Meditation** involves attaining a peaceful state of mind in which thoughts are not occupied by worry. The meditator is mindfully present to his or her thoughts and feelings but is not consumed by them.

There are many types of meditative practice (Kok, Waugh, & Fredrickson, 2013; Lumma, Kok, & Singer, 2015). They share at least two characteristics: *focused attention* and *open monitoring*. Focused attention means bringing awareness to one's inner life and attending to one's thoughts; it is being psychologically present as one thinks. Open monitoring refers to the capacity to observe one's thoughts as they happen without getting preoccupied by them. That is, through open monitoring, the person is able to reflect without becoming attached to a particular thought or idea. Let's take a closer look at two types of meditation: mindfulness meditation and lovingkindness meditation.

Mindfulness Meditation

Melissa Munroe, a Canadian woman diagnosed with Hodgkin lymphoma (a cancer of the immune system), was tormented by excruciating pain (Wijesiri, 2005). Seeking ways to cope with the agony, Munroe enrolled in a meditation program. She was skeptical at first. "What I didn't realize," she said, "is that if people have ever found themselves taking a walk in the countryside or in the forest or on a nice pleasant autumn day . . . and find themselves in a contemplative state, that's a form of meditation."

Munroe worked hard to use meditation to control her pain. Interestingly, she found that the way to handle her pain was not by trying to avoid thinking about it; instead, she harnessed the power of her mind to concentrate on the pain.

Using *mindfulness meditation,* a technique practiced by yoga enthusiasts and Buddhist monks, Munroe focused on her pain. By doing so, she was able to isolate the pain from her emotional response to it and to her cancer diagnosis. She grew to see her physical discomfort as bearable.

Munroe's success shows that contrary to what a non-meditator might think, meditation is not about avoiding one's thoughts. Indeed, the effort involved in avoidance steers the person away from the contemplative state. Munroe described her thoughts as like people striding by her on the street, walking in the other direction; she explained, "They come closer and closer, then they pass you by." Her comment reflects the open monitoring that is common to many forms of meditation.

Jon Kabat-Zinn (2006, 2009) has pioneered the use of meditation techniques in medical settings. Research by Kabat-Zinn and colleagues has demonstrated the beneficial effects of mindfulness meditation for a variety of conditions, including depression, panic attacks, and anxiety (Miller, Fletcher, & Kabat-Zinn, 1995), chronic pain (Kabat-Zinn, Lipworth, & Burney, 1985), and stress and the skin condition psoriasis (Kabat-Zinn & others, 1998). Many of these effects have also been shown to be long-lasting.

test yourself

1. What is hypnosis?
2. What are the four steps in hypnosis?
3. Name and describe two different theories about hypnosis.

● **meditation** The attainment of a peaceful state of mind in which thoughts are not occupied by worry; the meditator is mindfully present to his or her thoughts and feelings but is not consumed by them.

Among those practicing meditation are Zen monks who explore the Buddha-nature at the center of their being.

Richard Davidson and colleagues (including Jon Kabat-Zinn) studied the brain and immune system changes that might underlie the health and wellness effects of meditation (Davidson & others, 2003). They performed MRIs on the brains of individuals who were in a standard eight-week meditation-training program. After the training program and as compared to a control group, those in the meditation program reported reduced anxiety and fewer negative emotions. Furthermore, brain scans revealed that these individuals showed increased activation in the left hemisphere. In addition, the meditators showed better immune system response to a flu vaccine (Davidson & others, 2003; Kabat-Zinn & Davidson, 2012). Still, a great deal more research is needed to identify how mindfulness meditation is reflected in the brain (Tang, Hölzel, & Posner, 2015).

Lovingkindness Meditation

Another popular form of meditation is called *lovingkindness meditation*. The goal of this meditative practice is the development of loving acceptance of oneself and others. Lovingkindness fosters feelings of warmth, friendliness, compassion, and appreciative joy. At its highest level, the person experiences a sense of equanimity, or a feeling of openness to his or her thoughts and feelings without becoming preoccupied with them (Zeng & others, 2015). In lovingkindness meditation, the meditator begins by developing warm, accepting feelings toward himself or herself. Then, the person moves to meditate about a very close other, such as a family member one loves and respects. Over time, lovingkindness meditation widens to include an ever-broadening circle of people.

Research shows that lovingkindness meditation leads to heightened feelings of social connection, positive emotions (Engen & Singer, 2015), and better coping with stress (Hanley, Garland, & Black, 2014). People who engage in lovingkindness meditation enjoy personal benefits. Might this type of contemplative practice also have a positive impact on the social world? A recent study suggests that this form of meditation may help to combat prejudice—that is, unjustified negative views toward an individual based on his or her membership in a group. To read about the study, see the Intersection.

The Meditative State of Mind

What actually is the meditative state of mind? As a physiological state, meditation shows qualities of sleep *and* wakefulness, yet it is distinct from both. You may have experienced a state called *hypnagogic reverie*—an overwhelming feeling of wellness right before you fall asleep, the sense that everything is going to work out. Meditation has been compared to this relaxed sense that all is well (Friedman, Myers, & Benson, 1998).

In a study of Zen meditators, researchers examined what happens when people switch from their normal waking state to a meditative state (Ritskes & others, 2003). Using fMRI, the experimenters obtained images of the brain before and after the participants entered the meditative state. They found that the switch to meditation involved initial increases in activation in the basal ganglia and prefrontal cortex (the now familiar area that is often activated during consciousness). However, and interestingly, they also found that these initial activations led to decreases in the anterior cingulate, the brain area associated with conscious awareness and acts of will. These results provide a picture of the physical events of the brain that are connected with the somewhat paradoxical state of meditation—controlling one's thoughts in order to let go of the need to control.

Getting Started with Meditation

Would you like to experience the meditative state? If so, you can probably reach that state by following some simple instructions:

- Find a quiet place and a comfortable chair.
- Sit upright in the chair, rest your chin comfortably on your chest, and place your arms in your lap. Close your eyes.

Regular meditation can help you to clarify your goals and purpose in life, strengthen your values, and improve your outlook.

© Jules Frazier/Getty Images

INTERSECTION

Consciousness and Social Psychology: Can Lovingkindness Meditation Reduce Prejudice?

You are probably familiar with various forms of prejudice, such as racism (negative attitudes about people based on their skin color or ethnic background). And you are probably also aware that in contemporary society, it is considered offensive to hold racist views.

Interestingly, the concepts of controlled and automatic processes examined throughout this chapter apply to the topic of prejudice as well. Knowing that it is inappropriate to be prejudiced, people are often unwilling to admit that they hold such views if asked directly, reflecting controlled processing. Prejudice also has an automatic component. This component involves the ways we evaluate members of different groups, rapidly and without thought. These automatic evaluations are less affected by people's concerns about making a good impression.

Social psychologists have devised ways to measure such automatic prejudice by examining how quickly people are able to make associations between different groups (such as African Americans versus European Americans) and positive and negative stimuli (for instance, flowers versus spiders). When people are quicker to associate a group with negative compared to positive stimuli, they have shown *implicit bias*, an automatic form of prejudice. People can be high in implicit bias without knowing it, yet this bias predicts the ways people behave when interacting with members of other groups.

Reducing the tensions that exist among members of different groups is an important social goal. Could meditation have a role to play in achieving that goal? Recent studies suggest the answer to that question is yes (Parks, Birtel, & Crisp, 2014; Stell & Farsides, 2015).

In one of the first studies to test the possibility that lovingkindness mediation might reduce implicit prejudice, participants were assigned randomly to one of three groups (Kang, Gray, & Dovidio, 2014):

- The experimental group (lovingkindness practice): They attended six weekly meetings to engage in lovingkindness training and meditation and meditated on their own, 20 minutes a day, five days a week.

- Active control group (lovingkindness discussion): They met weekly but did not meditate.

© Ariel Skelley/Blend Images/Getty Images

- "Wait list" control group: They simply completed the dependent measures.

None of the participants knew that the study had anything to do with prejudice. Implicit measures of attitudes toward African Americans and homeless people were taken before the intervention and again afterward. Results showed that the lovingkindness meditation practice group showed lower implicit bias toward both African Americans and the homeless following the intervention (Kang, Gray, & Dovidio, 2014). Neither of the control groups showed changes in implicit bias.

What other social benefits might come from meditation?

These findings are remarkable because they show that, even without participants knowing that the study was about prejudice, meditation reduced bias toward two quite different groups. Indeed, lovingkindness meditation reduced biases that participants might not even have known they had. This research shows how activity inside the human mind may have important and positive implications for social behavior.

- Now focus on your breathing. Every time you inhale and every time you exhale, pay attention to the sensations of air flowing through your body, the feeling of your lungs filling and emptying.

- After you have focused on several breaths, begin to repeat silently to yourself a single word every time you breathe out. You can make a word up, use the word *one*, or try a word associated with an emotion you want to produce, such as *trust, love, patience*, or *happy*. Experiment with several different words to see which one works best for you.

- If you find that thoughts are intruding and you are no longer attending to your breathing, refocus on your breathing and say your chosen word each time you exhale.

176   CHAPTER 5   **States of Consciousness**

After you have practiced this exercise for 10 to 15 minutes, twice a day, every day for two weeks, you will be ready for a shortened version. If you notice that you are experiencing stressful thoughts or circumstances, simply meditate, on the spot, for several minutes. If you are in public, you do not have to close your eyes; just fix your gaze on a nearby object, attend to your breathing, and say your word silently every time you exhale.

Meditation is an age-old practice. Without explicitly mentioning meditation, some religions advocate related practices such as daily prayer and peaceful introspection. Whether the practice involves praying over rosary beads, chanting before a Buddhist shrine, or taking a moment to commune with nature, a contemplative state clearly has broad appeal and conveys many benefits (Kabat-Zinn & Davidson, 2012). Current research on the contemplative state suggests that there are good reasons why human beings have been harnessing its beneficial powers for thousands of years.

test yourself

1. What does the meditator experience during meditation?
2. Define mindfulness meditation and lovingkindness meditation.
3. On what body process does a meditator focus, and how is that focus maintained?

SUMMARY

1. THE NATURE OF CONSCIOUSNESS

Consciousness is the awareness of external events and internal sensations, including awareness of the self and thoughts about experiences. Most experts agree that consciousness is likely distributed across the brain. A global brain workspace that includes the association areas and prefrontal lobes is believed to play an important role in consciousness.

William James described the mind as a stream of consciousness. Consciousness occurs at different levels of awareness that include higher-level awareness (controlled processes and selective attention), lower-level awareness (automatic processes and daydreaming), altered states of consciousness (produced by drugs, trauma, fatigue, and other factors), subconscious awareness (waking subconscious awareness, sleep, and dreams), and no awareness (unconscious thought).

Psychologists refer to our understanding of other people's consciousness as theory of mind. Theory of mind is important to social capacities such as empathy, and some experts believe that deficits in theory of mind functioning are related to autism.

2. SLEEP AND DREAMS

The biological rhythm that regulates the daily sleep/wake cycle is the circadian rhythm. The part of the brain that keeps our biological clocks synchronized is the suprachiasmatic nucleus, a small structure in the hypothalamus that registers light. Biological clocks can become desynchronized by jet travel and work shifts; however, there are some helpful strategies for resetting the biological clock.

We need sleep for physical restoration, adaptation, growth, and memory. Research studies increasingly reveal that people do not function optimally when they are sleep-deprived.

Stages of sleep correspond to massive electrophysiological changes that occur in the brain and that can be assessed by an EEG. The human sleep cycle is defined by stages. In stage W, the person is awake. In the non-REM stages (stages N1 to N3), the person does not experience rapid eye movement but moves from light sleep to deep sleep. Stage N3 is the deepest sleep (also called slow wave sleep). Most dreaming occurs during stage R or REM sleep. A sleep cycle lasts about 90 to 100 minutes and recurs several times during the night. The REM stage lasts longer toward the end of a night's sleep.

The sleep stages are associated with distinct patterns of neurotransmitter activity. Levels of the neurotransmitters serotonin, norepinephrine, and acetylcholine decrease as the sleep cycle progresses from stage N1 through stage N3. Stage R, REM sleep, begins when the reticular formation raises the level of acetylcholine.

Sleep plays a role in a large number of diseases and disorders. Neurons that control sleep interact closely with the immune system, and when our body is fighting infection, our cells produce a substance that makes us sleepy. Individuals with depression often have sleep problems.

Many Americans suffer from chronic, long-term sleep disorders that can impair normal daily functioning. These include insomnia, sleepwalking and sleep talking, nightmares and night terrors, narcolepsy, and sleep apnea.

Contrary to popular belief, most dreams are not bizarre or strange. Freud thought that dreams express unconscious wishes in disguise. Cognitive theory attempts to explain dreaming in terms of the same concepts that are used in studying the waking mind. According to activation-synthesis theory, dreaming occurs when the cerebral cortex synthesizes neural signals emanating from activity in the lower part of the brain. In this view, the rising level of acetylcholine during REM sleep plays a role in neural activity in the brain stem that the cerebral cortex tries to make sense of.

3. PSYCHOACTIVE DRUGS

Psychoactive drugs act on the nervous system to alter states of consciousness, modify perceptions, and change moods. Some people are attracted to these drugs because they seem to help them deal with difficult life situations.

Addictive drugs activate the brain's reward system by increasing dopamine concentration. The reward pathway involves the ventral tegmental area and nucleus accumbens. The abuse of psychoactive drugs can lead to tolerance, psychological and physical dependence, and addiction—a pattern of behavior characterized by a preoccupation with using a drug and securing its supply.

Depressants slow down mental and physical activity. Among the most widely used depressants are alcohol, barbiturates, tranquilizers, and opiates.

After caffeine, alcohol is the most widely used drug in the United States. The high rate of alcohol abuse by high school and college students is especially alarming. Alcoholism is a disorder that involves long-term, repeated, uncontrolled, compulsive, and excessive use of alcoholic beverages that impairs the drinker's health and work and social relationships.

Stimulants increase the central nervous system's activity and include caffeine, nicotine, amphetamines, cocaine, and MDMA (Ecstasy). Hallucinogens modify a person's perceptual experiences and produce visual images that are not real. Marijuana has a mild hallucinogenic effect; LSD has a strong one.

4. HYPNOSIS

Hypnosis is a psychological state or possibly altered attention and awareness in which the individual is unusually receptive to suggestions. The hypnotic state is different from a sleep state, as EEG recordings confirm. Inducing hypnosis involves four basic steps, beginning with minimizing distractions and making the person feel comfortable and ending with the hypnotist's suggesting certain events or feelings that he or she knows will occur or observes occurring.

There are substantial individual variations in people's susceptibility to hypnosis. Two theories have been proposed to explain hypnosis. In Hilgard's divided consciousness view, hypnosis involves a divided state of consciousness, a splitting of consciousness into separate components. One component follows the hypnotist's commands; the other acts as a hidden observer. In the social cognitive behavior view, hypnotized individuals behave the way they believe hypnotized individuals are expected to behave.

5. CONSCIOUSNESS AND HEALTH AND WELLNESS: MEDITATION

Meditation refers to a state of quiet reflection; the practice has benefits for a wide range of psychological and physical illnesses. Meditation can also benefit the body's immune system. Mindfulness meditation is a powerful tool for managing life's problems. Lovingkindness meditation has both emotional and social benefits. Research using fMRI suggests that meditation allows an individual to control his or her thoughts in order to "let go" of the need to control. Seeking times of quiet contemplation can have a positive impact on our ability to cope with life's ups and downs.

key *terms*

activation-synthesis theory of dreaming	consciousness	manifest content	social cognitive behavior view of hypnosis
addiction	controlled processes	meditation	stimulants
alcoholism	depressants	opiates	stream of consciousness
automatic processes	divided consciousness view of hypnosis	physical dependence	suprachiasmatic nucleus (SCN)
barbiturates	executive function	psychoactive drugs	theory of mind
biological rhythms	hallucinogens	psychological dependence	tolerance
circadian rhythms	hypnosis	reticular activating system	tranquilizers
cognitive theory of dreaming	latent content	REM sleep	unconscious thought
		sleep	

apply your *knowledge*

1. Take 20 minutes and document your stream of consciousness. Just write whatever comes into your mind for this period. When you have finished, take a close look at what your stream of consciousness reveals. What topics came up that surprised you? Are the thoughts and feelings you wrote down reflective of your daily life? Your important goals and values? What is *not* mentioned in your stream of consciousness that is surprising to you?

2. Keep a sleep journal for several nights. Compare your sleep patterns with those described in the text. Do you have a sleep debt? If so, which stages of sleep are you most likely missing? Does a good night's sleep affect your behavior? Keep a record of your mood and energy levels after a short night's sleep and then after you have had at least 8 hours of sleep in one night. What changes do you notice, and how do they compare with the changes predicted by research on sleep deprivation described in the chapter?

3. Keep a dream diary for a few days. When you wake up in the morning, immediately write down all that you can remember about your dreams. Have you had many bizarre or unusual dreams? Are there themes in your dreams that reflect the concerns of your daily life? Compare the content of your dream diary with the stream-of-consciousness document you produced for question 1, above. Are there similarities in the content of your relaxed, waking mind and your dreams?

4. Go on a caffeine hunt. Check out the ingredients for the beverages, painkillers, and snacks you typically consume. Which contain caffeine? Are you surprised how much caffeine you ingest regularly?

5. Try out mindfulness meditation. Following the guidelines outlined in "Getting Started with Meditation", meditate once a day for a week. Keep track of your mood, health, and behaviors over the course of the week. How did mindfulness meditation work for you?

CHAPTER 6

Learning

Coach to the Rescue!

Elle Shaheen was diagnosed with type I diabetes at the age of 8. For the next five years, she and her parents felt constant worry. Elle's blood-glucose level might drop too low, leaving her vulnerable to a seizure or coma. Then, when she was 13, Elle's family adopted Coach, a yellow lab, who after almost 2,000 hours of training, had developed a nose for insulin (Shaheen, 2015). Coach has become Elle's trusty companion, specially trained to "alert" when, based on scent, he detects that Elle's glucose level is dangerously low. Coach's abilities are especially helpful at night, when a sleeping Elle might not notice any symptoms at all.

Many individuals with diabetes, which involves problems in regulating insulin and glucose in the blood, are not aware when their glucose levels are too low. Dogs can be trained to use their amazing sense of smell to sound an alarm when blood-glucose levels drop to a dangerous point.

Coach is just one of the estimated 30,000 assistance dogs working in the United States (Linebaugh, 2012). Service dogs are trained to aid people with a variety of disabilities. Their skills are amazing. They provide sound discrimination for the hearing impaired, assist those with limited mobility, and retrieve items; they locate people, bathrooms, elevators, and lost cell phones. They open and close doors, help people dress and undress, flush toilets, and even put clothes in a washer and dryer.

Truly, service dogs are highly skilled professionals. Anyone who has a lazy mutt at home might wonder how it is possible for dogs to acquire these skills. Service dogs are trained to perform these complex acts using the principles that psychologists have uncovered in studying the processes that underlie learning, the focus of this chapter. ●

PREVIEW

This chapter begins by defining learning and sketching out its main types: associative learning and observational learning. We then turn attention to two types of associative learning—classical conditioning and operant conditioning—followed by a close look at observational learning. Next, we consider the role of cognitive processes in learning before finally examining biological, cultural, and psychological constraints on learning. The close of the chapter looks at the role of learning in human health and wellness.

1. TYPES OF LEARNING

©Hello Lovely/Blend Images/Getty Images

● **learning** A systematic, relatively permanent change in behavior that occurs through experience.

● **behaviorism** A theory of learning that focuses solely on observable behaviors, discounting the importance of mental activity such as thinking, wishing, and hoping.

Learning anything new involves change. Once you learn the alphabet, it does not leave you; it becomes part of a "new you" who has been changed through the process of learning. Similarly, once you learn how to drive a car, you do not have to go through the process again at a later time. When you first arrived on campus at your school, you might have spent a lot of time lost. But once you got the lay of the land, you were able to navigate just fine. And perhaps you have a particular food that you know to avoid, because you once ate it, and it made you sick.

By way of experience, too, you may have learned that you have to study to do well on a test, that there usually is an opening act at a rock concert, and that there is a technique to playing a guitar chord. Putting these pieces together, we arrive at a definition of **learning:** a systematic, relatively permanent change in behavior that occurs through experience.

If someone were to ask you what you learned in class today, you might mention new ideas you heard about, lists you memorized, or concepts you mastered. However, how would you define learning if you could not refer to unobservable mental processes? You might follow the lead of behavioral psychologists. **Behaviorism** is a theory of learning that focuses solely on observable behaviors, discounting the importance of mental activity such as thinking, wishing, and hoping. Psychologists who examine learning from a behavioral perspective define learning as relatively stable, observable changes in behavior. The behavioral approach has emphasized general laws that guide behavior change and make sense of some of the puzzling aspects of human life (Greenwood, 2015).

Behaviorism maintains that the principles of learning are the same whether we are talking about humans or nonhuman animals. Because of the influence of behaviorism, psychologists' understanding of learning started with studies of rats, cats, pigeons, and even raccoons. A century of research on learning in animals and in humans suggests that many of the principles generated initially in research on animals also apply to humans (Burgos, 2015; Olmstead & Kuhlmeier, 2015).

In this chapter we look at two types of learning: associative learning and observational learning. Let's briefly review each of these before getting into the details.

● **associative learning** Learning that occurs when an organism makes a connection, or an association, between two events.

First, **associative learning** occurs when an organism makes a connection, or an association, between two events. *Conditioning* is the process of learning these associations. There are two types of conditioning—classical and operant—both of which have been studied by behaviorists (McSweeney & Murphy, 2014).

In *classical conditioning,* organisms learn the association between two stimuli. As a result of this association, organisms learn to anticipate events. For example, lightning is associated with thunder and regularly precedes it. Thus, when we see lightning, we anticipate that we will hear thunder soon afterward. In *operant conditioning,* organisms learn the association between a behavior and a consequence, such as a reward. As a result of this association, organisms learn to increase behaviors that are followed by rewards and to decrease behaviors that are followed by punishment. For example, children are likely to repeat their good manners if their parents reward them with candy after they have shown good manners. Also, if children's bad manners provoke scolding words and

Classical Conditioning	Operant Conditioning

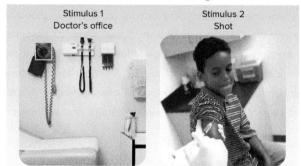

| Stimulus 1 | Stimulus 2 | Behavior | Consequences |
| Doctor's office | Shot | | |

FIGURE 1 Associative Learning: Comparing Classical and Operant Conditioning (*first*) In this example of classical conditioning, a child associates a doctor's office (stimulus 1) with getting a painful injection (stimulus 2). (*second*) In this example of operant conditioning, performing well in a swimming competition (behavior) becomes associated with getting awards (consequences).

(first) © PunchStock; (second) © Photodisc Collection/Getty Images; (third) © Ryan McVay/Getty Images; (fourth) © Photodisc Inc./Getty Images

harsh glances by parents, the children are less likely to repeat the bad manners. Figure 1 compares classical and operant conditioning.

Much of what we learn, however, is not a result of direct consequences but rather of exposure to models performing a behavior or skill (Legare & Nielsen, 2015; Meltzoff & Williamson, 2013). For instance, as you watch someone shoot baskets, you get a sense of how the shots are made. This brings us to our second type of learning: observational learning. **Observational learning** occurs when a person observes and imitates another's behavior. Observational learning is a common way that people learn in educational and other settings. Observational learning is different from the associative learning described by behaviorism because it relies on mental processes: The learner has to pay attention, remember, and reproduce what the model did. Observational learning is especially important to human beings. In fact, watching other people is another way in which human infants acquire skills.

Human infants differ from baby monkeys in their strong reliance on imitation (Bandura, 2009a, 2011a). After watching an adult model perform a task, a baby monkey will figure out its own way to do it, but a human infant will do exactly what the model did. Imitation may be the human baby's way to solve the huge problem it faces: to learn the vast amount of cultural knowledge that is part of human life. Many of our behaviors are rather arbitrary. Why do we clap to show approval or wave hello or bye-bye? The human infant has a lot to learn and may be well served to follow the old adage, "When in Rome, do as the Romans do."

Learning applies to many areas of acquiring new behaviors, skills, and knowledge (Barron & others, 2015). Our focus in this chapter is on the two types of associative learning—classical conditioning and operant conditioning—and on observational learning.

● **observational learning** Learning that occurs through observing and imitating another's behavior.

test yourself

1. What is associative learning?
2. What is conditioning? What two types of conditioning have behavioral psychologists studied?
3. What is observational learning? Give two examples of it.

2. CLASSICAL CONDITIONING

Early one morning, Bob is in the shower. While he showers, his wife enters the bathroom and flushes the toilet. Scalding hot water suddenly bursts down on Bob, causing him to yell in pain. The next day, Bob is back for his morning shower, and once again his wife enters the bathroom and flushes the toilet. Panicked by the sound of the toilet flushing, Bob yelps in fear and jumps out of the shower stream. Bob's panic at the sound of the toilet illustrates the learning process of **classical conditioning,** in which a neutral stimulus (the sound of a toilet flushing) becomes associated with an innately meaningful stimulus (the pain of scalding hot water) and acquires the capacity to elicit a similar response (panic).

● **classical conditioning** Learning process in which a neutral stimulus becomes associated with an innately meaningful stimulus and acquires the capacity to elicit a similar response.

Pavlov's Studies

Even before beginning this course, you might have heard about Pavlov's dogs. The work of the Russian physiologist Ivan Pavlov is well known. Still, it is easy to take its true significance for granted. Importantly, Pavlov demonstrated that neutral aspects of the environment can attain the capacity to evoke responses through pairing with other stimuli and that bodily processes can be influenced by environmental cues.

In the early 1900s, Pavlov was interested in the way the body digests food. In his experiments, he routinely placed meat powder in a dog's mouth, causing the dog to salivate. By accident, Pavlov noticed that the meat powder was not the only stimulus that caused the dog to drool. The dog salivated in response to a number of stimuli associated with the food, such as the sight of the food dish, the sight of the individual who brought the food into the room, and the sound of the door closing when the food arrived. Pavlov recognized that the dog's association of these sights and sounds with the food was an important type of learning, which came to be called *classical conditioning*.

Pavlov wanted to know *why* the dog salivated in reaction to various sights and sounds before eating the meat powder. He observed that the dog's behavior included both unlearned and learned components. The unlearned part of classical conditioning is based on the fact that some stimuli automatically produce certain responses apart from any prior learning; in other words, they are inborn (innate). *Reflexes* are such automatic stimulus–response connections. They include salivation in response to food, nausea in response to spoiled food, shivering in response to low temperature, coughing in response to throat congestion, pupil constriction in response to light, and withdrawal in response to pain.

An **unconditioned stimulus (US)** is a stimulus that produces a response without prior learning; food was the US in Pavlov's experiments. An **unconditioned response (UR)** is an unlearned reaction that is automatically elicited by the US. Unconditioned responses are involuntary; they happen in response to a stimulus without conscious effort. In Pavlov's experiment, drooling in response to food was the UR. In the case of Bob and the flushing toilet, Bob's learning and experience did not cause him to shriek when the hot water hit his body. His cry of pain was unlearned and occurred automatically. The hot water was the US, and Bob's panic was the UR.

In classical conditioning, a **conditioned stimulus (CS)** is a previously neutral stimulus that eventually elicits a conditioned response after being paired with the unconditioned stimulus. The **conditioned response (CR)** is the learned response to the conditioned

unconditioned stimulus (US) A stimulus that produces a response without prior learning.

unconditioned response (UR) An unlearned reaction that is automatically elicited by the unconditioned stimulus.

conditioned stimulus (CS) A previously neutral stimulus that eventually elicits a conditioned response after being paired with the unconditioned stimulus.

conditioned response (CR) The learned response to the conditioned stimulus that occurs after conditioned stimulus–unconditioned stimulus pairing.

Pavlov (the white-bearded gentleman in the center) is shown demonstrating the nature of classical conditioning to students at the Military Medical Academy in Russia.
© Universal Images Group/Getty Images

Before Conditioning

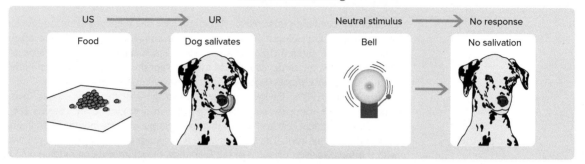

Conditioning

After Conditioning

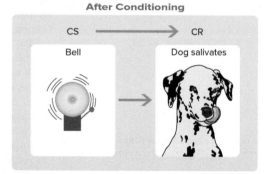

FIGURE 2   **Pavlov's Classical Conditioning** In one experiment, Pavlov presented a neutral stimulus (bell) just before an unconditioned stimulus (food). The neutral stimulus became a conditioned stimulus by being paired with the unconditioned stimulus. Subsequently, the conditioned stimulus (bell) by itself was able to elicit the dog's salivation.

stimulus that occurs after CS–US pairing (Pavlov, 1927). Sometimes conditioned responses are quite similar to unconditioned responses, but typically they are not as strong.

In studying a dog's response to various stimuli associated with meat powder, Pavlov rang a bell before giving meat powder to the dog. Until then, ringing the bell did not have a particular effect on the dog, except perhaps to wake the dog from a nap. The bell was a *neutral* stimulus, meaning that in the dog's world, this stimulus did not have any signal value at all. Prior to being paired with the meat powder, the bell was meaningless. However, the dog began to associate the sound of the bell with the food and salivated when it heard the bell. The bell had become a conditioned (learned) stimulus (CS), and salivation was now a conditioned response (CR). In the case of Bob's interrupted shower, the sound of the toilet flushing was the CS, and panicking was the CR after the scalding water (US) and the flushing sound (CS) were paired. Figure 2 summarizes how classical conditioning works.

Researchers have shown that salivation can be used as a conditioned response not only in dogs and humans but also in, of all things, cockroaches (Nishino & others, 2015; Watanabe & Mizunami, 2007). These researchers paired the smell of peppermint (the CS, which was applied to the cockroaches' antennae) with sugary water (the US). Cockroaches naturally salivate (the UR) in response to sugary foods, and after repeated pairings between peppermint smell and sugary water, the cockroaches salivated in response to the smell of peppermint (the CR). When they collected and measured the cockroach saliva, the researchers found that the cockroaches had slobbered over that smell for 2 minutes.

ACQUISITION

Whether it is human beings, dogs, or cockroaches, the first part of classical conditioning is called acquisition. **Acquisition** is the initial learning of the connection between the US and CS when these two stimuli are paired (as with the smell of peppermint and the sugary water). During acquisition, the CS is repeatedly presented followed by the US. Eventually, the CS will produce a response. Note that classical conditioning is a type of

● **acquisition** The initial learning of the connection between the unconditioned stimulus and the conditioned stimulus when these two stimuli are paired.

learning that occurs without awareness or effort, based on the presentation of two stimuli together. For this pairing to work, however, two important factors must be present: contiguity and contingency.

Contiguity simply means that the CS and US are presented very close together in time—even a mere fraction of a second (Gottlieb & Begej, 2014). In Pavlov's work, if the bell had rung 20 minutes before the presentation of the food, the dog probably would not have associated the bell with the food. However, pairing the CS and US close together in time is not all that is needed for conditioning to occur. Imagine that the bell not only rings just before the food is delivered, but it also rings many times when the food is not on its way. In such a situation, the dog would not associate the bell with the food, and no learning would occur. Why? Because the bell does not serve as a signal for the food.

Contingency means that the CS must not only precede the US closely in time, but it must serve as a reliable indicator that the US is on its way (Rescorla, 1966, 1988, 2009). To get a sense of the importance of contingency, imagine that the dog in Pavlov's experiment is exposed to a ringing bell at random times all day long. Whenever the dog receives food, the delivery of the food always immediately follows a bell ring. However, in this situation, the dog will not associate the bell with the food, because the bell is not a reliable signal that food is coming: It rings a lot when no food is on the way. Whereas *contiguity* refers to the fact that the CS and US occur close together in time, *contingency* refers to the information value of the CS relative to the US. When contingency is present, the CS provides a systematic signal that the US is on its way (Kringelbach & Berridge, 2015).

GENERALIZATION AND DISCRIMINATION

Pavlov found that the dog salivated in response not only to the tone of the bell but also to other sounds, such as a whistle. These sounds had not been paired with the unconditioned stimulus of the food. Pavlov discovered that the more similar the noise was to the original sound of the bell, the stronger the dog's salivary flow.

Generalization in classical conditioning is the tendency of a new stimulus that is similar to the original conditioned stimulus to elicit a response that is similar to the conditioned response (Dunsmoor & Murphy, 2015; Dunsmoor & Paz, 2015).

Generalization has value in preventing learning from being tied to specific stimuli. Once we learn the association between a given CS (say, flashing police lights behind our car) and a particular US (the dread associated with being pulled over), we do not have to learn it all over again when a similar stimulus presents itself (a police car with its siren howling as it cruises directly behind our car).

Stimulus generalization is not always beneficial. For example, the cat that generalizes from a harmless minnow to a dangerous piranha has a major problem; therefore, it is important to also discriminate among stimuli. **Discrimination** in classical conditioning is the process of learning to respond to certain stimuli and not others. To produce discrimination, Pavlov gave food to the dog only after ringing the bell and not after any other sounds. In this way, the dog learned to distinguish between the bell and other sounds.

EXTINCTION AND SPONTANEOUS RECOVERY

After conditioning the dog to salivate at the sound of a bell, Pavlov rang the bell repeatedly in a single session and did not give the dog any food. Eventually the dog stopped salivating. This result is **extinction,** which in classical conditioning is the weakening of the conditioned response when the unconditioned stimulus is absent (Dunsmoor & others, 2015; Vurbic & Boutin, 2014). Without continued association with the unconditioned stimulus (US), the conditioned stimulus (CS) loses its power to produce the conditioned response (CR). You might notice that although extinction weakens the link between the CS and the presence of the US, it can also be thought of as a second type of learning: learning that the CS means the US is *not* coming (Schyns & others, 2016).

Extinction is not always the end of a conditioned response. The day after Pavlov extinguished the conditioned salivation to the sound of a bell, he took the dog to the laboratory and rang the bell but still did not give the dog any meat powder. The dog salivated, indicating that an extinguished response can spontaneously recur. **Spontaneous recovery** is

● **generalization (in classical conditioning)** The tendency of a new stimulus that is similar to the original conditioned stimulus to elicit a response that is similar to the conditioned response.

● **discrimination (in classical conditioning)** The process of learning to respond to certain stimuli and not others.

● **extinction (in classical conditioning)** The weakening of the conditioned response when the unconditioned stimulus is absent.

● **spontaneous recovery** The process in classical conditioning by which a conditioned response can recur after a time delay, without further conditioning.

psychological *inquiry*

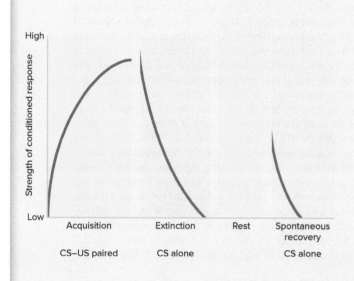

High

Strength of conditioned response

Low

Acquisition   Extinction   Rest   Spontaneous recovery

CS–US paired   CS alone   CS alone

From Acquisition to Extinction (to Spontaneous Recovery)

The figure illustrates the strength of a conditioned response (CR), shown on the Y or vertical axis, across the stages from acquisition, to extinction, to a rest period, and finally to spontaneous recovery. Using the graphs, answer the following questions.

1. What happens to the unconditioned stimulus (US) and the conditioned stimulus (CS) during acquisition, and how does this influence the conditioned response (CR)?

2. When is the CR strongest and when is it weakest?

3. What happens to the US and CS during extinction, and how does this influence the CR?

4. Notice that spontaneous recovery occurs after a rest period. Why is this rest necessary?

5. In your own life, what are some conditioned stimuli that are attached to conditioned responses for you? Trace them through these steps.

the process in classical conditioning by which a conditioned response can recur after a time delay, without further conditioning (Leising, Wong, & Blaisdell, 2015; Rescorla, 2005).

Consider an example of spontaneous recovery you may have experienced: You thought that you had forgotten about (extinguished) an old girlfriend or boyfriend, but then you found yourself in a particular context (perhaps the restaurant where you used to dine together), and you suddenly got a mental image of your ex, accompanied by an emotional reaction to him or her from the past (spontaneous recovery).

The steps in classical conditioning are reviewed in the Psychological Inquiry. The figure in the feature shows the sequence of acquisition, extinction, and spontaneous recovery. Spontaneous recovery can occur several times, but as long as the conditioned stimulus is presented alone (that is, without the unconditioned stimulus), spontaneous recovery becomes weaker and eventually ceases.

Not only do extinguished learned associations show spontaneous recovery, but they can be reinstated just by moving the organism to a new setting. **Renewal** refers to the recovery of the conditioned response when the organism is placed in a novel context (Revillo & others, 2014). Renewal can be a powerful problem to overcome—as it is when a person leaves a drug treatment facility to return to his or her previous living situation (Bouton, Winterbauer, & Vurbic, 2012).

● **renewal** The recovery of the conditioned response when the organism is placed in a novel context.

The processes of acquisition, extinction, spontaneous recovery, and renewal all demonstrate the important role of learned associations for the survival of all creatures. All animals, including humans, are, in some ways, on the look-out for survival-relevant connections, such as learning what cues signal food. Once such connections are made, they are difficult to break entirely as demonstrated in spontaneous recovery. Finally, those connections remain in the organism's repertoire and can pop back up in a new setting.

Classical Conditioning in Humans

Although the process of classical conditioning has often been studied in nonhuman animals, the human capacity to learn associations is extremely important for our survival (Krause, 2015). Here we review examples of classical conditioning at work in human life.

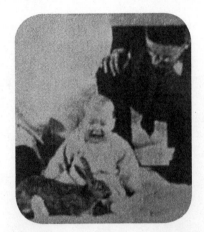

Watson and Rayner conditioned 11-month-old Albert to fear a white rat by pairing the rat with a loud noise. When little Albert was later presented with other stimuli similar to the white rat, such as the rabbit shown here with Albert, he was afraid of them too. This study illustrates stimulus generalization in classical conditioning.

Courtesy of Professor Benjamin Harris

EXPLAINING FEARS

Classical conditioning provides an explanation of fears (Field & Purkis, 2014). John B. Watson (who coined the term *behaviorism*) and Rosalie Rayner (1920) demonstrated classical conditioning's role in the development of fears with an infant named Albert. They showed Albert a white laboratory rat to see whether he was afraid of it. He was not. As Albert played with the rat, the researchers sounded a loud noise behind his head. The noise caused little Albert to cry. After only seven pairings of the loud noise with the white rat, Albert began to fear the rat even when the noise was not sounded. Albert's fear was generalized to a rabbit, a dog, and a sealskin coat.

Let's use Albert's example to review the key concepts of classical conditioning. In the beginning, Albert had no response to the rat. The rat, then, is a neutral stimulus—the conditioned stimulus (or CS). The rat was then paired with a loud noise. Note that the loud noise would startle Albert and make him cry: Loud noises upset babies. That makes the loud noise the unconditioned stimulus (US), because it evokes a response naturally without the need for learning. Albert's reaction to the loud noise is the unconditioned response (or UR). Again, being upset by loud noises is something that babies just do. The white rat (CS) and loud noise (US) were paired together in time, and each time the loud noise would upset little Albert (UR). This pairing is the process of acquisition. Then, the rat (the CS) was presented to Albert without the loud noise (the US), and Albert became alarmed and afraid even without the noise. Poor Albert's enduring fear of the rat is the conditioned response (CR).

Today, Watson and Rayner's (1920) study would violate the ethical guidelines of the American Psychological Association. In any case, Watson correctly concluded that we learn many of our fears through classical conditioning. We might develop fear of the dentist because of a painful experience, fear of driving after having been in a car crash, and fear of dogs after having been bitten by one.

If we can learn fears through classical conditioning, we also can possibly unlearn them through that process. In the chapter "Therapies", for example, we will examine the application of classical conditioning to therapies for treating phobias.

BREAKING HABITS

● **counterconditioning** A classical conditioning procedure for changing the relationship between a conditioned stimulus and its conditioned response.

● **aversive conditioning** A form of treatment that consists of repeated pairings of a stimulus with a very unpleasant stimulus.

Counterconditioning is a classical conditioning procedure for changing the relationship between a conditioned stimulus and its conditioned response. Therapists have used counterconditioning to break apart the association between certain stimuli and positive feelings (Engelhard & others, 2014). **Aversive conditioning** is a form of treatment that consists of repeated pairings of a stimulus with a very unpleasant stimulus. Electric shocks and nausea-inducing substances are examples of noxious stimuli that are used in aversive conditioning (Symonds & Hall, 2012).

To reduce drinking, for example, every time a person drinks an alcoholic beverage, he or she also consumes a mixture that induces nausea. In classical conditioning terminology, the alcoholic beverage is the conditioned stimulus, and the nausea-inducing agent is the unconditioned stimulus. Through a repeated pairing of alcohol with the nausea-inducing agent, alcohol becomes the conditioned stimulus that elicits nausea, the conditioned response. As a consequence, alcohol no longer is associated with something pleasant but rather with something highly unpleasant. Antabuse, a drug treatment for alcoholism since the late 1940s, is based on this association (Ullman, 1952). When someone takes this drug, ingesting even the smallest amount of alcohol will make the person quite ill, even if the exposure to the alcohol is through mouthwash or cologne. Antabuse continues to be used in the treatment of alcoholism today (Ellis & Dronsfield, 2013).

Classical conditioning is likely to be at work whenever we engage in mindless, habitual behavior (Wood & Rünger, 2016). Cues in the environment serve as conditioned stimuli, evoking feelings and behaviors without thought. These associations become implicit "if-then" connections: If you are sitting in front of your laptop, then you check your e-mail. These automatic associations can function for good (for instance, you get up every morning and go for a run without even thinking) or ill (you walk into the kitchen and open the fridge for a snack without even thinking).

INTERSECTION

Learning and Health Psychology: Can Classical Conditioning Be Used to Combat Obesity?

The rates of overweight and obesity in the United States are a public health crisis. Most Americans are over-weight, and approximately half of the U.S. adult population is obese (Ogden & others, 2014). Underlying these statistics is the simple fact that many people eat when they are not hungry. Eating in the absence of hunger (or EAH) is thought to be caused by reactions to food cues. The term *food cues* refers to the conditioned stimuli that are part of the eating experience, including the sight and smell of tasty food (Jansen, 1998). The conditioned response to these cues includes a desire to eat, salivation, and other bodily changes associated with preparing to eat. Essentially, when people look at and smell tasty food, the body automatically prepares to eat.

Some people, however, are more sensitive to food cues, showing a very strong response to these cues including the tendency to engage in more EAH (Boutelle & Bouton, 2015; Boutelle & others, 2015). Using the principles of classical conditioning, is it possible to extinguish the link between food cues and eating, thereby reducing EAH?

Now, the link between the sight and smell of a freshly baked chocolate chip cookie and eating that cookie might seem so strong that it would be next to impossible to extinguish. Can we separate food cues from eating?

A recent study examined this possibility (Schyns & others, 2016). Overweight women were randomly assigned to one of two conditions. Women in the experimental condition were exposed to the sights and smells of tasty food. These women sat at a table topped with a variety of delicious and decadent foods: chocolate mousse, whipped cream, strawberry mousse, custard, and chocolate cake. They were encouraged to look at the desserts, smell them, and fully imagine themselves eating them—but no tasting allowed. After 80 minutes of this exposure, the women were told to throw the desserts in the trash. For the control group, the experimenter presented standard information about body satisfaction and healthy weight for the same amount of time. Then, all participants were required to eat two sandwiches to

© D. Hurst/Alamy Stock Photo

Is your eating guided by food cues?

ensure that no participants were hungry. Finally, the dependent variables were measured.

A key dependent variable was EAH, operationalized by a phony "taste test." Participants were presented with the desserts and were told to taste each one and make ratings. They could eat as much as they wished, and the amount eaten was measured. Recall that because they had just eaten the sandwiches, none of the participants could be hungry, and so the amount of the desserts they ate is a measure of EAH. The results showed that the experimental group ate less than those in the control condition. In addition, compared to controls, those in the experimental group expressed less agreement with the belief that if tasty food is in front of them, then they must eat it. In short, staring at, smelling, and fantasizing about eating tasty food, but then not eating it, began the process of severing the link between those sights, smells, and thoughts and eating.

Pavlov's original discovery of classical conditioning occurred in the context of food and eating. We should not be surprised, then that classical conditioning holds a great deal of promise in developing interventions to combat overeating.

Let's consider an imaginary Pavlov's dog, called Bill. After years of service in Pavlov's lab, Bill is taken in by a caring family. Now, Bill is not kept in a state of hunger but is allowed to eat whenever he wants. But Bill's family might notice that he runs to his dish, salivating, and seems to want to eat whenever the doorbell rings—even if he is not hungry. Why? Because Bill has acquired an association in which ringing bells evoke food-related behaviors. Bill, our imaginary dog, eats when he is not hungry because of a learned association. Could such a link help explain overeating and obesity in humans? The principles of classical conditioning have been used to combat overweight and obesity in humans by targeting such links (Boutelle & Bouton, 2015). To read about this work, see the Intersection.

CLASSICAL CONDITIONING AND THE PLACEBO EFFECT

The chapter "Psychology's Scientific Method" defined the *placebo effect* as the effect of a substance (such as taking a pill orally) or a procedure (such as using a syringe to inject a substance) that researchers use as a control to identify the actual effects of a treatment. Placebo effects are observable changes (such as a drop in pain) that cannot be explained by the effects of an actual treatment. The principles of classical conditioning can help to explain some of these effects (Montgomery & Kirsch, 2013). In this case, the pill or syringe serves as a CS, and the actual drug is the US. After the experience of pain relief following the consumption of a drug, for instance, the pill or syringe might lead to a CR of lowered pain even in the absence of an actual painkiller. The strongest evidence for the role of classical conditioning on placebo effects comes from research on the immune system and the endocrine system.

CLASSICAL CONDITIONING AND THE IMMUNE AND ENDOCRINE SYSTEMS

Even the human body's internal organ systems can be classically conditioned. The immune system is the body's natural defense against disease. A number of studies reveal that classical conditioning can produce *immunosuppression,* a decrease in the production of antibodies, which can lower a person's ability to fight disease (Ader & Cohen, 1975; Sticht & others, 2015).

The initial discovery of this link between classical conditioning and immunosuppression came as a surprise. In studying classical conditioning, Robert Ader (1974) was examining how long a conditioned response would last in some laboratory rats. He paired a conditioned stimulus (saccharin solution) with an unconditioned stimulus, a drug called Cytoxan, which induces nausea. Afterward, while giving the rats saccharin-laced water without the accompanying Cytoxan, Ader watched to see how long it would take the rats to forget the association between the two.

Unexpectedly, in the second month of the study, the rats developed a disease and began to die off. In analyzing this unforeseen result, Ader looked into the properties of the nausea-inducing drug he had used. He discovered that one of its side effects was suppressed immune system functioning. It turned out that the rats had been classically conditioned to associate sweet water not only with nausea but also with the shutdown of the immune system. The sweet water apparently had become a conditioned stimulus for immunosuppression.

Researchers have found that conditioned immune responses also occur in humans (Kusnecov, 2014). For example, in one study, patients with multiple sclerosis were given a flavored drink prior to receiving a drug that suppressed the immune system. After this pairing, the flavored drink by itself lowered immune functioning, similarly to the drug (Giang & others, 1996).

Similar results have been found for the endocrine system. Recall from the chapter "Biological Foundations of Behavior" that the endocrine system is a loosely organized set of glands that produce and circulate hormones. Research has shown that placebo pills can influence the secretion of hormones if patients had previous experiences with pills containing actual drugs that affected hormone secretion (Benedetti & others, 2003; Piedimonte & Benedetti, 2015). Studies have revealed that the sympathetic nervous system (the part of the autonomic nervous system that responds to stress) plays an important role in the learned associations between conditioned stimuli and immune and endocrine functioning (Wager & Atlas, 2015).

TASTE AVERSION LEARNING

Consider this scenario. Mike goes out for sushi with some friends and eats spicy yellow tail, his favorite dish. He then proceeds to a jazz concert. Several hours later, he becomes very ill with stomach pains and nausea. A few weeks later, he tries to eat spicy yellow tail again but cannot stand it. Importantly, Mike does not experience an aversion to jazz, even though he attended the jazz concert that night before getting sick. Mike's experience exemplifies *taste aversion:* a special kind of classical conditioning involving the learned association between a particular taste and nausea (Bernal-Gamboa, Nieto, & Rosas, 2015; Garcia, Ervin, & Koelling, 1966; Martínez-Moreno, Rodríguez-Durán, & Escobar, 2016).

Taste aversion is special because it typically requires only one pairing of a neutral stimulus (a taste) with the unconditioned response of nausea to seal that connection, often for a very long time. As we consider later, it is highly adaptive to learn taste aversion in only one trial. An animal that required multiple pairings of taste with poison likely would not survive the acquisition phase. It is notable, though, that taste aversion can occur even if the "taste" had nothing to do with getting sick—perhaps, in Mike's case, he was simply coming down with a stomach bug. Taste aversion can even occur when a person has been sickened by a completely separate event, such as being spun around in a chair (Klosterhalfen & others, 2000).

Although taste aversion is often considered an exception to the rules of learning, Michael Domjan (2005, 2015) has suggested that this form of learning demonstrates how classical conditioning works in the natural world, where associations matter to survival. Remember, in taste aversion, the taste or flavor is the CS; the agent that made the person sick (it could be a rollercoaster ride or salmonella, for example) is the US; nausea or vomiting is the UR; and taste aversion is the CR.

Taste aversion learning is particularly important in the context of the traditional treatment of some cancers. Radiation and chemotherapy for cancer can produce nausea in patients, with the result that individuals sometimes develop strong aversions to foods they ingest prior to treatment (Coa & others, 2015; Davidson & Riley, 2015; Jacobsen & others, 1993). Consequently, they may experience a general tendency to be turned off by food, a situation that can lead to nutritional deficits (Coa & others, 2015).

The U.S. Fish and Wildlife Service is trying out taste aversion as a tool to prevent Mexican gray wolves from preying on cattle. To instill taste aversion for beef, the agency is deploying bait made of beef and cowhide that also contains odorless and flavorless substances that induce nausea (Bryan, 2012). The hope is that wolves that are sickened by the bait will no longer prey on cattle and might even rear their pups to enjoy alternative meals.

© Jeff Vanuga/Corbis

Researchers have used classical conditioning principles to combat these taste aversions, especially in children, for whom antinausea medication is often ineffective (Skolin & others, 2006) and for whom aversions to protein-rich food is particularly problematic (Ikeda & others, 2006). Early studies demonstrated that giving children a "scapegoat" conditioned stimulus prior to chemotherapy would help contain the taste aversion to only one specific type of food or flavor (Broberg & Bernstein, 1987). For example, children might be given a particular flavor of Lifesaver candy or ice cream before receiving treatment. For these children, the nausea would be more strongly associated with the Lifesaver or ice cream flavor than with the foods they needed to eat for good nutrition. These results show discrimination in classical conditioning—the kids developed aversions only to the specific scapegoat flavors.

CLASSICAL CONDITIONING AND ADVERTISING

Classical conditioning provides the foundation for many of the commercials that we are bombarded with daily. (Appropriately, when John Watson, whom you will recall from the baby Albert study, left the field of psychology, he went into advertising.) Think about it: Advertising involves creating an association between a product and pleasant feelings (buy that pumpkin spice latte and be happy). TV advertisers cunningly apply classical conditioning principles to consumers by showing ads that pair something positive—such as a beautiful woman (the US) producing pleasant feelings (the UR)—with a product (the CS) in hopes that you, the viewer, will experience those positive feelings toward the product (the CR).

Even when commercials are not involved, advertisers exploit classical conditioning principles—for instance, through the technique of product placement, or what is known as *embedded marketing*. For example, suppose that while viewing a TV show or movie, you notice that a character is drinking a particular brand of soft drink or eating a particular type of cereal. By placing their products in the context of a show or movie you like, advertisers are hoping that your positive feelings about the show, movie plot, or a character (the UR) rub off on their product (the CS). It may seem like a long shot, but all they need to do is enhance the chances that, say, navigating through a car dealership or a grocery store, you will feel attracted to their product.

DRUG HABITUATION

The chapter "States of Consciousness" noted how, over time, a person might develop a tolerance for a psychoactive drug and need a higher and higher dose of the substance to

190   CHAPTER 6   Learning

FIGURE 3   Drug Habituation The figure illustrates how classical conditioning is involved in drug habituation. As a result of conditioning, the drug user will need to take more of the drug to get the same effect as the person did before the conditioning. Moreover, if the user takes the drug without the usual conditioned stimulus or stimuli—represented in the middle panel by the bathroom and the drug tablets—overdosing is more likely. (first) © Thinkstock/JupiterImages; (second) © Brand X Pictures/PunchStock; (third) © Rick Gomez/Corbis

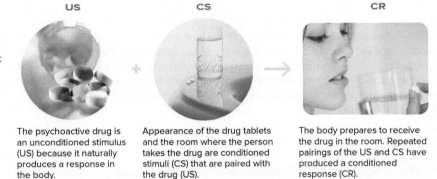

US   CS   CR

The psychoactive drug is an unconditioned stimulus (US) because it naturally produces a response in the body.

Appearance of the drug tablets and the room where the person takes the drug are conditioned stimuli (CS) that are paired with the drug (US).

The body prepares to receive the drug in the room. Repeated pairings of the US and CS have produced a conditioned response (CR).

● **habituation** Decreased responsiveness to a stimulus after repeated presentations.

get the same effect. Classical conditioning helps to explain **habituation,** which refers to the decreased responsiveness to a stimulus after repeated presentations. A mind-altering drug is an unconditioned stimulus: It naturally produces a response in the person's body. This unconditioned stimulus is often paired systematically with a previously neutral stimulus (CS). For instance, the physical appearance of the drug in a pill or syringe, and the room where the person takes the drugs, are conditioned stimuli that are paired with the unconditioned stimulus of the drug. These repeated pairings should produce a conditioned response, and they do—but it is different from those we have considered so far.

The conditioned response to a drug can be the body's way of *preparing* for the effects of a drug (Ettenberg & others, 2015; Rachlin & Green, 2009). In this case, the body braces itself for the effects of the drug with a CR that is the opposite of the UR. For instance, if the drug (the US) leads to an increase in heart rate (the UR), the CR might be a drop in heart rate. The CS serves as a warning that the drug is coming, and the conditioned response in this case is the body's compensation for the drug's effects (Figure 3). In this situation the conditioned response works to decrease the effects of the US, making the drug experience less intense. Some drug users try to prevent habituation by varying the physical location of where they take the drug.

This aspect of drug use can play a role in deaths caused by drug overdoses. How is classical conditioning involved? A user typically takes a drug in a particular setting, such as a bathroom, and acquires a conditioned response to this location (McClernon & others, 2015; Siegel, 1988). Because of classical conditioning, as soon as the drug user walks into the bathroom, the person's body begins to prepare for and anticipate the drug dose in order to lessen the effect of the drug. Essentially, the context in which the drug is taken (for example, the bathroom) becomes a conditioned stimulus that signals that the drug is coming. However, if the user takes the drug in a location other than the usual one, such as at a rock concert, the drug's effect is greater because no conditioned responses have built up in the new setting, and therefore the body is not prepared for the drug.

When you read about cases of deadly overdoses, note how often the person has taken the drug under unusual circumstances or after a visit to rehab. In these cases, with no CS signal, the body is unprepared for (and tragically overwhelmed by) the drug's effects. After time in rehab, the associative links have been extinguished and the individual is at risk of overdosing (Ravndal, Lauritzen, & Gossop, 2015).

test yourself

1. What is meant by an unconditioned stimulus (US) and an unconditioned response (UR)? In Pavlov's experiments with dogs, what were the US and the UR?

2. What is meant by a conditioned stimulus (CS) and a conditioned response (CR)? In Pavlov's experiments with dogs, what were the CS and the CR?

3. What learning principle does the Watson and Rayner study with baby Albert illustrate?

3. OPERANT CONDITIONING

Recall from early in the chapter that classical conditioning and operant conditioning are forms of associative learning, which involves learning that two events are connected. In classical conditioning, organisms learn the association between two stimuli (US and CS). Classical conditioning is a form of *respondent behavior,* behavior that occurs in automatic response to a stimulus such as a nausea-producing drug and later to a conditioned stimulus such as sweet water that was paired with the drug. Calling a behavior "respondent" means that it happens on auto pilot.

Classical conditioning explains how neutral stimuli become associated with unlearned, *involuntary responses*. Classical conditioning is not as effective, however, in explaining *voluntary behaviors* such as a student's studying hard for a test, a gambler's playing slot machines in Las Vegas, or a service dog fetching his owner's cell phone on command. Operant conditioning is usually much better than classical conditioning at explaining such voluntary behaviors. Whereas classical conditioning focuses on the association between stimuli, operant conditioning focuses on the association between behaviors and the stimuli that follow them.

Defining Operant Conditioning

Operant conditioning or instrumental conditioning is a form of associative learning in which the consequences of a behavior change the probability of the behavior's occurrence. The American psychologist B. F. Skinner (1938) chose the term *operant* to describe the behavior of the organism. An operant behavior occurs spontaneously. According to Skinner, the consequences that follow such spontaneous behaviors determine whether the behavior will be repeated.

Imagine, for example, that you spontaneously decide to take a different route while driving to campus one day. You are more likely to repeat that route on another day if you have a pleasant experience—for instance, arriving at school faster or finding a new coffee place to try—than if you have a lousy experience such as getting stuck in traffic. In either case, the consequences of your spontaneous act influence whether that behavior happens again.

Recall that *contingency* is an important aspect of classical conditioning in which the occurrence of one stimulus can be predicted from the presence of another one. Contingency also plays a key role in operant conditioning. For example, when a rat pushes a lever (behavior) that delivers food, the delivery of food (consequence) is contingent on that behavior. This principle of contingency helps explain why passersby should never praise, pet, or feed a service dog while he is working (at least without asking first). Providing rewards during such times might interfere with the dog's training.

● **operant conditioning or instrumental conditioning** A form of associative learning in which the consequences of a behavior change the probability of the behavior's occurrence.

Thorndike's Law of Effect

Although Skinner emerged as the primary figure in operant conditioning, the experiments of E. L. Thorndike (1898) established the power of consequences in determining voluntary behavior. At about the same time that Pavlov was conducting classical conditioning experiments with salivating dogs, Thorndike, another American psychologist, was studying cats in puzzle boxes. Thorndike put a hungry cat inside a box and placed a piece of fish outside. To escape from the box and obtain the food, the cat had to learn to open the latch inside the box. At first the cat made a number of ineffective responses. It clawed or bit at the bars and thrust its paw through the openings. Eventually the cat accidentally stepped on the lever that released the door bolt. When the cat returned to the box, it went through the same random activity until it stepped on the lever once more. On subsequent trials, the cat made fewer and fewer random movements until finally it immediately stepped on the lever to open the door (Figure 4). Thorndike's resulting **law of effect** states that behaviors followed by pleasant outcomes are strengthened and that behaviors followed by unpleasant outcomes are weakened.

The law of effect is profoundly important because it presents the basic idea that the consequences of a behavior influence the likelihood of that behavior's recurrence. Quite simply, a behavior can be followed by something good or something bad, and the probability of a behavior's being repeated depends on these outcomes. As we now explore, Skinner's operant conditioning model expands on this basic idea.

● **law of effect** Thorndike's law stating that behaviors followed by positive outcomes are strengthened and that behaviors followed by negative outcomes are weakened.

Skinner's Approach to Operant Conditioning

Skinner believed that the mechanisms of learning are the same for all species. This conviction led him to study animals in the hope that he could discover the components

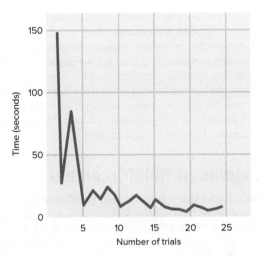

FIGURE 4   Thorndike's Puzzle Box and the Law of Effect (*left*) A box typical of the puzzle boxes Thorndike used in his experiments with cats to study the law of effect. Stepping on the lever released the door bolt; a weight attached to the door then pulled the door open and allowed the cat to escape. After accidentally pressing the lever as it tried to get to the food, the cat learned to press the lever when it wanted to escape the box. (*right*) One cat's learning curve over 24 separate trials. Notice that the cat escaped much more quickly after about five trials. It had learned the consequences of its behavior.

● **shaping** Rewarding successive approximations of a desired behavior.

of learning with organisms simpler than humans, including pigeons. During World War II, Skinner trained pigeons to pilot missiles. Naval officials just could not accept pigeons guiding their missiles in a war, but Skinner congratulated himself on the degree of control he was able to exercise over the pigeons (Figure 5).

Skinner and other behaviorists made every effort to study organisms under precisely controlled conditions so that they could examine the connection between the operant behavior and the specific consequences in minute detail. In the 1930s, Skinner created an operant conditioning chamber, also called a Skinner box, to control experimental conditions (Figure 6).

A device in the box delivered food pellets into a tray at random. After a rat became accustomed to the box, Skinner installed a lever and observed the rat's behavior. As the hungry rat explored the box, it occasionally pressed the lever, and a food pellet was dispensed. Soon the rat learned that the consequences of pressing the lever were positive: It would be fed. Skinner achieved further control by soundproofing the box to ensure that the experimenter was the only influence on the organism. In many of the experiments, the responses were mechanically recorded, and the food (the consequence) was dispensed automatically. These precautions were aimed at preventing human error.

Shaping

Imagine trying to teach even a really smart dog how to signal that her owner's blood-glucose level is low—or how to turn on the lights or do the laundry. These challenges might seem insurmountable, as it is unlikely that a dog will spontaneously perform any of these behaviors. You could wait a very long time for such feats to occur. Nevertheless, it *is* possible to train a dog or another animal to perform highly complex tasks through shaping.

Shaping refers to rewarding successive approximations of a desired behavior (Emer & others, 2015; Slater & Dymond, 2011). For example, shaping can be used to train a rat to press a bar to obtain food. When a rat is first placed in a Skinner box, it rarely presses the bar. Thus, the experimenter may start off by giving the rat a food pellet if it is in the same half of the cage as the bar. Then the experimenter might reward the rat's

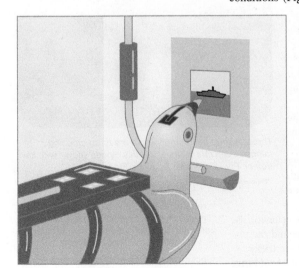

FIGURE 5   Skinner's Pigeon-Guided Missile Skinner wanted to help the military during World War II by using the tracking behavior of pigeons. A gold electrode covered the tip of the pigeons' beaks. Contact with the screen on which the image of the target was projected sent a signal informing the missile's control mechanism of the target's location. A few grains of food occasionally given to the pigeons maintained their tracking behavior.

behavior only when it is within 2 inches of the bar, then only when it touches the bar, and finally only when it presses the bar.

Returning to the service dog example, rather than waiting for the dog to spontaneously put the clothes in the washing machine, we might reward the dog for carrying the clothes to the laundry room and for bringing them closer and closer to the washing machine. Finally, we might reward the dog only when it gets the clothes inside the washer. Indeed, trainers use this type of shaping technique extensively in teaching animals to perform tricks. A dolphin that jumps through a hoop held high above the water has been trained to perform this behavior through shaping.

Principles of Reinforcement

We noted earlier that a behavior can be followed by something pleasant or something unpleasant. When behaviors are followed by a desirable outcome, the behaviors are likely to be repeated. When behaviors are followed by an undesirable outcome, they are less likely to occur. Now we can put some labels on these different patterns.

Reinforcement is the process by which a stimulus or event (a *reinforcer*) following a particular behavior increases the probability that the behavior will happen again. These desirable (or rewarding) consequences of a behavior fall into two types, called *positive reinforcement* and *negative reinforcement*. Both of these types of consequences are experienced as pleasant, and both increase the frequency of a behavior.

POSITIVE AND NEGATIVE REINFORCEMENT

In **positive reinforcement** the frequency of a behavior increases because it is followed by a desirable stimulus. For example, if someone you meet smiles at you after you say, "Hello, how are you?" and you keep talking, the smile has reinforced your talking. The same principle of positive reinforcement is at work when you teach a dog to "shake hands" by giving it a piece of food when it lifts its paw.

In contrast, in **negative reinforcement** the frequency of a behavior increases because it is followed by *the removal* of something undesirable. For example, if your father nagged you to clean out the garage and kept nagging until you cleaned out the garage, your response (cleaning out the garage) removed the unpleasant stimulus (your dad's nagging). Taking an aspirin when you have a headache works the same way: A reduction of pain reinforces the act of taking an aspirin. Similarly, if your laptop is making an irritating buzzing sound, you might give it a good smack on the side, and if the buzzing stops, you are more likely to smack it again if the buzzing resumes. Ending the buzzing sound rewards the laptop-smacking.

Notice that both positive and negative reinforcement involve rewarding behavior—but they do so in different ways. Positive reinforcement means following a behavior with the addition of something pleasant, and negative reinforcement means following a behavior with the removal of something unpleasant. So, in this case "positive" and "negative" have nothing to do with "good" and "bad." Rather, they refer to processes in which something is given (positive reinforcement) or removed (negative reinforcement).

Whether it is positive or negative, reinforcement is about increasing a behavior. Be sure to review Figure 7 as it provides further examples to help you understand the distinction between positive and negative reinforcement. These processes can be tricky.

A special kind of response to negative reinforcement is avoidance learning. **Avoidance learning** occurs when the organism learns that by making a particular response, a negative stimulus can be altogether avoided. For instance, a student who receives one bad grade might thereafter always study hard in order to avoid the negative outcome of bad grades in the future. Even when the bad grade is no longer present, the behavior pattern sticks. Avoidance learning is very powerful in the sense that the behavior is maintained even in the absence of any aversive stimulus. For example, animals that have been trained to avoid a negative stimulus, such as an electrical shock, by jumping

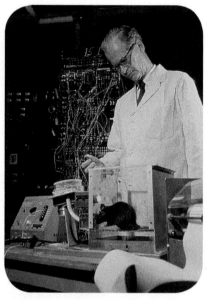

FIGURE 6   The Skinner Box B. F. Skinner conducting an operant conditioning study in his behavioral laboratory. The rat being studied is in an operant conditioning chamber, sometimes referred to as a Skinner box. © Nina Leen/Time & Life Pictures/Getty Images

Through shaping, animals can learn to do amazing things—even ride a wave, like this alpaca shown with its trainer, Peruvian surfer Domingo Pianezzi.
©Enrique Cuneo/AP Images

● **reinforcement** The process by which a stimulus or event (a reinforcer) following a particular behavior increases the probability that the behavior will happen again.

● **positive reinforcement** The presentation of a stimulus following a given behavior in order to increase the frequency of that behavior.

● **negative reinforcement** The removal of a stimulus following a given behavior in order to increase the frequency of that behavior.

● **avoidance learning** An organism's learning that it can altogether avoid a negative stimulus by making a particular response.

Positive Reinforcement

Behavior	Rewarding Stimulus Provided	Future Behavior
You turn in homework on time.	Teacher praises your performance.	You increasingly turn in homework on time.
You wax your skis.	The skis go faster.	You wax your skis the next time you go skiing.
You randomly press a button on the dashboard of a friend's car.	Great music begins to play.	You deliberately press the button again the next time you get into the car.

Negative Reinforcement

Behavior	Stimulus Removed	Future Behavior
You turn in homework on time.	Teacher stops criticizing late homework.	You increasingly turn in homework on time.
You wax your skis.	People stop zooming by you on the slopes.	You wax your skis the next time you go skiing.
You randomly press a button on the dashboard of a friend's car.	An annoying song shuts off.	You deliberately press the button again the next time the annoying song is on.

FIGURE 7 Positive and Negative Reinforcement Positive reinforcers involve adding something (generally something rewarding). Negative reinforcers involve taking away something (generally something aversive).

into a safe area may thereafter gravitate toward the safe area, even when the shock is no longer presented.

Experience with unavoidable negative stimuli can lead to a particular deficit in avoidance learning called learned helplessness. In **learned helplessness** the organism has learned that it has no control over negative outcomes. Learned helplessness was first identified by Martin Seligman and his colleagues (Altenor, Volpicelli, & Seligman, 1979; Hannum, Rosellini, & Seligman, 1976). Seligman and his associates found that dogs that were first exposed to inescapable shocks were later unable to learn to avoid those shocks, even when they could avoid them (Seligman & Maier, 1967). This inability to learn to escape was persistent: The dogs would suffer painful shocks hours, days, and even weeks later and never attempt to escape.

Exposure to unavoidable negative circumstances may also set the stage for humans' inability to learn avoidance, such as with the experience of depression and despair (Landgraf & others, 2015; Pryce & others, 2011). Learned helplessness has aided psychologists in understanding a variety of perplexing issues, such as why some victims of domestic violence fail to escape their terrible situation and why some students respond to failure at school by giving up trying.

TYPES OF REINFORCERS

Psychologists classify positive reinforcers as primary or secondary based on whether the rewarding quality of the consequence is innate or learned. A **primary reinforcer** is innately satisfying; that is, a primary reinforcer does not require any learning on the organism's part to make it pleasurable. Food, water, and sexual satisfaction are primary reinforcers.

A **secondary reinforcer** acquires its positive value through an organism's experience; a secondary reinforcer is a learned or conditioned reinforcer. Secondary reinforcers can be linked to primary reinforcers through classical conditioning. For instance, if someone wanted to train a cat to do tricks, the person might first repeatedly pair the sound of a whistle with food. Once the cat associates the whistle with food, the whistle can be used in training.

● **learned helplessness** An organism's learning through experience with negative stimuli that it has no control over negative outcomes.

● **primary reinforcer** A reinforcer that is innately satisfying; a primary reinforcer does not require any learning on the organism's part to make it pleasurable.

● **secondary reinforcer** A reinforcer that acquires its positive value through an organism's experience; a secondary reinforcer is a learned or conditioned reinforcer.

We encounter hundreds of secondary reinforcers in our lives, such as getting an *A* on a test and a paycheck for a job. Although we might think of these as positive outcomes, they are not innately positive. We learn through experience that *A*'s and paychecks are good. Secondary reinforcers can be used in a system called a *token economy*. In a token economy behaviors are rewarded with tokens (such as poker chips or stars on a chart) that can be exchanged later for desired rewards (such as candy or money).

GENERALIZATION, DISCRIMINATION, AND EXTINCTION

Not only are generalization, discrimination, and extinction important in classical conditioning, but they are also key principles in operant conditioning.

Generalization   In operant conditioning, **generalization** means performing a reinforced behavior in a different situation. For example, in one study pigeons were reinforced for pecking at a disk of a particular color (Guttman & Kalish, 1956). To assess stimulus generalization, researchers presented the pigeons with disks of varying colors. As Figure 8 shows, the pigeons were most likely to peck at disks closest in color to the original. When a student who gets excellent grades in a calculus class by studying the course material every night starts to study psychology and history every night as well, generalization is at work.

Discrimination   In operant conditioning, **discrimination** means responding appropriately to stimuli that signal that a behavior will or will not be reinforced. For example, you go to a restaurant that has a "University Student Discount" sign in the front window, and you enthusiastically flash your student ID with the expectation of getting the reward of a reduced-price meal. Without the sign, showing your ID might get you only a puzzled look, not cheap food.

The principle of discrimination helps to explain how a service dog "knows" when she is working. Typically, the dog wears a training harness while on duty but not at other times. Thus, when a service dog is wearing her harness, it is important to treat her like the professional that she is. Similarly, an important aspect of the training of service dogs is the need for selective disobedience. Selective disobedience means that in addition to obeying commands from her human partner, the service dog must at times override such commands if the context provides cues that obedience is not the appropriate response. So, if a guide dog is standing at the street corner with her visually impaired owner, and the person commands her to move forward, the dog might refuse if she sees the "Don't Walk" sign flashing. Stimuli in the environment serve as cues, informing the organism if a particular reinforcement contingency is in effect.

Extinction   In operant conditioning, **extinction** occurs when a behavior is no longer reinforced and decreases in frequency. If, for example, a soda machine that you frequently use starts "eating" your coins without dispensing soda, you quickly stop inserting more coins. Several weeks later, you might try to use the machine again, hoping that it has been fixed. Such behavior illustrates spontaneous recovery in operant conditioning (Bouton & Schepers, 2015).

CONTINUOUS REINFORCEMENT, PARTIAL REINFORCEMENT, AND SCHEDULES OF REINFORCEMENT

Most of the examples of reinforcement we have considered so far involve *continuous reinforcement,* in which a behavior is reinforced every time it occurs. When continuous reinforcement takes place, organisms learn rapidly. However, when reinforcement stops, extinction takes place quickly.

A variety of conditioning procedures have been developed that are particularly resistant to extinction. These involve *partial reinforcement,* in which a reinforcer follows a behavior only a portion of the time. Partial reinforcement characterizes most life experiences. For instance, a golfer does not win every tournament she enters; a chess whiz

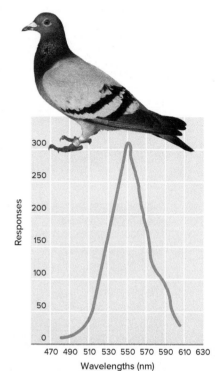

FIGURE 8   Stimulus Generalization
In the experiment by Norman Guttman and Harry Kalish (1956), pigeons initially pecked at a disk of a particular color (in this graph, a color with a wavelength of 550 nm) after they had been reinforced for this wavelength. Subsequently, when the pigeons were presented with disks of colors with varying wavelengths, they were likelier to peck at those with a similar color to the original disk. (photo) © Photodisc/Getty Images

● **generalization (in operant conditioning)**
Performing a reinforced behavior in a different situation.

● **discrimination (in classical conditioning)**
The process of learning to respond to certain stimuli and not others.

● **extinction (in operant conditioning)**
Decreases in the frequency of a behavior when the behavior is no longer reinforced.

● **schedules of reinforcement** Specific patterns that determine when a behavior will be reinforced.

does not win every match he plays; a student does not get a pat on the back each time she solves a problem.

Schedules of reinforcement are specific patterns that determine when a behavior will be reinforced (Bermúdez, Bruner, & Lattal, 2013; Craig & others, 2015). There are four main schedules of partial reinforcement: fixed ratio, variable ratio, fixed interval, and variable interval. With respect to these, *ratio schedules* involve the number of behaviors that must be performed prior to reward, and *interval schedules* refer to the amount of time that must pass before a behavior is rewarded. In a fixed schedule, the number of behaviors or the amount of time is always the same. In a variable schedule, the required number of behaviors or the amount of time that must pass changes and is unpredictable from the perspective of the learner. Let's look concretely at how each of these schedules of reinforcement influences behavior.

A *fixed-ratio schedule* reinforces a behavior after a set number of behaviors. For example, a child might receive a piece of candy or an hour of video-game play not *every* time he practices his piano, but after five days of practicing, at least an hour a day. A mail carrier must deliver mail to a fixed number of houses each day before he or she can head home. The business world often uses fixed-ratio schedules to increase production. For instance, a factory might require a line worker to produce a certain number of items in order to get paid a particular amount. As you can imagine, fixed-ratio schedules are not very mysterious, especially to human learners.

Consider, for instance, if you were playing the slot machines in Las Vegas, and they were on a fixed-ratio schedule, providing a $5 win every 20th time you put money in the machine. It would not take long to figure out that if you watched someone else play the machine 18 or 19 times, not get any money back, and then walk away, you should step up, insert your coin, and get back $5. Of course, if the reward schedule for a slot machine were that easy to figure out, casinos would not be so successful.

What makes gambling so tantalizing is the unpredictability of wins (and losses). Slot machines are on a *variable-ratio schedule,* a timetable in which behaviors are rewarded an average number of times but on an unpredictable basis. For example, a slot machine might pay off at *an average* of every 20th time, but the gambler does not know when this payoff will be. The slot machine might pay off twice in a row and then not again until after 58 coins have been inserted. This averages out to a reward for every 20 behavioral acts, but *when* the reward will be given is unpredictable.

Variable-ratio schedules produce high, steady rates of behavior that are more resistant to extinction than the other three schedules. Clearly, slot machines can make quite a profit. This is because not only are the rewards unpredictable, but they require behavior on the part of the person playing. One cannot simply wait around and then put in a coin after hours of not playing, hoping for a win. The machine requires that a certain *number* of behaviors occur; that is what makes it a *ratio* schedule.

In contrast to ratio schedules of reinforcement, *interval* reinforcement schedules are determined by the *time elapsed* since the last behavior was rewarded. A *fixed-interval schedule* reinforces the first appropriate behavior after a fixed amount of time has passed. If you take a class that has four scheduled exams, you might procrastinate most of the semester and cram just before each test. Fixed-interval schedules of reinforcement are also responsible for the fact that pets seem to be able to "tell time," eagerly sidling up to their food dish at 5 P.M. in anticipation of dinner. On a fixed-interval schedule, the rate of a behavior increases rapidly as the time approaches when the behavior likely will be reinforced. For example, suppose you are baking cookies, and when you put the cookie sheet into the oven, you set a timer. But before the timer goes off, you find yourself checking the cookies, over and over.

A *variable-interval schedule* is a timetable in which a behavior is reinforced after a variable amount of time has elapsed. Pop quizzes occur on a variable-interval schedule. Random drug testing follows a variable-interval schedule as well. So does fishing—you do not know if the fish will bite in the next minute, in a half hour, in an hour, or ever. Because it is difficult to predict when a reward will come, behavior is *slow and consistent* on a variable-interval schedule (Gaucher, Forget, & Clément, 2015; Romani &

Slot machines are on a variable-ratio schedule of reinforcement.

© David Sacks/The Image Bank/Getty Images

psychological *inquiry*

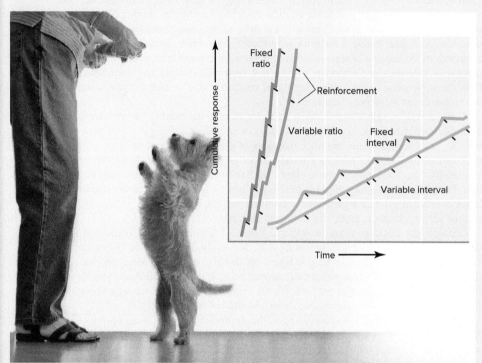

(photo) © Cardinal/Corbis

Schedules of Reinforcement and Different Patterns of Responding

This figure shows how the different schedules of reinforcement result in different rates of responding. The X or horizontal axis represents time. The Y or vertical axis represents the cumulative responses. That means that as the line goes up, the total number of responses are building and building. In the figure, each hash mark indicates the delivery of reinforcement. That is, each of those little ticks indicates that a reward is being given.

Look closely at the pattern of responses over time for each schedule of reinforcement. On the fixed-ratio schedule, notice the dropoff in responding after each response; on the variable-ratio schedule, note the high, steady rate of responding. On the fixed-interval schedule, notice the immediate dropoff in responding after reinforcement and the increase in responding just before reinforcement (resulting in a scalloped curve); and on the variable-interval schedule, note the slow, steady rate of responding.

1. Which schedule of reinforcement represents the "most bang for the buck"? That is, which one is associated with the most responses for the least amount of reward?

2. Which schedule of reinforcement is most similar to pop quizzes?

3. Which reinforcement schedule is most similar to regular tests on a course syllabus?

4. Which schedule of reinforcement would be best if you have very little time for training?

5. Which schedule of reinforcement do you think is most common in your own life? Why?

others, 2015). This is why pop quizzes lead to more consistent levels of studying compared to the cramming that might be seen with scheduled tests.

Let's take a closer look at the responses associated with each schedule of reinforcement in the Psychological Inquiry feature.

PUNISHMENT

We began this section by noting that behaviors can be followed by something good or something bad. So far, we have explored only the good things—reinforcers that are meant to increase behaviors. Sometimes, however, the goal is to decrease a behavior, and in such cases the behavior might be followed by something unpleasant. **Punishment** is a consequence that decreases the likelihood that a behavior will occur. For instance, a child plays with matches and gets burned when he lights one; the child consequently is less likely to play with matches in the future. As another example, a student interrupts the instructor, and the instructor scolds the student. This consequence—the teacher's verbal reprimand—makes the student less likely to interrupt in the future. In punishment, a response decreases because of its unpleasant consequences.

● **punishment** A consequence that decreases the likelihood that a behavior will occur.

● **positive punishment** The presentation of a stimulus following a given behavior in order to decrease the frequency of that behavior.

● **negative punishment** The removal of a stimulus following a given behavior in order to decrease the frequency of that behavior.

Just as the positive–negative distinction applies to reinforcement, it can also apply to punishment. As was the case for reinforcement, "positive" means adding something, and "negative" means taking something away. Thus, in **positive punishment** a behavior decreases when it is followed by the presentation of a stimulus, whereas in **negative punishment** a behavior decreases when a stimulus is removed. Examples of positive punishment include spanking a misbehaving child and scolding a spouse who forgot to call when she was running late at the office; the coach who makes his team run wind sprints after a lackadaisical practice is also using positive punishment. *Time-out* is a form of negative punishment in which a child is removed from a positive reinforcer, such as her toys. Getting grounded is also a form of negative punishment as it involves taking a teenager away from the fun things in his life. Figure 9 compares positive reinforcement, negative reinforcement, positive punishment, and negative punishment.

TIMING, REINFORCEMENT, AND PUNISHMENTS

How does the timing of reinforcement and punishment influence behavior? And does it matter whether the reinforcement is small or large?

Immediate Versus Delayed Reinforcement As is the case in classical conditioning, in operant conditioning learning is more efficient when the interval between a behavior and its reinforcer is a few seconds rather than minutes or hours, especially in lower animals (Freestone & Church, 2010). If a food reward is delayed for more than 30 seconds after a rat presses a bar, it is virtually ineffective as reinforcement (McNamara & others, 2015). Humans have the ability to connect their behaviors to delayed reinforcers. We can, for instance, study hard knowing that a test is a few weeks away (as there is the reward of the grade we will earn).

Sometimes important life decisions involve whether to seek and enjoy a small, immediate reinforcer or to wait for a delayed but more highly valued reinforcer (Murray, Theakston, & Wells, 2016). For example, you might spend your money now on clothes, concert tickets, and the latest smartphone, or you might save your money and buy a car

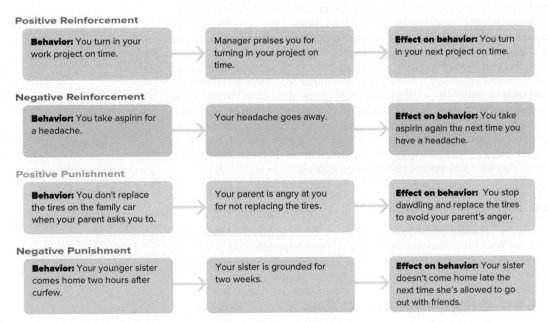

Positive Reinforcement

| **Behavior:** You turn in your work project on time. | Manager praises you for turning in your project on time. | **Effect on behavior:** You turn in your next project on time. |

Negative Reinforcement

| **Behavior:** You take aspirin for a headache. | Your headache goes away. | **Effect on behavior:** You take aspirin again the next time you have a headache. |

Positive Punishment

| **Behavior:** You don't replace the tires on the family car when your parent asks you to. | Your parent is angry at you for not replacing the tires. | **Effect on behavior:** You stop dawdling and replace the tires to avoid your parent's anger. |

Negative Punishment

| **Behavior:** Your younger sister comes home two hours after curfew. | Your sister is grounded for two weeks. | **Effect on behavior:** Your sister doesn't come home late the next time she's allowed to go out with friends. |

FIGURE 9 **Positive Reinforcement, Negative Reinforcement, Positive Punishment, and Negative Punishment** The fine distinctions here can sometimes be confusing. With respect to reinforcement, note that both types of reinforcement are intended to increase behavior, either by presenting a stimulus (in positive reinforcement) or by taking away a stimulus (in negative reinforcement). Punishment is meant to decrease a behavior either by presenting something (in positive punishment) or by taking away something (in negative punishment). The words *positive* and *negative* mean the same things in both cases.

later. You might choose to enjoy yourself now in return for immediate small reinforcers, or you might opt to study hard in return for delayed stronger reinforcers such as good grades, admittance to professional school, and a better job.

Immediate Versus Delayed Punishment   As with reinforcement, in most instances of research with lower animals, immediate punishment is more effective than delayed punishment in decreasing the occurrence of a behavior. However, also as with reinforcement, delayed punishment can have an effect on human behavior. Not studying at the beginning of a semester can lead to poor grades much later, and humans have the capacity to notice that this early behavior contributed to the negative outcome.

Immediate Versus Delayed Reinforcement and Punishment   Many daily behaviors revolve around rewards and punishments, both immediate and delayed. We might put off going to the dentist to avoid a small punisher (such as the discomfort that comes with getting a cavity filled). However, this procrastination might contribute to greater pain later (such as the pain of having a tooth pulled). Sometimes life is about enduring a little pain now to avoid a lot of pain later.

How does receiving immediate small reinforcement versus delayed strong punishment affect human behavior? One reason that obesity is such a major health problem is that eating is a behavior with immediate positive consequences—food tastes great and quickly provides a pleasurable, satisfied feeling. Although the potential delayed consequences of overeating are negative (obesity and other possible health risks), the immediate consequences are difficult to override. When the delayed consequences of behavior are punishing and the immediate consequences are reinforcing, the immediate consequences usually win, even when the immediate consequences are minor reinforcers, and the delayed consequences are major punishers.

Smoking and drinking follow a similar pattern. The immediate consequences of smoking are reinforcing for most smokers—the powerful combination of positive reinforcement (enhanced attention, energy boost) and negative reinforcement (tension relief, removal of craving). The primarily long-term effects of smoking are punishing and include shortness of breath, a chronic sore throat and/or coughing, chronic obstructive pulmonary disease (COPD), heart disease, and cancer. Likewise, the immediate pleasurable consequences of drinking override the delayed consequences of a hangover or even alcoholism and liver disease.

Now think about the following situations. Why are some of us so reluctant to take up a new sport, try a new dance step, run for office on campus or in local government, or do almost anything different? One reason is that learning new skills often involves minor punishing consequences, such as initially looking and feeling stupid, not knowing what to do, and having to put up with sarcastic comments from others. In these circumstances, reinforcing consequences are often delayed. For example, it may take a long time to become a good enough golfer or a good enough dancer to enjoy these activities, but persevering through the rough patches just might be worth it.

Applied Behavior Analysis

Some thinkers have criticized behavioral approaches for ignoring mental processes and focusing only on observable behavior. Nevertheless, these approaches do provide an optimistic perspective for individuals interested in changing their behaviors. That is, rather than concentrating on factors such as the type of person you are, behavioral approaches imply that you can modify even longstanding habits by changing the reward contingencies that maintain those habits (Craighead & others, 2013; Miltenberger, Miller, & Zerger, 2015).

One real-world application of operant conditioning principles to promote better functioning is applied behavior analysis. **Applied behavior analysis,** also called **behavior modification,** is the use of operant conditioning principles to change human behavior. In applied behavior analysis, the rewards and punishers that exist in a particular setting are carefully analyzed and manipulated to change behaviors (Horner & Sugai, 2015;

● **applied behavior analysis or behavior modification** The use of operant conditioning principles to change human behavior.

200   CHAPTER 6   Learning

©Sam Edwards/age fotostock

test yourself

1. What is operant conditioning?
2. Define shaping and give two examples of it.
3. What is the difference between positive reinforcement and negative reinforcement? Between positive punishment and negative punishment?

Miltenberger, Miller, & Zerger, 2015). Applied behavior analysis seeks to identify the rewards that might be maintaining unwanted behaviors and to enhance the rewards of more appropriate behaviors. From this perspective, we can understand all human behavior as being influenced by rewards and punishments. If we can figure out what rewards and punishers are controlling a person's behavior, we can change them—and eventually the behavior itself.

A manager who rewards staff members with a casual-dress day or a half day off if they meet a particular work goal is employing applied behavior analysis. So are a therapist and a client when they establish clear consequences of the client's behavior in order to reinforce more adaptive actions and discourage less adaptive ones (Miltenberger, Miller, & Zerger, 2015). A teacher who notices that a troublesome student seems to enjoy the attention he receives—even when that attention is scolding—might use applied behavior analysis by changing her responses to the child's behavior, ignoring it instead (an example of negative punishment). These examples show how attending to the consequences of behavior can be used to improve performance in settings such as the workplace and a classroom.

Applied behavior analysis has been effective in a wide range of situations. Practitioners have used it, for example, to treat individuals with autism (McMillin & others, 2015; Otero & others, 2015), children and adolescents with psychological problems (Ahmann, 2014; Pelham & others, 2016), and residents of mental health facilities (Kahng & others, 2015); to instruct individuals in effective parenting (Phaneuf & McIntyre, 2007); to enhance environmentally conscious behaviors such as recycling and properly disposing of garbage (Geller, 2002; Norton & others, 2015); to get people to wear seatbelts (Streff & Geller, 1986) and speed less (Mullen, Maxwell, & Bédard, 2015); and to promote workplace safety (Geller & Robinson, 2015). Applied behavior analysis can help people improve their self-control in many aspects of mental and physical health (Levy, 2013; Mazur, 2013).

4. OBSERVATIONAL LEARNING

Would it make sense to teach a 15-year-old girl how to drive with either classical conditioning or operant conditioning procedures? Driving a car is a voluntary behavior, so classical conditioning would not apply. In terms of operant conditioning, we could ask her to try to drive down the road and then reward her positive behaviors. Not many of us would want to be on the road, though, when she makes mistakes. Consider, as well, how many things human beings do that are arbitrary but important. We wave to say hello or good-bye, we eat certain foods for breakfast and not others. These conventions are learned through observational learning (Lindström & Olsson, 2015).

Albert Bandura (2011a) believes that if all our learning were conducted in such a trial-and-error fashion, learning would be exceedingly tedious and at times hazardous. Instead, he says, many complex behaviors are the result of exposure to competent models. By observing other people, we can acquire knowledge, skills, rules, strategies, beliefs, and attitudes (Meltzoff & Williamson, 2013). The capacity to learn by observation eliminates trial-and-error learning, and often such learning takes less time than operant conditioning.

Bandura's *observational learning,* also called *imitation* or *modeling,* is learning that occurs when a person observes and imitates behavior. Perhaps the most famous example of observational learning is the Bobo doll study (Bandura, Ross, & Ross, 1961). Bandura and his colleagues randomly assigned some children to watch an adult behaving aggressively and other children to watch an adult behaving nonaggressively. In the experimental condition, children saw the model hit an inflated Bobo doll with a mallet, kick it in the air, punch it, and throw it, all the while hollering aggressive phrases such as "Hit him!" "Punch him in the nose!" and "Pow!" In the control condition, the model played with Tinkertoys and ignored the Bobo doll. Children who watched the aggressive model were much more likely to engage in aggressive behavior when left alone with Bobo (Bandura, Ross, & Ross, 1961).

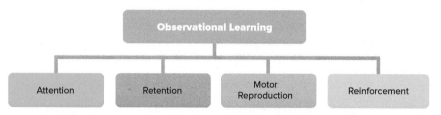

FIGURE 10 **Bandura's Model of Observational Learning** In terms of Bandura's model, if you are learning to ski, you need to attend to the instructor's words and demonstrations. You need to remember what the instructor did and said about how to avoid disasters. You also need the motor abilities to reproduce what the instructor has shown you. Praise from the instructor after you have completed a few moves on the slopes should improve your motivation to continue skiing.

Bandura (1986) described four main processes that are involved in observational learning: attention, retention, motor reproduction, and reinforcement. The first process that must occur is *attention* (which we considered in the chapter "Sensation and Perception" due to its crucial role in perception). To reproduce a model's actions, you must attend to what the model is saying or doing. You might not hear what a friend says if music is blaring, and you might miss your instructor's analysis of a problem if you are admiring someone sitting in the next row. As a further example, imagine that you decide to take a class to improve your drawing skills. To succeed, you need to attend to the instructor's words and hand movements. Characteristics of the model can influence whether we pay attention to him or her. Warm, powerful, atypical people, for example, command more attention than do cold, weak, typical people.

Retention is the second process required for observational learning to occur. Retention means you must hold the information in memory. To reproduce a model's actions, you must encode the information and keep it in memory so that you can retrieve it. A simple verbal description, or a vivid image of what the model did, assists retention. (Memory is such an important cognitive process that we devote the chapter "Memory" exclusively to it.) In the example of taking a class to sharpen your drawing skills, you will need to remember what the instructor said and did in modeling good drawing skills.

Motor reproduction, a third element of observational learning, is the process of imitating the model's actions. People might pay attention to a model and encode what they have seen, but limitations in motor development might make it difficult for them to reproduce the model's action. A 13-year-old might see a professional basketball player do a reverse two-handed dunk but be unable to reproduce the pro's play. Similarly, in your drawing class, if you lack fine motor reproduction skills, you might be unable to follow the instructor's example.

Reinforcement is a final component of observational learning. In this case, the question is whether the model's behavior is followed by a consequence. Seeing a model attain a reward for an activity increases the chances that an observer will repeat the behavior—a process called *vicarious reinforcement*. On the other hand, seeing the model punished makes the observer less likely to repeat the behavior—a process called *vicarious punishment*. Unfortunately, vicarious reinforcement and vicarious punishment are often absent in, for example, media portrayals of violence and aggression.

Observational learning has been studied in a variety of contexts. Researchers have explored observational learning, for example, as a means by which gorillas learn from one another about motor skills (Byrne, Hobaiter, & Klailova, 2011). They have also studied it as a process by which people learn whether stimuli are likely to be painful (Helsen & others, 2011) and as a tool individuals use to make economic decisions (Beshears & others, 2015).

Observational learning can be an important factor in the functioning of role models in inspiring people and changing their perceptions. Whether a model is similar to us can influence that model's effectiveness in modifying our behavior. The shortage of role models for women and minorities in science and engineering has often been suggested as a reason for the lack of women and minorities in these fields. After the election of Barack Obama as president of the United States, many commentators noted that for the first time, African American children could see concretely that they might also attain the nation's highest office some day. Figure 10 summarizes Bandura's model of observational learning.

test yourself

1. What are the four processes involved in observational learning?
2. What are two other names for observational learning?
3. What are vicarious reinforcement and vicarious punishment?

5. COGNITIVE FACTORS IN LEARNING

In learning about learning, we have looked at cognitive processes only as they apply in observational learning. Skinner's operant conditioning perspective and Pavlov's classical conditioning approach focus on the environment and observable behavior, not what is going on in the head of the learner. Many contemporary psychologists, including some behaviorists, recognize the importance of cognition and believe that learning involves more than environment–behavior connections. A good starting place for considering cognitive influences in learning is the work of E. C. Tolman.

Purposive Behavior

E. C. Tolman (1932) emphasized the *purposiveness* of behavior—the idea that much of behavior is goal-directed. Tolman believed that it is necessary to study entire behavioral sequences in order to understand why people engage in particular actions. For example, high school students whose goal is to attend a leading college or university study hard in their classes. If we focused only on their studying, we would miss the purpose of their behavior. The students do not always study hard because they have been reinforced for studying in the past. Rather, studying is a means to intermediate goals (learning, high grades) that in turn improve their likelihood of getting into the college or university of their choice. To understand human behavior, we sometimes need to place it in a larger context.

We can see Tolman's legacy today in the extensive interest in the role of goal setting in human behavior (Berson & others, 2015; Stetler & Magnusson, 2015). Researchers are especially curious about how people self-regulate and self-monitor their behavior to reach a goal (Bridgett & others, 2015).

EXPECTANCY LEARNING AND INFORMATION

In studying the purposiveness of behavior, Tolman went beyond the stimuli and responses of Pavlov and Skinner to focus on cognitive mechanisms. Tolman said that when classical conditioning and operant conditioning occur, the organism acquires certain expectations. In classical conditioning, the young boy fears the rabbit because he expects it will hurt him. In operant conditioning, a woman works hard all week because she expects a paycheck on Friday. Expectancies are acquired from people's experiences with their environment. Expectancies influence a variety of human experiences. We set the goals we do because we believe that we can reach them.

Expectancies also play a role in the placebo effect, described earlier. Many painkillers have been shown to be more effective in reducing pain if patients can see the intravenous injection sites (Price, Finniss, & Benedetti, 2008). If patients can observe that they are getting a drug, they can harness their own expectations for pain reduction.

Tolman (1932) emphasized that the information value of the conditioned stimulus is important as a signal or an expectation that an unconditioned stimulus will follow. Anticipating contemporary thinking, Tolman believed that the information that the CS provides is the key to understanding classical conditioning.

One contemporary view of classical conditioning describes an organism as an information seeker, using logical and perceptual relations among events, along with preconceptions, to form a representation of the world (Rescorla, 2003, 2004, 2005, 2006a, 2006b, 2006c, 2009).

A classic experiment conducted by Leon Kamin (1968) illustrates the importance of an organism's history and the information provided by a conditioned stimulus in classical conditioning. Kamin conditioned a rat by repeatedly pairing a tone (CS) and a shock (US) until the tone alone produced fear (CR). Then he continued to pair the tone with the shock, but he turned on a light (a second CS) each time the tone sounded. Even though he repeatedly paired the light (CS) and the shock (US), the rat showed no conditioning to the light (the light by itself produced no CR). Conditioning to the light was blocked, almost as if the rat had not paid attention. The rat apparently used the tone as a signal to predict that a shock would be coming; information about the light's pairing with the shock was redundant with the information already learned about the tone's pairing with the shock. In this experiment, conditioning was governed not by the contiguity of the CS and US but instead by the rat's history and the informational value of the stimuli it encountered. The rat already possessed a good signal for the shock; the additional CS was not useful.

LATENT LEARNING

Experiments on latent learning provide other evidence to support the role of cognition in learning. **Latent learning** or **implicit learning** is unreinforced learning that is not immediately reflected in behavior.

● **latent learning or implicit learning** Unreinforced learning that is not immediately reflected in behavior.

In one study, researchers put two groups of hungry rats in a maze and required them to find their way from a starting point to an end point (Tolman & Honzik, 1930). The first group found food (a reinforcer) at the end point; the second group found nothing there. In the operant conditioning view, the first group should learn the maze better than the second group, which is exactly what happened. However, when the researchers subsequently took some of the rats from the nonreinforced group and gave them food at the end point of the maze, they quickly began to run the maze as effectively as the reinforced group. The nonreinforced rats apparently had learned a great deal about the maze as they roamed around and explored it. However, their learning was *latent,* stored cognitively in their memories but not yet expressed behaviorally. When these rats were given a good reason (reinforcement with food) to run the maze speedily, they called on their latent learning to help them reach the end of the maze more quickly.

Outside a laboratory, latent learning is evident when you walk around a new setting to get "the lay of the land." The first time you visited your college campus, you may have wandered about without a specific destination in mind. Exploring the environment made you better prepared when the time came to find that 8 A.M. class.

Insight Learning

Like Tolman, the German gestalt psychologist Wolfgang Köhler believed that cognitive factors play a significant role in learning. Köhler spent four months in the Canary Islands during World War I observing the behavior of apes. There he conducted two fascinating experiments—the stick problem and the box problem. Although these two experiments are basically the same, the solutions to the problems are different. In both situations, the ape discovers that it cannot reach an alluring piece of fruit, either because the fruit is too high or because it is outside of the ape's cage and beyond reach. To solve the stick problem, the ape has to insert a small stick inside a larger stick to reach the fruit. To master the box problem, the ape must stack several boxes to reach the fruit (Figure 11).

According to Köhler (1925), solving these problems does not involve trial and error or simple connections between stimuli and responses. Rather, when the ape realizes that its customary actions are not going to help it get the fruit, it often sits for a period of time and appears to ponder how to solve the problem. Then it quickly rises, as if it has had a sudden flash of insight, piles the boxes on top of one another, and gets the fruit. **Insight learning** is a form of problem solving in which the organism develops a sudden insight into or understanding of a problem's solution.

● **insight learning** A form of problem solving in which the organism develops a sudden insight into or understanding of a problem's solution.

The idea that insight learning is essentially different from learning through trial and error or through conditioning has always been controversial (Spence, 1938). Insight learning appears to entail both gradual and sudden processes, and understanding how these lead to problem solving continues to fascinate psychologists (Chu & MacGregor, 2011; Weisberg, 2015).

Research has documented that nonhuman primates are capable of remarkable learning that certainly appears to be insightful (Manrique, Völter, & Call, 2013). In one study,

FIGURE 11   **Insight Learning** Sultan, one of Köhler's brightest chimps, was faced with the problem of reaching a cluster of bananas overhead. He solved the problem by stacking boxes on top of one another to reach the bananas. Köhler called this type of problem solving "insight learning." (all) ©SuperStock

researchers observed orangutans trying to figure out a way to get a tempting peanut out of a clear plastic tube (Mendes, Hanus, & Call, 2007). The primates wandered about their enclosures, experimenting with various strategies. Typically, they paused for a moment before finally landing on a solution: Little by little they filled the tube with water that they transferred by mouth from their water dishes to the tube. Once the peanut floated to the top, the clever orangutans had their snack. More recent research shows that chimps can solve the floating peanut task through observational learning (Tennie, Call, & Tomasello, 2010).

Insight learning requires that we think "outside the box," setting aside previous expectations and assumptions. One way to enhance insight learning and creativity in human beings is through multicultural experiences (Leung & others, 2008). Correlational studies have shown that time spent living abroad is associated with higher insight learning performance among MBA students (Maddux & Galinsky, 2007). Experimental studies have also demonstrated this effect. In one study, U.S. college students were randomly assigned to view one of two slide shows—one about Chinese and U.S. culture and the other about a control topic. Those who saw the multicultural slide show scored higher on measures of creativity and insight, and these changes persisted for a week (Leung & others, 2008).

Importantly, we can gain the benefits of multicultural exposure even without travel abroad or particular slide shows. One of the most dramatic changes in U.S. higher education is the increasing diversity of the student body. Might this growing diversity benefit students? Research suggests that it does. For instance, in a study of over 53,000 undergraduates at 124 colleges and universities, students' reported interactions with individuals from other racial and ethnic backgrounds predicted a variety of positive outcomes, including academic achievement, intellectual growth, and social competence (Hu & Kuh, 2003).

Many universities recognize that as U.S. society becomes more multiculturally diverse, students must be prepared to interact in a diverse community as they enter the job market. Participation in diversity courses in college is related to cognitive development (Bowman, 2010) and civic involvement (Gurin & others, 2002), with outcomes especially positive for non-Latino White students (Byrd, 2015; Hu & Kuh, 2003). Diverse groups provide broader knowledge and more varied perspectives than do homogeneous groups, to the positive benefit of all group members. As university communities become more diverse, they offer students an ever-greater opportunity to share and to benefit from those differences.

test yourself

1. What did Tolman mean by the purposiveness of behavior?
2. How do expectancies develop through classical and operant conditioning?
3. Define latent learning and insight learning and give an example of each.

6. BIOLOGICAL, CULTURAL, AND PSYCHOLOGICAL FACTORS IN LEARNING

Albert Einstein had many special talents. He combined enormous creativity with keen analytic ability to develop some of the twentieth century's most important insights into the nature of matter and the universe. Genes obviously endowed Einstein with extraordinary intellectual skills that enabled him to think and reason on a very high plane, but cultural factors also contributed to his genius. Einstein received an excellent, rigorous European education, and later in the United States he experienced the freedom and support believed to be important in creative exploration. Would Einstein have been able to develop his skills fully and to make such brilliant insights if he had grown up in a less advantageous environment? It is unlikely. Clearly, both biological *and* cultural factors contribute to learning.

Biological Constraints

Human beings cannot breathe under water, fish cannot ski, and cows cannot solve math problems. The structure of an organism's body permits certain kinds of learning and inhibits others. For example, chimpanzees cannot learn to speak human languages because they lack the necessary vocal equipment. In animals, various aspects of their physical makeup can influence what they can learn. Sometimes, species-typical behaviors (or instincts) can override even the best reinforcers, as we now consider.

INSTINCTIVE DRIFT

Keller and Marion Breland (1961), students of B. F. Skinner, used operant conditioning to train animals to perform at fairs and conventions and in television advertisements. They applied Skinner's techniques to teach pigs to cart large wooden nickels to a piggy bank and deposit them. They also trained raccoons to pick up a coin and drop it into a metal tray.

Although the pigs and raccoons, as well as chickens and other animals, performed most of the tasks well (raccoons became adept basketball players, for example—see Figure 12), some of the animals began acting strangely. Instead of picking up the large wooden nickels and carrying them to the piggy bank, the pigs dropped the nickels on the ground, shoved them with their snouts, tossed them in the air, and then repeated these actions. The raccoons began to hold on to their coins rather than dropping them into the metal tray. When two coins were introduced, the raccoons rubbed them together in a miserly fashion. Somehow these behaviors overwhelmed the strength of the reinforcement. This example of biological influences on learning illustrates **instinctive drift,** the tendency of animals to revert to instinctive behavior that interferes with learning.

Why were the pigs and the raccoons misbehaving? The pigs were rooting, an instinct that is used to uncover edible roots. The raccoons were engaging in an instinctive food-washing response. Their instinctive drift interfered with learning.

PREPAREDNESS

Some animals learn readily in one situation but have difficulty learning in slightly different circumstances (Garcia & Koelling, 1966, 2009). The difficulty might result not from some aspect of the learning situation but from the organism's biological predisposition (Seligman, 1970). **Preparedness** is the species-specific biological predisposition to learn in certain ways but not others.

Much of the evidence for preparedness comes from research on taste aversion (Garcia, 1989; Garcia & Koelling, 2009). Recall that taste aversion involves a single trial of learning the association between a particular taste and nausea. Rats that experience low

● **instinctive drift** The tendency of animals to revert to instinctive behavior that interferes with learning.

● **preparedness** The species-specific biological predisposition to learn in certain ways but not others.

FIGURE 12 **Instinctive Drift** This raccoon's skill in using its hands made it an excellent basketball player, but because of instinctive drift, the raccoon had a much more difficult time dropping coins into a tray. Cute. ©Keystone-France/Getty Images

levels of radiation after eating show a strong aversion to the food they were eating when the radiation made them ill. This aversion can last for as long as 32 days. Such long-term effects cannot be accounted for by classical conditioning, which would argue that a single pairing of the conditioned and unconditioned stimuli would not last that long (Garcia, Ervin, & Koelling, 1966). Taste aversion learning occurs in animals, including humans, that choose their food based on taste and smell. Other species are prepared to learn rapid associations between, for instance, colors of foods and illness.

Another example of preparedness comes from research on conditioning humans and monkeys to associate snakes with fear. Susan Mineka and Arne Öhman have investigated the fascinating natural power of snakes to evoke fear in many mammals (Mineka & Öhman, 2002; Öhman & Mineka, 2003). Many monkeys and humans fear snakes, and both monkeys and humans are very quick to learn the association between snakes and fear. In classical conditioning studies, when pictures of snakes (CS) are paired with electrical shocks (US), the snakes are likely to quickly and strongly evoke fear (CR). Interestingly, pairing pictures of, say, flowers (CS) with electrical shocks produces much weaker associations (Mineka & Öhman, 2002; Öhman & Soares, 1998). More significantly, pictures of snakes can serve as conditioned stimuli for fearful responses, even when the pictures are presented so rapidly that they cannot be consciously perceived (Öhman & Mineka, 2001).

The link between snakes and fear has been demonstrated not only in classical conditioning paradigms. Monkeys that have been raised in the lab and that have never seen a snake rapidly learn to fear snakes, even entirely by observational learning. Lab monkeys that see a videotape of a monkey expressing fear toward a snake learn to be afraid of snakes faster than monkeys seeing the same fear video spliced so that the feared object is a rabbit, a flower, or a mushroom (Öhman & Mineka, 2003).

Mineka and Öhman (2002) suggest that these results demonstrate preparedness among mammals to associate snakes with fear and aversive stimuli. They suggest that this association is related to the amygdala (the part of the limbic system that is related to emotion) and is difficult to modify. These researchers suggest that this preparedness for fear of snakes has emerged out of the threat that reptiles likely posed to our evolutionary ancestors.

Cultural Influences

Traditionally, interest in the cultural context of human learning has been limited, partly because the organisms in those contexts typically were animals. The question arises, how might culture influence human learning? Most psychologists agree that the principles of classical conditioning, operant conditioning, and observational learning are universal and are powerful learning processes in every culture. However, culture can influence the *degree* to which these learning processes are used (Matsumoto & Juang, 2017). For example, Mexican American students may learn more through observational learning, while non-Latino White students may be more accustomed to learn through direct instruction (Mejía-Arauz, Rogoff, & Paradise, 2005).

In addition, culture can determine the *content* of learning (Mistry, Contreras, & Dutta, 2013; Zhang & Sternberg, 2013). We cannot learn about something we do not experience. The 4-year-old who grows up among the Bushmen of the Kalahari Desert is unlikely to learn about taking baths and eating with a knife and fork. Similarly, a child growing up in Chicago is unlikely to be skilled at tracking animals and finding water-bearing roots in the desert. Learning often requires practice, and certain behaviors are practiced more often in some cultures than in others. In Bali, many children are skilled dancers by the age of 6, whereas Norwegian children are much more likely to be good skiers and skaters by that age.

On the Indonesian island of Bali, young children learn traditional dances, whereas in Norway children commonly learn to ski early in life. As cultures vary, so does the content of learning.

(first) © Paul Chesley/Stone/Getty Images; (second) ©Paul A. Souders/Getty Images

Psychological Constraints

Are there psychological constraints on learning? For animals, the answer is probably no. For humans, the answer may well be yes. This section opened with the claim that fish cannot ski. The truth of this statement is clear. Biological circumstances make it impossible. If we put biological considerations aside, we might ask ourselves about

CRITICAL CONTROVERSY

Do Learning Styles Matter to Learning?

The term *learning styles* refers to the idea that people differ in regard to which method of instruction will be most effective for them. You may have heard, for example, that someone can be a visual learner (he or she learns by seeing), an aural learner (the person learns by listening), or a kinesthetic learner (the individual learns through hands-on experience).

The notion that people have different learning styles is extremely popular. Many educational training programs and school districts advise teachers to take such differences into account in the classroom, tailoring their methods to fit students' learning styles. This advice is, of course, based on the assumption that individuals will learn better when instructions are targeted to their particular learning style.

Is there sound evidence for this assumption? Does tailoring instruction to different learning styles improve learning? A number of experts have examined research on this question (Pashler & others, 2008; Rohrer & Pashler, 2012), and their answer might surprise you. The scientific evidence shows that although children and adults report consistent preferences for particular learning styles, there is no evidence that tailoring instructional methods to "visual," "auditory," or "kinesthetic" learners produces better learning (Pashler & others, 2008).

Consider one study, in which researchers first measured whether participants were verbal or visual learners and then had them study a list of words presented verbally or visually. This study period was followed by a memory test. Results showed that all participants did better in the visual condition, and there was no relationship between preferred learning styles and memory for the material (Constantinidou & Baker, 2002).

In another series of studies, participants who identified themselves as visual or verbal learners were given the option to use visual or verbal help materials as they completed a computer-based learning unit. Although learning styles predicted the kind of materials participants preferred, the match between a person's learning style and the mode of instruction was unrelated to learning (Massa & Mayer, 2006). The investigators concluded that there was no evidence that different

© Purestock

© Steve Hix/Fuse/Getty Images

instructional methods should be used for different learners (Massa & Mayer, 2006). Based on these and other studies, Harold Pashler, an expert on human learning, and his colleagues concluded that the disconnect between the popularity of the learning styles approach within education and the lack of credible evidence for its usefulness was both "striking and disturbing" (2008, p. 117).

The notion of learning styles is appealing at least in part because it reflects something we know to be true: People learn differently. However, the different ways humans learn do not seem to be well captured by learning styles (Willingham, 2011). The effectiveness of particular methods of teaching may depend more on the material to be covered, a student's prior knowledge, motivation, and other factors. Coming at any topic from many different angles may improve student learning. Teachers may reach more students more effectively when they try different ways of approaching material—for instance, coming up with a hands-on tool to demonstrate a problem—but that is just good instruction, not instruction that is tailored to particular styles. Our senses work together to connect us to the external world. The brain and our sensory organs are not specialized to learn in specific ways.

Is there any harm in our trying to determine our preferred learning style? Perhaps, if the outcome constrains learning—if we assume, for example, that our personal learning style tells us what we cannot do or should not try. Sometimes the most meaningful learning experiences are those that push us beyond our comfort zone. Teachers and topics that challenge us to put in extra effort, to see the world and ourselves in different ways, may be the key to meaningful learning. Sometimes the easiest path is not the one most likely to lead to life-changing learning.

WHAT DO YOU THINK?

- Do you think that you have a particular learning style? If so, how does it influence your learning?
- Even if evidence supported the effectiveness of tailoring teaching methods to specific types of learning styles, how would we implement a program based on these ideas?

times in our lives when we feel like a fish trying to ski—when we feel that we just do not have what it takes to learn a skill or master a task. Some people believe that humans have particular learning styles that make it easier for them to learn in some ways but not others. To read about this possibility, see the Critical Controversy.

Carol Dweck (2006; Rattan & others, 2015) uses the term *mindset* to describe the way our beliefs about ability dictate what goals we set for ourselves, what we think we *can* learn, and ultimately what we *do* learn. Individuals have one of two mindsets: a *fixed mindset,* in which they believe that their qualities are carved in stone and cannot change; or a *growth mindset,* in which they believe their qualities can change and improve through their effort. These two mindsets have implications for the meaning of failure. From a fixed mindset, failure means lack of ability. From a growth mindset, however, failure tells the person what he or she still needs to learn. Your mindset influences whether you will be optimistic or pessimistic, what your goals will be, how hard you will strive to reach those goals, and how successful you are in college and after.

Dweck (2006) studied first-year pre-med majors taking their first chemistry class in college. Students with a growth mindset got higher grades than those with a fixed mindset. Even when they did not do well on a test, the growth-mindset students bounced back on the next test. Fixed-mindset students typically read and re-read the text and class notes or tried to memorize everything verbatim. The fixed-mindset students who did poorly on tests concluded that chemistry and maybe pre-med were not for them. By contrast, growth-mindset students took charge of their motivation and learning, searching for themes and principles in the course and going over mistakes until they understood why they made them. In Dweck's analysis, "They were studying to learn, not just ace the test. And, actually, this is why they got higher grades—not because they were smarter or had a better background in science" (Dweck, 2006, p. 61).

Dweck and her colleagues have continued to explore ways to improve students' motivation to achieve and succeed (Rattan & others, 2015). In one study, they assigned two groups of students to eight sessions of either (1) study skills instruction or (2) study skills instruction plus information about the importance of developing a growth mindset (called *incremental theory* in the research) (Blackwell, Trzesniewski, & Dweck, 2007).

One of the exercises in the growth-mindset group was titled "You Can Grow Your Brain," and it emphasized that the brain is like a muscle that can change and grow as it gets exercised and develops new connections. Students were informed that the more they challenged their brain to learn, the more their brain cells would grow. Prior to the intervention, both groups had a pattern of declining math scores. Following the intervention, the group that received only the study skills instruction continued to decline, but the group that received the study skills instruction *plus* the growth-mindset emphasis reversed the downward trend and improved their math achievement.

Following are some effective strategies for developing a growth mindset (Dweck, 2006):

- *Understand that your intelligence and thinking skills are not fixed but can change.* Even if you are extremely bright, with effort you can increase your intelligence.
- *Become passionate about learning and stretch your mind in challenging situations.* It is easy to withdraw into a fixed mindset when the going gets tough. However, as you bump up against obstacles, keep growing, work harder, stay the course, and improve your strategies; you will become a more successful person.
- *Think about the growth mindsets of people you admire.* Possibly you have a hero, someone who has achieved something extraordinary. You may have thought his or her accomplishments came easily because the person is so talented. If you find out more about this person, though, you likely will discover that hard work and effort over a long period of time were responsible for his or her achievements.
- *Begin now.* If you have a fixed mindset, commit to changing now. Think about when, where, and how you will begin using your new growth mindset.

Dweck's work challenges us to consider the limits we place on our own learning. Our beliefs about ability profoundly influence what we try to learn. As any 7-year-old with a growth mindset would tell you, you never know what you can do until you try.

7. LEARNING AND HEALTH AND WELLNESS

In this chapter, we have examined the main psychological approaches to learning. In this final section, we consider specific ways that research on learning has shed light on human health and wellness. We examine in particular the factors that animal learning models

test yourself

1. What are two biological constraints on learning?
2. How does culture influence learning?
3. What is the difference between a fixed mindset and a growth mindset?

have identified as playing an important role in the experience of stress—which, as you will recall from the chapter "Biological Foundations of Behavior", is the organism's response to a threat in the environment. A great deal of research in learning has relied primarily on models of animals, such as rats, to examine the principles that underlie human learning. Research on the stress response in rats provides useful insights into how we humans can deal with stress.

STRESS AND PREDICTABILITY

One very powerful aspect of potentially stressful experiences is their predictability. For a rat, predictability might depend on getting a warning buzzer before receiving a shock. Although the rat still experiences the shock, a buzzer-preceded shock causes less stress than a shock that is received with no warning (Abbott, Schoen, & Badia, 1984). Even having *good* experiences on a predictable schedule is less stressful than having good things happen at random times. For example, a rat might do very well receiving its daily chow at specific times during the day, but if the timing is random, the rat experiences stress. Similarly, when you receive a gift on your birthday or a holiday, the experience feels good. However, if someone surprises you with a present out of the blue, you might feel some stress as you wonder, "What is this person up to?"

© Image100 Ltd

Also relevant is classic research by Judith Rodin and her colleagues. In this study, nursing home residents showed better adjustment if they experienced a given number of visits at predictable times rather than the same number of visits at random times (Langer & Rodin, 1976).

STRESS AND CONTROL

Feeling in control may be a key to avoiding feelings of stress over difficulties (Carver & Scheier, 2013). Specifically, once you have experienced control over negative events, you may be "protected" from stress, even during trying times.

Returning to an animal model, suppose that a rat has been trained to avoid a shock by pressing a lever. Over time, even when the lever is no longer related to the shock, the rat presses it during the shock—and experiences less stress. We might imagine the rat thinking, "Gee, it would be really worse if I weren't pressing this lever!" Researchers have also found links between having control and experiencing stress in humans. For example, as mentioned above with the nursing home study (Langer & Rodin, 1976), residents are more likely to thrive if they receive visits at times they personally choose. In addition, simply having a plant to take care of is associated with living longer for nursing home residents.

A lack of control over aversive stimuli can be particularly stressful. For example, individuals exposed to uncontrollable loud blasts of noise show lowered immune system function (Sieber & others, 1992). One result of exposure to uncontrollable negative events is *learned helplessness,* which we examined earlier in this chapter. In learned helplessness, the organism has learned through experience that outcomes are not controllable. As a result, the organism stops trying to exert control.

Research has shown that, to break the lock of learned helplessness, dogs and rats have to be forcibly moved to escape an aversive shock (Seligman, Rosellini, & Kozak, 1975). From such animal studies, we can appreciate how difficult it may be for individuals who find themselves in situations in which they have little control—for example, women who are victims of domestic violence (Walker, 2009)—to take action. We can also appreciate the helplessness sometimes experienced by students with learning difficulties who withdraw from their coursework because they feel unable to influence outcomes in school (Gwernan-Jones & Burden, 2010).

STRESS AND IMPROVEMENT

Imagine that you have two mice, both of which are receiving mild electrical shocks. One of them, Jerry, receives 50 shocks every hour, and the other, Chuck-E, receives 10 shocks every hour. The next day both rats are switched to 25 shocks every hour. Which one is more stressed out at the end of the second day? The answer is that even though Jerry has experienced more shocks in general, Chuck-E is more likely to show the wear and tear of stress. In Jerry's world, even with 25 shocks an hour, *things are better*. The perception of improvement, even in a situation that is objectively worse than another, is related to lowered stress (Sapolsky, 2004).

OUTLETS FOR FRUSTRATION

When things are not going well for us, it often feels good to find an outlet, such as going for a run or, perhaps even better, taking a kickboxing class. Likewise, for a rat, having an outlet for life's frustrations is related to lowered stress symptoms. Rats that have a wooden post to gnaw on or even a furry little friend to complain to are less stressed out in response to negative circumstances.

Although studies using rats and dogs may seem far afield of our everyday experiences, researchers' observations provide important clues for avoiding stress. When we cultivate predictable environments and take control of circumstances, stress decreases. Further, when we can see improvement, even in difficult times, stress is likely to diminish. Finally, when we have an outlet for our frustrations in life—whether it is physical exercise, writing, or art—we can relieve our stress. When it comes to stress, humans have a lot to learn from rats.

test yourself

1. Based on research involving animal models, what are four ways in which human beings can reduce stress?
2. What is the main effect of learned helplessness on an organism?
3. Why do individuals who are experiencing domestic violence often have difficulty in overcoming their troubles?

SUMMARY

1. TYPES OF LEARNING

Learning is a systematic, relatively permanent change in behavior that occurs through experience. Associative learning involves learning by making a connection between two events. Observational learning is learning by watching what other people do. Conditioning is the process by which associative learning occurs. In classical conditioning, organisms learn the association between two stimuli. In operant conditioning, they learn the association between behavior and a consequence.

2. CLASSICAL CONDITIONING

Classical conditioning occurs when a neutral stimulus becomes associated with a meaningful stimulus and comes to elicit a similar response. Pavlov discovered that an organism learns the association between an unconditioned stimulus (US) and a conditioned stimulus (CS). The US automatically produces the unconditioned response (UR). After conditioning (CS–US pairing), the CS elicits the conditioned response (CR) by itself. Acquisition in classical conditioning is the initial linking of stimuli and responses, which involves a neutral stimulus being associated with the US so that the CS comes to elicit the CR. Two important aspects of acquisition are contiguity and contingency.

Generalization in classical conditioning is the tendency of a new stimulus that is similar to the original conditioned stimulus to elicit a response that is similar to the conditioned response. Discrimination is the process of learning to respond to certain stimuli and not to others. Extinction is the weakening of the CR in the absence of the US. Spontaneous recovery is the recurrence of a CR after a time delay without further conditioning. Renewal is the occurrence of the CR (even after extinction) when the CS is presented in a novel environment.

In humans, classical conditioning has been applied to eliminating fears, treating addiction, understanding taste aversion, and explaining different experiences such as pleasant emotions and drug overdose.

3. OPERANT CONDITIONING

Operant conditioning is a form of learning in which the consequences of behavior produce changes in the probability of the behavior's occurrence. Skinner described the behavior of the organism as operant: The behavior operates on the environment, and the environment in turn operates on the organism. Whereas classical conditioning involves respondent behavior, operant conditioning involves operant behavior. In

most instances, operant conditioning is better at explaining voluntary behavior than is classical conditioning.

Thorndike's law of effect states that behaviors followed by pleasant outcomes are strengthened, whereas behaviors followed by unpleasant outcomes are weakened. Skinner built on this idea to develop the notion of operant conditioning.

Shaping is the process of rewarding approximations of desired behavior in order to shorten the learning process. Principles of reinforcement include the distinction between positive reinforcement (the frequency of a behavior increases because it is followed by a rewarding stimulus) and negative reinforcement (the frequency of behavior increases because it is followed by the removal of an aversive, or unpleasant, stimulus). Positive reinforcement can be classified as primary reinforcement (using reinforcers that are innately satisfying) and secondary reinforcement (using reinforcers that acquire positive value through experience).

Reinforcement can also be continuous (a behavior is reinforced every time) or partial (a behavior is reinforced only a portion of the time). Schedules of reinforcement—fixed ratio, variable ratio, fixed interval, and variable interval—determine when a behavior will be reinforced.

Operant, or instrumental, conditioning involves generalization (giving the same response to similar stimuli), discrimination (responding to stimuli that signal that a behavior will or will not be reinforced), and extinction (a decreasing tendency to perform a previously reinforced behavior when reinforcement is stopped).

Punishment is a consequence that decreases the likelihood that a behavior will occur. In positive punishment, a behavior decreases when it is followed by a (typically unpleasant) stimulus. In negative punishment, a behavior decreases when a positive stimulus is removed from it.

Applied behavior analysis, or behavior modification, involves the application of operant conditioning principles to a variety of real-life behaviors.

4. OBSERVATIONAL LEARNING

Observational learning occurs when a person observes and imitates someone else's behavior. Bandura identified four main processes in observational learning: attention (paying heed to what someone is saying or doing), retention (encoding that information and keeping it in memory so that you can retrieve it), motor reproduction (imitating the actions of the person being observed), and reinforcement (seeing the person attain a reward for the activity).

5. COGNITIVE FACTORS IN LEARNING

Tolman emphasized the purposiveness of behavior. His belief was that much of behavior is goal-directed. In studying purposiveness, Tolman went beyond stimuli and responses to discuss cognitive mechanisms; he believed that expectancies, acquired through experiences with the environment, are an important cognitive mechanism in learning.

Latent learning is unreinforced learning that is not immediately reflected in behavior. Latent learning may occur when a rat or a person roams a particular location and shows knowledge of the area when that knowledge is rewarded.

Köhler developed the concept of insight learning, a form of problem solving in which the organism develops a sudden insight into or understanding of a problem's solution.

6. BIOLOGICAL, CULTURAL, AND PSYCHOLOGICAL FACTORS IN LEARNING

Biology restricts what an organism can learn from experience. These constraints include instinctive drift (the tendency of animals to revert to instinctive behavior that interferes with learned behavior), preparedness (the species-specific biological predisposition to learn in certain ways but not in others), and taste aversion (the biological predisposition to avoid foods that have caused sickness in the past).

Although most psychologists agree that the principles of classical conditioning, operant conditioning, and observational learning are universal, cultural customs can influence the degree to which these learning processes are used. Culture also often determines the content of learning.

In addition, what we learn is determined in part by what we believe we can learn. Dweck emphasizes that individuals benefit enormously from having a growth mindset rather than a fixed mindset.

7. LEARNING AND HEALTH AND WELLNESS

Research using rats and other animals has demonstrated four important variables involved in the human stress response: predictability, perceived control, perceptions of improvement, and outlets for frustration.

key *terms*

acquisition
applied behavior analysis or behavior modification
associative learning
aversive conditioning
avoidance learning
behaviorism
classical conditioning
conditioned response (CR)
conditioned stimulus (CS)
counterconditioning

discrimination (in classical conditioning)
discrimination (in operant conditioning)
extinction (in classical conditioning)
extinction (in operant conditioning)
generalization (in classical conditioning)
generalization (in operant conditioning)
habituation
insight learning

instinctive drift
latent learning or implicit learning
law of effect
learned helplessness
learning
negative punishment
negative reinforcement
observational learning
operant conditioning or instrumental conditioning
positive punishment
positive reinforcement

primary reinforcer
punishment
preparedness
reinforcement
renewal
schedules of reinforcement
secondary reinforcer
shaping
spontaneous recovery
unconditioned response (UR)
unconditioned stimulus (US)

apply your *knowledge*

1. Enlist some of your classmates to play this mind game on your professor. Every time your instructor moves to the right side of the room during lecture, be more attentive, smile, and nod. Start out by shaping—every time he or she moves even a little to the right, give a smile or nod. See how far you can get the instructor to go using this simple reward. In one introductory psychology class, students got their professor to move all the way to the right wall of the classroom, where she leaned, completely clueless.

2. The next time you are alone with a friend, try your best to use shaping and the principles of operant conditioning to get the person to touch the tip of his or her nose. Can you do it?

3. Demonstrate Pavlov's work with your friends. First buy some lemons and slice them. Then gather a group of friends to watch something on TV together, maybe the Academy Awards or the Super Bowl. Pick a conditioned stimulus that you know will come up a lot on the show—for example, someone saying "thank you" during the Oscars or a soft drink or beer ad during the Super Bowl. For the first half hour, everyone has to suck on a lemon slice (the US) when the CS is presented. After the first half hour, take the lemons away. Have everyone report on their salivation levels (the CR) whenever the CS is presented later in the show. What happens?

4. Positive reinforcement and negative reinforcement can be difficult concepts to grasp. The real-world examples and accompanying practice exercises on the following website should help to clarify the distinction:

   http://psych.athabascau.ca/html/prtut/reinpair.htm

5. Imagine that you are about to begin an internship in an organization where you would like to have a permanent position someday. Use the processes of observational learning to describe your strategy for making the most of your internship.

CHAPTER **8**

Thinking, Intelligence, and Language

A Real Power Plant

Sometimes crises lead to incredible inventions. Consider the plight of the residents of Nuevo Saposoa, a village in the Amazon rainforest in Peru. In March 2015, a flood laid waste to the electrical cables that provided power to the 173 people living there (Ahmed, 2016). These people were forced to use kerosene lanterns to see at night. Those lanterns are not only expensive but dangerous, as they involve, of course, open flames and toxic fumes. Building a power plant was simply too costly. Fixing the cables was not appealing either. These folks needed a durable solution to their problem. What to do?

Science came to the rescue in the form of researchers and students from the university in Lima. Their idea was to use what the rainforest offers—namely, soil and plants—to produce electricity. The team created the *Plantalámparas* ("lamp that runs on plant power") (Ahmed, 2016). Lamps are attached to a wooden box containing a plant in soil. Electrodes in the soil convert plant waste and microorganisms into energy. That energy is stored in a battery that produces light for 2 hours per charge. The plant-powered lamp is a brilliant idea that has brought light to the darkness for the people of Nuevo Saposoa.

Think about this amazing lamp for a moment. It is surprisingly simple and makes use of what scientists and engineers have known for a long time. Yet no one put it all together until calamity struck. Sometimes it takes a crisis to motivate the human capacity to devise a creative solution. ●

PREVIEW

Cognitive psychology is the study of mental processes. This chapter investigates the basic cognitive processes of thinking, intelligence, and language. We first define cognition and look at the cognitive revolution that led to new understanding about the workings of the human mind. Thinking refers to the process of cognition itself. We examine types of thinking, including problem solving, reasoning, critical thinking, and creativity. We then examine the quality of mental processes, focusing on a central indicator of cognitive ability—intelligence. We next explore the way that thoughts are typically expressed as we focus on the unique contribution of language to mental processes. Finally, we close by considering the role of thinking in health and wellness.

1. THE COGNITIVE REVOLUTION IN PSYCHOLOGY

● **cognition** The way in which information is processed and manipulated in remembering, thinking, and knowing.

Cognitive psychologists study **cognition**—the way in which information is processed and manipulated in remembering, thinking, and knowing. Cognitive psychology is a relatively young field, scarcely more than a half century old. We begin by tracing its history.

After the first decade of the twentieth century, behaviorism dominated the thinking of experimental psychologists. Behaviorists such as B. F. Skinner believed that the human mind is a black box best left to philosophers, and they considered observable behavior to be psychologists' proper focus. The behaviorist perspective had little use for the mental processes occurring in that place between your ears.

In the 1950s, psychologists' views began to change. The advent of computers provided a new way to think about the workings of the human mind. If we could "see" what computers were doing internally, maybe we could use our observations to study human mental processes, scientists reasoned. Indeed, computer science was a key motivator in the birth of the study of human cognition.

The first modern computer, developed by mathematician John von Neumann in the late 1940s, showed that machines could perform logical operations. In the 1950s, researchers speculated that computers might model some mental operations, and they believed that such modeling might shed light on how the human mind works (Virues-Ortega & Pear, 2015).

Cognitive psychologists often use the computer as an analogy to help explain the relationship between cognition and the brain (Gershman, Horvitz, & Tenenbaum, 2015; Griffiths, 2015). They describe the physical brain as the computer's hardware and cognition as its software.

Herbert Simon (1969) was among the pioneers in comparing the human mind to computer processing systems. In this analogy, the sensory and perceptual systems provide an "input channel," similar to the way data are entered into the computer (Figure 1). As input (information) comes into the mind, mental processes, or operations, act on it, just as the computer's software acts on the data. The transformed input generates information that remains in memory much in the way a computer stores what it has worked on. Finally, the information is retrieved from memory and "printed out" or "displayed" (so to speak) as an observable response.

Computers provide a logical and concrete, but oversimplified, model of human information processing. Inanimate computers and human brains function quite differently in some respects. For example, most computers receive information from a human who has already coded the information and removed much of its ambiguity. In contrast, each brain cell, or neuron, can respond to ambiguous information transmitted through sensory receptors such as the eyes and ears.

Computers can do some things better than humans. For instance, computers can perform complex numerical calculations much faster and more accurately than humans could

Artificial intelligence (AI) researchers are currently exploring frontiers that were once the context for science fiction. Shown here is ASIMO ("Advanced Step in Innovative Mobility"), a humanoid robot designed by Honda.

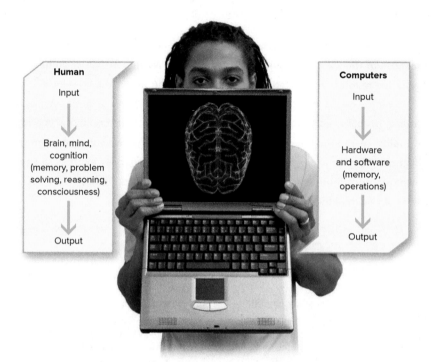

ever hope to (Liu & others, 2012). Computers can also apply and follow rules more consistently and with fewer errors than humans and can represent complex mathematical patterns better than humans.

Still, the brain's extraordinary capabilities will probably not be mimicked completely by computers any time in the near future. Attempts to use computers to process visual information or spoken language have achieved only limited success in specific situations. The human brain also has an incredible ability to learn new rules, relationships, concepts, and patterns that it can generalize to novel situations. In comparison, computers are quite limited in their ability to learn and generalize. Although a computer can improve its ability to recognize patterns or use rules of thumb to make decisions, it does not have the means to develop new learning goals.

Furthermore, the human mind is aware of itself; the computer is not. Indeed, no computer is likely to approach the richness of human consciousness (Agnati & others, 2012; Lewis & others, 2015; Nunez, 2012).

Nonetheless, the computer's role in cognitive psychology continues to increase. An entire scientific field called **artificial intelligence (AI)** focuses on creating machines capable of performing activities that require intelligence when people do them. AI is especially helpful in tasks requiring speed, persistence, and a vast memory (Goel & Davies, 2011; Hermundstad & others, 2011). AI systems also assist in diagnosing medical illnesses and prescribing treatment, examining equipment failures, evaluating loan applicants, and advising students about which courses to take (A. C. Chang, 2012). Computer scientists continue to develop computers that more closely approximate human thinking (Fleuret & others, 2011).

By the late 1950s the cognitive revolution was in full swing, and it peaked in the 1980s. The term *cognitive psychology* became a label for approaches that sought to explain observable behavior by investigating mental processes and structures that we cannot directly observe (Leahey, 2013; Robinson-Riegler & Robinson-Riegler, 2012; Sternberg, 2013a).

Cognitive psychology is a broad field that includes the study of consciousness, memory, as well as cognitive neuroscience. In this chapter we delve into three additional important aspects of cognition—thinking, intelligence, and language. We begin by examining the processes of problem solving, decision making, and critical thinking.

● **artificial intelligence (AI)** A scientific field that focuses on creating machines capable of performing activities that require intelligence when they are done by people.

test yourself

1. On what did behaviorists believe that psychology should properly focus?
2. What technological development gave psychologists a new way to look at the human mind?
3. How is the human mind superior to computers?

● **thinking** The process of manipulating information mentally by forming concepts, solving problems, making decisions, and reflecting critically or creatively.

● **concepts** Mental categories that are used to group objects, events, and characteristics.

● **prototype model** A model emphasizing that when people evaluate whether a given item reflects a certain concept, they compare the item with the most typical item(s) in that category and look for a "family resemblance" with that item's properties.

2. THINKING

When you save a file on a computer, you hear a sound from inside, and you know the computer is processing the work you have just done. Unlike a computer, the brain does not make noise to let us know it is working. Rather, the brain's processing is the silent operation of thinking. Formally defined, **thinking** involves manipulating information mentally by forming concepts, solving problems, making decisions, and reflecting in a critical or creative manner.

In this section we probe the nature of concepts—the basic components of thinking. We then explore the cognitive processes of problem solving, reasoning, and decision making. We also examine two capacities related to enhanced problem solving: critical thinking and creativity.

Concepts

A fundamental aspect of thinking is the notion of concepts. **Concepts** are mental categories that are used to group objects, events, and characteristics. Humans have a special ability for creating categories to help us make sense of information in our world (Ferry, Hespos, & Gentner, 2015; Lake, Salakhutdinov, & Tenenbaum, 2015; Rawson, Thomas, & Jacoby, 2015; Rips, Smith, & Medin, 2012). We know that apples and oranges are both fruits. We know that poodles and collies are both dogs and that cockroaches and ladybugs are both insects. These items differ from one another in various ways, and yet we recognize that they belong together because we have concepts for fruits, dogs, and insects.

Concepts are important for four reasons. First, concepts allow us to generalize. If we did not have concepts, each object and event in our world would be unique and brand new to us each time we encountered it. Second, concepts allow us to associate experiences and objects. Basketball, ice hockey, and track are sports. The concept *sport* gives us a way to compare these activities. Third, concepts aid memory by making it more efficient so that we do not have to reinvent the wheel each time we come across a piece of information. Imagine having to think about how to sit in a chair every time we find ourselves in front of one. Fourth, concepts provide clues about how to react to a particular object or experience. Perhaps you have had the experience of trying an exotic new cuisine and feeling puzzled as you consider the contents of your plate. If a friend tells you reassuringly, "That's food!" you know that given the concept *food*, it is okay to dig in.

Psychologists have developed a variety of ways to understand the structure and function of concepts. One of these is known as the prototype model. The **prototype model** emphasizes that when people evaluate whether a given item reflects a certain concept, they compare the item with the most typical item(s) in that category and look for a "family resemblance" with that item's properties. Birds generally fly, sing, and build nests, so we know that robins and sparrows are both birds. We recognize exceptions to these properties, however—we know that a penguin is still a bird even though it does not fly, sing, and build a nest.

The prototype model maintains that people use characteristic properties to create a representation of the average or ideal member—the prototype—for each concept. Comparing individual cases to our mental prototypes may be a good way to decide quickly whether something fits a particular category. As we will see later in this chapter, concepts can have particularly negative effects when they are applied to *people* rather than to objects.

Although it has a ducklike bill and lays eggs, the platypus is nevertheless a mammal like the tiger, as platypus females produce milk with which they feed their young. The prototypical birdlike characteristics of the platypus can lead us to think mistakenly that the platypus is a bird. Its atypical properties place the platypus on the extreme of the concept mammal.

Problem Solving

Concepts tell us *what* we think about but not *why* we think. *Why* do we bother to engage in the mental effort of thinking? Consider Levi Hutchins, an ambitious young man who sought to wake up at 4 A.M. every morning. Levi had a specific goal—he wanted to beat the sun up every day. To solve this problem (and achieve his goal), he invented the alarm clock in 1787. **Problem solving** means finding an appropriate way to attain a goal when the goal is not readily available (Bassok & Novick, 2012). Problem solving entails following several steps and overcoming mental obstacles.

● **problem solving** The mental process of finding an appropriate way to attain a goal when the goal is not readily available.

FOLLOWING THE STEPS IN PROBLEM SOLVING

Psychological research points to four steps in the problem-solving process.

1. Find and Frame Problems   Recognizing a problem is the first step toward a solution (Mayer, 2000). Finding and framing problems involves asking questions in creative ways and "seeing" what others do not.

It is not easy to learn how to recognize and frame a problem. Furthermore, many real-world problems are not well defined or are vague and have no clear-cut solutions (Moreau & Engeset, 2016). It can be difficult to recognize and work on ill-defined problems as they may require a great deal of creativity, a capacity we will discuss further below. The visionaries who developed the many inventions that influence our daily lives—such as the computer, telephone, and light bulb—all saw problems that everyone else was content to live with. Recognizing problems involves being aware of and open to experiences (two mental habits we will examine later). It also means listening carefully to that voice in your head that occasionally sighs, "There must be a better way."

2. Develop Good Problem-Solving Strategies   Once we find a problem and clearly define it, we need to develop strategies for solving it. Among the effective strategies are subgoals, algorithms, and heuristics.

Subgoals are intermediate goals or intermediate problems that we devise to put us in a better position for reaching a final goal or solution. Imagine that you are writing a paper for a psychology class. What are some subgoaling strategies for approaching this task? One might be locating the right books and research journals on your chosen topic. At the same time that you are searching for the right publications, you will likely benefit from establishing some subgoals within your time frame for completing the project. If the paper is due in two months, you might set a subgoal of a first draft of the paper two weeks before it is due, another subgoal of completing your reading for the paper one month before it is due, and still another subgoal of starting your library research tomorrow. Notice that in establishing the subgoals for meeting the deadline, you worked backward. Working backward in establishing subgoals is a good strategy. You first create the subgoal that is closest to the final goal and then work backward to the subgoal that is closest to the beginning of the problem-solving effort.

● **subgoals** Intermediate goals or intermediate problems devised to put the individual in a better position for reaching the final goal or solution.

Algorithms are strategies that guarantee a solution to a problem. Algorithms come in different forms, such as formulas, instructions, and the testing of all possible solutions. We use algorithms in cooking (by following a recipe) and driving (by following directions to an address). What all of these strategies have in common is that they lead to a single answer: the right one.

● **algorithms** Strategies—including formulas, instructions, and the testing of all possible solutions—that guarantee a solution to a problem.

An algorithmic strategy might take a long time. Staring at a rack of letters during a game of Scrabble, for example, you might find yourself moving the tiles around and trying all possible combinations to make a high-scoring word. Instead of using an algorithm to solve your Scrabble problem, however, you might rely on some rules of thumb about words and language. You know that if you have a *Q*, you are going to need a *U*. If you have an *X* and a *T*, the *T* is probably not going to come right before the X. So, in this example, rather than using an algorithm, you are using some quick rules that provide possible solutions to the problem. These shortcuts are called heuristics.

Heuristics are shortcut strategies or guidelines that suggest a solution to a problem but do not guarantee an answer (Stanovich, 2016). In the real world, we are more likely to solve the types of problems we face with heuristics than with algorithms (Boutang & De Lara, 2016). Heuristics help us to narrow down the possible solutions and to find one

● **heuristics** Shortcut strategies or guidelines that suggest a solution to a problem but do not guarantee an answer.

quickly that works. Heuristics are different from algorithms because they are fast, can lead to different answers to a given problem, and do not always lead to a clear right answer.

3. Evaluate Solutions Once we think we have solved a problem, we will not know how effective our solution is until we find out if it works. It helps to have in mind a clear criterion, or standard against which to judge the effectiveness of the solution. For example, what will your criterion be for judging the effectiveness of your solution to the assignment of writing a psychology paper? Will you judge your solution to be effective if you simply complete the paper? If you get an *A*? If the instructor says that it is one of the best papers a student ever turned in on the topic?

4. Rethink and Redefine Problems and Solutions over Time An important final step in problem solving is to rethink and redefine problems continually. Good problem solvers tend to be more motivated than the average person to improve on their past performances and to make original contributions. Can we make the computer faster and more powerful? Can we make the iPod Shuffle even smaller?

AN OBSTACLE TO PROBLEM SOLVING: BECOMING FIXATED

A key ingredient of being a good problem solver is to acknowledge that you do not know everything—that your strategies and conclusions are always open to revision. Optimal problem solving may require a certain amount of humility, or the ability to admit that you are not perfect and that there may be better ways to solve life's problems. It is easy to fall into the trap of becoming fixated on a particular strategy for solving a problem.

Fixation involves using a prior strategy and failing to look at a problem from a fresh new perspective. **Functional fixedness** occurs when individuals fail to solve a problem because they are fixated on a thing's usual functions (Wright, Boot, & Brockmole, 2015). Imagine having to hammer a nail but lacking a hammer. What to do? The functionally fixed person is stuck. If you have ever used a shoe to hammer a nail, you have overcome functional fixedness to solve a problem.

An example of a problem that requires overcoming functional fixedness is the Maier string problem, depicted in Figure 2 (Maier, 1931). The problem is to figure out how to tie two strings together when you must stand in one spot and cannot reach both strings at the same time. It seems as though you are stuck. However, there is a pair of pliers on a table. Can you solve the problem?

The solution is to use the pliers as a weight, tying them to the end of one string (Figure 3). Swing this string back and forth like a pendulum and grasp the stationary

● **fixation** Using a prior strategy and failing to look at a problem from a fresh new perspective.

● **functional fixedness** Failing to solve a problem as a result of fixation on a thing's usual functions.

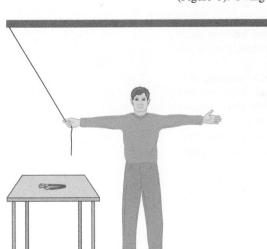

FIGURE 2 Maier String Problem How can you tie the two strings together if you cannot reach them both at the same time?

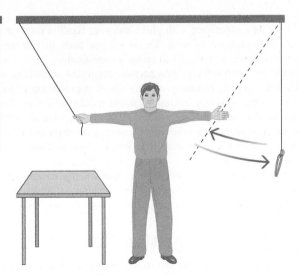

FIGURE 3 Solution to the Maier String Problem Use the pliers as a weight to create a pendulum motion that brings the second string closer.

Thinking   **255**

psychological *inquiry*

The Candle Problem

How would you mount a candle on a wall so that it won't drip wax on a table or a floor while it is burning?

The Nine-Dot Problem

Take out a piece of paper and copy the arrangement of dots shown below. Without lifting your pencil, connect the dots using only four straight lines.

The Six-Matchstick Problem

Arrange six matchsticks of equal length to make four equilateral triangles, the sides of which are one matchstick long.

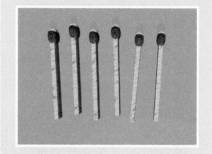

Thinking Outside the Box

The following are examples of how fixation impedes problem solving. These tasks help psychologists measure creative problem solving.

Each of the problems calls for a special kind of thinking—breaking out of your usual assumptions and looking at objects in a different way. Try your hand at solving each one and then answer the questions. Solutions to the problems can be found at the end of the chapter.

1. Which of the problems was most difficult to solve? Why?

2. Do you think these problems capture an important ability, or are they more like trick questions? Why?

3. Are these problems best solved by effortful thinking or by just going with your hunches? Explain.

string. Your past experience with pliers and your fixation on their usual function make this a difficult problem to solve. To do so, you need to find an unusual use for the pliers—in this case, as a weight to create a pendulum.

Effective problem solving often necessitates trying something new, or thinking out-side the box—that is, exploring novel ways of approaching tasks and challenges and finding solutions. This way of thinking might require admitting that your past strategies were not ideal or do not readily translate to a particular situation. Students who are used to succeeding in high school by cramming for tests and relying on parental pres-sure to get homework done may find that in college these strategies are no longer viable ways to succeed.

Sometimes successful problem solving means being *cognitively flexible*—recognizing that options are available and adapting to the situation. To explore how fixation might play a role in your own problem solving, try out the questions in the Psychological Inquiry.

Reasoning and Decision Making

In addition to forming concepts and solving problems, thinking includes the higher-order mental processes of reasoning and decision making. These activities require rich connec-tions among neurons and the ability to apply judgment. The end result of this type of thinking is an evaluation, a conclusion, or a decision.

256 CHAPTER 8 Thinking, Intelligence, and Language

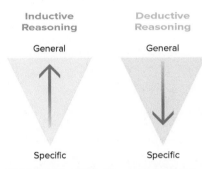

FIGURE 4 **Inductive and Deductive Reasoning** (*left*) The triangle represents inductive reasoning—going from specific to general. (*right*) The triangle represents deductive reasoning—going from general to specific.

● **reasoning** The mental activity of transforming information to reach conclusions.

● **inductive reasoning** Reasoning from specific observations to make generalizations.

● **deductive reasoning** Reasoning from a general case that is known to be true to a specific instance.

● **decision making** The mental activity of evaluating alternatives and choosing among them.

REASONING

Reasoning is the mental activity of transforming information to reach a conclusion. This type of thinking uses *reason*—weighing arguments, applying rules of logic, and coming up with sound conclusions. Reasoning is involved in problem solving and decision making. It is also a skill closely tied to critical thinking (Aizikovitsh-Udi & Cheng, 2015; Leighton & Sternberg, 2013). Reasoning can be either inductive or deductive (Figure 4).

Inductive reasoning involves reasoning from specific observations to make generalizations. You can think of inductive reasoning as "bottom-up processing" that we discussed in the "Sensation and Perception" chapter when talking about perception. Inductive reasoning means starting with incoming information and then drawing conclusions.

Inductive reasoning is an important way that we form beliefs about the world. For instance, having turned on your cell phone many times without having it explode, you have every reason to believe that it will not explode the next time you turn it on. From your prior experiences with the phone, you form the general belief that it is not likely to become a dangerous object. Or, imagine taking a sip of milk from a container and finding that it tastes sour. You are using inductive reasoning when you throw out the whole container even though you have not tasted every drop.

A great deal of scientific knowledge is the product of inductive reasoning. We know, for instance, that men and women are genetically different, with women having two X chromosomes and men having an X and a Y chromosome, though no one has actually tested every single human being's chromosomes to verify this generalization. Inductive reasoning is always involved when we make generalizations. Psychological research is often inductive as well, studying a *sample* of participants in order to yield conclusions about the population from which the sample is drawn.

In contrast, **deductive reasoning** is reasoning from a general principle that we know to be true to a specific instance. Using deductive reasoning, we draw conclusions based on facts. For example, we might start with the general premise that all Texans love the Dallas Cowboys. Thus, if John is a Texan, we logically might surmise that John loves the Dallas Cowboys. Notice, however, that the logic of this deductive reasoning requires that the first statement be true; if all Texans do not love the Cowboys, John just might be a Philadelphia Eagles fan.

When psychologists and other scientists use theories to make predictions and then evaluate their predictions by making further observations, deductive reasoning is at work. When psychologists develop a hypothesis from a theory, they are using a form of deductive reasoning, because the hypothesis is a specific, logical extension of the general theory. If the theory is true, then the hypothesis will be true as well.

The terms *inductive* and *deductive* are very similar, but they refer to different things. Remember that *in*ductive means going from a specific *in*stance to a general case. *D*eductive means reasoning from a general principle *d*own to a specific case.

DECISION MAKING

Think of all the decisions, large and small, that you have to make in life. Should you major in biology, psychology, or business? Should you go to graduate school right after college or get a job first? Should you establish yourself in a career before settling down to have a family? Do you want fries with that? **Decision making** involves evaluating alternatives and choosing among them (LeBoeuf & Shafir, 2012).

Decision making differs from reasoning. Reasoning involves following established rules to reach a sound conclusion. In decision making, such rules may not exist, and we may not know the consequences of the decisions (Ackermann & Landy, 2015). Some of the information might be missing, and we might not trust all of the information we have. In this sense, decision making is less certain than reasoning. Making decisions means weighing information and coming to some conclusion that we feel will maximize our outcome: Yes, we will be able to see the movie from this row in the theater; no, we will not run that red light to get to class on time.

TWO SYSTEMS OF REASONING AND DECISION MAKING

Recall the idea of automatic and controlled processes in consciousness. Many psychologists similarly divide reasoning and decision making into two levels—one that is automatic (often referred to as *system 1*) and one that is controlled (*system 2*) (Evans & Stanovich, 2013). The automatic system involves processing that is rapid, heuristic, associative, and intuitive; it entails following one's hunches about a particular decision or problem (Barr & others, 2015; Pennycook, Fugelsang, & Koehler, 2015). Intuitive judgment means knowing that something feels right even if the reason why is unknown (Horr, Braun, & Volz, 2014). In contrast, the controlled system is slower, effortful, and analytical. It involves conscious reflection. This is the kind of thinking that might be required to solve a difficult math problem, for example.

Although conscious effortful thinking is invaluable for solving many problems, research has shown that intuitive processing may also have an important role to play in decision making (Gigerenzer, 2014; Hertwig, Hoffrage, & the ABC Research Group, 2013). Studies have shown that, compared to effortful reflection, at times intuitive decision making can be less biased and more efficient in decision making. For example, in one study participants were told that their job was to rate the popularity of particular songs (Halberstadt & Catty, 2008). Participants listened to brief snippets of the songs. Half of the participants were asked to first reflect on the reasons a particular song might be popular. The other half simply rendered their judgments intuitively, without much thought. Those who rendered their judgments intuitively were actually more accurate in their popularity ratings, because they based these ratings on how familiar the song was to them. Basing judgments on the feeling of familiarity was a good idea in this case, as popular songs are likely to be familiar to everyone. Those who analyzed their reasons were less accurate because thinking about reasons disrupted this natural association.

The popular media sometimes portray intuitive hunches as sort of magical. However, these gut feelings do not emerge out of thin air. Rather, they are the product of learned associations such as those described in the "Learning" chapter (Kahneman & Klein, 2009; Unkelbach, 2007); of overlearned automatic processes (Halberstadt, 2010); and of implicit memory (Cheng & Huang, 2011). Your gut feelings about the right answer on a test are certainly more likely to be accurate if you have put in the requisite hours of conscious effortful study. The accuracy of intuitive judgments, then, may depend on the hours of conscious effort, even if the judgment feels like a gut feeling.

Keep in mind that system 1 processes are as rapid as they are because they often rely on heuristics. As noted above, unlike algorithms, heuristics do not guarantee a right answer. Although following these quick rules of thumb can often lead to a satisfying decision, it can also lead to mistakes (Bednark & others, 2013; D. Griffin, 2012; Kahneman, Lovallo, & Sibony, 2011), as we now consider.

BIASES AND HEURISTICS

In many cases, our decision-making strategies are well adapted to deal with a variety of problems (Hertwig, Hoffrage, & the ABC Research Group, 2013). However, at times, reliance on heuristics can lead to biased decisions and outright errors. In addition, sometimes we are simply unaware of the influence that heuristics may have on our decisions (Nisbett & Ross, 1980; Tversky & Kahneman, 1974). Here we look at a few biases and heuristic errors, summarized in Figure 5.

One of the most powerful biases in human decision making is loss aversion. **Loss aversion** refers to the tendency to strongly prefer to avoid losses compared to acquiring gains. We dislike the prospect of losing something we have more than we enjoy the prospect of gaining something new, even with the prospect of a gain outweighs the loss (Kahneman & Tversky, 1984). Imagine that you have a *B+* in a class with an optional, but likely very challenging, final exam. If you do well on the final, you could nudge your grade to an *A−*. But if you do poorly, your *B+* could plummet to a *C*. Would you risk what you already have for the chance to get a better grade. Perhaps not.

Loss aversion helps to explain a variety of phenomena in psychology and economics (Wang, Rieger, & Hens, 2016). For example, the *endowment effect* means that people ascribe

● **loss aversion** The tendency to strongly prefer to avoid losses compared to acquiring gains.

Loss Aversion	Confirmation Bias	Base Rate Neglect	Hindsight Bias	Representativeness Heuristic	Availability Heuristic
Description Tendency to weigh potential losses more heavily than potential gains **Example:** An investor decides not to buy stock in a new company even though the chances of financial gain outweigh the chances of financial loss.	**Description** Tendency to search for and use information that supports rather than refutes one's ideas **Example:** A politician accepts news that supports his views and dismisses evidence that runs counter to these views.	**Description** Tendency to ignore factual information based on numbers in favor of very specific but vivid information **Example:** You read a favorable statistics about a TV you are intending to buy, but you decide not to buy it when a friend tells you about a bad experience with that model.	**Description** Tendency to report falsely, after the fact, that one accurately predicted an outcome **Example:** You read about the results of a particular psychological study and say, "I always knew that," though in fact you have little knowledge about the issues examined in the study.	**Description** Tendency to make judgments about group membership based on physical appearances or one's stereotype of a group rather than available base rate information **Example:** The victim of a holdup, you view police photos of possible perpetrators. The suspects look very similar to you, but you choose the individual whose hair and clothing look dirtiest and most disheveled.	**Description** Prediction about the probability of an event based on the ease of recalling or imagining similar events **Example:** A girl from an extended family in which no family member ever attended college tells her mother that she wants to be a doctor. Her mother cannot imagine her daughter in such a career and suggests that she become a nurse.

FIGURE 5 **Decision-Making Problems: Biases and Heuristics** Biases and heuristics (rules of thumb) affect the quality of many of the decisions we make. (first photo) © Digital Vision/SuperStock; (second photo) © Brand X Pictures

greater value to things they already own, compared to objects owned by someone else. For example, in one study (Kahneman, Knetsch, & Thaler, 1990), some participants were shown a mug and were asked how much they would be willing to pay for it. Other participants were actually given the mug to keep and then were asked how much they would be willing to sell it for. In both groups the mugs were identical, simple coffee mugs with the university insignia on them. However, those who owned the mug believed it was worth over 3 dollars more than those who just looked it over. Somehow, just by owning it, it became more valuable.

Loss aversion also explains why sometimes it is so hard to cut our losses when we are in a losing battle. The *sunk cost fallacy* refers to the fact that people are reluctant to give up on a venture because of past investment. If we were perfectly rational, we would make decisions based only on current circumstances, maximizing the benefits and minimizing costs. However, past investment biases our judgments. Economically, sunk cost fallacy means "throwing good money after bad."

Imagine that you have just suffered through two years of training to become an accountant. What you have discovered is that you neither enjoy accounting nor are you good at it. The courses have been a struggle and you have just managed to pass. Should you stick with it? If you were making a decision rationally based on current circumstances alone, you might decide to change course and switch majors. However, doing so would also mean recognizing that the last two years have been "wasted." You have sunk a lot of resources into something you no longer even want. But sunk costs may spur you to stick it out, or even try harder. Sunk costs reflect loss aversion in that we dread the thought of losing the effort, time, and money we have already put into a venture if we give up.

Confirmation bias is the tendency to search for and use information that supports our ideas rather than refutes them (McKee & Stuckler, 2016; Yousaf & Gobet, 2016). Our decisions can also become further biased because we tend to seek out and listen to people whose views confirm our own while we avoid those with dissenting views (Mintz & Wayne, 2016).

● **confirmation bias** The tendency to search for and use information that supports one's ideas rather than refutes them.

Confirmation bias is sometimes also referred to as *myside bias,* as it involves seeking out and believing information that supports one's own beliefs. For instance, during the 2012 U.S. presidential elections, many polling experts agreed that President Obama would win reelection. Nevertheless, pundits who supported Mitt Romney argued forcefully that the polls were wrong and were quite surprised by the outcome. Members of Romney's staff were described as "utterly 'shellshocked'" (Firestone, 2012). Avoiding confirmation bias means seeking out disconfirming information and applying the same rigorous analysis to both sides of an argument, even when the information seems to point in a direction we dread.

Hindsight bias is our tendency to report falsely, after the fact, that we accurately predicted an outcome. It is sometimes referred to as the "I knew it all along effect." With this type of bias, people tend to view events that have happened as more predictable than they were and to represent themselves as being more accurate in their predictions than they actually were (Yopchick & Kim, 2012). For instance, at the end of a long baseball season, fans might say they knew all along that a particular team would win the World Series.

● **hindsight bias** The tendency to report falsely, after the fact, that one has accurately predicted an outcome.

Although the hindsight bias might sound self-serving in the sense that it means remembering ourselves as having known more than we really did know, cognitive psychologists recognize that this bias may be based on new learning and on updating our knowledge about the world (Nestler, Blank, & Egloff, 2010; Pezzo, 2011). One reason for hindsight bias is that actual events are more vivid in our minds than all those things that failed to happen, an effect called the availability heuristic.

The **availability heuristic** refers to a prediction about the probability of an event based on the ease of recalling or imagining similar events (Fiedler & Kutzner, 2015). Essentially, this heuristic means we think that events that are *cognitively available* are more likely to happen. Have you ever experienced a sudden fear of flying right after hearing about an airplane crash? Shocking events such as plane crashes stick in our minds, making it seem as if such disasters are common. The chance of dying in a plane crash in a given year, however, is tiny (1 in 400,000) compared to the chance of dying in a car accident (1 in 6,500). Because car accidents are less newsworthy, they are less likely to catch our attention and remain in our awareness. The availability heuristic is one reason people seem to have a difficult time believing that violent crime rates have declined. When they hear about single acts of violence, the vividness of these in memory is mistaken for their frequency.

● **availability heuristic** A prediction about the probability of an event based on the ease of recalling or imagining similar events.

The availability heuristic can reinforce generalizations about other people (Fiedler & Kutzner, 2015). Imagine, for instance, that Elvedina, a Mexican American girl, tells her mother that she wants to be a doctor. Her mother, who has never seen a Latina doctor, finds it hard to conceive of her daughter's pursuing such a career and might suggest that she try nursing instead.

Also reflective of the impact of vivid cases on decision making is **base rate neglect,** the tendency to ignore information about general principles in favor of very specific but vivid information. Let's say that as a prospective car buyer, you read *Consumer Reports* and find that a panel of experts rates a particular vehicle exceptionally well. You might still be swayed in your purchasing decision, however, if a friend tells you about her bad experiences with that car. Similarly, imagine being told that the average exam score for a test in your psychology class was 75 percent. If you were asked to guess a random student's score, 75 percent would be a good answer—the mean tells us the central tendency of any distribution. Yet if the student provided just a little bit of information, such as how many hours he studied, you might give too much weight to that specific information, losing sight of the valuable base rate information you have—namely, the class mean.

● **base rate neglect** The tendency to ignore statistical information in favor of very specific but vivid information.

To experience another heuristic in action, consider the following example. Your psychology professor tells you she has assembled 100 men, all in their 20s, in the hallway outside your classroom. The group consists of 5 members of the U.S. National Swim Team and 95 engineers. She is going to randomly select one man and bring him into the room, and you can win $100 if you accurately guess whether he is an engineer or an Olympic-caliber swimmer. The man stands before you. Tall and lanky, he is wearing a tight T-shirt, jeans, and flip-flops. He has sunglasses perched on his clean-shaven head.

● **representativeness heuristic** The tendency to make judgments about group membership based on physical appearance or the match between a person and one's stereotype of a group rather than on available base rate information.

Is he an engineer or an elite swimmer? If you guessed Olympic swimmer, you have just fallen victim to the representativeness heuristic.

The **representativeness heuristic** is the tendency to make judgments about group membership based on physical appearance or the match between a person and one's stereotype of a group rather than on available base rate information (Nilsson, Juslin, & Olsson, 2008). Essentially, a stereotype is the use of concepts to make generalizations about a group of people. We will examine stereotypes in some detail in the chapter "Social Psychology". In the example just described, the base rate information tells you that, 95 times out of 100, the man in your class is likely to be an engineer. The optimal approach to winning the $100 is simply to shut your eyes and guess engineer, no matter what the man looks like.

The representativeness heuristic can be particularly damaging in the context of social judgments. Consider a scenario where a particular engineering corporation seeks to hire a new chief executive officer (CEO). Lori, a top-notch candidate with an undergraduate engineering degree and an MBA from an outstanding business school, applies. If there are few women in upper management at the firm, the company's board of directors might inaccurately view Lori as "not fitting" their view of the prototypical CEO—and miss the chance to hire an exceptional candidate.

Heuristics help us make decisions rapidly, but to solve problems accurately and make the best decisions, we must sometimes override these shortcuts and think more deeply, critically, and creatively. Now that you have learned about heuristics and their potential to lead to biased and inaccurate conclusions, you might be wondering if this learning will pay off. Will you be less likely to be influenced by such biases in the future? Some people seem more likely to use heuristics whereas others are more likely to apply careful thought to decisions, overriding the influence of these shortcuts. Intelligence, interest in thinking through complex problems carefully, and maintaining an open mind are associated with less susceptibility to the biases promoted by heuristics (Chiesi, Primi, & Morsanyi, 2011; Toplak, West, & Stanovich, 2011). Still, such biases can influence us without our knowledge. Very bright people who can recognize biases in others may miss them in their own decisions, a phenomenon called *bias blind spot* (West, Meserve, & Stanovich, 2012).

Many of the cognitive biases we have reviewed seem to have a self-serving component. It makes us feel better (and smarter) to think that we "knew all along" which team was going to win the Super Bowl even though we did not. It may ease anxiety to avoid information indicating that our favored candidate is losing an election. These tendencies represent wishful thinking: beliefs and ideas that are colored by our hopes, desires, and goals.

A fascinating question is whether children engage in such thinking. Studying children's cognition provides an interesting window into system 1 processing. Very young children do not have highly developed capacities for reflection, and so studying how they think offers us insight into the foundations of the ways adults think. Do children engage in wishful thinking? To find out, see the Intersection.

Thinking Critically and Creatively

Problem solving and decision making are basic cognitive processes that we use multiple times each day. Certain strategies lead to better solutions and choices than others, and some people are particularly good at these cognitive exercises. In this section we examine two skills associated with superior problem solving: critical thinking and creativity.

CRITICAL THINKING

Critical thinking means thinking reflectively and productively and evaluating the evidence. Recall from the chapter "What Is Psychology?" that scientists are critical thinkers. Critical thinkers grasp the deeper meaning of ideas, question assumptions, and decide for themselves what to believe or do (Zoller, 2016). Critical thinking requires maintaining a sense of humility about what we know (and what we do not know). It means being motivated to see past the obvious.

INTERSECTION

Cognitive Psychology and Developmental Psychology: Do Children Engage in Wishful Thinking?

With her eyes shut tight, a 3-year-old makes a wish and blows out her birthday candles. For children, wishing has magical properties: Just making a wish can make it come true (Schneider, 1998).

When children make judgments, do they let their wishes color their thinking? Research to date has had difficulty answering this question because, when predicting outcomes, children often rely on the *effort heuristic*. This heuristic means that the likelihood of getting what you want is determined by how hard you work (Stipek & Mac Iver, 1989). This heuristic (which is, of course, often true), might lead children to overestimate their performance on tasks, simply because they imagine themselves working very hard. A recent (and very clever) study examined the question of childhood wishful thinking while avoiding this overestimation problem. Let's take a closer look at the study.

Preschoolers (ages 3 to 5), who participated one at a time, were shown four very fun little toys (such as colorful balloons and magnetic letters) by an experimenter (Bernard, Clément, &

© Jamie Grill/The Image Bank/Getty Images

Mercier, 2016). The toys were placed in two plastic eggs: three toys in one egg and one in the other. The eggs were closed up. The experimenter then put the eggs in a box, gave them a good shake, and announced that he would close his eyes and pull one egg out. The child's task was to guess whether that egg contained three toys or just one toy. Notice that this task involves no effort at all, just guessing.

The experimenter repeated this procedure over eight trials. For half of the trials, the child was told that the eggs and toys would eventually be put away for another child. For the other half of the trials, the child was told that he or she could keep whatever toys were found. The key question is whether the children's guesses depended on whether they got to keep the toys. Wishful thinking would be revealed if children guessed that the egg contained three toys more often when they got to keep the toys.

Results showed plenty of wishful thinking: Among the 3- and 4-year-olds especially, the guesses were about 50–50 when the children knew they would not get to keep the toys but were higher (as high as 75 percent) when they knew they would get to keep the toys. Interestingly, 5-year-olds did not share this overly optimistic view. Instead, they showed a naive theory of randomness, assuming that overall the three-toy egg should be found half the time (Bernard, Clément, & Mercier, 2016).

These results suggest that even young children's predictions about the future are colored by what they hope will happen. Wishful thinking seems to be a characteristic of very basic cognitive processes.

Even young children's predictions about the future are colored by what they hope will happen.

Clearly, wishful thinking continues, in varied ways, into adulthood. Of course, wishful thinking can be problematic when it prevents a person from facing challenges head on. Nevertheless, it is interesting to think about how such thinking might be adaptive, for children and adults, allowing us to maintain a sense of optimism about what might be just around the corner.

Critical thinking is vital to effective problem solving. However, it can be difficult to teach students to think critically, and schools must often balance other priorities (McCombs, 2013). The goal of maximizing students' scores on standardized tests can prompt teachers to concentrate on getting students to give a single correct answer in an imitative way rather than on encouraging new ideas (Lucariello & others, 2016). Further, many people are inclined to stay on the surface of problems rather than to stretch their minds. The cultivation of two mental habits is essential to critical thinking: mindfulness and open-mindedness.

Mindfulness means being alert and mentally present for one's everyday activities. The mindful person maintains an active awareness of the circumstances of his or her life.

● **mindfulness** The state of being alert and mentally present for one's everyday activities.

When we are mindful, we are engaged mentally in what is happening to us. According to Ellen Langer (1997, 2000, 2005), mindfulness is a key to critical thinking. Langer distinguishes *mindful* behavior from *mindless* behavior—automatic activities we perform without thought.

In a classic study, Langer found that people (as many as 90 percent) would mindlessly give up their place in line for a copy machine when someone asked, "Can I go first? I need to make copies" as compared to when the same person simply said, "Can I go first?" (just 60 percent) (Langer, Blank, & Chanowitz, 1978). For the mindless people in the study, even a completely meaningless justification—after all, everyone in line was there to make copies—was reason enough to step aside. A mindless person engages in automatic behavior without careful thinking. In contrast, a mindful person is engaged with the environment, responding in a thoughtful way to various experiences.

Open-mindedness means being receptive to other ways of looking at things. People often do not even know that there is another side to an issue or evidence contrary to what they believe. Simple openness to other viewpoints can help to keep individuals from jumping to conclusions. As Socrates once said, knowing what it is you do not know is the first step to true wisdom. *Actively open-minded thinking* refers to thinking that is flexible and open to questioning; it is not dogmatic or categorical (West, Toplak, & Stanovich, 2008). Individuals who engage in active open-minded thinking tend to be less susceptible to biases in their conclusions (Stanovich, 2016; West, Meserve, & Stanovich, 2012).

Being mindful and maintaining an open mind may be more difficult than the alternative of going through life on auto pilot. Critical thinking is valuable, however, because it allows us to make better predictions about the future, to evaluate situations objectively, and to effect appropriate changes. In some sense, critical thinking requires courage. When we expose ourselves to a broad range of perspectives, we risk finding out that our assumptions might be wrong. When we engage our critical minds, we may discover problems, but we are also more likely to have opportunities to make positive changes.

CREATIVE THINKING

In addition to thinking critically, coming up with the best solution to a problem may involve thinking creatively. The word *creative* can apply to an activity or a person, and creativity as a process may be open even to people who do not think of themselves as creative. When we talk about **creativity** as a characteristic of a person, we are referring to the ability to think about something in novel and unusual ways and to devise unconventional solutions to problems (Simonton, 2016).

Creative thinking is sometimes characterized as *divergent* and *convergent*. **Divergent thinking** produces many solutions to the same problem. **Convergent thinking** produces the single best solution to a problem. Perhaps you can see how these two types of thinking might work together in creativity. Divergent thinking occurs during *brainstorming*, which happens when people openly throw out a range of possible solutions to a problem, even some that might seem crazy. Having a lot of possible solutions, however, still requires that they come up with the solution that is best (An, Song, & Carr, 2016). That is where convergent thinking comes in. Convergent thinking means taking all of those possibilities and finding the right one for the job. Convergent thinking is best when a problem has only one right answer. Of course, for many problems we use both convergent and divergent thinking.

Individuals who think creatively also show the following characteristics (Perkins, 1994):

- *Flexibility and playful thinking:* Creative thinkers are flexible and play with problems. This trait gives rise to the paradox that, although creativity takes hard work, the work goes more smoothly if it is taken lightly. In a way, humor greases the wheels of creativity (Goleman, Kaufman, & Ray, 1993). When you are joking around, you are more likely to consider any possibility and to ignore the inner censor who can condemn your ideas as off base.

● **open-mindedness** The state of being receptive to other ways of looking at things.

● **creativity** The ability to think about something in novel and unusual ways and to devise unconventional solutions to problems.

● **divergent thinking** Thinking that produces many solutions to the same problem.

● **convergent thinking** Thinking that produces the single best solution to a problem.

■ *Inner motivation:* Creative people often are motivated by the joy of creating. They tend to be less motivated by grades, money, or favorable feedback from others. Thus, creative people are inspired more internally than externally (Hennessey, 2011).

■ *Willingness to face risk:* Creative people make more mistakes than their less imaginative counterparts because they come up with more ideas and more possibilities. They win some; they lose some. Creative thinkers know that being wrong is not a failure—it simply means that they have discovered that one possible solution does not work.

■ *Objective evaluation of work:* Most creative thinkers strive to evaluate their work objectively. They may use established criteria to make judgments or rely on the judgments of respected, trusted others. In this manner, they can determine whether further creative thinking will improve their work.

test yourself

1. What are four reasons why concepts are important?
2. Name and explain the key steps in solving a problem.
3. Name at least two biases and two heuristics that affect the quality of our decisions and give an example of each.

3. INTELLIGENCE

Like *creative,* the word *intelligent* can apply to a behavior or a person. We might say that someone who decides to quit smoking has made an intelligent choice. When we apply the word to a person, however, defining *intelligent* can be trickier.

Cultures vary in the ways they define intelligence (Zhang & Sternberg, 2013). Most European Americans think of intelligence in terms of reasoning and thinking skills, but people in Kenya consider responsible participation in family and social life an integral part of intelligence. An intelligent person in Uganda is someone who knows what to do and follows through with appropriate action. Intelligence to the Iatmul people of Papua New Guinea involves the ability to remember the names of 10,000 to 20,000 clans. The residents of the widely dispersed Caroline Islands incorporate the talent of navigating by the stars into their definition of intelligence (Figure 6).

In the United States, we generally define **intelligence** as an all-purpose ability to do well on cognitive tasks, to solve problems, and to learn from experience. Consider the ways we have described thinking—as problem solving, reasoning, decision making, critical analysis, and creativity. Intelligence refers to *how well* a person is able to perform these various cognitive activities.

The idea that intelligence captures a common general ability that is reflected in performance on various cognitive tests was introduced in 1904 by Charles Spearman (1904). Spearman noted that schoolchildren who did well in math also did well in reading, and he came up with the idea that intelligence is a general ability, which he

● **intelligence** An all-purpose ability to do well on cognitive tasks, to solve problems, and to learn from experience.

FIGURE 6   Culturally Defined Intelligence The intelligence of the Iatmul people of Papua New Guinea involves the ability to remember the names of many clans. For the residents of the 680 Caroline Islands in the Pacific Ocean east of the Philippines, intelligence includes the ability to navigate by the stars. (first) © Images of Africa Photobank/Alamy; (second) © Guido Alberto Rossi/age fotostock

called *g*. This view of intelligence suggests that general intelligence underlies performance in a variety of areas, whether it is mathematics, verbal ability, or abstract reasoning. Spearman's *g* essentially assumes that the intelligent person is a jack-of-all-cognitive trades.

Measuring Intelligence

Psychologists measure intelligence using tests that produce a score known as the person's *intelligence quotient (IQ)*. To understand how IQ is derived and what it means, let's first examine the criteria for a good intelligence test: validity, reliability, and standardization.

● **validity** The extent to which a test measures what it is intended to measure.

In the realm of testing, **validity** refers to the extent to which a test measures what it is intended to measure. If a test is supposed to measure intelligence, then it should measure intelligence, not some other characteristic, such as anxiety. One of the most important indicators of validity is the degree to which it predicts an individual's performance when that performance is assessed by *other measures,* or criteria, of the attribute. For example, if an intelligence test is valid, we might expect it to predict other variables, such as grades in school or work performance (Cucina & others, 2016). When the scores on a measure relate to important outcomes, we say the test has high *criterion validity.*

● **reliability** The extent to which a test yields a consistent, reproducible measure of performance.

Reliability is the extent to which a test yields a consistent, reproducible measure of performance. That is, a reliable test is one that produces the same score over time and repeated testing.

Reliability and validity are related, but they are not the same thing. If we think that the characteristic a test measures is stable, then for a test of that characteristic to be valid, it must be reliable. However, a test can be quite reliable but not valid. A person can get the same score on a test, over and over, and yet those scores may be wrong, each and every time. Imagine that someone proposes that eye color is a good measure of intelligence. Certainly, a person's eye color is not likely to change so this measure will be very reliable. The question for validity, though, is whether eye color bears any relationship to intelligence. It does not. So, we have a reliable measure that is not valid. To keep these important terms clear, remember that *reliability* refers only to the stability of scores on a test over time. *Validity,* in contrast, refers to the extent to which a scale measures what it purports to measure.

● **standardization** The development of uniform procedures for administering and scoring a test and the creation of norms (performance standards) for the test.

Good intelligence tests are not only reliable and valid but also standardized. **Standardization** involves developing uniform procedures for administering and scoring a test, as well as creating *norms,* or performance standards, for the test.

Uniform testing procedures require that the testing environment be as similar as possible for all individuals. Norms are created by giving the test to a large group of people who are representative of the population for whom the test is intended. Norms tell us which scores are considered high, low, or average. Many tests of intelligence are designed for individuals from diverse groups. So that the tests are applicable to such different groups, they may have different norms for individuals of different ages, socioeconomic statuses, and ethnic groups (Urbina, 2011). Figure 7 summarizes the criteria for test construction and evaluation.

Validity

Does the test measure what it purports to measure?

Reliability

Is test performance consistent?

Standardization

Are uniform procedures for administering and scoring the test used?

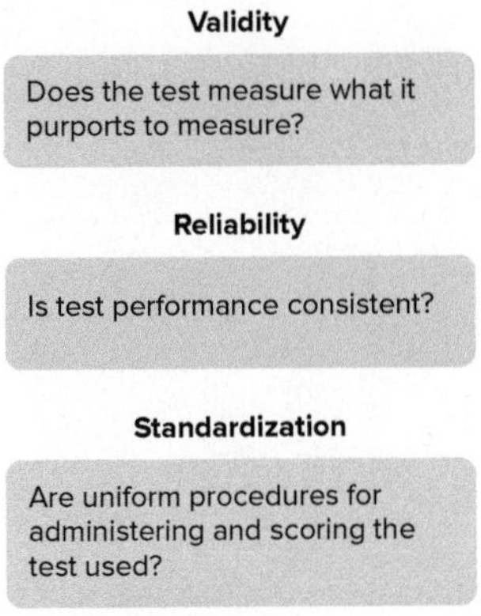

FIGURE 7   Test Construction and Evaluation Tests are a tool for measuring important abilities such as intelligence. Good tests show high reliability and validity and are standardized so that people's scores can be compared.

IQ TESTS

In 1904, the French Ministry of Education asked psychologist Alfred Binet to devise a method that would determine which students did not learn effectively from regular classroom instruction. School officials wanted to reduce overcrowding by placing such students in special schools. Binet and a student (Theophile Simon) developed an intelligence test to meet this request. Test items ranged from the ability to touch one's nose or ear on command to the ability to draw designs from memory and to define abstract concepts. Binet's test is now known as the Stanford-Binet, and it is still widely used.

To measure intelligence, Binet came up with the idea of comparing a person's mental abilities to the mental abilities that are typical for a particular age group. Binet developed the concept of **mental age (MA),** which is an individual's level of mental development relative to that of others. Binet reasoned that, because cognitive ability increases with age, we might expect a child with an intellectual disability to perform like a normally developing child *of a younger age*. To think about a person's level of intelligence, then, we might compare the person's mental age (MA) to his or her chronological age (CA), or age from birth. A very bright child has an MA considerably above CA; a less bright child has an MA considerably below CA.

The German psychologist William Stern devised the term **intelligence quotient (IQ)** in 1912. IQ consists of an individual's mental age divided by chronological age multiplied by 100:

$$IQ = (MA/CA) \times 100$$

If mental age is the same as chronological age, then the individual's IQ is 100 (average); if mental age is above chronological age, the IQ is more than 100 (above average); if mental age is below chronological age, the IQ is less than 100 (below average). For example, a 6-year-old child with a mental age of 8 has an IQ of 133, whereas a 6-year-old child with a mental age of 5 has an IQ of 83.

In childhood, mental age increases as the child ages, but once the child reaches about age 16, the concept of mental age loses its meaning. That is why many experts today prefer to examine IQ scores in terms of how unusual a person's score is when compared to the scores of other adults. For this purpose, researchers and testers use standardized norms that they have identified in the many people who have been tested.

Another measure of intelligence is the Wechsler scales, developed by David Wechsler (1939). There are three versions of the scale. For those ages 16 and older, the Wechsler Adult Intelligence Scale (the WAIS) includes items such as vocabulary, working memory capacity, math problems, and the ability to complete jigsaw puzzles. For children between the ages of 6 and 16, the Wechsler Intelligence Scale for Children (the WISC) includes vocabulary and comprehension but also tasks such as putting together blocks to fit a particular pattern. Finally, a version developed for children as young as 2½ is the Wechsler Pre-School and Primary Scale of Intelligence (the WPPSI, pronounced "whipsy"). On this measure, children are asked, for instance, to point to a picture that depicts a word the examiner says, to complete a block design, and to answer basic knowledge questions.

If you have taken an IQ test, chances are it was one of the Wechsler scales. It is currently the most popular measure of intelligence. In addition to summary scores for general IQ, the Wechsler scales include scores for areas such as verbal comprehension, perceptual reasoning, working memory, and processing speed. These scales provide scores on various subscales rather than a single IQ score. In addition, items were designed specifically for adults or for children.

Both the Stanford-Binet and the Wechsler scales provide measures of Spearman's *g*. Both of these measures of intelligence have a long history of research demonstrating their reliability, and they both feature standardized administration procedures and norms. Finally, they predict results that we would expect, including academic performance and a variety of life outcomes such as economic success (Damian & others, 2015; Hafer, 2016; Herrnstein & Murray, 1994).

Over the years, IQ tests like the Stanford-Binet and the Wechsler scales have been given to thousands upon thousands of children and adults of difference ages. When the scores for many people are examined, they approximate a normal distribution. A *distribution* refers to the frequencies of various scores on a scale—basically, how many people receive each of the possible scores. A **normal distribution** is a symmetrical, bell-shaped curve, with a majority of the scores falling in the middle of the possible range and few scores appearing toward the extremes of the range. To master the important idea of a normal distribution, complete the Psychological Inquiry.

Alfred Binet (1857–1911) Binet constructed the first intelligence test after being asked to create a measure to determine which children would benefit from instruction in France's schools.

© Everett Collection Inc/Alamy

● **mental age (MA)** An individual's level of mental development relative to that of others.

● **intelligence quotient (IQ)** An individual's mental age divided by chronological age multiplied by 100.

● **normal distribution** A symmetrical, bell-shaped curve, with a majority of the scores falling in the middle of the possible range and few scores appearing toward the extremes of the range.

psychological *inquiry*

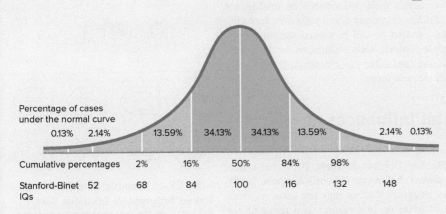

Percentage of cases
under the normal curve

| 0.13% | 2.14% | | 13.59% | 34.13% | 34.13% | 13.59% | | 2.14% | 0.13% |

Cumulative percentages   2%   16%   50%   84%   98%

Stanford-Binet   52   68   84   100   116   132   148
IQs

The Normal Curve

This figure shows the normal curve and Stanford-Binet IQ scores. The distribution of IQ scores approximates a normal distribution. Answer the following questions, keeping in mind that the area under the curve represents the number of people who obtain a given score on the test.

1. Do most people fall in the low, medium, or high range? How do you know?

2. If someone scored a 132 on the test, how many people scored below that person's score?

3. What is the mean or average on the IQ test? Where does the mean fall on the bell-shaped curve?

4. Notice that in a normal distribution, extremely high and extremely low scores are rare. What other human characteristics might follow this pattern?

CULTURAL BIAS IN TESTING

Many early intelligence tests were culturally biased, favoring people who were from urban rather than rural environments, of middle rather than low socioeconomic status, and non-Latino White rather than African American (Provenzo, 2002). For example, a question on an early test asked what one should do if one finds a 3-year-old child in the street. The correct answer was "call the police." However, children from inner-city families who perceive the police as scary are unlikely to choose this answer. Similarly, children from rural areas might not choose this answer if there is no police force nearby. Such questions clearly do not measure the knowledge necessary to adapt to one's environment or to be "intelligent" in an inner-city or a rural neighborhood. In addition, members of minority groups may not speak English or may speak nonstandard English. Consequently, they may be at a disadvantage in trying to understand verbal questions that are framed in standard English, even if the content of the test is appropriate (Cathers-Shiffman & Thompson, 2007).

Researchers have sought to develop tests that accurately reflect a person's intelligence, regardless of cultural background (Reynolds, Livingston, & Willson, 2006); te Nijenhuis & others, 2016). The effects of language bias and cultural bias estimated using the method of correlated. **Culture-fair tests** are intelligence tests that are intended to be culturally unbiased. One type of culture-fair test includes questions that are familiar to people from all socioeconomic and ethnic backgrounds. A second type contains no verbal questions. Figure 8 shows a sample question from the Raven Progressive Matrices test. Even though tests such as the Raven are designed to be culture-fair, people with more education still score higher than do those with less education.

Why is it so hard to create culture-fair tests? Just as the definition of intelligence may vary by culture, most tests of intelligence reflect what is important to the dominant culture. If tests have time limits, the test will be biased against groups not concerned with time. If languages differ, the same words might have different meanings for different language groups. Even pictures can produce bias, because some cultures have less

● **culture-fair tests** Intelligence tests that are intended to be culturally unbiased.

experience with drawings and photographs (Urbina, 2011). Because of such difficulties, Robert Sternberg and his colleagues conclude that there are no culture-fair tests, only *culture-reduced tests* (Sternberg, 2012a; Zhang & Sternberg, 2013).

Moreover, within the same culture, different groups can have different attitudes, values, and motivation, and these variations can affect their performance on intelligence tests (Ang & van Dyne, 2009; Sternberg, 2012a). Questions about railroads, furnaces, seasons of the year, distances between cities, and so on can be biased against groups who have less experience than others with these contexts. One explanation for the effects of education on IQ test scores is that education (and other environmental factors) may influence intelligence, a possibility to which we now turn.

Genetic and Environmental Influences on Intelligence

There is no doubt that genes influence intelligence (Bohlken & others, 2016), but understanding how and how much they do so has proved challenging (Chabris & others, 2012). Indeed, recently psychologists have come to recognize that we may not know as much as we thought we did about the influence of genes on intelligence, as a result of our growing understanding of genes themselves.

In the chapter "Biological Foundations of Behavior" we described the concepts of genotype and phenotype. Genotype refers to an organism's genetic material. Phenotype refers to the actual characteristics the organism possesses. When we are talking about genetic influences on intelligence, we are interested in understanding how differences at the level of the genotype predict differences in the phenotype of intelligence.

For quite some time, scientists relied on a statistic called heritability to describe the extent to which the observable differences among people in a group (the phenotype) can be explained by the genetic differences of the group's members (the genotype). **Heritability** is the proportion of observable differences in a group that can be explained by differences in the genes of the group's members. For intelligence, that means that heritability tells us how much of the differences we observe in intelligence is attributable to differences in genes. Because heritability is a proportion, the highest degree of heritability is 100 percent. Research on heritability has typically involved comparing the similarity of the phenotypes of identical or monozygotic twins to that of fraternal or dizygotic twins. Assuming that identical twins share 100 percent of their genetic material, and fraternal twins 50 percent of theirs, scientists have estimated the heritability of intelligence to be as high as 75 percent (Shakeshaft & others, 2015; Trzaskowski & others, 2014).

However, this conclusion, and others based on heritability estimates, has been called into question (Charney, 2012; Crusio, 2012). A key assumption of the heritability estimate—that twins share a specific amount of genetic material—is, it turns out, not completely accurate. Research suggests that the human genome possesses some degree of *plasticity*. Essentially, after conception, our genes can change. Identical twins might have identical DNA at the moment of conception, but DNA can move around prenatally (Xing & others, 2009) and postnatally, especially in the brain (Baillie & others, 2011).

Such findings have led some to call for heritability to be discarded as a measure of genetic influence on behaviors (Charney, 2012; Crusio, 2012). Other researchers have suggested that these discoveries may simply help to explain some of the errors in heritability estimates (Battaglia, 2012); that they do not justify complete dismissal of heritability studies (Miller, DeYoung, & McGue, 2012; Vilarroya, 2012); or that the frequency of genetic change is not so great as to call into question the validity of heritability estimates (MacDonald & LaFreniere, 2012). At the very least, we might be wise to consider the 75 percent heritability estimate for intelligence with some skepticism.

Even if we believe that 75 percent is a reasonable estimate of the amount of variability in intelligence that is explained by genetics, there are some important points to keep in mind. First and most important, heritability is a statistic that provides information about a group, not a single individual. This means that finding out that heritability for intelligence is 75 percent tells us nothing at all about the source of an individual person's intelligence.

FIGURE 8 Sample Item from the Raven Progressive Matrices Test For this item, the respondent must choose which of the numbered figures would come next in the order. Can you explain why the right answer is number 6? Adapted from *Raven's Progressive Matrices* (Advanced Progressive Matrices), 1998.

● **heritability** The proportion of observable differences in a group that can be explained by differences in the genes of the group's members.

We cannot dissect your intelligence and determine that you got 75 percent of it from your parents and 25 percent from your schooling. Heritability has no meaning when applied to a single case. Recall from the chapter "Psychology's Scientific Method" that group statistics do not apply to a specific case. That is, *statistics describe groups*, not individuals.

Certainly, heritability estimates can change over time and across different groups (Nisbett & others, 2012; Turkheimer & others, 2003). If a group of individuals lives in the same advantageous setting (with good nutrition, supportive parents, great schools, stable neighborhoods, and plenty of opportunities), heritability estimates for intelligence might be quite high, as this optimal environment allows genetic characteristics to flourish to their highest potential. However, if a group of individuals lives in a highly variable environment (with some individuals experiencing rich, nurturing environments full of opportunity and others experiencing less supportive contexts), genetic characteristics may be less predictive of differences in intelligence in that group, relative to environmental factors.

Finally, even if the heritability of a characteristic is very high, the environment still matters. Take height, for example. Heritability estimates suggest that more than 90 percent of the variation in height is explained by genetic variation. Generally speaking, humans continue to get taller and taller, however, and this trend demonstrates that environmental factors such as nutrition have an impact. Similarly, in the case of intelligence, most researchers agree that for most people, modifications in environment can change their IQ scores considerably (Esposito, Grigorenko, & Sternberg, 2012; Nisbett & others, 2012).

Indeed, research provides strong support for the conclusion that childhood experiences can profoundly affect IQ. The Database of Raising Intelligence is a continuously updated collection of research on the effects of various interventions on children's intelligence, ranging from infancy to age 5. Psychologists John Protzko, Joshua Aronson, and Clancy Blair (2013) published the results of an analysis of over 74 interventions including more than 37,000 children. All of the studies included were experiments, meaning that participants were randomly assigned to receive the intervention, and then researchers compared the IQs (the dependent variable) to those in the control groups. The analysis provided strong evidence for four environmental interventions that affect childhood IQ (Protzko, Aronson, & Blair, 2013):

- *Dietary supplements:* One type of dietary supplement that has been found to positively influence childhood IQ is long-chain polyunsaturated fatty acids, commonly referred to as Omega-3 fatty acids. These acids are found in breast milk, fish oil, salmon, walnuts, spinach, and avocados. When pregnant women, nursing mothers, and infants received 1,000 milligram supplements of Omega-3 fatty acids, the supplements led to an increase of about 3.5 IQ points.

- *Educational interventions:* Research shows that early childhood education can improve the IQ of economically disadvantaged young children: Early educational interventions, especially those that involved training on complex tasks, led to an increase in IQ of more than 4 points.

- *Interactive reading:* Interactive reading means that parents ask open-ended questions, encourage a child to read, and engage with the child actively about what they are reading together. Interactive reading raised a child's IQ by over 6 points, and this was especially true if the interventions occurred at younger ages.

- *Preschool:* Sending a child to preschool increased IQ by more than 4 points (Protzko, Aronson, & Blair, 2013). Socioeconomic status played an important role in these results. For economically disadvantaged children (those whose parents might not have been able to afford preschool except for the studies in which they were enrolled), attending preschool raised IQs by as much as 7 points. Preschool curricula including language development were especially effective. The researchers noted that the effects of preschool may not be maintained if children are not continually exposed to complex cognitive challenges in their environments as they move to grade school.

One effect of education on intelligence is evident in rapidly increasing IQ test scores around the world, a phenomenon called the *Flynn effect* (Flynn, 1999, 2006, 2013; Woodley of Menie & others, 2016; Trahan & others, 2014). Scores on these tests have been rising so fast that a high percentage of people regarded as having average intelligence in

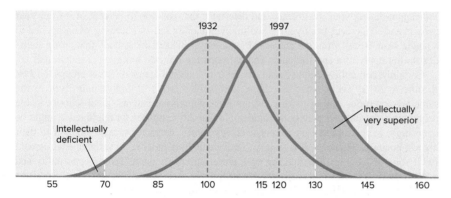

FIGURE 9 **The Increase In IQ Scores from 1932 to 1997** As measured by the Stanford-Binet intelligence test, U.S. children seem to be getting smarter. Scores of a group tested in 1932 fell along a bell-shaped curve, with half below 100 and half above. Studies show that if children took that same test today, using the 1932 scale, half would score above 120. Few of them would score in the "intellectually deficient" range, and about one-fourth would rank in the "very superior" range. Such findings suggest that IQ tests may require new norms to continue to be useful. Data from "The Increase in IQ Scores from 1932–1997" by Ulric Neisser.

1932 would be regarded as having below-average intelligence today (Figure 9). Because the increase has taken place in a relatively short period of time, it cannot be due to heredity but rather may be due to rising levels of education attained by a much greater percentage of the world's population or to other environmental factors, such as the explosion of information to which people are now exposed.

Environmental influences are complex (Trahan & others, 2014). Growing up with all the advantages does not guarantee success. Children from wealthy families may have easy access to excellent schools, books, tutors, and travel, but they may take such opportunities for granted and not be motivated to learn and to achieve. Alternatively, poor or disadvantaged children may be highly motivated and successful. Caregivers who themselves lacked educational opportunities may instill a strong sense of the value of learning and achievement in their children.

Let's return to the idea that the word *intelligent* describes not only people but also behaviors. Mastering skills, thinking about life actively, and making decisions thoughtfully are intelligent behaviors in which people can engage regardless of the numerical intelligence quotient on their permanent record. Intelligent behavior is always an option, no matter one's IQ score. As we saw in the chapter "Learning", our beliefs about cognitive ability, specifically whether it is fixed or changeable, have important implications for the goals we set for learning new skills (Dweck, 2006, 2013). We never know what we might accomplish if we try, and no one is doomed because of a number, no matter how powerful that number may seem.

● **gifted** Possessing high intelligence (an IQ of 130 or higher) and/or superior talent in a particular area.

Extremes of Intelligence

Intelligence, then, appears to emerge from a combination of genetic heritage and environmental factors. As we have seen, scores on IQ tests generally conform to the bell-shaped normal curve. We now examine the implications of falling on either tail of that curve.

GIFTEDNESS

There are people whose abilities and accomplishments outshine those of others—the *A+* student, the star athlete, the natural musician. People who are **gifted** have high intelligence (an IQ of 130 or higher) and/or superior talent in a particular area. Lewis Terman (1925) conducted a study of 1,500 children whose Stanford-Binet IQs averaged 150, a score that placed them in the top 1 percent. A popular myth is that gifted children are maladjusted, but Terman found that his participants ("Termites") were not only academically gifted but also socially well adjusted. Many of them later became successful

©Rawpixel.com/Shutterstock

doctors, lawyers, professors, and scientists. Do gifted children grow to be gifted and highly creative adults? In Terman's research, gifted children typically did become experts in a well-established domain, such as medicine, law, or business; but the Termites did not become major creators or innovators (Winner, 2000, 2006).

In light of the sweeping social and economic changes of the digital age, are today's gifted children perhaps better able than the Termites to use their gifts in innovative and important ways in adulthood? The results from a longitudinal study of profoundly gifted children at Johns Hopkins University in 1971 seem to indicate just that. The Study of Mathematically Precocious Youth (SMPY) includes 320 participants whom researchers recruited before age 13 based on IQ scores, with the group's average IQ estimated at 180. This group is said to represent the top 1 in 10,000 IQ scores (Lubinski & others, 2001).

Following up on these individuals in their 20s, David Lubinski and colleagues (2006) found that these strikingly gifted young people were doing remarkable things. At age 23, they were pursuing doctoral degrees at a rate 50 times higher than the average. Some reported achievements such as receiving writing awards, creating original music and art, publishing in scholarly journals, and developing commercially viable software and video games. Thus, unlike the Termites, this group has been quite creative and innovative (Wai, Lubinski, & Benbow, 2005).

Interestingly, the Flynn effect appears to apply to even those with very high IQs. Studies of individuals at the very highest level of intelligence show that their scores are also getting higher (Wai, Putallaz, & Makel, 2012). For this reason, newer studies similar to the SMPY research have begun to incorporate cognitive ability measures that have more "headroom." In other words, the tests are even more challenging (often designed for older youth or adults) to allow extraordinarily intelligent children to show their stuff (Wai & others, 2010).

Like intelligence itself, giftedness is likely a product of both heredity and environment. A study of nearly 400,000 sibling pairs and 9,000 twin pairs that included DNA sequencing showed that the genes and environmental experiences that explain normal-range intelligence also explain exceptional intelligence (Shakeshaft & others, 2015). Certainly, individuals who enjoy world-class status in the arts, mathematics, science, and sports not only demonstrate genetic heritage but also strong family support and years of training and practice (Bloom, 1985). Deliberate practice is an important characteristic of individuals who become experts in a particular domain (Ericsson & Moxley, 2012).

Of course, providing educational opportunities for youth who possess exceptionally high intelligence is just one of the many priorities faced by the educational system. For some talented students, it may be necessary to seek out opportunities outside of the regular classroom. Bill Gates, Microsoft's founder, took college math classes at 13, and famed cellist Yo-Yo Ma graduated from high school at 15 and then attended the Juilliard School of Music.

One important factor in gifted education is identifying children as gifted. Although many standardized tests are used to screen all children for IQ, parents or teachers might also nominate students as likely candidates for gifted instruction (Kornmann & others, 2015). These students are tested and then might enter into such programs. What this means is that, for some students, qualifying for gifted instruction involves someone else's *social perception*. Being recognized as possibly gifted depends on an adult noticing that a child might be highly intelligent.

Social perception can be influenced by stereotypes. Stereotypes are generalizations about people based on their group membership, and these beliefs do not take into account all the variability among group members. The notion that stereotypes about gifted children exist and affect who is included in gifted programs is suggested by the fact that ethnic groups (such as African Americans and Latino Americans), as well as individuals for whom English is a second language and those with physical and learning disabilities, are underrepresented in U.S. gifted programs (Carman, 2011; Gari, Mylonas, & Portešová, 2015).

Viewers of *The Big Bang Theory* will certainly recognize the stereotype of gifted individuals. On the show, characters with very high IQs are seen bumbling through social situations and having difficulty navigating many mundane everyday tasks, to great comic effect. These TV geniuses are shown as lovable social misfits.

Do gifted children also get labeled with these stereotypes? And do teachers themselves hold such stereotypes? To answer these questions, researchers have begun to study teachers' beliefs about children identified as gifted using methods developed in social psychology. To read about this work, see the Critical Controversy.

CRITICAL CONTROVERSY

Do Teachers Have Stereotypes About Gifted Children?

Research shows that intellectually gifted children are quite similar to average-ability children on various personality characteristics, social relationships, and well-being (Bergold & others, 2015). Yet, there are two (opposing) stereotypes of gifted students. One suggests that these students possess more desirable characteristics: Gifted students are friendlier, kinder, and more conscientious than average students. The other stereotype is that gifted students have less desirable characteristics: They are social misfits and are less creative, more introverted, less gregarious, less friendly, and socially incompetent (Preckel & others, 2015).

People in general may hold such stereotypes, but a key question is whether teachers, who are most likely to encounter these children and know of their gifted status, hold a stereotype about gifted children. Do teachers hold stereotyped beliefs about gifted kids? Unfortunately research suggests that they do.

For example, in one experiment, 321 teachers and students studying education were presented with vignettes describing identical situations in which they were called in to be the substitute teacher for a class (Baudson & Preckel, 2013). One student in the class was described as either gifted or average. The participants then rated the target child on various personality traits. There were no differences between raters who were actual teachers and those in training. In both groups, gifted students were rated as less extraverted, less emotionally stable, and less agreeable—that is, less nice. Clearly, then, teachers and prospective teachers in these studies appear to hold the social misfit stereotype of gifted students.

Why do these stereotypes exist? One reason may be an *illusory correlation*. Illusory correlations occur when two vivid

(first) © Aleksander Kaczmarek/iStock/Getty Images; (second) © Lane Oatey/Blue Jean Images/Getty Images

events happen together and become linked in memory. Individuals who have very high IQs are likely to be vivid, as are those who are socially awkward. When these characteristics occur together, we are more likely to notice them and think they are related. Of course, they are not (hence the term *illusory*).

The fact that even teachers hold these stereotypes is troubling. If a student does not fit the stereotype for giftedness, will he or she be less likely to be identified by teachers or parents and therefore less likely to benefit from special instruction? This stereotype might also affect how children who do not fit the stereotype are treated in gifted programs. Guidebooks for parents of gifted children sometimes warn them that their children may be socially awkward and emotionally unstable (Preckel & others, 2015). In a sense, these guidebooks treat high intelligence as a social disability, potentially perpetuating the stereotype.

Nurturing intelligence in all people is an important goal for society. An intellectually gifted child, no matter his or her ethnicity or disability status, deserves the chance to realize his or her potential. Even if a child is a star athlete, a popular social butterfly, or a gregarious class clown, maximizing his or her intellectual abilities is vital not only to the child but to society at large.

WHAT DO YOU THINK?
- When you think of a gifted child, what are the first characteristics to come to mind?
- How might ethnic and gender stereotypes influence whether a child receives gifted education?

INTELLECTUAL DISABILITY

Just as some individuals are at the high extreme of intelligence, others are at the lower end. **Intellectual disability** (or **intellectual developmental disorder**) is a condition of limited mental ability that affects functioning in three domains:

- *Conceptual skills,* including language, reading, writing, math, reasoning, and memory
- *Social skills,* including empathy, social judgment, interpersonal communication, and the ability to make friends
- *Practical skills,* including self-management of personal care, job responsibilities, money management, recreation, and organizing school and work tasks

Assessment of capacities in these areas can be used to determine the amount of care the person requires for daily living—not as a function of IQ but as a gauge of the person's ability to negotiate life's challenges.

● **intellectual disability or intellectual developmental disorder** A condition of limited mental ability that affects an individual's functioning in everyday life.

Individuals with Down syndrome may excel in sensitivity toward others. The possibility that other strengths or intelligences coexist with cognitive ability (or disability) has led some psychologists to propose the need for expanding the concept of intelligence.
©Denis Kuvaev/Shutterstock

Intellectual disability may have an organic cause, or it may be cultural and social in origin (Peters-Scheffer, Didden, & Lang, 2016). *Organic intellectual disability* is caused by a genetic disorder or brain damage; *organic* refers to the tissues or organs of the body, so there is some physical damage in organic retardation. Down syndrome, one form of organic intellectual disability, occurs when an extra chromosome is present in the individual's genetic makeup. Most people who suffer from organic retardation have an IQ between 0 and 50.

Cultural-familial intellectual disability is a mental deficit with no evidence of organic brain damage. Individuals with this type of disability have an IQ between 55 and 70. Psychologists suspect that such mental deficits result at least in part from growing up in a below-average intellectual environment. As children, individuals with this disability can be identified in school, where they often fail, need tangible rewards (candy rather than grades, for example), and are highly sensitive to what peers and adults expect of them (Vaughn, Bos, & Schumm, 2003). As adults, however, these individuals usually go unnoticed, perhaps because their environments do not tax their cognitive skills as much. It may also be that the intelligence of such individuals increases as they move toward adulthood.

There are several classifications of intellectual disability (Hodapp & others, 2011). In one classification system, disability ranges from mild, to moderate, to severe or profound, according to the person's IQ (Heward, 2013). The large majority of individuals diagnosed with intellectual disability fall in the mild category. Most school systems still use this system. However, these categories, based on IQ ranges, are not perfect predictors of functioning. Indeed, it is not unusual to find clear *functional* differences between two people who have the same low IQ. For example, looking at two individuals with a similarly low IQ, we might find that one of them is married, employed, and involved in the community while the other requires constant supervision in an institution. Such differences in social competence have led psychologists to include deficits in adaptive behavior in their definition of intellectual disability (Turnbull & others, 2013).

A person with Down syndrome may never accomplish the amazing academic feats of gifted individuals. However, he or she may be capable of building close, warm relations with others, serving as an inspiration to loved ones, and bringing smiles into an otherwise gloomy day (Van Riper, 2007). Moreover, individuals with Down syndrome might possess different kinds of intelligence, even if they are low on general cognitive ability. The possibility that other intelligences exist alongside cognitive ability (or disability) has inspired some psychologists to suggest that we need more than one concept of intelligence.

Theories of Multiple Intelligences

Is it more appropriate to think of an individual's intelligence as a general ability or as a number of specific abilities? Traditionally, most psychologists have viewed intelligence as a general, all-purpose problem-solving ability, termed *g* by Spearman (1904). Others have proposed that we think about different kinds of intelligence, such as *emotional intelligence,* the ability to perceive emotions in oneself and others accurately (Brackett, Rivers, & Salovey, 2011; Mayer & others, 2011). Robert Sternberg and Howard Gardner have developed influential theories presenting the viewpoint that there are *multiple intelligences.*

STERNBERG'S TRIARCHIC THEORY AND GARDNER'S MULTIPLE INTELLIGENCES

● **triarchic theory of intelligence** Sternberg's theory that intelligence comes in three forms: analytical, creative, and practical.

Robert J. Sternberg developed the **triarchic theory of intelligence,** which says that intelligence comes in multiple (specifically, three) forms (2011, 2012c, 2013a, 2013b). These forms are

- *Analytical intelligence:* The ability to analyze, judge, evaluate, compare, and contrast.
- *Creative intelligence:* The ability to create, design, invent, originate, and imagine.
- *Practical intelligence:* The ability to use, apply, implement, and put ideas into practice.

Howard Gardner suggests there are nine types of intelligence, or "frames of mind" (1983, 1993, 2002). These are described here, with examples of the types of vocations in which they are reflected as strengths (Campbell, Campbell, & Dickinson, 2004):

- *Verbal:* The ability to think in words and use language to express meaning. Occupations: author, journalist, speaker.
- *Mathematical:* The ability to carry out mathematical operations. Occupations: scientist, engineer, accountant.
- *Spatial:* The ability to think three-dimensionally. Occupations: architect, artist, sailor.
- *Bodily-kinesthetic:* The ability to manipulate objects and to be physically adept. Occupations: surgeon, craftsperson, dancer, athlete.
- *Musical:* The ability to be sensitive to pitch, melody, rhythm, and tone. Occupations: composer, musician.
- *Interpersonal:* The ability to understand and interact effectively with others. Occupations: teacher, mental health professional.
- *Intrapersonal:* The ability to understand oneself. Occupations: theologian, psychologist.
- *Naturalist:* The ability to observe patterns in nature and understand natural and human-made systems. Occupations: farmer, botanist, ecologist, landscaper.
- *Existentialist:* The ability to grapple with the big questions of human existence, such as the meaning of life and death, with special sensitivity to issues of spirituality. Gardner has not identified an occupation for existential intelligence, but one career path would likely be philosopher.

According to Gardner, everyone has all of these intelligences to varying degrees. As a result, we prefer to learn and process information in different ways. People learn best when they can do so in a way that uses their stronger intelligences.

EVALUATING THE MULTIPLE-INTELLIGENCES APPROACHES

Sternberg's and Gardner's approaches have stimulated teachers to think broadly about what makes up children's competencies. They have motivated educators to develop programs that instruct students in multiple domains. These theories have also contributed to interest in assessing intelligence and classroom learning in innovative ways, such as by evaluating student portfolios (Woolfolk, 2013).

Doubts about multiple intelligences persist, however. A number of psychologists think that the proponents of multiple intelligences have taken the concept of specific intelligences too far (Reeve & Charles, 2008). Some critics argue that a research base to support the three intelligences of Sternberg or the nine intelligences of Gardner has not yet emerged. One expert on intelligence, Nathan Brody (2007), observes that people who excel at one type of intellectual task are likely to excel at others. Thus, individuals who do well at memorizing lists of digits are also likely to be good at solving verbal problems and spatial layout problems. Other critics ask, if musical skill, for example, reflects a distinct type of intelligence, why not also label the skills of outstanding chess players, prizefighters, painters, and poets as types of intelligence? In sum, controversy still characterizes whether it is more accurate to conceptualize intelligence as a general ability, specific abilities, or both (Brody, 2007; Nisbett & others, 2012; Sternberg, 2013a, 2013b).

One question that remains is whether and how we can enhance our cognitive abilities. Although there is some controversy about whether these abilities can be changed (Melby-Lervåg & Hulme, 2016), there is some evidence that challenging ourselves in two different ways may enhance cognition. First, you might be surprised to learn that challenging physical activity is associated with improved cognitive performance (Moreau, 2015). Second, engaging in complex cognitive tasks can improve reasoning ability over time (Au & others, 2015). Importantly, for either type of activity to pay off, we must seek out ever-more challenging activities—no resting on our laurels.

Our examination of cognitive abilities has highlighted how individuals differ in the quality of their thinking and how thoughts themselves differ. Some thoughts reflect critical thinking, creativity, or intelligence. Other thoughts are perhaps less inspired. One thing thoughts have in common is that they usually involve language. Even when we talk to ourselves, we do so with words. The central role of language in cognitive activity is the topic to which we now turn.

© Dance By Beytan/Alamy

test yourself

1. With respect to testing, what do validity, reliability, and standardization mean?
2. What two terms respectively define individuals at the high end and at the low end of intelligence?
3. How does Spearman's *g* compare to approaches to multiple intelligences?

4. LANGUAGE

language A form of communication—whether spoken, written, or signed—that is based on a system of symbols.

Language is a form of communication—whether spoken, written, or signed—that is based on a system of symbols. We need language to speak with others, listen to others, read, and write. In this section we first examine the fundamental characteristics of language and then trace the links between language and cognition.

The Basic Properties of Language

All human languages have *infinite generativity,* the ability to produce an endless number of meaningful sentences. This superb flexibility comes from five basic rule systems:

phonology A language's sound system.

- **Phonology:** a language's sound system. Language is made up of basic sounds, or *phonemes.* Phonological rules ensure that certain sound sequences occur (for example, *sp, ba,* or *ar*) and others do not (for example, *zx* or *qp*) (Kuhl & Damasio, 2012). A good example of a phoneme in the English language is /k/, the sound represented by the letter *k* in the word *ski* and the letter *c* in the word *cat.* Although the /k/ sound is slightly different in these two words, the /k/ sound is described as a single phoneme in English.

morphology A language's rules for word formation.

- **Morphology:** a language's rules for word formation. Every word in the English language is made up of one or more morphemes. A morpheme is the smallest unit of language that carries meaning. Some words consist of a single morpheme—for example, *help.* Others are made up of more than one; for example, *helper* has two morphemes, *help + er.* The morpheme *-er* means "one who"—in this case, "one who helps." As you can see, not all morphemes are words; for example, *pre-, -tion,* and *-ing* are morphemes. Just as the rules that govern phonemes ensure that certain sound sequences occur, the rules that govern morphemes ensure that certain strings of sounds occur in particular sequences (Rizzi & Cinque, 2016).

syntax A language's rules for combining words to form acceptable phrases and sentences.

- **Syntax:** a language's rules for combining words to form acceptable phrases and sentences (de Villiers & de Villiers, 2013; Dixon, 2012). If someone says, "John kissed Emily" or "Emily was kissed by John," you know who did the kissing and who was kissed in each case because you share that person's understanding of sentence structure. You also understand that the sentence "You didn't stay, did you?" is a grammatical sentence but that "You didn't stay, didn't you?" is unacceptable.

semantics The meaning of words and sentences in a particular language.

- **Semantics:** the meaning of words and sentences in a particular language. Every word has a unique set of semantic features (Pan & Uccelli, 2009). *Girl* and *woman,* for example, share many semantic features (for instance, both signify a female human being), but they differ semantically in regard to age. Words have semantic restrictions on how they can be used in sentences. The sentence "The bicycle talked the boy into buying a candy bar" is syntactically correct but semantically incorrect. The sentence violates our semantic knowledge that bicycles do not talk.

pragmatics The useful character of language and the ability of language to communicate even more meaning than is verbalized.

- **Pragmatics:** the useful character of language and the ability of language to communicate even more meaning than is said (Al-Wer, 2014; Bryant, 2012). The pragmatic aspect of language allows us to use words to get the things we want. If you ever find yourself in a country in which you know only a little of the language, you will certainly take advantage of pragmatics. Wandering the streets of, say, Madrid, you might approach a stranger and ask, simply, "Autobus?" (the Spanish word for *bus*). You know that given your inflection and perhaps your desperate facial expression, the person will understand that you are looking for the bus stop.

With this basic understanding of language in place, we can examine the connections between language and cognition.

Language and Cognition

Language is a vast system of symbols capable of expressing most thoughts; it is the vehicle for communicating most of our thoughts to one another. Although we do not always think in words, our thinking would be greatly impoverished without words.

The connection between language and thought has been of considerable interest to psychologists. Some have even argued that we cannot think without language. This proposition has produced heated controversy. Is thought dependent on language or is language dependent on thought?

THE ROLE OF LANGUAGE IN COGNITION

Recall from the chapter "Memory" that memory is stored not only in the form of sounds and images but also in words. Language helps us think, make inferences, tackle difficult decisions, and solve problems (Gleitman & Papafragou, 2012; Novak & Goldin-Meadow, 2015). It is also a tool for representing ideas.

Today, most psychologists would accept these points. However, linguist Benjamin Whorf (1956) went a step further: He argued that language determines the way we think, a view that has been called the *linguistic relativity hypothesis*. Whorf and his student Edward Sapir were specialists in Native American languages, and they were fascinated by the possibility that people might perceive the world differently as the result of the different languages they speak. The Inuit people in Alaska, for instance, have a dozen or more words to describe the various textures, colors, and physical states of snow. In contrast, English has relatively few words to describe snow, and thus, according to Whorf's view, English speakers *cannot see* the different kinds of snow because they have no words for them.

Whorf's bold claim appealed to many scholars. Some even tried to apply Whorf's view to gender differences in color perception. Asked to describe the colors of two sweaters, a woman

Whorf's view is that our cultural experiences with a particular concept shape a catalog of names that can be either rich or poor. Consider how rich your mental library of names for camels might be if you had extensive experience with camels in a desert world, and how poor your mental library of names for snow might be if you lived in a tropical world of palm trees and parrots. Despite its intriguing appeal, Whorf's view likely overstates the role of language in shaping thought.

(first) © SuperStock; (second) ©White Fox/AGF/Universal Images Group/Getty Images

might say, "One is mauve and the other is magenta," while a man might say, "They're both pink." Whorf's view of the influence of language on perceptual ability might suggest that women are able to see more colors than men simply because they have a richer color vocabulary (Hepting & Solle, 1973). It turns out, however, that men can learn to discriminate among the various hues that women use, and this outcome suggests that Whorf's view is not quite accurate.

Indeed, critics of Whorf's ideas say that words merely reflect, rather than cause, the way we think. The Inuits' adaptability and livelihood in Alaska depend on their capacity to recognize various conditions of snow and ice. A skier or snowboarder who is not Inuit might also know numerous words for snow, far more than the average person, and a person who does not know the words for the different types of snow might still be able to perceive these differences. Interestingly, research has shown that Whorf might have been accurate for information that is presented to the left hemisphere of the brain. That is, when colors were presented in the right visual field (and therefore went to the left brain), having names for the colors enhanced perception of and discrimination among those colors (Gilbert & others, 2006).

Although the strongest form of Whorf's hypothesis—that language determines perception—seems doubtful, research has continued to demonstrate the influence of language on how we think. For instance, a recent set of studies showed that people were more lenient in their moral judgments when the activities were described in a foreign language (Geipel, Hadjichristidis, & Surian, 2015). Many people who are bilingual (that is, fluent in two languages) report feeling different while speaking each (Dewaele, 2016).

In fact, a set of studies demonstrated language could influence something as fundamental as our own personalities. In those studies, researchers interviewed bilingual individuals (fluent in Spanish and English) (Ramírez-Esparza & others, 2006) rated their personality characteristics, once in Spanish and once in English. Across all studies, and regardless of whether the individuals lived in a Spanish-speaking or an English-speaking country, respondents reported themselves as more outgoing, nicer, and more responsible when responding to the survey in English.

THE ROLE OF COGNITION IN LANGUAGE

Clearly, then, language can influence cognition. Researchers also study the possibility that cognition is an important foundation for language (Jackendoff, 2012).

One feature of human language that separates it from animal communication is the capacity to talk about objects that are not currently present (Hockett, 1960). A study comparing 12-month-old infants (who had not yet begun to talk) to chimpanzees suggests that this cognitive skill may underlie eventual language (Liszkowski & others, 2009). In this study, infants were more likely to communicate their desire for a toy by pointing to the place where the toy used to be. For many infants, this was the first thing they did to get their point across to another person who was present. In contrast, chimpanzees rarely pointed to where their desired object (food) had been, except as they desperately started pointing all over the place. So, even before they can talk, humans are communicating with others about what they want. Sometimes that communication demonstrates an appreciation of shared knowledge even about objects that are no longer present.

If language is a reflection of cognition in general, we would expect to find a close link between language ability and general intellectual ability. In particular, we would expect that problems in cognition are paralleled by problems in language. We would anticipate, for example, that general intellectual disability is accompanied by lowered language abilities. It is often but not always the case that individuals with intellectual disability have a reduced language proficiency. For instance, individuals with Williams syndrome—a genetic disorder that affects about 1 in 20,000 births—tend to show extraordinary verbal, social, and musical abilities while having an extremely low IQ and difficulty with motor tasks and numbers (Asada & Itakura, 2012). Williams syndrome demonstrates that intellectual disability is not always accompanied by poor language skills.

Another research topic that involves the influence of language on cognition is the association between bilingualism and cognitive capacities, especially executive function. Recall that **executive function** refers to an array of complex abilities including exerting control over one's mental processes. A number of studies have indicated that those who are bilingual show improved executive function compared to those who are monolingual (that is, who speak only one language) (Bialystok, 2015). However, this conclusion has come under extreme scrutiny as some researchers have not found a cognitive advantage for bilingualism at all or have found it to be limited to very narrow tasks—not the all-purpose toolbox of executive function (Papp, Johnson, & Sawi, 2015).

● **executive function** Higher-order, complex cognitive processes, including thinking, planning, and problem solving.

The controversy over this issue highlights the important role of rigorous scientific methods in research. Consider, for example, that comparing bilingual to monolingual individuals in a study often involves comparing individuals who have immigrated at some point in their lives to those who have always lived in the same place. Immigrant status, then, is often confounded with language group. Moreover, and interestingly, immigrants tend to have higher IQs than nonimmigrants, suggesting that bilingual individuals might have had higher executive function to start with (Bak, 2015). The issue is even more complicated than that, however. Socioeconomic status, parental education, and a host of other issues can also affect second-language acquisition, training, and executive function.

Clearly, this controversy is far from resolved. At the very least, it demonstrates that the relationship between language and cognition is complex. In summary, although thought influences language and language influences thought, there is increasing evidence that language and thought are not part of a single system. Instead, they seem to have evolved as separate but related components of the mind.

Biological and Environmental Influences on Language

Everyone who uses language in some way "knows" its rules and has the ability to create an infinite number of words and sentences. Is this knowledge the product of biology, or is language learned and influenced by experiences in the environment?

BIOLOGICAL INFLUENCES

Scientists believe that humans acquired language about 100,000 years ago. In evolutionary time, then, language is a very recent human ability. A number of biological systems are required for language, including the brain, nervous system, and vocal apparatus. Physically equipped to do so, *Homo sapiens* went beyond grunting and shrieking to develop abstract speech. This sophisticated language ability gave humans an enormous edge over other animals and increased their chances of survival (Arbib, 2012). Think about our distant ancestors, how they needed one another to survive, and how survival required communication.

Research indicates that language (and teaching) evolved along with toolmaking (Morgan & others, 2015). At some point, it was no longer enough to simply watch someone do what needed to be done and then imitate that model. Early humans who could actually tell one another what to do won the evolutionary sweepstakes and survived to produce all of us. For them, language solved an enormous problem.

Language Universals American linguist Noam Chomsky (1975) has argued that humans come into the world biologically prewired to learn language at a certain time and in a certain way. According to Chomsky and many other language experts, the strongest evidence for language's biological basis is the fact that children all over the world reach language milestones at about the same time and in about the same order, despite vast variations in the language input they receive from their environment. For example, in some cultures, such as some Samoan tribes (Schieffelin & Ochs, 1986), parents snuggle their babies but rarely talk to infants under 1 year of age, yet these infants still acquire language (Sterponi, 2010).

In Chomsky's view, children cannot possibly learn the full rules and structure of languages by only imitating what they hear. Rather, nature must provide children with a biological, prewired, universal grammar, allowing them to understand the basic rules of all languages and to apply these rules to the speech they hear. They learn language without an awareness of its underlying logic.

Think about it: The terms we used above to define the characteristics of language—*phonology, morphology, semantics,* and so forth—may be new to you, but on some level you have mastered these principles. This mastery is demonstrated by your reading of this material, writing a paper for class, texting a friend, and talking to your parents. Like all

Noam Chomsky (b. 1928) MIT linguist Noam Chomsky was one of the early architects of the view that children's language development cannot be explained by environmental input. In Chomsky's opinion, language has strong biological underpinnings, with children biologically prewired to learn language at a certain time and in a certain way.

other humans, you are engaged in the use of a rule-based language system even without knowing that you know those rules.

Language and the Brain   There is strong evidence to back up experts who believe language has a biological foundation. Neuroscience research has shown that the brain contains particular regions that are predisposed to language use (Griffiths & others, 2013; Hugdahl & Westerhausen, 2016; Mirman & others, 2015; Price, 2012).

As we saw in the chapter "Biological Foundations of Behavior", accumulating evidence suggests that language processing, such as speech and grammar, mainly occurs in the brain's left hemisphere (McGettigan & others, 2012). Recall the importance of two areas in the left hemisphere in terms of language: Wernicke's area (toward the middle and front) for language comprehension and Broca's area (toward the back) for speech production. Recently, scientists used direct cortical recordings to illuminate the role of Broca's area in speech. They found that this area is not directly involved in talking (Flinker & others, 2015). Instead, Broca's area sends and coordinates messages to sensory neurons (representing words) and motor neurons (for articulation) in preparation for speaking. Yet, during the actual talking, Broca's area is relatively inactive. These fascinating results point to the complex process involved in speech. Simply saying a word involves a great deal of preparatory work in the brain.

Using brain-imaging techniques such as PET scans, researchers have found that when an infant is about 9 months old, the hippocampus, the part of the brain that stores and indexes many kinds of memory, becomes fully functional (Bauer, 2009, 2013). This is also the time at which infants appear to be able to attach meaning to words—for instance, to look at the ball if someone says "ball"—suggesting links among language, cognition, and the development of the brain.

ENVIRONMENTAL INFLUENCES

Decades ago, behaviorists opposed Chomsky's hypothesis and argued that language represents nothing more than chains of responses acquired through reinforcement (Skinner, 1957). A baby happens to babble "ma-ma," mama rewards the baby with hugs and smiles, the baby says "mama" more and more. Bit by bit, said the behaviorists, the baby's language is built up. According to behaviorists, language is a complex learned skill, much like playing the piano or dancing.

Such a view of language development is simply not tenable. Children learn language rapidly, and once they start talking their skills take off. In addition, there is no evidence that social environments carefully reinforce language skills (R. Brown, 1973). This is not to say the environment has no role in language development. Many language experts argue that a child's experiences, the particular language to be learned, and the context in which learning takes place can strongly influence language acquisition (Casillas, Bobb, & Clark, 2016; Chang & others, 2015; Tamis-LeMonda & Song, 2013).

Evidence for the important role of the environment in language development comes from case histories of children who have lacked exposure to language. In 1970, a California social worker made a routine visit to the home of a partially blind woman who had applied for public assistance. The social worker discovered that the woman and her husband had kept their 13-year-old daughter, Genie, locked away in almost total isolation during her childhood. Genie could not speak or stand erect. She had spent every day bound naked to a child's potty seat. She could move only her hands and feet. At night, she had been placed in a kind of straightjacket and caged in a crib with wire mesh sides and a cover. Whenever Genie had made a noise, her father had beaten her. He had never communicated with her in words; he had growled and barked at her instead (Rymer, 1993).

After she was rescued from her parents, Genie spent a number of years in extensive rehabilitation programs, including speech and physical therapy (Curtiss, 1977). She eventually learned to walk, although with a jerky motion, and to use the toilet. Genie also learned to recognize many words and to speak in rudimentary sentences. Gradually, she was able to string together two-word combinations such as "big teeth," "little marble," and "two hand" and then three-word combinations such as "small two cup." As far as we know, unlike normal children, Genie did not learn to ask questions and did not develop a language system that allowed her to understand English grammar. As an adult, she speaks in short, mangled phrases such as "father hit leg," "big wood," and "Genie hurt."

Children who, like Genie, are abused and lack exposure to language for many years rarely speak normally. Some language experts have argued that these cases support the idea that there is a critical period for language development, a special time in a child's life (usually the preschool years) during which language must develop or it never will. Because these children also suffer severe emotional trauma and possible neurological deficits, however, the issue is still far from clear. Whether or not these cases suggest such a critical period, they certainly support the idea that the environment is crucial for the development of language.

Clearly, most humans do not learn language in a social vacuum. From infancy, most children are bathed in language from a very early age (Kuhl, 2012). And infants' attention to the conversations going on around them predicts language development (Vouloumanos & Curtin, 2014).

FIGURE 10   **The Power of Smile and Touch** Research has shown that when mothers immediately smiled and touched their 8-month-old infants after they babbled, the infants subsequently made more complex speechlike sounds than when mothers responded randomly to their infants. © Camille Tokerud/Getty Images

The ways adults interact with children can facilitate language learning (Golinkoff & others, 2015). For example, one study showed that when mothers immediately smiled and touched their 8-month-old infants after they had babbled, the infants subsequently made more complex speechlike sounds than when mothers responded to their infants in a random manner (Goldstein, King, & West, 2003) (Figure 10).

The influence of environment on language acquisition was also demonstrated in an older study examining family backgrounds, language exposure, and language acquisition. In that study, researchers observed the language environments of children from two different backgrounds: families of middle-income professionals and families living on welfare (Hart & Risley, 1995; Risley & Hart, 2006). Then they examined the children's language development. All of the children developed normally in terms of learning to talk and acquiring the basic rules of English and a fundamental vocabulary. However, the researchers found enormous differences in the sheer amount of language to which the children were exposed and in the level of the children's language development.

For example, in a typical hour, the middle-income professional parents spent almost twice as much time communicating with their children as did the parents in the lower socioeconomic families. The children from the middle-income professional families heard about 2,100 words an hour; the children in the poorer families heard only 600 words an hour. The researchers estimated that by 4 years of age, the average child from the poorer family group would have 13 million fewer words of cumulative language experience than the average child from the middle-income professional family group. Amazingly, some of the 3-year-old children from middle-class professional families had a recorded vocabulary that exceeded the recorded vocabulary of some of the parents from the poorer families.

Research findings about environmental influences on language learning complicate our understanding of its foundations. In the real world of language learning, children appear to be neither exclusively biologically programmed linguists nor exclusively socially driven language experts. Children are biologically prepared to learn language but benefit enormously from being immersed in a competent language environment from an early age.

Language Development over the Life Span

Most individuals develop a clear understanding of their language's structure, as well as a large vocabulary, during childhood. Most adults in the United States have acquired a vocabulary of nearly 50,000 words. Researchers have taken a great interest in the process by which these aspects of language develop (Parrish-Morris, Golinkoff, & Hirsh-Pasek, 2013). Their many studies have provided an understanding of the milestones of language development (Figure 11).

Language researchers are fascinated by babies' speech even before the little ones say their first words (Goldin-Meadow & Alibali, 2013). *Babbling*—endlessly repeating

FIGURE 11 Language Milestones
All children are different and acquire language at varying rates, but these milestones provide a general sense of how language emerges in human life.

(text) John W. Santrock, *Educational Psychology*. Fig. 2.14 Copyright © 2001 by McGraw-Hill Education. Used with permission. (mother and baby) © Blend Images/SuperStock; (woman reading) © Veer

0–6 Months	Cooing Discrimination of vowels Babbling present by 6 months
6–12 Months	Babbling expands to include sounds of spoken language Gestures used to communicate about objects First words spoken 10–13 months
12–18 Months	Understands 50+ words on average
18–24 Months	Vocabulary increases to an average of 200 words Two-word combinations
2 Years	Vocabulary rapidly increases Correct use of plurals Use of past tense Use of some prepositions
3–4 Years	Mean length of utterances increases to 3–4 morphemes in a sentence Use of yes and no questions, wh- questions Use of negatives and imperatives Increased awareness of pragmatics
5–6 Years	Vocabulary reaches an average of about 10,000 words Coordination of simple sentences
6–8 Years	Vocabulary continues to increase rapidly More skilled use of syntactical rules Conversational skills improve
9–11 Years	Word definitions include synonyms Conversational strategies continue to improve
11–14 Years	Vocabulary increases with addition of more abstract words Understanding of complex grammar forms Increased understanding of function a word plays in a sentence Understands metaphor and satire
15–20 Years	Understands adult literary works

sounds and syllables, such as "bababa" or "dadada"—begins at the age of about 4 to 6 months and is determined by biological readiness, not by the amount of reinforcement or the ability to hear (Menn & Stoel-Gammon, 2009). Even babies who are deaf babble for a time (Lenneberg, Rebelsky, & Nichols, 1965). Babbling probably allows babies to exercise their vocal cords and helps develop the ability to articulate different sounds.

Patricia Kuhl's research reveals that long before they begin to learn words, infants can sort through a number of spoken sounds in search for the ones that have meaning for their culture (1993, 2000, 2011, 2012, 2015). Kuhl argues that from birth to about 6 months of age, children are "universal linguists" who are capable of distinguishing each of the sounds that make up the various different human languages. By about 6 months of age, they have started to specialize in the speech sounds (or phonology) of their native language (Figure 12).

A child's first words, uttered at the age of 10 to 13 months, name important people ("dada," "mama"), familiar animals ("kitty"), vehicles ("car"), toys ("ball"), food ("milk"), body parts ("eye"), clothes ("hat"), household items ("clock"), and greetings ("bye"). These were babies' first words a century ago, and they are babies' first words still (Bloom, 2004).

By the time children reach the age of 18 to 24 months, they usually utter two-word statements. They quickly grasp the importance of expressing concepts and the role that language plays in communicating with others (Sachs, 2009). To convey meaning in two-word statements, the child relies heavily on gesture, tone, and context. Although these two-word sentences omit many parts of speech, they are remarkably effective in conveying many messages. When a toddler demands, "Pet doggie!" parents know he means, "May I please pet the doggie?" Very young children learn that language is a good way to get what they want, suggesting that they grasp another aspect of language—its pragmatics.

Although childhood is an important time for language learning, we continue to learn language (new words, new skills) throughout life. For many years, it was claimed that if individuals did not learn a second language prior to puberty, they would never reach native-language learners' levels in the second language (Johnson & Newport, 1991). However, recent research indicates a more complex conclusion: Sensitive periods likely vary across different language systems (Thomas & Johnson, 2008). Thus, for late second-language learners, such as adolescents and adults, new vocabulary is easier to learn than new sounds or new grammar (Neville, 2006). For example, children's ability to pronounce words with a native-like accent in a second language typically decreases with age, with an especially sharp drop occurring after about 10 to 12 years of age.

For adults, learning a new language requires a special kind of cognitive exercise. As we have seen, a great deal of language learning in infancy and childhood involves recognizing the sounds that are part of one's native tongue. This process also entails learning to ignore sounds that are *not* important to one's first language. For instance, in Japanese, the phonemes /l/ and /r/ are not distinguished from each other, so that, for a Japanese adult, the word *lion* is not distinguishable from the name *Ryan* (Werker & Hensch, 2015).

Research suggests that mastering a new language in adulthood may involve overriding such learned habits and learning to listen to sounds that one previously ignored (Linebaugh & Roche, 2015). Indeed, adults can learn to hear and discriminate sounds that are part of a new language, and this learning can contribute to speech fluency and language skill (Evans & Iverson, 2007; Huensch & Tremblay, 2015). Research suggests that the cerebellum, located at the base of the brain, plays a role in perceiving new sounds (Guediche & others, 2015). Thus, learning a new language in adulthood involves cognitively stretching ourselves away from our assumptions and opening up to new experiences.

Around the world, young children learn to speak in two-word utterances at 18 to 24 months of age.
© Anita van Zyl/age fotostock

FIGURE 12   From Universal Linguist to Language-Specific Listener A baby is shown in Patricia Kuhl's research laboratory. In this research, babies listen to recorded voices that repeat syllables. When the sounds of the syllables change, the babies quickly learn to look at the bear. Using this technique, Kuhl has demonstrated that babies are universal linguists until about 6 months of age, but in the next 6 months they become language-specific listeners. (first) © 2003 University of Washington, Institute for Learning and Brain Sciences (I-LABS); (second) © 2003 University of Washington, Institute for Learning and Brain Sciences (I-LABS)

5. THINKING, PROBLEM SOLVING, AND HEALTH AND WELLNESS

The way we think about life events can have a profound impact on our experience of stress. Recall that stress refers to our response to changes in the environment and that stressors are those changes. Consider the stressors in your life. They can be anything from losing irreplaceable notes from a class, to being yelled at by a friend, to failing a test, to being in a car wreck. Although everyone's body may have a similar response to stressors, not everyone perceives the same events as stressful, as we consider in this final section.

Cognitive Appraisal and Stress

Whether an experience "stresses us out" depends on how we think about that experience. For example, you may perceive an upcoming job interview as a threatening obligation, whereas your roommate may perceive it as a challenging opportunity. He or she might feel some anxiety but see the experience as a chance to shine. You might view a *D* on a paper as threatening; your roommate may view the same grade as an incentive to work harder. To some degree, then, what is stressful depends on how we think about events—what psychologists call cognitive appraisal (Gianaros & Wager, 2015; Schwarzer & Luszczynska, 2013).

Cognitive appraisal refers to a person's interpretation of a situation. This appraisal includes whether the event or situation is viewed as harmful and threatening, or challenging, and the person's determination of whether he or she has the resources to cope effectively with the events. Is moving to a new apartment stressful? It depends on how you look at it and whether you have the resources you need to handle the challenge effectively.

Coping is essentially a kind of problem solving. It involves managing taxing circumstances, expending effort to solve life's problems, and seeking to master or reduce stress (Neupert & others, 2015). Richard Lazarus (1993, 2000) most clearly articulated the importance of cognitive appraisal to stress and coping. In Lazarus's view, people appraise events in two steps: primary appraisal and secondary appraisal.

In *primary appraisal,* individuals interpret whether an event involves *harm or loss* that has already occurred, a *threat* of some future danger, or a *challenge* to be overcome. Lazarus believed that perceiving a stressor as a challenge to be overcome, rather than as a threat, is a good strategy for reducing stress. To understand Lazarus's concept of primary appraisal, consider two students, each of whom has a failing grade in a psychology class at midterm. Sam is almost frozen by the stress of the low grade and looks at the rest of the term as a threatening prospect. In contrast, Pam does not become overwhelmed by the harm already done and the threat of future failures. She looks at the low grade as a challenge that she can address and overcome. This initial appraisal of an event as threatening or challenging can have profound impact on health and wellness (Fosco & Feinberg, 2015; Luyten, Boddez, & Hermans, 2015; Seery, 2011; Wang, Jackson, & Cai, 2016).

Primary appraisal involves our immediate reactions to an event. What happens next? We need to figure out if we can handle whatever we are facing. Do we have what it takes to deal with the situation? *Secondary appraisal* means evaluating our resources and determining how effectively they can be used to cope with the event (Slattery & others, 2013; Timmerman & others, 2016).

This appraisal is secondary for two reasons: It comes after primary appraisal, and it depends on the degree to which the event is appraised as harmful/threatening or challenging. For example, Sam might have some helpful resources for coping with his low midterm grade, but he views the stressful circumstance as so harmful and threatening that he does not take stock of and use his resources. Pam, in contrast, evaluates the resources she can call on to improve her grade during the second half of the term. These include asking the instructor for suggestions about how to study better for the tests in the course, setting up a time management program to include more study hours, and consulting with several high-achieving classmates about their strategies. Importantly, *rethinking* our appraisals of potential stressors can influence health and wellness.

Cognitive Reappraisal

Once an event or experience has been appraised, it need not be set in stone. Indeed, one way of dealing with potentially stressful situations is to reappraise the event actively and come up with a new way of thinking about it.

© Ariel Skelley/The Image Bank/Getty Images

Cognitive reappraisal involves regulating our feelings about an experience by reinterpreting it or thinking about it in a different way or from a different angle (Roseman & Smith, 2009). Research has shown that reappraising an event can change not only the way people feel about it, but also the brain activity linked to the experience (Holz & others, 2016).

● **cognitive reappraisal** Regulating one's feelings about an experience by reinterpreting that experience or thinking about it in a different way or from a different angle.

For example, in one brain-imaging study, participants were shown images that were likely to produce negative feelings, such as a driver standing beside a car that has been in an accident (McRae & others, 2010). To examine the effects of cognitive reappraisal, the researchers told participants to look at the pictures and think about them in a way that would reduce their negative feelings. Results showed that reappraising the stimuli resulted in decreased negative feelings, decreased activation in the amygdala, and increased activation in prefrontal regions.

Reappraising negative life events can involve a process called *benefit finding*. Benefit finding means looking at a stressful life event in a particular way, focusing on the good that has arisen in one's life as a result. Finding benefits in negative life events can be a way to make meaning out of those experiences (Mock & Boerner, 2010; C. L. Park, 2010, 2012). Finding benefits in negative life events has been related to better physical health (Bower, Moskowitz, & Epel, 2009) and better psychological functioning in the context of a variety of illnesses (Gianinazzi & others, 2016; C. L. Park, 2010, 2012; C. L. Park & others, 2009).

It may be challenging to think of negative life events as opportunities. However, the capacity to think about such events differently—to engage creatively with the notion that even objectively negative life events have helped us to become more compassionate, wiser, or better able to meet the challenges of the future—can be a powerful tool for staving off stress (King & Hicks, 2007).

test yourself

1. What is cognitive appraisal?
2. What is cognitive reappraisal?
3. How does benefit finding relate to physical health and to body function in a variety of illnesses?

The Candle Problem

The solution requires a unique perception of the function of the box in which the matches came. It can become a candleholder when tacked to the wall.

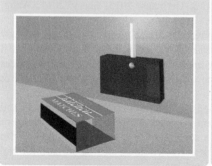

The Nine-Dot Problem

Most people have difficulty with this problem because they try to draw the lines within the boundaries of the dots. Notice that by extending the lines beyond the dots, the problem can be solved.

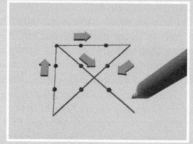

The Six-Matchstick Problem

Nothing in the instructions said that the solution had to be two-dimensional.

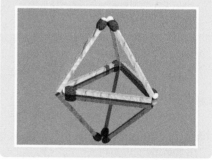

Solutions to problems from the Psychological Inquiry feature "Thinking Outside the Box."

SUMMARY

1. THE COGNITIVE REVOLUTION IN PSYCHOLOGY

Cognition is the way in which information is processed and manipulated in remembering, thinking, and knowing. The advent of the computer in the mid-twentieth century spurred a cognitive revolution in which psychologists took on the challenge of understanding human information processing. Artificial intelligence (AI), the science of creating machines capable of performing activities that require intelligence when people do them, is a byproduct of the cognitive revolution.

2. THINKING

Concepts are mental categories used to group objects, events, and characteristics. Concepts help us to generalize; they improve our memories; and they keep us from having to learn new things with every new instance or example of a concept. The prototype model suggests that members of a concept vary in terms of their similarity to the most typical item.

Problem solving is an attempt to find a way to attain a goal when the goal is not readily available. The four steps in problem solving are to (1) find and frame the problem, (2) develop good problem-solving strategies, (3) evaluate solutions, and (4) rethink and redefine problems and solutions over time. Among effective strategies for solving problems are setting subgoals (intermediate goals that put us in a better position to reach our goal), devising algorithms (strategies that guarantee a solution), and using heuristics (shortcuts that suggest, but do not guarantee, a solution to a problem).

Reasoning is the mental activity of transforming information to reach conclusions. Inductive reasoning is reasoning from the specific to the general. Deductive reasoning is reasoning from the general to the specific. Decision making involves evaluating alternatives and making choices among them. Biases and heuristics that may lead to problematic decision making include loss aversion, confirmation bias, hindsight bias, the availability heuristic, and the representativeness heuristic.

Critical thinking and creativity improve problem solving. Critical thinking involves thinking productively, evaluating the evidence, being mindful, and keeping an open mind. Creativity is the ability to think in novel and unusual ways and to come up with unconventional solutions. Creative thinkers are flexible and playful, self-motivated, willing to face risk, and objective in evaluating their work.

3. INTELLIGENCE

Intelligence consists of the ability to solve problems and to adapt to and learn from everyday experiences. Traditionally, intelligence has been measured by tests designed to compare people's performance on cognitive tasks.

A good test of intelligence meets three criteria: validity, reliability, and standardization. Validity is the extent to which a test measures what it is intended to measure. Reliability is how consistently an individual performs on a test. Standardization focuses on uniform procedures for administering and scoring a test and establishing norms.

Binet developed the first intelligence test. Individuals from age 2 through adulthood may take the current Stanford-Binet test or the age-appropriate Wechsler scale. Some intelligence tests are unfair to individuals from different cultures. Culture-fair tests are intelligence tests that are intended to be culturally unbiased.

Genes are clearly involved in intelligence. The proportion of differences in intelligence that is explained by genetic variation (or heritability) is substantial, although critics have questioned the heritability estimate. Environmental influences on intelligence have also been demonstrated. A number of interventions including interactive reading have been shown to influence children's IQ. The fact that intelligence test scores have risen considerably around the world in recent decades—called the Flynn effect—supports the role of environment in intelligence.

At the extreme ends of intelligence are giftedness and intellectual disability. People who are gifted have high intelligence (IQ of 130 or higher) and/or superior talent for a particular domain. Research has shown that individuals who are gifted are likely to make important and creative contributions. Intellectual disability (or intellectual learning disorder) is a condition of limited mental ability affecting a person's daily functioning. Intellectual disability can have an organic cause or can be cultural and social in origin.

Instead of focusing on intelligence as a single, broad cognitive ability, some psychologists view intelligence as a variety of life skills. Sternberg's triarchic theory states there are three main types of intelligence: analytical, creative, and practical. Gardner identifies nine types of intelligence, involving skills that are verbal, mathematical, spatial, bodily-kinesthetic, musical, interpersonal, intrapersonal, naturalist, and existential. The multiple-intelligences approaches have broadened the definition of intelligence and motivated educators to develop programs that instruct students in different domains.

Critics maintain that multiple-intelligences theories include factors that really are not part of intelligence, such as musical skills, and that people who are highly intelligent are likely to excel in many different areas, not just one. Skeptics also argue that there is not enough research to support the concept of multiple intelligences.

4. LANGUAGE

Language is a form of communication that is based on a system of symbols. All human languages have common aspects, including infinite generativity and organizational rules about structure. Also, all languages have five characteristics: phonology (the sound system of a language); morphology (the rules for combining morphemes, which are meaningful strings of sounds that contain no smaller meaningful parts); syntax (the ways words are combined to form acceptable phrases and sentences); semantics (the meaning of words and sentences); and pragmatics (the uses of language).

Although language and thought influence each other, there is increasing evidence that they evolved as separate, modular, biologically prepared components of the mind. Evolution shaped humans into linguistic creatures. Chomsky said that humans are biologically prewired to learn language at a certain time and in a certain way. In addition, there is strong evidence that particular regions in the left hemisphere of the brain are predisposed to be used for language. Experience is also crucial to language development. It is important for children to interact with language-skilled people. Children are biologically prepared to learn language but benefit enormously from being in a competent language environment from early in development.

Although we often think of language, thinking, and intelligence as fixed when we are adults, research shows that we can continue to master skills and even increase intelligence by engaging in challenging mental tasks.

5. THINKING, PROBLEM SOLVING, AND HEALTH AND WELLNESS

The way individuals think about life events determines whether they experience them as stressful. Cognitive appraisal is individuals' interpretation of the events in their lives as either threatening (and stressful) or challenging (and not stressful). Coping refers to people's attempts to handle situations that they perceive as stressful. Cognitive reappraisal can be a powerful tool for coping with negative life events. One type of reappraisal, benefit finding, relates to enhanced psychological and physical health.

key *terms*

algorithms	decision making	intelligence	prototype model
artificial intelligence (AI)	deductive reasoning	intelligence quotient (IQ)	reasoning
availability heuristic	divergent thinking	language	reliability
base rate neglect	executive function	loss aversion	representativeness heuristic
cognition	fixation	mindfulness	semantics
cognitive appraisal	functional fixedness	mental age (MA)	standardization
cognitive reappraisal	gifted	morphology	subgoals
concepts	heritability	normal distribution	syntax
confirmation bias	heuristics	open-mindedness	thinking
convergent thinking	hindsight bias	phonology	triarchic theory of intelligence
coping	inductive reasoning	pragmatics	validity
creativity	intellectual disability or intellectual	problem solving	
culture-fair tests	developmental disorder		

apply your *knowledge*

1. To get a sense of the roles of divergent and convergent thinking in creativity, try the following exercise. First take 10 minutes and jot down all of the uses that you can think of for a cardboard box. Don't hold back—include every possibility that comes to mind. That list represents divergent thinking. Now look over the list. Which of the possible uses are most unusual or most likely to be worthwhile? That is convergent thinking.

2. Ask a few friends to define the term *intelligent*. Do they mostly describe intelligent people or intelligent behaviors? Do their definitions focus on cognitive ability or other abilities?

3. Many different intelligence tests are available online, such as www .iqtest.com/. Give this one a try and then do a web search for intelligence tests and see if you get the same results when you take a different test. Do the websites tell you how reliable the tests are? Do they provide information on standardization or validity? If your scores on the two tests are very different, what might account for this difference?

CHAPTER 10

Motivation and Emotion

"Training. Guts. Teamwork."

The Medal of Honor is the highest military honor in the United States. It is awarded for acts of enormous personal bravery that must involve risking one's own life. On November 12, 2015, President Barack Obama presented the Medal of Honor to Army Captain Florent Groberg.

Groberg had been a champion long-distance runner in high school and college. But, on the worst day of his life, he nearly lost a leg. On that day in 2012, Groberg was on security detail in Afghanistan with five other soldiers. Seeing a man in dark clothing, Groberg had a weird feeling, what he called his "Spidey sense," that something was just not right: That man was a threat (Scott, 2015). Yet, Groberg immediately ran to the man. As Groberg grabbed him, he could feel the suicide vest under the man's clothing. Groberg pulled the man closer, trying to keep him away from the others. As the man fell to the ground, he detonated the bomb, sending Groberg flying 20 feet. He lost consciousness.

Imagine having the same feeling deep in your gut that Captain Groberg felt—that things were not right. Can you imagine running toward that threat, rather than away? How could he do it? President Obama remarked that "what made Flo a great runner also made him a great soldier." Those characteristics? "Training. Guts. Teamwork." (Office of the Press Secretary, 2015). Although filled with dread, Captain Groberg forged ahead to complete his mission and try to save his fellow soldiers, even if it meant losing his own life.

The terms *motivation* and *emotion* come from the Latin word *movere,* which means "to move." Motivation is the why of what we do. When we are committed to goals, we may achieve amazingly courageous acts. Motivation and emotion are the "go" of human life, propelling us forward. ●

PREVIEW

This chapter examines the ways psychologists study motivation and emotion. We first review some general approaches to motivation and consider one important physiological source of motivation: hunger. We then examine motivation as it applies to everyday life. Next, we explore the rich topic of emotion. To close, we consider the ways that motivation and emotion intertwine in the pursuit of happiness.

1. THEORIES OF MOTIVATION

● **motivation** The force that moves people to behave, think, and feel the way they do.

Motivation is the force that moves people to behave, think, and feel the way they do. Motivated behavior is energized, directed, and sustained. Psychologists have proposed a variety of theories about why organisms are motivated to do what they do. In this section we explore some of the main theoretical approaches to motivation.

The Evolutionary Approach

● **instinct** An innate (unlearned) biological pattern of behavior that is assumed to be universal throughout a species.

Early evolutionary accounts of motivation emphasized the role of instincts. An **instinct** is an innate (unlearned) biological pattern of behavior that is assumed to be universal throughout a species. Generally, an instinct is set in motion by a *sign stimulus*— something in the environment that turns on a fixed pattern of behavior. Instincts may explain a great deal of nonhuman animal behavior. In addition, some human behavior is instinctive. Recall, for example, the discussion of infant reflexes in the chapter "Human Development". Babies do not have to learn to suck; they instinctively do it when something is placed in their mouth. So, for infants, an object touching the lips is a sign stimulus. After infancy, though, it is hard to think of specific behaviors that all human beings engage in when presented with a particular stimulus.

More recently, evolutionary psychologists have emphasized how human motivation is rooted in our evolutionary past (Maner, 2016). Because evolutionary approaches emphasize the passing on of one's genes, these theories focus on domains of life that are especially relevant to reproduction, such as sexual behavior and behaviors relevant to competition among members of a species, such as aggression and achievement.

In general, even these behaviors are far too complex to be explained on the basis of instinct. Indeed, it would hardly seem adaptive for humans to have a fixed action pattern that is invariably set in motion by a particular signal in the environment. To understand human behavior, psychologists have developed a variety of other approaches, as we now consider.

Drive Reduction Theory

● **drive** An aroused state that occurs because of a physiological need.

● **need** A deprivation that energizes the drive to eliminate or reduce the deprivation.

Another way to think about motivation is through the constructs of drive and need. A **drive** is an aroused state of tension that occurs because of a physiological need. You can think of a drive as a psychological itch that requires scratching. A **need** is a deprivation that energizes the drive to eliminate or reduce the deprivation. Generally, psychologists think of needs as underlying our drives. You may have a need for water; the drive that accompanies that need is your feeling of being thirsty. Drive pertains to a psychological state, whereas need involves a physiological one.

Usually but not always, needs and drives are closely associated. Drives do not always follow from needs. For example, if you are deprived of oxygen because of a gas leak, you have a need for oxygen. You may feel lightheaded but never experience the drive for oxygen that might lead you to open a window. Moreover, drives sometimes seem to come out of nowhere. Having eaten a fine meal and feeling full to the point of not wanting another bite, you might nevertheless feel ready to tackle the Double Chocolate Oblivion when the waiter wheels over the dessert cart.

psychological *inquiry*

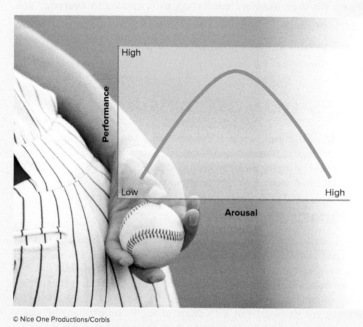

© Nice One Productions/Corbis

Obeying the (Yerkes–Dodson) Law

The graph displays the relationship between arousal (shown on the X, or horizontal, axis) and performance (shown on the Y, or vertical, axis). Note that the curve is an inverted *U*.

Using the figure as a reference, answer the questions below.

1. What was your arousal level the last time you took an exam? If you were very nervous, your arousal level would be considered high. If you were excited and engaged but not too worried, your level would be in the medium range. If you were feeling sluggish, your arousal level would be low.

2. How did you actually do on that test? Plot your performance on the graph. Does it fit with the Yerkes–Dodson prediction?

3. Now think about performance in sports or the arts. Imagine your favorite athlete, musician, or actor. How might that person feel when he or she is on the spot, trying to sink a winning free throw, strike out the last batter, or impress an audience? How might arousal influence performance in those cases?

4. In many professions, individuals are forced to perform under conditions of very high arousal. These include EMTs, lifeguards, and emergency room staff. (Name some others.) How might such individuals train themselves to perform even under conditions of extreme arousal?

Drive reduction theory explains that as a drive becomes stronger, we are motivated to reduce it. The goal of drive reduction is **homeostasis,** the body's tendency to maintain an equilibrium, or a steady state or balance. Hundreds of biological states in the body must be maintained within a certain range; these include temperature, blood-sugar level, potassium and sodium levels, and oxygenation. When you dive into an icy swimming pool, your body uses energy to maintain its normal temperature. When you step into the heat of a summer day, your body releases excess heat by sweating. These physiological changes occur automatically to keep your body in an optimal state of functioning.

Most psychologists conclude that drive reduction theory does not provide a comprehensive framework for understanding motivation because people often behave in ways that increase rather than reduce a drive. Many things we do involve increasing (not decreasing) tensions—for example, taking a challenging course in school, raising a family, and working at a difficult job.

Optimum Arousal Theory

When psychologists talk about arousal, they are generally referring to a person's feelings of being alert and engaged. When we are very excited, our arousal levels are high. When

● **homeostasis** The body's tendency to maintain an equilibrium, or a steady state or balance.

Performance under high-arousal conditions, such as those faced by Captain Groberg in Afghanistan, requires being trained to the point of overlearning.

© Chip Somodevilla/Getty Images

we are bored, they are low. Optimal arousal theory suggests that there should be a level of arousal that is ideal for facilitating goal attainment.

You have probably noticed that motivation influences arousal levels. Sometimes you can want something (for example, to do well on a test) so much that you can become overly motivated and anxious. On the other hand, you might be so unmotivated for a task (such as doing the dishes) that you can hardly force yourself to complete it. Sometimes, to do well, you need to have an arousal level that is "just right" (Keeley, Zayac, & Correia, 2008).

Early in the twentieth century, two psychologists described how arousal can influence performance. According to their formulation, known as the **Yerkes–Dodson law**, performance is best under conditions of moderate arousal rather than either low or high arousal. At the low end of arousal, you may be too lethargic to perform tasks well; at the high end, you may not be able to concentrate. To master the Yerkes–Dodson law, check out the Psychological Inquiry.

The link between arousal and performance is one reason that individuals in many professions are trained to overlearn important procedures. **Overlearning** means learning to perform a task so well that it becomes automatic. Recall Captain Florent Groberg who grabbed a suicide bomber or consider the Navy SEALS who conducted the raid on Osama bin Laden's compound in Pakistan in 2011.

For individuals who must perform at their best in a crisis, success depends on knowing what to do so well that it requires little or no thought. With this extra learning, when these individuals are under conditions of high arousal, they can rely on auto pilot to do what needs to be done.

- **Yerkes–Dodson law** The psychological principle stating that performance is best under conditions of moderate arousal rather than either low or high arousal.

- **overlearning** Learning to perform a task so well that it becomes automatic.

test yourself

1. What is motivation?
2. What are three theoretical approaches to motivation?
3. What is overlearning, and how can it help an individual who must perform at his or her best?

2. HUNGER, OBESITY, AND EATING DISORDERS

Part of the power of motivation in life is tied to physiological needs. We experience strong motivational forces, for example, when we are hungry or thirsty. Furthermore, the physiological state of being hungry has often been used as a path toward understanding a variety of human motivations. We use words about hunger in contexts that are not physiological, such as when we say that someone is "craving" attention or "starving" for affection. In this section we examine the basic motivational processes underlying hunger and eating, including the related topic of eating disorders.

The Biology of Hunger

You know you are hungry when your stomach growls and you feel hunger pangs. What role do such signals play in hunger?

GASTRIC SIGNALS

Over a century ago, Walter Cannon and A. L. Washburn conducted an experiment that revealed a close association between stomach contractions and hunger (1912) (Figure 1). In one step of the procedure, a partially inflated balloon was passed through a tube inserted in Washburn's mouth and pushed down into his stomach. A machine that measures air pressure was connected to the balloon to monitor Washburn's stomach contractions. Every time Washburn reported hunger pangs, his stomach was also contracting.

Sure enough, a growling stomach needs food. The stomach tells the brain not only how full it is but also how much nutrient is present. That is why rich foods stop hunger faster than the same amount of water. The hormone cholecystokinin (CCK) helps start the digestion of food, travels to the brain through the bloodstream, and signals us to stop eating (Moss & others, 2012). Hunger involves a lot more than an empty stomach, however.

BLOOD CHEMISTRY

Three key chemical substances play a role in hunger, eating, and *satiety* (the state of feeling full): glucose, insulin, and leptin.

Glucose (blood sugar) is an important factor in hunger, probably because the brain critically depends on sugar for energy. One set of sugar receptors, located in the brain, triggers hunger when sugar levels fall too low. Another set of sugar receptors is in the liver, which stores excess sugar and releases it into the blood when needed. The sugar receptors in the liver signal the brain when its sugar supply falls, and this signal also can make you hungry.

The hormone *insulin* also plays a role in glucose control. When we eat complex carbohydrates such as bread and pasta, insulin levels go up and fall off gradually. When we consume simple sugars such as candy, insulin levels rise and then fall sharply—the all-too-familiar "sugar low" (Rodin, 1984). This difference explains why we are more likely to eat again within the next several hours after eating simple sugars than after eating complex carbohydrates.

Released by fat cells, the chemical *leptin* (from the Greek word *leptos,* meaning "thin") decreases food intake and increases energy expenditure or metabolism (Friedman, 2015). Leptin's functions were discovered in a strain of genetically obese mice, called *ob mice* (Pelleymounter & others, 1995). Because of a genetic mutation, the fat cells of ob mice cannot produce leptin. The ob mouse has a low metabolism, overeats, and gets extremely fat. Leptin appears to act as an anti-obesity hormone (Davis, Mudd, & Hawkins, 2014; Procaccini, Jirillo, & Matarese, 2012). If ob mice are given daily injections of leptin, their metabolic rate increases, and they become more active, eat less, and lose weight. Figure 2 shows an untreated ob mouse and an ob mouse that has received injections of leptin.

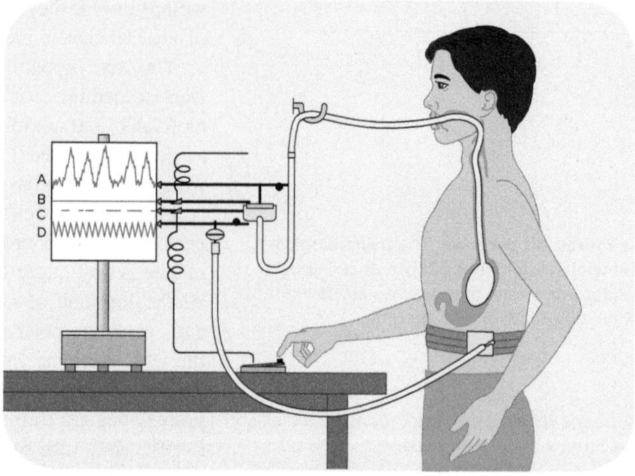

In humans, high concentrations of leptin have been linked with lower weight, less body fat, and weight loss in response to dieting (Lopez & Knudson, 2012; Rosenbaum & Leibel, 2014). Scientists continue to explore the possibility that disorders in the production and uptake of leptin may explain human obesity (Carnell & others, 2012; Dougkas & others, 2013).

BRAIN PROCESSES

The chapter "Biological Foundations of Behavior" described the central role of the hypothalamus in regulating important body functions, including hunger. More specifically, activity in two areas of the hypothalamus plays a role in hunger. The *lateral hypothalamus* (located on the outer portions) is involved in stimulating eating. When this area is electrically stimulated in a well-fed animal, the animal begins to eat. If this part of the hypothalamus is destroyed, even a starving animal will show no interest in food. The *ventromedial hypothalamus* (located more in the middle) is involved in reducing hunger and restricting eating. When this area of an animal's brain is stimulated, the animal stops eating. When the area is destroyed, the animal eats profusely and quickly becomes obese.

It might be confusing that these regions of the hypothalamus have very different functions but very similar names. Remember that *lateral* here refers to the outer sides (and you might *go out* to eat when hungry), whereas *ventromedial* refers to the inner portions (and you might *stay in* if you are already full).

Although the lateral and ventromedial hypothalamuses both influence hunger, there is much more to the brain's role in determining hunger than these on/off centers in the

FIGURE 1 **Cannon and Washburn's Classic Experiment on Hunger** In this experiment, the researchers demonstrated that stomach contractions, which were detected by the stomach balloon, accompany a person's hunger feelings, which were indicated by pressing the key. Line A in the chart records increases and decreases in the volume of the balloon in the participant's stomach. Line B records the passage of time. Line C records the participant's manual signals of feelings of hunger. Line D records a reading from the belt around the participant's waist to detect movements of the abdominal wall and ensure that such movements are not the cause of changes in stomach volume.

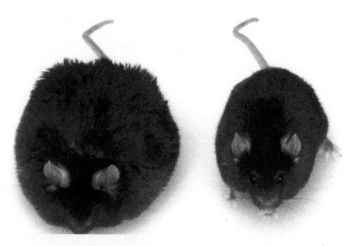

FIGURE 2 **Leptin and Obesity** The ob mouse on the left is untreated; the one on the right has been given injections of leptin.
©The Rockefeller University/AP Images

hypothalamus. Neurotransmitters (the chemical messengers that convey information from neuron to neuron) and neural circuits (clusters of neurons that often involve different parts of the brain) also function in hunger (Marston & others, 2011). Leptin influences eating by inhibiting the production of a neurotransmitter in the hypothalamus that induces eating. The neurotransmitter serotonin is partly responsible for the satiating effect of CCK, and serotonin antagonists have been used to treat obesity in humans (Ellis & others, 2013; Rozenblit-Susan & others, 2016).

Obesity

Given that the brain and body are so elegantly wired to regulate eating behavior, why do so many people in the United States overeat and suffer the effects of this behavior? According to the Centers for Disease Control and Prevention (CDC), 60 percent of Americans are overweight, and one-third of adults in the United States are considered obese (dangerously overweight) (CDC, 2015d). The National Health and Nutrition Examination Survey (NHANES) projected that 86 percent of Americans will be overweight or obese by 2030 if current weight trends continue (Beydoun & Wang, 2009). An international comparison of 33 developed countries revealed that the United States had the highest percentage of obese adults (OECD, 2010).

Obesity and overweight raise one's risk for a host of health problems, including cardiovascular disease, type II diabetes (Mozaffarian, 2016; Wong & others, 2016), and even cancer (Hsueh, & Deng, 2016). Currently, the number of people considered overweight around the world is 20 percent higher than the number suffering from hunger. Overweight and obesity are global health problems.

Why so many people overeat to the point of becoming obese is a motivational puzzle, because it involves eating when one is not in need of nutrition. As is the case with much behavior, biological, psychological, and sociocultural factors interact in diverse ways to produce eating and overeating.

THE BIOLOGY OF OBESITY

Obesity clearly has a genetic component (Ehrlich & Friedenberg, 2016). After the discovery of an ob gene in mice, researchers found a similar gene in humans. Only 10 percent of children who do not have obese parents become obese themselves, whereas 40 percent of children who have one obese parent become obese, and 70 percent of children who have two obese parents become obese.

• set point The weight maintained when the individual makes no effort to gain or lose weight.

Another factor in weight is **set point,** the weight maintained when the individual makes no effort to gain or lose weight. Set point is determined in part by the number of *adipose cells,* or fat cells, stored in the body (Speakman & others, 2011). When these cells are filled, the person does not get hungry. When people gain weight, they add fat cells, and even if they later lose weight, they may not be able to get rid of these extra ones. A normal-weight individual has 10 to 20 billion fat cells. An obese individual can have up to 100 billion fat cells (Hellmich, 2008). Consequently, an obese individual has to eat more to feel satisfied.

PSYCHOLOGICAL FACTORS IN EATING AND OBESITY

Psychologists used to think that obesity stemmed from factors such as unhappiness and external food cues. These ideas make some sense; drowning one's sorrows in chocolate or eating some cookies just because they are there seems common enough to explain overeating. However, many psychological factors affect what, when, and how much we eat.

From an evolutionary perspective, human taste preferences developed at a time when reliable food sources were scarce. Our earliest ancestors needed a lot of calories to survive in challenging circumstances. They likely developed a preference for sweet and fatty foods. Today, many people still have a taste for such foods although modern sweet and fatty foods provide far more calories than we need with far

less nutritional value. In addition, learned associations of food with a particular time and place are characteristic of many organisms, including humans. If it is noon, we eat lunch; in a movie theater, we eat popcorn.

Of particular concern in the battle over obesity is *how much* people eat. Indeed, growing portion sizes have been implicated in the alarming rates of obesity in the United States (Kling & others, 2016; Ledikwe, Ello-Martin, & Rolls, 2005). It is puzzling, though, that portion size should matter. After all, a person does not have to eat all of the food on the plate. Interestingly, research shows that smaller portions of snacks can be just as satisfying as larger portions (van Kleef, Shimizu, & Wansink, 2013). So, why do people eat an entire portion of food when just a bit of it might have led to the same feeling of fullness?

Of course, parents often teach their children to "finish what's on your plate." Many people eat automatically and rely not on a feeling of fullness but rather on the sight of an empty plate or bowl as the cue to stop eating (Wansink, 2013; Wansink, Painter, & North, 2005). Increasingly, however, cleaning one's plate has involved eating more and more food. Why might this be the case?

A fascinating body of research by Brian Wansink (2013) and his colleagues has examined the factors that influence how much food people eat. One surprising factor that influences portion size is plate size. Since 1900, the width of the average plate has increased from about 9½ inches to nearly a foot (van Ittersum & Wansink, 2012). Larger plates often lead to larger portions and more eating (Wansink & Cheney, 2005). A study at an ice cream social found that larger bowls led even experts in nutrition to serve larger portions and to eat more (Wansink, van Ittersum, & Painter, 2006).

What steps can be taken to reduce mindless eating? One possibility is to segment food in a way that alerts eaters to how much they are eating. In one study, participants ate tubes of stacked potato chips while watching a movie. The control group ate regular chips. The experimental group was given tubes of chips in which a potato chip that had been dyed red appeared every seventh chip. Participants who encountered the red chips (which were otherwise identical to the other chips) ate less than half the number of chips and were more accurate in their estimates of how much they had eaten compared to the control group (Geier, Wansink, & Rozin, 2012). The red chips allowed eaters to be less mindless in their consumption.

Dieting is a continuing U.S. obsession (Dulloo, Jacquet, & Montani, 2012). However, some people trying to lose weight are doing so not to improve their health but because they have an eating disorder, the topic we turn to next.

Disordered Eating

For some people, concerns about weight and body image become a serious, debilitating disorder. For such individuals, the very act of eating is an arena where a variety of complex biological, psychological, and cultural issues are played out, often with tragic consequences.

A number of famous people have coped with eating disorders, including Paula Abdul, Mary-Kate Olsen, Kelly Clarkson, and Demi Lovato. Eating disorders are characterized by extreme disturbances in eating behavior—from eating very, very little to eating a great deal. In this section we examine three eating disorders—anorexia nervosa, bulimia nervosa, and binge eating disorder.

ANOREXIA NERVOSA

Anorexia nervosa is an eating disorder that involves the relentless pursuit of thinness through starvation. According to the National Institute of Mental Health (NIMH), anorexia nervosa is much more common in girls and women than boys and men and affects between 0.5 and 3.7 percent of young women (NIMH, 2016a). The American Psychiatric Association (2013a) lists these main characteristics of anorexia nervosa:

- Severely restricted food intake in the pursuit of significantly low body weight compared to what is considered normal for age and height, and refusal to maintain weight at a healthy level.

● **anorexia nervosa** An eating disorder that involves the relentless pursuit of thinness through starvation.

Uruguayan model Eliana Ramos posed for the camera in her native country. Tragically, the super-thin Eliana died at age 18 in February 2007, two years after this picture was taken, reportedly from health problems associated with anorexia nervosa.

©Ricardo Figueredo/AP Images

● **bulimia nervosa** An eating disorder in which the individual (typically female) consistently follows a binge-and-purge eating pattern.

- An intense fear of gaining weight that does not decrease with weight loss.
- A distorted body image. Even when individuals with anorexia nervosa are extremely thin, they never think they are thin enough.

Over time, anorexia nervosa can lead to physical changes, such as the growth of fine hair all over the body, thinning of bones and hair, severe constipation, and low blood pressure (NIMH, 2016a; Westmoreland, Krantz, & Mehler, 2016). Dangerous and even life-threatening complications of anorexia nervosa include damage to the heart and thyroid. Anorexia nervosa is said to have the highest mortality rate (about 5.6 percent of individuals with anorexia nervosa die within 10 years of diagnosis) of any psychological disorder (Hoek, 2006; NIMH, 2016a).

Anorexia nervosa typically begins in the teenage years, often following an episode of dieting and some type of life stress (Nagl & others, 2016). Most individuals with anorexia nervosa are non-Latino White female adolescents or young adults from well-educated middle- and upper-income families (Darcy, 2012; Dodge, 2012). They are often high-achieving perfectionists (Forbush, Heatherton, & Keel, 2007). In addition to perfectionism, obsessive thinking about weight and compulsive exercise are related to anorexia nervosa (Hildebrant & others, 2012; Simpson & others, 2013).

BULIMIA NERVOSA

Bulimia nervosa is an eating disorder in which an individual (typically female) consistently follows a binge-and-purge eating pattern. The individual goes on an eating binge and then purges by self-induced vomiting or the use of laxatives. Most people with bulimia nervosa are preoccupied with food, have a strong fear of becoming overweight, and are depressed or anxious (Accurso & others, 2016). Because bulimia nervosa occurs within a normal weight range, the disorder is often difficult to detect. A person with bulimia nervosa usually keeps the disorder a secret and experiences a great deal of self-disgust and shame.

Bulimia nervosa can lead to complications such as a chronic sore throat, kidney problems, dehydration, gastrointestinal disorders, and dental problems, as persistent exposure to the stomach acids in vomit can wear away tooth enamel (Westmoreland, Krantz, & Mehler, 2016).

Bulimia nervosa typically begins in late adolescence or early adulthood (Uher & Rutter, 2012). The disorder affects between 1 and 4 percent of young women (NIMH, 2016a). Many young women who develop bulimia nervosa are highly perfectionistic (Lampard & others, 2012). At the same time, they tend to have low levels of self-efficacy (Bardone-Cone & others, 2006). In other words, these are young women with very high standards but very low confidence that they can achieve their goals.

Impulsivity, negative emotion, and childhood obsessive-compulsive tendencies (see the chapter "Psychological Disorders") are also related to bulimia (Roncero, Perpiñá, & García-Soriano, 2011; Tchanturia & others, 2004; Vervaet, van Heeringen, & Audenaert, 2004). Bulimia nervosa is associated, too, with sexual and physical abuse in childhood (Lo Sauro & others, 2008).

ANOREXIA NERVOSA AND BULIMIA NERVOSA: CAUSES AND TREATMENTS

What is the etiology (cause) of anorexia nervosa and bulimia nervosa? For many years researchers thought that sociocultural factors, such as media images of very thin women and family pressures, were the central determinant of these disorders (Le Grange, 2016). Media images that glorify extreme thinness can influence women's body image, and emphasis on the thin ideal is related to anorexia nervosa and bulimia nervosa (Carr & Peebles, 2012). However, as powerful as these media messages might be, countless girls and women are exposed to media images of unrealistically thin women, but relatively few develop eating disorders; and many young women embark on diets, but comparatively few of them develop eating disorders.

Furthermore, eating disorders occur in cultures that do not emphasize the ideal of thinness, although the disorders may differ from Western descriptions. For instance, in Eastern cultures, individuals can show the symptoms of anorexia nervosa, but they lack the fear of getting fat that is common in North Americans with the disorder (Pike, Yamamiya, & Konishi, 2011).

Since the 1980s, researchers have moved beyond a sole focus on sociocultural factors and have increasingly probed the potential biological underpinnings of these disorders. This research has examined the interplay of social and biological factors in eating disorders. Genes play a substantial role in both anorexia nervosa and bulimia nervosa (Brandys & others, 2015; Peterson & others, 2016). In fact, genes influence many psychological characteristics (for example, perfectionism, impulsivity, obsessive-compulsive tendencies, thinness drive) and behaviors (restrained eating, binge eating, self-induced vomiting) that are associated with anorexia nervosa and bulimia nervosa (Slof-Op't Landt & others, 2013). These genes are also factors in the regulation of serotonin, and problems in regulating serotonin are related to both anorexia nervosa and bulimia nervosa (Yilmaz, Hardaway, & Bulik, 2015).

Keep in mind that even as biological factors play a role in the emergence of eating disorders, eating disorders themselves affect the body, including the brain (Lavagnino & others, 2016). Although social factors and experiences may play a role in triggering dieting, the physical effects of dieting, bingeing, and purging may change the neural networks that then sustain the disordered pattern, in a kind of vicious cycle. In terms of social factors, problems in family functioning are increasingly thought to be involved in the appearance of eating disorders in adolescence (Stiles-Shields & others, 2012).

Although anorexia and bulimia nervosa are serious disorders, recovery is possible (Thaler & others, 2016). Anorexia nervosa may require hospitalization. The first target of intervention is promoting weight gain, in extreme cases through the use of a feeding tube. A common obstacle in the treatment of anorexia nervosa is that individuals with the disorder deny that anything is wrong (Dalle Grave & others, 2016; Wilson, Grilo, & Vitousek, 2007). Psychotherapy, family therapy, and drug treatments have been shown to be effective in treating anorexia nervosa and bulimia nervosa (Couturier, Kimber, & Szatmari, 2013; Hagman & Frank, 2012).

BINGE EATING DISORDER

Binge eating disorder (BED) is characterized by recurrent episodes of eating more food in a short period of time than most people would eat and during which the person feels a lack of control over eating (Schulte, Grilo, & Gearhardt, 2016). Individuals with BED do not try to compensate for what they have eaten by purging (APA, 2013a). Most individuals with BED are overweight or obese (Carrard, Van der Linden, & Golay, 2012).

Individuals with BED frequently eat alone because of embarrassment or guilt, and they feel ashamed and disgusted with themselves after bingeing. The most common of all eating disorders, BED affects men, women, and ethnic groups within the United States more similarly than anorexia nervosa or bulimia nervosa (Azarbad & others, 2010). An estimated 2 to 5 percent of Americans will suffer from BED in their lifetime (NIMH, 2016a).

Binge eating disorder is thought to characterize approximately 8 percent of individuals who are obese. Unlike obese individuals who do not suffer from BED, binge eaters are more likely to place great value on their physical appearance, weight, and body shape (Grilo, Masheb, & White, 2010). The complications of BED are those of obesity more generally, including diabetes, hypertension, and cardiovascular disease.

BINGE EATING DISORDER: CAUSES AND TREATMENTS

Researchers are examining the role of biological and psychological factors in BED (Schulte, Grilo, & Gearhardt, 2016). Genes play a role, as does dopamine, the neurotransmitter related to reward pathways in the brain (Kessler & others, 2016). The fact that binge eating often occurs after stressful events suggests that binge eaters use food to regulate their emotions (Wilson, Grilo, & Vitousek, 2007). The areas of the brain and endocrine system that respond to stress are overactive in individuals with BED (Lo Sauro & others, 2008). Individuals with BED may be more likely to perceive events as stressful and then seek to manage that stress by binge eating. Research using fMRI also found that the areas of

● **binge eating disorder (BED)** An eating disorder characterized by recurrent episodes of eating more food in a short period of time than most people would eat and during which the person feels a lack of control over eating.

Unlike individuals with anorexia nervosa or bulimia nervosa, most people with binge eating disorder (BED) are overweight or obese.
© Digital Vision/Getty Images

334   CHAPTER 10 Motivation and Emotion

the brain involved in self-regulation and impulse control, especially the prefrontal cortex, showed diminished activity in individuals with binge eating disorder (Balodis & others, 2013; Kessler & others, 2016).

Little research has examined the sociocultural factors in binge eating disorder. One study examined whether exposure to U.S. culture might increase the risk of developing BED (Swanson & others, 2012). With the research controlled for a variety of factors, the results showed that Mexicans who immigrated to the United States and Mexican Americans were more likely to develop BED than were Mexicans who lived in Mexico (Swanson & others, 2012).

Just as treatment for anorexia nervosa first focuses on weight gain, some believe that treatment for BED should first target weight loss (De Angelis, 2002). Others argue that individuals with BED must be treated for disordered eating per se, and they insist that if the underlying psychological issues are not addressed, weight loss will not be successful or permanent (de Zwaan & others, 2005; Hay & others, 2009). Research indicates that drugs targeting the functioning of neurotransmitters serotonin and norepinephrine show some promise in treating BED (Marazziti & others, 2012).

Food is unquestionably necessary for survival. Individuals struggling with disordered eating must change their relationship with this vital resource in order to survive and, eventually, thrive. Clearly, though, thriving involves more than food. We next turn to the broader implications of motivation in everyday life.

3. APPROACHES TO MOTIVATION IN EVERYDAY LIFE

Think about the wide range of human actions and achievements, such as Captain Groberg's heroism from the opening of this chapter. Such behaviors are not easily explained by motivational approaches that focus on physiological needs. Increasingly, psychologists are recognizing the role of goals that people set for themselves in motivation. In this section, we explore the ways that psychologists have come to understand the processes that underlie everyday human behavior.

Maslow's Hierarchy of Human Needs

Humanistic theorist Abraham Maslow (1954, 1971) proposed a **hierarchy of needs** that must be satisfied in the following sequence: physiological needs, safety, love and belongingness, esteem, and self-actualization (Figure 3). The strongest needs are at the base of the hierarchy (physiological), and the weakest are at the top (self-actualization).

According to this hierarchy, people are motivated to satisfy their need for food first and to fulfill their need for safety before their need for love. If we think of our needs as calls for action, hunger and safety needs shout loudly, whereas the need for self-actualization beckons with a whisper. Maslow asserted that each lower need in the hierarchy comes from a deficiency—such as being hungry, afraid, or lonely—and that we can only see the higher-level needs in a person who has satisfied to some extent these most basic needs. Such an individual can then turn his or her attention to the fulfillment of a higher calling.

Self-actualization, the highest and most elusive of Maslow's needs, is the motivation to develop one's full potential as a human being. According to Maslow, self-actualization is possible only after the other needs in the hierarchy are met. Maslow cautions that most people stop moving up the hierarchy after they have developed a high level of esteem and do not become self-actualized.

The idea that human motives are hierarchically arranged is appealing; however, Maslow's ordering of the needs is debatable (Kenrick & others, 2010). Some people, for example, might seek greatness in a career to achieve self-esteem, while putting on hold their needs for love and belongingness. Certainly history is full of examples of individuals who, in the most difficult circumstances, were still able to engage in acts of

● **hierarchy of needs** Maslow's theory that human needs must be satisfied in the following sequence: physiological needs, safety, love and belongingness, esteem, and self-actualization.

● **self-actualization** The motivation to develop one's full potential as a human being—the highest and most elusive of Maslow's proposed needs.

● **self-determination theory** Deci and Ryan's theory asserting that all humans have three basic, innate organismic needs: competence, relatedness, and autonomy.

kindness that seem to come from higher-level needs. Often, the individuals with the least financial resources are most likely to give generously to others.

Perhaps Maslow's greatest contribution to our understanding of motivation is that he asked the key question about motivation for modern people: How can we explain what humans do, once their bellies are full? That is, how do we explain the "why" of human behavior when survival is not the most pressing need? This is the kind of questioning that inspired *self-determination theory* (Deci & Ryan, 2002; Ryan & Deci, 2009; Weinstein, Deci, & Ryan, 2011).

Self-Determination Theory

Psychologists Edward Deci and Richard Ryan have explored the role of motivation in optimal human functioning from a perspective that emphasizes particular kinds of needs as factors in psychological and physical well-being (Deci & Ryan, 2000; Ryan & Deci, 2009). Their **self-determination theory** asserts that there are three basic organismic needs: competence, relatedness, and autonomy. The word *organismic* here means that these psychological needs are innate and exist in every person. They are basic to human growth and functioning, just as water, soil, and sunshine are necessary for plant growth. This metaphor is especially apt, because once we plant a seed, all it requires to thrive and grow is a supportive environment. Similarly, self-determination theory holds that we all have the capacity for growth and fulfillment in us, ready to emerge if given the right context.

Importantly, from the perspective of self-determination theory, these organismic needs do

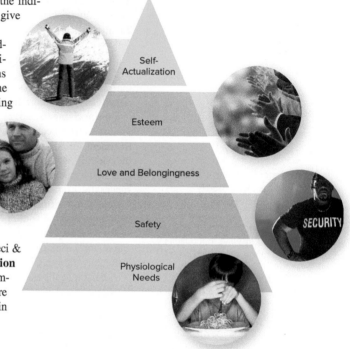

FIGURE 3   Maslow's Hierarchy of Needs Abraham Maslow developed the hierarchy of human needs to show that we have to satisfy basic physiological needs before we can satisfy other, higher needs. Later in his career, Maslow added self-transcendence to the top of the hierarchy. With this stage, he indicated that the very highest level of motivation involved service to others. (mountaintop photo) © Photogl/iStock/Getty Images; (clapping photo) © Brand X Pictures/PunchStock; (couple photo) © Digital Vision; (security guard photo) © Brand X Pictures; (boy with plate of food photo) © Brooke Fasani/Corbis

not arise from deficits. Self-determination theory is not a drive reduction theory. Deci and Ryan (2000) argue that these needs concern personal growth, not the filling of deficiencies. Let's examine each of these needs in depth.

The first organismic need described by self-determination theory, *competence,* is met when we feel that we are able to bring about desired outcomes (Reis & others, 2000). Competence motivation involves *self-efficacy* (the belief that you have the competence to accomplish a given goal or task) and *mastery* (the sense that you can gain skills and overcome obstacles). One domain in which competence needs may be met is in the realm of achievement. Some individuals are highly motivated to succeed and spend considerable effort striving to excel.

The second organismic need described by self-determination theory is *relatedness—* the need to engage in warm relations with other people. The need for relatedness is reflected in the importance of parents nurturing children's development, the intimate moments of sharing private thoughts in friendship, the uncomfortable feelings we have when we are lonely, and the powerful attraction we experience when we are in love.

The critical role of social bonds is also demonstrated in research examining the effects of being socially excluded (Hess & Pickett, 2010; K. D. Williams, 2007). When people are left out, they tend to engage in a variety of self-defeating behaviors, such as overeating and drinking to excess (Twenge, 2008). Research has shown that even when the exclusion is unintentional (for instance, when someone is ignored, though not purposely), it can lead to distress and the feeling that one's life is meaningless (K. D. Williams, 2012).

The third need proposed by self-determination theory is *autonomy—*the sense that we are in control of our own life. Autonomy means feeling that one's behavior is self-motivated and emerging from genuine interest (Weinstein, Deci, & Ryan, 2011). Of course, many of the behaviors we engage in may feel like things we are forced to do, but a sense of autonomy is strongly related to well-being (Sheldon & others, 2005).

© Rubberball/Getty Images

Research supports the idea that progress on goals that serve the three organismic needs is strongly related to well-being (Sheldon, 2013). Further, valuing more extrinsic qualities—such as money, prestige, and physical appearance—over these organismic concerns is associated with lowered well-being, lowered self-actualization, and physical illness (Kasser & Ryan, 1996; Kasser & others, 2004).

Self-determination theory maintains that one of the most important aspects of healthy motivation is the sense that we do the things we do because we have freely chosen to do them. When we can choose our behaviors and feel ownership over those choices, we are likely to experience heightened fulfillment (Koestner & others, 2012).

From the self-determination theory perspective, when our behaviors serve the needs for competence, autonomy, and relatedness, we experience intrinsic motivation. When our behavior, instead, serves needs for other values—such as prestige, money, or approval—our behavior is extrinsically motivated (Ryan & Deci, 2009). We examine this important distinction between intrinsic and extrinsic motivation next.

Intrinsic Versus Extrinsic Motivation

● **intrinsic motivation** Motivation based on internal factors such as organismic needs (competence, relatedness, and autonomy), as well as curiosity, challenge, and fun.

One way psychologists understand the "why" of our goals is by distinguishing between intrinsic and extrinsic motivation. **Intrinsic motivation** is based on internal factors such as organismic needs (competence, relatedness, and autonomy), as well as curiosity, challenge, and fun. When we are intrinsically motivated, we engage in a behavior because we enjoy it. **Extrinsic motivation** involves external incentives such as rewards and punishers. When we are extrinsically motivated, we engage in a behavior for some external payoff or to avoid an external punishment.

● **extrinsic motivation** Motivation that involves external incentives such as rewards and punishments.

Some students study hard because they are internally motivated to put forth considerable effort and achieve high quality in their work (intrinsic motivation). Other students study hard because they want to make good grades or avoid parental disapproval (extrinsic motivation). Many psychologists believe that intrinsic motivation leads to more positive outcomes than extrinsic motivation (Blumenfeld, Kempler, & Krajcik, 2006; Patall, Cooper, & Robinson, 2008; Ryan & Deci, 2009). They argue that intrinsic motivation is more likely to produce competent behavior and mastery.

Many very successful individuals are both intrinsically motivated (they have high personal standards of achievement and emphasize personal effort) and extrinsically motivated (they are strongly competitive) (Ciani & Sheldon, 2010). Indeed, many of us might think of the ideal occupation as one in which we get paid (an extrinsic reward) for doing something we love to do (intrinsic motivation).

Self-Regulation: The Successful Pursuit of Goals

Today many psychologists approach motivation in the way that you yourself might—by asking about the goals a person is trying to accomplish in everyday life.

● **self-regulation** The process by which an organism effortfully controls behavior in order to pursue important objectives.

Goal approaches to motivation include the concept of self-regulation. **Self-regulation** is the process by which an organism effortfully controls behavior in order to pursue important objectives (Carver & Scheier, 2013). A key aspect of self-regulation is getting feedback about how we are doing in our goal pursuits. Our daily mood has been proposed as a way that we may receive this feedback—that is, we feel good or bad depending on how we are doing in the areas of life we value. Note that the role of mood in self-regulation means that we cannot be happy all the time. In order to effectively pursue our goals, we have to be open to the bad news that might occasionally come our way (King, 2008).

Putting our personal goals into action is a potentially complex process that involves setting goals, planning for their implementation, and monitoring our progress. Individuals' success improves when they set goals that are specific and moderately challenging (Bandura, 1997; Schunk, 2012). A fuzzy, nonspecific goal is "I want to be successful." A concrete, specific goal is "I want to have a 3.5 average at the end of the semester."

Accomplishing long-term goals is facilitated by the pursuit of short-term goals. When you set long-term goals, such as "I want to be a clinical psychologist," make sure that you also create short-term goals as steps along the way, such as "I want to get an *A* on my next

CRITICAL CONTROVERSY

Do Superstars Inspire or Discourage?

Maybe you have seen the sign in the parking lot of a local department store: Reserved for the Employee of the Month. Perhaps a professor has pointed out particularly outstanding work completed by a classmate. These examples, and others like them, are meant to inspire the rest of us and help us to aspire to greatness.

Within social psychology, comparing ourselves to those who are better off than we are is called *upward social comparison.* Sometimes such consideration evokes admiration and inspires greater striving. But sometimes our reactions can be more complicated than that, including feelings of envy and inadequacy (Onu, Kessler, & Smith, 2016). Seeing someone else do well can be threatening to a person's ego (Kim & others, 2016).

A recent study (Rogers & Feller, 2016) examined the effect of being exposed to outstanding work by another and found that it can lead not only to poorer performance but to quitting altogether. First, researchers studied a massive online course of more than 150,000 students—only 2 percent of whom had actually completed the course with a passing grade. As part of the class, the students wrote essays and then were randomly assigned to grade the essay of another student. Following up at the end of the semester, the results showed that students who graded outstanding essays were more likely to quit the course! Those who graded the excellent essays but stayed in the course earned lower final

© Calaimage/Paul Bradbur/OJO+/Getty Images

grades (Rogers & Feller, 2016). These results were especially strong if the essays had been exceptionally good.

Why would being exposed to someone who does exceptionally well be associated with giving up and performing poorly? In a second study, the researchers found that exposure to excellence led to feelings of discouragement and inadequacy. These feelings, in turn, were associated with withdrawing from the goal of doing well (Rogers & Feller, 2016).

Can we avoid these negative feelings in response to superstars? One key issue is that when people are presented with an outstanding performance, they might not realize how rare that performance is. Teachers and others might reduce the threat posed by examples of excellence by acknowledging that these examples are not typical. Another strategy is to build up levels of happiness and personal satisfaction prior to presenting such exemplars. Happy people tend to be less threatened by those who might be superior in skill (Kim & others, 2016; Lyubomirsky & Ross, 1997). Being happy with ourselves might be the first step to being truly inspired by others.

WHAT DO YOU THINK?

- Do you find examples of excellence inspiring or threatening? Why?
- How might publicly awarding excellent performance influence intrinsic motivation?

---

psychology test." Planning how to reach a goal and monitoring progress toward the goal are critical aspects of achievement. Make commitments in manageable chunks. High-achieving individuals monitor their own learning and systematically evaluate their progress toward their goals more than do low-achieving individuals (Harkin & others, 2016).

Even as we keep our nose to the grindstone in pursuing short-term goals, it is also important to have a sense of the big picture. Dedication to a long-term dream or personal mission can enhance one's sense of purpose in life. Although short-term goals can provide a feeling of accomplishment, attaching these goals to a future dream can allow individuals to experience a sense of meaning and to maintain their efforts in the face of short-term failure (Houser-Marko & Sheldon, 2008).

One way we can witness the payoff of goal pursuit is to look to individuals who have achieved the life dreams we seek. A young girl trying to become a great soccer midfielder might watch Carli Lloyd in action. A budding politician running for campus office might watch great speeches by John F. Kennedy, Ronald Reagan, or Barack Obama. Role models can be powerful sources of inspiration (Babey, Wolstein, & Diamant, 2016; Shin, Levy, & London, 2016).

Perhaps because role models can be motivating, teachers, parents, and bosses often hold up high-achieving students, siblings, or coworkers as exemplars of excellence (perhaps couched within a question, "Why can't you be more like . . .?"). Does thinking about a high-achieving person encourage or discourage achievement? To read about research addressing this question, see the Critical Controversy.

A key concept in understanding how individuals successfully pursue goals is *delay of gratification*—putting off a pleasurable experience in the interest of some larger but later reward. Successful delay of gratification is evident in the student who does not go out with friends but instead stays in and studies for an upcoming test, perhaps thinking, "There will be plenty of time to party after this test is over."

Delay of gratification is challenging. Think about it—future payoffs are simply much less certain than current rewards. In a situation where rewards are few and far between, it might make sense to eat, drink, or be merry based on whatever is around right now (Logue, 1995).

Walter Mischel and his colleagues examined how children managed to delay gratification, in what have become known as the Stanford marshmallow experiments (Mischel, Cantor, & Feldman, 1996; Mischel & Moore, 1980). They placed children in a difficult situation—alone in a room with a very tempting marshmallow within reach. The children were told that if they wanted to, at any time they could ring a bell and eat the marshmallow. Otherwise, they could wait until the experimenter returned, and then they would get two marshmallows. The children were then left alone to face this self-control dilemma. In truth, the experimenter was not coming back. The researchers were interested in measuring how long the children could wait before giving in to temptation and eating the marshmallow.

There were a variety of responses to this unusual situation. Some children sat dead still, focused on the tempting marshmallow. Some stared the marshmallow down. Some smelled the marshmallow. Others turned away, sang songs, picked their nose, or did anything but pay attention to the marshmallow.

How did the children who were able to resist temptation do it? Mischel and colleagues found that the kids who were able to distract themselves from the marshmallow by focusing on "cool thoughts" (that is, non-marshmallow-related things) were better able to delay gratification. In contrast, children who remained focused on the marshmallow and all its delightful qualities—what Mischel called "hot thoughts"—ate the marshmallow sooner (Metcalfe & Mischel, 1999).

These findings have implications for self-control. Imagine that you are in a long-term romantic relationship that you wish to continue, and you meet an appealing new person to whom you are physically attracted. Should you cultivate a friendship with him or her? Maybe not, if you want to avoid temptation and preserve your current relationship. Think about all the current and potential "marshmallows" in your life—those things that have the power to distract you from achieving your long-term plans. Mischel's research with children demonstrates that avoiding these hot issues might be a good way to see a long-term plan through to its completion.

Interestingly, Mischel and his colleagues continued to study those children for many years. They found that the amount of time the children were able to delay gratification predicted their academic performance in high school and college (Mischel, 2004) and even their self-regulation skills in their 40s (Casey & others, 2011; Mischel & others, 2011).

Self-regulation can be challenging. Two things that are associated with particularly poor self-regulation are impulsivity and procrastination. *Impulsivity* is the tendency to act rashly, without thinking or planning. Impulsive individuals have trouble dealing with temptation and successfully sticking to their long-term goals in a variety of domains (Haw, 2016; MacKillop & others, 2014).

Evolutionary explanations for the existence of impulsivity suggest that, in the harsh environments where they lived, early humans had to meet their survival needs quickly (Steel, 2010). The modern world, however, poses different challenges, requiring people to manage multiple long-term goals. In such a context, impulsivity may lead to negative self-regulatory outcomes. But impulsivity paid off for our ancestors. This evolutionary explanation is supported by the fact that impulsivity is moderately heritable. Genetic variation explains about half of the differences we see in impulsivity (Gustavson & others, 2014, 2015).

Procrastination means intentionally putting off actions on a goal (Ferrari, 1993; Rebetez, Rochat, & Van der Linden, 2015; Tibbett & Ferrari, 2015). We have all experienced it: You really wanted tickets to that concert, but you waited until the last minute and it sold out. Although it is common, procrastination is a bit of a puzzle. If we really want something, why would we deliberately not act to get it?

INTERSECTION

Motivation and Behavior Genetics: Why Do We Procrastinate?

Course syllabi state the dates of all the exams for a term, providing the information required to prepare for these, well in advance. Yet, some students will find themselves pulling all-nighters, having spent the prior days (and weeks) wanting to study, thinking about studying, but somehow not ever actually studying. What explains this irrational behavior? There are likely a variety of contributors to procrastination, but until recently research had not addressed the possibility that genes might predispose individuals to procrastination.

Recent large-scale studies comparing adult twins have demonstrated that not only is procrastination explained in part by genes, but that the same genetic origins are linked to procrastination, impulsivity, and low levels of executive function (Gustavson & others, 2014, 2015). In the studies, participants completed questionnaires to measure procrastination that included items like, "I don't get started until time is about to run out." In one study, they completed measures of impulsivity and in another study measures of executive function (the capacity to think carefully, set goals, and plan). Results showed procrastination was positively linked with impulsivity and negatively related to executive function (Gustavson & others, 2014, 2015). In addition, differences in these traits were explained by the same genetic variation.

© Michael Blann/Getty Images

Who is the worst procrastinator you know? Is he or she also impulsive?

Although correlational, these results suggest that procrastination may be a byproduct of impulsivity and low executive function. How might this work?

Think about all the things you do while you are procrastinating. Often, procrastination is not doing nothing. Rather, it involves doing lots of things irrelevant to the goal. Yes, you will study, but first you might finish those dishes in the sink, or text that friend, or finally answer those e-mails. While we procrastinate, we are often attending to more immediate tasks that take us away from our long-term pursuits. Sounds a lot like impulsivity!

At first blush, it might seem that impulsivity and procrastination are almost opposites. After all, impulsivity means doing something quickly without thought, and procrastination means thinking about it but not doing anything. Yet, these two characteristics are related, with procrastinators scoring highly on measures of impulsivity (Steel, 2007). A recent investigation examined the genetic underpinnings of procrastination and provided a fascinating explanation for the link between procrastination and impulsivity. To read about this work, see the Intersection.

4. EMOTION

The concept of self-regulation suggests that motivation and emotion are closely linked. We feel happy or sad depending on how events influence the likelihood of our getting the things we want in life. Our emotions tell us what really matters to us. We might think, for instance, that we have lost interest in a romantic partner until that person initiates a breakup. Suddenly, we realize how much the person really means to us.

Emotions are complex. The body, the mind, and the face play key roles in emotion, although psychologists debate which of these components is most significant in emotion and how they mix to produce emotional experiences (Christenfeld & Mandler, 2013; Kalat & Shiota, 2012). For our purposes, **emotion** is feeling, or affect, that can involve physiological arousal (such as a fast heartbeat), conscious experience (feeling joy), and behavioral expression (a smile).

test yourself

1. What is Maslow's hierarchy of needs? Explain.
2. What is self-actualization, according to Maslow, and on what does it depend?
3. How do intrinsic motivation and extrinsic motivation differ?

● **emotion** Feeling, or affect, that can involve physiological arousal (such as a fast heartbeat), conscious experience (thinking about being in love with someone), and behavioral expression (a smile or grimace).

Biological Factors in Emotion

A friend whom you have been counseling about a life problem texts you, "r u home? On my way over." You get nervous. What could be going on? You feel burdened—you have a lot of work to do, and you do not have time for a talk session. When she arrives with a gift-wrapped package and a big smile, your nerves give way to relief. She announces, "Here's a present to say thanks for all your help." Your heart warms, and you feel a strong sense of your enduring bond with her. As you moved through the emotions of worry, relief, and joy, your body changed. Indeed, the body is a crucial part of our emotional experience.

THE AUTONOMIC NERVOUS SYSTEM

Recall from the chapter "Biological Foundations of Behavior" that the *autonomic nervous system (ANS)* takes messages to and from the body's internal organs, monitoring such processes as breathing, heart rate, and digestion. The ANS is divided into the sympathetic and the parasympathetic nervous systems (Figure 4). The *sympathetic nervous system (SNS)* is responsible for rapid reactions to threats. SNS arousal causes increased blood pressure, faster heart rate, more rapid breathing, and more efficient blood flow to the brain and major muscle groups. These changes prepare us for action, the "fight or flight" response. In contrast, the *parasympathetic nervous system (PNS)* calms the body, promoting processes of maintenance and healing. When the PNS is activated, blood pressure drops, heart rate and breathing slow, and food digestion increases, which is the "rest and digest" response. These two sides of the autonomic nervous system can be easy to confuse. Be sure to closely review Figure 4.

　The sympathetic and parasympathetic nervous systems evolved to improve the human species' likelihood for survival. It does not take a life-threatening situation to activate the SNS response. *Emotions* are associated with SNS arousal as well, suggesting that such arousal plays a role in emotional experience.

MEASURING SNS ACTIVITY

Clearly, when the SNS is active, the body jumps into action. How might we measure these changes? One way psychologists have measured this arousal is *skin conductance level (SCL),* a rise in the skin's electrical conductivity when sweat gland activity increases.

FIGURE 4 **The Autonomic Nervous System and Its Role in Arousing and Calming the Body** The two parts of the autonomic nervous system work in different ways. The sympathetic nervous system arouses the body in reaction to a stressor, evoking the "fight or flight" response. In contrast, the parasympathetic nervous system calms the body, promoting relaxation and healing. Remember, the latter system functions to "rest and digest."
(photo) © James Woodson/Getty Images

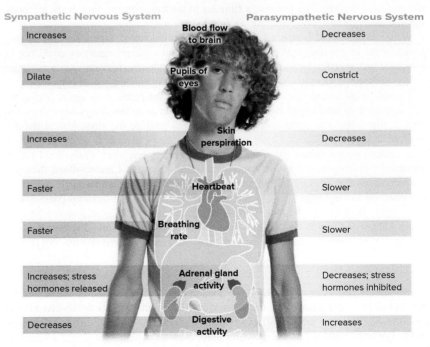

Sympathetic Nervous System		Parasympathetic Nervous System
Increases	Blood flow to brain	Decreases
Dilate	Pupils of eyes	Constrict
Increases	Skin perspiration	Decreases
Faster	Heartbeat	Slower
Faster	Breathing rate	Slower
Increases; stress hormones released	Adrenal gland activity	Decreases; stress hormones inhibited
Decreases	Digestive activity	Increases

A sweaty palm conducts electricity better than a dry one. This difference provides the basis for SCL as a measure of autonomic arousal.

Another measure of arousal is the **polygraph** or lie detector, a machine examiners use to try to determine whether someone is lying. The polygraph monitors changes in the body—heart rate, breathing, and SCL—thought to be influenced by emotional states. In a typical polygraph test, the examiner asks the individual a number of neutral questions and several key, less neutral questions. If the individual's heart rate, breathing, and SCL responses increase substantially when the key questions are asked, the individual is assumed to be lying (Grubin, 2010).

> ● **polygraph** A machine, commonly called a lie detector, that monitors changes in the body, used to try to determine whether someone is lying.

How accurate is the lie detector? Experts argue that the polygraph errs just under 50 percent of the time (Iacono & Lykken, 1997; Lykken, 1987, 2001; Seymour & others, 2000). The problem with the polygraph is that heart rate, breathing, and SCL can increase for reasons other than lying—for instance, because a person is *nervous* (not necessarily guilty). For this reason, the Employee Polygraph Protection Act of 1988 restricts polygraph testing outside of government agencies, and most courts do not accept the results of polygraph testing.

THEORIES OF EMOTION

Imagine that you and your date are enjoying a picnic in the country. Suddenly, a bull runs across the field toward you. Why are you afraid? Two well-known theories of emotion that involve physiological processes provide answers to this question.

Common sense tells you that you are trembling and running away from the bull because you are afraid, but William James (1950) and Carl Lange (pronounced "Long-uh") (1922) said emotion works in the opposite way. According to the **James–Lange theory,** emotion results from physiological states triggered by stimuli in the environment: Emotion occurs *after* physiological reactions. This perspective holds that emotions are not mental events that lead to reactions but rather that those physiological reactions are what lead to emotional states. Lange especially emphasized that each emotion—from anger to rapture—has a distinct set of physiological changes, evident in changes in heart rate, breathing patterns, sweating, and other responses.

> ● **James–Lange theory** The theory that emotion results from physiological states triggered by stimuli in the environment.

Let's apply the James–Lange theory to the situation with the bull. You see the bull scratching its hoof on the ground, and you begin to run away. Your aroused body then sends sensory messages to your brain, at which point emotion is perceived. According to this theory, you do not run away because you are afraid; rather, you are afraid because you are running away. You perceive a stimulus in the environment, your body responds, and you interpret the body's reaction as emotion.

Walter Cannon (1927) rejected the idea that each emotional experience has its own particular set of physiological changes. He argued that different emotions could not be associated with specific physiological changes because autonomic nervous system responses are too diffuse and slow to account for rapid and differentiated emotional responses.

To understand Cannon's view, imagine the bull and the picnic once again. Seeing the bull scratching its hoof causes the thalamus of your brain to do two things simultaneously: First, it stimulates your autonomic nervous system to produce the physiological changes involved in emotion (increased heart rate, rapid breathing); second, it sends messages to your cerebral cortex, where the experience of emotion is perceived. Philip Bard (1934) supported this analysis, and so the theory became known as the **Cannon–Bard theory**— the proposition that emotion and physiological reactions occur *simultaneously.*

> ● **Cannon–Bard theory** The proposition that emotion and physiological reactions occur simultaneously.

Unlike the James–Lange theory, which proposes that the physical reactions come first, in the Cannon–Bard theory, the body plays a less important role. Figure 5 shows how the James–Lange and Cannon–Bard theories differ. Whether emotions involve discrete autonomic nervous system responses, as Lange expected, continues to be debated (Barrett, 2011).

NEUROTRANSMITTERS AND NEURAL CIRCUITS

Contemporary researchers are keenly interested in discovering the role of neurotransmitters and charting the neural circuitry of emotions. Research suggests the involvement of neurotransmitters in emotional experience (Amano & others, 2011; Klimecki, 2015; Lövheim, 2012). For instance, dopamine and endorphins are linked to positive

342 🦐 CHAPTER 10 **Motivation and Emotion**

FIGURE 5 **James–Lange and Cannon–Bard Theories** From the James–Lange perspective, the experience of fear is an outcome of physiological arousal. In the Cannon–Bard view, fear occurs at the same time as the physiological response. (longhorn) © Brand X Pictures/PunchStock; (nervous system) © M. Freeman/PhotoLink/Getty Images; (surprised face) © Tim Hall/Getty Images

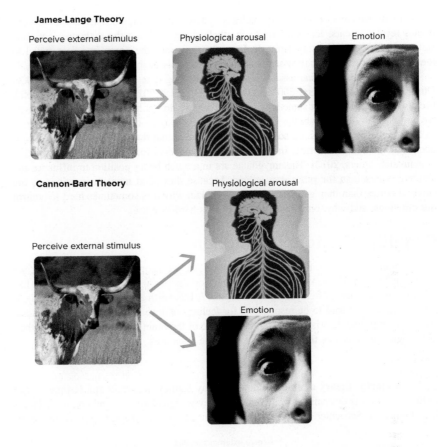

James-Lange Theory

Perceive external stimulus → Physiological arousal → Emotion

Cannon-Bard Theory

Perceive external stimulus → Physiological arousal / Emotion

emotions, such as happiness (Koepp & others, 2009), and norepinephrine functions in regulating arousal and anxiety (Berridge & Kringelbach, 2008; Greeson & others, 2009).

With regard to the brain structures involved in emotional experience, research has focused on the limbic system and especially the amygdalae, the almond-shaped structures in the limbic system that we considered in the chapter "Biological Foundations of Behavior". The limbic system, including the amygdalae, is involved in the experience of positive emotions (Hurleman & others, 2010; Koepp & others, 2009; Ritchey, LaBar, & Cabeza, 2011). However, most research has focused on the important role of the amygdalae in the experience of negative emotion, particularly fear.

Research by Joseph LeDoux and his colleagues demonstrates that the amygdalae play a central role in fear (Johansen & others, 2012; LeDoux, 2009, 2012, 2013). When the amygdalae determine that danger is present, they shift into high gear, marshaling the brain's resources in an effort to protect the organism from harm. This fear system evolved to detect and respond to natural dangers that threaten survival or territory.

The brain circuitry for fear can follow two pathways: a direct pathway from the thalamus to the amygdalae or an indirect pathway from the thalamus through the sensory cortex to the amygdalae (Figure 6). The direct pathway does not convey detailed information about the stimulus, but it has the advantage of speed—and speed is a vital characteristic of information for an organism facing a

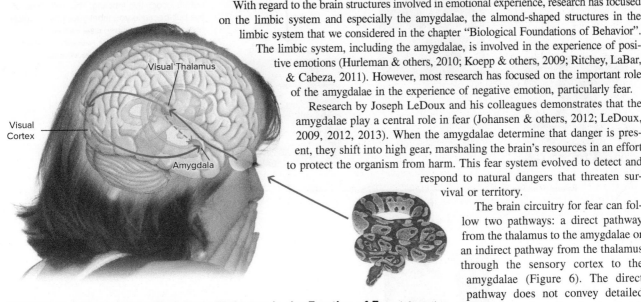

FIGURE 6 **Direct and Indirect Brain Pathways in the Emotion of Fear** Information about fear can follow two pathways in the brain when an individual sees a snake. The direct pathway (*broken arrow*) conveys information rapidly from the thalamus to the amygdala. The indirect pathway (*solid arrows*) transmits information more slowly from the thalamus to the sensory cortex (here, the visual cortex) and then to the amygdala. (snake photo) © IT Stock/PunchStock

threat to its survival. The indirect pathway carries nerve impulses from the sensory organs (eyes and ears, for example) to the thalamus (recall that the thalamus is a relay station for incoming sensory stimuli); from the thalamus, the nerve impulses travel to the sensory cortex, which then sends appropriate signals to the amygdalae.

The amygdalae retain fear associations for a very long time (Debiec & LeDoux, 2006; Duvarci, Nader, & LeDoux, 2008; LeDoux, 2009, 2012, 2013). This quality is useful, because once we learn that something is dangerous, we do not have to relearn it. However, we pay a penalty for this ability. Once acquired, fears may be quite difficult to unlearn.

Part of the reason fears are so difficult to change is that the amygdalae are well connected to the cerebral cortex, in which thinking and decision making primarily occur (Linnman & others, 2012). The amygdalae are in a much better position to influence the cerebral cortex than the other way around, because they send more connections to the cerebral cortex than they get back. This may explain why it is sometimes hard to control our emotions, and why, once fear is learned, it is hard to erase.

Cognitive Factors in Emotion

Does emotion depend on the tides of the mind? Are we happy only when we think we are happy? Cognitive theories of emotion center on the premise that emotion always has a cognitive component (Derryberry & Reed, 2002; Ellsworth & Dougherty, 2016; Frijda, 2007). Thinking is said to be responsible for feelings of love and hate, joy and sadness. Although cognitive theorists do recognize the role of the brain and body in emotion, they give cognitive processes the main credit for these responses.

THE TWO-FACTOR THEORY OF EMOTION

In the **two-factor theory of emotion** developed by Stanley Schachter and Jerome Singer (1962), emotion is determined by two factors: physiological arousal and cognitive labeling (Figure 7). Schachter and Singer argued that we look to the external world for an

● **two-factor theory of emotion** Schachter and Singer's theory that emotion is determined by two factors: physiological arousal and cognitive labeling.

FIGURE 7   Schachter and Singer's Two-Factor Theory of Emotion The two-factor theory includes not only arousal but also cognitive labeling: You feel afraid of the bull because you label your physiological response "fear." (longhorn) © Brand X Pictures/PunchStock; (nervous system) © M. Freeman/PhotoLink/Getty Images; (open mouth face) © BananaStock/PictureQuest; (surprised face) © Tim Hall/Getty Images

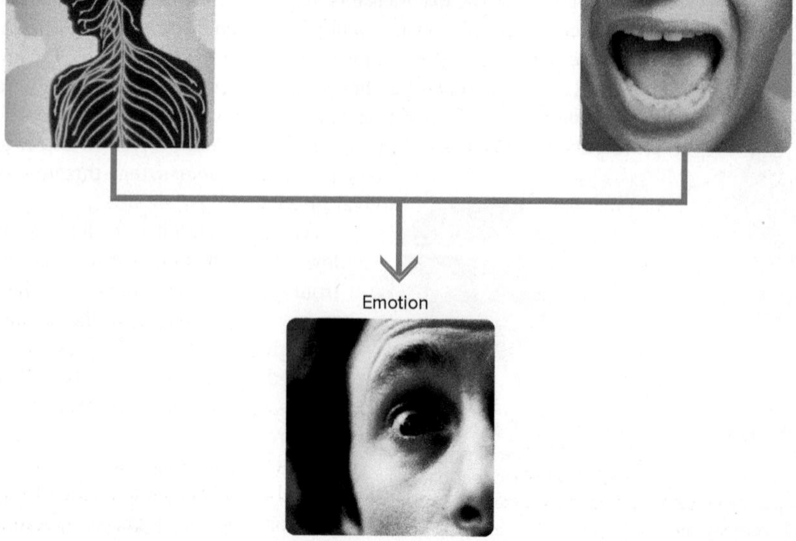

Perceive external stimulus

Physiological arousal

Cognitive labeling

Emotion

explanation of *why* we are aroused. We interpret external cues and label the emotion. For example, if you feel good after someone has made a pleasant comment to you, you might label the emotion "happy." If you feel bad after you have done something wrong, you may label the feeling "guilty."

To test their theory of emotion, Schachter and Singer (1962) injected volunteer participants with epinephrine, a drug that produces high arousal. After participants received the drug, they observed someone else behave in either a euphoric way (shooting papers at a wastebasket) or an angry way (stomping out of the room). As predicted, the euphoric and angry behavior influenced the participants' cognitive interpretation of their own arousal. When they were with a happy person, they rated themselves as happy; when they were with an angry person, they said they were angry. This effect occurred, however, only when the participants were not told about the true effects of the injection. When they were told that the drug would increase their heart rate and make them jittery, they said the reason for their own arousal was the drug, not the other person's behavior. Notice, then, how external cues were only consulted if participants' feelings were ambiguous and required explanation.

The two-factor theory of emotion tells us that often our bodies send us ambiguous messages about what is going on in the world. We take those messages and look for explanations in our immediate circumstances, and that is what produces emotions. Imagine that you are late for class on an important exam day. You sprint across campus as fast as you can, arriving just in time for the test. As you look over the questions, your heart is racing, your breathing is fast, and you feel sweaty. Are you nervous about the test or just recovering from your run to the classroom? The two-factor theory suggests that you just might mistake your bodily sensations as indications that you are scared of the test.

THE PRIMACY DEBATE: COGNITION OR EMOTION?

Which comes first, thinking or feeling? Fans of vintage episodes of TV's *Star Trek* may recognize this theme from the frequent arguments between Mr. Spock, the logical Vulcan, and Dr. McCoy, the emotional doctor on the *Enterprise*. In the 1980s and 1990s, two eminent psychologists, Richard Lazarus and Robert Zajonc, debated which was more central—cognition or emotion?

Recall from the chapter "Thinking, Intelligence, and Language" that Lazarus said that we cognitively appraise ourselves and our circumstances and that these appraisals determine how we feel about events and experiences. For Lazarus (1991), then, thinking is primary—he believed cognitive activity causes our feelings. Our appraisals—which are guided by values, goals, beliefs, and expectations—determine our emotions (Urry, 2010; Wilkowski & Robinson, 2010). Consider a student who fails a test. This event would seem to be negative to everyone. But Lazarus would say that the emotions that follow depend on appraisal. If the class is important to the student's goals, she might feel distress, but if she had been looking for a reason to change her major, she might feel relief.

Zajonc (1984) disagreed with Lazarus. Emotions are primary, he said, and our thoughts are a result of them. Zajonc famously argued that "preferences need no inferences," meaning that the way we feel about something requires no thought.

Which of the two psychologists is right? *Both* are likely correct. Lazarus talked mainly about a cluster of related events that occur over a period of time, whereas Zajonc described single events or a preference for one stimulus over another. Lazarus was concerned with love over the course of months and years, a sense of value to the community, and plans for retirement; Zajonc spoke about a car accident, an encounter with a snake, and a penchant for ice cream over spinach.

Some of our emotional reactions are virtually instantaneous and probably do not involve cognitive appraisal, such as shrieking upon detecting a snake (Young & Claypool, 2010). Other emotional circumstances, especially long-term feelings

Vintage Star Trek *episodes explored the question, what comes first—thinking or feeling?*

such as a depressed mood or anger toward a friend, are more likely to involve cognitive appraisal (Smith & Kirby, 2009). Indeed, the direct and indirect brain pathways described earlier support the idea that some of our emotional reactions do not involve deliberate thinking, whereas others do (LeDoux, 2012).

Behavioral Factors in Emotion

Remember that our definition of emotion includes not only physiological and cognitive components but also a behavioral component. The behavioral component can be verbal or nonverbal. Verbally, a person might show love for someone by professing it in words or might display anger by saying nasty things. Nonverbally, a person might smile, frown, show a fearful expression, or slouch.

The most interest in the behavioral dimension of emotion has focused on the nonverbal behavior of facial expressions (Sacco & Hugenberg, 2009; Todd & others, 2011). Emotion researchers have been intrigued by people's ability to detect emotion from a person's facial expression (Geangu & others, 2016; Yan & others, 2016). In a typical research study, participants, when shown photographs like those in Figure 8, are usually able to identify six emotions: happiness, anger, sadness, surprise, disgust, and fear (Ekman & O'Sullivan, 1991).

Might our facial expressions not only reflect our emotions but also influence them? According to the **facial feedback hypothesis,** facial expressions can influence emotions as well as reflect them (Davis, Senghas, & Ochsner, 2009). In this view, facial muscles send signals to the brain that help us to recognize the emotion we are experiencing (Keillor & others, 2002; Liu & others, 2016). For example, we feel happier when we smile and sadder when we frown. The facial feedback hypothesis provides support for the James–Lange theory of emotion discussed earlier—namely, that emotional experiences can be generated by changes in and awareness of our own bodily states.

● **facial feedback hypothesis** The idea that facial expressions can influence emotions as well as reflect them.

FIGURE 8   Recognizing Emotions in Facial Expressions Look at the six photographs and determine the emotion reflected in each of the six faces: (*top*) happiness, anger, sadness; (*bottom*) surprise, disgust, fear. (first) ©sirtravelalot/Shutterstock; (second) ©Royalty-free/Corbis; (third) ©Image Source; (fourth) ©gulfimages/Alamy Stock Photo; (fifth) ©Paul Burns/Getty Images; (sixth) ©Masterfile

Sociocultural Factors in Emotion

Are the facial expressions that are associated with different emotions largely innate, or do they vary across cultures? Answering this question requires a look at research findings on sociocultural influences in emotions.

CULTURE AND THE EXPRESSION OF EMOTION

In 1872 Charles Darwin stated in *The Expression of the Emotions in Man and Animals* that the facial expressions of human beings are innate, not learned; are the same in all cultures around the world; and have evolved from the emotions of animals (Darwin, 1965). Many psychologists still believe that emotions, and especially how they are expressed facially, have strong biological ties (de Gelder & others, 2006; Peleg & others, 2006). For example, children who are blind from birth, and have never observed the smile or frown on another person's face, smile or frown in the same way that children with normal vision do (Shariff & Tracy, 2011). If emotions and the facial expressions that go with them are unlearned, then they should be the same the world over. Are they?

Extensive research has examined the universality of facial expressions and the ability of people from different cultures accurately to label the emotion that lies behind facial expressions (Sauter & others, 2010). Paul Ekman's careful observations reveal that the many faces of emotion do not differ significantly from one culture to another (Ekman, 1980, 1996, 2003).

For example, Ekman and Wallace Friesen photographed people expressing emotions such as happiness, fear, surprise, disgust, and grief. When they showed the photographs to people from the United States, Chile, Japan, Brazil, and Borneo (an Indonesian island in the western Pacific), the participants recognized the emotions the faces were meant to show, across the various cultures (Ekman & Friesen, 1969). Similarly, in another study, members of the Fore tribe, an isolated Stone Age culture in New Guinea, were able to match descriptions of emotional situations with photographs of faces expressing fear, happiness, anger, and surprise (Ekman & Friesen, 1971). Figure 9 shows the similarity of facial expressions of emotions by persons in New Guinea and the United States.

FIGURE 9 Disgust or Happiness?
Disgust and happiness activate specific facial muscles, no matter who is making the face. As quickly as you can, go through these diverse faces and identify which of these folks look like they just smelled sour milk (disgust) and which look like they are definitely getting the joke (happiness).
(first) ©DRB Images, LLC/E+/Getty Images; (second) ©digitalskillet/E+/Getty Images; (third) ©SIBSA Digital Pvt. Ltd./Alamy Stock Photo; (fourth) ©Vladimir Wrangel/Alamy Stock Photo; (fifth) ©themacx/iStock/Getty Images; (sixth) ©Joan Vicent Canto Roig/Getty Images

Not all psychologists believe that facial expressions of basic emotions are universal (Barrett, 2011), but all would certainly agree that cultures have different norms that govern the expression of emotion (Fischer, 2006; Fok & others, 2008; Matsumoto, Yoo, & Fontaine, 2008). **Display rules** are sociocultural standards that determine when, where, and how emotions should be expressed. For example, although happiness is a universally expressed emotion, when, where, and how people display it may vary from one culture to another (Engelmann & Pogosyan, 2013; Sauter & others, 2010). The same is true for other emotions, such as fear, sadness, and anger.

The importance of display rules is especially evident when we evaluate the emotional expression of another. Does that grieving husband on a morning talk show seem appropriately distraught over his wife's murder? Or might he be a suspect?

Many nonverbal signals of emotion vary from one culture to another (Mesquita, 2002). For example, male-to-male kissing is commonplace in Yemen, but it is not so common in the United States. The "thumbs up" sign, which in most cultures means either that everything is okay or that one wants to hitch a ride, is an insult in Greece, similar to a raised third finger in the United States—a cultural difference to keep in mind if you find yourself backpacking through Greece.

In the Middle Eastern country of Yemen, male-to-male kissing is commonplace, but in the United States it is less common.
© Adam Jan/AFP/Getty Images

● **display rules** Sociocultural standards that determine when, where, and how emotions should be expressed.

EMOTIONAL EXPRESSION IN COMPUTER COMMUNICATIONS

A fairly recent area of interest to psychologists is the expression of emotion in computer-mediated communications, including e-mails, blogs, and instant messages. Emoticons are used to express a variety of feelings, from joy **:D** to sadness **:-(** to silliness **;P** to great shock and dismay **: - O.**

Emoticons allow us to compensate for the loss of information from other expressive channels, such as vocal tone and facial expression (Derks, Bos, & von Grumbkow, 2008; Lo, 2008). People use emoticons as they do other displays of emotion, such as laughter, often at the end of the statement they are trying to clarify (Provine, Spencer, & Mandell, 2007).

Just as culture influences emotional expressions, it influences emoticons. For instance, East Asian emoticons are less likely to be presented sideways, so that a Japanese student might convey her level of exhaustion with **(-.-)Zzzzz** rather than **l-)Zzzzz.** Even with emoticons, display rules can be important. A Japanese student expressing a thumbs up **d(^_^)b** might encounter an American who thinks he is saying he has big ears.

Emoticons reveal a potentially unique aspect of computer-mediated communication. Consider that back when people often communicated by writing letters (an art that would seem to share the limitations of e-mail and texting), emoticons were not used. Looking at the letters of great writers, we do not find smileys and frownies explaining their feelings. Of course, contemporary messaging is currently as likely to contain emojis as emoticons.

Classifying Emotions

There are more than 200 words for emotions in the English language, indicating the complexity and variety of emotions. Not surprisingly, psychologists have created ways to classify emotions—to summarize these many emotions along various dimensions (Izard, 2009), including their valence, arousal, and motivational quality.

VALENCE

The *valence* of an emotion refers to whether it feels pleasant or unpleasant. You probably are not surprised to know that happiness, joy, pleasure, and contentment are positively valenced emotions. In contrast, sadness, anger, and worry are negatively valenced emotions. Research has shown that emotions tend to go together based on their valence, so that if someone is sad, he or she is also likely to be angry or worried, and if a person is happy, he is or she is also likely to be feeling confident, joyful, and content (Watson, 2001).

348   CHAPTER 10   Motivation and Emotion

psychological *inquiry*

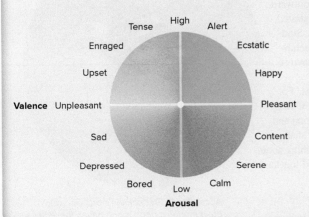

The Full Circle of Emotions

The figure shows a commonly used representation of human emotions—the circumplex model. Note that the circle is created by two independent dimensions: valence and arousal. Emotions that are similar are closer together, and those that differ are farther apart. Using the figure as a reference, answer the following questions.

1. Locate the emotions "upset" and "sad" on the circumplex. According to the circumplex, these two feelings differ primarily in terms of their arousal. Which is higher in arousal? Do you agree with this placement of these emotions? Explain.

2. According to the model, which emotion is the exact opposite of "serene"?

3. Where would you place the following feelings on the circle: worried, proud, angry, embarrassed?

● **negative affect** Negative emotions such as anger, guilt, and sadness.

● **positive affect** Positive emotions such as joy, happiness, and interest.

We can classify many emotional states on the basis of valence. Indeed, according to some experts in emotion (Watson, 2001), there are two broad dimensions of emotional experience: negative affect and positive affect. **Negative affect** refers to emotions such as anger, guilt, and sadness. **Positive affect** refers to emotions such as joy, happiness, and interest.

Although it seems essential to consider the valence of emotions as a way to classify them, valence does not fully capture all that we need to know about emotional states. The joy a person experiences at the birth of a child and the mild high at finding a $5 bill are both positive states, but they clearly differ. One way in which they differ is in their level of arousal.

AROUSAL LEVEL

The *arousal level* of an emotion (sometimes called *activation level*) is the degree to which the emotion is reflected in an individual's being active, engaged, or excited versus passive, disengaged, or calm. Positive and negative emotions can be high or low in arousal. Ecstasy and excitement are examples of high-arousal positive emotions, whereas contentment and tranquility are low-arousal positive emotions. Examples of high-arousal negative emotions are rage, fury, and panic, whereas irritation and boredom represent low-arousal negative emotions.

Valence and arousal level are independent dimensions that together describe a vast number of emotional states. Using these dimensions, psychologists have created a wheel of mood states that they call a *circumplex model of emotions* (Posner, Russell, & Peterson, 2005). A circumplex is a graph that creates a circle from two independent dimensions. Using the dimensions of valence and arousal level, we can arrange emotional states in an organized fashion. To view the circumplex model and grasp its usefulness, see the Psychological Inquiry.

THE MOTIVATIONAL QUALITY OF EMOTIONS

The notion that emotions can motivate action has been recognized since Darwin, who proposed that emotional expressions are themselves remnants of the actions an emotion would provoke. You can probably think of actions that are associated with emotions, even if you do not engage in those actions literally. For instance, anger might engender the behavior of striking out at another person. Joy might move us to seek out other people (in a friendlier manner). Fear might tell us to run away from whatever is making us afraid.

© Peter Griffith/Getty Images

Recently, psychologists have begun to classify emotions based on their relevance to motivations—as either emotions to *avoid* punishers or to *approach* rewards (Carver & Harmon-Jones, 2009). Fear, for instance, is thought of as an avoidance-motivating emotion because it tells us to escape the threatening stimulus. In contrast, anger is thought to be an approach-related emotion because it directs our behavior outward. Moreover, anger is concerned with rewards: When we feel angry or frustrated, it is because something (or someone) is blocking us from what we want. Studies have shown that viewing pictures of fearful facial expressions foster behaviors that suggest avoidance and pictures of angry faces foster approach behaviors (Wilkowski & Meier, 2010).

Thinking about emotions in this way can lead to unexpected predictions. For instance, consider the emotions anger and joy. Clearly, these emotions differ in their valence, but in terms of their motivational pull, both involve approach motivation and rewards. Interestingly, research suggests that positive emotions and anger share an approach motivational tendency (Pettersson & Turkheimer, 2013). When we think about emotions in a motivational context, even very different feelings can be linked together.

The Adaptive Functions of Emotions

In considering the functions of emotions, it is fairly easy to come up with a good reason for us to have emotions such as fear and anger. Negative emotions carry direct and immediate adaptive benefits in situations that threaten survival (Lench, Tibbett, & Bench, 2016). Negative emotions indicate clearly that something is wrong and that we must take action. Positive emotions do not signal a problem. So, what is the adaptive function of positive emotions?

Confronting this question, Barbara Fredrickson proposed the **broaden-and-build model** of positive emotion (Fredrickson, 1998, 2001, 2006, 2009, 2013b). This model states that the function of positive emotions is to broaden the scope of attention and foster the building of resources.

The model begins with the influence of positive emotion on attention. Positive moods, such as contentment and humor, have been shown to broaden our attentional focus; they allow us to see the forest for the trees. As a result, when in a good mood, we may be more disposed to think outside the box—to see unusual possibilities that escaped us before.

The "building" part of the model comes in as positive mood signals that there is no immediate threat in the environment, and we can explore without concern. We can take the time to make friends, to exercise to promote our health, to branch out in new ways. These activities allow us to build up strengths that we can use when we encounter life's difficulties (Kok, Catalino, & Fredrickson, 2008; Papousek & others, 2010). For example, joy creates the urge to play, push the limits, and be creative. Interest creates the motivation to explore, absorb new information and experiences, and expand the self (Csikszentmihalyi, 1990; Ryan & Deci, 2000).

The adaptive function of positive emotions can be seen in the quality of *resilience*. Recall from the chapter "Human Development" that resilience is the ability to bounce back from negative experiences, to be flexible and adaptable when things are not going well. Resilient individuals might be thought of as tall trees with the ability to bend but not break in response to strong winds. In contrast, people who lack resilience might be characterized as more brittle—more likely to snap or break in the face of adversity (Block & Kremen, 1996).

Positive emotions play an important role in the ability of resilient individuals to cope successfully with life's challenges. Resilient individuals are zestful, optimistic, and energetic in their approach to life (Block & Kremen, 1996). They cultivate positive emotion through the use of humor (Segerstrom, 2006). Michelle Tugade, Barbara Fredrickson, and Lisa Feldman Barrett (2004) found that the superior coping of resilient individuals came from their ability to use positive emotions to bounce back from negative emotional experiences. Using measures of cardiovascular activity, the researchers found that resilient individuals were better able to regulate their responses to stressful situations (for instance, being told they were about to give an important speech) by strategically experiencing positive emotion.

According to Fredrickson's broaden-and-build model, a good mood paves the way for building resources such as close friends and health-promoting activities.
© Brand X/JupiterImages

● **broaden-and-build model** Fredrickson's model of positive emotion, stating that the function of positive emotions lies in their effects on an individual's attention and ability to build resources.

Resilient individuals seem to show a kind of emotional wisdom; they capitalize on the power of positive emotions to reverse the stress of negative feelings. This skill was demonstrated in a study of responses to the terrorist attacks of September 11, 2001. Resilient individuals were found to be less likely to fall prey to depression after 9/11, and this capacity to flourish in the face of the crisis was a result of their attention to positive emotions (Fredrickson & others, 2003).

In sum, although they are aware of and feel negative emotions, resilient individuals are better able to regulate their feelings. They boost their functioning by capitalizing on positive emotions even in the context of distress.

5. MOTIVATION, EMOTION, AND HEALTH AND WELLNESS: THE PURSUIT OF HAPPINESS

Motivation is about what people want, and a quick scan of the bestseller list or the self-help section of any bookstore would seem to indicate that one thing people want very much is to be happy—or happier.

There might be good reasons to pursue happiness. The experience of negative emotions is related to disease, heart attack, and death (Cohen, Janicki-Deverts, & Miller, 2007; Hemingway & Marmot, 1999). In contrast, the experience of positive emotions has been linked to lower levels of pain and disease (Pressman & Cohen, 2005) as well as improved disease survival (Moskowitz, 2003) and longer lives (Chida & Steptoe, 2008; Diener & Chan, 2011). A study examining individuals from 42 countries showed that self-reported health was strongly related to both negative and positive emotional experiences, even in developing nations (Pressman, Gallagher, & Lopez, 2013).

So, perhaps becoming happier is a worthwhile goal. Can people become happier? Let's consider the evidence.

Biological Factors in Happiness

As we have seen, the brain is certainly at work in the experience of positive emotions. Genes also play a role. For instance, research on the heritability of well-being has tended to show that a substantial proportion of well-being differences among people can be explained by genetics. The heritability estimates for happiness range from 50 to 80 percent (Lykken, 1999). Remember from the chapter "Human Development" that heritability is a statistic that describes characteristics of a group, that heritability estimates can vary across groups and over time, and that even highly heritable characteristics can be influenced by experience. Thus, a person is not necessarily doomed to an unhappy life, even if the person has particularly miserable parents.

Recall the concept of *set point* in our discussion of weight. As it happens, there may also be a happiness set point—a person's basic level of happiness when the individual is not intentionally trying to increase his or her happiness (Sheldon & Lyubomirsky, 2007, 2012). Like weight, the happiness level may fluctuate around this set point. In investigating how to increase happiness, we must consider the role of this powerful starting spot, which is likely the result of genetic factors and personal disposition.

Other factors also complicate the pursuit of happiness. As we shall see, these include getting caught up on the hedonic treadmill and making happiness itself the direct goal.

Obstacles in the Pursuit of Happiness

The first key challenge individuals encounter in trying to increase their happiness is the hedonic (meaning "related to pleasure") treadmill (Brickman & Campbell, 1971; Fredrick & Loewenstein, 1999). The term *hedonic treadmill* captures the idea that any aspect of life that enhances one's positive feelings is likely to do so for only a short time, because individuals generally adapt to any life change that would presumably influence their happiness.

Winning the lottery, moving into a dream home, or falling in love may lead to temporary gains in the experience of joy, but eventually people go back to their baseline (Schkade & Kahneman, 1998). What a person first experiences as a life-changing improvement eventually fades to a routine (but still necessary) aspect of life, all too soon to be taken for granted. How can individuals increase their happiness if such pleasure enhancers lose their power?

A second obstacle in the goal of enhancing happiness is that pursuing happiness for its own sake is rarely a good way to get happy or happier. When happiness is the goal, the pursuit is likely to backfire (Schooler, Ariely, & Loewenstein, 2003). Indeed, those who explicitly link the pursuit of their everyday goals to happiness fare quite poorly (McIntosh, Harlow, & Martin, 1995).

In light of this difficult path, how can we enhance our happiness without having any new capacity for joy become ho-hum? How might we achieve happiness *without trying to* pursue it?

© SW Productions/Getty Images

Happiness Activities and Goal Striving

Sonja Lyubomirsky and her colleagues have suggested a promising approach to enhancing happiness (Lyubomirsky, 2011, 2013; Sheldon & Lyubomirsky, 2007, 2012; Sin & Lyubomirsky, 2009). Lyubomirsky proposes beginning with intentional activities. For example, she notes that physical activity, kindness, and positive self-reflection all enhance positive affect (Lyubomirsky & others, 2011a, 2011b; Sheldon & Lyubomirsky, 2007). Engaging in altruistic behavior—habitually helping others, especially through a wide range of acts of service—is another powerful way to enhance happiness, according to Lyubomirsky (2008, 2013).

One technique for engaging in positive self-reflection is to keep a gratitude journal. Studies by Robert Emmons and Michael McCullough (2004) have demonstrated the ways that being grateful can lead to enhanced happiness and psychological well-being. In one study, they asked individuals to keep a diary in which the participants counted their blessings every day. Those who counted their blessings were better off on various measures of well-being. Although some individuals seem to be naturally more grateful than others, experimental evidence indicates that even people who are not naturally grateful can benefit from taking a moment to count their blessings (Emmons & McCullough, 2003).

Another potentially useful approach to enhancing happiness is to commit to the pursuit of personally meaningful goals. Stop for a minute and write down the things you are typically trying to accomplish in your everyday behavior. You might identify a goal such as "to get better grades" or "to be a good friend (or partner or parent)." Such everyday goals and the pursuit of them have been shown to relate strongly to subjective well-being (Brunstein, 1993; Sheldon, 2002). Goal pursuit provides the glue that meaningfully relates a chain of life events, endowing life with beginnings, middles, and ends (King, 2008).

The scientific literature on goal investment offers a variety of ideas about the types of goals that are likely to enhance happiness. To optimize the happiness payoffs of goal pursuit, one ought to set goals that are important and personally valuable and that reflect the intrinsic needs of relatedness, competence, and autonomy (Sheldon, 2002). These goals also should be moderately challenging and should share an instrumental relationship with each other—so that the pursuit of one goal facilitates the accomplishment of another (Emmons & King, 1988).

With regard to the hedonic treadmill, goal pursuit has a tremendous advantage over many other ways of trying to enhance happiness. Goals change and are changed by life experience. As a result, goal pursuit may be less susceptible to the dreaded hedonic treadmill over time. Goals accentuate the positive but do not necessarily eliminate the negative. When we fail to reach our goals, we may experience momentary increases in unhappiness (Pomerantz, Saxon, & Oishi, 2000), which can be a very good thing. Because goals can make us happy and unhappy, they keep life emotionally interesting, and their influence on happiness does not wear off over time.

Overall, goal pursuit may lead to a happier life. Goals keep the positive possible and interesting. The conclusion to be drawn from the evidence, assuming that you want to enhance your happiness, is to strive mightily for the goals that you value. You may fail now and then, but missing the mark will only make your successes all the sweeter.

test yourself

1. Explain the term *hedonic treadmill* and give some real-world examples of it.

2. According to Lyubomirsky, how can individuals cultivate positive emotion?

3. How does committing oneself to personally meaningful goals relate to well-being?

SUMMARY

1. THEORIES OF MOTIVATION

Motivated behavior is energized, directed, and sustained. Early evolutionary theorists considered motivation to be based on instinct—the innate biological pattern of behavior.

A drive is an aroused state that occurs because of a physiological need or deprivation. Drive reduction theory was proposed as an explanation of motivation, with the goal of drive reduction being homeostasis: the body's tendency to maintain equilibrium.

Optimum arousal theory focuses on the Yerkes–Dodson law, which states that performance is best under conditions of moderate rather than low or high arousal. Moderate arousal often serves us best, but there are times when low or high arousal is linked with better performance.

2. HUNGER, OBESITY, AND EATING DISORDERS

Stomach signals are one factor in hunger. Glucose (blood sugar) and insulin both play an important role in hunger. Glucose is needed for the brain to function, and low levels of glucose increase hunger. Insulin can cause a rise in hunger.

Leptin, a protein secreted by fat cells, decreases food intake and increases energy expenditure. The hypothalamus plays an important role in regulating hunger. The lateral hypothalamus is involved in stimulating eating; the ventromedial hypothalamus, in restricting eating.

Obesity is a serious problem in the United States. Heredity, basal metabolism, set point, and fat cells are biological factors involved in obesity. Time and place affect eating. Our early ancestors ate fruits to satisfy nutritional needs, but today we fill up on the empty calories in sweets.

Three eating disorders are anorexia nervosa, bulimia nervosa, and binge eating disorder. Anorexia nervosa is characterized by extreme underweight and starvation. Anorexia nervosa is related to perfectionism and obsessive-compulsive tendencies. Bulimia nervosa involves a pattern of binge eating followed by purging through self-induced vomiting or laxatives. Binge eating disorder involves binge eating without purging.

Anorexia nervosa and bulimia nervosa are much more common in women than men, but there is no gender difference in binge eating disorder. Although sociocultural factors were once thought to be primary in explaining eating disorders, more recent evidence points to the role of biological factors.

3. APPROACHES TO MOTIVATION IN EVERYDAY LIFE

According to Maslow's hierarchy of needs, our main needs are satisfied in this sequence: physiological needs, safety, love and belongingness, esteem, and self-actualization. Maslow gave the most attention to self-actualization: the motivation to develop to one's full potential.

Self-determination theory states that intrinsic motivation occurs when individuals are engaged in the pursuit of organismic needs that are innate and universal. These needs include competence, relatedness, and autonomy. Intrinsic motivation is based on internal factors. Extrinsic motivation is based on external factors, such as rewards and punishments.

Self-regulation involves setting goals, monitoring progress, and making adjustments in behavior to attain desired outcomes. Research

suggests that setting intermediate goals on the path toward a long-term goal is a good strategy.

4. EMOTION

Emotion is feeling, or affect, that has three components: physiological arousal, conscious experience, and behavioral expression. The biology of emotion focuses on physiological arousal involving the autonomic nervous system and its two subsystems. Skin conductance level and the polygraph have been used to measure emotional arousal.

The James–Lange theory states that emotion results from physiological states triggered by environmental stimuli: Emotion follows physiological reactions. The Cannon–Bard theory states that emotion and physiological reactions occur simultaneously. Contemporary biological views of emotion increasingly highlight neural circuitry and neurotransmitters. LeDoux has charted the neural circuitry of fear, which focuses on the amygdalae and consists of two pathways, one direct and the other indirect. It is likely that positive and negative emotions use different neural circuitry and neurotransmitters.

Schachter and Singer's two-factor theory states that emotion is the result of both physiological arousal and cognitive labeling. Lazarus believed that cognition always directs emotion, but Zajonc argued that emotion directs cognition. Both probably were right.

Research on the behavioral component of emotion focuses on facial expressions. The facial feedback hypothesis states that facial expressions can influence emotions, as well as reflect them.

Many psychologists believe that facial expressions of basic emotions are the same across cultures. However, display rules—nonverbal signals of body movement, posture, and gesture—vary across cultures. Differences in emoticons across cultures reinforce the idea that display rules are culture-dependent.

Emotions can be classified based on valence (pleasant or unpleasant) and arousal (high or low). Using the dimensions of valence and arousal, emotions can be arranged in a circle, or circumplex model. Emotions may also be classified in terms of whether they suggest approach or avoidance motivation.

Positive emotions may play a role in well-being by broadening our focus and allowing us to build resources. Resilience is an individual's capacity to thrive even during difficult times. Research has shown that one way resilient individuals thrive is by experiencing positive emotions.

5. MOTIVATION, EMOTION, AND HEALTH AND WELLNESS: THE PURSUIT OF HAPPINESS

Happiness is highly heritable, and there is reason to consider each person as having a happiness set point. Still, many people would like to increase their level of happiness. One obstacle to changing happiness is the hedonic treadmill: the idea that we quickly adapt to changes that might enhance happiness. Another obstacle is that pursuing happiness for its own sake often backfires.

Ways to enhance happiness include engaging in physical activity, helping others, engaging in positive self-reflection, and experiencing meaning (such as by keeping a gratitude journal). Another way to enhance happiness is to pursue personally valued goals passionately.

key *terms*

anorexia nervosa	emotion	James–Lange theory	self-actualization
binge eating disorder (BED)	extrinsic motivation	motivation	self-determination theory
broaden-and-build model	facial feedback hypothesis	need	self-regulation
bulimia nervosa	hierarchy of needs	negative affect	set point
Cannon–Bard theory	homeostasis	overlearning	two-factor theory of emotion
display rules	instinct	polygraph	Yerkes–Dodson law
drive	intrinsic motivation	positive affect	

apply your *knowledge*

1. Ask your friends and your parents to define the word *motivation*. Compare your friends' and parents' definitions with the way psychologists define and approach motivation. What are the similarities? What are the differences? How do the definitions of your friends differ from those of your parents? Why do you think all of these variations exist?

2. To explore your own goals and sense of purpose, try the following activity. First list the top 5 or 10 goals that you are trying to accomplish in your everyday behavior. Then write your responses to the following questions that William Damon used in his interviews (Damon, 2008):

   - Do you have any long-term goals?
   - What does it mean to have a good life?
   - What does it mean to be a good person?
   - If you were looking back on your life now, how would you like to be remembered?

   Finally, consider: Are your everyday goals leading to the fulfillment of your long-term dream? How are you working in your everyday behavior to achieve your grander purposes?

3. Some psychologists believe that the ability to identify and regulate one's emotions is a kind of intelligence. Emotionally intelligent people are also thought to be better at reading the emotional expressions of others. Do a web search for "emotional intelligence tests" and take some online quizzes, or try the one at http://testyourself.psychtests.com/testid/3038. Do you think you are emotionally intelligent? Does your performance on the test seem to reflect your actual experience? What is your opinion of the test you tried? Is there information on the site showing its validity and reliability?

4. This chapter reviewed the use of autonomic nervous system activity in the detection of deception. Psychologists have devised various ways to detect lying. Go online and search for information on detecting deception and lies. Is there a good way to tell if someone is being truthful? Explain.

CHAPTER 12

Personality

Getting in Trouble Just Like in the Old Days

Thanks to social media, keeping track of long-lost friends is easier than it used to be. Looking at Facebook posts from someone you knew in first grade, you probably recognize that person as the friend you had from long ago.

Friendships are like that. Betty James and Joan Ellis were best friends at the age of 11 when they went to the same school in England, back in the 1930s. Together they had many great times, sometimes getting into trouble for being too noisy and disruptive. The girls drifted apart, however, and each went on to lead a long and happy life: marrying, having children, grandchildren, and great-grandchildren. They had not seen each other in 80 years when Joan spotted Betty walking by. These old friends, now age 92, were practically neighbors in their retirement community. Now, they spend at least two days a week together, chatting and laughing like always. And, they get complaints for being too loud and disruptive, just like old times (Butt, 2015).

How is it possible to feel that way, after eight decades? Surely, for Joan and Betty many things had changed, but something about each of them remained the same. There is something about each person that makes that person who he or she is—that makes the person recognizable as those who "knew them when," whether from the first day of school, at summer camp, or in college. Age and life experiences can change us, but something about us endures throughout life. That "something" is personality, the focus of this chapter. ●

394 CHAPTER 12 Personality

PREVIEW

Personality psychology explores the psychological attributes that underlie who we really are—the unified and enduring core characteristics that account for our existence as one and the same person throughout the life span. In this chapter, we survey the field of personality from a variety of perspectives. We begin with classic theories from psychodynamic and humanistic thinkers and then examine more contemporary approaches, including the trait, life story, social cognitive, and biological perspectives. We then look at personality assessment. Finally, we consider the role of personality in health and wellness.

1. PSYCHODYNAMIC PERSPECTIVES

● **personality** A pattern of enduring, distinctive thoughts, emotions, and behaviors that characterize the way an individual adapts to the world.

● **psychodynamic perspectives** Theoretical views emphasizing that personality is primarily unconscious (beyond awareness).

Personality is a pattern of enduring, distinctive thoughts, emotions, and behaviors that characterize the way an individual adapts to the world. Psychologists have approached these enduring characteristics in a variety of ways, focusing on different aspects of the person.

Psychodynamic perspectives on personality emphasize that personality is primarily unconscious. According to this viewpoint, the enduring patterns that make up personality are largely unavailable to our conscious awareness, and they powerfully shape our behaviors in ways that we cannot readily comprehend (Bornstein, Denckla, & Chung, 2013). Psychodynamic theorists use the word *unconscious* differently from how other psychologists do. From the psychodynamic perspective, aspects of our personality are unconscious because they *must* be: These mysterious, unconscious forces are simply too frightening to be part of our awareness (Barratt, 2015).

Psychodynamic theorists believe that behavior is only a surface characteristic and that to truly understand someone's personality, we have to explore the symbolic meanings of that behavior and the deep inner workings of the mind (Elliot, 2015). Psychodynamic theorists also stress that early childhood experience shapes adult personality. The psychodynamic view of personality was introduced by Sigmund Freud.

Freud's Psychoanalytic Theory

Sigmund Freud, one of the most influential thinkers of the twentieth century, was born in Freiberg, Moravia (today part of the Czech Republic), in 1856 and died in London at the age of 83. Freud spent most of his life in Vienna, leaving that city near the end of his career to escape the Holocaust.

Freud has had such a phenomenal impact that just about everyone has an opinion about him, even those who have never studied his work. If you ask others what they think of Freud, you will likely get a variety of interesting answers. Some might comment that Freud was a cocaine addict. Freud did use cocaine early in his career, but he stopped using the drug when he learned of its harmful effects. Others might claim that Freud hated women. As we will see, Freud's theory of development did include the notion that women are morally inferior to men. However, Freud was never satisfied with his approach to the psychology of women. He welcomed women interested in pursuing careers in psychoanalysis, and many of his earliest followers were women. Finally, people might declare that Freud thought everything was about sex. That claim, it turns out, is true, except that by *sex* Freud did not mean sexual activity in the usual sense. Freud defined sex as organ pleasure. *Anything* that is pleasurable is sex, according to Freud.

For Freud, the sexual drive was the most important motivator in human life. Freud thought that the human sex drive was the main determinant of personality development, and he felt that psychological disorders, dreams, and all human behavior represent the conflict between unconscious sexual drive and the demands of civilized human society.

Sigmund Freud (1856–1939) Freud's theories have strongly influenced how people in Western cultures view themselves and the world.

©Hulton-Deutsch Collection/Getty Images

Freud developed *psychoanalysis,* his approach to personality, through his work with patients suffering from hysteria. *Hysteria* refers to physical symptoms that have no physical cause. For instance, a person might be unable to see, even with perfectly healthy eyes, or unable to walk, despite having no physical injury.

In Freud's day (the Victorian era, a time marked by strict rules regarding sex), many young women suffered from hysterical symptoms, physical problems that could not be explained by actual physical illness. In his practice, Freud spent long hours listening to these women talk about their symptoms. Freud came to understand that the hysterical symptoms stemmed from unconscious conflicts, centered on experiences in which the person's drive for pleasure was thwarted by the social pressures of Victorian society. Moreover, the particular symptoms were related symbolically to these underlying conflicts.

For instance, one of Freud's patients, Fraulein Elisabeth Von R., suffered from leg pains that prevented her from standing or walking. Through analysis, Freud discovered that Fraulein Elisabeth had had a number of experiences in which she wanted nothing more than to take a walk but had been prevented from doing so by her duty to her ill father. Fraulein Elisabeth's symptoms were not due to a single experience, but rather to *many repeated* experiences, all related to walking.

Based on such observations, Freud concluded that hysterical symptoms were *overdetermined,* meaning that those symptoms had *many* causes in the unconscious. Eventually, Freud came to use hysterical symptoms as his metaphor for understanding dreams, slips of the tongue, and all human behavior. Everything we do, he said, has a multitude of unconscious causes.

Drawing from his analyses of patients (as well as himself), Freud developed a model of human personality. He saw personality as like an iceberg, existing mostly below the level of awareness, just as the massive part of an iceberg lies beneath the surface of the water. Figure 1 illustrates this analogy and depicts the extensiveness of the unconscious part of our mind, in Freud's view. Notice how only the tiniest bit of the personality is the conscious mind. Most of who we are is cloaked in the unconscious.

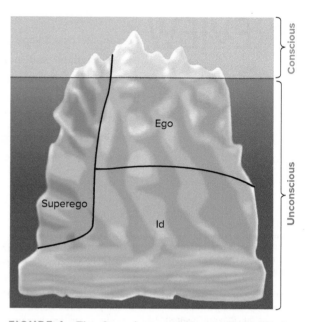

FIGURE 1 **The Conscious and Unconscious Mind** The iceberg can be used as an analogy to illustrate how much of the mind is unconscious in Freud's theory. The conscious mind is the part of the iceberg above water; the unconscious mind is the part below water. Notice that the id is totally unconscious, whereas the ego and the superego can operate at either the conscious or the unconscious level.

STRUCTURES OF PERSONALITY

The three structures of personality described by Freud are shown in Figure 1. Freud (1924) called these structures the id, the ego, and the superego. You can get a better feel for these Latin labels by considering their English translations: The id is literally the "it," the ego is the "I," and the superego is the "above-I."

The **id** consists of unconscious drives and is the individual's reservoir of sexual energy. This "it" is a pool of amoral and often vile urges pressing for expression. In Freud's view, the id has no contact with reality. The id works according to the *pleasure principle:* the Freudian concept that the id seeks immediate gratification.

The world would be pretty scary if personalities were all id. As young children mature, they learn that they cannot act on every impulse. They cannot snatch every candy or slug other children. They must negotiate with others to get the things they want. As children experience the constraints of reality, a new element of personality is formed—the **ego,** the Freudian structure of personality that deals with the demands of reality. According to Freud, the ego abides by the *reality principle.* It tries to get the id what it wants within the norms of society. Whereas the id is completely unconscious, the ego is partly conscious. It houses our higher mental functions—reasoning, problem solving, and decision making, for example.

The id and ego do not consider whether something is right or wrong. Rather, the **superego** is the harsh internal judge of our behavior. The superego is reflected in what we often call conscience and evaluates the morality of our behavior.

The ego acts as a mediator between the conflicting demands of the id and the superego, as well as the real world. Your ego might say, for example, "I will have sex only

• **id** The Freudian structure of personality consisting of unconscious drives; the individual's reservoir of sexual energy.

• **ego** The Freudian structure of personality that deals with the demands of reality.

• **superego** The Freudian structure of personality that serves as the harsh internal judge of our behavior; what we often call conscience.

in a committed relationship and always practice safe sex." Your id, however, screams, "Sex! Now!" and your superego commands, "Sex? Don't even think about it."

DEFENSE MECHANISMS

The conflicts that erupt among the demands of the id, the superego, and reality create a great deal of anxiety for the ego. The ego has strategies for dealing with this anxiety, called defense mechanisms. **Defense mechanisms** are tactics the ego uses to *reduce* anxiety by unconsciously *distorting* reality. For example, imagine that Jason's id is pressing to express an unconscious desire to have sex with his mother. Clearly, acting on this impulse would not please the superego or society at large. If he became aware of this impulse, Jason might recoil in horror. Instead, Jason's ego might use a defense mechanism of *displacement*. Displacement means directing unacceptable impulses at a less threatening target. So, Jason might develop a relationship with a girlfriend who looks and acts like his mother. Through displacement, the ego allows Jason to express his id impulse in a way that will not land him in trouble. Of course, Jason's friends might chuckle at the resemblance between his mother and his girlfriend, but you can bet that Jason will never notice.

Figure 2 describes several defense mechanisms, many of which were introduced and developed by Freud's daughter Anna, who followed in her father's career footsteps. All defense mechanisms reduce anxiety by distorting reality. Defense mechanisms are unconscious; we are not aware that we are calling on them.

Repression is the most powerful and pervasive defense mechanism. To reduce the anxiety caused by unacceptable id impulses, repression pushes these impulses back into the unconscious. Freud said, for example, that our early childhood experiences, many of which he believed were sexually laden, are too threatening for us to deal with consciously, so we reduce the anxiety of childhood conflict through repression.

● **defense mechanisms** The Freudian term for tactics the ego uses to reduce anxiety by unconsciously distorting reality.

Defense Mechanism	How It Works	Example
Repression	The master defense mechanism; the ego pushes unacceptable impulses out of awareness, back into the unconscious mind.	A young girl was sexually abused by her uncle. As an adult, she can't remember anything about the traumatic experience.
Rationalization	The ego replaces a less acceptable motive with a more acceptable one.	A college student does not get into the fraternity of his choice. He tells himself that the fraternity is very exclusive and that a lot of students could not get in.
Displacement	The ego shifts feelings toward an unacceptable object to another, more acceptable object.	A woman can't take her anger out on her boss, so she goes home and takes it out on her husband.
Sublimation	The ego replaces an unacceptable impulse with a socially acceptable one.	A man with strong sexual urges becomes an artist who paints nudes.
Projection	The ego attributes personal shortcomings, problems, and faults to others.	A man who has a strong desire to have an extramarital affair accuses his wife of flirting with other men.
Reaction Formation	The ego transforms an unacceptable motive into its opposite.	A woman who fears her sexual urges becomes a religious zealot.
Denial	The ego refuses to acknowledge anxiety-producing realities.	A man won't acknowledge that he has cancer even though a team of doctors has diagnosed his cancer.
Regression	The ego seeks the security of an earlier developmental period in the face of stress.	A woman returns home to mother every time she and her husband have a big argument.

FIGURE 2   Defense Mechanisms Defense mechanisms reduce anxiety in various ways, in all instances by distorting reality.

Defense mechanisms have been used to explain prejudice—that is, holding negative attitudes toward a group of people because of their race, ethnicity, or other characteristic. The defense mechanism of *projection* involves seeing the impulses a person fears in him- or herself in others. We might say that prejudicial attitudes involve projecting one's own impulses onto others.

PSYCHOSEXUAL STAGES OF PERSONALITY DEVELOPMENT

Freud believed that human beings go through universal stages of personality development and that at each developmental stage we experience sexual pleasure in one part of the body more than in others. Each stage is named for the location of sexual pleasure at that stage. *Erogenous zones* are parts of the body that have especially strong pleasure-giving qualities at particular stages of development.

- *Oral stage (first 18 months):* The infant's pleasure centers on the mouth. Sucking, chewing, and biting are the chief sources of pleasure that reduce tension in the infant.

- *Anal stage (18 to 36 months):* During a time when most children are experiencing toilet training, the child's greatest pleasure involves the anus and urethra and their functions. Freud recognized that there is pleasure in "going" and "holding it" as well as in the experience of control over one's parents in deciding when to do either.

- *Phallic stage (3 to 6 years):* The name of Freud's third stage comes from the Latin word *phallus,* which means "penis." Pleasure focuses on the genitals as the child discovers that self-stimulation is enjoyable.

  In Freud's view, the phallic stage has a special importance in personality development because it triggers the Oedipus complex. This name comes from the Greek tragedy in which Oedipus unknowingly kills his father and marries his mother. The **Oedipus complex** is the boy's intense desire to replace his father and enjoy the affections of his mother. Eventually, the boy recognizes that his father might punish him for these incestuous wishes, specifically by cutting off the boy's penis. *Castration anxiety* refers to the boy's intense fear of being mutilated by his father. To reduce this conflict, the boy identifies with his father, adopting the male gender role. The intense castration anxiety is repressed into the unconscious and serves as the foundation for the development of the superego.

  Freud recognized differences between boys and girls in the phallic stage. Because a girl does not have a penis, she cannot experience castration anxiety, Freud reasoned. Instead, she compares herself to boys and realizes that she is missing something—a penis—and thus experiences not castration anxiety but "castration completed," resulting in *penis envy*—the intense desire to obtain a penis by eventually marrying and bearing a son. Without castration anxiety, a girl cannot develop a superego in the same sense that boys do. In this way, for Freud, anatomy is destiny: The physical fact that girls lack a penis means they cannot develop a superego. Thus, Freud concluded, women are morally inferior to men.

  Although noting that his views ran counter to the feminist thinkers of his time, Freud stood firm that the sexes are not equal in every way. He considered women to be somewhat childlike in their development and thought it was good that fathers, and eventually husbands, should guide them through life. He asserted that the only hope for women's moral development is education.

- *Latency period (6 years to puberty):* This phase is not a developmental stage but rather a kind of psychic time-out. After the drama of the phallic stage, the child sets aside all interest in sexuality.

- *Genital stage (adolescence and adulthood):* The genital stage is the time of sexual reawakening, a point when the source of sexual pleasure shifts to someone outside the family. Freud believed that in adulthood, individuals become capable of the two hallmarks of maturity: love and work. However, Freud felt that human beings are inevitably subject to intense conflict, reasoning that everyone, no matter how well adjusted, still has an id pressing for expression. Adulthood, even in the best of circumstances, still involves reliving the unconscious conflicts of childhood.

● **Oedipus complex** According to Freud, a boy's intense desire to replace his father and enjoy the affections of his mother.

Stage	Adult Extensions (Fixations)	Sublimations	Reaction Formations
Oral	Smoking, eating, kissing, oral hygiene, drinking, chewing gum	Seeking knowledge, humor, wit, sarcasm, being a food or wine expert	Speech purist, food faddist, prohibitionist, dislike of milk
Anal	Notable interest in one's bowel movements, love of bathroom humor, extreme messiness; or, alternatively, extreme cleanliness, stubbornness, and a strong desire for simplicity and structure	Interest in painting or sculpture, being overly giving, great interest in statistics	Extreme disgust with feces, fear of dirt, prudishness, irritability
Phallic	Heavy reliance on masturbation, flirtatiousness, expressions of virility	Interest in poetry, love of love, interest in acting, striving for success	Puritanical attitude toward sex, excessive modesty

FIGURE 3 Defense Mechanisms and Freudian Stages If a person is fixated at a psychosexual stage, the fixation can color his or her personality in many ways, including the defense mechanisms the person might use to cope with anxiety.

Freud argued that the individual may become stuck in any of these developmental stages if he or she is overdisciplined or overindulged at a given stage. For example, a parent might wean a child too early (or not early enough) or be too strict (or too lax) in toilet training. *Fixation* occurs when a particular psychosexual stage colors an individual's adult personality. For instance, an *anal retentive* person (someone who is obsessively neat and organized) is fixated at the anal stage. The construct of fixation thus explains how, according to Freud, childhood experiences can have an enormous impact on adult personality. Figure 3 illustrates possible links between adult personality characteristics and fixation at the oral, anal, and phallic stages.

Psychodynamic Critics and Revisionists

Because Freud was among the first theorists to explore personality, some of his ideas have needed updating and revision over time, while others have been tossed out altogether. In particular, Freud's critics have said that his ideas about sexuality, early experience, social factors, and the unconscious mind were misguided (Adler, 1927; Erikson, 1968; Friedman, Alfonso, & Downey, 2015; Fromm, 1947; Horney, 1945; Jung, 1917; Kohut, 1977; Rapaport, 1967; Sullivan, 1953). They stress the following points:

- Sexuality is not the pervasive force that Freud believed it to be. Furthermore, the Oedipus complex is not as universal as Freud maintained. Freud's concepts were heavily influenced by the setting in which he lived—turn-of-the-century Vienna, a society that, compared with contemporary society, was sexually repressed and male-dominated.

- The first five years of life are not as powerful in shaping adult personality as Freud thought. Later experiences warrant attention.

- The ego and conscious thought processes play a larger role in personality than Freud believed. Achievement, thinking, and reasoning are not always tied to sexual impulses.

- Sociocultural factors are much more important than Freud believed. In stressing the id's dominance, Freud placed more emphasis on the biological basis of personality. More contemporary psychodynamic scholars have especially emphasized the interpersonal setting of the family and the role of early social relationships in personality development (Bornstein, Denckla, & Chung, 2013).

A number of dissenters and revisionists to Freud's theory have been influential in the development of psychodynamic theories. Erik Erikson, whose psychosocial stages we examined in the chapter "Human Development", is among these. Here we briefly consider three other thinkers—Karen Horney, Carl Jung, and Alfred Adler—who made notable revisions to Freud's approach.

HORNEY'S SOCIOCULTURAL APPROACH

Karen Horney (1885–1952) rejected the notion that anatomy is destiny. She argued that sociocultural influences on personality development should be investigated as well (Schultz & Schultz, 2016). Consider Freud's concept of penis envy. Horney pointed out that women might envy the penis not because of unconscious issues but because of the status that society bestows on those who have one. Further, she suggested that both sexes envy the attributes of the other, with men coveting women's reproductive capacities (Horney, 1967).

Horney believed that the need for security, not sex, is the prime motive in human existence. She reasoned that an individual whose needs for security are met should be able to develop his or her capacities to the fullest extent. She viewed psychological health as allowing the person to express talents and abilities freely and spontaneously.

JUNG'S ANALYTICAL THEORY

Freud's contemporary Carl Jung (1875–1961) shared Freud's interest in the unconscious, but he believed that Freud underplayed the role of the unconscious mind in personality. In fact, Jung believed that the roots of personality go back to the dawn of humanity.

The **collective unconscious** is Jung's term for the impersonal, deepest layer of the unconscious mind, shared by all human beings because of their common ancestral past. Describing the collective unconscious as "impersonal" emphasizes that it is the same, across all humanity. In Jung's theory, the experiences of a common past have made a deep, permanent impression on the human mind (Hunt, 2012).

Jung posited that the collective unconscious contains **archetypes,** emotionally laden ideas and images that have symbolic meaning for all people. Jung concluded that these archetypes emerge in art, literature, religion, and dreams (Faber & Mayer, 2009; Morgan, 2012; Neumann, 2015). Archetypes are essentially predispositions to respond to the environment in particular ways.

Jung used the terms *anima* and *animus* to identify two common archetypes. He believed each of us has a passive feminine side—the anima—and an assertive masculine side—the animus. The *persona* is another archetype. Jung thought that the persona represents the public mask that we all wear during social interactions; he believed that it is an essential archetype because the persona allows us always to keep some secret part of ourselves hidden from others.

ADLER'S INDIVIDUAL PSYCHOLOGY

Alfred Adler (1870–1937) was one of Freud's earliest followers, although his relationship with Freud was quite brief and his approach to personality was drastically different. In Adler's **individual psychology,** people are motivated by purposes and goals—thus, perfection, not pleasure, is the key motivator in human life. Adler argued that people have the ability to take their genetic inheritance and their environmental experiences and act upon them creatively to become the person they want to be.

Adler thought that everyone strives for superiority by seeking to adapt, improve, and master the environment (Kern & Curlette, 2015). Striving for superiority is our response to the uncomfortable feelings of inferiority that we experience as infants and young children when we interact with bigger, more powerful people. *Compensation* is Adler's term for the individual's attempt to overcome imagined or real inferiorities or weaknesses by developing one's own abilities. Adler believed that compensation is normal, and he said that we often make up for a weakness in one ability by excelling in a different one. For example, a person of small stature and limited physical abilities (like Adler himself) might compensate by excelling in academics (Abramson, 2015).

Adler (1928) believed that birth order could have a profound influence on personality. He viewed firstborn children to be in a particularly vulnerable state given that they begin life as the center of attention but then are knocked off their pedestal by their siblings.

Karen Horney (1885–1952) Horney developed the first feminist criticism of Freud's theory. Horney's view emphasizes women's positive qualities and self-evaluation.

©Bettmann/Getty Images

Carl Jung (1875–1961) Swiss psychoanalytic theorist Jung developed the concepts of the collective unconscious and archetypes.

© Douglas Glass/Paul Popper/Popperfoto/Getty Images

● **collective unconscious** Jung's term for the impersonal, deepest layer of the unconscious mind, shared by all human beings because of their common ancestral past.

● **archetypes** Jung's term for emotionally laden ideas and images in the collective unconscious that have rich and symbolic meaning for all people.

● **individual psychology** Adler's view that people are motivated by purposes and goals and that perfection, not pleasure, is thus the key motivator in human life.

CRITICAL CONTROVERSY

Does Birth Order Affect Personality?

Alfred Adler's ideas about birth order strike a chord with many people. Adler is certainly not the only person to posit an association between birth order and personality. Other psychologists have also proposed that being born first, second, or third can influence personality and behavior (Sulloway, 2010).

Here are some common beliefs about birth order: Firstborns are natural leaders; "babies of the family" are indulged; middle children are neglected (like Jan Brady). Ask yourself, what is the typical firstborn, middle, or youngest child like? Chances are, if you have siblings (and even if you do not), you have some hypotheses about the way birth order relates to personality. Do these naive theories have a kernel of truth? The answer to that question might surprise you. Let's take a look at the data.

The earliest studies of this research question were limited by a variety of issues. They often had small samples, which are unlikely to identify replicable results, and they failed to account for family size (Damian & Roberts, 2015b). Family size is an important potential "third variable" because it is entwined with birth order: You cannot be a middle child if you have no siblings.

Recent impressive research examining the relationship between birth order and personality characteristics has included very large samples: nearly 400,000 U.S. teenagers (Damian & Roberts, 2015a) as well as over 5,000 U.S. adults, nearly 5,000 British adults, and over 10,000 German teens and adults (Rohrer, Egloff, & Schmukle, 2015). For each of the samples, participants completed measures of personality characteristics. Information was collected about birth order, family size, socioeconomic status, and

© Tanya Little/Moment/Getty Images

other potential third variables. In addition, the studies compared individuals across different families (for example, comparing all firstborns to all secondborns) as well as within families (comparing siblings to each other). Because the research used very large samples, included a host of potential confounds, and employed the most sophisticated analytical tools, the investigators were very well positioned to find links between birth order and personality, if those links existed.

The results? For all of the samples, the relationship between birth order and personality was, essentially, *zero*. Birth order was unrelated to personality characteristics. For example, firstborns *were not* more likely to have leadership characteristics nor were they more responsible (Damian & Roberts, 2015a; Rohrer, Egloff, & Schmukle, 2015). The lack of associations held as well across genders: Whether older brothers or sisters were compared to younger brothers and sisters, no systematic differences in personality characteristics were found.

The results were very clear-cut, yet the intuition that birth order matters to personality seems to persist. In fact, some researchers refer to the idea that birth order predicts personality as "zombie theory," one that should die but somehow simply won't (Damian & Roberts, 2015b). Perhaps the biggest mystery of all is why the idea that personality is linked to birth order is so compelling.

WHAT DO YOU THINK?
- Are you convinced that birth order bears no relationship to personality? Why or why not?
- Where do your beliefs about personality and birth order originate?

Adler believed that the firstborn are more likely to suffer from psychological disorders and to engage in criminal behavior. Youngest children, however, also are potentially in trouble because they are most likely to be spoiled.

The healthiest birth order? According to Adler, those (including Adler) who are middle children are in a particularly advantageous situation because they have older siblings as built-in inspiration for superiority striving. Importantly, though, Adler did not believe that anyone is doomed by birth order. Rather, sensitive parents could help children in any position in the family to negotiate their needs for superiority.

Many students (but especially middle children) find Adler's approach to the effects of birth order on personality to be fascinating. Adler only *theorized* about birth order; he did not conduct empirical research to investigate whether birth order affects personality—either as he proposed or in any other way. To read about this topic, see the Critical Controversy.

Evaluating the Psychodynamic Perspectives

Although psychodynamic theories have diverged from Freud's original psychoanalytic version, they share some core principles:

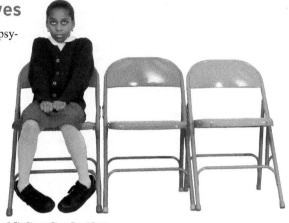

© Big Cheese Photo/PunchStock

- Personality is determined both by current experiences *and* by early life experiences.

- Personality can be better understood by examining it developmentally— as a series of stages that unfold with the individual's physical, cognitive, and socioemotional development.

- We mentally transform our experiences, giving them meaning that shapes our personality.

- The mind is not all conscious; unconscious motives lie behind some of our puzzling behavior.

- The individual's inner world often conflicts with the outer demands of reality, creating anxiety that is not easy to resolve.

- Personality and adjustment are important topics of psychological inquiry.

Psychodynamic perspectives have come under fire for a variety of reasons. Some critics say that psychodynamic theorists overemphasize the influence of early family experiences on personality and do not acknowledge that people retain the capacity for change and adaptation throughout life. Moreover, some psychologists believe that Freud and Jung put too much faith in the unconscious mind's ability to control behavior. Others complain that Freud placed too much importance on sexuality in explaining personality.

Some have argued, too, that psychoanalysis is not a theory that researchers can test through empirical studies. However, numerous empirical studies on concepts such as defense mechanisms and the unconscious have proved this criticism to be unfounded (Cramer, 2008a, 2008b, 2009a, 2009b; Weinstein & others, 2012). At the same time, we could look at this argument about empirical testing of psychoanalysis in a different way: Although it is certainly possible to test hypotheses derived from psychoanalytic theory through research, the question remains whether psychoanalytically oriented individuals who believe strongly in Freud's ideas would be open to research results that call for serious changes in the theory.

In light of these criticisms, it may be hard to appreciate why Freud continues to have an impact on psychology. It is useful to keep in mind that Freud made a number of important contributions, including being the first to propose that childhood is crucial to later functioning, that development might be understood in terms of stages, and that unconscious processes might play a significant role in human life (Benet-Martínez & others, 2015).

test yourself

1. What three structures of personality did Freud describe, and how did he define each?
2. What are Freud's psychosexual stages of personality development?
3. What criticisms have been leveled at psychodynamic theories of personality?

2. HUMANISTIC PERSPECTIVES

Humanistic perspectives stress a person's capacity for personal growth and positive human qualities. Humanistic psychologists believe that we all have the ability to control our lives and to achieve what we desire.

Such perspectives contrast with both psychodynamic perspectives and behaviorism, discussed in the chapter "Learning". Humanistic theorists sought to move beyond Freudian psychoanalysis and behaviorism to a theory that might capture the rich and potentially positive aspects of human nature.

● **humanistic perspectives** Theoretical views stressing a person's capacity for personal growth and positive human qualities.

Maslow's Approach

A leading architect of the humanistic movement was Abraham Maslow (1908–1970), whose hierarchy of needs we considered in the chapter "Motivation and Emotion". Maslow believed that we can learn the most about human personality by focusing on the very best examples of human beings—self-actualizers.

Carl Rogers (1902–1987) Rogers was a pioneer in the development of the humanistic perspective.

©Michael Rougier/The LIFE Picture Collection/Getty Images

● **unconditional positive regard** Rogers's construct referring to the individual's need to be accepted, valued, and treated positively regardless of the person's behavior.

● **conditions of worth** The standards that the individual must live up to in order to receive positive regard from others.

©Thorsten Indra/Alamy

Recall that at the top of Maslow's (1954, 1971) hierarchy was the need for self-actualization. Self-actualization is the motivation to develop to one's full potential as a human being. Maslow described self-actualizers as spontaneous, creative, and possessing a childlike capacity for awe. According to Maslow, a person at this optimal level of existence would be tolerant of others, have a gentle sense of humor, and be likely to pursue the greater good. Self-actualizers also maintain a capacity for "peak experiences," or breathtaking moments of spiritual insight. As examples of self-actualized individuals, Maslow included Pablo Casals (cellist), Albert Einstein (physicist), Ralph Waldo Emerson (writer), William James (psychologist), Thomas Jefferson (politician), Eleanor Roosevelt (humanitarian, diplomat), and Albert Schweitzer (humanitarian).

Created more than 40 years ago, Maslow's list of self-actualizers is limited. Because he concentrated on people who were successful in a particular historical context, Maslow's self-actualizers include only those who had opportunities for success in that setting. Maslow listed considerably more men than women, and mostly individuals from Western cultures and of European ancestry. Today, we might add to Maslow's list individuals such as the Dalai Lama (Tenzin Gyatso), Tibetan spiritual and political leader, and Malala Yousafzai, the Pakistani girl who defied the Taliban and, even after being shot in the head, became an activist for education for girls. Both of them are winners of the Nobel Peace Prize, with Yousafzai being the youngest winner of the prize to date, at just 17 years old.

Rogers's Approach

The other key figure in the development of humanistic psychology, Carl Rogers (1902–1987), began his career as a psychotherapist struggling to understand the unhappiness of the individuals he encountered in therapy. Rogers's work established the foundations for more contemporary studies of personal growth and self-determination.

Like Freud, Rogers began his inquiry into human nature with troubled people. Based on his clinical observations, Rogers (1961) devised his own approach to personality. He believed that we are all born with the raw ingredients of a fulfilling life. We simply need the right conditions to thrive. Just as a sunflower seed, once planted in rich soil and given water and sunshine, will grow into a strong and healthy flower, all humans will flourish in the appropriate environment.

This analogy is particularly apt and reveals the differences between Rogers's view of human nature and Freud's. A sunflower seed does not have to be shaped away from its dark natural tendencies by social constraints, nor does it have to reach a difficult compromise between its vile true impulses and reality. Instead, given the appropriate environment, it will grow into a beautiful flower. Rogers believed that, similarly, each person is born with natural capacities for growth and fulfillment. We are also endowed with an innate sense—a gut feeling—that allows us to evaluate whether an experience is good or bad for us. Finally, we are all born with a need for positive regard from others. We need to be loved, liked, or accepted by people around us. As children interacting with our parents, we learn early on to value the feeling that they value us, and we gain a sense of self-worth.

EXPLAINING UNHAPPINESS

If we have innate tendencies toward growth and fulfillment, why are so many people so unhappy? The problem arises when our need for positive regard from others is not met *unconditionally*. **Unconditional positive regard** means being accepted, valued, and treated positively regardless of one's behavior. Rogers noted that often others value us only when we behave in particular ways that meet particular standards. **Conditions of worth** are the standards we must live up to in order to receive positive regard. For instance, parents might give their son positive regard only when he achieves in school or chooses a profession that they themselves value. According to Rogers, as we grow up, people who are central to our lives condition us to move away from our genuine feelings, to earn their love by pursuing those goals that they value, even if those goals do not reflect our deepest wishes.

Rogers's theory includes the idea that we develop a *self-concept,* our conscious representation of who we are and who we wish to become, during childhood. This idea is quite different from Freud's ego. For Rogers, the self-concept is the hub of human functioning. Optimally, this self-concept reflects our genuine, innate desires. However, conditions of worth can become part of the self-concept. As a result, we can become alienated from our real feelings and strive to actualize a self that does not represent our authentic desires. A person who dedicates himself or herself to such goals might be very successful by outward appearances but might feel utterly unfilled. Such an individual might be able to check off all the important boxes in life's to-do lists, and complete all that he or she is "supposed to do," but never feel truly happy.

PROMOTING OPTIMAL FUNCTIONING

To remedy this situation, Rogers believed that the person must reconnect with his or her true feelings and desires. He proposed that to achieve this reconnection, the individual must experience a relationship that includes three essential qualities: unconditional positive regard, empathy, and genuineness. We consider each in turn.

First, Rogers said that regardless of what they do, people need unconditional positive regard. Although an individual might lack unconditional positive regard in childhood, he or she can experience this unconditional acceptance from others later, in friendships and/or romantic relationships or during sessions with a therapist. Even when a person's behavior is inappropriate, obnoxious, or unacceptable, he or she still needs the respect, comfort, and love of others. Research supports the notion that an enduring, stable sense of self-esteem is more likely to emerge if we feel good about ourselves, without having to live up to external standards (Crocker & Park, 2012; Didonato & Krueger, 2010; Franck & others, 2016; Goldner, Abir, & Sachar, 2016).

Second, Rogers said that individuals can become more fulfilled by interacting with people who are empathic toward them. Empathy involves being a sensitive listener and understanding another's true feelings.

Genuineness is a third requirement in the individual's path to become fully functioning. Being genuine means being open with one's feelings and dropping all pretenses and facades. The importance that Rogers placed on the therapist's acting genuinely in the therapeutic relationship demonstrates his strong belief in the positive character of human nature. For Rogers, we can help others simply by being present for them as the authentic individuals we really are. Research on being genuine or authentic supports Rogers's assertion that being true to ourselves is associated with stable self-esteem (Davis & others, 2015; Kernis, 2003; Showers, Ditzfeld, & Zeigler-Hill, 2015) and well-being more generally (Schlegel, Hirsch, & Smith, 2013; Schlegel & others, 2013; Wickham & others, 2016).

Thus, according to Rogers, unconditional positive regard, empathy, and genuineness are three essential ingredients of healthy human relations. Anyone—a manager, teacher, counselor, member of the clergy—who is interested in promoting optimal human functioning can apply these principles.

Evaluating the Humanistic Perspectives

The humanistic perspectives emphasize that the way we perceive ourselves and the world around us is an essential element of personality. Humanistic psychologists also stress that we need to consider the whole person and the positive side of human nature (Schneider, 2009; Schultz & Schultz, 2016). Their emphasis on conscious experience has given us the view that personality contains a well of potential that can be developed to its fullest.

Some critics believe that humanistic psychologists are too optimistic about human nature. Others argue that humanistic approaches do not hold individuals accountable for their behaviors, if all negative human behavior is seen as emerging out of negative situations.

Self-determination theory, which we considered in the chapter "Motivation and Emotion", demonstrates the way that psychologists have studied humanistic ideas (Kusurkar & others, 2013; Standage & others, 2012). Their work bears witness to the enduring impact of humanistic perspectives on contemporary personality psychology.

test yourself

1. What do the humanistic perspectives on personality emphasize?
2. What name did Maslow give to the motivation to develop to one's full human potential?
3. According to Rogers, what three qualities do individuals need in order to connect with their feelings and desires? How did Rogers define each?

3. TRAIT PERSPECTIVES

If you are setting up a friend on a blind date, you are likely to describe the person in terms of his or her *traits,* or lasting personality characteristics. Trait perspectives on personality have been the dominant approach for decades.

Trait Theories

● **trait theories** Theoretical views stressing that personality consists of broad, enduring dispositions (traits) that tend to lead to characteristic responses.

According to **trait theories,** personality consists of broad, enduring dispositions that tend to lead to characteristic responses. These enduring dispositions are called *traits.* In other words, we can describe people in terms of the ways they behave, such as whether they are outgoing, friendly, private, or hostile. People who have a strong tendency to behave in certain ways are referred to as "high" on the traits; those with a weak tendency to behave in these ways are "low" on the traits. Although trait theorists differ about which traits make up personality, they agree that traits are the fundamental building blocks of personality (Ashton, Lee, & Boies, 2015; Costa & McCrae, 2013; Knežević & others, 2016).

Gordon Allport (1897–1967), sometimes referred to as the father of American personality psychology, was particularly bothered by the negative view of humanity that psychoanalysis portrayed. He rejected the notion that the unconscious was central to an understanding of personality and believed that to understand healthy people, we must focus on their lives *in the present,* not on their childhood experiences. In defining personality, Allport (1961) stressed each person's uniqueness and capacity to adapt to the environment. He was dedicated to the idea that psychology should have relevance to issues facing modern society, and his scholarship has influenced not only personality psychology but also the psychology of religion and prejudice (Allport, 1954).

Allport (1961) believed that personality psychology should focus on understanding healthy, well-adjusted individuals. He described healthy mature people as having

- A positive but objective sense of self and others
- Interest in issues beyond their own experience
- A sense of humor
- Common sense
- A unifying philosophy of life—typically but not always provided by religious faith

Allport asserted that traits were the optimal way to understand personality. He defined traits as mental structures that make different situations the same for the person. For instance, if Carly is sociable, she is likely to behave in an outgoing fashion whether she is at a party or in a group study session. Allport's definition implies that behavior should be consistent across different situations.

We get a sense of the down-to-earth quality of Allport's approach to personality by looking at his study of traits. In the late 1930s, Allport and his colleague H. S. Odbert (1936) sat down with two big unabridged dictionaries and pulled out all the words that could be used to describe a person—a method called the *lexical approach.* This approach reflects the idea that if a trait is important to people in real life, it ought to be represented in the natural language people use to talk about one another. Allport and Odbert started with 18,000 words and gradually pared down that list to 4,500.

Clearly, 4,500 traits would make for a very long questionnaire. Do we really need them all? Imagine that you are asked to rate a person, Ignacio, on some traits. You use a scale from 1 to 5, with 1 meaning "not at all" and 5 meaning "very much." If you give Ignacio a 5 on "outgoing," what do you think you might give him on "shy"? So, we may not need 4,500 traits to summarize the way we describe personality. Still, how might we whittle down these descriptors further without losing something important?

With advances in statistical methods and the advent of computers, the lexical approach became considerably less cumbersome. Researchers began to analyze trait words to look for underlying structures that might explain their overlap. Specifically, a statistical procedure called *factor analysis* allowed researchers to identify the traits that go together. Factor analysis essentially tells us what items on a scale people are responding to as if they mean the same thing. For example, if Ignacio got a 5 on "outgoing," he probably would get a 5 on "talkative" and a 1 or 2 on "shy." Factor analysis involves taking the various ratings and reducing them down to a few underlying factors that explain their overlap.

One important characteristic of factor analysis is that it relies on the scientist to interpret the meaning of the factors, and the researcher must make some decisions about how many factors are enough to explain the data (Goldberg & Digman, 1994). In 1963, W. T. Norman reanalyzed the Allport and Odbert traits and concluded that only five factors were needed to summarize these traits. Norman's research set the stage for the dominant approach in personality psychology today: the five-factor model (Digman, 1990).

The Five-Factor Model of Personality

Pick a friend and jot down 10 of that friend's most notable personality traits. Did you perhaps list "reserved" or "a good leader"? "Responsible" or "unreliable"? "Sweet," "kind," or "friendly"? Maybe "creative"? Researchers in personality psychology have found that there are essentially five broad personality dimensions that are represented in the natural language; these dimensions also summarize the various ways psychologists have studied traits (Costa & McCrae, 2006, 2013).

The **big five factors of personality**—the broad traits that are thought to describe the main dimensions of personality—are neuroticism (the tendency to worry and experience negative emotions and is sometimes identified by its opposite, emotional stability), extraversion, openness to experience, agreeableness, and conscientiousness. Openness to experience is often the most difficult to understand. This trait refers to a tendency to enjoy intellectual pursuits, an interest in art and culture, and creative pursuits. Today it is most commonly labeled "openness to experience," but it was previously termed "intellect" and "culture." Personality psychologists typically refer to the traits as N, E, O, A, and C. If you scramble the first letters of the trait names, you can create an anagram and get the word *OCEAN*.

Figure 4 more fully defines the big five traits. To find out where you stand on these traits, see the Psychological Inquiry.

Each of the big five traits has been the topic of extensive research (Costa & McCrae, 2013; Karsten & others, 2012; King & Trent, 2013; Ozer & Benet-Martínez, 2006). The following is a just a sampling of the interesting work that the five-factor model has inspired:

- *Neuroticism* is related to feeling negative emotion more often than positive emotion in one's daily life (Widiger, 2009). Neuroticism predicts health complaints (Carver & Connor-Smith, 2010) and coronary heart disease risk (Dermody & others, 2016; Koelsch, Enge, & Jentschke, 2012). In a longitudinal study tracking older individuals for nearly seven years, neuroticism predicted dying during the study (Fry & Debats, 2009). In older adults, neuroticism is linked to higher levels of mortality following bereavement (Bratt, Stenström, & Rennemark, 2016). Neuroticism is associated with lowered psychological well-being (Sobol-Kwapinska, 2016) and with

● **big five factors of personality** The five broad traits that are thought to describe the main dimensions of personality: neuroticism (emotional instability), extraversion, openness to experience, agreeableness, and conscientiousness.

Openness	**C**onscientiousness	**E**xtraversion	**A**greeableness	**N**euroticism (emotional instability)
• Imaginative or practical	• Organized or disorganized	• Sociable or retiring	• Softhearted or ruthless	• Calm or anxious
• Interested in variety or routine	• Careful or careless	• Fun-loving or somber	• Trusting or suspicious	• Secure or insecure
• Independent or conforming	• Disciplined or impulsive	• Energetic or reserved	• Helpful or uncooperative	• Self-satisfied or self-pitying

FIGURE 4   The Big Five Factors of Personality Each of the broad traits encompasses more narrow traits and characteristics. Use the acronym *OCEAN* to remember the big five personality factors: openness, conscientiousness, extraversion, agreeableness, and neuroticism.

psychological *inquiry*

Your Personality Traits: Who Are You?

Use the following scale to rate yourself on the trait items listed below. Next to each item, write the number from the scale that best corresponds to how you rate yourself with respect to that trait.

Disagree strongly	Disagree moderately	Disagree a little	Neither agree nor disagree	Agree a little	Agree moderately	Agree strongly
1	2	3	4	5	6	7

I see myself as:

1. _____ extraverted, enthusiastic.
2. _____ critical, quarrelsome.
3. _____ dependable, self-disciplined.
4. _____ anxious, easily upset.
5. _____ open to new experiences, complex.
6. _____ reserved, quiet.
7. _____ sympathetic, warm.
8. _____ disorganized, careless.
9. _____ calm, emotionally stable.
10. _____ conventional, uncreative.

© PhotoAlto/PunchStock

You have just completed the Ten-Item Personality Inventory, or TIPI (Gosling, Rentfrow, & Swann, 2003), a measure of the big five traits. All of the even-numbered items are *reverse-scored,* meaning your ratings should be reversed for these. (Reverse items are included in scales to fully identify a characteristic and to make sure that respondents are reading items carefully.) So, if you gave item number 2 a rating of 7, it should be a 1; a rating of 6 should be a 2, and so on. The first step in calculating your scores is to reverse your scores on these even-numbered items. Then average together your ratings for the following items for each trait, using the steps in the table below.

Trait	Items	Sum of Your Ratings	Your Score (divide the sum by 2)	Low Score	Medium Score	High Score
Emotional Stability (the opposite of neuroticism)	4, 9	_____	_____	3.41	4.83	6.25
Extraversion	1, 6	_____	_____	2.99	4.44	5.89
Openness to Experience	5, 10	_____	_____	4.13	5.38	6.45
Agreeableness	2, 7	_____	_____	4.12	5.23	6.34
Conscientiousness	3, 8	_____	_____	4.08	5.40	6.72

The last three columns provide information about what those scores mean. The "medium scores" reflect the mean score found in a sample of more than 1,800 participants. The "low scores" are that mean minus 1 standard deviation. The "high scores" are the mean plus 1 standard deviation. Now answer the following questions.

1. Do your scores reflect your sense of who you really are? Explain.

2. Why do you think the researchers included one reverse-scored item for each trait?

3. The guides for low, medium, and high scores were provided by data from a sample of college students at the University of Texas. Do you think these norms might differ at your school? Why or why not?

4. Although this is a very short assessment, scores on this scale are highly correlated with scores on longer scales measuring the same traits (Ehrhart & others, 2009). What does it mean to say that the scores are highly correlated?

higher risk of a number of psychological disorders (Paulus & others, 2016). However, a fascinating recent study showed that neuroticism may have some healthy correlates. Among individuals who had been diagnosed with serious disease, neuroticism predicted lowered levels of smoking (Weston & Jackson, 2015).

- Individuals high in *extraversion* are more likely than others to engage in social activities (Emmons & Diener, 1986). People rate extraverts as smiling, standing energetically, and dressing stylishly (Durante & Griskevicius, 2016; Naumann & others, 2009). Extraverts report greater satisfaction with their relationships, and they tend to trust others (Tov, Nai, & Lee, 2016). Extraversion is a very strong correlate of psychological well-being (Womick & King, 2016) and is negatively related to symptoms of psychological disorders, especially depression (Watson & others, 2015).

- *Openness to experience* is related to liberal values, open-mindedness, tolerance (McCrae & Sutin, 2009), and creativity (Xu, Jiang, & Walsh, 2016). Openness is also associated with superior cognitive functioning and IQ across the life span (Sharp & others, 2010). Individuals who rate themselves as open to experience are more likely to dress distinctively (Naumann & others, 2009), to pursue entrepreneurial goals (for instance, starting their own business), and to experience success in those pursuits (Zhao, Seibert, & Lumpkin, 2010). Openness is associated with generating innovative ideas for product development (Stock, von Hippel, & Gillert, 2016). A meta-analysis found that openness to experience was linked to living longer (Ferguson & Bibby, 2012).

- *Agreeableness* is related to generosity, altruism (Caprara & others, 2010), religious faith (Haber, Koenig, & Jacob, 2011), and more satisfying social relationships (Tov, Nai, & Lee, 2016). In online dating profiles, agreeableness is negatively related to lying about oneself (J. A. Hall & others, 2010; Stanton, Ellickson-Larew, & Watson, 2016).

- *Conscientiousness* is a key factor in a variety of life domains. One meta-analysis found that a higher level of conscientiousness was linked to higher college grade-point averages (McAbee & Oswald, 2013). Conscientiousness also predicts better work performance (S. D. Brown & others, 2011). Conscientiousness is associated with dressing neatly, especially among men (Naumann & others, 2009) and, like openness, is related to entrepreneurial success (Zhao, Seibert, & Lumpkin, 2010). Conscientiousness relates to better-quality friendships (Jensen-Campbell & Malcolm, 2007) and higher levels of religious faith (Saroglou, 2010). Low levels of conscientiousness are linked with criminal behavior and substance abuse (Walton & others, 2016). Conscientiousness is the most consistent personality predictor of health and longevity (Jokela & others, 2013).

Keep in mind that because the five factors are theoretically independent of one another, a person can be any combination of them. Do you know a neurotic extravert or an agreeable introvert, for example? Reading about the correlates of personality traits can sometimes be dissatisfying. If you are low in conscientiousness, are you doomed to an unsuccessful career?

In many ways, the role of personality traits in our life depends on the situations in which we find ourselves. Traits can be strengths or weaknesses, depending on the types of situations we encounter and the kinds of situations we seek out for ourselves (King & Trent, 2013). Even a trait like agreeableness may be a liability when the situation calls for confrontational behavior. For instance, a woman whose marriage is breaking up might wish for a divorce lawyer who treats her kindly but might prefer one who is less than agreeable at the bargaining table. Eminent psychologist Lee Cronbach (1957, p. 679) once said, "If for each environment there is a best organism, for every organism there must be a best environment." If our personalities are not particularly well suited to a situation, we can change that situation or create one that fits better (King & Trent, 2013).

TRAITS AND PERSONALITY DEVELOPMENT

Although it is an assumption of the trait approach that these aspects of personality are relatively stable (Costa & McCrae, 2006), numerous studies show that personality traits can change throughout life (Durbin & others, 2016; Kandler & others, 2015; van

Scheppingen & others, 2016). Increasingly, psychologists have come to think of these changes in traits as representing personality development because they very often indicate a change from less to greater psychological maturity (Roberts, Donnellan, & Hill, 2013).

For example, in an important meta-analysis, Brent Roberts and his colleagues analyzed 92 different longitudinal studies that included thousands of participants, ranging from 12 years old to over 80, and that measured aspects of the big five across the life course (Roberts, Walton, & Viechtbauer, 2006). They found consistent evidence for trait changes throughout life, even into adulthood. Social dominance (a facet of extraversion), conscientiousness, and emotional stability (the opposite of neuroticism) were found to increase—especially between the ages of 20 and 40. Social vitality, another facet of extraversion, and openness to experience increased most during adolescence but then declined in old age. Agreeableness showed a steady rise over the life course. Especially between ages 17 and 24, individuals were likely to become more responsible and less distressed (Blonigen & others, 2008; Klimstra & others, 2009). In general, changes in personality traits across adulthood occur in a direction suggesting that people become more socially mature with time (Roberts & Mroczek, 2008).

THE BIG FIVE ACROSS CULTURES

If the traits identified in the big five truly capture human personality, they should do so in different cultures and in different languages. Do the big five show up in the assessment of personality in cultures around the world? Many studies suggest that they do. A version of the five factors appears in people in countries as diverse as Canada, Finland, Poland, China, and Japan (Paunonen & others, 1992; X. Zhou & others, 2009). Among the big five, the factors most likely to emerge across cultures and languages are extraversion, agreeableness, and conscientiousness (De Raad & others, 2010).

ANIMAL STUDIES ON THE BIG FIVE

Researchers have found evidence for at least some of the big five personality traits in animals, including domestic dogs (Gosling, 2008; Gosling, Kwan, & John, 2003) and hyenas (Gosling & John, 1999). In addition, studies have turned up evidence for general personality traits (such as overall outgoingness) in orangutans, geese, lizards (Weinstein, Capitanio, & Gosling, 2008), fish (Wilson & Godin, 2010), and cockatiels (Fox & Millam, 2010), among others. You might be surprised to learn that research using animals has provided insight into a classic question in personality: Do life experiences change personality? To read about this research, see the Intersection.

Evaluating the Trait Perspectives

As already noted, the trait approach is the dominant perspective on personality psychology today. The emergence of the five-factor model has provided personality psychologists with a common language and a set of tools for understanding a host of important topics, including the prediction of behavior, psychological well-being, psychological disorders, and health and illness (George, Helson, & John, 2011; Leary & Hoyle, 2009a; Turiano & others, 2012).

Despite strong evidence for the big five, some personality researchers say that these traits might not end up being the ultimate list of broad traits; they argue that more specific traits are better predictors of behavior. One alternative, the HEXACO model, incorporates a sixth dimension, honesty/humility, to capture the moral dimensions of personality (Ashton & Lee, 2008; Ashton, Lee, & Boies, 2015; K. Lee & others, 2013a). So, in this case personality is explained by the following traits: *h*onesty/*h*umility, *e*motional stability, *e*xtraversion, *a*greeableness, *c*onscientiousness, and *o*penness to experience.

The trait approach has been faulted for missing the importance of *situational* factors in personality and behavior (Engler, 2014; Kammrath & Scholer, 2013; Leary & Hoyle, 2009b). For example, a person might rate herself as introverted among new people but very outgoing with family and friends. Further, some have criticized the trait perspective for painting an individual's personality with very broad strokes. These critics say that although traits can tell us much about someone whom we have never met, they reveal little about the nuances of an individual's personality (Uher, 2015).

test yourself

1. How do trait theorists define personality?
2. What kind of work did the lexical approach of Allport and Odbert involve, and what key idea about personality traits did it reflect?
3. What traits are included in the big five factors of personality? Define them.

INTERSECTION

Personality Psychology and Comparative Psychology: Do Life Experiences Influence Personality?

If someone asked you how you became the person you are today, chances are you would mention experiences you have had: growing up in a small town (or a big city), falling in love (or having your heart broken) for the first time, the loss of a loved one, or a major accomplishment at work or school. You might feel like coming to college has made you a different person than you once were.

For personality psychologists, these interesting possibilities are very hard to study experimentally. It is impossible to randomly assign people to the significant experiences that might affect their personalities. Research on the influence of life events on personality characteristics in humans is largely correlational. Recently, however, scientists have begun to address this question in a different way, employing animals ranging from fish (Filipa & others, 2016) to guinea pigs (Finkemeier, Trillmich, & Guenther, 2016).

© age fotostock/Alamy Stock Photo

Because researchers can manipulate the kinds of experiences animals have, they are able to draw causal conclusions about how experiences shape personality.

One of the most important life events for an adult is becoming a parent. Does parenthood affect personality? Research on humans has produced mixed results (Jeronimus & others, 2014; van Scheppingen & others, 2016). A recent study addressed the effects of parenthood on personality in a species of fish called the threespine stickleback (Stein, Trapp, & Bell, 2016). Male sticklebacks are an interesting group for this research question because once they have mated, they build a nest, protect the eggs, and care for the offspring (for about five days before all are ready to go their own ways). Would the experience of reproduction affect the personalities of these little fish?

The researchers (Stein, Trapp, & Bell, 2016) randomly assigned 10 male sticklebacks to experience reproduction

and parenting (the experimental group) and 10 to see a female but not be permitted to mate with her (the control group). The personality trait of interest was boldness. Would parenting make the fish become more cautious and less risk-taking? To measure boldness, some tasty bloodworms were placed in each fish's tank. Then the skull of a model egret (a water bird that eats sticklebacks) was propped above the water line, just above the worms. Boldness was measured by how quickly the fish dared to swim over and eat the bloodworms, even after the researchers staged a fake attack by splashing the egret beak into the water. (To be certain that boldness was a stable trait, it was measured multiple times before and after the manipulation.)

The results? The experimental group was more timid, taking fewer risks to get the food compared to the control fish. The fish that experienced parenthood were more timid even well after offspring had left the nest. Moreover, the researchers found that personality differences were explained by changes in hormone levels between the groups (Stein, Trapp, & Bell, 2016).

Hearing about these results, you might think of Nemo's overly protective dad in the animated film. It is important to keep in mind that fish are not people. The urge to think of them as psychologically similar to us (or even to cartoon characters) is strong but not realistic. Nevertheless, this study shows how animals can be used to investigate even the very complicated questions posed by personality psychology.

> *Does parenting affect personality in fish?*

4. PERSONOLOGICAL AND LIFE STORY PERSPECTIVES

If two people have the same levels of the big five traits, do they essentially have the same personality? Researchers who approach personality from the personological and life story perspectives do not think so (Adler & others, 2016; McAdams & Manczak, 2015). One of the goals of personality psychology is to understand how each of us is unique. **Personological and life story perspectives** stress that the way to understand the uniqueness of each person is to focus on his or her life history and life story.

● **personological and life story perspectives** Theoretical views stressing that the way to understand the person is to focus on the person's life history and life story.

Henry Murray's psychological profile of Adolf Hitler, developed in 1943 during World War II, serves as a model for criminal profiling today.

© Hugo Jaeger/Timepix/Time Life Pictures/Getty Images

Murray's Personological Approach

Henry Murray (1893–1988) was a young biochemistry graduate student when he became interested in the psychology of personality after meeting Carl Jung and reading his work. Murray went on to become the director of the Psychological Clinic at Harvard at the same time that Gordon All-port was a member of that faculty. Murray and Allport saw personality very differently. Whereas Allport was most comfortable focusing on con-scious experience and traits, Murray embraced the psychodynamic notion of unconscious motivation.

Murray coined the word *personology* to refer to the study of the whole person. He believed that to understand a person, we have to know that per-son's history, including the physical, psychological, and sociological aspects of the person's life.

Murray applied his insights into personality during World War II, when he was called upon by the Office of Strategic Services (a precursor to the CIA) to develop a psychological profile of Adolf Hitler. That document, produced in 1943, accurately predicted that Hitler would commit suicide rather than be taken alive. Murray's analysis of Hitler was the first "offender profile," and it has served as a model for modern criminal profiling.

The aspect of Murray's research that has had the most impact on contemporary personality psychology is his approach to motivation. Murray believed that our motives are largely unknown to us. This circumstance complicates the study of motivation: Researchers cannot simply ask people to say what it is they want. To address the issue, Murray, along with Christiana Morgan, developed the Thematic Apperception Test (TAT), to which we return later in this chapter (Morgan & Murray, 1935).

For the TAT, a person looks at an ambiguous picture and writes or tells a story about what is going on in the scene. A variety of scoring procedures have been devised for analyzing the unconscious motives that are revealed in imaginative stories (C. P. Smith, 1992). These scoring procedures involve *content analysis,* a procedure in which a psy-chologist takes the person's story and codes it for different images, words, and so forth. Although Murray posited 22 different unconscious needs, three have been the focus of most current research:

- *Need for achievement:* an enduring concern for attaining excellence and overcoming obstacles
- *Need for affiliation:* an enduring concern for establishing and maintaining interper-sonal connections
- *Need for power:* an enduring concern for having impact on the social world

David Winter (2005) analyzed the motives revealed in inaugural addresses of U.S. presidents. He found that certain needs revealed in these speeches corresponded to later events during the person's presidency. For instance, presidents who scored high on need for achievement (such as Jimmy Carter) were less successful during their terms. Note that the need for achievement is about striving for personal excellence and may have little to do with playing politics, negotiating interpersonal relationships, or delegating responsibility. Presidents who scored high on need for power tended to be judged as more successful (John F. Kennedy, Ronald Reagan), and presidents whose addresses suggested a high need for affiliation tended to experience scandal during their presiden-cies (Richard M. Nixon).

The Life Story Approach to Identity

Following in the Murray tradition, Dan McAdams developed the *life story approach* to identity (McAdams, 2001, 2006, 2011, 2012). His work centers on the idea that each of us has a unique life story, representing our memories of what makes us who we are. This life story is a constantly changing narrative that provides us with a sense of coherence. For McAdams, our life story is our very identity.

McAdams (1989) also introduced the concept of intimacy motivation. The *intimacy motive* is an enduring concern for warm interpersonal encounters for their own sake. Intimacy motivation is revealed in the warm, positive interpersonal imagery in the stories people tell. Intimacy motive has been shown to relate to positive outcomes. For instance, college men who were high on intimacy motivation showed heightened levels of happiness and lowered work strain some 30 years later (McAdams & Bryant, 1987). A study of the coming-out stories of gay men and lesbians demonstrated that intimacy-related imagery (for example, experiencing falling in love or warm acceptance from others) was associated with well-being and personality development (King & Smith, 2005).

Other personality psychologists have relied on narrative accounts of experiences as a means of understanding how individuals create meaning in life events (King & others, 2000). In one study, parents of children with Down syndrome wrote down the story of how they found out about their child's diagnosis. Parents whose stories ended happily scored higher on measures of hap-

Research by David Winter (2005) has analyzed presidential motives in inaugural addresses such as those delivered by Richard M. Nixon (first) and John F. Kennedy (second). Winter found that certain needs revealed in these speeches corresponded to later events during these individuals' terms in office.

(first) © Pictorial Parade/Getty Images; (second) © Joseph Scherschel/Time Life Pictures/Getty Images

piness, life meaning, and personal growth than others. Parents who told stories about struggling to make sense of the experience tended to mature psychologically over time (King & others, 2000). By using narratives, personal documents (such as diaries), and even letters and speeches, personality psychologists search for the deeper meaning that cannot be revealed through tests that ask people directly about whether specific items capture their personality traits.

Finally, some personality psychologists use the life story approach to understand individual lives. *Psychobiography* is a type of inquiry in which personality psychologists attempt to apply personality theory to one person's life (Runyon, 2007; W. T. Schultz, 2005). Erik Erikson's study of Gandhi's life, described in the chapter "Psychology's Scientific Method", is an example of a psychobiography. Psychobiographies have been written about a diverse array of figures, including Sigmund Freud, Gordon Allport, George W. Bush, Osama bin Laden, and Elvis Presley (W. T. Schultz, 2005).

Evaluating the Personological and Life Story Perspectives

Studying individuals through narratives and personal interviews provides an extraordinarily rich opportunity for the researcher. Imagine having the choice of reading someone's diary versus seeing that person's scores on a questionnaire measuring traits. Not many would pass up the chance to read the diary.

However, such studies are difficult and time-consuming. Personologist Robert W. White (1992) referred to the study of narratives as exploring personality "the long way." Collecting interviews and narratives is often just the first step. Turning these personal stories into scientific data means transforming them into numbers, and that process involves extensive coding and content analysis. Further, for narrative studies to be worthwhile, they must tell us something we could not have found out in a much easier way (King, 2003). Moreover, psychobiographical inquiries are prone to the biases of the scholars who conduct them and may not serve the scientific goal of generalizability.

test yourself

1. What did Murray mean by personology, and what did he believe was essential to understanding who a person really is?
2. On what does McAdams say our identities are dependent?
3. What is the intimacy motive? What has research revealed about it?

5. SOCIAL COGNITIVE PERSPECTIVES

● **social cognitive perspectives** Theoretical views emphasizing conscious awareness, beliefs, expectations, and goals.

Social cognitive perspectives on personality emphasize conscious awareness, beliefs, expectations, and goals. While incorporating principles from behaviorism (see the chapter "Learning"), social cognitive psychologists explore the person's ability to reason; to think about the past, present, and future; and to reflect on the self. They emphasize the person's individual interpretation of situations and thus focus on the uniqueness of each person by examining how behavior is tailored to the diversity of situations in which people find themselves.

Social cognitive theorists are not interested in broad traits such as the big five. Rather, they investigate how more specific factors, such as beliefs, relate to behavior and performance. In this section we consider the two major social cognitive approaches, developed respectively by Albert Bandura and Walter Mischel.

Bandura's Social Cognitive Theory

In his social cognitive approach to learning, Albert Bandura took the basic tenets of behaviorism (see the chapter "Learning") and added a recognition of the role of mental processes in determining behavior (Bandura, 1986, 2011a). Applying these principles to personality, Bandura's social cognitive theory states that behavior, environment, and person/cognitive factors are *all* important in understanding personality.

Bandura coined the term *reciprocal determinism* to describe the way behavior, environment, and person/cognitive factors interact to create personality (Figure 5). Reciprocal determinism means that the relationships among the person, his or her behavior, and the environment are all two-way streets. The environment can determine a person's behavior, but the person can act to change the environment. Similarly, person/cognitive factors can both influence behavior and be influenced by behavior. Our behavior—for instance, doing well on a test—can influence our beliefs about ourselves and in turn influence future behaviors.

From Bandura's perspective, then, behavior is a product of a variety of forces—some of which come from the situation and some of which the person brings to the situation. We now review the important processes and variables Bandura uses to understand personality.

Albert Bandura (b. 1925) Bandura's practical, problem-solving social cognitive approach has made a lasting mark on personality theory and therapy.

© Jon Brenneis/Time & Life Pictures/Getty Images

OBSERVATIONAL LEARNING

Recall from the chapter "Learning" Bandura's belief that observational learning is a key aspect of how we learn. By observing how others behave and noticing the consequences of their actions, we might come to adopt the behavior ourselves. For example, a boy might observe that his mother's hostile exchanges with other people are an effective way to get what she wants. Later, when the boy is with his peers, he might adopt the same strategy. Social cognitive theorists believe that we acquire a wide range of behaviors, thoughts, and feelings by watching others' behavior and that our observations strongly shape our personality (Bandura, 2009a, 2011a).

PERSONAL CONTROL

Social cognitive theorists emphasize that we can regulate and control our own behavior despite our changing environment (Bandura, 2011a; Damen & others, 2015; Mischel, 2004). For example, a young executive who observes her boss behave in an overbearing and sarcastic manner toward his subordinates may find the behavior distasteful and go out of her way to encourage and support her own staff. Psychologists commonly describe a sense of behavioral control as coming from inside the person (an *internal locus of control*) or outside the person (an *external locus of control*). When we feel that we ourselves are controlling our choices and behaviors, the locus of control is internal, but when other influences are controlling them, the locus of control is external.

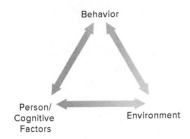

FIGURE 5 Bandura's Social Cognitive Theory Bandura's social cognitive theory emphasizes reciprocal influences of behavior, environment, and person/cognitive factors. Notice that from Bandura's perspective, all of those arrows are double-headed, meaning that causation goes in both directions.

Consider the question of whether you will perform well on your next test. With an internal locus of control, you believe that you are in command of your choices and behaviors, and your answer will depend on what you can realistically do (for example, study hard or attend a special review session). With an external locus of control, however, you might say that you cannot predict how things will go because so many outside factors influence performance, such as whether the test is difficult, how the curve is set in the course, and whether the instructor is fair. Feeling a strong sense of personal control is vital to many aspects of performance, behavior, and well-being (Bertrand, Graham, & Lachman, 2013; Tigani & others, 2012).

SELF-EFFICACY

Self-efficacy is the belief that one has the competence to accomplish a given goal or task and produce positive change. Bandura and others have shown that self-efficacy is related to a number of positive developments in people's lives, including solving problems and becoming more sociable (Bandura, 2011a).

● **self-efficacy** The belief that one can accomplish a given goal or task and produce positive change.

Self-efficacy influences whether people even try to develop healthy habits, as well as how much effort they expend in coping with stress, how long they persist in the face of obstacles, and how much stress and pain they experience (Becker, Kang, & Stuifbergen, 2012; Schutte & Malouff, 2016; Zahodne & others, 2015). We will return to the topics of personal control and self-efficacy at the end of this chapter.

Mischel's Contributions

Like Bandura, Walter Mischel is a social cognitive psychologist who has explored how personality influences behavior. Mischel has left his mark on the field of personality in two notable ways. First, his critique of the idea of consistency in behavior ignited a flurry of controversy. Second, he proposed the CAPS model, a new way of thinking about personality.

MISCHEL'S CRITIQUE OF CONSISTENCY

Whether we are talking about unconscious sexual conflicts, traits, or motives, all of the approaches we have considered so far maintain that these various personality characteristics are an enduring influence on behavior. In 1968 Walter Mischel's book *Personality and Assessment* shattered this assumption and nearly ended the psychological study of personality.

To understand Mischel's argument, recall Gordon Allport's definition of a trait as a characteristic that ought to make different situations equivalent for a given person. This quality of traits suggests that a person should behave consistently in different situations—in other words, the individual should exhibit *cross-situational consistency*. For example, an outgoing person should act highly sociably whether she is at a party or in the library. However, Mischel looked at the research compiled on trait prediction of behavior and found it to be lacking. He concluded that there was no evidence for cross-situational consistency in behavior—and thus no evidence for the existence of personality as it had been previously conceptualized.

Rather than understanding personality as consisting of broad, internal traits that produce consistent behavior across situations, Mischel said that personality often changes according to a given situation. Mischel asserted that behavior is discriminative; that is, a person looks at each situation and responds accordingly. Mischel's view is called *situationism*, the idea that personality and behavior often vary considerably from one context to another.

Personality psychologists responded to Mischel's situationist attack in various ways (Donnellan, Lucas, & Fleeson, 2009; Funder, 2009; Hogan, 2009). Researchers showed that it is not a matter of *whether* personality predicts behavior but *when and how* it does so, often in combination with situational factors (Sherman, Nave, & Funder, 2010). The research findings were that

■ The narrower and more limited a trait is, the more likely it will predict behavior.

■ Some people are consistent on some traits, and other people are consistent on other traits.

414 CHAPTER 12 Personality

■ Personality traits exert a stronger influence on an individual's behavior when situational influences are less powerful. A very powerful situation is one that contains many clear cues about how a person is supposed to behave. For example, even a highly talkative person typically sits quietly during a class lecture. In weaker situations, however, such as during leisure time, the person may spend most of the time talking.

Moreover, individuals select the situations they are in. Consequently, even if situations determine behavior, traits play a role by influencing which situations people choose—such as going to a party or staying home to study (Emmons & Diener, 1986).

Interestingly, one study showed that people *do* behave in a consistent fashion across different interpersonal situations. In that research, participants were videotaped as they interacted with different partners (Leikas, Lönnqvist, & Verkasalo, 2012). The partners were trained actors who served as confederates. The confederates were instructed to behave in different ways toward the participants across four different interactions; they were either friendly or quarrelsome and were either dominant or submissive. The way participants behaved in response to these different partners was coded afterward, based on the tapes.

The results showed that many of the participants' behaviors during the interactions were rather consistent, especially being talkative, using gestures, and expressing emotion (Leikas, Lönnqvist, & Verkasalo, 2012). Indeed, even when the type of treatment they received influenced their behavior, participants maintained a high level of cross-situational consistency in their *rank order*. This means that although an extraverted person might have been less talkative than usual when interacting with a dominant partner, he or she was still more talkative than an introvert in the same situation.

Interestingly, the judges—who rated the big five traits of the participants based on the videotapes—agreed with the participants' self-reports of the traits. In other words, even when observing a person in different situations, observers recognized whether the person was extraverted, agreeable, conscientious, neurotic, or open to experience.

Let's pause and reflect on what it means to be consistent. You might believe that being consistent is part of being a genuine, honest person and that tailoring behavior to different situations means being fake. On the other hand, consider that a person who never changes his or her behavior to fit a situation might be unpleasant to have around. For example, think about someone who cannot put aside his competitive drive even when playing checkers with a 4-year-old. Clearly, adaptive behavior might involve sometimes being consistent and sometimes tailoring behavior to the situation.

Over time, Mischel (2004, 2009) has developed an approach to personality that he feels is better suited to capturing the nuances of the relationship between the individual and situations in producing behavior. Imagine trying to study personality without using traits or broad motives. What would you focus on? Mischel's answer to this dilemma is his CAPS theory.

CAPS THEORY

Recall Mischel's work on delay of gratification from the chapter "Motivation and Emotion" (Mischel, Cantor, & Feldman, 1996; Mischel & Moore, 1980; Mischel & others, 2011). In that work, children were left in a room with a tempting marshmallow. Mischel measured the amount of time the kids were able to delay eating the marshmallow, and he and his colleagues continued to study those children for many years. They found that the amount of time the children were able to delay gratification predicted their academic performance in high school and even college (Mischel, 2004). These results indicate remarkable stability in personality over time (Casey & others, 2011).

Mischel's approach to personality is concerned with just such stability (or coherence) in the pattern of behavior *over time,* not with consistency across differing situations. That is, Mischel and his colleagues have studied how behaviors in very different situations have a coherent pattern, such as a child's waiting to eat the marshmallow and that same individual's (as a grown college student) deciding to stay home and study instead of going out to party.

© Image Source/Getty Images

In keeping with the social cognitive emphasis on the person's cognitive abilities and mental states, Mischel conceptualizes personality as a set of interconnected **cognitive affective processing systems (CAPS)** (Kross, Mischel, & Shoda, 2010; Mischel, 2004; Mischel & Ayduk, 2011; Mischel & Shoda, 1999; Shoda & others, 2013). This label captures how the CAPS approach understands personality: It involves information processing (cognitive) and emotional experience (affective) interacting to systematically determine behavior, as the person encounters different situations. According to this approach, our thoughts and emotions about ourselves and the world affect our behavior and become linked in ways that matter to behavior (Kammrath & Scholer, 2013).

● **cognitive affective processing systems (CAPS)** Mischel's theoretical model for describing how individuals' thoughts and emotions about themselves and the world affect their behavior and become linked in ways that matter to that behavior.

Personal control and self-efficacy are psychological connections that a person has made among situations, beliefs, and behaviors. For example, Raoul may be excited by the challenge of a new assignment from his boss and think about all the possible strategies to complete the project and get down to work immediately. Yet this go-getter may respond differently to other challenges, depending on who gives the assignment, what it is, or whether he feels he can do a good job.

From the CAPS perspective, it makes no sense to ask a person "How extraverted are you?" because the answer is always, "It depends." A person may be outgoing in one situation (on the first day of class) and not so in another (right before an exam), and that unique pattern of flexibility is what personality is all about.

Not surprisingly, CAPS theory focuses on how people behave in different situations and how they uniquely interpret situational features. Research using the CAPS approach generally involves observing individuals behaving in a variety of contexts in order to identify the patterns of associations that exist among beliefs, emotions, and behavior for each person across different situations (Romero-Canyas & others, 2010).

Evaluating the Social Cognitive Perspectives

Social cognitive theory focuses on the interactions of individuals with their environments. The social cognitive approach has fostered a scientific climate for understanding personality that highlights the observation of behavior. Social cognitive theory emphasizes the influence of cognitive processes in explaining personality and suggests that people have the ability to control their environment.

Critics of the social cognitive perspective on personality take issue with one or more aspects of the theory. For example, they charge that

- The social cognitive approach is too concerned with situational influences on personality. It ignores the role played by traits and other enduring qualities of personality.
- Social cognitive theory overlooks the role biology plays in personality.
- In its attempt to incorporate both the situation and the person into its view of personality, social cognitive psychology tends to lead to very specific predictions for each person in any given situation, making generalizations impossible.

test yourself

1. In what ways did Bandura react to and modify Skinner's approach to understanding human functioning?
2. What is self-efficacy, and to what kinds of positive life developments has research linked it?
3. With what is Mischel's cognitive affective processing systems (CAPS) approach centrally concerned?

6. BIOLOGICAL PERSPECTIVES

The notion that physiological processes influence personality has been around since ancient times. Around 400 B.C.E., Hippocrates, the father of medicine, described human beings as having one of four basic personalities based on levels of particular bodily fluids (called *humours*). For Hippocrates, a "sanguine" personality was a happy, optimistic individual who happened to have an abundance of blood. A "choleric" person was quick-tempered with too much yellow bile. A "phlegmatic" personality referred to a placid, sluggish individual with too much phlegm, and a "melancholic" pessimist had too much black bile.

Hippocrates' ideas about bodily fluids have fallen by the wayside, but personality psychologists have long acknowledged that personality involves the brain and biological processes. Psychologists' beliefs about these interacting processes in personality, though, were based on assumptions, not direct study. For instance, Freud's psychosexual stages demonstrate his strong belief in the connection between the mind (personality) and the body; Allport defined traits as "*neuro*psychic" structures, and personality as a "*psycho-physical*" system; and Murray once declared, "No brain, no personality." More recently, with advances in method and theory, biological perspectives on personality have become more prominent (Allen & DeYoung, 2016; Plomin & others, 2016). The biological approach to personality seeks to link personality processes with physical aspects of the person, including the brain and genes.

Personality and the Brain

The brain is clearly important in personality as in other psychological phenomena. Recall the case of Phineas Gage, described in the chapter "Biological Foundations of Behavior". A key effect of Gage's horrific accident was that it changed his personality. He went from being gentle, kind, and reliable to being angry, hostile, and untrustworthy.

A great deal of research is currently addressing the ways in which brain activity is associated with various personality traits (Beaty & others, 2016; DeYoung & others, 2010; Xu & Potenza, 2012). For example, research has shown that an extraverted person's left prefrontal cortex is more responsive to positive stimuli and that the same area in neurotic individuals is more responsive to negative stimuli (Canli, 2008a, 2008b; Haas & others, 2007; Schmidtke & Heller, 2004). More recently, researchers have begun to explore the ways that traits influence the meaning of brain structure or activity differences (Kong & others, 2015). Hans Eysenck and Jeffrey Gray have proposed two theoretical approaches to the biology of personality.

EYSENCK'S RETICULAR ACTIVATION SYSTEM THEORY

British psychologist Hans Eysenck (1967) was among the first to describe the role of a particular brain system in personality. He developed an approach to extraversion/introversion based on the role of arousal in personality and behavior. In the chapter "States of Consciousness", we discussed the meaning of arousal as a state of engagement with the environment. In the chapter "Biological Foundations of Behavior", we noted that reticular formation is located in the brain stem and plays a role in wakefulness or arousal. Eysenck focused on the *reticular activation system (RAS)*, which is the name given to the reticular formation and its connections.

Eysenck posited that all of us share an optimal arousal level, a level at which we feel comfortably engaged with the world. However, Eysenck proposed, the RAS of extraverts and introverts differs with respect to the baseline level of arousal. You know that an extravert tends to be outgoing, sociable, and dominant and that an introvert is quieter and more reserved and passive. According to Eysenck, these behavioral differences reflect different arousal regulation strategies (Figure 6). Extraverts wake up in the morning under-aroused, *below* the optimal level, whereas introverts start out *above* the optimal level.

FIGURE 6 Eysenck's Reticular Activation System Theory Eysenck viewed introversion and extraversion as characteristic behavioral patterns that aim to regulate arousal around the individual's baseline level. (first photo) © drbimages/E+/Getty Images; (second photo) © Stockbyte/Getty Images

Introversion

Quiet, reserved, passive

Above optimal level

Keeping distractions to a minimum
Being alone
Reading quietly

Personality Characteristics

Level of Arousal

Typical Activities

Extraversion

Outgoing, social, dominant

Below optimal level

Seeking out distractions
Spending time with friends
Listening to loud music

If *you* were feeling under-engaged with life, what might you do? You might listen to loud music or hang out with friends—in other words, behave like an extravert. If, on the other hand, you were feeling over-aroused or too stimulated, what would you do? You might spend time alone, keep distractions to a minimum, maybe sit quietly and read a book—in other words, you might act like an introvert. Thus, from Eysenck's perspective, we can understand the continuum of extraversion/introversion as demonstrating patterns of behavior aimed at regulating arousal around our baseline. According to Eysenck, extraverts experience a baseline that is below the optimal; introverts experience a baseline that is above the optimal.

Research has not shown that extraverts and introverts differ in terms of baseline arousal. Instead, researchers have found that a process similar to what Eysenck proposes for arousal—not involving the activation of RAS, but rather blood flow in the striatum, a part of the basal ganglia—plays a role in dopamine levels (Hermes & others, 2011; Wacker & Smillie, 2015). Recall that dopamine is the neurotransmitter linked with the experience of reward. From this approach, introverts have higher baseline blood flow, and extraverts have lower baseline blood flow to this region of the brain. Because extraverts are motivated to bring those dopamine levels up, they are more likely to seek out pleasurable experiences and thus behave in extraverted ways.

GRAY'S REINFORCEMENT SENSITIVITY THEORY

Jeffrey Gray proposed a neuropsychology of personality, called *reinforcement sensitivity theory,* that has been the subject of much research (Corr, 2016; Gray, 1987; Gray & McNaughton, 2000). On the basis of animal learning principles, Gray posited that two neurological systems—the *behavioral activation system (BAS)* and the *behavioral inhibition system (BIS)*—could be viewed as underlying personality, as Figure 7 shows.

According to Gray, these systems explain differences in an organism's attention to rewards and punishers in the environment. An organism sensitive to rewards is more likely to learn associations between behaviors and rewards and therefore to show a characteristic pattern of seeking out rewarding opportunities. In contrast, an organism with a heightened sensitivity to punishers in the environment is more likely to learn associations between behaviors and negative consequences. Such an organism shows a characteristic pattern of avoiding such consequences.

In Gray's theory, the BAS is sensitive to rewards in the environment, predisposes one to feelings of positive emotion, and underlies the trait of extraversion (Aluja & others, 2015). In contrast, the BIS is sensitive to punishments and is involved in avoidance learning; it predisposes the individual to feelings of fear and underlies the trait of neuroticism (Gray & McNaughton, 2000; Hirsh & Kang, 2016).

Gray's conceptual model of reinforcement sensitivity proposed interacting brain systems as primarily responsible for the behavioral manifestations of the BAS and BIS. Research has provided some evidence for the biological underpinnings of these systems. The amygdalae, the prefrontal cortex, and the anterior cingulated cortex appear to serve together as a system for affective style (Davidson, 2005; McNaughton & Corr, 2008) and are particularly implicated in the BAS or extraversion (Pickering & Smillie, 2008).

THE ROLE OF NEUROTRANSMITTERS

Neurotransmitters have also been implicated in personality in ways that fit Gray's model (Delvecchio & others, 2016). As noted above, the neurotransmitter dopamine functions in the experience of reward. Dopamine is vital to learning that certain behaviors are rewarding, sending the message, "Do it again!" Research has shown that dopamine is a factor in BAS or extraversion (Wacker & Smillie, 2015) suggesting that the dopaminergic system in extraverts is well prepared to learn associations between environmental cues and rewards.

Even stronger than the link between dopamine and extraversion is the relationship between the neurotransmitter serotonin and neuroticism (Brummett & others, 2008; Delvecchio & others, 2016). In this case, neuroticism is associated with low levels of circulating serotonin. As well, neuroticism may be related to a certain serotonin transporter gene and to the binding of serotonin in the thalamus (Hettema & others, 2015; Kruschwitz & others, 2015; Vinberg & others, 2010). Interestingly, the influence of this gene on personality may

Behavioral Activation System

Sensitive to
Environmental reward

Behavior
Seek positive
consequences/rewards

Character of emotion
Positive

Personality trait
Extraversion

Behavioral Inhibition System

Sensitive to
Environmental punishment

Behavior
Avoid negative
consequences/punishments

Character of emotion
Negative

Personality trait
Neuroticism

FIGURE 7   Gray's Reinforcement Sensitivity Theory Gray theorized that two neurological systems, the BAS and the BIS, explain differences in an organism's attention to environmental rewards and punishments and in this way shape personality. (top photo) © Photodisc/Getty Images; (bottom photo) © Photodisc/Getty Images

418   CHAPTER 12   Personality

© Greatstock Photographic Library/Alamy

● **behavioral genetics** The study of the inherited underpinnings of behavioral characteristics.

depend on experience. Whether individuals who have this genetic characteristic actually develop into worriers depends on their social experiences (Laceulle & others, 2015; Pluess & others, 2010).

Keep in mind that finding associations between neurotransmitters and personality does not tell us about the potential causal pathways between these variables. Extraversion is linked to dopamine, neuroticism to serotonin. Yet, behavior can influence brain processes, and patterns of behavior can determine brain activity and neurotransmitter levels. One thing that behavior cannot influence, at least not yet, is genes, another important biological factor in personality.

Personality and Behavioral Genetics

Behavioral genetics is the study of the inherited underpinnings of behavioral characteristics. A great deal of research in behavioral genetics has involved twin studies, and the hub of this work is, appropriately, the University of Minnesota, Twin Cities.

Twin studies show that genetic factors explain a substantial amount of the observed differences in each of the big five traits. Remember that to conduct these studies, researchers compare identical twins, who share 100 percent of their genes, with fraternal twins, who share just 50 percent. All of the participants complete questionnaires measuring their traits. Then the researchers see if the identical twins are more similar to each other than the fraternal twins.

Heritability estimates for the five factors are about 50 percent (Bouchard & Loehlin, 2001; Jang, Livesley, & Vernon, 1996; Keyes & others, 2015). As noted in the chapter "Biological Foundations of Behavior", heritability statistics have come into question (Charney, 2012; Crusio, 2012), and as such these estimates are likely higher than reality. Still, they suggest a substantial role of genes in explaining differences between people on personality traits.

Even aspects of personality that are not traits reveal genetic influence. For example, autobiographical memories about one's childhood and early family experiences (the kind of data that the personologist might find interesting) are influenced by genetics. Robert Krueger and his colleagues examined retrospective reports on the quality of family environments in a sample of twins who were reared apart (Krueger, Markon, & Bouchard, 2003). Participants rated their adoptive families on a variety of characteristics such as parental warmth, feelings of being wanted, and the strictness of their parents. These twins, though obviously sharing genetics, were reared by different families, so they were describing different experiences. Yet their recollections of their early family experiences were similar, and the heritability estimate for family cohesion ranged from 40 to 60 percent.

Understanding the role of genetic factors in personality is enormously complex. Research on non-twin samples often suggests much lower heritability, for reasons that are not well understood (South & Krueger, 2008). Furthermore, because genes and environment are often intertwined, it is very difficult to tease apart whether, and how, genes or experience explains enduring patterns of behavior. For instance, a little girl who is genetically predisposed to disruptive behavior may often find herself in a time-out or involved in arguments with parents or teachers. When that child emerges as an adult with a "fighting spirit" or lots of "spunk," are those adult traits the product of genes, experiences, or both? Finally, most traits are probably influenced by multiple genes (Costa & others, 2010), making the task of identifying specific molecular links very challenging.

Evaluating the Biological Perspectives

Exploring the biological aspects of personality is a vital continuing goal in personality psychology. This work ties the field of personality to animal learning models, advances in brain imaging, and evolutionary theory (Sefcek, Black, & Wolf, 2015). However, a few cautions are necessary in thinking about biological variables and their place in personality.

As we considered above, biology can be the effect, not the cause, of personality. To be sure that you grasp this idea, first recall that personality is the individual's characteristic pattern of behavior, thoughts, and feelings. Then recall from previous chapters that behavior, thoughts, and feelings are physical events in the body and brain. If traits predispose individuals to particular and consistent behaviors, thoughts, and emotional responses, traits may play a role in forging particular habitually used pathways in the brain. Recall, too, from the chapter "Memory" that memory may be thought of as patterns of activation among neurons. The autobiographical memories that interest personologists, then, might be viewed as well-worn patterns of activation. To the extent that personality represents a person's characteristic pattern of thought or the accumulation of memories over the life span, personality may not only be influenced by the brain—it may also play a role in the brain's very structure and functions.

7. PERSONALITY ASSESSMENT

One of the great contributions of personality psychology is its development of rigorous methods for measuring mental processes. Psychologists use a number of scientifically developed methods to evaluate personality. They assess personality for different reasons— from career counseling and job selection to clinical evaluation and criminal risk (Gardner & others, 2015; Loveland & others, 2015).

Self-Report Tests

The most commonly used method of measuring personality characteristics is the **self-report test** (also called an *objective test* or an *inventory*), which directly asks people whether specific items describe their personality traits. Self-report personality tests include items such as

- I am easily embarrassed.
- I love to go to parties.
- I like to watch cartoons on TV.

Respondents choose from a limited number of answers (yes or no, true or false, agree or disagree).

One problem with self-report tests is *social desirability*. To grasp the idea of social desirability, imagine answering the item "I am lazy at times." This statement is probably true for everyone, but would you feel comfortable admitting it? When motivated by social desirability, individuals say what they think will make them look better. One way to measure the influence of social desirability is to give individuals a questionnaire that is designed to tap into this tendency. Such scales typically contain universally true but threatening items ("I like to gossip at times," "I have never said anything intentionally to hurt someone's feelings"). If scores on a trait item correlate with this measure of social desirability, we know that the test takers were probably not being straightforward on their trait ratings.

Another way to get around social desirability issues is to design scales so that it is virtually impossible for the respondent to know what the researcher is trying to measure. One means of accomplishing this goal is to use an **empirically keyed test,** a type of self-report test that is created by first identifying two groups that are known to be different. The researcher would give these two groups a large number of questionnaire items and then see which items show the biggest differences between the groups. Those items would become part of the scale to measure the group difference. For instance, a researcher might want to develop a test that distinguishes between individuals with a history of substance abuse and those with no such history. The researcher might generate a long list of true/false items asking about a variety of topics but not mentioning substance abuse. These questions would be presented to the members of the two groups, and on the basis of the responses, the researcher can then select the items that best discriminate between the members of the differing groups. Empirically keyed tests require that we have two groups we know in advance differ on an important variable.

test yourself

1. According to Eysenck, what part of the brain influences whether a person is an introvert or an extravert?
2. How does Gray's reinforcement sensitivity theory of personality explain extraversion and neuroticism?
3. What is behavioral genetics, and what kind of study is commonly used in research in this area?

● **self-report test** A method of measuring personality characteristics that directly asks people whether specific items describe their personality traits; also called an objective test or an inventory.

● **empirically keyed test** A type of self-report test that presents many questionnaire items to two groups that are known to be different in some central way.

Note that an empirically keyed test avoids the issue of social desirability because the items that distinguish between the two groups are not related in any obvious way to the actual purpose of the test. For instance, those without a substance abuse history might typically respond "true" to the item "I enjoy taking long walks," whereas those with a history of substance abuse might respond "false"; but this item does not mention substance use, and there is no clear reason why it should distinguish between these groups.

Indeed, an important consideration with respect to empirically keyed tests is that researchers often do *not* know why a given test item distinguishes between two groups. Imagine, for example, that an empirically keyed test of achievement motivation includes an item such as "On TV, I prefer to watch sports, not romantic movies." A researcher might find that this item does a good job of distinguishing between higher-paid versus lower-paid managers in a work setting. However, does this item measure achievement motivation or, instead, simply the respondents' gender? Because empirically keyed tests depend on knowing in advance that two groups differ, there may be reasons other than the one the researcher is focusing on that might lead to differences on items.

MMPI

● **Minnesota Multiphasic Personality Inventory (MMPI)** The most widely used and researched empirically keyed self-report personality test.

The **Minnesota Multiphasic Personality Inventory (MMPI)** is the most widely used and researched empirically keyed self-report personality test. The MMPI was initially constructed in the 1940s to assess "abnormal" personality tendencies. The most recent version of the inventory, the MMPI-2, is still widely used around the world to assess personality and predict outcomes (Butcher & others, 2011; Schuder & others, 2016). The scale features 567 items and provides information on a variety of personality characteristics. The MMPI also includes items meant to assess whether the respondent is lying or trying to make a good impression (social desirability). The MMPI is used to assess mental health (Greene, 2011), as a tool in hiring decisions, to help people make career choices (Caillouet & others, 2010), and in forensic settings, assessing criminal risk (Bow, Flens, & Gould, 2010; Sellbom & others, 2010).

ASSESSMENT OF THE BIG FIVE FACTORS

Paul Costa and Robert McCrae (1992) constructed the Neuroticism Extraversion Openness Personality Inventory—Revised (or NEO-PI-R, for short), a self-report test assessing the five-factor model: neuroticism, extraversion, openness, agreeableness, and conscientiousness. Other measures of the big five traits have relied on the lexical approach and offer the advantage of being available without a fee.

● **face validity** The extent to which a test item appears to fit the particular trait it is measuring.

Unlike empirically keyed tests, measures of the big five generally contain straightforward items; for instance, the trait "talkative" might show up on an extraversion scale. These items have what psychologists call **face validity,** which means that the items seem on the surface to be testing the characteristic in question. Measures of the big five typically involve items that are obvious in terms of what they measure, but not all self-report assessments have this quality.

It is likely that you could give a reasonably good assessment of your own levels of traits such as neuroticism and extraversion. What about the more mysterious aspects of yourself and others? If you are like most people, you think of psychological assessments as tools to find out things you do not already know about yourself. For that objective, psychologists might turn to projective tests.

Projective Tests

● **projective test** A personality assessment test that presents individuals with an ambiguous stimulus and asks them to describe it or tell a story about it—to project their own meaning onto the stimulus.

A **projective test** presents individuals with an ambiguous stimulus and asks them to describe it or tell a story about it—in other words, to *project* their own meaning onto the stimulus. Projective tests are based on the assumption that the ambiguity of the stimulus allows individuals to interpret it based on their feelings, desires, needs, and attitudes. Based on the defense mechanism of projection, projective tests are especially designed to elicit the individual's unconscious feelings and conflicts, providing an assessment that goes deeper than the surface of personality (Sahly & others, 2011).

Projective tests attempt to get inside the mind to discover how the test taker really feels and thinks; that is, they aim to go beyond the way the individual overtly presents himself or herself. These tests are theoretically aligned with psychodynamic perspectives on personality, which give more weight to the unconscious than do other perspectives. Projective techniques require content analysis; the examiner must code the responses for the underlying motivations revealed in the story.

Perhaps the most famous projective test is the **Rorschach inkblot test,** developed in 1921 by Swiss psychiatrist Hermann Rorschach. The test consists of 10 cards, half in black-and-white and half in color, which the individual views one at a time (Figure 8). The test taker is asked to describe what he or she sees in each of the inkblots. The individual may say, for example, "I see two fairies having a tea party" or "This is a picture of the female reproductive organs." These responses are scored based on indications of various underlying psychological characteristics (Bornstein, 2012).

The Rorschach's usefulness in research is controversial. Both the test's reliability and validity have been criticized (Garb & others, 2001; Hunsley & Bailey, 2001; Weiner, 2004). If the Rorschach were reliable, two different scorers would agree on the personality characteristics of the individual being tested. If the Rorschach were valid, it would predict behavior outside of the testing situation; that is, it would predict, for example, whether an individual will attempt suicide, become severely depressed, cope successfully with stress, or get along well with others. Research shows that the Rorschach does not meet these criteria of reliability and validity (Lilienfeld, Wood, & Garb, 2000).

Although sometimes administered in clinical (Huprich, 2013) and applied settings (Piotrowski, 2015), the Rorschach is not commonly used in personality research. However, the projective method itself remains a tool for studying personality, especially in the form of the Thematic Apperception Test (TAT).

The **Thematic Apperception Test (TAT),** developed by Henry Murray and Christiana Morgan in the 1930s, is designed to elicit stories that reveal something about an individual's personality. The TAT consists of a series of pictures like the one in Figure 9, each on an individual card or slide. The TAT test taker is asked to tell a story about each of the pictures, including events leading up to the situation described, the characters' thoughts and feelings, and the way the situation turns out. The TAT is now more commonly referred to as a *Picture Story Exercise (PSE)*.

PSE methods are used in clinical practice and in research. The stories can be coded for motivational content, including need for achievement, affiliation, power, intimacy, and a variety of other needs (Schultheiss & Brunstein, 2005) as well as unconscious defense mechanisms (Cramer, 2015). In contrast to the Rorschach, TAT measures have shown reliability and validity (Aydinli & others, 2015; Schüler & others, 2015).

Other Assessment Methods

Self-report questionnaires and projective techniques are just two of the multitude of assessment methods developed and used by personality psychologists. Many personality psychologists incorporate interviews as well as friend or peer ratings of individuals' traits or other characteristics. Personality psychologists also measure behavior directly, by observing a person either live or in a video (Kelly & Agnew, 2012). In addition, cognitive assessments have become more common in personality psychology, as researchers investigate topics such as the relation between personality and processes of attention and memory. Personality psychologists also use a host of psychophysiological measures, such as heart rate and skin conductance. Increasingly, personality psychologists are incorporating brain imaging as well.

Whether personality assessments are being used by clinical psychologists, psychological researchers, or other practitioners, the choice of assessment instrument depends greatly on the researcher's theoretical perspective. Figure 10 summarizes which methods are associated with each of the theoretical perspectives. The figure also summarizes each approach, including its major assumptions, and gives a sample research question addressed by each. Personality psychology is a diverse field, unified by a shared interest in understanding those aspects of the person that make the individual who he or she really is.

FIGURE 8   Type of Stimulus Used in the Rorschach Inkblot Test What do you see in this figure? Do you see two green seahorses? Or a pair of blue spiders? A psychologist who relies on the Rorschach test would examine your responses to find out who you are. ©Science Museum/SSPL/The Image Works

● **Rorschach inkblot test** A famous projective test that uses an individual's perception of inkblots to determine his or her personality.

● **Thematic Apperception Test (TAT)** A projective test that is designed to elicit stories that reveal something about an individual's personality.

FIGURE 9   Picture from the Thematic Apperception Test (TAT) What are this man and woman thinking and feeling? How did they come to this situation, and what will happen next? A psychologist who uses the TAT would analyze your story to find out your unconscious motives. ©Bill Aron/PhotoEdit

Approach	Summary	Assumptions	Typical Methods	Sample Research Question
Psychodynamic	Personality is characterized by unconscious processes. Childhood experiences are of great importance to adult personality.	The most important aspects of personality are unconscious.	Case studies, projective techniques.	How do unconscious conflicts lead to dysfunctional behavior?
Humanistic	Personality evolves out of the person's innate, organismic motives to grow and actualize the self. These healthy tendencies can be undermined by social pressure.	Human nature is basically good. By getting in touch with who we are and what we really want, we can lead happier, healthier lives.	Questionnaires, interviews, observation.	Can situations be changed to support individuals' organismic values and enhance their well-being?
Trait	Personality is characterized by five general traits that are represented in the natural language that people use to describe themselves and others.	Traits are relatively stable over time. Traits predict behavior.	Questionnaires, observer reports.	Are the five factors universal across cultures?
Personological and Life Story	To understand personality, we must understand the whole person. We all have unique life experiences, and the stories we tell about those experiences make up our identities.	The life story provides a unique opportunity to examine the personality processes associated with behavior, development, and well-being.	Written narratives, TAT stories or PSE, autobiographical memories, interviews, and psychobiography.	How do narrative accounts of life experiences relate to happiness?
Social Cognitive	Personality is the pattern of coherence that characterizes a person's interactions with the situations he or she encounters in life. The individual's beliefs and expectations, rather than global traits, are the central variables of interest.	Behavior is best understood as changing across situations. To understand personality, we must understand what each situation means for a given person.	Multiple observations over different situations; video-recorded behaviors rated by coders; questionnaires.	When and why do individuals respond to challenging tasks with fear versus excitement?
Biological	Personality characteristics reflect underlying biological processes such as those carried out by the brain, neurotransmitters, and genes. Differences in behaviors, thoughts, and feelings depend on these processes.	Biological differences among individuals can explain differences in their personalities.	Brain imaging, twin studies, molecular genetic studies.	Do genes explain individual differences in extraversion?

FIGURE 10   **Approaches to Personality Psychology** This figure summarizes the broad approaches to personality described in this chapter. Many researchers in personality do not stick with just one approach but apply the various theories and methods that are most relevant to their research questions.

8. PERSONALITY AND HEALTH AND WELLNESS

Personality comprises a set of enduring characteristics that influence behavior. As such, personality affects many behaviors that impact physical health and psychological wellness, as we consider in this final section.

Personality and Physical Health

We first survey personality characteristics that are linked, respectively, to health and to illness.

CONSCIENTIOUSNESS

Conscientiousness is not the sexiest personality trait, but it might well be the most important of the big five when it comes to longevity and healthy living (Hampson & others, 2013; B. W. Roberts & others, 2009; Turiano & others, 2015). The capacity to follow a sensible plan may be just what it takes to do the mundane tasks required to live a long, healthy life.

A variety of studies show that conscientious people tend to do all the things that they are told are good for their health, such as getting regular exercise, avoiding drinking and smoking, wearing seatbelts, and checking smoke detectors (Hakulinen & others, 2015; O'Connor & others, 2009; Turiano & others, 2012). Conscientiousness is correlated with better health and lower stress (Gartland, O'Connor, & Lawton, 2012; Murphy, Miller, & Wrosch, 2013; Takahashi, Roberts, & Hoshino, 2012). Research has shown that conscientious individuals are less likely to die than their counterparts who are less conscientious (Turiano & others, 2015). A fascinating recent study found that teachers' ratings of the responsibility and studiousness of elementary schools students predicted lowered risk of death at age 52 (Spengler & others, 2016).

PERSONAL CONTROL

Another personality characteristic associated with taking the right steps toward a long, healthy life is personal control. Feeling in control can reduce stress during difficult times and can lead to the development of problem-solving strategies to deal with hardship (Milte & others, 2015; S. E. Taylor, 2015; S. C. Thompson, 2001). Personal control has been linked to lower risk of cancer and cardiovascular disease (Stürmer, Hasselbach, & Amelang, 2006; Williams & others, 2016). Personal control has been related to emotional well-being, successful coping with a stressful event, healthy behavior change, and good health (Aarts & others, 2015; Hughes, Berg, & Wiebe, 2012; Lefcourt, 2014; Sproesser & others, 2011).

SELF-EFFICACY

Self-efficacy is related to success in a wide variety of positive life changes, including achieving weight loss (Byrne, Barry, & Petry, 2012), exercising regularly (Clum & others, 2014), quitting smoking (de Hoog & others, 2016), reducing substance abuse (Goldsmith & others, 2012), and practicing safe sex (Boone, Cherenack, & Wilson, 2015). Evidence shows a link between self-efficacy and cardiovascular functioning following heart failure. Individuals high in self-efficacy are not only less likely to suffer a second hospitalization due to heart failure but also likely to live longer (Bachmann & others, 2015; Maeda & others, 2012; Sarkar, Ali, & Whooley, 2009).

If there is a problem to be fixed, self-efficacy—having a can-do attitude—is related to finding a solution. In one study, smokers were randomly assigned to one of three conditions. In the *self-efficacy condition,* individuals were told they had been chosen for the study because they had great potential to quit smoking (Warnecke & others, 2001). Then they participated in a 14-week program on smoking cessation. In the *treatment-alone condition,* individuals participated in the 14-week smoking cessation program but were told that they had been randomly selected for it. In the *no-treatment control condition,* individuals did not participate in the smoking cessation program. At the end of the 14 weeks, individuals in the self-efficacy condition were more likely to have quit smoking than their counterparts in the other two conditions. The Psychological Inquiry shows the results.

OPTIMISM

A factor that is often linked to positive functioning and adjustment is optimism (Carver & Connor-Smith, 2010). Researchers have found that optimism is associated with taking proactive steps to protect one's health (Carver, Scheier, & Segerstrom, 2010; Ramírez-Maestre, Esteve, & López, 2012).

Optimism has been studied in two different ways. First, some scientists, including Martin Seligman (1990), focus on how optimists and pessimists explain the causes of events in their lives. From this perspective, optimists explain the causes of bad events as external, unstable, and specific, whereas pessimists explain them as internal, stable, and global. Studies have associated explaining life events optimistically with a variety of positive outcomes (Jowsey & others, 2012; Reivich & Gillham, 2003).

Martin Seligman (b. 1942) Seligman went from pessimist to optimist and believes that others can, too. Seligman (1990) provided the details in his book *Learned Optimism.*

© Courtesy of Dr. Martin E. P. Seligman, University of Pennsylvania

psychological *inquiry*

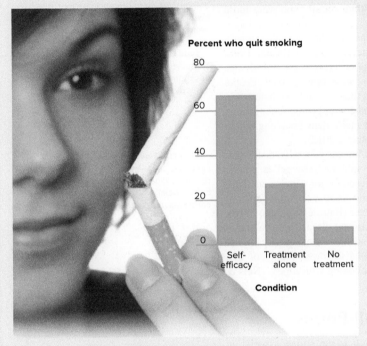

Percent who quit smoking

Condition

A Can-Do Attitude Means You Can Quit Smoking

The figure shows the results of the study on self-efficacy and smoking cessation (Warnecke & others, 2001). Smokers were randomly assigned to one of three conditions—self-efficacy, treatment alone, and no treatment. Notice that the Y, or vertical, axis shows the dependent variable, the percentage of participants who quit smoking. The X, or horizontal, axis shows the independent variable, the groups to which participants were assigned. Try your hand at the following questions.

1. Why were participants randomly assigned to groups?

2. If the researchers concluded that the self-efficacy manipulation caused these differences, would their conclusion be justified? Explain.

3. How might the results of this study be generalized to groups who wish to change other behaviors?

4. How would you design a correlational study that would examine the relationship between self-efficacy and smoking cessation?

A second approach focuses on optimists as having the general expectation that good things are more likely than bad things to occur in the future (Carver & Connor-Smith, 2010; Carver & Scheier, 2009). Numerous studies reveal that those who hold these positive expectancies for the future are physically and mentally healthier than pessimists (Boehm & Kubzansky, 2012; Gallagher, Lopez, & Pressman, 2013; Tindle & others, 2012). Optimism is related to effective immune system functioning (O'Donovan & others, 2009, 2012; Segerstrom & Sephton, 2010). Optimism is associated with better cardiovascular health (Hernandez & others, 2015) and better outcomes among individuals with coronary heart disease (Hevey, McGee, & Horgan, 2014).

As you think about the traits we have examined—conscientiousness, personal control, self-efficacy, and optimism—and their relationship to good health, keep in mind that you can *cultivate* these qualities. Studies show that even conscientiousness, the most stable of these characteristics, can increase, especially in young adulthood. Although these characteristics are generally associated with wellness, other aspects of personality are linked to health problems, as we now consider.

PERSONALITY TYPES: THE TYPE A/TYPE B AND TYPE D BEHAVIOR PATTERNS

In the late 1950s, a secretary for two cardiologists, Meyer Friedman and Ray Rosenman, observed that the chairs in their waiting rooms were tattered and worn, but only on the front edges. The cardiologists themselves had noticed the impatience of their cardiac patients, who often arrived exactly on time and were in a great hurry to leave. Intrigued by this consistency, they conducted a study of 3,000 healthy men between the ages of 35 and 59 over eight years to find out whether people with certain behavioral characteristics might be prone to heart problems (Friedman & Rosenman, 1974). During the eight years, one group of men had twice as many heart attacks or other forms of heart disease as the other men.

Friedman and Rosenman described the common personality characteristics of the men who developed coronary disease as the **Type A behavior pattern,** a cluster of characteristics—being excessively competitive, hard-driven, impatient, and hostile. Rosenman and Friedman labeled the behavior of the healthier group, who were more relaxed and easygoing, the **Type B behavior pattern.**

Subsequent research showed that the link between Type A behavior and coronary disease is not as strong as Friedman and Rosenman believed (Suls & Swain, 1998; R. B. Williams, 2001, 2002). However, certain components of Type A are linked with coronary risk (Spielberger, 2004), especially hostility (Mwendwa & others, 2013). People who are hostile are more likely to develop heart disease than their less angry counterparts (Eng & others, 2003; K. A. Matthews & others, 2004). People with hostile feelings tend to have strong physiological reactions to stress: Their heart races, their breathing quickens, and their muscles tense up (K. King, 2012; Vella & others, 2012).

The **Type D behavior pattern** describes individuals who are generally distressed, frequently experience negative emotions, and are socially inhibited (Beutel & others, 2012; Cosci, 2012; Molloy & others, 2012). Even after adjustment for depression, Type D individuals face a threefold increased risk of adverse cardiovascular (Denollet & Conraads, 2011) and may also be at increased risk of breast cancer (Batselé & others, 2016). A meta-analysis found that Type D individuals with cardiovascular disease are at a higher risk for major adverse cardiac events and have a lower health-related quality of life (O'Dell & others, 2011). Type D behavior pattern is related to lower quality of life, higher levels of depression, poor health behaviors, and poor coping with illness (Nefs & others, 2015; van Dooren & others, 2016).

Personality and Psychological Well-Being

Among the most consistent findings in personality research is the strong association between personality traits and psychological well-being. Specifically, neuroticism is strongly related to lower levels of well-being, whereas extraversion is related to higher levels (Ní Mhaoláin & others, 2012; Otonari & others, 2012; Wilt & Revelle, 2009). The links between these two traits and well-being have even been found in orangutans (Weiss, King, & Perkins, 2006). What explains these connections?

As defined by psychologists, **subjective well-being** is a person's assessment of his or her level of positive affect and negative affect and an evaluation of his or her life in general (Diener, 2012a). This definition provides a clue as to why the traits of neuroticism and extraversion are so strongly related to well-being. Neurotic individuals experience more negative affect than others, and their moods are more changeable. David Watson, a personality and clinical psychologist who specializes in the study of mood, has suggested that negative emotion is at the very core of the trait of neuroticism (Miller, Vachon, & Lynam, 2009; Watson & Clark, 1997).

Interestingly, however, research has shown that neurotics can be happy—especially if they are also extraverted (Hotard & others, 1989). Indeed, Watson suggests that positive emotion is the core of the trait of extraversion (Watson & Naragon, 2009). Research has shown that extraverts are happier than introverts even when they are alone (Lucas, 2008). In fact, research has supported the conclusion that extraverts are happier regardless of what they are doing or with whom they are doing it (Lucas, 2007; McNiel, Lowman, & Fleeson, 2010).

If you are not very conscientious, or you are a pessimist with an external locus of control, or you are hostile, or neurotic, or an introvert—or a hostile, neurotic introvert—you may be feeling your mood deflating. If personality is stable, what good is it to find out that your personality—who you really are—might put you at risk for illness and make you miserable?

A positive way to think about these issues is to focus on the difference between traits and states (Marine & others, 2006). Recall that traits are enduring characteristics—the way you generally are. In contrast, states (such as positive or negative moods) are briefer experiences. Having a trait, such as neuroticism, that predisposes you to feelings of worry (a state) does not mean that your overall well-being must suffer. Instead,

● **Type A behavior pattern** A cluster of characteristics—including being excessively competitive, hard-driven, impatient, and hostile—related to a higher incidence of heart disease.

● **Type B behavior pattern** A cluster of characteristics—including being relaxed and easygoing—related to a lower incidence of heart disease.

● **Type D behavior pattern** A cluster of characteristics—including being generally distressed, having negative emotions, and being socially inhibited—related to adverse cardiovascular outcomes.

● **subjective well-being** A person's assessment of his or her own level of positive affect relative to negative affect and an evaluation of his or her life in general.

test yourself

1. What are four personality characteristics that are associated with positive functioning and positive life changes?
2. How have various researchers defined optimism?
3. What is the Type A behavior pattern, and what specific aspect of it is most often linked to coronary disease?

recognizing that you tend to be neurotic may be an important step in noting when your negative moods are potentially being fed by this trait and are not necessarily the result of objective events. Finding out that you have a personality style associated with higher levels of stress or lower levels of happiness does not mean that you are doomed. Rather, you can use this information to cultivate good habits and to make the most of your unique qualities.

Remember, too, that personality characteristics influence health through their relationships to behaviors and the experience of stress. Even a person very low in conscientiousness can engage in healthy behaviors. Consider that characteristics such as locus of control and self-efficacy are about your beliefs about the world, and these aspects of personality are changeable. Recall that in the Psychological Inquiry in this section self-efficacy was manipulated by simply telling people they had high potential to change. Believing in *your own* potential may be the first step to enhancing your health and wellness.

SUMMARY

1. PSYCHODYNAMIC PERSPECTIVES

Freud developed psychoanalysis through his work with patients suffering from hysterical symptoms (physical symptoms with no physical cause). Freud viewed these symptoms as representing conflicts between sexual drive and duty. Freud believed that most personality—which, in his theory, includes the id, ego, and superego—is unconscious. The ego uses various defense mechanisms, Freud said, to reduce anxiety.

A number of theorists criticized and revised Freud's approach. Horney said that the need for security, not sex or aggression, is our most important need. Jung developed the concept of the collective unconscious, a storehouse of archetypes. Adler's individual psychology stresses that people are striving toward perfection.

Weaknesses of the psychodynamic perspectives include overreliance on reports from the past and overemphasis on the unconscious mind. Strengths of psychodynamic approaches include recognizing the importance of childhood, conceptualizing development through stages, and calling attention to the role of unconscious processes in behavior.

2. HUMANISTIC PERSPECTIVES

Humanistic perspectives stress a person's capacity for personal growth and positive human qualities. Maslow developed the concept of a hierarchy of needs, with self-actualization being the highest human need. In Rogers's approach, each of us is born with a tendency toward growth, a sense of what is good and bad for us, and a need for unconditional positive regard. Because we are often denied unconditional positive regard, we may become alienated from our innate growth tendencies. In order to reconnect with these innate tendencies, Rogers felt, a person requires a relationship that includes unconditional positive regard, empathy, and genuineness.

The humanistic perspectives recognize positive human capacities, but critics suggest the approach is too optimistic and may downplay personal responsibility.

3. TRAIT PERSPECTIVES

Trait theories emphasize that personality consists of traits—broad, enduring dispositions that lead to characteristic responses. Allport stated that traits should produce consistent behavior in different situations, and he used the lexical approach to personality traits, which involves using all the words in the natural language that could describe a person as a basis for understanding the traits of personality.

The current dominant perspective in personality psychology is the five-factor model. The big five traits include openness to experience, conscientiousness, extraversion, agreeableness, and neuroticism. Studying people in terms of their traits has value, but trait approaches are criticized for focusing on broad dimensions and not attending to each person's uniqueness.

4. PERSONOLOGICAL AND LIFE STORY PERSPECTIVES

Murray described personology as the study of the whole person. Contemporary followers of Murray study personality through narrative accounts and interviews. McAdams introduced the life story approach to identity, which views identity as a constantly changing story with a beginning, a middle, and an end. Psychobiography is a form of personological investigation that applies personality theory to one person's life. Life story approaches to personality reveal the richness of each person's unique life story, but it is difficult to carry out and is time-consuming.

5. SOCIAL COGNITIVE PERSPECTIVES

Social cognitive theory states that behavior, environment, and person/cognitive factors are important in understanding personality. In Bandura's view, these factors reciprocally interact.

Two important concepts in social cognitive theory are self-efficacy and personal control. Self-efficacy is the belief that one can master a situation and produce positive outcomes. Personal control refers to individuals' beliefs about whether the outcomes of their actions depend on their own acts (internal) or on events outside of their control (external).

Mischel's controversial book *Personality and Assessment* stressed that people do not behave consistently across different situations but rather tailor their behavior to suit particular situations. Personality psychologists countered that personality does predict behavior for some people some of the time. Mischel developed a revised approach to personality centered on cognitive affective processing systems (CAPS). According to CAPS, personality is best understood as a person's habitual emotional and cognitive reaction to specific situations.

A particular strength of social cognitive theory is its focus on cognitive processes. However, social cognitive approaches have not given adequate attention to enduring individual differences, to biological factors, and to personality as a whole.

6. BIOLOGICAL PERSPECTIVES

Eysenck suggested that introversion/extraversion can be understood as reflecting differences in arousal regulation. Gray developed a reinforcement sensitivity theory of personality, suggesting that extraversion and neuroticism can be understood as two neurological systems that respond to rewards (the behavioral activation system, or BAS) and punishments (the behavioral inhibition system, or BIS) in the environment.

Research has found that dopamine is associated with behavioral approach (extraversion) and serotonin with behavioral avoidance (neuroticism). Behavioral genetic studies have shown that the heritability of personality traits is approximately 50 percent. Studies of biological processes in personality are valuable but can overestimate the causal role of biological factors.

7. PERSONALITY ASSESSMENT

Self-report tests assess personality by asking participants about their preferences and behaviors. One problem in self-report research is the tendency for individuals to respond in socially desirable ways. Empirically keyed tests avoid social desirability problems by using items that distinguish between groups even if we do not know precisely why the items do so.

The Minnesota Multiphasic Personality Inventory (MMPI) is the most widely used empirically keyed personality test. The most popular test for assessing the big five traits is the NEO-PI-R, which uses self-report items to measure each of the traits.

Projective tests, designed to assess unconscious aspects of personality, present individuals with an ambiguous stimulus, such as an inkblot or a picture, and ask them to tell a story about it. Projective tests are based on the assumption that individuals will project their personalities onto these stimuli. The Thematic Apperception Test (TAT) is a projective test that has been used in personality research. Today, the TAT is more commonly termed the Picture Story Exercise (PSE). Other assessment methods include behavioral observation, reports from peers, and psychophysiological and neuropsychological measures.

8. PERSONALITY AND HEALTH AND WELLNESS

Conscientiousness and personal control relate to health and longevity through their association with healthy lifestyle choices. Self-efficacy is also related to the ability to make positive changes in lifestyle. Optimism is another personality characteristic that is related to better health.

The Type A behavior pattern is a set of characteristics including hostility, time urgency, and competitiveness. Type B behavior, in contrast, refers to a more easygoing style. With regard to predicting cardiovascular disease, the crucial aspect of Type A appears to be hostility. The Type D personality is prone to distress, and this type has been linked to poorer health outcomes.

Personality traits that are related to health and wellness can also be thought of as states. Thus, even if you are low on these wellness traits, you can still benefit by seeking out states that foster positive attributes.

key *terms*

archetypes	empirically keyed test	personological and life story perspectives	superego
behavioral genetics	face validity	projective test	Thematic Apperception Test (TAT)
big five factors of personality	humanistic perspectives	psychodynamic perspectives	trait theories
cognitive affective processing systems (CAPS)	id	Rorschach inkblot test	Type A behavior pattern
collective unconscious	individual psychology	self-efficacy	Type B behavior pattern
conditions of worth	Minnesota Multiphasic Personality Inventory (MMPI)	self-report test	Type D behavior pattern
defense mechanisms	Oedipus complex	social cognitive perspectives	unconditional positive regard
ego	personality	subjective well-being	

apply your *knowledge*

1. Consider a facet of your personality that you might want to change. From the perspective of Freud's psychoanalytic theory and Rogers's humanistic theory, could you change this aspect of your personality? If so, how?

2. How important has your childhood been in the development of your adult personality? Choose an experience or series of experiences in childhood and describe how they are represented in your current personality.

3. If you are a fan of reality television, try your hand at identifying the personality characteristics of the individuals involved. Are any of the folks from *Real Housewives* or *Survivor* particularly neurotic or conscientious? If you prefer fictional shows, consider your favorite characters: What are the traits these individuals express?

4. Look at your own social networking profile. Do you think you are expressing the "real you"? If so, how?

CHAPTER 13

CHAPTER OUTLINE

Social Psychology

Being Different in a Cool Way

We all differ from one another in important ways. But feeling different can be hard, especially for children. It can mean dealing with teasing and stares. Each year, hundreds of children in the United States are born without fingers, and others lose digits through accidents. Complicating matters, artificial limbs are too costly for youngsters who will grow out of them all too soon.

A remarkable group of kind strangers armed with 3-D printers has come up with a way to help. It turns out these devices are perfect for creating inexpensive prosthetics. Tailored for kids, the artificial limbs are not only useful, but they are colorful, creative, and even inspired by superhero hands.

Transforming the experience of being different is a job for a whole circle of people. Parents enter a child's measurements and needs on a website. From these measurements, a printer, often owned by a complete stranger, implements a custom design. The prosthetics then require about 20 hours of printing and a few more hours for assembly—similar to a challenging Lego project.

Eight-year-old Ethan Brown, born with two missing fingers, now has a Cyborg Beast hand in his school colors. Ethan used to be teased, but, as his mom noted, "Now he's different in a cool way" (Mroz, 2015). The experience is just as meaningful for those who own the printers. As one person commented, "What could be more rewarding than using your 3-D printer to make a hand for someone?" (Mroz, 2015). From the positive experiences of giving and getting extraordinary help from complete strangers to the negative experiences of stigma and stares, this example illustrates the diverse ways human beings are influenced by and influence their social world—the focus of social psychology. ●

PREVIEW

We begin our study of social psychology by examining social cognition and then exploring social behavior, including altruism and aggression. We next look at conformity, obedience, and social influence before considering how the groups to which we belong shape our interactions with other groups. We probe the world of close relationships, including attraction and love. Finally, we consider the vital role of social connections in health and wellness.

1. DEFINING SOCIAL PSYCHOLOGY

We need other people to survive. Our thoughts and emotions are often about the people we care about. Our goals and motives often include interpersonal relationships. Our behavior is often directed toward (or in response to) another person. It is hard to think of an aspect of our lives that is not in some way connected to other people. This fundamental property of human existence, its social nature, is the focus of social psychology. **Social psychology** is the study of how people think about, influence, and relate to other people.

Social psychology is sometimes confused with *sociology*. Sociology is the study of human societies, organizations, and institutions. Although both sociology and social psychology and are interested in human social behavior, sociology focuses on the group level. Social psychology, in contrast, is interested in how individuals influence groups and how groups influence individuals. Unlike sociologists, social psychologists often focus on the immediate social situation to understand what causes people to behave as they do. Social psychologists are interested in studying how a person's thoughts, feelings, and behaviors are influenced by the actual (or imagined) presence of others.

Within psychology, social psychology is most closely aligned with personality psychology. Social psychologists and personality psychologists are both interested in understanding and predicting behavior. What distinguishes them from each other is where they look for the causes of behavior. Typically, personality psychologists look within the person and his or her traits, motives, and so forth. Social psychologists typically focus on the situational factors that lead to behavior.

● **social psychology** The study of how people think about, influence, and relate to other people.

Features of Social Psychology

Social psychology shares many characteristics with other areas of psychology, but it is distinctive in at least two ways. These include its connection to real-life events and its reliance on experimental methods. Let's review each of these features.

SOCIAL PSYCHOLOGY IS CONNECTED TO REAL LIFE

There are few issues reported in the news today that social psychologists have not studied or will not study in the near future. Whether it is the latest political campaign or social media obsession, social psychologists have likely weighed in with scientific evidence (Forgas, Fiedler, & Crano, 2015). In fact, since it earliest days, social psychology has been inspired by real-life events.

The emergence of social psychology as a field can be traced back to the years after the U.S. Civil War in the late 1800s (Morawski & Bayer, 2013). Imagine what the country was like at that time. The nation was recovering from an incredibly bloody battle that almost ended the union. Former slaves and former slave owners had to find a way to live together in peace. There were many problems to be solved, to say the least. It was at this time that people began to consider whether the new science of psychology might be useful in solving these problems. To this day, racism, prejudice, and attitudes in general are central topics of inquiry in social psychology.

Similarly, after World War II, social psychology saw enormous growth as scientists dedicated themselves to understanding the events that led to the war, the rise of the Nazis, and the Holocaust. Later, during the civil rights movement in the United States, social psychologists were interested in studying all of the ways that changing situational factors might change a person's life for the better.

Not only do social psychologists take inspiration from real-life events, but their research has important implications for many aspects of everyday life. Social psychological research includes topics like leadership, organizational behavior, marketing, and persuasion. Social psychology places many topics from other areas of psychology—including neuroscience, perception, cognition, learning, motivation, and emotion—into a social context. From a social psychological perspective, because human beings are innately social creatures, it makes sense to always consider the social context of any psychological process.

SOCIAL PSYCHOLOGICAL RESEARCH IS (OFTEN) EXPERIMENTAL

Although some social psychological research is correlational in nature, more often than not social psychologists use experimental methods. That means that social psychologists are likely to manipulate an independent variable—for example, an aspect of the social context—to draw causal conclusions about its effects on some outcome (the dependent variable). These experiments are often inspired by observations of the phenomena in the social world.

An Example: The Bystander Effect

To give you a sense of the flavor of social psychology, let's review a classic study, which is drawn from real life and which uses experimental methods—the two distinctive features of social psychology. In 1964, a young woman named Kitty Genovese was brutally murdered in New York City. She was attacked at about 3 A.M. in a courtyard surrounded by apartment buildings. It took the slayer approximately 30 minutes to kill Genovese. Thirty-eight neighbors watched the gory scene from their windows and heard Genovese's screams. Media reports declared that no one helped or called the police. Those reports turned out to be erroneous (Manning, Levine, & Collins, 2007). Nevertheless, inspired by this case, social psychologists John Darley and Bibb Latané (1968) devised a number of studies to examine when the presence of others would lead individuals to be less likely to help a person in distress.

The studies involved randomly assigning participants to be alone or with other people and then staging various emergencies. For example, there might be a woman in the hallway in distress or smoke might begin to slowly fill the room from a vent. The independent variable was whether the participant was alone or with other people. The dependent measure was whether people acted to help the person or respond to the emergency (or how long it took them to do so). The studies showed that when alone, a person was likely to take action about 75 percent of the time, but when another bystander was present, the figure dropped to 50 percent. These results demonstrate the **bystander effect,** the tendency for an individual to be less likely to help in an emergency when other people are present.

Research continues to document the bystander effect. For instance, in a recent study, 5-year-old children were either alone coloring with an experimenter who was painting or were accompanied by two other children (Plötner & others, 2015). To operationalize helping, the experimenter staged an accidental spill of colored water. Results showed that nearly all of the children came to the aid of the experimenter when they were alone. However, they were far less likely to help if there were other (unhelpful) children present.

Unfortunately, the bystander effect is still in evidence today. Consider the case of an unconscious young woman who was sexually assaulted in broad daylight on a crowded Florida beach during spring break in 2015 (Geggel, 2015). The victim was not aware of the assault until she recognized herself in a video of the incident posted online. Sadly, today it often seems as though people are as likely to video a crime as to report it or get help for the victim.

● **bystander effect** The tendency of an individual who observes an emergency to help less when other people are present than when the observer is alone.

Why does the bystander effect occur? According to Darley and Latané (1970), there are five steps to helping in an emergency. The actor (that is, the person observing the event) must

- Notice the event
- Understand that it is an emergency
- Take responsibility for aiding the victim
- Know how to help
- Help

The presence of other people appears to short-circuit the process at some point, but where? Evidence suggests two factors may be at work. First, actors may use other people as a guide for behavior. If no one else is helping, maybe one ought not to help either. Perhaps, then, the presence of others who are not helping indicates that it is not an emergency or sends the message that people are not supposed to help. Second, diffusion of responsibility is a strong factor. The presence of others may have the effect of draining responsibility from each person present (Plötner & others, 2015).

2. SOCIAL COGNITION

● **social cognition** The area of social psychology that explores how people select, interpret, remember, and use social information.

Social cognition is the area of social psychology that explores how people select, interpret, remember, and use social information (Happé & Bird, 2017). Essentially, it is the way in which individuals think in social situations (Hamilton & Carlston, 2013).

Person Perception

Person perception refers to the processes by which we use social stimuli to form impressions of others (Greven, Downing, & Ramsey, 2016). One important social cue is the face (Hugenberg & Wilson, 2013; Watson, Huis In 't Veld, & de Gelder, 2016). Seeing only a face, we automatically process information about how trustworthy and dominant a person is likely to be (Rule & others, 2010).

Alexander Todorov and his colleagues (2005) examined how perception of faces can influence political elections. They asked people to rate the competence of individuals from photographs of their faces. The faces were of candidates in the 2000, 2002, and 2004 U.S. House and Senate elections. Respondents' ratings accurately predicted the outcome for about *70 percent* of the elections. Faces reveal information about the candidates, particularly how competent and trustworthy the perceivers felt each office-seeker would be (Franklin & Zebrowitz, 2016).

The trustworthiness of a face can have profound implications. In a recent study, participants were shown pictures of individuals who were convicted of violent crimes. Faces rated as untrustworthy were more likely to belong to individuals who had been sentenced to death (Wilson & Rule, 2016). Faces can have other important implications for social perception, as we now consider.

PHYSICAL ATTRACTIVENESS AND OTHER PERCEPTUAL CUES

You will not be surprised to learn that physical attractiveness is a powerful social cue. Research has shown that even infants as young as 3 to 6 months of age showed a preference for looking at attractive faces versus unattractive faces, as rated by adults (Ramsey & others, 2004; Rennels & others, 2016). Attractive individuals are generally assumed to have a variety of other positive characteristics, including being better adjusted, socially skilled, friendly, likable, extraverted, and likely to achieve superior job performance (Langlois & others, 2000; Putz & others, 2016). These positive expectations for physically attractive individuals have been referred to as the "beautiful is good" stereotype.

● **stereotype** A generalization about a group's characteristics that does not consider any variations from one individual to another.

A **stereotype** is a generalization about a group's characteristics that does not consider any variations from one individual to another. Stereotypes are a natural extension of the limits on human cognitive processing and our reliance on concepts in cognitive processing (Fiske & Tablante, 2015). We simplify the task of understanding people by classifying them as members of groups or categories with which we are familiar. It takes more mental effort to consider a person's individual characteristics than it does to label him or her as a member of a particular group or category. In this sense, stereotypes are heuristics, those mental shortcuts we reviewed in the chapter "Thinking, Intelligence, and Language". Keep in mind that just as we automatically use many mental shortcuts, so too are stereotypes often automatically part of the way we think about other people (Richeson & Sommers, 2016).

Is there any truth to the "beautiful is good" stereotype? Attractive people may indeed possess a number of positive characteristics (Langlois & others, 2000; Wolbring & Riordan, 2016). Does that mean that attractiveness is naturally related to, for example, better social skills? Not necessarily.

One way that stereotypes can influence individuals is through **self-fulfilling prophecy.** In a self-fulfilling prophecy, expectations cause individuals to act in ways that serve to make the expectations come true. Robert Rosenthal and Lenore Jacobson conducted a classic self-fulfilling prophecy study (1968). The researchers told grade-school teachers that five students were likely to be "late bloomers"—that these students had high levels of ability that would likely shine forth over time. In reality, however, the researchers had randomly selected the students. Nonetheless, a year later, the researchers found that teachers' expectations for the "late bloomers" were reflected in student performance: The academic performance of these five was beyond that of other students. Self-fulfilling prophecy shows the potential power of stereotypes and other sources of expectations on human behavior.

Let's apply self-fulfilling prophecy to physically attractive individuals. Attractive people may receive differential treatment from others throughout their lives. This special treatment increases the likelihood that the attractive individuals might well develop enhanced social skills and be more self-confident than others.

Another relevant question is, what makes a face attractive? *People* magazine's "50 Most Beautiful People" issue might lead you to conclude that attractiveness is about being exceptional in some physical way. Consider Beyoncé's radiant smile or Ryan Gosling's icy blue eyes. It turns out, though, that very attractive faces are actually *average*.

Using computer technology that allowed them to digitally "average" the faces of a large group of individuals of varying attractiveness, Langlois and her colleagues (1994) created composite faces. A large sample of college students then rated the individual faces and the composites. The results showed that individual faces were less attractive than faces that were created by averaging 8, 16, or 32 other faces. These researchers concluded that attractive faces are "just average." Although "averageness" is not the only predictor of attractiveness, Langlois and her colleagues suggest that being average is an essential component (along with variables such as symmetry and youthfulness) of facial attractiveness.

Recent research has added another fascinating contributor to what makes a face attractive: attention. The more we attend to a face, the more attractive it becomes, as compared to faces that have not captured our attention (Störmer & Alvarez, 2016).

FIRST IMPRESSIONS

When we first meet someone, typically the new acquaintance quickly makes an impression. That first impression can have lasting effects (North & Fiske, 2012; Uleman & Kressel, 2013). Why are they so powerful? One possibility is the primacy effect (see the chapter "Memory"): the tendency to attend to and remember what they learned first (N. H. Anderson, 1965). How quickly do we make these initial impressions of others? In one study, individuals needed just a 100-millisecond exposure time to unfamiliar faces to form an impression (Willis & Todorov, 2006).

Are first impressions correct? A number of studies have shown that they can be. Based on photographs or very brief interactions or videos, people are able to accurately discern a person's romantic interest in them (Place & others, 2012), propensity for violence

● **self-fulfilling prophecy** Social expectations that cause an individual to act in such a way that expectations are realized.

What makes a face attractive? Research has found that "averageness" is an essential component.

(Fowler, Lilienfeld, & Patrick, 2009; Stillman, Maner, & Baumeister, 2010), and sexual orientation (Ambady, Hallahan, & Conner, 1999; Stern & others, 2013b).

In addition, a large body of evidence suggests that even in cases where two people are only slightly acquainted, ratings of personality traits can be surprisingly accurate. In one study, participants watched video clips of a group of target individuals, and they rated the targets on various traits. After just *5 seconds,* those ratings related very well to the targets' self-reports for extraversion, conscientiousness, and intelligence. Neuroticism, openness to experience, and agreeableness took a little longer, but within 1 minute judges were reasonably good at producing ratings that agreed with the targets' self-ratings (Carney, Colvin, & Hall, 2007).

Of course, once you become acquainted with someone, you have a lot more information to use to form an opinion of the person. The process by which we come to understand the causes of others' behavior and form an impression of them as individuals is called *attribution.*

Attribution

Attributions are explanations of the causes of behavior (Reeder, 2013). We can observe someone's actions, such as a friend giving money to a homeless person. To determine the underlying cause of that behavior, what it means about that friend, we often have to make inferences. Making inferences means taking the information we have and coming up with a good guess about who someone is and what the person is likely to do in the future (Rudolph, 2016; Todorov & others, 2015). The results of those inferences are our attributions. What factors play a role in the attributions we make about behaviors? This question is addressed by attribution theory.

● **attribution theory** The view that people are motivated to discover the underlying causes of behavior as part of their effort to make sense of the behavior.

Attribution theory views people as motivated to discover the underlying causes of behavior as part of their effort to make sense of the behavior (Heider, 1958; Kelley, 1973; Weiner, 2006). Attributions vary along three dimensions:

- *Internal/external causes:* Internal attributions are causes inside and specific to the person, such as his or her traits and abilities. External attributions are causes outside the person, such as social pressure, aspects of the social situation, the weather, and luck. Did Beth get a *D* on the test because she didn't study or because the test was too hard?

- *Stable/unstable causes:* Whether the cause of behavior is relatively enduring and permanent or temporary influences attributions. Did Taylor honk her car horn because she is a hostile person or because she happens to be in a big hurry that day?

- *Controllable/uncontrollable causes:* We perceive that people have power over some causes (for instance, by preparing delicious food for a picnic) but not others (rain on picnic day). So, if a rainstorm spoils Henry's picnic, we would not hold that against him.

ATTRIBUTIONAL ERRORS

In attribution theory, the person who produces the behavior to be explained is called the *actor.* The person who offers a causal explanation of the actor's behavior is called the *observer.* Actors often explain their own behavior in terms of external causes. That means that Beth might say she did poorly on the test because it was, in fact, too hard. In contrast, observers frequently explain the actor's behavior in terms of internal causes. Taylor might explain that she honked at a car that was slow to move when the light turned green because she was in a hurry to get to the hospital to see her ill father, but the other driver might think she was rude.

● **fundamental attribution error** Observers' overestimation of the importance of internal traits and underestimation of the importance of external situations when they seek explanations of an actor's behavior.

The **fundamental attribution error** refers to the tendency of observers to overestimate the importance of internal traits and underestimate the importance of external factors when they explain an actor's behavior (Fiedler & Kutzner, 2016; Jones & Harris, 1967; Repacholi & others, 2016) (Figure 1).

Although it is called the *fundamental* attribution error, this error is not universal. Cross-cultural studies show that Westerners tend to attribute causes of behavior to the person. In contrast, those from collectivistic cultures are more likely to look to the situation to explain the behavior of others (Berry & Fredrickson, 2015; Imada, 2012; Morris & Peng, 1994; Rips, 2011).

HEURISTICS IN SOCIAL INFORMATION PROCESSING

When we make attributions, we are engaging in social information processing. Just as heuristics are useful in general information processing, they can play a role in *social* information processing (Rand & others, 2014). Heuristics can be helpful tools for navigating the complex social landscape, but they can lead to mistakes. Because these mistakes occur in the social context, their consequences can be serious. As an example, recall the **representativeness heuristic.** When we use this heuristic, we ignore unbiased information in favor of the resemblance between a person and our image of a typical member of a group. If a woman does not look like any of the other engineers we know, we may not view her as capable of the job.

One common heuristic is the false consensus effect. The **false consensus effect** means overestimating the degree to which everybody else thinks or acts the way we do. Ask yourself: "How many students at your school support the death penalty?" The false consensus effect tells us that your answer is likely to depend on whether *you* support the death penalty.

The fundamental attribution error and the false consensus effect are both related to the special significance of our own thoughts and circumstances. Both of these effects reflect the vast amount of information we have about ourselves relative to the more limited information we have about other people, and they suggest the special place of the self in social information processing.

The Self as a Social Object

Each of us carries around mental representations of ourselves. We can think of the self as our schema, as described in the chapter "Memory", for who we are, what we are like (and not like), and how we feel about these perceptions. The self is different from other social objects because we know so much more about ourselves than we do about others (Hoyle, 2013).

The self is special as well because we value ourselves. One of the most important self-related variables is *self-esteem,* the degree to which we have positive or negative feelings about ourselves (Brummelman, Thomaes, & Sedikides, 2016; Harter, 2013). In general, research has shown that it is good to feel good about oneself, especially if those feelings are stable and not overly inflated (Koch, 2013; Orth & others, 2016).

Individuals with high self-esteem often possess a variety of **positive illusions**—rosy views of themselves that are not necessarily rooted in reality. Indeed, research shows that many of us think of ourselves as "above average" on valued characteristics, including how trustworthy, objective, and capable we are (Gregg & Sedikides, 2010; Hepper & Sedikides, 2012; Hepper, Sedikides, & Cai, 2013; Sedikides & Skowronski, 2012).

Shelley Taylor and her colleagues have demonstrated that those who hold positive illusions about themselves are psychologically healthier and more likely to be judged positively by others (S. E. Taylor, 2011c, 2013; Taylor & Sherman, 2008; Taylor & others, 2003a, 2003b, 2007).

Self-serving bias refers to the tendency to take credit for our successes and to deny responsibility for our failures when we make attributions about our own behavior. Think about taking an exam. If you do well, you are likely to take credit for that success ("I'm smart"); you tend to make internal attributions. If you do poorly, however, you are more likely to blame situational factors ("The test was too hard"); you tend to make external attributions. You might note that self-serving bias suggests a twist on the fundamental attribution error. We look to situational factors to explain our failures (as in the fundamental attribution error). However, we are happy to take credit for our successes, making personal attributions for these.

Observer Tends to give internal, trait explanations of actor's behavior

"She's late with her report because she can't concentrate on her own responsibilities."

Actor Tends to give external, situational explanations of own behavior

"I'm late with my report because other people keep asking me to help them with their projects."

FIGURE 1 **The Fundamental Attribution Error** In this situation, the supervisor is the observer, and the employee is the actor. (top photo) © Kris Timken/ Blend Images LLC; (bottom photo) © John Dowland/Getty Images

● **representativeness heuristic** The tendency to make judgments about group membership based on physical appearance or the match between a person and one's stereotype of a group rather than on available base rate information.

● **false consensus effect** A person's overestimation of the degree to which everybody else thinks or acts the way he or she does.

● **positive illusions** Favorable views of the self that are not necessarily rooted in reality.

● **self-serving bias** The tendency to take credit for one's successes and to deny responsibility for one's failures.

© Blue Jean Images/Getty Images

● **self-objectification** The tendency to see oneself primarily as an object in the eyes of others.

SELF-OBJECTIFICATION

Self-objectification refers to the tendency to see oneself as an object in others' eyes. Researchers have focused on how women have been socialized to think of themselves and their bodies as objects in the social world (Fredrickson & Roberts, 1997). Making women aware of their status as sexual objects can induce body image concerns, shame, and restricted eating (Moradi & Huang, 2008). Chronic feelings of objectification are associated with lower self-esteem and higher levels of depression (Miner-Rubino, Twenge, & Fredrickson, 2002). Women who feel objectified are less likely to reject sexism and less likely to engage in social activism (Calogero, 2013).

Self-objectification can interfere with task performance. For example, in a series of studies, men and women were asked first to try on either a sweater or a swimsuit and then to complete a math test. After trying on a swimsuit, women performed much more poorly on the math test. The researchers surmised that trying on the swimsuit heightened women's experience of self-objectification and body shame, reducing their mental resources for completing the math test (Fredrickson & others, 1998).

Self-objectification research suggests that reminding women of the fact that they are often judged based on their appearance has important implications for their feelings and behavior. A similar process has been found for members of stereotyped groups.

STEREOTYPE THREAT

● **stereotype threat** An individual's fast-acting, self-fulfilling fear of being judged based on a negative stereotype about his or her group.

Stereotype threat is an individual's fast-acting, self-fulfilling fear of being judged based on a negative stereotype about his or her group. A person who experiences stereotype threat is well aware of stereotypical expectations for him or her as a member of a group. In stereotype-relevant situations, the individual experiences anxiety about living "down" to expectations and consequently underperforms (Aronson & others, 2013; Hartley & Sutton, 2013; Spencer, Logel, & Davies, 2016). Research has shown that when a test is presented to African American and European American students who have first simply checked a box indicating their ethnicity, the African Americans perform more poorly (Steele & Aronson, 1995, 2004). When attention is not drawn to ethnicity, no differences in performance emerged.

Stereotype threat affects performance on math tests by women compared to men, even when both groups have equally strong math training (Spencer, Steele, & Quinn, 1999). Women can experience stereotype in leadership positions as well (Hoyt & Murphy, 2016). European American men, too, can fall prey to stereotype threat; in a study of golf ability, European American men performed more poorly than African American men when they were told the test measured "natural athletic ability" (Stone, 2002). Studies have also shown that boys, compared to girls, can be affected by stereotype threat in academic endeavors, especially reading, that are more stereotypically associated with girls (Pansu & others, 2016).

How exactly does stereotype threat interfere with performance? There are likely many processes at work, including anxiety, distraction, loss of motivation and effort (Davies & others, 2016; Spencer, Logel, & Davies, 2016). What factors might help prevent the consequences of stereotype threat? In one study, African American schoolchildren who were asked their race prior to a math test did not perform as well unless the test was presented to them as a challenge, not as a threat (Alter & others, 2010).

SOCIAL COMPARISON

● **social comparison** The process by which individuals evaluate their thoughts, feelings, behaviors, and abilities in relation to others.

Have you ever felt great about getting a *B* on a test, only to feel deflated after finding out a friend got an *A*? Comparing ourselves to other people is one way we come to understand our own behavior. **Social comparison** is the process by which we evaluate our thoughts, feelings, behaviors, and abilities in relation to others. Social comparison tells us what our distinctive characteristics are and aids us in building an identity.

Over 60 years ago, Leon Festinger (1954) proposed a theory of social comparison. The theory states that when no objective means are available to evaluate our opinions and abilities, we compare ourselves with others. Extended and modified over the years, Festinger's theory continues to provide an important rationale for how individuals come to know themselves. *Upward* social comparisons—when we compare ourselves to those who are better off than we are—can foster feelings of envy and inadequacy. Social media can lead to these feelings, as most people post only very positive portrayals of their lives on Instagram or Facebook (Appel, Gerlach, & Crusius, 2016). *Downward* social comparisons—that is, comparing ourselves with others who are less fortunate—can make us feel better about our own lives (Huang, 2016).

Attitudes

Attitudes are our opinions and beliefs about people, objects, and ideas—how we feel about the world. Social psychologists are interested in how attitudes relate to behavior and in whether and how attitudes can change (Arpan, Rhodes, & Roskos-Ewoldsen, 2012; Briñol & Petty, 2012; Wegener & Petty, 2013).

● **attitudes** An individual's opinions and beliefs about people, objects, and ideas—how the person feels about the world.

CAN ATTITUDES PREDICT BEHAVIOR?

People sometimes say one thing but do another. On a survey, you might report positive attitudes about recycling but still pitch an aluminum soda can in the trash. Studies over the past half-century indicate some of the conditions under which attitudes guide actions (Briñol & Petty, 2012):

- *When the person's attitudes are strong:* If you are very passionate about recycling, you are less likely to pitch that soda can in the trash compared to someone who has only a weak attitude (Ajzen, 2001).

- *When the person shows a strong awareness of an attitude and rehearses and practices it:* For example, a person who has been asked to give a speech about the benefits of recycling is more likely to recycle than is an individual with the same attitude about recycling who has not done so (Fazio & Olsen, 2007; Fazio & others, 1982).

- *When the person has a vested interest:* People are more likely to act on attitudes when the issue at stake is something that will affect them personally. A classic study examined whether students would show up for a rally protesting a change that would raise the legal drinking age from 18 to 21 (Sivacek & Crano, 1982). Although generally students were against the change, only those in the critical age group (from 18 to 20) were likely to show up to protest.

In sum, if an attitude is strong, if it is one a person has thought about a great deal, and if it is about an issue that has direct implications for a person's life, that attitude is likely to predict behavior.

Attitudes are an important topic for the field of social psychology. Social psychologists are interested in just about every question you can imagine asking about attitudes, including where they come from, what they predict, and whether they can be changed.

Attitude researchers assume that most of the way we feel about something is determined by that thing, itself. For example, you like skiing because of the speed or you like summer days because they are fun. Based on this assumption, there should be things that just about everyone hates or loves. Who doesn't like puppies or chocolate? But, recently, researchers who study attitudes noticed that there seem to be some people whose attitudes tend to be positive (or negative), no matter what the attitudes are about. Could it be that some people just like (or dislike) everything? To find out read the Intersection.

CAN BEHAVIOR PREDICT ATTITUDES?

Does the link between attitudes and behaviors run in both directions? Social psychologists offer two main explanations for how behavior influences attitudes: cognitive dissonance theory and self-perception theory.

INTERSECTION

Social Psychology and Personality Psychology: Do Some People Just Hate Everything?

You probably know someone who just seems to complain about everything: Winter is too cold; summer is too hot. The new smartphone is too slow. The food is too salty, or not salty enough. Perhaps you also know someone who seems incapable of having a negative opinion about anything. For this person, mosquitoes aren't so bad and pop quizzes are fun. If you wanted to verify, scientifically, that such people exist, how would you do it?

Researchers in personality and social psychology have developed questionnaires to measure these global negative and positive attitudes—what are called *dispositional attitudes*—because they refer to attitudes that people carry with them, like personality traits (Eschleman, Bowling, & Judge, 2015; Hepler & Albarracín, 2013; Judge & Bretz, 1993). These scales ask participants to rate their feelings about a variety of completely unrelated objects, like "cold showers," "camping," "taxes," "modern art," "bicycles," or "how people drive." Strangely enough, even though these items have

© Elenathewise/IStock/Getty Images

nothing to do with one another, there are indeed people who express relatively positive (or negative) attitudes about all of them, regardless of what they are. The findings suggest that there are people who just like or dislike everything. Can these dispositional attitudes be tapping into something real?

Research shows that individuals who hold dispositional attitudes express positive (or negative) attitudes toward new objects they have never encountered before (Eschelman, Bowling, & Judge, 2015). These attitudes are not simply extensions of personality traits, mood, or optimism (Hepler & Albarracín, 2013). Interestingly, dispositional attitudes do predict behavior. People who like everything tend to be more likely to engage in a variety of different activities (Hepler & Albarracín, 2014).

Do you know someone who has a negative (or positive) attitude about everything?

Would it be a lovely world if everyone just had positive dispositional attitudes? Maybe not. These dispositional attitudes may not be a boon to social interactions. Imagine a person unable to see the negatives in unfairness, poverty, or suffering. To the extent that these attitudes are unlikely to change, they could lead to conflicts with others (Hepler, 2015). If your romantic partner tells you he or she loves your new haircut, might it mean a little less if you know that your partner likes everything?

● **cognitive dissonance** An individual's psychological discomfort (dissonance) caused by two inconsistent thoughts.

Cognitive Dissonance Theory   **Cognitive dissonance,** another concept introduced by Festinger (1957), is the psychological discomfort (*dissonance*) caused by two inconsistent thoughts. According to the theory, we feel uneasy when we notice an inconsistency between what we believe and what we do.

In a classic study, Festinger and J. Merrill Carlsmith (1959) asked college students to engage in a series of very boring tasks, such as sorting spools into trays and turning wooden pegs. These participants were later asked to persuade another student (who was in fact a confederate) to participate in the study by telling him that the task was actually interesting and enjoyable. Half of the participants were randomly assigned to be paid $1 for telling this white lie, and the other half received $20. Afterward, all of the participants rated how interesting and enjoyable the task really was.

Those who were paid only $1 to tell the lie rated the task as significantly more enjoyable than those who were paid $20. Festinger and Carlsmith reasoned that those paid $20 to tell the lie could attribute their behavior to the high value of the money they received. On the other hand, those who were paid $1 experienced cognitive dissonance: "How could I *lie* for just $1? If I said I liked the task, I must have really liked it." The inconsistency between what they *did* (tell a lie) and what they *were paid for it* (just $1) moved these individuals to change their attitudes about the task.

When attitudes and behavior conflict, we can reduce cognitive dissonance in one of two ways: change our behavior to fit our attitudes or change our attitudes to fit our behavior. In the classic study above, participants changed their attitudes about the task to match their behavior. If you pitched that soda can, for example, you might feel dissonance ("Wait, I believe in recycling, yet I just pitched that can") and relieve that dissonance by telling yourself, "Recycling is not really *that* important." Through cognitive dissonance, your behavior changed your attitude.

One type of dissonance reduction is called effort justification. *Effort justification* means coming up with a rationale for the amount of work we put into getting something, typically by increasing the value associated with things that are difficult to attain.

Effort justification explains the strong group loyalty that emerges after enduring difficult experiences to get into groups, such as initiation rites for Greek organizations, boot camp in the Marines, and the rigors of medical school en route to becoming a physician. From a cognitive dissonance perspective, individuals in these situations are likely to think, "If it's this tough to get into, it must be worth it." Working hard to get into a group can change our attitudes about that group. In some U.S. presidential elections, many voters have to wait in line for hours to cast their votes. You can imagine that many of them feel that the right to vote is extraordinarily important to them, after the long wait.

Working hard to get into a group inspires loyalty through cognitive dissonance.
©Andrew Lichtenstein/The Image Works

Self-Perception Theory   **Self-perception theory** is Daryl Bem's (1967) take on how behavior influences attitudes. According to self-perception theory, individuals make inferences about their attitudes by observing their behavior. That is, behaviors can cause attitudes, because when we are questioned about our attitudes, we think back on our behaviors for information. If you stood in line for five hours to vote and someone asked about your attitude toward voting, for example, you might think, "Well, I have waited all this time, it must be very important to me." Your behavior has led you to recognize something about yourself that you had not noticed before. According to Bem, we are especially likely to look to our behavior to determine our attitudes when those attitudes are unclear.

Figure 2 compares cognitive dissonance theory and self-perception theory. Both theories have merit in explaining the connection between attitudes and behavior, and

● **self-perception theory** Bem's theory on how behaviors influence attitudes, stating that individuals make inferences about their attitudes by perceiving their behavior.

Festinger's Cognitive Dissonance Theory

We are motivated toward consistency between attitudes and behavior and away from inconsistency.

Example: "I hate my job. I need to develop a better attitude toward it or else quit."

Bem's Self-Perception Theory

We make inferences about our attitudes by perceiving and examining our behavior and the context in which it occurs, which might involve inducements to behave in certain ways.

Example: "I am spending all of my time thinking about how much I hate my job. I really must not like it."

FIGURE 2   Two Theories of the Connections Between Attitudes and Behavior Although we often think of attitudes as causing behavior, *behavior* can change *attitudes*, through either dissonance reduction or self-perception.
(photo) ©Photodisc/Getty Images

Senator Elizabeth Warren has used her persuasive power to get elected and to advocate for her stance on economic issues.

© Chip Somodevilla/Getty Images

these opposing views bring to light the complexity that may exist in this connection. Both theories suggest that behavior can change attitudes. Another route to attitude change is persuasion.

PERSUASION

Persuasion involves trying to change someone's attitude—and often his or her behavior as well (Petty & Briñol, 2015). Teachers, lawyers, and sales representatives study techniques that will help them sway their audiences (children, juries, and buyers). Presidential candidates have arsenals of speechwriters and image consultants to help ensure that their words are persuasive. Advertisers are skilled persuaders, who draw on a full array of techniques to sell everything from cornflakes to carpets to cars.

Carl Hovland and his colleagues originally identified the various elements of persuasion (Hovland, Janis, & Kelley, 1953; Janis & Hovland, 1959):

- *The communicator (source):* A key factor in persuasion is the person doing the persuading. Is the person delivering the message (or the source of the message) viewed as credible (or believable)? Trustworthiness, expertise, power, attractiveness, likability, and similarity are all credibility characteristics that help a communicator change people's attitudes or convince them to act.

- *The medium:* Another persuasion factor is the medium or technology used to get the message across. Is the message presented in print, on TV, on Twitter, or YouTube? Because it presents live images, television is generally a more powerful medium than print sources for changing attitudes. Of course, the effects of the medium of a message may depend on who is receiving it. When Missouri Senator Claire McCaskill announced her support for same-sex marriage, she did so on Tumblr, perhaps suggesting the age group she was trying to reach.

- *The target (audience):* The audience or target of a message can play a role in message persuasiveness. Younger people are more likely to change their attitudes than older ones. And individuals with weak attitudes are more easily persuaded than those with strong ones.

- *The message:* The final aspect of persuasion is the message itself. What kind of message is persuasive? Some messages involve strong logical arguments, and others focus on exciting emotions such as fear and anger in the audience. Which is more likely to work and when? The elaboration likelihood model addresses this question.

● **elaboration likelihood model** Theory identifying two ways to persuade: a central route and a peripheral route.

The **elaboration likelihood model** identifies two pathways of persuasion: a central route and a peripheral route (Briñol & Petty, 2015; Petty & Cacioppo, 1986). The *central route* works by engaging the audience thoughtfully with a sound, logical argument. The *peripheral route* involves factors such as the source's attractiveness or the emotional power of an appeal. The peripheral route is effective when people are not paying close attention or lack the time or energy to think about the message. As you might guess, television advertisers often use the peripheral route to persuasion on the assumption that during the commercials you are probably not paying full attention to the screen. The central route is more persuasive when people have the ability and the motivation to pay attention.

Successful Persuasion　Sooner or later, nearly everyone will be in a position of selling someone something. Social psychologists have studied ways in which social psychological principles influence whether a salesperson makes that sale (Cialdini, 1993).

One strategy is called the *foot-in-the-door* technique (Freedman & Fraser, 1966). The foot-in-the-door strategy involves making a smaller request ("Would you be interested in a three-month trial subscription to a magazine?") at the beginning, saving the biggest demand ("How about a full year?") for last. The foot-in-the-door strategy relies on the notion that in agreeing to the smaller offer, the customer has created a relationship with the seller, expressing a level of trust.

A different strategy is called the *door-in-the-face* technique (Cialdini & others, 1975). The door-in-the-face technique involves making the biggest pitch first ("Would you be interested in a full-year subscription?"), which the customer probably will reject, and then making a smaller, "concessionary" demand ("Okay, then, how about a three-month trial?"). This technique relies on the fact that the customer feels a sense of obligation: You let him off the hook with that big request, maybe he should be nice and take the smaller offer.

Resisting Persuasion   Advertisers and salespeople work their hardest to persuade us to buy their products. How do we resist their appeals? According to William McGuire, one way to resist persuasion is through *inoculation* (McGuire, 2003; McGuire & Papageorgis, 1961). McGuire proposed that just as administering a vaccine inoculates individuals from a virus by introducing a weakened or dead version of that virus to the immune system, giving people a weak version of a persuasive message and allowing them time to argue against it can help individuals avoid persuasion.

Such "inoculation" helps college students resist plagiarism (Compton & Pfau, 2008) as well as credit card marketing appeals (Compton & Pfau, 2004). When individuals are warned that they are going to be hit with persuasive appeals and are given arguments to help them resist these pitches, they are able to do so.

test yourself

1. What do psychologists mean by a stereotype, and how do they define a stereotype threat?
2. What is involved in making a fundamental attribution error? Give an example of such an error.
3. Identify and briefly explain the four elements of persuasion.

3. SOCIAL BEHAVIOR

We do not just think socially; we also behave in social ways. Two particular types of behavior that have interested psychologists represent the extremes of human social activity: altruism and aggression.

Altruism

High school junior Meghan Vogel was running the 3,200-meter race in the 2012 Ohio Division III State Track Championships. Ahead of her was Arden McMath, a sophomore from another school. With just 20 meters to go, Arden collapsed, and then something amazing happened. Instead of passing her, Meghan stopped and helped. Putting Arden's arm around her own neck, Meghan supported her to the finish line, ensuring that Arden crossed the line before she did (Binder, 2012). This simple act of kindness gained widespread praise, though for Meghan it was nothing special.

People engage in a surprising range of extreme acts of kindness. Some give away nearly every cent they own to charities. Others donate kidneys to complete strangers or adopt more than 20 children out of a simple sense of kindness (MacFarquhar, 2015).

In everyday life, we witness and perform "random acts of kindness"—maybe adding a quarter to someone's expired parking meter or giving up our seat on a bus to someone in need. All of these acts are *prosocial behaviors*—they all involve helping another person (Schroeder & Graziano, 2015). Such acts of kindness bear the markings of altruism. **Altruism** means giving to another person with the ultimate goal of benefiting that person, even if it incurs a cost to oneself. Are acts of kindness truly altruistic?

Psychologists debate whether human behavior is ever truly altruistic. Altruistic motives contrast with selfish or egoistic motives (Cialdini, 1991; Maner & others, 2002). **Egoism** means helping another person for personal gain, such as to feel good or avoid guilt. Kindness might also serve selfish purposes by ensuring *reciprocity*, meaning that we help another person to increase the chances that the person will return the favor. When a person behaves kindly toward another and expects something in return (reciprocity), that is not altruism. Rather, altruism means doing something good for another even if it poses a cost to oneself and even if the act can never be repaid.

Altruism has presented a puzzle for evolutionary psychologists (André & Morin, 2011; Kurzban, Burton-Chellew, & West, 2015; Simpson & Willer, 2015). How can behavior that rewards others, and not oneself, be adaptive? One way to explain this puzzle is to note that prosocial behavior is often extended among family members, because helping a relative also means promoting the survival of the family's genes (Kurzban, Burton-Chellew, & West, 2015). Evolutionary theorists believe that reciprocity in relationships with nonfamily members is essentially the mistaken application of a heuristic that made

● **altruism** Unselfish interest in helping another person.

● **egoism** Giving to another person to ensure reciprocity; to gain self-esteem; to present oneself as powerful, competent, or caring; or to avoid censure from oneself and others for failing to live up to society's expectations.

© Mel Curtis/Getty Images

sense in human evolutionary history—to engage in selfless acts of kindness to one's own family (Nowak, Page, & Sigmund, 2000).

Acts of kindness seem to have one powerful payoff for those who do them: Helping others strongly and consistently leads to increased positive mood (Aknin & others, 2015; Dunn, Aknin, & Norton, 2008; Schaller & Cialdini, 1988). Prosocial spending, or spending money on others rather than oneself, is linked to greater well-being, potentially universally (Aknin & others, 2013). Does the fact that behaving prosocially leads to feelings of pleasure mean that such behavior is always selfish?

Feelings of pleasure are linked with adaptive behaviors, those things we need to do to survive and reproduce. We enjoy eating. We enjoy sex. Is it possible that the strong link between pleasure and kindness demonstrates that prosocial behavior is an important adaptation for humans who depend on one another for survival? Interestingly, kindness is not exclusive to humans. Ethology—the study of animal behavior—has examined whether acts of kindness occur in nonhuman animals. Ethologists have found that nonhuman primates demonstrate altruistic acts of kindness (Engelmann & Hermann, 2016).

Setting aside the question of whether such acts are altruistic, in this section we review biological, psychological, and sociocultural factors that predict prosocial behavior. As you read, consider whether you think altruism is a problem to be solved or a natural aspect of human life.

BIOLOGICAL FACTORS IN PROSOCIAL BEHAVIOR

Research has shown that genetics play a role in prosocial behavior. Genetic factors explain between 30 and 69 percent of the differences we see in the tendency to engage in kind acts (Knafo, Israel, & Ebstein, 2011; Knafo-Noam & others, 2015). Prosociality is linked as well to the oxytocin receptor gene (Wu & Su, 2015). Such a link makes sense as oxytocin is associated with social bonding (Johnson & Young, 2015). High levels of serotonin are associated with prosocial behavior (Crockett, 2009). In addition, dopamine receptors in the brain are associated with prosocial behavior (Knafo, Israel, & Ebstein, 2011).

In terms of brain structures, research suggests that when we feel compassion for another person, areas of the midbrain associated with the perception of pain are likely to be active (Simon-Thomas & others, 2012). These same areas are associated with nurturing parental behaviors, suggesting that neural factors associated with the parent–child relationship are involved in kindness toward others.

PSYCHOLOGICAL FACTORS IN PROSOCIAL BEHAVIOR

Among the psychological factors thought to play a role in prosocial behavior are empathy, personality, and mood.

Empathy As we discussed in the chapter "Gender, Sex, and Sexuality", *empathy* is a person's feeling of oneness with the emotional state of another. When we feel empathy for someone, we feel what that person is feeling. Empathy allows us to put ourselves in another person's shoes. We can feel empathy even for those we do not particularly like, as demonstrated by the playing of "Sweet Caroline" (a tradition of the Boston Red Sox) at Yankee Stadium during the game with their arch rivals following the Boston Marathon bombing in 2013.

Daniel Batson has spent the better part of his career searching for proof that true altruism does exist, and he argues that empathy is the key to altruism (Batson, 2002, 2006, 2012; Batson & others, 2007). When we are feeling empathy for someone else's plight, we are moved to action—not to make ourselves feel better but out of genuine concern for the other person.

Personality Agreeableness (see the chapter "Personality") is the personality trait most strongly associated with prosocial behaviors (Graziano & Habashi, 2015). The association between agreeableness and brain structures helps to illuminate its role in acts of kindness. Agreeableness is related to greater volume in the posterior cingulate cortex (DeYoung & others, 2010), a brain area associated with understanding other people's beliefs and associated with empathy (Saxe & Powell, 2006).

Mood   Our mood can determine whether or not we engage in kind behaviors. The research literature strongly concludes that happy people are more likely than unhappy people to help others (Snyder & Lopez, 2007). Does it then follow that being in a bad mood makes people less helpful? Not necessarily, because adults (especially) generally understand that doing good for another person can be a mood booster. When people are in a bad mood, they might be likely to help if they think that doing so will improve their mood.

SOCIOCULTURAL FACTORS IN PROSOCIAL BEHAVIOR

Two sociocultural factors that influence prosocial behavior are socioeconomic status and the media.

Socioeconomic Status   Socioeconomic status is a sociocultural factor in prosocial behavior. Although they have less, those of lower socioeconomic status tend to be more likely to help than those who have more (Piff & others, 2010). Even children from lower socioeconomic backgrounds are more generous (Miller, Kahle, & Hastings, 2015). Compared to wealthier individuals, those from poorer backgrounds tend be more attuned to the suffering of others (Stellar & others, 2012). It may be that relative wealth promotes a focus on maintaining one's standing in the world to the detriment of reaching out to help those in need (Kraus & others, 2012).

Media Influences   Media—including music, TV, film, and video games—can influence prosocial behavior. Whether it is on YouTube or TV, seeing someone perform an act of kindness can move us to behave kindly as well (Ellithorpe, Ewoldsen, & Oliver, 2015). Listening to music with prosocial lyrics can promote kindness (Greitemeyer, 2009). Watching television shows with positive content predicts prosocial behavior (de Leeuw & others, 2015). Playing prosocial video games enhances prosocial thoughts (Greitemeyer & Osswald, 2011) and acts of kindness (Greitemeyer & Osswald, 2010; Whitaker & Bushman, 2012).

The human ability to engage in kindness sits alongside the capacity to cause others harm. Some evolutionary scientists have suggested that altruism, especially when it is directed at the members of one's own group, may coexist with hostile actions toward other groups (Arrow, 2007). A soldier may perform selfless acts of altruism for his or her country, but for a person on the other side of the combat, that behavior is harmful. Thus, altruism within a group may be linked to aggression.

Aggression

Aggression refers to social behavior with the objective of harming someone, either physically or verbally. Ethologists note aggression in nonhuman animals (Lorenz, 1965; Tinbergen, 1969). However, in the animal kingdom, most hostile encounters do not escalate to killing or even severe harm. Much of the fighting is ritualistic and involves threat displays—for example, a bear's laid-back ears, lowered head, and bellowing.

● **aggression** Behavior that is intended to harm another person.

Evolutionary theorists believe that human beings are not much different from other animals. A basic theme of their theory is the survival of the fittest (Barber, 2009; Cosmides, 2013; Wrangham & Glowacki, 2012). Thus, they conclude that early in human evolution the survivors were probably aggressive individuals. In this section we will review biological, psychological, and sociocultural influences on aggression.

BIOLOGICAL INFLUENCES IN AGGRESSION

Researchers who approach aggression from a biological viewpoint examine the influence of genetics and neurobiological factors.

Genes   The importance of genes to aggression is clear in selective breeding of animals. After a number of breedings among only aggressive animals and among only docile animals, vicious and timid strains of animals emerge. The vicious strains attack nearly anything in sight; the timid strains rarely fight, even when attacked.

In the animal world, aggression often is ritualistic and typically involves threat displays, such as a bear's laid-back ears, lowered head, and bellowing.

© LOOK-foto/Superstock

The genetic basis for aggression is more difficult to demonstrate in humans than nonhuman animals and may depend on the type of aggression studied (Brendgen & others, 2008; Porsch & others, 2016). Specifically, twin studies have shown that physical aggression that is proactive in nature (that is, unprovoked aggression) may be more influenced by genes, but more reactive aggression may be more susceptible to environmental effects.

Neurobiological Factors   Although humans do not have a specific aggression center in the brain, aggressive behavior often results when areas such as the limbic system are stimulated by electric currents (Aaronson & Lloyd, 2015; Herbert, 1988; Wood & Liossi, 2006). The frontal lobes of the brain—the areas most involved in executive functions such as planning and self-control—have also been implicated in aggression. Research has examined the brains of individuals who have committed the ultimate act of violence: murder (Nordstrom & others, 2011; Raine, 2008). The results indicate that murderers may differ from others in deficits in the functioning of these areas of the brain.

Neurotransmitters—particularly, lower levels of serotonin—have been linked to aggressive behavior (Coccaro & others, 2015; Glick, 2015). However, the link between serotonin and aggression is small (Duke & others, 2013).

Hormones are another biological factor that may play a role in aggression, as noted in the chapter "Gender, Sex, and Sexuality". The hormone that is typically implicated in aggressive behavior is testosterone (Nguyen & others, 2016). Animal research has shown that testosterone relates to aggression (Cunningham & McGinnis, 2007), but the link between testosterone and aggression in humans is likely more complex (Carré & Olmstead, 2015).

PSYCHOLOGICAL INFLUENCES IN AGGRESSION

Psychological influences on aggression include personality characteristics, frustrating and aversive circumstances, cognitive determinants, and observational learning factors.

Personality Characteristics   Some people are more likely to behave aggressively than others. Not surprisingly, low levels of agreeableness are associated with more aggressive behavior (Wang & others, 2016). In addition, a constellation of traits—including low agreeableness, low conscientiousness, and high levels of neuroticism—is associated with aggression (Settles & others, 2012). A meta-analysis showed that individuals who are high on hostility and irritability are more likely to behave aggressively, whether provoked or not (Bettencourt & others, 2006). Other personality characteristics are associated with greater aggressive behavior only when individuals are provoked. For instance, individuals who ruminate over interpersonal slights are more likely to aggress when provoked (Bettencourt & others, 2006).

Frustrating and Aversive Circumstances   Many years ago, John Dollard and his colleagues (1939) proposed that *frustration,* the blocking of an individual's attempts to reach a goal, triggers aggression. The *frustration-aggression hypothesis* states that frustration always leads to aggression. When people are frustrated in their desires, they will lash out.

Psychologists later recognized that frustration is just one of many aversive experiences can lead to aggression. You might notice that you are more grumpy and short-tempered when you have a headache or a toothache, for example. Circumstances like physical pain, personal insults, crowding, and unpleasant events can all lead to aggression. Aversive circumstances also include factors in the physical environment, such as the weather. Murder, rape, and assault increase when temperatures are the highest, as well as in the hottest years and the hottest cities (Anderson & Bushman, 2002).

Cognitive Determinants   Aggressive behavior often starts with aggressive thoughts. Aspects of the environment can put aggressive thoughts in our heads through priming. Recall from the chapter "Memory" that priming can involve making something salient to a person, even subliminally or without the person's awareness. Research by Leonard Berkowitz and others has shown that the mere presence of a weapon (such as a gun) may prime hostile thoughts and produce aggression (Anderson, Benjamin, & Bartholow, 1998; Berkowitz, 1990; Berkowitz & LePage, 1996). The tendency for the presence of firearms to enhance aggression is known as the *weapons effect*. In support of Berkowitz's ideas, a well-known study found

Aversive circumstances that might stimulate aggression include factors in the physical environment such as noise and crowding.

© Sandy Huffaker/Getty Images

that individuals who lived in a household with a gun were 2.7 times more likely to be murdered than those dwelling in a household without a gun (Kellermann & others, 1993).

Observational Learning Factors   Social cognitive theorists believe that individuals learn aggression through reinforcement and observational learning. Watching others engage in aggressive actions can evoke aggression, as you might recall from the classic Bobo doll study described in the chapter "Learning" (Bandura, Ross, & Ross, 1961). One of the strongest predictors of aggression is witnessing aggression in one's own family (Ferguson & others, 2008). Watching television provides a ready opportunity to observe aggression in our culture, which we consider further in the discussion below on media violence.

SOCIOCULTURAL INFLUENCES IN AGGRESSION

Aggression and violence are more common in some cultures than others. In this section, we review sociocultural influences on aggression including the culture of honor and media influences.

The Culture of Honor   Dov Cohen has examined how cultural norms about masculine pride and family honor may foster aggressive behavior (Cohen, 2001; Vandello & Cohen, 2004, 2008; Vandello & others, 2009). In *cultures of honor,* a man's reputation is thought to be an essential aspect of his economic survival. Such cultures see insults to a man's honor as diminishing his reputation and view violence as a way to compensate for that loss. In these cultures, family pride might lead to so-called honor killings in which, for example, a female rape victim is slain by her male family members so that they, in turn, are not "contaminated" by the rape.

Cohen has examined how, in the United States, southerners are more likely than northerners to be aggressive when honor is at stake. In one study, Cohen and his colleagues (1996) had men who were from either the North or the South take part in an experiment that required them to walk down a hallway. A member of the study passed all the men, bumping against them and quietly calling them a derogatory name. The southerners were more likely than the northerners to think their masculine reputation was threatened, to become physiologically aroused by the insult, and to engage in actual aggressive or dominant acts. In contrast, the northerners were less likely to perceive a random insult as "fightin' words."

Media   Images of violence pervade U.S. popular media: newscasts, television shows, sports broadcasts, movies, video games, Internet videos, and song lyrics. Do portrayals of violence lead to aggression?

Social psychologists sometimes ask participants in a study to assign the amount of hot sauce a person must drink as a measure of aggression. Do you think that is a good operational definition of aggression?

© flashgun/IStock/Getty Images

test yourself

1. What is the difference between altruism and egoism?
2. What are the various psychological influences contributing to aggression?
3. What have researchers found about the influence of prosocially oriented video games? What have they learned about the effects of violent video games?

Although some critics reject the conclusion that TV violence causes aggression (Savage & Yancey, 2008), many scholars insist that TV violence can prompt aggressive or antisocial behavior in children (Brown & Tierney, 2011; Bushman & Huesmann, 2012; Comstock, 2012). Of course, television violence is not the only cause of aggression in children or adults. Like all social behaviors, aggression has multiple determinants (Matos, Ferreira, & Haase, 2012). The link between TV violence and aggression in children is influenced by children's personality traits and attitudes toward violence.

Another type of media that has interested psychologists is violent pornography. Violent pornography includes films, videos, websites, and magazines portraying the degradation of women in a sexual context. Do such media foster violence toward women? Based on several meta-analyses and on research of their own, Neil Malamuth and his colleagues concluded that pornography consumption does have a small effect on male sexual aggression and is related to more tolerance of violence toward women (Hald, Malamuth, & Yuen, 2010; Malamuth, Addison, & Koss, 2000). Yet Malamuth and his colleagues caution that pornography is only one of a number of factors that may lead to sexual violence against women (Hald, Malamuth, & Yuen, 2010; Vega & Malamuth, 2007). The most problematic materials are those that depict women enjoying being the victims of male sexual violence (Hald, Malamuth, & Yuen, 2010). Such violent pornography reinforces the *rape myth*—the false belief that women desire coercive sex.

As we discussed earlier, research shows that prosocial video games foster prosocial behavior. Do violent video games foster aggression? Experimental evidence shows that playing a violent video game can lead to more aggressive thoughts and behaviors in children (Saleem, Anderson, & Gentile, 2012) and adults (Hasan, Bègue, & Bushman, 2013). Correlational studies demonstrate an association between playing violent video games and a number of negative outcomes (Boxer, Groves, & Docherty, 2015). A meta-analysis concluded that children and adolescents who play violent video games extensively are more aggressive, less sensitive to real-life violence, and more likely to engage in delinquent acts than their counterparts who spend less time playing the games or do not play them at all (C. A. Anderson & others, 2010).

Critics of the conclusion that violent video-game exposure leads to aggression have pointed out that the acts of aggression studied in the laboratory are not generalizable to real-world criminal violence (Ritter & Elsea, 2005; Savage, 2008; Savage & Yancey, 2008). Operationalizing aggression in the laboratory is challenging. Researchers might provide participants the opportunity to "aggress" against another, for instance, by subjecting the individual to a blast of loud noise, dispensing a mild electrical shock, or administering a large dose of Tabasco to swallow. Whether these operational definitions of aggression are applicable to real-life violence is a matter of much debate (Savage & Yancey, 2008).

Perhaps more importantly, critics of research on the link between violent video games and aggression argue that this research often employs small samples and does not equalize gaming experiences across both violent and nonviolent games (Hilgard & others, 2016). For example, violent games are often more challenging and difficult than nonviolent games. In addition, many studies have not consistently measured important third variables, such as family violence, in predicting both video-game use and aggression (Ferguson, 2015; Ferguson & Kilburn, 2010; Ferguson & others, 2008).

4. SOCIAL INFLUENCE

Another topic of interest to social psychologists is how our behavior is influenced by other individuals and groups. This section explores key aspects of social influence: conformity, obedience, and group influence.

Conformity and Obedience

After World War II, psychologists sought answers to the disturbing question of how ordinary people could be influenced to commit the atrocities inflicted on Jews, Gypsies, and other minorities during the Holocaust. Many people engaged in terrible actions because everyone else was doing it or because they were told to do it by an authority figure. Researchers wanted to understand the processes by which people allowed themselves to be controlled by the social situation in this way. This interest gave rise to research on conformity and obedience as well as to three classic studies in social psychology that we will encounter along the way.

CONFORMITY

Conformity is a change in a person's behavior to coincide more closely with a group standard. When we conform, we do something we might not have done otherwise because everyone else is doing it. Conformity takes many forms and affects many aspects of people's lives, in positive and negative ways. Conformity is at work when we obey the rules and regulations that allow society to run smoothly. Consider how chaotic it would be if people did not conform to social norms such as stopping at a red light, driving on the correct side of the road, and not punching others in the face.

Conformity can also be a powerful way to increase group cohesion. Even something as simple as marching in step together or singing a song along with a group can lead to enhanced cooperation among group members (Wiltermuth & Heath, 2009). Some of the most important rituals in which humans participate involve conforming to particular actions: We march, stand, kneel, dance—in unison. Such behaviors increase our sense of belonging (Tarr, Launay, & Dunbar, 2016; Wen, Herrmann, & Legare, 2016).

Conformity can also be destructive. Conformity is at work, for example, when a person comes to college and starts to drink heavily at parties, even though he or she might have never consumed alcohol before. Conformity is a powerful social force. You can feel the pressure of conformity for yourself if, the next time you get on an elevator with other people, you do not turn around to face the door. We begin our exploration of conformity by considering a classic study by Solomon Asch.

Asch's Experiment   Put yourself in this situation: You are taken into a room where you see five other people seated along a table. A person in a white lab coat enters the room and announces that you are about to participate in an experiment on perceptual accuracy. The group is shown two cards—the first having only a single vertical line on it and the second having three vertical lines of varying length. You are told that the task is to determine which of the three lines on the second card is the same length as the line on the first card. You look at the cards and think, "What a snap. It's so obvious which is the same."

What you do not know is that the other people in the room are confederates who are working with the experimenter. On the first several trials, everyone agrees about which line matches the standard. Then on the fourth trial, each of the others picks the same *incorrect* line. As the last person to make a choice, you have the dilemma of responding as your eyes tell you or conforming to what the others before you said. How would you answer?

Solomon Asch conducted this classic experiment on conformity in 1951. Asch instructed the confederates to give incorrect responses on 12 of 18 trials. To his surprise, Asch (1951) found that participants conformed to the incorrect answers 35 percent of the time.

Why would people go along with a group even when they have clear-cut information disputing the others, such as the lines in the Asch experiment? Next we review biological, psychological, cultural answers to this question.

Biological Factors in Conformity   Research on how the brain responds to moments when we do not fit in with a group suggest that the brain may actually "feel better" when we fit in. Using fMRI, one study examined what happens in the brain when people find out that their opinions conflict with those of others (Klucharev & others, 2009). Women were asked to rate a variety of female faces for attractiveness, and their brains were scanned while they received feedback about whether their ratings agreed with those of the other group members. When participants were told that their ratings differed from the group's ratings, they showed enhanced activation in the brain area typically associated with monitoring for errors. In other words, the brain responded to judgments that differed from the group's as if they were mistakes.

● **conformity** A change in a person's behavior to coincide more closely with a group standard.

Further, when their ratings differed from the group's, women experienced less activation in the nucleus accumbens and the ventral tegmental area—the brain's reward centers. The greater the degree to which women's brains responded to being different as an error and as not rewarding, the more they tended to conform when given a chance to re-rate the faces at the end of the study.

Another biological factor in conformity is oxytocin, the neurotransmitter and hormone associated with social bonding. In a double-blind experiment, participants were randomly assigned to receive oxytocin or a placebo and were then placed in groups to make ratings about the attractiveness of various symbols. Those who were given oxytocin were more likely produce preferences that matched the ratings of members of their groups—that is, to conform (Stallen & others, 2012).

Psychological Factors in Conformity   Imagine walking into the first meeting of a group you have just joined. You do not know the members very well and are unfamiliar with how they run things. You are very likely to use the behavior of others to direct your own: When in Rome, do as the Romans do. But why, precisely, would you do that? For one thing, you lack knowledge of the group's customs. For another, you are new and want them to like you. These two reasons are the two main psychological factors identified as contributing to conformity: informational social influence and normative social influence.

Informational social influence refers to the influence other people have on us because we want to be right. The social group can provide us with information that we do not have or may help us see things in ways that had not occurred to us. As a result, we may conform because we have come to agree with the group. The tendency to conform based on informational social influence depends especially on two factors: how confident we are in our own judgment and how well informed we perceive the group to be. For example, if you know little about computers and three of your acquaintances who are IT geeks tell you not to buy a particular brand of computer, you are likely to conform to their recommendation. They have knowledge you lack, and you want to make the right choice.

In contrast, **normative social influence** is the influence others have on us because we want them to like us. Whether the group is an inner-city gang or members of a profession such as medicine or law, if a particular group is important to us, we might adopt the clothing style of the group, use the same slang words, and assume the attitudes that characterize the group's members (Hewlin, Kim, & Song, 2016). On your first day of work at a new job, you might remind yourself what you saw others wearing on your interview and follow suit because you want to fit in. That's normative social influence.

In sum, we have two reasons for conformity: Informational social influence means we conform to be right; normative social influence means we conform to be liked.

Cultural Factors in Conformity   As we have reviewed previously, individualistic cultures value independence and individual accomplishments and emphasize differences and uniqueness. Collectivistic cultures value the group, emphasize group harmony, and believe that accomplishments depend on individuals' carrying out their roles in the larger social network. It is not surprising, then, that collectivism has been associated with greater levels of conformity. One research review, summarizing 133 experiments following Asch's design, found that individualism within cultures was negatively correlated with conformity (Bond & Smith, 1996).

OBEDIENCE

Obedience is behavior that complies with the explicit demands of the individual in authority. We are obedient when an authority figure demands that we do something, and we do it. Note that in conformity, people change their thinking or behavior so that it will be more like that of others, while in obedience, there is an explicit demand made on the person.

Obedient behavior sometimes can be distressingly cruel. One of the most infamous examples of the destructive nature of obedience is the Nazi crimes against Jews and others during World War II. More recent examples include the obedience of radical Muslims instructed to participate in suicide attacks against Israelis and westerners (McCauley & Segal, 2009) and that of U.S. military personnel at Abu Ghraib prison in

● **informational social influence** The influence other people have on us because we want to be right.

● **normative social influence** The influence others have on us because we want them to like us.

● **obedience** Behavior that complies with the explicit demands of the individual in authority.

Iraq, who justified their horrendous abuse of detainees by asserting that they were "just following orders" (A. G. Miller, 2004).

Millions of people throughout history have obeyed commands to commit terrible acts. Two classic experiments in social psychology provide insight into obedience.

Milgram's Experiment   Stanley Milgram (1965, 1974) was a social psychologist interested in how susceptible people can be to following orders. Initially, Milgram was interested in finding out if Americans would be as likely as Germans were to obey commands to harm another person. The studies he conducted demonstrated the profound effect of obedience.

To get a sense for his studies, imagine that, as part of a psychology experiment on the effects of punishment on memory, you are asked to deliver a series of electric shocks to another person. Your role is to be the "teacher" and to punish the mistakes made by the "learner." Each time the learner makes a mistake, you are to increase the intensity of the shock.

You are introduced to the learner, a nice 50-year-old man who mumbles something about having a heart condition. Strapped to a chair in the next room, he communicates with you through an intercom. The apparatus in front of you has 30 switches, ranging from 15 volts (slight) to 450 volts (marked as beyond dangerous: "XXX").

As the trials proceed, the learner quickly runs into trouble and is unable to give the correct answers. As you increase the intensity of the shock, the learner says that he is in pain. At 150 volts, he demands to have the experiment stopped. At 180 volts, he cries out that he cannot stand it anymore. At 300 volts, he yells about his heart condition and pleads to be released. If you hesitate in shocking the learner, however, the experimenter tells you, "You must go on. The experiment requires that you continue."

Eventually the learner stops responding altogether, and the experimenter tells you that not responding is the same as a wrong answer. The learner is unresponsive. He might be injured or even dead. Would you keep going? Do you think most people would? As shown in Figure 3, when Milgram conducted this study, the majority of the teachers obeyed the experimenter: Almost two-thirds delivered the full 450 volts. By the way, the 50-year-old man was a confederate and was not being shocked at all. Of course, the teachers were unaware that the learner was only pretending to be shocked.

"You must go on. The experiment requires that you continue." Imagine that with those simple statements the experimenter was able to calmly command people (as far as they knew) to shock a man to unconsciousness and possibly death. Such is the power of obedience to authority.

Milgram's studies have been an ethical controversy since they began. Under today's ethical guidelines, it is unlikely that these experiments would have been approved. Nonetheless, we are still learning from Milgram's data. A meta-analysis of his experiments suggested that the critical decision was at the 150-volt level, when the learner first requested that the experiment be halted. At that point, 80 percent of those who were going to stop did so (Packer, 2008). Apparently, individuals who were going to disobey were those who responded not to the later anguished cries of pain but to the learner's first request to be set free.

You might wonder whether Milgram's results would apply today. To examine this question, Jerry Burger (2009) recreated Milgram's study. His study was very similar to Milgram's with a key exception: Burger's participants were never allowed to go higher than 150 volts. At 150 volts, the confederate asked to end the study, and immediately after participants decided whether to continue, the experiment was ended. Surprisingly, Burger's participants were only slightly less likely to obey than Milgram's had been. The *Psychological Inquiry* probes the results of Burger's study.

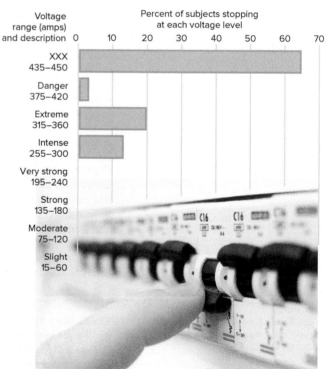

FIGURE 3   **Milgram Obedience Study** A 50-year-old man, the "learner," is strapped into a chair. The experimenter makes it look as if a shock generator is being connected to his body through several electrodes. The chart shows the percentage of "teachers" who stopped shocking the learner at each voltage level. © BernardaSv/iStock/Getty Images

psychological *inquiry*

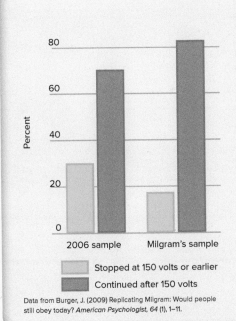

Stopped at 150 volts or earlier
Continued after 150 volts

Data from Burger, J. (2009) Replicating Milgram: Would people still obey today? *American Psychologist, 64* (1), 1–11.

Obedience Then and Now

The figure shows the results of Burger's obedience study, conducted in 2006 and published in 2009, and the results of one of Milgram's studies. The vertical, or Y axis, shows the percent of participants who stopped or continued shocking the learner after that individual first expressed a desire to end the study. Try answering the questions below the figure.

1. Does this comparison surprise you? Why or why not?
2. Burger did not allow participants who knew of Milgram's study to take part in his study. How might the results have differed if these individuals had been permitted to participate?
3. If you had been a "teacher" in this study, what do you think you would have done?

The Stanford Prison Experiment   Another controversial demonstration of the power of obedience is provided by the famous Stanford prison experiment, conducted by Philip Zimbardo in 1971. This study illustrates the potentially horrific effects of obedience, not only on those who obey but on those who wield authority.

For the study, Zimbardo and his students created a simulated prison in the basement of a Stanford University building (Haney, Banks, & Zimbardo, 1973; Zimbardo, 1972, 1973, 2007). Newspaper ads recruited men for a two-week study of prison life that would pay $15 per day (about $86 in 2016). After undergoing screening to ensure they were psychologically healthy, 24 men were assigned to the role of either "prisoner" or "guard."

Prisoners were "arrested" at their homes, booked and fingerprinted at the local police station, and brought to the prison. They were strip-searched, given uncomfortable uniforms, and assigned three to a cell where they spent most of their time, night and day. The guards wore uniforms and mirrored sunglasses (to prevent eye contact with prisoners) and wielded wooden batons. They could leave the prison between their eight-hour shifts. Zimbardo, acting as the prison superintendent, told the guards that they had all the power in the prison (Zimbardo, 1989). He informed the guards that they would be taking away each prisoner's individuality.

The course of the study surprised even Zimbardo. Things got ugly very quickly. During the first two days, one prisoner had to be released when he started raging uncontrollably, and a group of prisoners blockaded themselves in their cells. Additional guards were brought in to control the uprising. Some guards attacked prisoners with fire extinguishers while not being watched by the research staff. One-third of the guards behaved in extremely sadistic ways, forcing prisoners to stand naked in their cells or allowing them only a bucket in which to urinate and defecate. The study was cut short after just six days, prompted by a graduate student's concern for participant safety (Zimbardo, Maslach, & Haney, 2000).

Zimbardo concluded that situational factors powerfully affect human behavior. To explain why prisoners did not quit the study, he argued that they had internalized their roles. To explain the guards' cruelty, Zimbardo reasoned that when an authority figure removes personal responsibility, when other people are dehumanized, and when norms support otherwise horrifying behavior, true evil can emerge. The conclusions drawn from this work are similar to those of the Milgram obedience studies: Anyone would do vile things if put in the same situation, and good people will do evil things to other good people if the situation supports those deeds (Zimbardo, Maslach, & Haney, 2000).

Scholars have questioned whether Zimbardo's study provides evidence of human nature's potential for shocking and inhumane behavior (Haslam & Reicher, 2003). For instance, recall that Zimbardo recruited participants with an ad that mentioned "prison life." Thomas Carnahan and Sam McFarland (2007) placed two ads in a newspaper—one that mentioned prison life and one that did not. Individuals who answered the first ad differed from those who answered the second: They were higher on characteristics such as aggression and exploitativeness and lower in altruism and empathy.

Like Milgram's studies, the Stanford prison experiment has been criticized on ethical grounds (De Vos, 2010; Fromm, 1973; Savin, 1973). Participants in the experiment (and Milgram's studies, for that matter) did not express regret and felt the study was worthwhile (Zimbardo, 2007). Perhaps you can see how cognitive dissonance might explain such responses. Still, the Stanford prison experiment is an influential study in social psychology. It continues to inform our understanding of human behavior in prison contexts (Zimbardo, 1971, 2007) and to inspire controversy (McAdams, 2007).

EXERTING PERSONAL CONTROL

After reading about these landmark studies by Asch, Milgram, and Zimbardo, you may be questioning the value of conformity and obedience and wondering what it might take for people to stand up to group pressure or against the demands of an authority figure. It can be difficult to go against the crowd and risk being wrong or rejected. When people believe that they have control over their own actions, they are less likely to conform (Alquist, Ainsworth, & Baumeister, 2013).

Reactance refers to the motivation to reject attempts to control us (Brehm, 2000). Reactance occurs when a person feels that someone or something is taking away his or her choices. Sometimes when authority figures overreach, reactance propels people to defy those authorities. Reactance might explain the high levels of voter turnout in the 2016 presidential primaries in places where authorities had attempted to limit voting.

Daily life requires some amount of conformity and obedience, but there are times when all of us must exert personal control over our actions. Although it may not be easy to resist the group or authority, living with the knowledge that you compromised your own moral integrity may be more difficult in the long run.

Group Influence

Scenes of mobs rioting are all too common in the media. A team wins a championship, and fans who would never otherwise break the law can be seen setting fire to cars and looting businesses. People at a political rally who might otherwise never even raise their voices to someone else are captured on video punching individuals who favor a different candidate. Teammates, fraternity and sorority members, bandmates, and members of various clubs harm and even kill new members during hazing rituals. Make no mistake, the perpetrators in these instances are often people with no history of violence who genuinely have no hostility toward the person harmed. None of them, acting alone, would have performed destructive, even murderous, acts. Why does being in a group lead to such behavior? This central question has driven research in the social psychology of group influence.

DEINDIVIDUATION

One process that sheds light on the behavior of individuals in groups is **deindividuation,** which occurs when being part of a group reduces personal identity and erodes the sense of personal responsibility (Levine, Cassidy, & Jentzsch, 2010; Zimbardo, 2007). An example of the effects of deindividuation is the wild street celebrations that erupt after a team's victory in the World Series or Super Bowl.

One explanation for the effects of deindividuation is that groups give us anonymity. When we are part of a group, we may act in an uninhibited way because we believe that no one will be able to identify us. The Ku Klux Klan demonstrates a variety of

● **deindividuation** The reduction in personal identity and erosion of the sense of personal responsibility when one is part of a group.

Why do individuals who would never perform destructive acts when alone perpetrate them when in a group?

©Patrick Fallon/Cal Sport Media/Newscom

● **social contagion** Imitative behavior involving the spread of actions, emotions, and ideas.

ways that human beings can deindividuate: acting in groups, often under cover of darkness, and wearing white hoods to conceal identity.

Nowhere is the deindividuating cloak of anonymity more apparent than in anonymous online communication (Coles & West, 2016; Mikal & others, 2016). Indeed, cyberbullying is highest when people feel they are completely anonymous online (Bartlett, 2015).

SOCIAL CONTAGION

Have you ever noticed that a movie you watched in a crowded theater seemed funnier than it did when you watched it alone at home? People laugh more when others are laughing. Babies cry when other babies are crying. The effects of others on our behavior can take the form of **social contagion,** imitative behavior involving the spread of actions, emotions, and ideas (Kiuru & others, 2012; Poirier & Cobb, 2012). Social contagion effects have been observed in varied phenomena, including shopping online or in stores (Bilgicer & others, 2015), gun shot injuries (Papachristos, Wildeman, & Roberto, 2015), the popularity of dog breeds (Herzog, 2006), the spread of unhealthy behaviors such as smoking and drinking among adolescents (Rodgers, 2007), and the way members of sports teams seem to all have bad performances during the same game (Boss & Kleinart, 2015).

One way to observe social contagion is to sit in a quiet but crowded library and start coughing. You will soon notice others doing the same thing. Similarly, imagine that you are walking down the sidewalk and come upon a group of people who are all looking up. How likely is it that you can avoid the temptation of looking up to see what is so interesting?

GROUP PERFORMANCE

Are two or three heads better than one? Some studies reveal that we do better in groups; others show that we are more productive when we work alone (Meyer, Schermuly, & Kauffeld, 2016; Wolf & others, 2015). Social psychologists use the terms *social facilitation* and *social loafing* to describe the varying ways the presence of others can influence performance.

● **social facilitation** Improvement in an individual's performance because of the presence of others.

Social Facilitation   If you have ever given a presentation in a class, you might have noticed that you did a much better job standing in front of your classmates than during any of your practice runs. **Social facilitation** occurs when an individual's performance improves because of the presence of others. Robert Zajonc (1965) argued that the presence of other individuals arouses us. The arousal produces energy and facilitates our performance in groups. If our arousal is too high, however, we are unable to learn new or difficult tasks efficiently. Social facilitation, then, improves our performance on well-learned tasks. For new or difficult tasks, we might be best advised to work things out on our own before trying them in a group.

● **social loafing** Each person's tendency to exert less effort in a group because of reduced accountability for individual effort.

Social Loafing   Another factor in group performance is the degree to which one's behavior is monitored. **Social loafing** refers to each person's tendency to exert less effort in a group because of reduced accountability for individual effort. The effect of social loafing is lowered group performance. The larger the group, the more likely it is that an individual can loaf without detection. Social loafing can be reduced by making individuals' contributions more identifiable and unique, simplifying the evaluation of these contributions, and making the group's task more attractive (Karau & Williams, 1993).

GROUP DECISION MAKING

Many of the decisions we make take place in groups—juries, teams, families, clubs, school boards, and the U.S. Senate, for example. What happens when people put their minds to the task of making a group decision? How do they decide whether a criminal is guilty, whether a country should attack another, where a family should go on vacation, or whether sex education should be part of a school curriculum? Three aspects of group decision making bear special mention: risky shift and group polarization; groupthink; and majority and minority influence.

Risky Shift and Group Polarization   Imagine that you have a friend, Ann, who works as an accountant. All her life Ann has longed to be a writer. In fact, she believes that she has the next great American novel in her head; she just needs time and energy to devote to writing it. Would you advise Ann to quit her job and go for it? What if you knew beforehand that her chances of success were 50–50? How about 60–40? How much risk would you advise Ann to take?

In one investigation, participants were presented with fictitious dilemmas like this one and were asked how much risk the characters in the scenarios should take (Stoner, 1961). When the individuals discussed the dilemmas as a group, they endorsed riskier decisions than when they were queried alone. The so-called **risky shift** is the tendency for a group decision to be riskier than the average decision made by the individual group members (Westfall, Judd, & Kenny, 2015). Essentially, risky shift means that after group discussion, people start to move toward a riskier choice than their first decision.

However, people do not always make riskier decisions in a group than when alone. Instead, a group discussion can move individuals more strongly in the direction of the position they initially held (Moscovici, 1985). The **group polarization effect** is the solidification and further strengthening of an individual's position as a consequence of a group discussion or interaction. For example, in 2013, a YouTube clip surfaced of (now former) Rutgers men's basketball coach Mike Rice abusing players during a practice. Administrators had seen the video months earlier and had decided that a fine, suspension, and anger management courses would be appropriate consequences. However, after the wider public saw and discussed the clip, it became clear that a more extreme punishment was required, and Rice was fired.

Why would conversation lead to more extreme opinions? First, during the discussion, new, more persuasive arguments can strengthen an original position. Second, social comparison can have influence. The administrators at Rutgers certainly wanted to see themselves as standing up for what was right. Comparing their response to the public outcry revealed they needed to do more to achieve that goal.

Groupthink: Getting Along but Being Very Wrong   Groupthink refers to the impaired group decision making that occurs when making the right decision is less important than maintaining group harmony. Instead of engaging in an open discussion of all the available information, in groupthink, members of a group place the highest value on conformity and unanimity. Members are encouraged to "get with the program." Those who dissent are met with very strong disapproval. Groupthink can occur in different types of groups, ranging from government (Kelman, Sanders, & Pandit, 2016) to medical decision-making teams (Madigosky & Schaik, 2016) to street gangs (Caya, 2015). Symptoms of groupthink include overestimating the power and morality of one's group, close-mindedness and unwillingness to hear all sides of an argument, and pressure for uniformity. Groupthink can occur whenever groups value conformity over accuracy.

Groupthink can result in disastrous decisions. Irving Janis (1972) introduced the concept of groupthink to explain a number of enormous decision-making errors throughout history. Such errors include the lack of U.S. preparation for the Japanese bombing of Pearl Harbor during World War II, the escalation of the Vietnam War in the 1960s, the Watergate coverup in 1974, and the *Challenger* space shuttle disaster in 1986.

Groupthink has also been suggested as being involved in the failure to heed warnings of the 9/11 terrorist attacks, the abuse of prisoners at Abu Ghraib, the lack of action to circumvent activities leading to the recession of 2008, and the unresponsiveness of officials to allegations that former assistant football coach Jerry Sandusky of Penn State University engaged in many acts of child abuse. If you look at your favorite news source today, you will likely find some evidence of groupthink lurking behind negative events.

Groupthink can be prevented if groups avoid isolation, allow the airing of all sides of an argument, have an impartial leader, include outside experts in the debate, and encourage

● **risky shift** The tendency for a group decision to be riskier than the average decision made by the individual group members.

● **group polarization effect** The solidification and further strengthening of an individual's position as a consequence of a group discussion or interaction.

● **groupthink** The impaired group decision making that occurs when making the right decision is less important than maintaining group harmony.

© Scott Olson/Getty Images

members who are strongly identified with the group to speak out in dissent (Packer, 2009). The decision in 2011 for the Navy SEALS to conduct an assassination raid on Osama bin Laden's compound involved an open discussion. Although most of President Obama's advisors hedged their bets, Vice President Biden specifically advised against the raid, whereas then–CIA Director Leon Panetta explicitly recommended going in (Landler, 2012).

Majority and Minority Influence   Most groups make decisions by voting, and, even in the absence of groupthink, the majority usually wins. The majority exerts influence on group decision making through both informational influence (they have greater opportunity to share their views) and normative influence (they set group norms). Those who do not go along may be ignored or even given the boot.

Prospects might seem dim for minority opinion holders, but they *can* make a difference. Because it is outnumbered, the minority cannot win through normative pressure. Instead, it must do its work through informational pressure. If the minority presents its views consistently and confidently, then the majority is more likely to listen to the minority's perspectives. A powerful way that minority opinion holders can have influence is by winning over former majority members to their points of view.

5. INTERGROUP RELATIONS

Conflicts between groups, especially ethnic and cultural groups, are rampant around the world. The terrorist organization ISIS attacks Paris and Brussels; the wronged nations retaliate. Israelis and Palestinians fight over territory in the Middle East, each claiming religious and historical rights to the disputed land. In countries across Africa, tribal chiefs try to craft a new social order favorable to their own rule.

A variety of concepts introduced by social psychologists can help us understand the intensity of conflicts between groups and can provide insight into how to reduce them (Campon & Yzerbyt, 2016; Devine & others, 2012; Vázquez & others, 2016).

Group Identity

Think about the groups of which you are a member—your religious and social organizations, your ethnic group, your nationality. When someone asks you to identify yourself, how often do you respond by mentioning these group memberships? And how much does it matter whether the people you associate with are members of the same groups as you?

SOCIAL IDENTITY

Social identity refers to the way we define ourselves in terms of our group membership. In contrast to personal identity, which can be highly individualized, social identity assumes some commonalities with others (Richeson & Sommers, 2016). A person's social identity might include identifying with a religious group, a country, a social organization, a political party, and many other groups. These diverse forms of social identity reflect the numerous ways people connect to groups and social categories (Hogg, 2012). Social psychologist Kay Deaux (2001) identified five distinct types of social identity: ethnicity and religion, personal relationships, vocations and avocations, political affiliations, and stigmatized groups (Figure 4).

For many people, ethnic identity and religious identity are central to their social identity (Hughes & others, 2015; Rivas-Drake, 2012). Ethnic identity can be a source of pride (Serrano-Villar & Calzada, 2016; Smith & Trimble, 2016). In the United States,

test yourself

1. Compare and contrast informational social influence and normative social influence.
2. What is the difference between conformity and obedience?
3. What do the concepts of risky shift and group polarization have to say about decision making in a group context?

● **social identity** The way individuals define themselves in terms of their group membership.

Ethnicity & Religion	Relationships	Vocations & Avocations	Political Affiliation	Stigmatized Identities
Jewish Asian American Southern Baptist West Indian	Parent Mother Son Widow	Artist Athlete Psychologist Military veteran	Environmentalist Feminist Republican	Overweight person Person with AIDS Homeless person Alcoholic

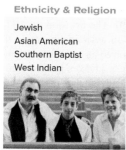   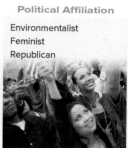 

FIGURE 4   **Types of Identity** When we identify ourselves, we draw on a host of different characteristics associated with the various social groups to which we belong. (first photo) © Rob Melnychuk/Getty Images; (second photo) © Trinette Reed/Brand X Pictures/JupiterImages; (third photo) © Digital Vision/Getty Images; (fourth photo) © moodboard/Corbis; (fifth photo) © Stockbyte/PunchStock

special events celebrate the rich cultural contributions of many different groups to the society. Such experiences may provide individuals with an important resource in coping with biases they encounter (Ikram & others, 2016). Feeling connected to one's ethnic group may buffer individuals from the stressful effects of injustice (Mroczkowski & Sánchez, 2015).

Social psychologist Henry Tajfel (1978), a Holocaust survivor, wanted to explain the extreme violence and prejudice that his religious group (Jews) experienced. Tajfel developed **social identity theory** that states that our social identities are a crucial part of our self-image and a valuable source of positive feelings about ourselves. To feel good about ourselves, we need to feel good about the groups to which we belong. For this reason, individuals invariably think of the group to which they belong as an *ingroup,* a group that has special value in comparison with other groups, called *outgroups.* To improve our self-image, we continually compare our ingroups with outgroups. In the process, we often focus more on the differences between the two groups than on their similarities. Moreover, we begin to see outgroups as more similar to each other: "They" are all the same (Savitsky & others, 2016).

Research by Tajfel (and many others who have used his theory) shows how easy it is to lead people to think in terms of "us" and "them" (Tajfel, 1978). In one experiment, Tajfel had participants look at a screen featuring a huge number of dots and estimate how many dots were displayed. He then assigned the participants to groups based on an arbitrary situation—whether they overestimated or underestimated the number of dots. Once assigned to one of the two groups, the participants were asked to award money to other participants. Tajfel found that individuals awarded money to members of their ingroup, not to participants in the outgroup, even though the group assignment had been essentially arbitrary. If we favor the members of a group that was formed on such a trivial basis, it is no wonder that we show intense ingroup favoritism when differences are not so trivial.

● **social identity theory** Tajfel's theory that social identity, based on group membership, is a crucial part of self-image and a valuable source of positive feelings about oneself.

ETHNOCENTRISM

Ethnocentrism is the tendency to favor one's own ethnic group over other groups. Ethnocentrism is not simply taking pride in one's group; it involves asserting the group's superiority over other groups. As such, ethnocentrism encourages ingroup/outgroup or we/they thinking (Dovidio, Newheiser, & Leyens, 2012). Consequently, ethnocentrism implies that ethnic outgroups are not just different; they are worse than one's group. Hence, ethnocentrism may underlie prejudice.

● **ethnocentrism** The tendency to favor one's own ethnic group over other groups.

PREJUDICE

Prejudice is an unjustified negative attitude toward an individual based on the individual's membership in a particular group. The group can be made up of people of a specific ethnicity, sex, age, religion—essentially, people who are different in some way from a prejudiced person (Monteith, Woodcock, & Lybarger, 2013; Richeson & Sommers, 2016).

● **prejudice** An unjustified negative attitude toward an individual based on the individual's membership in a group.

Ethnic identity evokes ethnic pride. Here, Chinese American children touch the "lion" in the streets of New York City's Chinatown on the day of Chinese New Year, in hopes of receiving good luck and prosperity.

© Roberto Soncin Gerometta/Getty Images

Prejudice is a worldwide phenomenon that can be seen in eruptions of hatred throughout human history. In the Balkan Peninsula of eastern Europe, the Serbs' prejudice against Bosnians prompted the Serb policy of "ethnic cleansing." The prejudice of the Hutus against the Tutsis in Rwanda led them to go on a murderous rampage, attacking the Tutsis with machetes.

A powerful example of destructive prejudice within U.S. society is racial prejudice against African Americans. When Africans were brought to colonial America as slaves, they were considered property and treated inhumanely. In the first half of the twentieth century, most African Americans still lived in the South and remained largely segregated based on skin color; restaurants, movie theaters, and buses had separate areas for Whites and Blacks.

It is useful at this point to note that talking openly about race and ethnicity can be awkward. Even coming up with labels to use to describe different groups of people can be difficult. In the United States, typical labels have changed from "Black" and "White" to "African American" and "European American." But even these labels are not without problems. Many times labels are based not on information about the person's origins, but solely on the color of the person's skin. Nelson Mandela, for instance, was not African American. He was African. How do we distinguish between Mandela and F. W. de Klerk, the former (White) South African president who shared the Nobel Peace Prize with Mandela in 1993 for abolishing apartheid? In our discussion here, we will use the terms *Black* and *White* when in a particular study the actual ethnic background of targets of social judgment is not specified. In these instances, the only cue to the person's background, or anything else about that person, is skin color. Unfortunately, skin color can have a remarkably negative effect on how people are treated.

Despite progress over the years, there remain notable racial disparities among Americans, in terms of poverty, employment, education, and healthcare. Research continues to demonstrate the influence of race in U.S. life. In one study, researchers sent out 5,000 résumés in response to 1,200 job ads placed in newspapers in Chicago and Boston. The résumés were identical in qualifications. They differed only in whether the candidates' names were stereotypically White or Black. "White" names included Meredith, Emily, Brad, and Greg. "Black" names included Tamika, Lakisha, Darnell, and Kareem.

The researchers found that even with identical qualifications, the applicants with White-sounding names were 50 percent more likely to be called for an interview (Bertrand & Mullainathan, 2004; Patacchini, Ragusa, & Zenou, 2015). Results like these have prompted some to consider banning names of applicants on résumés. Such effects are not limited to employment. Churches are most likely to respond to e-mails from individuals with White-sounding names, compared to those with Black- or Latino-sounding names and especially compared to those with Asian-sounding names (Wright & others, 2015).

Another study examined the way race influenced the advice that bankruptcy attorneys gave to clients. During the financial crisis that began in 2008, many Americans resorted to bankruptcy. Declaring bankruptcy means that a person is admitting that he or she is unable to repay debts. This legal claim can allow people to start the arduous process of regaining financial solvency. The two ways of declaring bankruptcy are Chapter 7 and Chapter 13. Chapter 7 bankruptcy is less expensive and often less burdensome than Chapter 13. An analysis of bankruptcy cases across the United States showed that African Americans were more likely than Whites to file Chapter 13 rather than Chapter 7 bankruptcy (Braucher, Cohen, & Lawless, 2012).

© David Maung/Bloomberg via Getty Images

Why would a group of individuals choose the more difficult and expensive form of bankruptcy? Could attorneys be steering African Americans toward this more burdensome path? To address these questions, the researchers conducted an experiment involving a random sample of bankruptcy lawyers. Participants read scenarios in which potential clients were identified as either "Reggie and Latisha" or "Todd and Alison." Even when all other aspects of the cases were identical, lawyers were more likely to recommend that Todd and Alison declare Chapter 7 and that Reggie and Latisha pursue Chapter 13 (Braucher, Cohen, & Lawless, 2012).

Such results are troubling. It is important to keep in mind that these responses to Black-sounding names might not reflect intentional biases but instead subtle and potentially unconscious racial biases. Because racial prejudice is socially unacceptable, few people today would readily admit to racist or prejudicial views. Today, prejudiced individuals are more likely than before to appear unprejudiced on the surface while nevertheless holding racist views at a deeper, potentially unconscious, level.

To confront this problem, social psychologists examine prejudicial attitudes on two levels—explicit racism and implicit racism. *Explicit racism* is a person's conscious and openly shared attitude, which might be measured using a questionnaire. *Implicit racism* refers to attitudes that exist on a deeper, hidden level. Implicit attitudes must be measured with a method that does not require awareness (Perry & others, 2015). For example, implicit racism is sometimes measured using the Implicit Associations Test (IAT), a computerized survey that assesses the ease with which a person can associate a Black or White person with good things (for example, flowers) or bad things (for example, misery) (Greenwald & others, 2009; Sriram & Greenwald, 2009). This test is based on the idea that preexisting biases may make it easier to associate some social stimuli with positive rather than negative items. Although the IAT is widely used, scholars have raised concerns about its validity (Blanton, Jaccard, & Burrows, 2015; Blanton & others, 2009).

Implicit prejudice can influence behavior. In one study, White college students completed measures of explicit and implicit attitudes toward Black people using an implicit measure similar to the IAT (Dovidio, Kawakami, & Gaertner, 2002). The students then interacted with a Black student partner. Explicit prejudice predicted what people said to a person of a different race—that is, White students who said they were not prejudiced were unlikely to say overtly racist things. However, implicit prejudice related to nonverbal aspects of the interaction, such as White students' facial expressions and how close they sat to their partners.

Another terrible example of the potential influence of implicit racial prejudice on behavior is the shootings of unarmed Black men by police. To read about research addressing this issue, see the Critical Controversy.

CRITICAL CONTROVERSY

Why Does a Cell Phone Look Like a Gun?

A cell phone. Car keys. A driver's license. A billfold. A bottle of water. A toy gun in a toy aisle.

What all of these mundane objects have in common is that they have all, in various tragic cases, been mistaken for a gun by a police officer who has opened fire on the men holding them. In all of these cases, the police officers were cleared of wrongdoing. Juries and judges concluded that they had made terrible but honest mistakes. Such cases have incited critical public and media interest. Could it be a coincidence that the unarmed dead men were all African Americans? What role did race play in these honest mistakes?

Inspired by such cases, social psychologist Keith Payne (2006) examined how ethnicity might influence the tendency to misperceive harmless objects such as wallets, car keys, and cell phones as handguns. Participants were told that they would see two pictures on a computer screen. Their job was to decide, as quickly and accurately as possible, whether the second picture was a gun or a tool. The first picture—always a picture of an African American man or a White man—cued the participants that the judgment was coming. After seeing an African American man's face, participants were quicker to recognize guns accurately in the second picture. In a second study using the same sequence of images, participants

(cell phone) © McGraw-Hill Education/Mark Dierker, photographer; (billfold) © Stockbyte/ PunchStock; (bottle) © McGraw-Hill Education; (keys) © Photographer's Choice/Getty Images; (toy gun) © Stockbyte/Getty Images

were required to respond very quickly. Like the police officers in the real-life cases, participants were more likely to misperceive tools as guns when the tools were shown after a picture of an African American man.

How can we understand such results? Social psychologists suggest that when what we see is ambiguous, stereotypes can fill in the gaps (Correll & others, 2015). Essentially, this means that the faces of African American men are acting as *primes,* or cognitive cues, that facilitate access to stereotypical information indicating the person is dangerous. Perhaps most disturbing, a recent set of studies showed that even when Black male faces were those of children as young as 5 years old, participants were quicker to recognize weapons (Todd, Thiem, & Neel, 2016). Even the faces of children primed weapons.

Could such associations help us understand shootings of unarmed Black men? Research suggests that it might (Kahn & McMahon, 2015). In these studies, participants play a video game in which they must decide whether to shoot or not shoot a potential suspect who is holding either a gun or some harmless object. In these studies, both African American and White participants have been found to decide to shoot more quickly at an armed African American man and to decide not to shoot more quickly at an unarmed White man (Correll & others, 2011). Because African Americans and Whites were equally disposed to react in these ways, the researchers concluded that personal prejudice cannot explain the tendency to let ethnicity guide the decision to shoot or not shoot a suspect. Instead, the explanation may lie in knowledge of stereotypes—or generalizations—about different ethnicities.

The mistakes police have made in shooting unarmed men and boys may be innocent, but they are not inevitable. Individuals who live in a society that does not view ethnic minority individuals as dangerous, aggressive, or likely to be criminals might be less inclined to misperceive a wallet, car keys, or cell phone as a weapon.

WHAT DO YOU THINK?

- How might this research be used to prevent future tragic mistakes?

- How does this research influence your views of police use of deadly force?

Why do people develop prejudice? Social psychologists have explored a number of possible reasons. One contributor is realistic conflict between groups, especially when resources are scarce. For example, immigrants often compete with established low-income members of a society for jobs—a situation that can lead to persistent conflict between the two groups. Cultural learning is also clearly involved. Children can adopt the prejudicial attitudes of their families and friends before they even meet a person from an outgroup. In addition, when people feel bad about themselves, they might bolster their self-esteem by demeaning outgroup members.

A final factor that might underlie prejudice comes from the limits on our information-processing abilities. As already noted, individuals have a limited capacity for effortful thought, but we face a complex social environment. To simplify the challenge of understanding others' behavior, people use categories or stereotypes. Stereotypes can be a powerful force in developing and maintaining prejudicial attitudes.

Recall that stereotypes are generalizations about a group that deny variations within the group. At the root of prejudice is a particular kind of stereotype: a negative generalization about a group that is applied to all members of that group (Richeson & Sommers, 2016; Wetherell, 2012).

DISCRIMINATION

Discrimination is an unjustified negative or harmful action toward a member of a group simply because the person belongs to that group. Discrimination occurs when negative emotional reactions combine with prejudicial beliefs and are translated into behavior (Pattachini, Ragusa, & Zenou, 2015). Since the Civil Rights Act of 1964 (revised in 1991), it has been unlawful to deny someone employment on the basis of gender or ethnicity, as we will review in the chapter "Industrial and Organizational Psychology".

● **discrimination** An unjustified negative or harmful action toward a member of a group simply because the person belongs to that group.

Ways to Improve Intergroup Relations

People show bias against others based on innumerable characteristics: race, gender, gender identification, sexuality, disability status, weight, socioeconomic status, to name just a few. Considering the evidence described so far, one might feel a bit hopeless. Why can't we all just get along? Social psychologists have not simply documented the existence of prejudice and discrimination; they have also tried to devise ways to improve relations among different groups. Here we consider two of these—optimal group contact and changing the prejudice habit.

OPTIMAL GROUP CONTACT

One way to improve intergroup relations might be for people to come to know one another better. However, in daily life many people interact with individuals from other ethnic groups, and this contact does not necessarily lead to tolerance or warm relations. Indeed, researchers have consistently found that contact by itself—attending the same school or working in the same company—does not necessarily improve relations among people of different ethnic backgrounds. So, rather than focusing on contact per se, researchers have examined how *various features* of a contact situation may be optimal for reducing prejudice and promoting intergroup harmony (Kenworthy & others, 2016).

Gordon Allport (1954), whose contributions to personality psychology we examined in the chapter "Personality", theorized that particular aspects of the contact between groups could help to reduce prejudice. According to Allport, intergroup contact is likely to reduce prejudice when group members

■ Think that they are of equal status

■ Feel that an authority figure sanctions their positive relationships

■ Believe that friendship might emerge from the interaction

■ Engage in cooperative tasks in which everyone has something to contribute

Research supports many of Allport's ideas (Pettigrew & Tropp, 2006). In particular, studies have examined the role of *task-oriented cooperation*—working together on a shared goal—in reducing tensions between groups. Two examples of the power of task-oriented cooperation are Sherif's Robbers Cave Study and Aronson's jigsaw classroom.

It may be hard to imagine in our post-*Survivor* era, but even before Jeff Probst started handing out color-coded "buffs" on the TV show *Survivor*, Muzafer Sherif and his colleagues (1961) had the idea of exploring group processes by assigning 11-year-old boys to two competitive groups (the "Rattlers" and the "Eagles") in a summer camp called Robbers Cave (see the Psychological Inquiry). Sherif, disguised as a janitor so that he could observe the boys, arranged for the two groups to compete in baseball, touch football, and tug-of-war. If you have watched reality television, you have some idea how this experiment went. In short order,

psychological *inquiry*

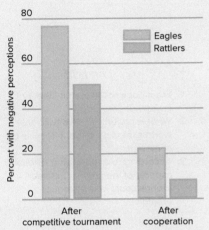

Data from Sherif, M., Harvey, O.J., White, B.J., Hood, W.R., & Sherif, C.W. (1961) *Intergroup cooperation and competition: The Robbers Cave experiment.* Norman: University of Oklahoma Press

Improving Group Relations Through Cooperative Activities

The figure illustrates the results of Sherif's (1961) Robbers Cave Study. The graph shows the negative feelings expressed by members of the Eagles and Rattlers toward the other group (the outgroup) after a competitive tournament and after cooperative activity. Try your hand at these questions.

1. When did hostility between the groups peak? When did it drop?

2. What is up with the Eagles? What are some reasons why they might be more negative about the Rattlers?

3. In your own life, are there examples of holding particular attitudes toward a group different from your own? How have your attitudes changed, and what events preceded these changes?

relations between the groups deteriorated. Members of each group expressed negative opinions of members of the other group, and the Rattlers and Eagles became battling factions.

What would bring these clashing groups together? Sherif created tasks that required the joint efforts of both groups, such as working together to repair the camp's only water supply. When the groups were required to work cooperatively to solve problems, the Rattlers and Eagles developed more positive relationships.

Sherif's idea was later tested in the real world in Austin, Texas, when ethnic tensions and violence erupted among African Americans, Mexican Americans, and European Americans in desegregated schools. Social psychologist Eliot Aronson was asked to help address the problem, and he devised the *jigsaw classroom* (1986), where all of the students had to pull together to get the "big picture."

Let's say there is an ethnically diverse class of 30 students. The academic goal for all students is to learn about the life of Rosa Parks. The class might be broken up into five study groups of six students each, with the groups being as equal as possible in ethnic composition and academic achievement level. Learning about Parks's life becomes a class project divided into six parts, with one part given to each member of the six-person group. The components might be various books about Parks or information about different aspects of her life. The parts are like the pieces of a jigsaw puzzle: They have to be put together to form the complete puzzle.

U.S. teachers have used the jigsaw approach in their classrooms, and it has been associated with increased self-esteem, better academic performance, friendships among classmates, and improved interethnic perceptions (Slavin, 2006). Indeed, one meta-analysis found that real-life contact interventions, such as jigsaw classrooms, do lead to lowered prejudice and that such changes are long-lasting (Lemmer & Wagner, 2015).

BREAKING THE PREJUDICE HABIT

Given that much of prejudice in contemporary life is likely to be implicit—meaning that it happens automatically and can occur unconsciously—it is important to ask whether we can change not only explicit attitudes but implicit ones as well. Implicit prejudice rests on automatic associations: You see a person from a different ethnic, racial, or religious group, and stereotypical thoughts pop into your head. In this sense, prejudice is a habitual way of thinking.

Can we short-circuit these automatic connections and reduce implicit prejudice? A study by Patricia Devine and her colleagues (2012) suggests that we can. Non–African

American participants were randomly assigned to an experimental group that received an intervention to reduce implicit prejudice or a control group that simply completed the dependent measures. Based on the idea that to change racial attitudes people must be aware of them, the first step was to measure implicit racial prejudice using the IAT and give the participants their scores. These scores can be surprising to many people who feel they are not prejudiced against people of color.

Next, participants in the experimental group were trained in various ways to break the prejudice habit. This training to introduce new habits of the mind included noticing stereotypic thoughts about African Americans and replacing them with more individualized information about the person. Participants were also trained to think about individuals who do not fit the stereotype of various outgroups, and they were encouraged to put themselves in the other's position and consider things from that person's perspective. Finally, participants were urged to seek out contact with members of the outgroup. The results showed that, six weeks later, participants who had experienced this intervention did show reductions in implicit bias against African Americans. In addition, these individuals were more likely to express concerns about the problems of discrimination in U.S. society.

These results, and those of contact interventions, suggest that even though the problem of racial tension in the United States and across the world may seem insurmountable, it is possible to improve relations among groups.

6. CLOSE RELATIONSHIPS

Along with good health and happiness, close relationships figure prominently in people's notions of a good life. Because close romantic relationships are so crucial for most of us, it is no wonder that social psychologists are interested in studying this vital part of human existence. A vast literature has accumulated in social psychology, examining attraction, love, and intimacy.

Attraction

At the beginning of this chapter, we discussed one key factor in interpersonal attraction, namely, physical attractiveness. Research on interpersonal attraction has illuminated a variety of other factors that play a role in the dynamic of attraction.

PROXIMITY AND SIMILARITY

Even in the age of Internet dating, it is very unlikely that you are going to become attracted to someone without meeting the person. *Proximity,* or physical closeness, is a strong predictor of attraction. You are more likely to become attracted to someone you pass in the hall every day than to a person you rarely see. One potential mechanism for the role of proximity in attraction is the mere exposure effect (Zajonc, 1968, 2001). The **mere exposure effect** is the phenomenon that the more we encounter someone or something (a person, a word, an image), the more probable it is that we will start liking the person or thing even if we do not realize we have seen it before.

In addition to proximity, similarity plays an important role in attraction (Finkel & others, 2015). We have all heard that opposites attract, but what is true of magnets is not usually true of human beings. We like to associate with people who are similar to us (Berscheid, 2000). Our friends and lovers are much more like us than unlike us. We share similar attitudes, behavior patterns, taste in clothes, intelligence, personality, other friends, values, lifestyle, and physical attractiveness.

The concept of *consensual validation* explains why people are attracted to others who are similar to them. Our own attitudes and behavior are supported when someone else's attitudes and behavior are familiar—their attitudes and behavior validate ours. Another reason that similarity matters is that we tend to shy away from the unknown. Similarity implies that we will enjoy doing things with another person who has comparable tastes and attitudes.

test yourself

1. What does social identity theory say about groups?
2. What is prejudice? Give two real-world examples, either historical or contemporary.
3. According to Allport, what particular aspects of the contact between groups could help to reduce prejudice?

● **mere exposure effect** The phenomenon that the more individuals encounter someone or something, the more probable it is that they will start liking the person or thing even if they do not realize they have seen it before.

As love matures, passionate love tends to give way to affectionate love.

© Digital Vision/Getty Images

● **romantic love or passionate love** Love with strong components of sexuality and infatuation, often dominant in the early part of a love relationship.

● **affectionate love or companionate love** Love that occurs when individuals desire to have another person near and have a deep, caring affection for the person.

● **social exchange theory** The view of social relationships as involving an exchange of goods, the objective of which is to minimize costs and maximize benefits.

● **investment model** A model of long-term relationships that examines the ways that commitment, investment, and the availability of attractive alternative partners predict satisfaction and stability in relationships.

Love

Some relationships never progress much beyond the attraction stage. Others deepen to friendship and perhaps even to love. Social psychologists have long puzzled over exactly what love is (Berscheid, 2006, 2010; Sternberg, 2013c). One way to think about love is to consider the types of love that characterize different human relationships—for instance, friendships versus romantic relationships (Hendrick & Hendrick, 2009; Rawlins & Russell, 2013). Here we consider two types of love: romantic love and affectionate love.

Poets, playwrights, and musicians through the ages have celebrated the fiery passion of romantic love—and lamented the searing pain when it fails. Think about songs and books that hit the top of the charts. Chances are, they are about romantic love. **Romantic love,** also called **passionate love,** is love with strong components of sexuality and infatuation, and it often predominates in the early part of a love relationship (Hendrick & Hendrick, 2006). This is the kind of sexually charged feeling we usually mean when we talk about being "in love" (Berscheid, 1988).

Love is more than just passion, however (Fitness & Williams, 2013; Prager & others, 2013). **Affectionate love,** also called **companionate love,** is the type of love that occurs when individuals desire to have the other person near and have a deep, caring affection for the person. There is a growing belief that the early stages of love have more romantic ingredients and that as love matures, passion tends to give way to affection (Berscheid & Regan, 2005).

Models of Close Relationships

What makes long-term romantic relationships last? Two theoretical approaches to this sometimes bewildering question include social exchange theory and the investment model.

SOCIAL EXCHANGE THEORY

The social exchange approach to close relationships focuses on the costs and benefits of one's romantic partner. **Social exchange theory** is based on the notion of social relationships as involving an exchange of goods, the objective of which is to minimize costs and maximize benefits. This theory looks at human relations as an exchange of rewards between actors.

From the social exchange perspective, the most important predictor of a relationship's success is *equity*—a feeling on the part of the individuals in the relationship that each is doing his or her "fair share." Essentially, social exchange theory asserts that the partners keep a mental balance sheet, tallying the pluses and minuses associated with each other—what they put in ("I paid for our last date") and what they get out ("He brought me flowers").

As relationships progress, equity may no longer apply. In fact, research shows that over time, this kind of accounting not only is less likely to explain what happens in a relationship but also becomes distasteful to the partners. Happily married couples are less likely to keep track of "what I get versus what I give," and they avoid thinking about the costs and benefits of their relationships (Buunk & Van Yperen, 1991; Clark & Chrisman, 1994). Surely we can all think of long-term relationships in which one partner remains committed even when the benefits are hard for the outsider to see—as in the case where the person's romantic partner is gravely ill for a long time.

THE INVESTMENT MODEL

Another way to think about long-term romantic relationships is to focus on the underlying factors that characterize stable, happy relationships compared to others. The **investment model** examines the ways that commitment, investment, and the availability of attractive alternative partners predict satisfaction and stability in relationships (Rusbult, Agnew, & Arriaga, 2012).

From the investment model perspective, long-term relationships are likely to continue when both partners are committed to the relationship and both have invested a great deal; in addition, relationships are more enduring when there are few tempting alternatives for the partners. For example, college students who are committed to their romantic partners are less likely to cheat on them sexually during spring break (Drigotas, Safstrom, & Gentilia, 1999).

Commitment to a relationship also predicts a willingness to sacrifice for a romantic partner. In one study, individuals were given a chance to climb up and down a short staircase, over and over, to spare their partner from having to do so. Those who were more committed to their partner worked harder climbing up and down to spare their loved one the burden (Van Lange & others, 1997). When two partners are deeply invested in a relationship, they can also bring the best out in each other, mutually helping themselves grow into their best possible selves (Rusbult, Finkel, & Kumashiro, 2009).

7. SOCIAL PSYCHOLOGY AND HEALTH AND WELLNESS

The principles of social psychology have provided a strong foundation for ongoing research in the areas of health and wellness (S. E. Taylor, 2015). In this concluding section, we glimpse some of the significant connections that researchers have uncovered among social contacts, physical health, and psychological wellness.

A long list of studies has shown that social ties are an important, if not the *most* important, variable in predicting health. For example, in a landmark study, social isolation had six times the effect on mortality rates that cigarette smoking had (House, Landis, & Umberson, 1988). In another study involving 1,234 heart attack patients, those living alone were nearly twice as likely to have a second heart attack (Case & others, 1992). Loneliness is linked with impaired physical health (Hawkley, Preacher, & Cacioppo, 2010) and death (Julsing & others, 2016). Without a doubt, being connected to others is crucial to human survival.

Having many different social ties may be especially important during difficult times (S. E. Taylor, 2015). Individuals who participate in more diverse social networks—for example, having a close relationship with a partner; interacting with family members, friends, neighbors, and fellow workers; and belonging to social and religious groups—live longer than those with a narrower range of social relationships (Valente, 2017; Vogt & others, 1992).

One study investigated the effects of diverse social ties on susceptibility to getting a common cold (S. Cohen & others, 1998). Individuals reported the extent of their participation in 12 types of social ties. Then they were given nasal drops containing a cold virus and monitored for the appearance of a cold. Individuals with more diverse social ties were less likely to get a cold than their counterparts with less diverse social networks.

Each of us has times in our life when we feel lonely, particularly when we are going through major life transitions. For example, when individuals leave the familiar world of their hometown and family to begin college, they can feel especially lonely. Indeed, experiencing loneliness at the beginning of one's college career is quite common and normal (Cutrona, 1982).

If you are lonely, there are strategies you can use to become better connected with others. You might consider joining activities, such as volunteering your time for a cause in which you believe. When interacting with others, you will improve your chances of developing enduring relationships if you are considerate, honest, trustworthy, and cooperative. If you cannot get rid of your loneliness on your own, you might want to contact the counseling services at your college.

Having completed this chapter's survey of social psychology, you may be surprised to learn that we have barely scratched the surface of this broad and deep field: The branch of psychology that focuses on the ways human beings relate to one another is a rich, intriguing area of study. In the next few days, think about the stories that are making the headlines and that you are talking about with your friends. Reflecting back on this chapter, you might notice that social psychology would have something to say about most of these topics.

test yourself

1. Explain the concept of consensual validation.
2. What is the difference between romantic love and affectionate love, and what is another name for each?
3. What does social exchange theory say about happy romantic relationships?

test yourself

1. What are some physical illnesses in which social isolation plays a significant role, according to researchers?
2. What kinds of social networks are especially important in times of trouble?
3. If a friend were struggling with loneliness, what strategy would you recommend for coping with it?

SUMMARY

1. DEFINING SOCIAL PSYCHOLOGY

Social psychology is the scientific study of how people think about, influence, and relate to other people. This broad subfield of psychology is relevant to everyday life and typically relies on experimental methods. An example of social psychology in action is provided by classic research on the bystander effect. The bystander effect means that individuals who observe an emergency are less likely to help when someone else is present than when they are alone.

2. SOCIAL COGNITION

The face conveys information to social perceivers, including attractiveness. Self-fulfilling prophecy means that our expectations of others can have a powerful impact on their behavior.

Attributions are our thoughts about why people behave as they do and about who or what is responsible for the outcome of events. Attribution theory views people as motivated to discover the causes of behavior as part of their effort to make sense of it. The dimensions used to make sense of the causes of human behavior include internal/external, stable/unstable, and controllable/uncontrollable.

The fundamental attribution error is observers' tendency to overestimate traits and to underestimate situations when they explain an actor's behavior. Self-serving bias means attributing our successes to internal causes and blaming our failures on external causes. Heuristics are used as shortcuts in social information processing. One such heuristic is a stereotype—a generalization about a group's characteristics that does not consider any variations among individuals in the group.

The self is our mental representation of our own characteristics. Self-esteem refers to the attitude we take toward ourselves. Stereotype threat is an individual's fast-acting, self-fulfilling fear of being judged based on a negative stereotype about his or her group. In order to understand ourselves better, we might engage in social comparison, evaluating ourselves by comparison with others.

Attitudes are our feelings—about people, objects, and ideas. Attitudes predict behavior when an individual's attitudes are strong, when the person is aware of his or her attitudes and expresses them often, and when the person has a vested interest in the attitude. Sometimes changes in behavior precede changes in attitude.

According to cognitive dissonance theory, our strong need for cognitive consistency causes us to change our behavior to fit our attitudes or to change our attitudes to fit our behavior. Self-perception theory stresses the importance of making inferences about attitudes by observing our own behavior, especially when our attitudes are not clear.

3. SOCIAL BEHAVIOR

Altruism is an unselfish interest in helping someone else. Reciprocity often is involved in altruism. Genes play a role in prosocial behavior, along with neurotransmitters serotonin, dopamine, and oxytocin. The experience of empathy is linked to helping as is the personality trait of agreeableness. Individuals who are in a good mood are more helpful.

Aggression is behavior meant to harm another person. Evidence for genetic and neurobiological factors are mixed and generally less clear-cut than that suggested by research with animals. Psychological factors in aggression include frustrating and aversive circumstances. Sociocultural factors include cross-cultural variation, the culture of honor, and violence in the media.

4. SOCIAL INFLUENCE

Conformity involves a change in behavior to coincide with a group. Factors that influence conformity include informational social influence (going along to be right) and normative social influence (going along to be liked). Asch conducted a classic experiment on conformity in 1951.

Obedience is behavior that complies with the explicit demands of an authority. Milgram's experiments demonstrated the power of obedience. Another such demonstration is the Stanford prison experiment, illustrating the potential effects of obedience not only on individuals who obey but also on those who exercise authority.

People often change in their behavior when they are in a group. Deindividuation refers to the lack of inhibition and diffusion of responsibility that can occur in groups. Social contagion refers to imitative behaviors involving the spread of behavior, emotions, and ideas. Our performance in groups can be improved through social facilitation and lowered because of social loafing.

Risky shift refers to the tendency for a group decision to be riskier than the average decision made by the individual group members. The group polarization effect is the solidification and further strengthening of a position as a consequence of group discussion or interaction. Groupthink involves impaired decision making resulting from valuing group harmony over accuracy.

5. INTERGROUP RELATIONS

Social identity is our definition of ourselves in terms of our group memberships. Social identity theory states that when individuals are assigned to a group, they invariably think of it as the ingroup. Identifying with the group allows the person to have a positive self-image. Ethnocentrism is the tendency to favor one's own ethnic group over others.

Prejudice is an unjustified negative attitude toward an individual based on membership in a group. The underlying reasons for prejudice include competition between groups over scarce resources, a person's motivation to enhance his or her self-esteem, cognitive processes that tend to categorize and stereotype others, and cultural learning. Prejudice is also based on stereotypes. The cognitive process of stereotyping can lead to discrimination, an unjustified negative or harmful action toward a member of a group simply because he or she belongs to that group. Discrimination results when negative emotional reactions combine with prejudicial beliefs and are translated into behavior.

An effective strategy for enhancing the effects of intergroup contact is to set up task-oriented cooperation among individuals from different groups.

6. CLOSE RELATIONSHIPS

We tend to be attracted to people whom we see often and who are similar to us. Romantic love (passionate love) includes feelings of infatuation and sexual attraction. Affectionate love (companionate love) is more akin to friendship and includes deep, caring feelings for another.

Social exchange theory states that a relationship is likely to be successful if individuals feel that they get out of the relationship what they put in. The investment model focuses on commitment, investment, and the availability of attractive alternatives in predicting relationship success.

7. SOCIAL PSYCHOLOGY AND HEALTH AND WELLNESS

Social isolation is a strong risk factor for a range of physical illnesses. Loneliness relates to a number of negative health outcomes, including impaired physical health and early death. Individuals who participate in more diverse social networks live longer than those with a narrower range of social relationships. Loneliness often emerges when people make life transitions, so it is not surprising that loneliness is common among college freshmen. Strategies that can help to reduce loneliness include participating in activities with others and taking the initiative to meet new people.

key *terms*

affectionate love or
  companionate love
aggression
altruism
attitudes
attribution theory
bystander effect
cognitive dissonance
conformity
deindividuation
discrimination

egoism
elaboration likelihood model
ethnocentrism
false consensus effect
fundamental attribution error
group polarization effect
groupthink
informational social influence
investment model
mere exposure effect
normative social influence

obedience
positive illusions
prejudice
representativeness heuristic
risky shift
romantic love or passionate love
self-fulfilling prophecy
self-objectification
self-perception theory
self-serving bias
social cognition

social comparison
social contagion
social exchange theory
social facilitation
social identity
social identity theory
social loafing
social psychology
stereotype
stereotype threat

apply your *knowledge*

1. Check out this website to see how the averaging of faces works: www.faceresearch.org/demos/average. Pick some faces you consider unattractive. What happens when you average them together? If you have a digital photograph of yourself and some friends, see what happens when you average those faces. Do you agree that average faces are more attractive than any single face?

2. Many people are surprised by the results of the IAT when they take this implicit measure. Try it out at https://implicit.harvard.edu/implicit. Do you think your results are valid? Explain.

3. We are often unaware of how many attributions we make about the behavior of others. To demonstrate this point to yourself, spend some time in a crowded area observing the interactions of others (alternatively, watch some scenes in television shows or movies). Take careful notes about the social behaviors that occur and then document your impression of why the individuals behaved as they did. What cues did you use in making your attributions about their behavior? Did your knowledge of the fundamental attribution error influence your attributions? Why or why not?

4. Take a day and engage in altruistic behavior. Act as kindly toward others as you can without telling anyone what you are up to. Keep track of your thoughts and feelings as you experience this day of kindness. How does it influence your feelings about altruism?

5. Interview the happiest couple you know. Ask the partners individually about the things that they think help make their relationship work. Then examine your notes. How do the characteristics of your "ideal" couple's relationship compare with the findings of research on close relationships?

CHAPTER 15

CHAPTER OUTLINE

© Andersen Ross/Media Bakery

Psychological Disorders

What's It Like to Be You?

When her 18-year-old son was diagnosed with schizophrenia, psychologist Lynda Crane learned a hard lesson: Once they heard about her son's diagnosis, people stopped seeing the person he was.

"They just saw the diagnosis and a collection of symptoms. Doug, my son, was forgotten" (Saker, 2014).

Moved by her experience, Crane and psychologist Tracy McDonough founded the Schizophrenia Oral History Project (http://www.schizophreniaoralhistories.com/) to collect and share the life stories of people suffering from the potentially devastating psychological disorder. Crane and McDonough pose the question, "What's it like to be you?" Many individuals in the project have noted that, actually, no one had asked them this simple question before. Their answers provide a glimpse into their sometimes surprisingly normal lives. After hearing some of the stories, a nursing student confessed, "I would not have been surprised to learn that a patient with cancer or heart disease loved organic gardening or painting. Why in the world should I be surprised that someone with schizophrenia has hobbies, too?"

Individuals with psychological disorders are not so different from the rest of us. They are brothers, sisters, grandparents, uncles, aunts, and parents, classmates, and coworkers: people with life stories to share. Psychological disorders may make their lives more difficult and our relationships with them more challenging, but they cannot take away the humanity that binds them to us. ●

PREVIEW

This chapter surveys psychological disorders. We first explore the meaning of the word *abnormal* and examine approaches to understanding abnormal behavior. We then survey a number of disorders. In the concluding section, we consider the influence of the stigma associated with psychological disorders on the health and wellness of those who experience with them.

1. DEFINING AND EXPLAINING ABNORMAL BEHAVIOR

What makes behavior normal or abnormal? Abnormal behavior is certainly statistically unusual or atypical. Alicia Keyes, Cam Newton, and Mark Zuckerberg are atypical—but we do not categorize them as abnormal. Three criteria help distinguish normal from abnormal behavior. **Abnormal behavior** is behavior that is deviant, maladaptive, or personally distressful over a relatively long period of time. Let's examine each of the three criteria more closely:

● **abnormal behavior** Behavior that is deviant, maladaptive, or personally distressful over a relatively long period of time.

- Abnormal behavior is *deviant*. Deviant means that a behavior does not conform to accepted social standards. When atypical behavior deviates from what is acceptable in a culture, it often is considered abnormal. A woman who washes her hands four times an hour and takes seven showers a day is abnormal because her behavior deviates from what we consider acceptable. The *context* of a behavior may determine whether it is deviant. If the woman who washes her hands three or four times an hour and takes repeated showers works in a sterile lab with live viruses or radioactive material, her behavior might be quite acceptable.

- Abnormal behavior is *maladaptive*. Maladaptive behavior interferes with a person's ability to function effectively in the world. A man who believes that he can endanger other people through his breathing may go to great lengths to avoid people, isolating himself from others, for what he believes is their own good. His belief separates him from society and prevents his everyday functioning; thus, his behavior is maladaptive. Importantly, behavior that presents a danger to the person or to those around him or her would be considered maladaptive (and abnormal).

- Abnormal behavior involves *personal distress* over a long period of time. The person engaging in the behavior finds it troubling. A woman who secretly makes herself vomit after every meal may never be seen by others as deviant (because they do not know about it), but this pattern of behavior may cause her to feel intense shame and guilt.

Only one of the three criteria described above needs to be present for behavior to be labeled "abnormal," but typically two or all three may be present. When abnormal behavior persists, it may lead to the diagnosis of a psychological disorder.

Accomplished people—such as singer-songwriter Alicia Keys, NFL superstar Cam Newton, and Facebook CEO Mark Zuckerberg—are atypical but not abnormal. However, when atypical behavior deviates from cultural norms, it often is considered abnormal.

(first) © Allstar Picture Library/Alamy; (second) © Maddie Meyer/ Getty Images; (third) © Simon Dawson/Bloomberg via Getty Images

Theoretical Approaches to Psychological Disorders

What causes people to develop a psychological disorder, that is, to behave in deviant, maladaptive, and personally distressful ways? Theorists have suggested various approaches to this question.

THE BIOLOGICAL APPROACH

The biological approach attributes psychological disorders to organic, internal causes. This approach primarily focuses on the brain, genetic factors, and neurotransmitter functioning as the sources of abnormality. The American Psychiatric Association (2001, 2006, 2013) defines abnormal behavior in medical terms—as a mental illness that affects or is manifested in a person's brain and can affect the way the individual thinks, behaves, and interacts with others. This approach is part of the **medical model,** which describes psychological disorders as medical diseases with a biological origin.

● **medical model** The view that psychological disorders are medical diseases with a biological origin.

THE PSYCHOLOGICAL APPROACH

The psychological approach emphasizes the contributions of experiences, thoughts, emotions, and personality characteristics in explaining psychological disorders. Psychologists might focus, for example, on the influence of childhood experiences or personality traits in the development and course of psychological disorders. Behavioral psychologists probe the rewards and punishers in the environment that determine abnormal behavior, whereas social cognitive psychologists focus on observational learning, cognitions, and beliefs as factors that foster or maintain abnormal behavior.

THE SOCIOCULTURAL APPROACH

The sociocultural approach emphasizes the social contexts in which a person lives, including the individual's culture. Using the criterion of deviance to describe a behavior as abnormal suggests the important role of sociocultural factors in psychological disorders. Cultures establish the norms by which people evaluate behavior, telling us whether it is socially acceptable (Bassett & Baker, 2015; Hansen, 2016). In evaluating behavior as deviant, culture matters in complex ways (Sue & others, 2014).

Importantly, cultural norms can be mistaken. Such norms can be limiting, oppressive, and prejudicial (Kent, 2016; Potter, 2012). Individuals who fight to change the established social order sometimes face being labeled "deviant" or even "mentally ill." In the late nineteenth and early twentieth centuries, for instance, women in Britain who demonstrated for women's right to vote were widely considered mentally ill. When individuals' behavior challenges social expectations, we must be open to the possibility that such actions are an adaptive response to injustice. Challenging what everyone thinks is true and expressing ideas that seem strange, they may make others feel uncomfortable. However, justifiable demands for social change ought not to be labeled abnormal. Further, definitions of normal change as societal norms change. Consider that cigarette smoking was not only an acceptable habit in the 1960s, but it was also promoted as a healthy way to relax.

Cultural variation in what it means to be normal or abnormal makes it very difficult to compare different psychological disorders across different cultures. Many of the diagnostic categories we trace in this chapter primarily reflect Western (and often U.S.) notions of normality, and applying these to other cultures can be inappropriate (Agorastos, Haasen, & Huber, 2012; Rubington & Weinberg, 2015). As individuals move from one culture to another, evaluations of their behavior must take into account the norms in their culture of origin (Bourque & others, 2012; Hassan & others, 2016; Lee, Choi, & Matejkowski, 2013). Historically, people entering the United States from other countries were examined at Ellis Island, and many were judged to be mentally impaired simply because of differences in their language and customs.

The sociocultural perspective stresses the ways that cultures influence the understanding and treatment of psychological disorders. The frequency and intensity of psychological

Disorder	Culture	Description/Characteristics
Amok	Malaysia, Philippines, Africa	This disorder involves sudden, uncontrolled outbursts of anger in which the person may injure or kill someone. Amok is often found in males who are emotionally withdrawn before the onset of the disorder. After the attack on someone, the individual feels exhausted and depressed and does not remember the rage and attack.
Anorexia Nervosa	Western cultures, especially the United States	This eating disorder involves a relentless pursuit of thinness through starvation and can eventually lead to death.
Koro	China and Southeast Asia	This disorder in China and Southeast Asia involves the terrifying belief that one's genitalia are retracting into one's abdomen.

FIGURE 1 **Some Culture-Related Disorders** Although many psychological disorders are universal, some are associated with specific cultures, as this figure illustrates.

disorders vary and depend on social, economic, technological, and religious aspects of cultures (Baxter & others, 2013; Collado, Lim & MacPherson, 2016; Polanczyk & others, 2015). Some disorders are culture-related, as indicated in Figure 1.

In addition to recognizing the role of culture in definitions of normality, sociocultural researchers stress the role of social factors—such as gender, ethnicity, socioeconomic status, and family relationships—on psychological disorders. For instance, poverty creates stressful circumstances that can contribute to the development of a psychological disorder (Chen & Miller, 2013; Lund, 2015).

THE BIOPSYCHOSOCIAL MODEL

Abnormal behavior can be influenced by biological factors (such as genes), psychological factors (such as childhood experiences), and sociocultural factors (such as gender). These factors can operate alone, but they often act in combination with one another (Forero, Castro-Rodríguez, & Alonso, 2015). From the biopsychosocial perspective, none of the factors considered is necessarily viewed as more important than another; rather, biological, psychological, and social factors are *all* significant ingredients in producing both normal and abnormal behavior. Furthermore, these ingredients may combine in unique ways, so that one depressed person might differ from another in terms of the key factors associated with the development of the disorder.

Why do we need to consider these multiple factors? As you will see throughout this chapter, generally speaking, there is no one gene or experience that leads inevitably to the development of a psychological disorder. Two people can share the same gene—one develops a disorder, but another does not. Similarly two people might have the same experience, such as childhood neglect, and one might develop a disorder, but the other does not. Thus, to understand the development of psychological disorders, we must consider a variety of *interacting* factors from each of the domains of experience.

An important concept that has helped psychologists understand the ways different factors influence the development of psychological disorders is the **vulnerability-stress hypothesis** (also called the **diathesis-stress model**). The vulnerability-stress hypothesis suggests that preexisting conditions (such as genetic characteristics, personality dispositions, or experiences) may put a person at risk of developing a psychological disorder. This vulnerability in combination with stressful experiences can lead to a psychological disorder.

● **vulnerability-stress hypothesis or diathesis-stress model** Theory suggesting that preexisting conditions—such as genetic characteristics, personality dispositions, or experiences—may put a person at risk of developing a psychological disorder.

One way that psychologists study these processes is by examining the interactions between genetic characteristics and environmental circumstances or gene × environment (G × E) interactions (Peeters & others, 2015). Scientists continue to probe the ways genetic characteristics might produce a vulnerability to psychological disorders in the face of difficult life experiences (Hankin & others, 2015; Lickliter, 2013; Shapero & others, 2016).

Classifying Abnormal Behavior

To understand, prevent, and treat abnormal behavior, psychiatrists and psychologists have devised systems classifying those behaviors into specific psychological disorders. Classifying psychological disorders provides a common basis for communicating. If one psychologist says that her client is experiencing depression, another psychologist understands that a particular pattern of abnormal behavior has led to this diagnosis. A classification system can also help clinicians make predictions about the likelihood of a particular disorder's occurrence, which individuals would be most susceptible to it, and what the best treatment might be (Blashfield & others, 2014). Further, a classification system may benefit the person suffering from psychological symptoms. The fact that an individual's disorder has a name can be a comforting signal that the person may reasonably expect relief.

On the other hand, officially labeling a problem can also have serious negative implications because of the potential for creating *stigma,* a mark of shame that may cause others to avoid or to act negatively toward a person (Hipes & others, 2016). Indeed, being diagnosed with a psychological disorder can profoundly influence a person's life because of what the diagnosis means to the person, his or her family, and the larger social world. We return to the important issue of stigma at the end of this chapter.

THE *DSM* CLASSIFICATION SYSTEM

In 1952, the American Psychiatric Association (APA) published the first major classification of psychological disorders in the United States, the *Diagnostic and Statistical Manual of Mental Disorders.* Its current version, ***DSM-5,*** was approved in 2013. Throughout the history of the *DSM,* the number of diagnosable disorders has increased dramatically. For example, *DSM-5* includes new diagnoses such as binge eating disorder and gambling addiction.

The *DSM* is not the only diagnostic system. The World Health Organization devised the *International Classification of Diseases and Related Health Problems (ICD-10),* which includes a chapter on mental and behavioral disorders. One of the goals of *DSM-5* was to bring diagnoses closer to the *ICD-10* though the two manuals remain different in important ways.

CRITIQUES OF THE *DSM*

Even before it was published, *DSM-5* was criticized on a number of bases (Wakefield, 2016). A central criticism that applies to all versions of the *DSM* is that it treats psychological disorders as if they are medical illnesses, taking an overly biological view of conditions that may have their roots in social experience (Blashfield & others, 2014). Even as research has shed light on the complex interaction of genetic, neurobiological, cognitive, social, and environmental factors in psychological disorders, *DSM-5* continues to reflect the medical model, neglecting factors such as poverty, unemployment, and trauma (Surís, Holliday, & North, 2016).

Another general criticism of the *DSM* is that it focuses strictly on problems. Critics argue that emphasizing *strengths* as well as weaknesses might help to destigmatize psychological disorders (Roten, 2007). Other criticisms of *DSM-5* include:

- It relies too much on social norms and subjective judgments.
- Too many new categories of disorders have been added, some of which do not yet have consistent research support and would lead to a significant increase in the number of people being labeled as having a mental disorder.
- Loosening the standards for some existing diagnoses will add to the already very high rates of these.

In thinking about critiques of the *DSM*, you might be wondering what all the fuss is about. One reason for these concerns is that generally U.S. insurance companies will only reimburse for treatments of diagnoses that appear in *DSM-5.* Another key reason for concern is that part of the medical model is the assumption that, optimally, disorders would be treated through medical means. Generally, that means prescribing medications. If diagnostic criteria are loosened, many more individuals might be given powerful psychoactive drugs, perhaps unnecessarily. Thus, it is imperative that the *DSM* get it right, and many critics argue that it falls short in this high-stakes context (Blashfield & others, 2014; Paris, 2012; Pickersgill, 2104; D. Watson & others, 2013).

Figure 2 shows some of the changes that are part of the newest formulation of the *DSM.* As you can see, concerns are likely to erupt especially around disorders that pertain to children. One of these is autism spectrum disorder, which we reviewed previously in the chapter "States of Consciousness". Another is somatic symptom disorder. Let's take a closer look at these changes.

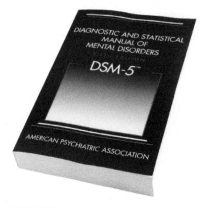

© Studio 101/Alamy

● ***DSM-5*** The fifth edition of the *Diagnostic and Statistical Manual of Mental Disorders;* the major classification of psychological disorders in the United States.

Disorder	Changes	Sources of Concern
Major Depressive Disorder	In the past, those experiencing grief due to the loss of a loved one generally have not been considered depressed. This grief exclusion has been dropped.	This change may result in those experiencing normal grief to be labeled with depression.
Attention-Deficit/ Hyperactivity Disorder (ADHD)	Some of the diagnostic requirements have been loosened, and the age of diagnosis has been changed.	Overdiagnosis of ADHD is already a concern, as is the proliferation of drugs used to treat the condition.
Autism Spectrum Disorder	The diagnosis of Asperger syndrome, which was given to high-functioning individuals with autistic characteristics, has been dropped.	Those who were previously diagnosed with Asperger's may not be diagnosed at all and may not receive treatment.
Post-Traumatic Stress Disorder (PTSD)	Previously, a person had to have experienced or witnessed a trauma. Now, PTSD can be diagnosed even for those who only hear about a trauma.	The change may lead to a huge increase in those with this disorder.
Disruptive Mood Regulation Disorder	This is a new diagnosis for children with wild mood swings.	Adding diagnoses targeting children is concerning.
Mild Neurocognitive Impairment	This new diagnosis is for adults experiencing cognitive decline.	Many adults experience mild cognitive decline with age, and this diagnosis may pathologize normal aging.

FIGURE 2   **Sample of Changes in *DSM-5***

AUTISM SPECTRUM DISORDER

Autism spectrum disorder refers to a range of neurodevelopmental disorders involving impaired social interaction and communication, repetitive behavior, and restricted interests. Like many other neurodevelopmental conditions, autism spectrum disorder refers to a *range* of symptoms, and there is no single identified cause for the disorder. Those on the autism spectrum are a diverse group, and their level of disability can be relatively mild to quite severe.

It is likely that the disabilities shared by these individuals have numerous complex causes, including genetic and neurological factors (T. Thompson, 2013; Tick & others, 2016). Some previously considered causes of this disorder have been discounted thoroughly, including cold or rejecting parents (Rimland, 1964) and childhood vaccinations (Committee to Review Adverse Effects of Vaccines, 2011).

According to estimates by the Centers for Disease Control and Prevention (CDC), in the United States 1 in 68 children born in 2004 have been identified with autism spectrum disorder (CDC, 2016b). This estimate suggests higher prevalence than in earlier times. The increase is likely due to greater awareness by parents and healthcare providers and wider availability of reliable diagnostic tests (T. Thompson, 2013). Such awareness is important, as early interventions are particularly helpful in treating children on the autism spectrum.

SOMATIC SYMPTOM DISORDER

somatic symptom disorder A psychological disorder in which a person experiences one or more bodily (somatic) symptoms and experiences excessive thoughts and feelings about these symptoms that interfere with everyday functioning.

Another major change to the *DSM* occurred for a disorder that was formerly called *somatoform disorder*. The disorder is now called somatic symptom disorder. In **somatic symptom disorder** a person experiences one or more bodily (somatic) symptoms and experiences excessive thoughts and feelings about these symptoms (APA, 2013a). The changes that have been made to this diagnostic category demonstrate not only the relationship between the mind and the body but also changes to the way the psychiatric community views patients (Barsky, 2016; Eliason & others, 2016).

First, somatic symptom disorder involves the person experiencing a physical symptom, such as chronic pain. Previously, a key feature of this kind of disorder was the fact that no medical explanation could be found for the symptom. That is, the person must have demonstrated efforts to find a medical explanation for the symptom, and the focus was on the fact that these symptoms are not physically "real." As you can imagine, patients often found this aspect of the diagnosis insulting, as if doctors were saying "It's all in your head."

Instead, now the focus is on the experience of distressing thoughts and feelings related to the symptoms. Individuals diagnosed with somatic symptom disorder may be wary of medical professionals because they have often endured many medical procedures (including surgeries and medications) in an effort to treat their physical symptoms. These experiences can, understandably, lead to a lack of trust (Luytan & Fonagy, 2016). By focusing on psychological symptoms (rather than the absence of physical causes associated with the bodily symptoms experienced), it is hoped that psychologists and psychiatrists might begin to regain that trust.

Another controversial disorder is **attention-deficit/hyperactivity disorder (ADHD).** To read more, see the Critical Controversy.

Before we begin our survey of the various psychological disorders, consider this caution. It is very common for individuals who are learning about psychological disorders to recognize the symptoms and behaviors of disorders in themselves or in people around them. Only trained professionals can diagnose a psychological disorder.

● **attention-deficit/hyperactivity disorder (ADHD)** A common psychological disorder in which the individual exhibits one or more of the following: inattention, hyperactivity, and impulsivity.

test yourself

1. What three main criteria distinguish abnormal behavior from normal behavior?
2. Why is it important to have formal systems for classifying abnormal behavior into specific psychological disorders?
3. What are some criticisms of *DSM-5*?

2. ANXIETY AND ANXIETY-RELATED DISORDERS

Think about how you felt before a make-or-break exam or a big presentation—or perhaps as you noticed police lights flashing behind your speeding car. Did you feel jittery and nervous and experience tightness in your stomach? These are moments of anxiety, an unpleasant feeling of fear and dread.

Individuals with high levels of anxiety worry a lot, but their anxiety does not necessarily impair their ability to function. In contrast, **anxiety disorders** involve fears that are uncontrollable, disproportionate to the actual danger the person might be in, and disruptive of ordinary life (Bomyea & others, 2015; Gallo & others, 2013). They feature motor tension (jumpiness, trembling), hyperactivity (dizziness, a racing heart), and apprehensive expectations and thoughts.

DSM-5 recognizes 12 types of anxiety disorders. In this section, we survey four of the most common anxiety disorders:

● **anxiety disorders** Disabling (uncontrollable and disruptive) psychological disorders that feature motor tension, hyperactivity, and apprehensive expectations and thoughts.

- Generalized anxiety disorder
- Panic disorder
- Specific phobia
- Social anxiety disorder

We also consider two disorders that are not classified by *DSM-5* as anxiety disorders but are related to the experience of anxiety:

- Obsessive-compulsive disorder (categorized under obsessive-compulsive and related disorders)
- Post-traumatic stress disorder (categorized under trauma- and stressor-related disorders)

Generalized Anxiety Disorder

When you are worrying about getting a speeding ticket, you know why you are anxious; there is a specific cause. **Generalized anxiety disorder** is different from such everyday

● **generalized anxiety disorder** An anxiety disorder marked by persistent anxiety for at least six months, and in which the individual is unable to specify the reasons for the anxiety.

CRITICAL CONTROVERSY

Does Everyone *Have ADHD?*

Chances are you know someone who suffers from ADHD. You might have been diagnosed with it yourself. ADHD involves inattention, hyperactivity, and impulsivity. ADHD diagnoses have skyrocketed. In the United States, in 1988 just 500,000 cases of ADHD were diagnosed. By 2011 that number had grown to over 6 million (Visser & others, 2014). The percentage of American children diagnosed increased from less than 8 percent in 2003 to 11 percent in 2011.

Experts previously thought that most children "grow out" of ADHD. However, many adolescents and adults diagnosed as children continue to experience ADHD symptoms (Salomone & others, 2016; van Lieshout & others, 2016); as a result, *DSM-5* recognizes ADHD in adults.

The number of ADHD diagnoses has prompted speculation that psychiatrists, parents, and teachers are labeling normal childhood behavior "psychopathology" (Mash & Wolfe, 2013; Molina & Pelham, 2014; Wakefield, 2016). Scholars argue that the spread of ADHD is primarily a function of *overpathologizing* normal behavior, confusing ADHD for other disorders, and aggressive marketing by pharmaceutical companies (Moncrieff & Timimi, 2010).

One reason for concern about overdiagnosing ADHD is that the treatment in most cases is drugs such as Ritalin and Adderall (Pelham & others, 2016). Animal research shows that in the absence of ADHD, exposure to such stimulants can predispose the brain to later addiction problems (Leo, 2005). Moreover, as more and more young adults are diagnosed, the availability of these drugs has become widespread. A special concern is that college students provide one another with these drugs, not as a treatment, but to boost academic performance (Schwarz, 2013). These individuals may not realize that supplying others with these drugs

is, in fact, a felony. Moreover, having so many powerful drugs widely available increases the chances of overdose and injury (Cairns & others, 2016).

Is ADHD overdiagnosed? In one study, child psychologists, psychiatrists, and social workers were sent case descriptions of children and were asked to diagnose the children described (Bruchmüller, Margraf, & Schneider, 2012). Some of the descriptions fit the diagnostic criteria for ADHD, but others lacked key features of the disorder. In addition, in the case descriptions the researchers varied on whether the child was identified as male or female. The dependent variable was whether these professionals gave a case an ADHD diagnosis. The results? Participants overdiagnosed ADHD, giving an ADHD diagnosis to cases that specifically lacked important aspects of the disorder about 17 percent of the time. Further, regardless of symptoms, boys were twice as likely as girls to receive such a diagnosis.

There is concern as well about overdiagnosis of adults (Paris, Bhat, & Thombs, 2016). A recent experiment showed that, compared to a control group, adults who were randomly assigned to receive feedback that they showed signs of adult ADHD scored significantly higher on a measure of ADHD symptoms (Privitera & others, 2015).

Untreated, ADHD makes adjustment difficult, so it is critical that diagnoses of the disorder be accurate (Molina & Pelham, 2014). Childhood ADHD is associated with conduct problems that in turn predict poorer adjustment in young adulthood (Owens & Hinshaw, 2016). Children with ADHD are at heightened risk of dropping out of school, teen pregnancy, and antisocial behavior (von Polier, Vloet, & Herpertz-Dahlmann, 2012).

ADHD is not the only controversial diagnosis, nor is it the only one given a great deal of attention by pharmaceutical companies (Mash & Wolfe, 2013). Drug companies commonly fund research that focuses on a disease model of psychological disorders. The controversy over ADHD is a reminder of the important role of research in clarifying and defining diagnostic categories. Nobody wants to label inappropriately, to misdiagnose, or to mistreat people who are already suffering.

© ParkerDeen/Vetta/Getty Images

WHAT DO YOU THINK

- Would ADHD be as controversial if the treatment did not involve drugs? Why or why not?

- Do you think ADHD would be diagnosed as often as it is if drugs were not readily available for its treatment?

- If a teacher suggested that your child be tested for ADHD, what would you do?

feelings of anxiety in that sufferers experience persistent anxiety for at least six months and are unable to specify the reasons for the anxiety (APA, 2013a). People with generalized anxiety disorder are nervous most of the time and worry a great deal. That worry can take a physical toll, so that individuals with generalized anxiety disorder may suffer from fatigue, muscle tension, stomach problems, and difficulty sleeping.

What biopsychosocial factors play a role in generalized anxiety disorder? Among the biological factors are genetic predisposition, deficiency in the neurotransmitter GABA (the brain's brake pedal), respiratory system abnormalities, and problems in regulating the sympathetic nervous system (Möhler, 2012; Pittig & others, 2013; Reeves & others, 2016; Zhang & others, 2015). The psychological and sociocultural factors include having harsh (or even impossible) self-standards; overly strict, critical, or cold parents; automatic negative thoughts when feeling stressed; and a history of uncontrollable traumas or stressors (such as an abusive parent) (Fergusson, McLeod, & Horwood, 2013; Long & others, 2015).

Panic Disorder

Much like everyone else, you might have a specific experience that sends you into a panic. For example, you work all night on a paper, only to have your computer crash before you save your last changes, or you are just about to dash across a street when you see a large truck coming right at you. Your heart races, your hands shake, and you might break into a sweat. In these situations, you know why you are experiencing feelings of panic.

In **panic disorder,** however, a person experiences recurrent, sudden onsets of intense terror, often without warning and with no specific cause. Panic attacks can produce severe palpitations, extreme shortness of breath, chest pains, trembling, sweating, dizziness, and a feeling of helplessness (Oral & others, 2012). People with panic disorder may feel that they are having a heart attack.

Charles Darwin, the scientist who proposed the theory of evolution, suffered from intense panic disorder (Barloon & Noyes, 1997), as has former NFL running back Earl Campbell.

What factors underlie panic disorder? In terms of biological factors, individuals may have a genetic predisposition to the disorder (Hohoff & others, 2015). Of particular interest to researchers are genes that direct the action of neurotransmitters such as norepinephrine, GABA, and serotonin (Howe & others, 2016). Another brain chemical, lactate, which plays a role in brain metabolism, is elevated in individuals with panic disorder (Vollmer, Strawn, & Sah, 2015). Interestingly, experimental research has shown that increasing lactate levels can produce panic attacks (Leibold & others, 2015; Reiman & others 1989).

Other research points to the involvement of a wider range of genes and bodily systems, implicating genes involved in hormone regulation (Wilson, Markie, & Fitches, 2012) and responses to stress (Esler & others, 2009). Panic disorder appears to share biological characteristics with physical illnesses, such as asthma (Domschke & others, 2011), hypertension (Esler & others, 2009), and cardiovascular disease (Tully & others, 2015).

With respect to psychological influences, learning processes, as described in the chapter "Learning", are one factor that has been considered in panic disorder. Classical conditioning research has shown that learned associations between bodily cues of respiration and fear can play a role in panic attacks (Acheson, Forsyth, & Moses, 2012). Interestingly, in humans carbon dioxide (CO_2) is a very strong conditioned stimulus for fear

Many experts interpret Edvard Munch's painting The Scream *as an expression of the terror brought on by a panic attack.*

© Universal Images Group/Getty Images

● **panic disorder** An anxiety disorder in which the individual experiences recurrent, sudden onsets of intense terror, often without warning and with no specific cause.

(Feinstein & others, 2013), suggesting that humans may be biologically prepared to learn an association between high concentrations of CO_2 and fear (Acheson, Forsyth, & Moses, 2012; De Cort & others, 2012). Thus, some learning researchers have suggested that at the heart of panic attacks are such learned associations (De Cort & others, 2012; Duits & others, 2015).

In addition, the learning concept of *generalization* may apply to panic attack. Recall that in classical conditioning generalization means showing a conditioned response (in this case, fear) to stimuli other than the particular one used in learning. Individuals who suffer from panic attacks are more likely to display overgeneralization of fear learning (Duits & others, 2015; Lissek & others, 2010). Why might those who suffer from panic attacks be more likely to show stronger and more generalized fear associations? It may be that genetic characteristics predispose individuals to develop such associations when they encounter particularly stressful life events, especially involving separation (Choe & others, 2013). Such an explanation represents a vulnerability-stress prediction.

In terms of sociocultural factors, women are nearly twice as likely as men to have panic attacks (Boyd & others, 2015). Possible reasons for this difference include biological differences in hormones and neurotransmitters (Fodor & Epstein, 2002), as well as the different ways men and women cope with anxiety-provoking situations (Schmidt & Koselka, 2000).

Specific Phobia

Many people are afraid of spiders and snakes; indeed, thinking about letting a tarantula crawl over one's face is likely to give anyone the willies. It is not uncommon to be afraid of particular objects or specific environments such as extreme heights. For most of us, these fears do not interfere with daily life. A fear becomes a phobia when a situation is so dreaded that an individual goes to almost any length to avoid it. A fear of snakes that keeps a city-dweller from leaving his apartment is clearly disproportionate to the actual chance of encountering a snake. **Specific phobia** is an anxiety disorder in which an individual has an irrational, overwhelming, persistent fear of a particular object or situation.

● **specific phobia** An anxiety disorder in which the individual experiences an irrational, overwhelming, persistent fear of a particular object or situation.

Specific phobias come in many forms, as shown in Figure 3. John Madden—former NFL coach, football commentator, and video-game consultant—is also known for a fear of flying that led him to take a bus to the games that he broadcast.

Where do specific phobias come from? Answering this question typically involves first acknowledging that fear plays an important role in adaptive behavior. Fear tells us when we are in danger and need to take to action. The importance of this function suggests that fears should be relatively quickly learned, because learning to fear things that

Acrophobia	Fear of high places	Arachnophobia	Fear of spiders	Mysophobia	Fear of dirt
Aerophobia	Fear of flying	Astrapophobia	Fear of lightning	Nyctophobia	Fear of darkness
Ailurophobia	Fear of cats	Cynophobia	Fear of dogs	Ophidiophobia	Fear of nonpoisonous snakes
Algophobia	Fear of pain	Gamophobia	Fear of marriage		
Amaxophobia	Fear of vehicles, driving	Hydrophobia	Fear of water	Thanatophobia	Fear of death
		Melissophobia	Fear of bees	Xenophobia	Fear of strangers

FIGURE 3 Specific Phobia This figure features examples of specific phobias—psychological disorders characterized by irrational, overwhelming, and persistent fear of a particular object or situation. photos (first) ©Fuse/Getty Images; (second) ©Flying Colors Ltd./Getty Images; (third) ©Digital Archive Japan/Alamy; (fourth) ©Comstock Images/Alamy; (fifth) ©Jurkos/Getty Images (sixth) ©IStock/Getty Images; (seventh) ©Creatas/PunchStock; (eighth) ©Funzen/iStock/Getty Images; (spider) ©Photodisc/Getty Images

will hurt us keeps us out of harm's way. Specific phobias might be viewed, then, as an extreme and unfortunate variant on this adaptive process (Coelho & Purkis, 2009; Muris & Merckelbach, 2012). Women are more likely than men to experience specific phobias (Steinhausen & others, 2016).

Many explanations of specific phobias view these as based on experiences, memories, and learned associations (Veale & others, 2013). Perhaps, for example, the individual with a fear of heights experienced a fall from a high place earlier in life and therefore associates heights with pain (a classical conditioning explanation). Alternatively, he or she may have heard about or watched others who demonstrated terror of high places (an observational learning explanation), as when a little girl develops a fear of heights after sitting next to her terrified mother and observing her clutch the handrails, white-knuckled, as the roller coaster creeps steeply uphill.

Not all people who have a specific phobia can easily identify experiences that explain them, so other factors may also be at play (Coelho & Purkis, 2009). Each specific phobia may have its own neural correlates (Lueken & others, 2011), and some people may be especially prone to phobias (Burstein & others, 2012). One risk factor for developing a specific phobia is having a parent who has a psychological disorder, even if that disorder is not a specific phobia (Steinhausen & others, 2016)

Social Anxiety Disorder

Imagine how you might feel just before you first meet the parents of the person you hope to marry. You might dread the thought of making some awful gaffe, ruining their first impression of you. Or imagine getting ready to give a big speech before a crowd and suddenly realizing you have forgotten your notes. **Social anxiety disorder (SAD)** (also called **social phobia**) is an intense fear of being humiliated or embarrassed in social situations (Lampe & Sunderland, 2013; Morrison & Heimberg, 2013).

Where does social anxiety disorder come from? Genes appear to play a role (Torvik & others, 2016), along with neural circuitry involving the thalamus, amygdalae, and cerebral cortex (Heitmann & others, 2016; Weidt & others, 2016). Also, a number of neurotransmitters may be involved, including oxytocin (Ma & others, 2016). Social anxiety disorder may involve vulnerabilities, such as genetic characteristics or overprotective or rejecting parenting, that lay a foundation of risk, combined with learning experiences in a social context (Higa-McMillan & Ebesutani, 2011; Pejic & others, 2013; Sharma & others, 2016).

Individuals with social anxiety disorder often feel that their anxiety prevents them from letting others know who they really are. You can imagine that if you are extremely anxious, it is difficult to just be with another person authentically. Research demonstrates that authenticity is strongly related to well-being (Davis & others, 2015; Wang, 2016). Being who we really are can even buffer the effects of social conflicts (Wickham & others, 2016). Might it be that missing out on being authentic creates a vicious cycle for individuals with social anxiety disorder? To find out, read the Intersection.

In *DSM-5*, generalized anxiety disorder, panic disorder, specific phobia, and social anxiety disorder are all classified as anxiety disorders (APA, 2016; Gallo & others, 2013; Kupfer, 2015). Our next topics—obsessive-compulsive disorder and post-traumatic stress disorder—are not included under the umbrella of anxiety disorders. Instead, these disorders have their own separate categories. Nonetheless, as we will see, anxiety is relevant to these disorders.

● **social anxiety disorder (SAD) or social phobia** An anxiety disorder in which the individual has an intense fear of being humiliated or embarrassed in social situations.

Obsessive-Compulsive Disorder

Just before leaving on a long road trip, you find yourself checking to be sure you locked the front door. Going to bed the night before an early flight, you check your alarm clock a few times to be sure it will wake you for your 8 A.M. plane. This kind of checking behavior is a normal part of worrying.

In contrast, **obsessive-compulsive disorder (OCD)** involves anxiety-provoking thoughts that will not go away and/or urges to perform repetitive, ritualistic behaviors to

● **obsessive-compulsive disorder (OCD)** Psychological disorder in which the individual has anxiety-provoking thoughts that will not go away and/or urges to perform repetitive, ritualistic behaviors to prevent or produce some future situation.

INTERSECTION

Clinical Psychology and Social Psychology: Can Authentic Interactions Help Those with Social Anxiety?

One way that close relationships enhance our lives is by giving us a chance to express who we really are. We know that we have found a true friend when we have revealed our authentic selves and found someone who (still) loves us. In contrast, when our behavior involves hiding who we really are, it is difficult to feel good about ourselves (Gino, Kouchaki, & Galinsky, 2015) or our relationships (Gordon & Chen, 2016).

One of the worst consequences of social anxiety disorder (SAD) is its effect on people's relationships. Those with SAD have fewer friends and report less satisfaction with their social relationships (Alden & Taylor, 2004; Dryman & others, 2016; Levine & others, 2015).

Individuals with SAD, who are terrified of being humiliated in social interactions, engage in what are called safety behaviors (Grumet & Fitzpatrick, 2016; Plasencia, Taylor, & Alden, 2016). Safety behaviors involve protecting oneself from

feared outcomes by avoiding self-disclosure and putting up a false front. Such behavior makes sense: If you are extremely afraid of dreaded outcomes, keeping your true self hidden probably seems like a good idea. But note that as a result of their intense fear, those with SAD are robbed of the opportunity to be themselves around others as well as the other benefits that come with authentic self-expression.

What "safety behaviors" do you engage in?

A simple but elegant study (Plasencia, Taylor, & Alden, 2016) examined whether reducing safety behaviors would allow those with SAD to be more authentic and to enjoy a social interaction more. Individuals seeking treatment for SAD had a conversation with a member of the opposite sex (who was a confederate of the experimenters). Prior to the interaction, participants were randomly assigned to an experimental group or to a control group. In the experimental group, they were told that during the coming interaction, they should not do anything intended to hide their true feelings or their genuine selves. Even though they might be afraid, they needed to stay in the interaction and not engage in safety behaviors. The control group was told that simply engaging in social interactions for a longer time than usual was important. After the interaction, participants rated the quality of the interaction as well as their level of experienced authenticity.

The results showed that, compared to controls, those in the experimental group used fewer safety behaviors, reported more authenticity, and enjoyed the interaction more. Importantly, these outcomes were all related. The fewer safety behaviors, the more authentic participants felt. In turn, the more authentic they felt, the higher their ratings of interaction quality (Plasencia, Taylor, & Alden, 2016).

These results paint a poignant portrait of the prison that SAD can be for those struggling with it. Their anxiety leads to behaviors that keep them separate from others, denying them the warm light of authenticity.

© JackF/iStock/Getty Images

prevent or produce some future situation. *Obsessions* are recurrent thoughts, and *compulsions* are recurrent behaviors. Individuals with OCD dwell on normal doubts and repeat their behavioral routines sometimes hundreds of times a day.

The most common compulsions are excessive checking, cleansing, and counting. An individual with OCD might believe that she has to touch the doorway with her left hand whenever she enters a room and count her steps as she walks across the room. If she does not complete this ritual, she may be overcome with fear that something terrible will happen. Indeed, most individuals feel extraordinarily anxious if they do not act out their compulsions (Laposa & others, 2015; Yap, Mogan, & Kyrios, 2012). Actor and reality show host Howie Mandel has coped with OCD.

FACTORS CONTRIBUTING TO OCD

Among the theories about the causes of OCD, most researchers agree that there seems to be a genetic component (Alonso & others, 2012, 2013; Matthiesen & others, 2015).

Research also points to low levels of the neurotransmitters serotonin and dopamine (Goljevscek & Carvalho, 2011; D. L. Murphy & others, 2013; Soomro, 2012) and high levels of glutamate (S. E. Stewart & others, 2013) in the brain pathways linked with OCD.

Brain-imaging and EEG studies and animal research suggest neurological links for OCD (Millet & others, 2013; Montiero & Feng, 2016). Research shows that the brain seems to engage in a hyperactive monitoring of behavior in those with OCD (Endrass & others, 2013), and brain activation during learning may predispose individuals with OCD to a chronic feeling that something is not quite right (Gehring, Himle, & Nisenson, 2000).

One interpretation of these data is that the frontal cortex or basal ganglia are so active in OCD that numerous impulses reach the thalamus, generating obsessive thoughts or compulsive actions (Rotge & others, 2009). Essentially, the brain fails to get the "finished" message (Montiero & Feng, 2016).

Learning processes are also implicated in OCD (Endrass & others, 2013). A person who engages in compulsive behaviors often feels like doing so is an important way to fend off some dreaded outcome. For instance, consider a woman who feels compelled to check the locks on her apartment door 10 times so that she knows she has not put herself in danger by leaving the door unlocked. Having locked the door once, she is, of course, safe from this feared result. But she checks nine more times just to be sure.

Can you see the vicious cycle of her compulsion? Over and over again, she performs the ritual and nothing bad happens. As long as she performs this ritual, she will never discover that the terrible outcome would not have happened anyway. This example suggests that *avoidance learning* might be an important contributor to the maintenance of compulsive symptoms. Recall that avoidance learning is a particularly powerful form of negative reinforcement that occurs when the organism learns that by making a particular response, an unpleasant or aversive stimulus can be avoided completely. That response is maintained even in the absence of any aversive stimulus. The unpleasant stimulus is no longer around, but the avoiding organism will never discover that fact.

The notion that those with OCD may get "stuck" in the vicious cycle of avoidance learning is supported by studies showing that OCD is associated with reduced flexibility in picking up on changes in the rules of learning tasks (Bradbury, Cassin, & Rector, 2011).

Not surprisingly, individuals with OCD show a cognitive bias associated with overestimating threats, particularly when those threats are personally relevant (Moritz & others, 2011). Just as noted above, from the cognitive perspective, individuals with OCD show an inability to turn off negative, intrusive thoughts by ignoring or effectively dismissing them.

Thus, the science of OCD suggests that these individuals are preoccupied with avoiding a dreaded outcome, are prone to see that outcome as worse and more likely than it actually is, and are likely to be bothered by lingering doubts about whether they have actually avoided it. Once they find a way to fend off the feared result, they are likely to have difficulty unlearning that strategy. Some psychologists propose that, fundamentally, OCD symptoms reflect intolerance of uncertainty (Boelen & Carleton, 2012; Giele & others, 2016).

OCD-RELATED DISORDERS

DSM-5 expanded the disorders that are thought to be related to OCD (Abramowitz & Jacoby, 2015; Nissen & others, 2016). All of these disorders involve repetitive behavior, and like OCD, issues with uncertainty and anxiety. Some of the new additions are listed here:

- *Hoarding disorder* involves compulsive collecting, poor organization skills, and difficulty discarding, but also cognitive deficits in information-processing speed, decision making, and procrastination (Kress & others, 2016). Individuals with hoarding disorder find it difficult to throw things away; they are troubled by the feeling of uncertainty—the sense that they might need, for instance, old newspapers, at a later time (Wheaton & others, 2016).

510   CHAPTER 15   **Psychological Disorders**

- *Excoriation disorder* (or skin picking) refers to a particular compulsion, picking at one's skin, sometimes to the point of injury (Schumer, Bartley, & Bloch, 2016). Skin picking is more common among women than men and is seen as a symptom of autism spectrum disorder. Infections and complications with healing are issues with this disorder.

- *Trichotillomania* (hair pulling) is a disorder in which the person compulsively pulls at his or her hair, from the scalp, eyebrows, and other body areas (Keijsers & others, 2016). Hair pulling from the scalp can lead to patches of baldness that the person may go to great lengths to disguise.

- *Body dysmorphic disorder* involves a distressing preoccupation with imagined or slight flaws in one's physical appearance (Summers & others, 2016). Individuals with the disorder cannot stop thinking about their appearance, comparing their appearance to others, checking themselves in the mirror, and so forth. Occurring about equally in men and women, this disorder can involve maladaptive behaviors such as compulsive exercise and bodybuilding and repeated cosmetic surgery.

Prior to deployment, troops receive stress-management training aimed at helping to prevent PTSD and other disorders that might be triggered by the high-stress conditions of war.

© John Moore/Getty Images

● **post-traumatic stress disorder (PTSD)**
Psychological disorder that develops through exposure to a traumatic event, a severely oppressive situation, cruel abuse, or a natural or an unnatural disaster.

Post-Traumatic Stress Disorder

If you have ever been in even a minor car accident, you may have had a nightmare or two about it. You might have even found yourself reliving the experience for some time. This normal recovery process takes on a particularly devastating character in post-traumatic stress disorder. **Post-traumatic stress disorder (PTSD)** is a disorder that develops through exposure to a traumatic event that has overwhelmed the person's abilities to cope (Bisson, 2013).

In a controversial move, *DSM-5* expanded the experiences that might foster PTSD, recognizing that PTSD can occur not only in those who directly experience a trauma but also in those who witness it and those who only *hear* about it (APA, 2013a). The symptoms of PTSD vary but include:

- Flashbacks in which the individual relives the event as if it is happening all over again. A flashback can make the person lose touch with reality and reenact the event for seconds, hours, or (very rarely) days.

- Avoidance of emotional experiences and of talking about emotions with others as well as emotional numbing.
- Feelings of anxiety, nervousness, excessive arousal, and an inability to sleep.
- Difficulties with memory and concentration.
- Impulsive behavior.

PTSD symptoms can follow a trauma immediately or can occur after months or years (Welch & others, 2016). It is not uncommon for people who are exposed to a traumatic event to experience some of the symptoms in the days and weeks following the event. Traumatic life events can alter the delicate balance of neurotransmitters and hormones and other biological systems, such that PTSD can color the way the brain and body react to stress (Bremner & Pearce, 2016).

Clearly, one cause of PTSD is the traumatic event itself. However, not every individual exposed to the same event develops PTSD (Whitman & others, 2013). Therefore, other factors must influence a person's vulnerability to the disorder (Logue & others, 2015). These include a history of previous traumatic events and conditions, such as abuse and psychological disorders (Rudenstine & others, 2015), cultural background (Koo & others, 2016), and genetic predisposition (Castro-Vale & others, 2016; Telch & others, 2015). These preexisting conditions make individuals more vulnerable to PTSD when they are combined with stressful events.

test yourself

1. Define four anxiety disorders.
2. What are the central features of obsessive-compulsive disorder?
3. Describe the symptoms of post-traumatic stress disorder (PTSD).

3. DISORDERS INVOLVING EMOTION AND MOOD

Imagine that you have studied hard for a notoriously difficult class. With an *A* on the final, you will ace the course. If you end up with a *C* on the final, you might feel sad or disappointed. If you get an *A+*, you might feel ecstatic. Our emotions tell us how we are doing in life. We feel good or bad depending on our progress on important goals. For some individuals, the link between life experiences and emotions is off-kilter. They may feel sad for no reason at all or a sense of elation in the absence of any great accomplishment. Many psychological disorders involve this kind of dysregulation in a person's emotional life. In this section we examine two such disorders: depressive disorders and bipolar disorders.

Depressive Disorders

Everyone feels blue sometimes. A romantic breakup, the death of a loved one, or a personal failure can cast a dark cloud over life. Sometimes, however, a person might feel unhappy and not know why. **Depressive disorders** are disorders in which the individual suffers from *depression*—an unrelenting lack of pleasure in life.

Depressive disorders are common. In 2014, nearly 16 million American adults had at least one major depressive episode in the last 12 months. That is about the combined populations of Missouri and North Carolina or 6.7 percent of all U.S. adults (NIMH, 2016b).

A number of successful individuals have been diagnosed with depression, including musicians Sheryl Crow, Eric Clapton, and Peter Gabriel; actors Drew Barrymore and Jim Carrey; and artist Pablo Picasso, photographer Diane Arbus, astronaut Buzz Aldrin (the second man to walk on the moon), famed architect Frank Lloyd Wright, and J. K. Rowling, the author of the Harry Potter series.

Major depressive disorder (MDD) involves a significant depressive episode and depressed characteristics, such as lethargy and hopelessness, for at least two weeks. MDD impairs daily functioning, and it has been called the leading cause of disability in the United States (NIMH, 2016b). The symptoms of major depressive disorder may include:

- Depressed mood most of the day
- Reduced interest or pleasure in activities that were once enjoyable
- Significant weight loss or gain or significant decrease or increase in appetite
- Trouble sleeping or sleeping too much
- Fatigue or loss of energy
- Feeling worthless or guilty in an excessive or inappropriate manner
- Problems in thinking, concentrating, or making decisions
- Recurrent thoughts of death and suicide
- No history of manic episodes (periods of euphoric mood)

Individuals who experience less extreme depressive mood for over two months may be diagnosed with *persistent depressive disorder*. This disorder includes symptoms such as hopelessness, lack of energy, poor concentration, and sleep problems. A variety of biological, psychological, and sociocultural factors have been implicated in the development of depressive disorders.

BIOLOGICAL FACTORS

The biological factors implicated in depressive disorders include genes, brain structure and function, and neurotransmitters. Genes appear to play a role in depression, but they may do so in conjunction with experiences, again suggesting a vulnerability-stress association. For instance, depression has been linked to particular features of the serotonin transporter gene, called the 5-HTTLPR (Schneck & others, 2016). Importantly, research shows that these features do not inevitably lead to depression. Rather, they are associated with depression

● **depressive disorders** Psychological disorders in which the individual suffers from depression—an unrelenting lack of pleasure in life.

● **major depressive disorder (MDD)** Psychological disorder involving a significant depressive episode and depressed characteristics, such as lethargy and hopelessness, for at least two weeks.

This painting by Vincent Van Gogh, Portrait of Dr. Gachet, *reflects the extreme melancholy that characterizes the depressive disorders.*
© Art Reserve/Alamy

512 CHAPTER 15   Psychological Disorders

only if the person's social environment is stressful (Arpawong & others, 2016; Juhasz & others, 2015). In fact, individuals who possess these features are at a *decreased* risk for depression if they are also in a warm, positive social environment (Eley & others, 2004).

In addition, specific brain structures are involved in depression (Tozzi & others, 2016). For example, depressed individuals show lower levels of brain activity in a section of the prefrontal cortex that is involved in generating actions (Duman & others, 2012) and in regions of the brain associated with the perception of rewards in the environment (Howland, 2012; Zahavi & others, 2016). A depressed person's brain may not recognize opportunities for pleasurable experiences.

Depression also likely involves problems in neurotransmitter regulation, particularly serotonin, norepinephrine, and others. As we will see in the chapter "Therapies", medical treatments for depression seek to increase the amount of circulating serotonin in the brain. However, and interestingly, the research is far from straightforward in indicating a relationship between depression and the amount of these neurotransmitters (or receptors for them) in the brain. Some evidence indicates that individuals with depressive disorder appear to have too few receptors for the neurotransmitters serotonin and norepinephrine (Healy, 2015). The relationship of neurotransmitters to depression is likely complex and involves many of these chemicals in concert.

The incidence of depression is high among people living in poverty, as well as single women who are the heads of households.

PSYCHOLOGICAL FACTORS

Psychological explanations of depression have drawn on behavioral learning theories and cognitive theories. One behavioral view of depression focuses on learned helplessness (see the chapter "Learning"), an individual's feelings of powerlessness following exposure to aversive circumstances, such as prolonged stress, over which the individual has no control. When people cannot control negative circumstances, they may feel helpless and stop trying to change their situation. This helplessness spirals into a feeling of hopelessness (Huys, Daw, & Dayan, 2015). One advantage of the learned helplessness approach is that, because scientists can induce learned helplessness in animals, animal models can be used to examine how such experiences affect the brain and body (Shirayama & others, 2015).

Cognitive explanations of depression focus on thoughts and beliefs that can contribute to and prolong this sense of hopelessness (Hommel, Carey, & Jaillard, 2015; Ruscio & others, 2015). From this perspective, automatic negative thoughts reflect illogical self-defeating beliefs that shape the experiences of individuals who are depressed (Beck, 1967; Beck & Haigh, 2014). These habitual negative thoughts magnify negative experiences (Dozois & Rnic, 2015). For example, a person who is depressed might overgeneralize about a minor occurrence—say, turning in a work assignment late—and think that he or she is worthless. The accumulation of cognitive distortions can lead to depression.

The course of depression can be influenced by not only what people think but also *how* they think. Depressed individuals may ruminate on negative experiences and negative feelings, playing them over and over again in their mind (Hsu & others, 2015; Wang & others, 2015). This tendency to ruminate is associated with the development of depression (Stone & Gibb, 2015).

Another cognitive view of depression focuses on the *attributions* people make—their attempts to explain the cause of what happens. Research from this perspective examines how particular styles of attributions relate to depression (Moore & others, 2016; Rubenstein & others, 2016).

Attributional style is a person's habitual way of explaining events in their lives. *Pessimistic* attributional style means blaming oneself for negative events and expecting the negative events to recur in the future (Abramson, Seligman, & Teasdale, 1978). The pessimist explains negative events as having internal causes ("It is my fault I failed the exam"), stable causes ("I'm going to fail again and again"), and global causes ("Failing this exam shows that I won't do well in any of my courses").

This pessimistic attributional style can be contrasted with an optimistic attributional style. Optimists make external attributions for bad things that happen ("I did badly on the test because it's hard to know what a professor wants on the first exam"). They also recognize that these causes can change ("I'll do better on the next one") and that they are specific ("It was only one test"). Optimistic attributional style has been related to better outcomes, ranging from lowered depression, less distress, and decreased suicide risk in a variety of samples (Hirsch & Rabon, 2015; Rasmussen & Wingate, 2011; Stein & others, 2016; Tindle & others, 2012).

Combining the cognitive perspective with research on the brain, we might say that individuals with depression have a brain that is wired for attention to negative information and that their habitual patterns of thought and attributions produce well-worn neurological pathways for maintaining that unhappiness.

SOCIOCULTURAL FACTORS

Individuals with a low socioeconomic status (SES), especially people living in poverty, are more likely to develop depression than their higher-SES counterparts (Groffen & others, 2013; Kim & others, 2016; Williams, Priest, & Anderson, 2016). Depression increases as standards of living and employment circumstances worsen (Lorant & others, 2007). Studies have found very high rates of depression in Native American groups, among whom poverty, hopelessness, and alcoholism are widespread (Garrett & others, 2015; LaFromboise, Albright, & Harris, 2010; Roh & others, 2015).

Women are nearly twice as likely as men to be diagnosed with depression (Boyd & others, 2015; Doyle & others, 2015), a gender difference that is consistent across many cultures. The Psychological Inquiry provides a closer look at gender differences in depression.

Bipolar Disorder

Just as we all have down times, there are times when things seem to be going phenomenally well. For individuals with bipolar disorder, the ups and downs of life take on an extreme and often harmful tone. **Bipolar disorder** is characterized by extreme mood swings that include one or more episodes of *mania*—an overexcited, unrealistically optimistic state. During a manic episode, the person feels euphoric and energetic and might sleep very little. A manic state also features an impulsivity that can lead to trouble, such as spending one's life savings on a foolish business venture.

The severity of manic episodes is used to distinguish between two types of bipolar disorder. *Bipolar I disorder* refers to individuals who have extreme manic episodes during which they may experience hallucinations—that is, seeing or hearing things that are not there. *Bipolar II disorder* refers to the milder version in which the individual may experience a less extreme level of euphoria.

Most individuals with bipolar disorder experience multiple cycles of depression interspersed with mania. These people can have manic and depressive episodes four or more times a year, but they usually are separated by six months to a year. Bipolar disorder is equally common in women and men. Academy Award–winning actor Catherine Zeta-Jones, famed dancer and choreographer Alvin Ailey, and actor Carrie Fisher (Princess Leia in *Star Wars*) have been diagnosed with bipolar disorder.

What factors play a role in the development of bipolar disorder? Genetic influences are stronger predictors of bipolar disorder than of depressive disorder (Ament & others, 2015; Fabbri & Serretti, 2016; Song & others, 2015). An individual with an identical twin who has bipolar disorder has about a 70 percent probability of also having the disorder, and a fraternal twin has a more than 10 percent probability (Figure 4).

● **bipolar disorder** Psychological disorder characterized by extreme mood swings that include one or more episodes of mania—an overexcited, unrealistically optimistic state.

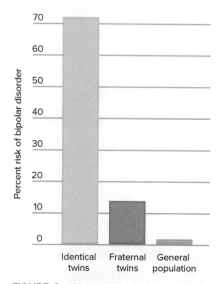

FIGURE 4   Risk of Bipolar Disorder in Identical and Fraternal Twins If One Twin Has the Disorder, and in the General Population Notice how much stronger the similarity of bipolar disorder is in identical twins, compared with fraternal twins and the general population. These statistics suggest a strong genetic role in the disorder. Data from *Annual Review of Neuroscience*, vol. 20, 1997. Annual Reviews. www.annualreviews.org

514 CHAPTER 15 Psychological Disorders

psychological *inquiry*

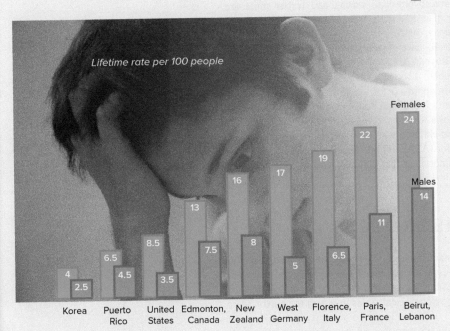

Lifetime rate per 100 people

| | Korea | Puerto Rico | United States | Edmonton, Canada | New Zealand | West Germany | Florence, Italy | Paris, France | Beirut, Lebanon |

Females: 24 (Beirut)
Males: 14 (Beirut)

(photo) © McGraw-Hill Education/Gary He, photographer
Data from Weissman, M. & Olfson, M. (1995) "Depression in women: Implications for health care research" *Science, 269,* 99–801

Depression Among Women and Men Across Cultures

The graph shows the rates of depression for women and men in nine different cultures (Weissman & Olfson, 1995). The rates represent the number of diagnosed cases per 100 people.

1. Which cultures have the highest and lowest levels of depression overall? What might account for these differences?

2. Which places have the biggest gender difference in depression? What might account for these differences?

3. In order to be diagnosed with depression, a person has to seek treatment for the disorder. How might gender influence a person's willingness to seek treatment?

4. How does your answer to question 3 influence the conclusions you would draw from the data illustrated in the graph?

Other biological processes are also a factor. Bipolar disorder is associated with differences in brain activity. Figure 5 shows the metabolic activity in the cerebral cortex of an individual cycling through depressive and manic phases. Notice the decrease in metabolic activity in the brain during depression and the increase in metabolic activity during

FIGURE 5 Brain Metabolism in Mania and Depression These images are of PET scans for an individual with bipolar disorder, who is described as a rapid cycler because of how quickly severe mood changes occur. The scans on the top and the bottom show the person's brain in a depressed state. The scans in the middle show the person in a manic state. The PET scans reveal how the brain's energy consumption falls in depression and rises in mania. The red areas in the middle row reflect rapid consumption of glucose.
Courtesy of Dr. Michael Phelps, UCLA School of Medicine

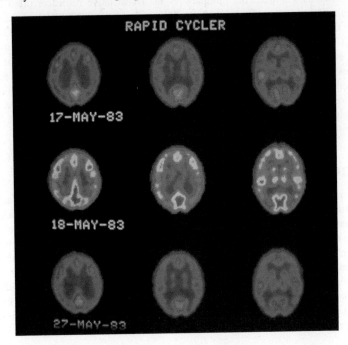

mania (Baxter & others, 1995). In addition to high levels of norepinephrine and low levels of serotonin, studies link high levels of the neurotransmitter glutamate to bipolar disorder (Dhillon, 2012; Ehrlich & others, 2015; Liu & others, 2016).

In addition to these biological factors, experience can influence bipolar disorder as well. For instance, childhood experiences with physical, sexual, and verbal abuse are associated with earlier onset of bipolar disorder, with more difficulty in treatment (Agnew-Blais & Danese, 2016; Post & others, 2015).

In recent years, mental health professionals have noted cases of children who appear to suffer from bipolar disorder (Cosgrove, Roybal, & Chang, 2013; DeFilippis & Wagner, 2015). A key dilemma is that treating bipolar disorder in adults involves psychoactive drugs, and these medications have not been approved for use in children. The potential side effects of these drugs could put children's health and development at risk. To address this issue, *DSM-5* included a new diagnosis, *disruptive mood dysregulation disorder*, which is considered a depressive disorder in children who show persistent irritability and recurrent episodes of out-of-control behavior (APA, 2013a). This decision is not without controversy. As we saw with ADHD, it is not clear that children who are prone to wild mood swings are not, simply, children.

test yourself

1. What are the features of major depressive disorder?
2. Give at least two biological, two psychological, and two sociocultural factors in depression.
3. What are the essential characteristics of bipolar disorder, and how are they different in bipolar I versus bipolar II?

4. DISSOCIATIVE DISORDERS

Have you ever been on a long car ride and completely lost track of time, so that you could not even remember a stretch of miles along the road? Have you been so caught up in a daydream that you were unaware of the passage of time? These are examples of normal dissociation. *Dissociation* refers to psychological states in which the person feels disconnected from immediate experience.

At the extreme of dissociation are individuals who feel a sense of disconnection *persistently*. **Dissociative disorders** are psychological disorders that involve a sudden loss of memory or change in identity. Under extreme stress or shock, the individual's conscious awareness becomes *dissociated* (separated or split) from previous memories and thoughts (Espirito-Santo & Pio-Abreu, 2009; Spiegel & others, 2013).

Psychologists believe that dissociation is an individual's way of dealing with extreme stress (Spiegel & others, 2013). Through dissociation the individual mentally protects his or her conscious self from the traumatic event. Dissociative disorders often occur in individuals who also show signs of PTSD (Lanius & others, 2012). Both of these disorders are thought to be rooted, in part, in extremely traumatic life events (Dorahy & others, 2015). The notion that dissociative disorders are related to problems in pulling together emotional memories is supported by findings showing lower volume in the hippocampus and amygdala in individuals with dissociative disorders (Chalavi & others, 2015; Vermetten & others, 2006). The hippocampus is especially involved in consolidating memory and organizing life experience into a coherent whole (Sar, Akyuz, & Dogan, 2007; Spiegel, 2006). Two kinds of dissociative disorders are dissociative amnesia and dissociative identity disorder.

● **dissociative disorders** Psychological disorders that involve a sudden loss of memory or change in identity due to the dissociation (separation) of the individual's conscious awareness from previous memories and thoughts.

Dissociative Amnesia

Recall from the chapter "Memory" that *amnesia* is the inability to recall important events (Markowitsch & Staniloiu, 2012). **Dissociative amnesia** is a type of amnesia characterized by extreme memory loss that stems from extensive psychological stress (Dell, 2013). A person experiencing dissociative amnesia still remembers things like how to hail a cab or use a phone. Only aspects of the individual's own identity and autobiographical experiences are forgotten.

Sometimes individuals suffering from dissociative amnesia will unexpectedly travel away from home, even assuming a new identity. For instance, on August 28, 2008, Hannah Upp, a 23-year-old middle schoolteacher in New York City, disappeared while out for a run (Marx & Didziulis, 2009). She had no wallet, identification, cell phone, or

● **dissociative amnesia** Dissociative disorder characterized by extreme memory loss that is caused by extensive psychological stress.

money. Her family and friends posted flyers around the city and messages on the Internet. As days went by, they became increasingly concerned that something terrible had happened. Finally, Hannah was found floating face down in the New York harbor on September 16, sunburned and dehydrated but alive. She remembered nothing of her experiences. To her, it felt like she had gone out for a run and 10 minutes later was being pulled from the harbor. To this day, she does not know what event might have led to her dissociative amnesia nor does she remember how she survived during her two-week disappearance. At one point while she was missing, someone approached her and asked if she was the Hannah everyone was looking for. She answered no.

Dissociative Identity Disorder

● **dissociative identity disorder (DID)**
Dissociative disorder in which the individual has two or more distinct personalities or selves, each with its own memories, behaviors, and relationships; formerly called multiple personality disorder.

Dissociative identity disorder (DID), formerly called *multiple personality disorder,* is the most dramatic, least common, and most controversial dissociative disorder. Individuals with this disorder have two or more distinct personalities or identities (Belli & others, 2012). Each identity has its own memories, behaviors, and relationships. One identity dominates at one time; another takes over at another time.

A famous real-life example of dissociative identity disorder (DID) is the "three faces of Eve" case, based on the life of a woman named Chris Sizemore (Thigpen & Cleckley, 1957) (Figure 6). Eve White was the original dominant personality. She had no knowledge of her second personality, Eve Black, although Eve Black had been alternating with Eve White for a number of years. Eve White was quiet and serious, Eve Black was carefree and mischievous. Eve Black would emerge at the most inappropriate times, leaving Eve White with hangovers, bills, and a reputation in local bars that she could not explain. During treatment, Jane, a third personality, emerged.

The factors that contribute to DID remain something of a mystery (Boysen & VanBergen, 2013). Research suggests that a high rate of extraordinarily severe sexual or physical abuse during early childhood is related to the condition (Ross & Ness, 2010). Some psychologists believe that a child can cope with intense trauma by dissociating from the experience and developing alternate selves as protectors. Sexual abuse is thought to be extremely common in these individuals (Jacobson & others, 2015); however, the majority of individuals who have been sexually abused do not develop DID. The vast majority of individuals with DID are women.

Dissociative identity disorder is a controversial diagnosis (Freeland & others, 1993; Sar, Akyuz, & Dogan, 2007; Spiegel, 2006). Until the 1980s, only about 300 cases of DID had ever been reported, but in the years since hundreds more have been diagnosed (Gentile, Dillon, & Gillig, 2013). Between 2000 and 2010, some 1,171 new cases were identified (Boysen & VanBergen, 2013).

Social cognitive theorists point out that DID has tended to increase whenever the popular media present a case, such as the film *The Three Faces of Eve,* the miniseries *Sybil,* or the Showtime drama *The United States of Tara.* From this perspective, after exposure to these examples, people may be more likely to view multiple identities as a real condition and develop the disorder through a process of social contagion (as described in the chapter "Social Psychology"). However, research comparing China (a culture in which DID is not widely publicized) and Canada (where it is) shows that dissociative experiences (and traumatic events) were similar across both groups (Ross & others, 2008), casting some doubt on the notion that dissociative experiences are entirely a product of social contagion.

Some experts believe that dissociative identity disorder is a *social construction*—that it represents a category some

FIGURE 6   The Three Faces of Eve Chris Sizemore, the subject of the 1950s book and film *The Three Faces of Eve,* is shown here with a work she painted titled *Three Faces in One.* © Gerald Martineau/The Washington Post/ Getty Images

people adopt to make sense out of their experiences (Spanos, 1996). Rather than being a single person with many conflicting feelings, wishes, and potentially awful experiences, the individual compartmentalizes different aspects of the self into independent identities. In some cases, therapists have been accused of creating alternate personalities. Encountering an individual who appears to have a fragmented sense of self, the therapist may begin to treat each fragment as its own "personality" (Spiegel, 2006).

5. SCHIZOPHRENIA

Have you had the experience of watching a movie and suddenly noticing that the film bears an uncanny resemblance to your life? Have you ever listened to a radio talk show and realized that the host was saying exactly what you were just thinking? Do these moments mean something special about you or are they coincidences? For individuals with severe psychological disorders, such random experiences take on special and personal meaning.

Psychosis refers to a state in which a person's perceptions and thoughts are fundamentally removed from reality. *DSM-5* recognizes a class of disorders called "schizophrenia spectrum and other psychotic disorders." Within this group is one of the most debilitating psychological disorders and our focus in this section: schizophrenia.

Schizophrenia is a severe psychological disorder that is characterized by highly disordered thought processes. Individuals with schizophrenia may see things that are not there, hear voices inside their heads, and live in a terrifying world of twisted logic. They may say odd things, show inappropriate emotion, and move their bodies in peculiar ways. Often, they are socially withdrawn and isolated.

Schizophrenia is usually diagnosed in early adulthood, around age 18 for men and 25 for women. The suicide risk for individuals with schizophrenia is eight times that for the general population (Depp & others, 2016; Pompili & others, 2007).

Symptoms of Schizophrenia

Psychologists classify the symptoms of schizophrenia into positive symptoms, negative symptoms, and cognitive deficits (NIMH, 2016c).

POSITIVE SYMPTOMS

Positive symptoms involve a distortion or an excess of normal function. They are "positive" because they reflect something added above and beyond normal behavior. Positive symptoms of schizophrenia include hallucinations, delusions, thought disorders, and movement disorders.

Hallucinations are sensory experiences that occur in the absence of real stimuli. Hallucinations are usually auditory—the person might complain of hearing voices—or visual, and much less commonly they take the form of smells or tastes (Winton-Brown & others, 2015). Visual hallucinations involve seeing things that are not there. For example, at the age of 21, while serving in Vietnam as a medical corpsman for the Marines, Moe Armstrong experienced a psychotic break. Dead Vietcong soldiers appeared to talk to him, beg him for help, and did not seem to realize that they were dead. Armstrong, now a successful businessman and a sought-after public speaker who holds two master's degrees, relies on medication to keep such experiences at bay (Bonfatti, 2005).

Delusions are false, unusual, and sometimes magical beliefs that are not part of an individual's culture. A delusional person might think that he is Jesus Christ or Muhammad; another might imagine that her thoughts are being broadcast over the radio. Delusions can be difficult to change.

For individuals with schizophrenia, delusional beliefs that might seem completely illogical to the outsider are experienced as all too real. At one point in his life, Bill Garrett, a college student with schizophrenia, was convinced that a blister on his hand was a sign of gangrene. So strong was his belief that he tried to cut off his hand with a knife, before being stopped by his family (M. Park, 2009).

test yourself

1. What are the main characteristics of dissociative disorders? What does the word *dissociative* mean in reference to them?
2. Identify the characteristics of dissociative amnesia.
3. What explanations have experts given for the development of dissociative identity disorder in individuals?

● **psychosis** Psychological state in which a person's perceptions and thoughts are fundamentally removed from reality.

● **schizophrenia** Severe psychological disorder characterized by highly disordered thought processes; individuals suffering from schizophrenia may be referred to as psychotic because they are so far removed from reality.

● **hallucinations** Sensory experiences that occur in the absence of real stimuli.

● **delusions** False, unusual, and sometimes magical beliefs that are not part of an individual's culture.

● **thought disorder** The unusual, sometimes bizarre thought processes that are characteristic positive symptoms of schizophrenia.

Thought disorder refers to the unusual, sometimes bizarre thought processes that are characteristic positive symptoms of schizophrenia. The thoughts of individuals with schizophrenia can be disorganized and confused. Often those with schizophrenia do not make sense when they talk or write. For example, someone with schizophrenia might say, "Well, Rocky, babe, happening, but where, when, up, top, side, over, you know, out of the way, that's it. Sign off." Such speech has no meaning for the listener. The individual might also make up new words (*neologisms*) (Fineberg & others, 2015; Senkowski & Gallinat, 2015).

● **referential thinking** Ascribing personal meaning to completely random events.

In addition, a person with schizophrenia can show **referential thinking,** which means ascribing personal meaning to completely random events. For instance, the individual might believe that a dead bird on the sidewalk is a sign from God or that a person walking nearby is an agent from the government. Molly Watson was diagnosed with schizophrenia in her 30s. Recently, she described how during her first psychotic episode she was convinced that car license plate numbers were important messages to be followed or avoided (Watson, 2015).

● **movement disorders** The unusual mannerisms, body movements, and facial expressions that are characteristic positive symptoms of schizophrenia.

Movement disorders are a final positive symptom of schizophrenia, involving unusual mannerisms, body movements, and facial expressions. The individual may repeat certain motions over and over or, in extreme cases, may become catatonic. **Catatonia** is a state of immobility and unresponsiveness that lasts for long periods of time.

● **catatonia** State of immobility and unresponsiveness lasting for long periods of time.

NEGATIVE SYMPTOMS

Whereas schizophrenia's positive symptoms are characterized by a distortion or an excess of normal functions, schizophrenia's *negative symptoms* reflect social withdrawal, behavioral deficits, and the loss or decrease of normal functions. One negative symptom is **flat affect,** which means the display of little or no emotion (Ventura & others, 2015). Individuals with schizophrenia also may be lacking in the ability to read the emotions of others (Frajo-Apor & others, 2016). They may show a deficient ability to plan, initiate, and engage in goal-directed behavior.

● **flat affect** The display of little or no emotion—a common negative symptom of schizophrenia.

COGNITIVE SYMPTOMS

Cognitive symptoms of schizophrenia include deficits in executive functioning (Kluwe-Schiavon & others, 2013), including difficulty sustaining attention, problems holding information in memory, and inability to interpret information and make decisions (Harvey & Bowie, 2013; Marin & others, 2015).

Causes of Schizophrenia

A great deal of research has investigated schizophrenia's causes, including biological, psychological, and sociocultural factors.

BIOLOGICAL FACTORS

Research provides strong support for biological explanations of schizophrenia. Particularly compelling is the evidence for a genetic predisposition (Kavanagh & others, 2015; Ruzzo & Geschwind, 2016), but structural brain abnormalities and problems with neurotransmitter regulation also are linked to this disorder.

Genes Research supports the notion that schizophrenia is at least partially explained by genetic factors (Kavanagh & others, 2015). The Psychological Inquiry shows the results of research examining the role of genetics in schizophrenia.

Structural Brain Abnormalities Studies have found structural brain abnormalities in people with schizophrenia, specifically enlarged ventricles (Kubota & others, 2015; Rais & others, 2012). Ventricles are fluid-filled spaces, and enlargement of the ventricles indicates deterioration in other brain tissue. These changes can occur over time, suggesting that as schizophrenia progresses, the brain deteriorates.

psychological *inquiry*

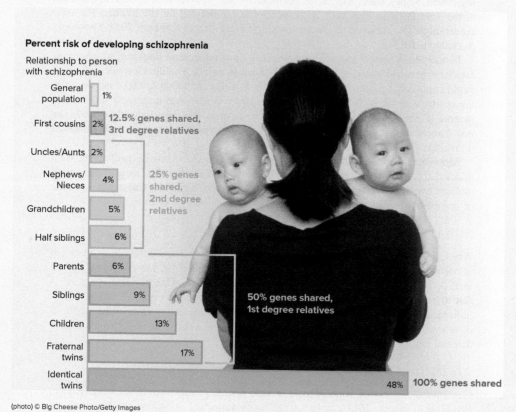

Percent risk of developing schizophrenia

Relationship to person with schizophrenia

- General population — 1%
- First cousins — 2% — 12.5% genes shared, 3rd degree relatives
- Uncles/Aunts — 2%
- Nephews/Nieces — 4% — 25% genes shared, 2nd degree relatives
- Grandchildren — 5%
- Half siblings — 6%
- Parents — 6%
- Siblings — 9% — 50% genes shared, 1st degree relatives
- Children — 13%
- Fraternal twins — 17%
- Identical twins — 48% — 100% genes shared

(photo) © Big Cheese Photo/Getty Images

The Association of Genes with Schizophrenia

This figure shows that as genetic relatedness to an individual with schizophrenia increases, so does the lifetime risk of developing schizophrenia. Using the graph, answer these questions:

1. Which familial relations have the lowest and highest level of genetic overlap (shared genes)?

2. What is the difference in genetic overlap between identical twins and non-twin siblings?

3. What is the difference in risk of schizophrenia between identical twins and non-twin siblings of individuals with schizophrenia?

4. What do you think accounts for the differences in your answers to questions 2 and 3?

Individuals with schizophrenia also have a smaller prefrontal cortex and lower activity in this area of the brain than healthy individuals (Pillai & others, 2016). The prefrontal cortex is the region where thinking, planning, and decision making take place. Recall from the chapter "Human Development" that the prefrontal cortex continues to develop throughout adolescence and into early adulthood. It may be telling that the emergence of symptoms of schizophrenia, which typically occurs in young adulthood, happens during the time when the prefrontal cortex becomes fully connected.

Still, differences between the brains of healthy individuals and those with schizophrenia are small. Microscopic studies of brain tissue after death reveal small changes in the distribution or characteristics of brain cells in persons with schizophrenia. At least some of these changes seem to have occurred prenatally because they are not accompanied by glial cells, which are always present when a brain injury occurs after birth (Vuillermot & others, 2010). Problems in prenatal development may predispose a brain to developing schizophrenic symptoms later in life (Fatemi & Folsom, 2009).

Neurotransmitter Regulation   Whether it is differences in amount of dopamine, its production, or its uptake, there is good evidence that problems regulating the neurotransmitter dopamine play a role in schizophrenia (Slifstein & others, 2015).

A link between dopamine and psychotic symptoms was first noticed when the drug L-dopa (which increases dopamine levels) was given to individuals as a treatment for Parkinson disease. In addition to relieving Parkinson symptoms, L-dopa caused some to experience psychosis (Janowsky, Addario, & Risch, 1987; Madras, 2013). Further, drugs that reduce psychotic symptoms often block dopamine (Howes, McCutcheon, & Stone, 2015).

Previously we have encountered dopamine as the "feel good" neurotransmitter that helps us recognize rewarding stimuli in the environment and relates to being outgoing and sociable. How can a neurotransmitter that is associated with good things play a crucial role in schizophrenia?

One way to think about this puzzle is to view dopamine as a neurochemical messenger that shouts out, "Hey! This is important!" whenever we encounter opportunities for reward. Imagine what it might be like to be bombarded with such messages about even the smallest details of life (Roiser & others, 2010). Private thoughts might take on such dramatic proportions that they sound like someone else's voice talking inside the person's head. Fleeting ideas, such as "The traffic lights are turning red *because* I am in a hurry," suddenly seem not silly but true. Hallucinations, delusions, and referential thinking may be expressions of the individual's attempts to make sense of such extraordinary feelings (Kapur, 2003).

Another neurotransmitter that is thought to play a role in schizophrenia is glutamate. In the brain, the majority of excitatory messages are sent by glutamate, a neurotransmitter that sends the message for other neurons to fire. Some of the drugs used to treat schizophrenia have the effect of increasing glutamate. Although initially, it was hypothesized that low levels of glutamate led to schizophrenia, it appears that schizophrenia is associated with abnormalities in specific types of glutamate receptors (Howes, McCutcheon, & Stone, 2015).

PSYCHOLOGICAL FACTORS

Psychologists used to explain schizophrenia as rooted in childhood experiences with unresponsive parents. Such explanations have fallen by the wayside. Contemporary theorists do recognize that stress may contribute to the development of this disorder. Experiences are now viewed through the lens of the vulnerability-stress hypothesis, suggesting that individual with schizophrenia may have biological risk factors that interact with experience to produce the disorder.

SOCIOCULTURAL FACTORS

Sociocultural background is not considered a *cause* of schizophrenia, but sociocultural factors do appear to affect the *course* of the disorder, or how it progresses. Across cultures, individuals with schizophrenia in developing, nonindustrialized nations tend to have better outcomes than those in developed, industrialized nations (Jablensky, 2000; Myers, 2010). This difference may be due to the fact that in developing nations, family and friends are more accepting and supportive of individuals with schizophrenia. In Western samples, marriage, warm supportive friends (Jablensky & others, 1992; Wiersma & others, 1998), and employment are related to better outcomes for individuals diagnosed with schizophrenia (Rosen & Garety, 2005).

Some experts have called for a focus on preventing schizophrenia by identifying those at risk and then intervening early to reduce the level of disability they experience (Addington & others, 2011; Walder & others, 2012). Early intervention can be important because a strong predictor of relapse (that is, having symptoms again after treatment) is the amount of time a person spends in a psychotic state without treatment (Hegelstad & others, 2012; Karson & others, 2016). Intervening after a person's first psychotic break and preventing further such experiences is an important goal.

Is there a way to know who might be at risk for schizophrenia? One study showed that among those with a family history of schizophrenia, lower levels of *social* functioning distinguished those who went on to develop schizophrenia from others (Cornblatt & others, 2012).

test yourself

1. What is schizophrenia?
2. What are some positive and negative symptoms of schizophrenia?
3. How is dopamine thought to be involved in schizophrenia?

6. PERSONALITY DISORDERS

Are there aspects of your personality that you would like to change? Maybe you worry too much or fall in love too easily. Imagine that your very personality—who you really are—is the core of your life difficulties. **Personality disorders** are chronic, maladaptive cognitive-behavioral patterns that are thoroughly integrated into an individual's personality. Personality disorders affect a person's sense of self and capacity for relationships with others (Trull, Carpenter, & Widiger, 2013). Such disorders are relatively common. In a study of a representative U.S. sample, researchers found that 15 percent had a personality disorder (Grant & others, 2004). One study found that among problem gamblers, nearly half had a personality disorder (Dowling & others, 2015).

DSM-5 lists 10 personality disorders (Figure 7). Below, we survey the two personality disorders that have been studied most extensively: antisocial personality disorder and borderline personality disorder. As we review below, both of these disorders are associated with dire consequences.

● **personality disorders** Chronic, maladaptive cognitive-behavioral patterns that are thoroughly integrated into an individual's personality.

Antisocial Personality Disorder

Antisocial personality disorder (ASPD) is characterized by guiltlessness, law-breaking, exploitation of others, irresponsibility, and deceit. Those with this disorder are aggressive

● **antisocial personality disorder (ASPD)** Psychological disorder characterized by guiltlessness, law-breaking, exploitation of others, irresponsibility, and deceit.

Personality Disorder	Description
Paranoid Personality Disorder	Paranoia, suspiciousness, and deep distrust of others. People with this disorder are always on the lookout for danger and the slightest social mistreatment. They may be socially isolated.
Schizoid Personality Disorder	Extreme lack of interest in interpersonal relationships. People with this disorder are emotionally cold and apathetic, and they are generally detached from interpersonal life.
Schizotypal Personality Disorder	Socially isolated and prone to odd thinking. People with this disorder often have elaborate and strange belief systems and attribute unusual meanings to life events and experiences.
Antisocial Personality Disorder	Manipulative, deceitful, and amoral. People with this disorder lack empathy for others, are egocentric, and are willing to use others for their own personal gain.
Borderline Personality Disorder	Emotionally volatile and unstable sense of self. These individuals are prone to mood swings, excessive self-criticism, extreme judgments of others, and are preoccupied with being abandoned.
Histrionic Personality Disorder	Attention-seeking, dramatic, lively, and flirtatious. These individuals are inappropriately seductive in their interactions with others.
Narcissistic Personality Disorder	Self-aggrandizing yet overly dependent on the evaluations of others. People with this disorder view themselves as entitled and better than others. They show deficits in empathy and in understanding the feelings of others.
Avoidant Personality Disorder	Socially inhibited and prone to feelings of inadequacy, anxiety, and shame. These individuals feel inadequate and hold back in social situations. They have unrealistic standards for their own behavior and avoid setting goals, taking personal risks, or pursuing new activities.
Dependent Personality Disorder	Dependent on others for emotional and physical needs. People with this disorder perceive others as powerful and competent and themselves as childlike and helpless.
Obsessive-Compulsive Personality Disorder	Conforming rigidly to rules. These individuals show an excessive attachment to moral codes and are excessively orderly in daily life.

FIGURE 7   The 10 Personality Disorders Included in *DSM-5* Diagnoses of these disorders require that the person be over the age of 18, and all involve pervasive aspects of the person that color their cognition, emotion, and behavior. Note that some of the labels are potentially confusing. Schizoid and schizotypal personality disorders are not the same thing as schizophrenia (though schizotypal personality disorder may proceed to schizophrenia). Further, obsessive-compulsive personality disorder is not the same thing as obsessive-compulsive disorder.

John Wayne Gacy (top) and Ted Bundy (bottom) exemplify the subgroup of people with ASPD who are also psychopathic.

©Bettmann/Getty Images

(Lobbestael, Cima, & Arntz, 2013) and potentially violent (Yiend & others, 2013). ASPD is far more common in men than in women (Cale & Lilienfeld, 2002).

ASPD is characterized by

- Failure to conform to social norms or obey the law
- Deceitfulness, lying, or conning others for personal profit or pleasure
- Impulsivity
- Irritability and aggressiveness, getting into physical fights or perpetrating assaults
- Reckless disregard for the safety of self or others
- Consistent irresponsibility, inconsistent work behavior, not paying bills
- Lack of remorse, showing indifference to the pain of others, or rationalizing, having hurt or mistreated another

ASPD is related to criminal behavior, but not all individuals with ASPD engage in crime, and not all criminals suffer from ASPD. Individuals with ASPD can be successful. There are antisocial physicians, clergy, journalists, law enforcement officers, and just about any other occupation. Still, such individuals tend to exploit others, lack empathy, and break the rules.

A number of factors intertwine to produce ASPD. Research has linked ASPD to low levels of activation in the prefrontal cortex and has related these brain differences to poor decision making and problems in learning (Yang & Raine, 2009). Both genetic factors and childhood abuse are associated with ASPD (Reichborn-Kjennerud & others, 2015; Werner, Few, & Bucholz, 2015), but there is evidence that genetic differences may distinguish abused children who go on to commit violent acts from those who do not (Caspi & others, 2002; Lynam & others, 2007).

Individuals with ASPD show lower levels of autonomic nervous system arousal and are less stressed than others by aversive circumstances, including punishment (Fung & others, 2005; Portnoy & Farrington, 2015). They have the ability to keep their cool while engaging in deception (Verschuere & others, 2005), suggesting that those with ASPD might be able to fool a polygraph. The underaroused autonomic nervous system may be a key difference between adolescents who become antisocial adults and those whose behavior improves during adulthood (Raine, Venables, & Williams, 1990).

Psychopaths are one subgroup of individuals with ASPD (Strickland & others, 2013). They are remorseless predators who engage in violence to get what they want. Examples include serial killers John Wayne Gacy (who murdered 33 boys and young men) and Ted Bundy (who confessed to murdering at least 30 young women).

Research on prison inmates with ASPD (all of whom committed violent offenses) shows that those who are classified as psychopaths have lower levels of gray matter than those who are not (Decety, Skelly, & Kiehl, 2013; Gregory & others, 2012). Recall from the chapter "Gender, Sex, and Sexuality" that gray matter is thought to be associated with empathy. Not surprisingly, psychopaths show deficits in theory of mind (Shamay-Tsoory & others, 2010).

A key challenge in treating individuals with ASPD, including psychopaths, is their ability to con even sophisticated mental health professionals. Those with ASPD may resist engaging in a therapeutic relationship because it involves giving up a sense of power or control (McRae, 2013). Many never seek therapy, and others end up in prison, where treatment is rarely an option.

Borderline Personality Disorder

● **borderline personality disorder (BPD)**
Psychological disorder characterized by a pervasive pattern of instability in interpersonal relationships, self-image, and emotions and by marked impulsivity beginning by early adulthood and present in a variety of contexts.

Borderline personality disorder (BPD) is a pervasive pattern of instability in interpersonal relationships, self-image, and emotions. Individuals with BPD are impulsive, insecure, and emotional. BPD is related to self-harming behaviors, such as cutting (Gratz & others, 2012) and suicide (D. L. Turnbull & others, 2013).

At the very core of borderline personality disorder is profound instability—in mood, in sense of self, in relationships. Four essential features characterize BPD (Trull & Brown, 2013):

- Unstable affect
- Unstable sense of self and identity, including self-destructive impulsive behavior and chronic feelings of emptiness
- Negative interpersonal relationships, which are unstable, intense, and characterized by extreme shifts between idealization and devaluation
- Self-harm, including recurrent suicidal behavior, gestures, or threats or self-mutilating behavior

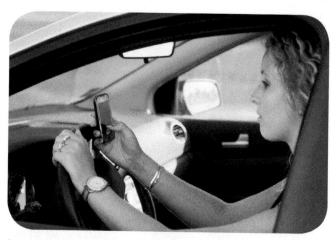

Impulsivity of the type that can lead to self-harm can be a symptom of borderline personality disorder.
© Martinan/iStock/Getty Images

To cope with their unstable emotional lives, individuals with BPD may engage in a variety of maladaptive behaviors, among them drinking alcohol and using illicit substances (Barker & others, 2015). BPD is more common in women than men, among those in low-income brackets, and among those younger than 30 (Tomko & others, 2013). A renowned expert on BPD, Marsha Linehan revealed that she herself has struggled with the disorder (Carey, 2011a).

The potential causes of BPD are complex and likely include biological factors and childhood experiences. The role of genes in BPD has been demonstrated in a variety of studies and across cultures (Distel & others, 2012; Mulder, 2012; Reichborn-Kjennerud & others, 2015). Many individuals with BPD report experiences of childhood sexual abuse, physical abuse, and neglect (De Fruyt & De Clercq, 2012; Fossati & others, 2016). It is not clear, however, whether abuse is a primary cause of the disorder (Trull, Carpenter, & Widiger, 2013). Rather, childhood abuse experiences may combine with genetic factors in promoting BPD.

Cognitive factors associated with BPD include a tendency to hold the irrational beliefs that one is powerless and innately unacceptable (Leahy & McGinn, 2012) and that other people are dangerous and hostile (Arntz, 2005). Individuals with BPD also display *hypervigilance:* the tendency to be constantly on the alert, looking for threatening information in the environment (Izurieta Hidalgo & others, 2016).

Individuals with BPD are very sensitive to how others treat them. They tend to see the world in either-or terms, a thinking style called *splitting.* For example, they typically view other people as either hated enemies with no positive qualities or as beloved, idealized friends who can do no wrong.

Up until about 25 years ago, experts thought that BPD was untreatable, but evidence suggests that many individuals with BPD show improvement over time. As many as 50 percent of individuals with BPD improve within two years, and once improved they are not likely to relapse (Gunderson, 2008). One key aspect of improvement appears to be reducing social stress, such as leaving an abusive romantic partner or establishing a sense of trust in a therapist (Gunderson & others, 2003). In the chapter "Therapies", we will review dialectical therapy that has shown effectiveness for BPD (Linehan & others, 2015).

test yourself

1. How are personality disorders defined?
2. To what sorts of behaviors is antisocial personality disorder related?
3. How is borderline personality disorder defined, and what are four features that characterize it?

7. SUICIDE

Thinking about suicide is not necessarily abnormal, but attempting or completing the act of suicide is. Sadly, many individuals who, to the outside eye, seem to be leading successful lives have committed suicide. Examples include poet Sylvia Plath, novelist Ernest Hemingway, grunge icon Kurt Cobain, and actor Robin Williams.

According to the Centers for Disease Control and Prevention (CDC), in 2013, 41,149 people in the United States committed suicide, and suicide was the 10th-leading cause of death in the country for all ages (CDC, 2015e). Suicide is the second-leading cause of death (after accidents) for U.S. adolescents ages 13 through 19 (CDC, 2016a).

What to Do

1. Ask direct, straightforward questions in a calm manner. For example, "Are you thinking about hurting yourself?"

2. Be a good listener and be supportive. Emphasize that unbearable pain can be survived.

3. Take the suicide threat very seriously. Ask questions about the person's feelings, relationships, and thoughts about the type of method to be used. If a gun, pills, rope, or other means is mentioned and a specific plan has been developed, the situation is dangerous. Stay with the person until help arrives.

4. Encourage the person to get professional help and assist him or her in getting help. If the person is willing, take the person to a mental health facility or hospital.

What Not to Do

1. Don't ignore the warning signs.

2. Don't refuse to talk about suicide if the person wants to talk about it.

3. Don't react with horror, disapproval, or repulsion.

4. Don't offer false reassurances ("Everything will be all right") or make judgments ("You should be thankful for . . .").

5. Don't abandon the person after the crisis seems to have passed or after professional counseling has begun.

FIGURE 8 **When Someone Is Threatening Suicide** Do not ignore the warning signs if you think someone you know is considering suicide. Talk to a counselor if you are reluctant to say anything to the person yourself. (photo) © Nathan Lau/Design Pics/Corbis

Given these grim statistics, psychologists work with individuals to reduce the frequency and intensity of suicidal impulses. You can do your part. Figure 8 provides good advice on what to do and what not to do if you encounter someone who is threatening suicide.

What might prompt an individual to end his or her own life? Biological, psychological, and sociocultural circumstances can be contributing factors.

Biological Factors

Genetic factors appear to play a role in suicide, which tends to run in families (Althoff & others, 2012; Peñas-Lliedó, Naranjo, & Llierena, 2013). One famous family that has been plagued by suicide is the Hemingways. Five members of that family, spread across generations, committed suicide, including the writer Ernest Hemingway and his granddaughter Margaux, a model and actor. Similarly, in 2009, Nicholas Hughes—a successful marine biologist and the son of Sylvia Plath, a poet who had killed herself—tragically hanged himself. In considering these examples, you might note that Margaux Hemingway and Nicholas Hughes had experienced the suicide of a family member and might therefore have been more likely than most people to view suicide as a way to cope with life's difficulties.

A number of studies link suicide with low levels of serotonin and serotonin-linked genes (Enoch & others, 2013; H. Y. Lee & others, 2015; Lyddon & others, 2013). Poor physical health, especially when it is chronic, is another risk factor for suicide (Webb & others, 2012).

Psychological Factors

Psychological factors that can contribute to suicide include psychological disorders and traumatic experiences (Barr & others, 2016; Pompili & others, 2015). Approximately 90 percent of individuals who commit suicide are estimated to have a diagnosable mental disorder (American Foundation for Suicide Prevention, 2016; NIMH, 2013). The most common disorders among individuals who commit suicide are depression and anxiety (Bentley & others, 2016; Zalpuri & Rothschild, 2016). An immediate and highly stressful circumstance—such as the loss of a loved one, losing one's job, flunking out of school, or an unwanted pregnancy—can lead people to threaten and/or to commit suicide (Kumar & George, 2013). In addition, substance abuse is linked with suicide (Carmel & others, 2016).

An expert on suicide, Thomas Joiner (2005) has proposed a comprehensive theory of the phenomenon. His *interpersonal theory of suicide* states that suicide involves two factors (Hames, Hagan, & Joiner, 2013; Joiner, 2005; Joiner & Ribeiro, 2011; A. R. Smith & others, 2013):

- A desire to die

- The acquired capability for suicide

The desire to die, from this perspective, emerges when a person's social needs are not met. Individuals who feel they do not belong, are chronically lonely, and who perceive themselves to be a burden on others are more likely to experience a desire to die (Barzilay & others, 2015; Hames, Hagan, & Joiner, 2013; Van Orden & others, 2008).

Even among those with a desire to die, however, a key variable is the person's acquired capability to complete a suicide attempt. For most people, a fear of death and a strong desire to avoid feeling pain prevent us from suicide. Research suggests that one way individuals might overcome these natural motivations is to develop a tolerance for pain through previous experiences of injury (Joiner, Ribeiro, & Silva, 2012). Through past experiences, then, the interpersonal theory asserts that individuals are able to extinguish the fear response, allowing them to complete the horrific act of suicide.

The interpersonal theory continues to be tested. Research has supported the ideas that feeling burdensome and not belonging predict suicidal intentions in samples of adolescents (Barzilay & others, 2015) as well as middle-aged adults (Van Orden & others, 2016). However, support for the idea that people acquire the capacity to commit suicide is mixed (Bryan, Sinclair, & Heron, 2016).

Sociocultural Factors

Suicide rates vary worldwide; the lowest rates occur in countries with cultural and religious norms against ending one's own life. According to the World Health Organization (WHO), among the nations with the highest suicide rates are Guyana, South Korea, Sri Lanka, and Lithuania. Among the nations with the lowest rates are Saudi Arabia, Lebanon, Kuwait, and Haiti (WHO, 2015). Of the 171 nations ranked by the WHO, the United States ranks 50th.

Within cultures, economic conditions and ethnic contexts may contribute to suicide risk. Research has also linked suicide to the culture of honor. Recall that in honor cultures, individuals are more likely to interpret insults as fighting words and to defend their personal honor with aggression. One set of studies examined suicide and depression in the United States, comparing geographic regions that are considered to have a culture of honor (for example, the South in the United States) with other areas. Even accounting for a host of other factors, suicide rates were found to be higher in states with a culture of honor (Osterman & Brown, 2011).

There are gender differences in suicide as well. Men are four times more likely to complete suicide than women (CDC, 2015e). According to the CDC, men are more likely to use a firearm while women are more likely to use poison in a suicide attempt.

Suicide tends to run in families. Five suicides occurred in different generations of the Hemingway family, including author Ernest and his granddaughter Margaux.

(first) ©Bettmann/Getty Images (second) ©Vauthey Pierre/Getty Images

8. PSYCHOLOGICAL DISORDERS AND HEALTH AND WELLNESS

Putting a label on a person with a psychological disorder can make the disorder seem like something that happens only to other people. The truth is that psychological disorders are not just about *other* people; they are about people, period. Between 18 and 32 percent of Americans ages 18 and older suffer from a diagnosable psychological disorder in a given year—at least 43.6 million U.S. adults (Bagalman & Napili, 2015; Center for Behavioral Health Statistics and Quality, 2015).

Chances are that you or someone you know will experience a psychological disorder. Figure 9 shows how common many psychological disorders are in the United States.

Psychological disorders present a challenge to living a healthy, fulfilling life. For the many individuals who are diagnosed with one or more such disorders, a significant obstacle in the pursuit of that life is the fear of stigma, stereotypes, prejudice, and discrimination.

To appreciate the power of the labels that are attached to individuals with psychological disorders, consider a classic and controversial study by David Rosenhan (1973). He recruited eight adults (including a stay-at-home mother, a psychology graduate student, a pediatrician, and some psychiatrists), none with a psychological disorder, to see a psychiatrist at various hospitals. These "pseudo-patients" were instructed to act in a normal way except to complain about hearing voices that said things like "empty" and "thud." All eight expressed an interest in leaving the hospital and behaved cooperatively. Nevertheless, all eight were labeled with schizophrenia and kept in the hospital from 3 to 52 days. None of the mental health professionals they encountered ever questioned the diagnosis that had been given to these individuals, and all were discharged with the label "schizophrenia in remission." The label "schizophrenia" had stuck to the pseudo-patients

test yourself

1. What are the two requirements for suicide as described by the interpersonal theory of suicide?
2. Give at least two biological, two psychological, and two sociocultural factors in suicide.
3. From the perspective of the three criteria for abnormal behavior, how does *thinking* about suicide compare to *attempting* suicide?

526 CHAPTER 15 Psychological Disorders

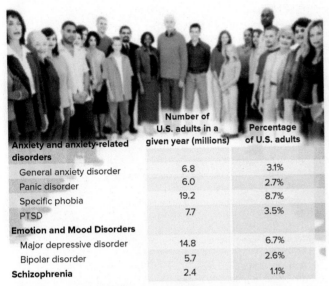

	Number of U.S. adults in a given year (millions)	Percentage of U.S. adults
Anxiety and anxiety-related disorders		
General anxiety disorder	6.8	3.1%
Panic disorder	6.0	2.7%
Specific phobia	19.2	8.7%
PTSD	7.7	3.5%
Emotion and Mood Disorders		
Major depressive disorder	14.8	6.7%
Bipolar disorder	5.7	2.6%
Schizophrenia	2.4	1.1%

FIGURE 9 **The 12-Month Prevalence of the Most Common Psychological Disorders.** Psychological disorders are more common than you might expect. (photo) © Ryan McVay/Getty Images

and caused the professionals around them to interpret their quite normal behavior as abnormal. Once a person has been labeled with a psychological disorder, that label colors how others perceive everything else he or she does.

If a person is diagnosed with a psychological disorder, can he or she still be a good friend? A good parent? A competent worker? A significant concern for individuals with psychological disorders is the negative attitudes that others might have about people struggling with mental illness (Phelan & Basow, 2007). Stigma can be a significant barrier for individuals coping with a psychological disorder and for their families and loved ones (Corrigan, 2007; Hinshaw, 2007). Fear of stigma can prevent individuals from seeking treatment and from talking about their problems with family and friends. To test your own attitudes about people with psychological disorders, complete the exercise in Figure 10.

Consequences of Stigma

The stigma attached to psychological disorders can provoke prejudice and discrimination toward individuals who are struggling with these problems, complicating an already difficult situation (Hipes & others, 2016; Pescosolido & others, 2013). Having a disorder and experiencing the stigma associated with it can also negatively affect the physical health of such individuals.

PREJUDICE AND DISCRIMINATION

Labels of psychological disorders can be damaging because they may lead to negative stereotypes, which, as reviewed in the chapter "Social Psychology", play a role in prejudice. For example, the label "schizophrenic" often has negative connotations such as "frightening" and "dangerous."

Vivid cases of extremely harmful behavior by individuals with psychological disorders can perpetuate the stereotype that people with such disorders are violent. You have probably heard of such cases. In 2007, Cho Seung-Hui, a college student, murdered 32 students and faculty at Virginia Tech University before killing himself. In December 2012, Adam Lanza killed his mother and then killed 20 children and 6 adults at Sandy Hook Elementary School in Newtown, Connecticut, before killing himself. James Eagan Holmes committed a mass shooting in an Aurora, Colorado, movie theater in July 2012, leaving 12 dead and 70 injured.

Aside from having committed these notorious acts of violence, these three individuals have something else in common: They all have been described as having a history of psychological disorders. For Cho, it was depression and anxiety; for Lanza, it was a type of autism spectrum disorder; Holmes has been reported to suffer from schizophrenia or a personality disorder. Such vivid cases may give the erroneous impression that individuals who suffer from psychological disorders are prone to violence. That impression is called an *illusory correlation*, because it is an illusion. Consider that these young men share other qualities as well. For instance, they were all young men. They are no more representative of people with psychological disorders than they are representative of young men.

Consider, too, that after the Sandy Hook killings, many commentators noted that to do such a thing, one *must* have a psychological disorder, by definition (Estes, 2012; Solomon, 2012). Whether or not one believes that statement is true, it leads to at least two unfortunate potential inferences. First, it suggests that individuals who commit acts that are widely condemned cannot be held responsible for those acts, because their behaviors are, by definition, symptoms of a disorder. Second, it suggests that such acts are something that people with psychological disorders do. This conclusion is not true. The fact is people with psychological disorders (especially those in treatment) are no more likely to commit violent acts than the general population. In fact, individuals with psychological disorders are more likely to be the *victims* of violence than the perpetrators (Corrigan & others, 2002; Hiroeh & others, 2001).

Individuals with psychological disorders are often aware of the stigma attached to these conditions (Brohan & others, 2010; Corrigan, 2015; Moses, 2010). They themselves may have previously held such negative attitudes. People with psychological disorders need help, but seeking that assistance may involve sacrificing their status as mentally healthy for a new, stigmatized identity (Thornicroft & others, 2009; Yen & others, 2009).

Among the most feared aspects of stigma is discrimination. As we saw in the chapter "Social Psychology", discrimination means acting prejudicially toward a person who is a member of a stigmatized group. In the workplace, discrimination against a person with a psychological disorder is illegal. The Americans with Disabilities Act (ADA) of 1990 forbids employers from refusing employment or a promotion to someone with a psychological disorder when the person's condition does not prevent performance of the job's essential functions (Cleveland, Barnes-Farrell, & Ratz, 1997). A person's appearance or behavior may be unusual or irritating, but as long as that individual is able to complete the duties required of a position, he or she cannot be denied employment or promotion.

PHYSICAL HEALTH

Compared to their psychologically healthy counterparts, individuals with psychological disorders are more likely to be physically ill (Gittelman, 2008), to be obese, to smoke, to drink excessively, and to lead sedentary lives (Beard, Weisberg, & Keller, 2010; Chou & others, 2013; H.-Y. Lin & others, 2013).

You might be thinking that these physical health issues are the least of their worries. If people with schizophrenia want to smoke, why not let them? This type of thinking reveals the subtle way that prejudice toward those with psychological disorders can affect their lives. It sells short the capacity of treatments to help those with psychological disorders, and, more importantly, it fails to acknowledge that individuals with serious mental disorders can lead healthy, meaningful lives.

Research has shown that health-promotion programs can work for individuals with a psychological disorder (Farholm & Sørensen, 2016; Robson & others, 2013; Rosenbaum & others, 2014). When we disregard the potential of physical health interventions for people with psychological disorders to make positive life changes, we reveal our own biases.

Rate the following items using a scale of 1–5, with 1 indicating that you completely *disagree* with the statement and 5 indicating that you completely *agree* with the statement.

1 = completely disagree   2 = slightly agree
3 = moderately agree   4 = strongly agree
5 = completely agree

_____ 1. I would rather not live next door to a person with a psychological disorder.

_____ 2. A person with a psychological disorder is unfit to raise children.

_____ 3. I would be afraid to be around a person with a psychological disorder.

_____ 4. I would not want to live in the same neighborhood as a group home for persons with psychological disorders.

_____ 5. A person with a psychological disorder cannot hold a job.

_____ 6. A person with a psychological disorder is dangerous or potentially violent.

Total _____

Add up your score and divide by 6. If your score is 3 or higher, you may want to rethink your attitudes about individuals with psychological disorders.

It may be revealing to ask yourself how you would respond to these statements if the words "person with a psychological disorder" were replaced with "woman," "African American," or "gay man or lesbian." Sometimes even individuals who would not think of themselves as being prejudiced against other groups find themselves biased against the mentally ill.

FIGURE 10   Test Your Attitudes About People with Psychological Disorders Take the survey to discover and evaluate your own attitudes.
(photos) © Ingram Publishing/AGE Fotostock

Overcoming Stigma

How can we effectively combat the stigma of psychological disorders? One obstacle to changing people's attitudes toward individuals with psychological disorders is that mental illness is often invisible. That is, sometimes a person can have a disorder without others ever knowing. Indeed, we may be unaware of *many* courageous lives around us that are being lived within the challenging context of psychological disorders, because worries about being stigmatized keep the affected individuals from "coming out" (Corrigan & others, 2015). Thus, stigma leads to a catch-22: Positive examples of individuals coping with psychological disorders are often missing from our experience because those who are doing well shun public disclosure of their disorders.

A critical step toward eliminating stigma is to resist thinking of people with disorders as limited individuals whose disorder colors everything they do. Instead, it is vital to recognize their strengths—both in confronting their disorder and in carrying on despite their problems—and their achievements. By creating a positive environment for people with disorders, we encourage more of them to become visible and empower them to be positive role models for others. We must recognize that those with psychological disorders have strengths to offer, creating a context for them to be open about their struggles (Corrigan & others, 2015).

After reading this chapter, you know that many admired individuals have dealt with psychological disorders. Their diagnoses do not detract from their accomplishments. To the contrary, their accomplishments are all the more remarkable in the context of the challenges they have faced.

test yourself

1. What did the classic study by Rosenhan reveal about the power of labels that are applied to individuals?
2. What social and physical effects can result from the stigma with which some people view psychological disorders?
3. What are some critical considerations in efforts to eliminate stigma toward individuals with psychological disorders?

SUMMARY

1. DEFINING AND EXPLAINING ABNORMAL BEHAVIOR

Abnormal behavior is deviant, maladaptive, or personally distressful. Theoretical perspectives on the causes of psychological disorders include biological, psychological, sociocultural, and biopsychosocial approaches.

Biological approaches to disorders view psychological disorders as diseases with origins in neurological, biochemical, and genetic factors. Psychological approaches include the behavioral, social cognitive, and trait perspectives. Sociocultural approaches place emphasis on the larger social and cultural context and factors such as marriage, socioeconomic status, ethnicity, gender, and culture. Biopsychosocial approaches view the interactions among biological, psychological, and social factors as significant forces in producing both normal and abnormal behavior. The vulnerability-stress hypothesis (or the diathesis-stress model) suggests that some factors may predispose a person to developing a psychological disorder in response to stressful experiences.

Classifying disorders facilitates communication, allowing clinicians to make predictions and decide on treatment. The *Diagnostic and Statistical Manual of Mental Disorders (DSM)* is the classification system clinicians use to diagnose psychological disorders. Some psychologists contend that *DSM-5* perpetuates the medical model of psychological disorders, that it labels everyday problems as psychological disorders, and that it fails to address strengths.

2. ANXIETY AND ANXIETY-RELATED DISORDERS

Anxiety disorders involve unrealistic and debilitating high levels of anxiety. Generalized anxiety disorder involves a high level of anxiety with no specific reason for the anxiety. Panic disorder involves attacks marked by the sudden onset of intense terror. Specific phobia is irrational, overwhelming fear of a particular object, such as snakes, or a situation, such as flying. Social anxiety disorder refers to the intense fear that one will do something embarrassing or humiliating in public.

Obsessive-compulsive disorder involves anxiety-provoking thoughts that will not go away (obsession) and/or urges to perform repetitive, ritualistic behaviors to prevent or produce some future situation (compulsion). Post-traumatic stress disorder (PTSD) is a disorder that develops through exposure to traumatic events. Symptoms include flashbacks, emotional avoidance, emotional numbing, and excessive arousal.

3. DISORDERS INVOLVING EMOTION AND MOOD

In depressive disorder, the individual experiences a serious depressive episode and depressed characteristics such as lethargy and hopelessness. Biological explanations of depressive disorders focus on heredity, neurophysiological abnormalities, and neurotransmitter deregulation. Psychological explanations include behavioral and cognitive perspectives. Sociocultural explanations emphasize socioeconomic and ethnic factors, as well as gender.

Bipolar disorder is characterized by extreme mood swings that include one or more episodes of mania (an overexcited, unrealistic, optimistic state). Individuals with bipolar I disorder have more extreme manic episodes, while those with bipolar II disorder have less extreme episodes.

4. DISSOCIATIVE DISORDERS

Dissociative amnesia involves memory loss caused by extensive psychological stress. In dissociative identity disorder, formerly called multiple personality disorder, two or more distinct personalities are present in the same individual; this disorder is rare.

5. SCHIZOPHRENIA

Schizophrenia is a severe psychological disorder characterized by highly disordered thought processes. Positive symptoms of schizophrenia are behaviors and experiences that are present in individuals with schizophrenia but absent in healthy people; they include hallucinations, delusions, thought disorder, and disorders of movement. Negative symptoms are behaviors and experiences that are part of healthy human life that are absent for those with this disorder; they include flat affect and an inability to plan or engage in goal-directed behavior.

Biological, psychological, and sociocultural factors may be involved in schizophrenia. Biological factors include genes and the neurotransmitter dopamine. Psychological and sociocultural factors are not viewed as stand-alone causes of schizophrenia, but they are related to the course of the disorder.

6. PERSONALITY DISORDERS

Personality disorders are chronic, maladaptive cognitive-behavioral patterns that are thoroughly integrated into an individual's personality. Antisocial personality disorder (ASPD) is characterized by guiltlessness, law-breaking, exploitation of others, irresponsibility, and deceit. Individuals with this disorder often lead a life of crime and violence. Psychopaths—remorseless predators who engage in violence to get what they want—are a subgroup of individuals with ASPD. Biological factors for ASPD include genetic, brain, and autonomic nervous system differences.

Borderline personality disorder is a pervasive pattern of instability in interpersonal relationships, self-image, and emotions. This disorder is related to self-harming behaviors such as cutting and suicide. The potential causes of BPD are complex and include biological and cognitive factors and childhood experiences.

7. SUICIDE

Severe depression and other psychological disorders can cause individuals to want to end their lives. Theorists have proposed biological, psychological, and sociocultural explanations of suicide. The interpersonal theory of suicide suggests that it requires the desire to die and the acquired capability to kill oneself.

8. PSYCHOLOGICAL DISORDERS AND HEALTH AND WELLNESS

Stigma can create a significant barrier for people coping with a psychological disorder, and for their loved ones. Fear of being labeled can prevent individuals from getting treatment and from talking about their problems with family and friends. In addition, the stigma attached to psychological disorders can lead to prejudice and discrimination toward individuals who are struggling with these problems.

We can help to combat stigma by acknowledging the strengths and the achievements of individuals coping with psychological disorders. By creating a positive environment for people with disorders, we encourage them to be open about their struggles and to thrive, with the result that they can become positive role models for others.

key *terms*

- abnormal behavior
- antisocial personality disorder (ASPD)
- anxiety disorders
- attention-deficit/hyperactivity disorder (ADHD)
- bipolar disorder
- borderline personality disorder (BPD)
- catatonia

- delusions
- depressive disorders
- dissociative amnesia
- dissociative disorders
- dissociative identity disorder (DID)
- *DSM-5*
- flat affect
- generalized anxiety disorder
- hallucinations

- major depressive disorder (MDD)
- medical model
- movement disorders
- obsessive-compulsive disorder (OCD)
- panic disorder
- personality disorders
- post-traumatic stress disorder (PTSD)

- psychosis
- referential thinking
- schizophrenia
- social anxiety disorder (SAD) or social phobia
- somatic symptom disorder
- specific phobia
- thought disorder
- vulnerability-stress hypothesis or diathesis-stress model

apply your *knowledge*

1. Spend 15 to 20 minutes observing an area with a large number of people, such as a mall, a cafeteria, or a stadium during a game. Identify and make a list of behaviors you would classify as abnormal. How does your list of behaviors compare with the definition of abnormal provided in the chapter? What would change in the list if you were in a different setting, such as a church, a bar, or a library? What does this exercise tell you about the meaning of abnormal?

2. If you have never encountered anyone with schizophrenia, meet Moe Armstrong by checking out this YouTube video: www.youtube.com/watch?v=p-_j1ZNKzsg

3. Although we might think of people who contend with psychological disorders as troubled and downtrodden, they (like all people) have the capacity to be astonishingly creative. Check out the website maintained by the National Art Exhibitions of the Mentally Ill (NAEMI) to experience some amazing creations of artists who suffer from mental illness. Go to www.naemi.org and click on "Enter" to view each artist's work. How does your exploration of this artwork influence your feelings about mental illness?

4. Go online and search for message boards where individuals with different psychological disorders share with one another. How do the discussion boards reflect what you have learned about these disorders?

GLOSSARY

360-degree feedback A method of performance appraisal whereby an employee's performance is rated by a variety of individuals, including himself or herself, a peer, a supervisor, a subordinate, and perhaps a customer or client.

abnormal behavior Behavior that is deviant, maladaptive, or personally distressful over a relatively long period of time.

absolute threshold The minimum amount of stimulus energy that a person can detect.

accommodation An individual's adjustment of his or her schemas to new information.

acquired immune deficiency syndrome (AIDS) A sexually transmitted infection, caused by the human immunodeficiency virus (HIV), which destroys the body's immune system.

acquisition The initial learning of the connection between the unconditioned stimulus and the conditioned stimulus when these two stimuli are paired.

action potential The brief wave of positive electrical charge that sweeps down the axon.

activation-synthesis theory of dreaming Theory that dreaming occurs when the cerebral cortex synthesizes neural signals generated from activity in the lower part of the brain and that dreams result from the brain's attempts to find logic in random brain activity that occurs during sleep.

addiction Either a physical or a psychological dependence, or both, on a drug.

adrenal glands Glands at the top of each kidney that are responsible for regulating mood, energy level, and the ability to cope with stress.

aerobic exercise Sustained activity—jogging, swimming, or cycling, for example—that stimulates heart and lung functioning.

affectionate love or companionate love Love that occurs when individuals desire to have another person near and have a deep, caring affection for the person.

affective commitment A kind of job commitment deriving from the employee's emotional attachment to the workplace.

afferent nerves or sensory nerves Nerves that carry information about the external environment *to* the brain and spinal cord via sensory receptors.

aggression Behavior that is intended to harm another person.

alcoholism A disorder that involves long-term, repeated, uncontrolled, compulsive, and excessive use of alcoholic beverages and that impairs the drinker's health and social relationships.

algorithms Strategies—including formulas, instructions, and the testing of all possible solutions—that guarantee a solution to a problem.

all-or-nothing principle The principle that once the electrical impulse reaches a certain level of intensity (its threshold), it fires and moves all the way down the axon without losing any intensity.

altruism Unselfish interest in helping another person.

amnesia The loss of memory.

amygdala An almond-shaped structure within the base of the temporal lobe that is involved in the discrimination of objects that are necessary for the organism's survival, such as appropriate food, mates, and social rivals. There is one amygdala in each hemisphere of the brain.

androgens The class of sex hormones that predominate in males, produced by the testes in males and by the adrenal glands in both males and females.

androgynous Having attributes that are typically associated with both genders.

anorexia nervosa An eating disorder that involves the relentless pursuit of thinness through starvation.

anterograde amnesia A memory disorder that affects the retention of new information and events.

antianxiety drugs Drugs that reduce anxiety by making the individual calmer and less excitable; commonly known as tranquilizers.

antidepressant drugs Drugs that regulate mood.

antipsychotic drugs Powerful drugs that diminish agitated behavior, reduce tension, decrease hallucinations, improve social behavior, and produce better sleep patterns in individuals with a severe psychological disorder, especially schizophrenia.

antisocial personality disorder (ASPD) Psychological disorder characterized by guiltlessness, law-breaking, exploitation of others, irresponsibility, and deceit.

anxiety disorders Disabling (uncontrollable and disruptive) psychological disorders that feature motor tension, hyperactivity, and apprehensive expectations and thoughts.

apparent movement The perception that a stationary object is moving.

applied behavior analysis or behavior modification The use of operant conditioning principles to change human behavior.

archetypes Jung's term for emotionally laden ideas and images in the collective unconscious that have rich and symbolic meaning for all people.

artificial intelligence (AI) A scientific field that focuses on creating machines capable of performing activities that require intelligence when they are done by people.

assimilation An individual's incorporation of new information into existing knowledge.

association cortex or association area The region of the cerebral cortex that is the site of the highest intellectual functions, such as thinking and problem solving.

associative learning Learning that occurs when an organism makes a connection, or an association, between two events.

Atkinson–Shiffrin theory Theory stating that memory storage involves three separate systems: sensory memory, short-term memory, and long-term memory.

attention The process of focusing awareness on a narrow aspect of the environment.

attention-deficit/hyperactivity disorder (ADHD) A common psychological disorder in which the individual exhibits one or more of the following: inattention, hyperactivity, and impulsivity.

attitudes An individual's opinions and beliefs about people, objects, and ideas—how the person feels about the world.

attribution theory The view that people are motivated to discover the underlying causes of behavior as part of their effort to make sense of the behavior.

auditory nerve The nerve structure that receives information about sound from the hair cells of the inner ear and carries these neural impulses to the brain's auditory areas.

authoritarian parenting A restrictive, punitive style in which the parent exhorts the child to follow the parent's directions.

authoritative parenting A parenting style that encourages the child to be independent but that still places limits and controls on behavior.

autobiographical memory A special form of episodic memory, consisting of a person's recollections of his or her life experiences.

automatic processes States of consciousness that require little attention and do not interfere with other ongoing activities.

autonomic nervous system The body system that takes messages to and from the body's internal organs, monitoring such processes as breathing, heart rate, and digestion.

availability heuristic A prediction about the probability of an event based on the ease of recalling or imagining similar events.

aversive conditioning A form of treatment that consists of repeated pairings of a stimulus with a very unpleasant stimulus.

avoidance learning An organism's learning that it can altogether avoid a negative stimulus by making a particular response.

axon The part of the neuron that carries information away from the cell body toward other cells.

barbiturates Depressant drugs, such as Nembutal and Seconal, that decrease central nervous system activity.

basal ganglia Large neuron clusters located above the thalamus and under the cerebral cortex that work with the cerebellum and the cerebral cortex to control and coordinate voluntary movements.

base rate neglect The tendency to ignore statistical information in favor of very specific but vivid information.

behavior Everything we do that can be directly observed.

behavior therapies Treatments, based on the behavioral and social cognitive theories of learning, that use principles of learning to reduce or eliminate maladaptive behavior.

behavioral approach An approach to psychology focusing on the scientific study of observable behavioral responses and their environmental determinants.

behavioral genetics The study of the inherited underpinnings of behavioral characteristics.

behavioral medicine An interdisciplinary field that focuses on developing and integrating behavioral and biomedical knowledge to promote health and reduce illness; overlaps with health psychology.

behaviorism A theory of learning that focuses solely on observable behaviors, discounting the importance of mental activity such as thinking, wishing, and hoping.

big five factors of personality The five broad traits that are thought to describe the main dimensions of personality: neuroticism (emotional instability), extraversion, openness to experience, agreeableness, and conscientiousness.

binding In the sense of vision, the bringing together and integration of what is processed by different neural pathways or cells.

binge eating disorder (BED) An eating disorder characterized by recurrent episodes of eating more food in a short period of time than most people would eat and during which the person feels a lack of control over eating.

binocular cues Depth cues that depend on the combination of the images in the left and right eye and on the way the two eyes work together.

biological approach An approach to psychology focusing on the body, especially the brain and nervous system.

biological rhythms Periodic physiological fluctuations in the body, such as the rise and fall of hormones and accelerated and decelerated cycles of brain activity, that can influence behavior.

biological therapies or biomedical therapies Treatments that reduce or eliminate the symptoms of psychological disorders by altering aspects of bodily functioning.

bipolar disorder Psychological disorder characterized by extreme mood swings that include one or more episodes of mania—an overexcited, unrealistically optimistic state.

bisexual Referring to a sexual orientation in which the individual is sexually attracted to people of both sexes.

borderline personality disorder (BPD) Psychological disorder characterized by a pervasive pattern of instability in interpersonal relationships, self-image, and emotions and by marked impulsivity beginning by early adulthood and present in a variety of contexts.

bottom-up processing The operation in sensation and perception in which sensory receptors register information about the external environment and send it up to the brain for interpretation.

brain stem The stemlike brain area that includes much of the hindbrain (excluding the cerebellum) and the midbrain; it connects with the spinal cord at its lower end and then extends upward to encase the reticular formation in the midbrain.

broaden-and-build model Fredrickson's model of positive emotion, stating that the function of positive emotions lies in their effects on an individual's attention and ability to build resources.

bulimia nervosa An eating disorder in which the individual (typically female) consistently follows a binge-and-purge eating pattern.

burnout A distressed psychological state in which a person experiences emotional exhaustion and little motivation for work.

bystander effect The tendency of an individual who observes an emergency to help less when other people are present than when the observer is alone.

Cannon–Bard theory The proposition that emotion and physiological reactions occur simultaneously.

case study or case history An in-depth look at a single individual.

catatonia State of immobility and unresponsiveness lasting for long periods of time.

cell body The part of the neuron that contains the nucleus, which directs the manufacture of substances that the neuron needs for growth and maintenance.

central nervous system (CNS) The brain and spinal cord.

cerebral cortex Part of the forebrain, the outer layer of the brain, responsible for the most complex mental functions, such as thinking and planning.

chromosomes In the human cell, threadlike structures that come in 23 pairs, one member of each pair originating from each parent, and that contain the remarkable substance DNA.

circadian rhythms Daily behavioral or physiological cycles that involve the sleep/wake cycle, body temperature, blood pressure, and blood sugar level.

classical conditioning Learning process in which a neutral stimulus becomes associated with an innately meaningful stimulus and acquires the capacity to elicit a similar response.

client-centered therapy A form of humanistic therapy, developed by Rogers, in which the therapist provides a warm, supportive atmosphere to improve the client's self-concept and to encourage the client to gain insight into problems; also called Rogerian therapy or nondirective therapy.

clinical psychology The area of psychology that integrates science and theory to prevent and treat psychological disorders.

cognition The way in which information is processed and manipulated in remembering, thinking, and knowing.

cognitive affective processing systems (CAPS) Mischel's theoretical model for describing how individuals' thoughts and emotions about themselves and the world affect their behavior and become linked in ways that matter to that behavior.

cognitive appraisal Interpreting the events and experiences in one's life as harmful and threatening, or as challenging, and determining whether one has the resources to cope effectively.

cognitive approach An approach to psychology focusing on the mental processes involved in knowing: how we direct our attention, perceive, remember, think, and solve problems.

cognitive dissonance An individual's psychological discomfort (dissonance) caused by two inconsistent thoughts.

cognitive reappraisal Regulating one's feelings about an experience by reinterpreting that experience or thinking about it in a different way or from a different angle.

cognitive theory of dreaming Theory proposing that dreaming can be understood by applying the same cognitive concepts used to study the waking mind.

cognitive therapies Treatments emphasizing that cognitions (thoughts) are the main source of psychological problems and that attempt to change the individual's feelings and behaviors by changing cognitions.

cognitive-behavior therapy A therapy that combines cognitive therapy and behavior therapy with the goal of developing self-efficacy.

collective unconscious Jung's term for the impersonal, deepest layer of the unconscious mind, shared by all human beings because of their common ancestral past.

concepts Mental categories that are used to group objects, events, and characteristics.

concrete operational stage Piaget's third stage of cognitive development, lasting from about 7 to 11 years of age, during which the individual uses operations and replaces intuitive reasoning with logical reasoning in concrete situations.

conditioned response (CR) The learned response to the conditioned stimulus that occurs after conditioned stimulus–unconditioned stimulus pairing.

conditioned stimulus (CS) A previously neutral stimulus that eventually elicits a conditioned response after being paired with the unconditioned stimulus.

conditions of worth The standards that the individual must live up to in order to receive positive regard from others.

cones The receptor cells in the retina that allow for color perception.

confederate A person who is given a role to play in an experiment so that the social context can be manipulated.

confirmation bias The tendency to search for and use information that supports one's ideas rather than refutes them.

conformity A change in a person's behavior to coincide more closely with a group standard.

connectionism or parallel distributed processing (PDP) The theory that memory is stored throughout the brain in connections among neurons, several of which may work together to process a single memory.

consciousness An individual's awareness of external events and internal sensations under a condition of arousal, including awareness of the self and thoughts about one's experiences.

continuance commitment A kind of job commitment deriving from the employee's perception that leaving the organization would be too costly, both economically and socially.

control group The participants in an experiment who are as much like the experimental group as possible and who are treated in every way like the experimental group except for a manipulated factor, the independent variable.

controlled processes The most alert states of human consciousness, during which individuals actively focus their efforts toward a goal.

convergence A binocular cue to depth and distance in which the muscle movements in an individual's two eyes provide information about how deep and/or far away something is.

convergent thinking Thinking that produces the single best solution to a problem.

coping Managing taxing circumstances, expending effort to solve life's problems, and seeking to master or reduce stress.

corpus callosum The large bundle of axons that connects the brain's two hemispheres, responsible for relaying information between the two sides.

correlational research Research that examines the relationship between variables with the purpose of determining whether and how two variables change together.

counterconditioning A classical conditioning procedure for changing the relationship between a conditioned stimulus and its conditioned response.

couples therapy Group therapy with married or unmarried couples whose major problem lies within their relationship.

creativity The ability to think about something in novel and unusual ways and to devise unconventional solutions to problems.

critical thinking The process of reflecting deeply and actively, asking questions, and evaluating the evidence.

cross-cultural competence A therapist's assessment of his or her ability to manage cultural issues in therapy and the client's perception of those abilities.

cross-sectional design A type of correlational study in which variables are measured at a single point in time.

culture-fair tests Intelligence tests that are intended to be culturally unbiased.

decay theory Theory stating that when an individual learns something new, a neurochemical memory trace forms, but over time this trace disintegrates; suggests that the passage of time always increases forgetting.

decision making The mental activity of evaluating alternatives and choosing among them.

deductive reasoning Reasoning from a general case that is known to be true to a specific instance.

deep brain stimulation A procedure for treatment-resistant depression that involves the implantation of electrodes in the brain that emit signals to alter the brain's electrical circuitry.

defense mechanisms The Freudian term for tactics the ego uses to reduce anxiety by unconsciously distorting reality.

deindividuation The reduction in personal identity and erosion of the sense of personal responsibility when one is part of a group.

delusions False, unusual, and sometimes magical beliefs that are not part of an individual's culture.

demand characteristic Any aspect of a study that communicates to the participants how the experimenter wants them to behave.

dendrites Treelike fibers projecting from a neuron, which receive information and orient it toward the neuron's cell body.

deoxyribonucleic acid (DNA) A complex molecule in the cell's chromosomes that carries genetic information.

dependent variable The outcome; the variable that may change in an experiment in response to changes in the independent variable.

depressants Psychoactive drugs that slow down mental and physical activity.

depressive disorders Psychological disorders in which the individual suffers from depression—an unrelenting lack of pleasure in life.

depth perception The ability to perceive objects three-dimensionally.

descriptive research Research that determines the basic dimensions of a phenomenon—defining what it is, how often it occurs, and so on.

descriptive statistics Mathematical procedures that are used to describe and summarize sets of data in a meaningful way.

development The pattern of continuity and change in human capabilities that occurs throughout life, involving both growth and decline.

difference threshold The degree of difference that must exist between two stimuli before the difference is detected.

discrimination An unjustified negative or harmful action toward a member of a group simply because the person belongs to that group.

discrimination (in classical conditioning) The process of learning to respond to certain stimuli and not others.

discrimination (in operant conditioning) Responding appropriately to stimuli that signal that a behavior will or will not be reinforced.

disorders of sexual development (DSD) Congenital conditions in which the development of chromosomal, gonadal, or anatomical sex is atypical; formerly called intersex conditions or hermaphroditism.

display rules Sociocultural standards that determine when, where, and how emotions should be expressed.

dissociative amnesia Dissociative disorder characterized by extreme memory loss that is caused by extensive psychological stress.

dissociative disorders Psychological disorders that involve a sudden loss of memory or change in identity due to the dissociation (separation) of the individual's conscious awareness from previous memories and thoughts.

dissociative identity disorder (DID) Dissociative disorder in which the individual has two or more distinct personalities or selves, each with its own memories, behaviors, and relationships; formerly called multiple personality disorder.

divergent thinking Thinking that produces many solutions to the same problem.

divided attention Concentrating on more than one activity at the same time.

divided consciousness view of hypnosis Hilgard's view that hypnosis involves a splitting of consciousness into two separate components: one that follows the hypnotist's commands and the other that acts as a "hidden observer."

dominant-recessive genes principle The principle that, if one gene of a pair is dominant and one is recessive, the dominant gene overrides the recessive gene. A recessive gene exerts its influence only if both genes of a pair are recessive.

double-blind experiment An experimental design in which neither the experimenter nor the participants are aware of which participants are in the experimental group and which are in the control group until the results are calculated.

downsizing A dramatic cutting of the workforce that has become a popular business strategy to enhance profitability.

dream analysis A psychoanalytic technique for interpreting a person's dreams.

drive An aroused state that occurs because of a physiological need.

DSM-5 The fifth edition of the *Diagnostic and Statistical Manual of Mental Disorders;* the major classification of psychological disorders in the United States.

efferent nerves or motor nerves Nerves that carry information *out of* the brain and spinal cord to other areas of the body.

ego The Freudian structure of personality that deals with the demands of reality.

egoism Giving to another person to ensure reciprocity; to gain self-esteem; to present oneself as powerful, competent, or caring; or to avoid censure from oneself and others for failing to live up to society's expectations.

elaboration The formation of a number of different connections around a stimulus at any given level of memory encoding.

elaboration likelihood model Theory identifying two ways to persuade: a central route and a peripheral route.

electroconvulsive therapy (ECT) A treatment, sometimes used for depression, that sets off a seizure in the brain; also called shock therapy.

emerging adulthood The transitional period from adolescence to adulthood, spanning approximately 18 to 25 years of age.

emotion Feeling, or affect, that can involve physiological arousal (such as a fast heartbeat), conscious experience (thinking about being in love with someone), and behavioral expression (a smile or grimace).

emotion-focused coping The coping strategy that involves responding to the stress that one is feeling—trying to manage one's emotional reaction—rather than focusing on the problem itself.

empathy A feeling of oneness with the emotional state of another person.

empirical method Gaining knowledge through the observation of events, the collection of data, and logical reasoning.

empirically keyed test A type of self-report test that presents many questionnaire items to two groups that are known to be different in some central way.

empirically supported treatment An approach to treating psychological disorders that advocates making treatment decisions based on the body of research that has shown which type of therapy works best.

encoding The first step in memory; the process by which information gets into memory storage.

endocrine system The body system consisting of a set of glands that regulate the activities of certain organs by releasing their chemical products into the bloodstream.

episodic memory The retention of information about the where, when, and what of life's

happenings—that is, how individuals remember life's episodes.

ergonomics or human factors A field that combines engineering and psychology and that focuses on understanding and enhancing the safety and efficiency of the human–machine interaction.

estrogens The class of sex hormones that predominate in females, produced mainly by the ovaries.

ethnocentrism The tendency to favor one's own ethnic group over other groups.

evidence-based practice Integration of the best available research with clinical expertise in the context of client characteristics, culture, and preferences.

evolutionary approach An approach to psychology focusing on evolutionary ideas such as adaptation, reproduction, and natural selection as the basis for explaining specific human behaviors.

executive function Higher-order, complex cognitive processes, including thinking, planning, and problem solving.

exercise Structured activities whose goal is to improve health.

experiment A carefully regulated procedure in which the researcher manipulates one or more variables that is believed to influence some other variable.

experimental group The participants in an experiment who receive the drug or other treatment under study; those who are exposed to the change that the independent variable represents.

experimenter bias The influence of the experimenter's expectations on the outcome of the research.

explicit memory or declarative memory The conscious recollection of information, such as specific facts or events and, at least in humans, information that can be verbally communicated.

extinction (in classical conditioning) The weakening of the conditioned response when the unconditioned stimulus is absent.

extinction (in operant conditioning) Decreases in the frequency of a behavior when the behavior is no longer reinforced.

extrinsic motivation Motivation that involves external incentives such as rewards and punishments.

face validity The extent to which a test item appears to fit the particular trait it is measuring.

facial feedback hypothesis The idea that facial expressions can influence emotions as well as reflect them.

false consensus effect A person's overestimation of the degree to which everybody else thinks or acts the way he or she does.

family therapy Group therapy with family members.

feature detectors Neurons in the brain's visual system that respond to particular features of a stimulus.

fetish An object or activity that arouses sexual interest and desire.

figure-ground relationship The principle by which we organize the perceptual field into stimuli that stand out (figure) and those that are left over (ground).

fixation Using a prior strategy and failing to look at a problem from a fresh new perspective.

flashbulb memory The memory of emotionally significant events that people often recall with more accuracy and vivid imagery than everyday events.

flat affect The display of little or no emotion—a common negative symptom of schizophrenia.

flow The optimal experience of a match between one's skills and the challenge of a task.

forebrain The brain's largest division and its most forward part.

formal operational stage Piaget's fourth stage of cognitive development, which begins at 11 to 15 years of age and continues through the adult years; it features thinking about things that are not concrete, making predictions, and using logic to come up with hypotheses about the future.

frequency theory Theory on how the inner ear registers the frequency of sound, stating that the perception of a sound's frequency depends on how often the auditory nerve fires.

frontal lobes The portions of the cerebral cortex behind the forehead that are involved in personality, intelligence, and the control of voluntary muscles.

functional fixedness Failing to solve a problem as a result of fixation on a thing's usual functions.

functionalism James's approach to mental processes, emphasizing the functions and purposes of the mind and behavior in the individual's adaptation to the environment.

fundamental attribution error Observers' overestimation of the importance of internal traits and underestimation of the importance of external situations when they seek explanations of an actor's behavior.

gender The social and psychological aspects of being female or male; gender goes beyond biological sex to include an individual's personal understanding of the meaning of being male or female.

gender identity An individual's multifaceted sense of belonging to the male or female sex.

gender roles Roles that reflect the individual's expectation for how a female person and how a male person should think, act, and feel.

gender similarities hypothesis Hyde's proposition that men and women (and boys and girls) are much more similar than they are different.

gender stereotypes Overly general beliefs and expectations about what women and men are like.

general adaptation syndrome (GAS) Selye's term for the common effects of stressful demands on the body, consisting of three stages: alarm, resistance, and exhaustion.

generalization (in classical conditioning) The tendency of a new stimulus that is similar to the original conditioned stimulus to elicit a response that is similar to the conditioned response.

generalization (in operant conditioning) Performing a reinforced behavior in a different situation.

generalized anxiety disorder An anxiety disorder marked by persistent anxiety for at least six months, and in which the individual is unable to specify the reasons for the anxiety.

genes The units of hereditary information, consisting of short segments of chromosomes composed of DNA.

genotype An individual's genetic heritage; one's actual genetic material.

gestalt psychology A school of thought interested in how people naturally organize their perceptions according to certain patterns.

gifted Possessing high intelligence (an IQ of 130 or higher) and/or superior talent in a particular area.

glands Organs or tissues in the body that create chemicals that control many bodily functions.

glial cells or glia The second of two types of cells in the nervous system; glial cells provide support, nutritional benefits, and other functions and keep neurons running smoothly.

gonads Glands that produce sex hormones and generate ova (eggs) in females and sperm in males; collectively called gametes, the ova and sperm are the cells that eventually will be used in reproduction.

group polarization effect The solidification and further strengthening of an individual's position as a consequence of a group discussion or interaction.

group therapy A sociocultural approach to the treatment of psychological disorders that brings together individuals who share a particular psychological disorder in sessions that are typically led by a mental health professional.

groupthink The impaired group decision making that occurs when making the right decision is less important than maintaining group harmony.

habituation Decreased responsiveness to a stimulus after repeated presentations.

hallucinations Sensory experiences that occur in the absence of real stimuli.

hallucinogens Psychoactive drugs that modify a person's perceptual experiences and produce visual images that are not real.

halo effect A bias, common in performance appraisals, that occurs when a rater gives an employee the same rating on all of the items being evaluated, even though the individual varies across the dimensions being assessed.

hardiness A personality trait characterized by a sense of commitment rather than alienation and of control rather than powerlessness; a perception of problems as challenges rather than threats.

Hawthorne effect The tendency of individuals to perform better simply because of being singled out and made to feel important.

health behaviors Practices that have an impact on physical well-being, such as adopting a healthy approach to stress, exercising, eating right, brushing one's teeth, performing breast and testicular exams, not smoking, drinking in moderation (or not at all), and practicing safe sex.

health psychology A subfield of psychology that emphasizes psychology's role in establishing and maintaining health and preventing and treating illness.

heritability The proportion of observable differences in a group that can be explained by differences in the genes of the group's members.

heterosexual Referring to a sexual orientation in which the individual is generally sexually attracted to members of the opposite sex.

heuristics Shortcut strategies or guidelines that suggest a solution to a problem but do not guarantee an answer.

hierarchy of needs Maslow's theory that human needs must be satisfied in the following sequence: physiological needs, safety, love and belongingness, esteem, and self-actualization.

hindbrain Located at the skull's rear, the lowest portion of the brain, consisting of the medulla, cerebellum, and pons.

hindsight bias The tendency to report falsely, after the fact, that one has accurately predicted an outcome.

hippocampus The structure in the limbic system that has a special role in the storage of memories.

homeostasis The body's tendency to maintain an equilibrium, or a steady state or balance.

homosexual Referring to a sexual orientation in which the individual is generally sexually attracted to members of the same sex.

hormones Chemical messengers that are produced by the endocrine glands and carried by the bloodstream to all parts of the body.

human relations approach A management approach emphasizing the psychological characteristics of workers and managers, stressing the importance of factors such as morale, attitudes, values, and humane treatment of workers.

human sexual response pattern Masters and Johnson's model of human sexual response, consisting of four phases—excitement, plateau, orgasm, and resolution.

humanistic approach An approach to psychology focusing on a person's positive qualities, the capacity for positive growth, and the freedom to choose one's destiny.

humanistic perspectives Theoretical views stressing a person's capacity for personal growth and positive human qualities.

humanistic therapies Treatments, unique in their emphasis on clients' self-healing capacities, that encourage clients to understand themselves and to grow personally.

hypnosis An altered state of consciousness or a psychological state of altered attention and expectation in which the individual is unusually receptive to suggestions.

hypothalamic-pituitary-adrenal axis (HPA axis) The complex set of interactions among the hypothalamus, the pituitary gland, and the adrenal glands that regulates various body processes and controls reactions to stressful events.

hypothalamus A small forebrain structure, located just below the thalamus, that monitors three pleasurable activities—eating, drinking, and sex—as well as emotion, stress, and reward.

hypothesis An educated guess that derives logically from a theory; a prediction that can be tested.

id The Freudian structure of personality consisting of unconscious drives; the individual's reservoir of sexual energy.

implementation intentions Specific strategies for dealing with the challenges of making a life change.

implicit memory or nondeclarative memory Memory in which behavior is affected by prior experience without a conscious recollection of that experience.

independent variable A manipulated experimental factor; the variable that the experimenter changes to see what its effects are.

individual psychology Adler's view that people are motivated by purposes and goals and that perfection, not pleasure, is thus the key motivator in human life.

inductive reasoning Reasoning from specific observations to make generalizations.

industrial and organizational (I-O) psychology The field of psychology that applies the science of human behavior to work and the workplace.

infant attachment The close emotional bond between an infant and its caregiver.

inferential statistics Mathematical methods that are used to indicate whether the data sufficiently support a research hypothesis.

informational social influence The influence other people have on us because we want to be right.

inner ear The part of the ear that includes the oval window, cochlea, and basilar membrane and whose function is to convert sound waves into neural impulses and send them to the brain.

insecure attachment Infants do not use the caregiver as a secure base from which to explore; instead, they experience their relationship with the caregiver as unstable and unreliable. The two types of insecure attachment are avoidant and anxious/ambivalent (also called preoccupied).

insight learning A form of problem solving in which the organism develops a sudden insight into or understanding of a problem's solution.

instinct An innate (unlearned) biological pattern of behavior that is assumed to be universal throughout a species.

instinctive drift The tendency of animals to revert to instinctive behavior that interferes with learning.

integrative therapy Use of a combination of techniques from different therapies based on the therapist's judgment of which particular methods will provide the greatest benefit for the client.

integrity test A type of job-screening examination that is designed to assess whether a candidate will be honest on the job.

intellectual disability or intellectual developmental disorder A condition of limited mental ability that affects an individual's functioning in everyday life.

intelligence An all-purpose ability to do well on cognitive tasks, to solve problems, and to learn from experience.

intelligence quotient (IQ) An individual's mental age divided by chronological age multiplied by 100.

interference theory The theory that people forget not because memories are lost from storage but because other information gets in the way of what they want to remember.

internal validity The degree to which changes in the dependent variable are due to the manipulation of the independent variable.

intrinsic motivation Motivation based on internal factors such as organismic needs (competence, relatedness, and autonomy), as well as curiosity, challenge, and fun.

investment model A model of long-term relationships that examines the ways that commitment, investment, and the availability of attractive alternative partners predict satisfaction and stability in relationships.

James–Lange theory The theory that emotion results from physiological states triggered by stimuli in the environment.

job analysis The process of generating a description of what a job involves, including the knowledge and skills that are necessary to carry out the job's functions.

job crafting The physical and cognitive changes individuals can make within the constraints of a task to make the work "their own."

job satisfaction The extent to which a person is content in his or her job.

job stress The experience of stress on the job and in the workplace setting.

kinesthetic senses Senses that provide information about movement, posture, and orientation.

KSAOs or KSAs Common elements in a person-oriented job analysis; an acronym for *k*nowledge, *s*kills, *a*bilities, and *o*ther characteristics.

language A form of communication—whether spoken, written, or signed—that is based on a system of symbols.

latent content According to Freud, a dream's hidden content; its unconscious and true meaning.

latent learning or implicit learning Unreinforced learning that is not immediately reflected in behavior.

law of effect Thorndike's law stating that behaviors followed by positive outcomes are strengthened and that behaviors followed by negative outcomes are weakened.

learned helplessness An organism's learning through experience with negative stimuli that it has no control over negative outcomes.

learning A systematic, relatively permanent change in behavior that occurs through experience.

leisure The pleasant times before or after work when individuals are free to pursue activities and interests of their own choosing, such as hobbies, sports, and reading.

levels of processing A continuum of memory processing from shallow to intermediate to deep, with deeper processing producing better memory.

limbic system A loosely connected network of structures under the cerebral cortex, important in both memory and emotion. Its two principal structures are the amygdala and the hippocampus.

lithium The lightest of the solid elements in the periodic table of elements, widely used to treat bipolar disorder.

long-term memory A relatively permanent type of memory that stores huge amounts of information for a long time.

longitudinal design A special kind of systematic observation, used by correlational researchers, that involves obtaining measures of the variables of interest in multiple waves over time.

loss aversion The tendency to strongly prefer to avoid losses compared to acquiring gains.

major depressive disorder (MDD) Psychological disorder involving a significant depressive episode and depressed characteristics, such as lethargy and hopelessness, for at least two weeks.

manifest content According to Freud, the surface content of a dream, containing dream symbols that disguise the dream's true meaning.

mean A measure of central tendency that is the average for a sample.

median A measure of central tendency that is the middle score in a sample.

medical model The view that psychological disorders are medical diseases with a biological origin.

meditation The attainment of a peaceful state of mind in which thoughts are not occupied by worry; the meditator is mindfully present to his or her thoughts and feelings but is not consumed by them.

memory The retention of information or experience over time as the result of three key processes: encoding, storage, and retrieval.

mental age (MA) An individual's level of mental development relative to that of others.

mental processes The thoughts, feelings, and motives that each of us experiences privately but that cannot be observed directly.

mentoring A relationship between an experienced employee—a mentor—and a novice, in which the more experienced employee serves as an advisor, a sounding board, and a source of support for the newer employee.

mere exposure effect The phenomenon that the more individuals encounter someone or something, the more probable it is that they will start liking the person or thing even if they do not realize they have seen it before.

meta-analysis A statistical procedure that summarizes a large body of evidence from the research literature on a particular topic, allowing the researcher to assess the strength of the relationship between the variables.

midbrain Located between the hindbrain and forebrain, an area in which many nerve-fiber systems ascend and descend to connect the higher and lower portions of the brain; in particular, the midbrain relays information between the brain and the eyes and ears.

middle ear The part of the ear that channels sound through the eardrum, hammer, anvil, and stirrup to the inner ear.

mindfulness The state of being alert and mentally present for one's everyday activities.

Minnesota Multiphasic Personality Inventory (MMPI) The most widely used and researched empirically keyed self-report personality test.

mirror neurons Nerve cells in the brain that are activated (in human and nonhuman primates) both when an action is performed and when the organism observes the action being performed by another.

mode A measure of central tendency that is the most common score in a sample.

monocular cues Powerful depth cues available from the image in one eye, either the right or the left.

morphology A language's rules for word formation.

motivated forgetting Forgetting that occurs when something is so painful or anxiety-laden that remembering it is intolerable.

motivation The force that moves people to behave, think, and feel the way they do.

motor cortex A region in the cerebral cortex that processes information about voluntary movement, located just behind the frontal lobes.

movement disorders The unusual mannerisms, body movements, and facial expressions that are characteristic positive symptoms of schizophrenia.

myelin sheath A layer of fat cells that encases and insulates most axons.

natural selection Darwin's principle of an evolutionary process in which organisms that are better adapted to their environment will survive and produce more offspring.

naturalistic observation The observation of behavior in a real-world setting.

nature An individual's biological inheritance, especially his or her genes.

need A deprivation that energizes the drive to eliminate or reduce the deprivation.

negative affect Negative emotions such as anger, guilt, and sadness.

negative punishment The removal of a stimulus following a given behavior in order to decrease the frequency of that behavior.

negative reinforcement The removal of a stimulus following a given behavior in order to increase the frequency of that behavior.

neglectful parenting A parenting style characterized by a lack of parental involvement in the child's life.

neocortex The outermost part of the cerebral cortex, making up 80 percent of the cortex in the human brain.

nervous system The body's electrochemical communication circuitry.

neural networks Networks of nerve cells that integrate sensory input and motor output.

neurons One of two types of cells in the nervous system; neurons are the type of nerve cell that handles the information-processing function.

neuroscience The scientific study of the structure, function, development, genetics, and biochemistry of the nervous system, emphasizing that the brain and nervous system are central to understanding behavior, thought, and emotion.

neurotransmitters Chemical substances that are stored in very tiny sacs within the terminal buttons and involved in transmitting information across a synaptic gap to the next neuron.

noise Irrelevant and competing stimuli—not only sounds but also any distracting stimuli for the senses.

normal distribution A symmetrical, bell-shaped curve, with a majority of the scores falling in the middle of the possible range and few scores appearing toward the extremes of the range.

normative commitment A kind of job commitment deriving from the employee's sense of obligation to the organization for the investment it has made in the individual's personal and professional development.

normative social influence The influence others have on us because we want them to like us.

nurture An individual's environmental and social experiences.

obedience Behavior that complies with the explicit demands of the individual in authority.

object permanence Piaget's term for the crucial accomplishment of understanding that objects and events continue to exist even when they cannot directly be seen, heard, or touched.

observational learning Learning that occurs through observing and imitating another's behavior.

obsessive-compulsive disorder (OCD) Psychological disorder in which the individual has anxiety-provoking thoughts that will not go away and/or urges to perform repetitive, ritualistic behaviors to prevent or produce some future situation.

occipital lobes Structures located at the back of the head that respond to visual stimuli.

Oedipus complex According to Freud, a boy's intense desire to replace his father and enjoy the affections of his mother.

olfactory epithelium The lining of the roof of the nasal cavity, containing a sheet of receptor cells for smell.

open-mindedness The state of being receptive to other ways of looking at things.

operant conditioning or instrumental conditioning A form of associative learning in which the consequences of a behavior change the probability of the behavior's occurrence.

operational definition A definition that provides an objective description of how a variable is going to be measured and observed in a particular study.

operations Piaget's term for mental representations of changes in objects that can be reversed.

opiates Opium and its derivatives; narcotic drugs that depress the central nervous system's activity and eliminate pain.

opponent-process theory Theory stating that cells in the visual system respond to complementary pairs of red-green and blue-yellow colors; a given cell might be excited by red and inhibited by green, whereas another cell might be excited by yellow and inhibited by blue.

optic nerve The structure at the back of the eye, made up of axons of the ganglion cells, that carries visual information to the brain for further processing.

organizational citizenship behavior (OCB) Discretionary actions on the part of an employee that promote organizational effectiveness but are not included in the person's formal responsibilities.

organizational culture An organization's shared values, beliefs, norms, and customs.

organizational identity Employees' feelings of oneness with the organization and its goals.

orientation A program by which an organization introduces newly hired employees to the organization's goals, familiarizes them with its rules and regulations, and lets them know how to get things done.

outer ear The outermost part of the ear, consisting of the pinna and the external auditory canal.

ovaries Sex-related endocrine glands that produce hormones involved in female sexual development and reproduction.

overlearning Learning to perform a task so well that it becomes automatic.

overt aggression Physically or verbally harming another person directly.

pain The sensation that warns an individual of damage to the body.

pancreas A dual-purpose gland under the stomach that performs both digestive and endocrine functions.

panic disorder An anxiety disorder in which the individual experiences recurrent, sudden onsets of intense terror, often without warning and with no specific cause.

papillae Rounded bumps above the tongue's surface that contain the taste buds, the receptors for taste.

parallel processing The simultaneous distribution of information across different neural pathways.

paraphilic disorders Sexual disorders that feature recurrent sexually arousing fantasies, urges, or behaviors involving nonhuman objects; the suffering or humiliation of oneself or one's partner; or children or other nonconsenting individuals.

parasympathetic nervous system The part of the autonomic nervous system that calms the body.

parietal lobes Structures at the top and toward the rear of the head that are involved in registering spatial location, attention, and motor control.

pedophilic disorder A paraphilic disorder in which an adult or an older adolescent sexually fantasizes about or engages in sexual behavior with individuals who have not reached puberty.

perception The process of organizing and interpreting sensory information so that it makes sense.

perceptual constancy The recognition that objects are constant and unchanging even though sensory input about them is changing.

perceptual set A predisposition or readiness to perceive something in a particular way.

performance appraisal The evaluation of a person's success at meeting his or her organization's goals.

peripheral nervous system (PNS) The network of nerves that connects the brain and spinal cord to other parts of the body.

permissive parenting A parenting style characterized by the placement of few limits on the child's behavior.

personality A pattern of enduring, distinctive thoughts, emotions, and behaviors that characterize the way an individual adapts to the world.

personality disorders Chronic, maladaptive cognitive-behavioral patterns that are thoroughly integrated into an individual's personality.

personological and life story perspectives Theoretical views stressing that the way to understand the person is to focus on the person's life history and life story.

phenotype An individual's observable characteristics.

phonology A language's sound system.

physical dependence The physiological need for a drug that causes unpleasant withdrawal symptoms such as physical pain and a craving for the drug when it is discontinued.

pituitary gland A pea-sized gland just beneath the hypothalamus that controls growth and regulates other glands.

place theory Theory on how the inner ear registers the frequency of sound, stating that each frequency produces vibrations at a particular spot on the basilar membrane.

placebo In a drug study, a harmless substance that has no physiological effect, given to participants in a control group so that they are treated identically to the experimental group except for the active agent.

placebo effect A phenomenon in which the expectation of the participants, rather than actual treatment, produces an outcome.

plasticity The brain's special physical capacity for change.

polygraph A machine, commonly called a lie detector, that monitors changes in the body, used to try to determine whether someone is lying.

population The entire group about which the investigator wants to draw conclusions.

positive affect Positive emotions such as joy, happiness, and interest.

positive illusions Favorable views of the self that are not necessarily rooted in reality.

positive psychology A branch of psychology that emphasizes human strengths.

positive punishment The presentation of a stimulus following a given behavior in order to decrease the frequency of that behavior.

positive reinforcement The presentation of a stimulus following a given behavior in order to increase the frequency of that behavior.

post-traumatic stress disorder (PTSD) Psychological disorder that develops through exposure to a traumatic event, a severely oppressive situation, cruel abuse, or a natural or an unnatural disaster.

pragmatics The useful character of language and the ability of language to communicate even more meaning than is verbalized.

prediction A statement about the specific expectation for the outcome of a study.

preferential looking A research technique that involves giving an infant a choice of what object to look at.

prejudice An unjustified negative attitude toward an individual based on the individual's membership in a group.

preoperational stage Piaget's second stage of cognitive development, lasting from about 2 to 7 years of age, during which thought is more symbolic than sensorimotor thought.

preparedness The species-specific biological predisposition to learn in certain ways but not others.

primary reinforcer A reinforcer that is innately satisfying; a primary reinforcer does not require any learning on the organism's part to make it pleasurable.

priming The activation of information that people already have in storage to help them remember new information better and faster.

proactive interference Situation in which material that was learned earlier disrupts the recall of material that was learned later.

problem solving The mental process of finding an appropriate way to attain a goal when the goal is not readily available.

problem-focused coping The coping strategy of squarely facing one's troubles and trying to solve them.

procedural memory Memory for skills.

projective test A personality assessment test that presents individuals with an ambiguous stimulus and asks them to describe it or tell a story about it—to project their own meaning onto the stimulus.

prosocial behavior Behavior that is intended to benefit other people.

prospective memory Remembering information about doing something in the future; includes memory for intentions.

prototype model A model emphasizing that when people evaluate whether a given item reflects a certain concept, they compare the item with the most typical item(s) in that category and look for a "family resemblance" with that item's properties.

psychoactive drugs Drugs that act on the nervous system to alter consciousness, modify perception, and change mood.

psychoanalysis Freud's therapeutic technique for analyzing an individual's unconscious thoughts.

psychodynamic approach An approach to psychology focusing on unconscious thought, the conflict between biological drives (such as the drive for sex) and society's demands, and early childhood family experiences.

psychodynamic perspectives Theoretical views emphasizing that personality is primarily unconscious (beyond awareness).

psychodynamic therapies Treatments that stress the importance of the unconscious mind, extensive interpretation by the therapist, and the role of early childhood experiences in the development of an individual's problems.

psychological dependence The strong desire to repeat the use of a drug for emotional reasons, such as a feeling of well-being and reduction of stress.

psychology The scientific study of behavior and mental processes.

psychoneuroimmunology A new field of scientific inquiry that explores connections among psychological factors (such as attitudes and emotions), the nervous system, and the immune system.

psychopathology The scientific study of psychological disorders and the development of diagnostic categories and treatments for those disorders.

psychosis Psychological state in which a person's perceptions and thoughts are fundamentally removed from reality.

psychosurgery A biological therapy, with irreversible effects, that involves removal or destruction of brain tissue to improve the individual's adjustment.

psychotherapy A nonmedical process that helps individuals with psychological disorders recognize and overcome their problems.

puberty A period of rapid skeletal and sexual maturation that occurs mainly in early adolescence.

punishment A consequence that decreases the likelihood that a behavior will occur.

random assignment The assignment of participants to experimental groups by chance, to reduce the likelihood that a study's results will be due to preexisting differences between groups.

random sample A sample that gives every member of the population an equal chance of being selected.

range A measure of dispersion that is the difference between the highest and lowest scores.

reasoning The mental activity of transforming information to reach conclusions.

referential thinking Ascribing personal meaning to completely random events.

reflective speech A technique in which the therapist mirrors the client's own feelings back to the client.

reinforcement The process by which a stimulus or event (a reinforcer) following a particular behavior increases the probability that the behavior will happen again.

relapse A return to former unhealthy patterns.

relational aggression Behavior that is meant to harm the social standing of another person.

reliability The extent to which a test yields a consistent, reproducible measure of performance.

REM sleep An active stage of sleep during which dreaming occurs.

renewal The recovery of the conditioned response when the organism is placed in a novel context.

representativeness heuristic The tendency to make judgments about group membership based on physical appearance or the match between a person and one's stereotype of a group rather than on available base rate information.

research participant bias In an experiment, the influence of participants' expectations, and of their thoughts on how they should behave, on their behavior.

resilience A person's ability to recover from or adapt to difficult times.

resting potential The stable, negative charge of an inactive neuron.

reticular activating system A network of structures including the brain stem, medulla, and thalamus that are involved in the experience of arousal and engagement with the environment.

reticular formation A system in the midbrain comprising a diffuse collection of neurons involved in stereotyped patterns of behavior such as walking, sleeping, and turning to attend to a sudden noise.

retina The multilayered, light-sensitive surface in the eye that records electromagnetic energy and converts it to neural impulses for processing in the brain.

retrieval The memory process that occurs when information that was retained in memory comes out of storage.

retroactive interference Situation in which material that was learned later disrupts the retrieval of information that was learned earlier.

retrograde amnesia Memory loss for a segment of the past but not for new events.

retrospective memory Remembering information from the past.

risky shift The tendency for a group decision to be riskier than the average decision made by the individual group members.

rods The receptor cells in the retina that are sensitive to light but not very useful for color vision.

role conflict The kind of stress that arises when a person tries to meet the demands of more than one important life role, such as worker and mother.

romantic love or passionate love Love with strong components of sexuality and infatuation, often dominant in the early part of a love relationship.

Rorschach inkblot test A famous projective test that uses an individual's perception of inkblots to determine his or her personality.

sample The subset of the population chosen by the investigator for study.

schedules of reinforcement Specific patterns that determine when a behavior will be reinforced.

schema A preexisting mental concept or framework that helps people to organize and interpret information. Schemas from prior encounters with the environment influence the way individuals encode, make inferences about, and retrieve information.

schizophrenia Severe psychological disorder characterized by highly disordered thought processes; individuals suffering from schizophrenia may be referred to as psychotic because they are so far removed from reality.

science The use of systematic methods to observe the natural world and to draw conclusions.

scientific management The managerial philosophy that emphasizes the worker as a well-oiled machine and the determination of the most efficient methods for performing any work-related task.

script A schema for an event, often containing information about physical features, people, and typical occurrences.

secondary reinforcer A reinforcer that acquires its positive value through an organism's experience; a secondary reinforcer is a learned or conditioned reinforcer.

secondary sex characteristics Traits that differ between the two sexes but are not part of the reproductive system; they include breasts in females and facial hair in males.

secure attachment The ways that infants use their caregiver, usually their mother, as a secure base from which to explore the environment.

selective attention The act of focusing on a specific aspect of experience while ignoring others.

self-actualization The motivation to develop one's full potential as a human being—the highest and most elusive of Maslow's proposed needs.

self-determination theory Deci and Ryan's theory asserting that all humans have three basic, innate organismic needs: competence, relatedness, and autonomy.

self-efficacy The belief that one can accomplish a given goal or task and produce positive change.

self-fulfilling prophecy Social expectations that cause an individual to act in such a way that expectations are realized.

self-objectification The tendency to see oneself primarily as an object in the eyes of others.

self-perception theory Bem's theory on how behaviors influence attitudes, stating that individuals make inferences about their attitudes by perceiving their behavior.

self-regulation The process by which an organism effortfully controls behavior in order to pursue important objectives.

self-report test A method of measuring personality characteristics that directly asks people whether specific items describe their personality traits; also called an objective test or an inventory.

self-serving bias The tendency to take credit for one's successes and to deny responsibility for one's failures.

semantic memory A person's knowledge about the world, including his or her areas of expertise; general knowledge, such as of things learned in school, and everyday knowledge.

semantics The meaning of words and sentences in a particular language.

semicircular canals Three fluid-filled circular tubes in the inner ear containing the sensory receptors that detect head motion caused when an individual tilts or moves the head and/or the body.

sensation The process of receiving stimulus energies from the external environment and transforming those energies into neural energy.

sensorimotor stage Piaget's first stage of cognitive development, lasting from birth to about 2 years of age, during which infants construct an understanding of the world by coordinating sensory experiences with motor (physical) actions.

sensory adaptation A change in the responsiveness of the sensory system based on the average level of surrounding stimulation.

sensory memory Memory system that involves holding information from the world in its original sensory form for only an instant, not much longer than the brief time it is exposed to the visual, auditory, and other senses.

sensory receptors Specialized cells that detect stimulus information and transmit it to sensory (afferent) nerves and the brain.

serial position effect The tendency to recall the items at the beginning and end of a list more readily than those in the middle.

set point The weight maintained when the individual makes no effort to gain or lose weight.

sex The properties of a person that determine his or her classification as male or female.

sex chromosomes In humans, the pair of genes that differs between the sexes and determines a person's sex as male or female.

sexual harassment Unwelcome behavior or conduct of a sexual nature that offends, humiliates, or intimidates another person.

sexual orientation The direction of an individual's erotic interests.

sexual selection According to Darwin's theory of evolution, the differentiation between the male and female members of a species because of the differences between the two in competition and choice.

sexuality The ways people experience and express themselves as sexual beings.

sexually transmitted infection (STI) An infection that is contracted primarily through sexual activity—vaginal intercourse as well as oral and anal sex.

shaping Rewarding successive approximations of a desired behavior.

short-term memory Limited-capacity memory system in which information is usually retained for only as long as 30 seconds unless the individual uses strategies to retain it longer.

signal detection theory An approach to perception that focuses on decision making about stimuli under conditions of uncertainty.

situational judgment test A type of job-screening examination that presents job candidates with realistic, hypothetical scenarios and asks them to identify the most appropriate response.

sleep A natural state of rest for the body and mind that involves the reversible loss of consciousness.

social anxiety disorder (SAD) or social phobia An anxiety disorder in which the individual has an intense fear of being humiliated or embarrassed in social situations.

social cognition The area of social psychology that explores how people select, interpret, remember, and use social information.

social cognitive behavior view of hypnosis The perspective that hypnosis is a normal state in which the hypnotized person behaves the way the individual believes that a hypnotized person should behave.

social cognitive perspectives Theoretical views emphasizing conscious awareness, beliefs, expectations, and goals.

social comparison The process by which individuals evaluate their thoughts, feelings, behaviors, and abilities in relation to others.

social contagion Imitative behavior involving the spread of actions, emotions, and ideas.

social exchange theory The view of social relationships as involving an exchange of goods, the objective of which is to minimize costs and maximize benefits.

social facilitation Improvement in an individual's performance because of the presence of others.

social identity The way individuals define themselves in terms of their group membership.

social identity theory Tajfel's theory that social identity, based on group membership, is a crucial part of self-image and a valuable source of positive feelings about oneself.

social loafing Each person's tendency to exert less effort in a group because of reduced accountability for individual effort.

social psychology The study of how people think about, influence, and relate to other people.

social role theory Eagly's theory of gender development that, while acknowledging the physical differences between the sexes, argues that these differences color social expectations and create social structures that limit opportunities for both sexes.

social support Information and feedback from others indicating that one is loved and cared for, esteemed and valued, and included in a network of communication and mutual obligation.

sociocultural approach An approach to psychology focusing on the ways in which social and cultural environments influence behavior.

somatic nervous system The body system consisting of the sensory nerves, whose function is to convey information from the skin and muscles to the CNS about conditions such as pain and temperature, and the motor nerves, whose function is to tell muscles what to do.

somatic symptom disorder A psychological disorder in which a person experiences one or more bodily (somatic) symptoms and experiences excessive thoughts and feelings about these symptoms that interfere with everyday functioning.

somatosensory cortex A region in the cerebral cortex that processes information about body sensations, located at the front of the parietal lobes.

specific phobia An anxiety disorder in which the individual experiences an irrational, overwhelming, persistent fear of a particular object or situation.

spontaneous recovery The process in classical conditioning by which a conditioned response can recur after a time delay, without further conditioning.

stages of change model Theoretical model describing a five-step process by which individuals give up bad habits and adopt healthier lifestyles.

standard deviation A measure of dispersion that indicates how much the scores in a sample differ from the mean in the sample.

standardization The development of uniform procedures for administering and scoring a test and the creation of norms (performance standards) for the test.

stem cells Unique primitive cells that have the capacity to develop into most types of human cells.

stereotype A generalization about a group's characteristics that does not consider any variations from one individual to another.

stereotype threat An individual's fast-acting, self-fulfilling fear of being judged based on a negative stereotype about his or her group.

stimulants Psychoactive drugs—including caffeine, nicotine, amphetamines, and cocaine—that increase the central nervous system's activity.

storage The retention of information over time and how this information is represented in memory.

stream of consciousness Term used by William James to describe the mind as a continuous flow of changing sensations, images, thoughts, and feelings.

strengths-based management A management style emphasizing that maximizing an employee's existing strengths is much easier than trying to build such attributes from the ground up.

stress The responses of individuals to environmental stressors.

stress management program A regimen that teaches individuals how to appraise stressful events, how to develop skills for coping with stress, and how to put these skills into use in everyday life.

stressors Circumstances and events that threaten individuals and tax their coping abilities and that cause physiological changes to ready the body to handle the assault of stress.

structuralism Wundt's approach to discovering the basic elements, or structures, of mental processes; so called because of its focus on identifying the structures of the human mind.

structured interview A kind of interview in which candidates are asked specific questions that methodically seek to obtain truly useful information for the interviewer.

subgoals Intermediate goals or intermediate problems devised to put the individual in a better position for reaching the final goal or solution.

subjective well-being A person's assessment of his or her own level of positive affect relative to negative affect and an evaluation of his or her life in general.

subliminal perception The detection of information below the level of conscious awareness.

superego The Freudian structure of personality that serves as the harsh internal judge of our behavior; what we often call conscience.

suprachiasmatic nucleus (SCN) A small brain structure that uses input from the retina to synchronize its own rhythm with the daily cycle of light and dark; the body's way of monitoring the change from day to night.

sustained attention or vigilance The ability to maintain attention to a selected stimulus for a prolonged period of time.

sympathetic nervous system The part of the autonomic nervous system that arouses the body to mobilize it for action and thus is involved in the experience of stress.

synapses Tiny spaces between neurons; the gaps between neurons are referred to as synaptic gaps.

syntax A language's rules for combining words to form acceptable phrases and sentences.

systematic desensitization A method of behavior therapy that treats anxiety by teaching the client to associate deep relaxation with increasingly intense anxiety-producing situations.

temperament An individual's behavioral style and characteristic ways of responding.

temporal lobes Structures in the cerebral cortex that are located just above the ears and are involved in hearing, language processing, and memory.

testes Sex-related endocrine glands in the scrotum that produce hormones involved in male sexual development and reproduction.

thalamus The forebrain structure that sits at the top of the brain stem in the brain's central core and serves as an important relay station.

Thematic Apperception Test (TAT) A projective test that is designed to elicit stories that reveal something about an individual's personality.

theory A broad idea or set of closely related ideas that attempts to explain observations and to make predictions about future observations.

theory of mind Individuals' understanding that they and others think, feel, perceive, and have private experiences.

theory of planned behavior Theoretical model that includes the basic ideas of the theory of reasoned action but adds the person's perceptions of control over the outcome.

theory of reasoned action Theoretical model stating that effective change requires individuals to have specific intentions about their behaviors, as well as positive attitudes about a new behavior, and to perceive that their social group looks favorably on the new behavior as well.

Theory X managers Managers who assume that work is innately unpleasant and that people have a strong desire to avoid it; such managers believe that employees need direction, dislike responsibility, and must be kept in line.

Theory Y managers Managers who assume that engaging in effortful behavior is natural to human beings; they recognize that people seek out responsibility and that motivation can come from allowing employees to suggest creative and meaningful solutions.

therapeutic alliance The relationship between the therapist and client; an important element of successful psychotherapy.

thermoreceptors Sensory nerve endings under the skin that respond to changes in temperature at or near the skin and provide input to keep the body's temperature at 98.6 degrees Fahrenheit.

thinking The process of manipulating information mentally by forming concepts, solving problems, making decisions, and reflecting critically or creatively.

third variable problem The circumstance in which a variable that has not been measured accounts for the relationship between two other variables. Third variables are also known as confounds.

thought disorder The unusual, sometimes bizarre thought processes that are characteristic positive symptoms of schizophrenia.

tip-of-the-tongue (TOT) phenomenon A type of effortful retrieval associated with a person's feeling that he or she knows something (say, a word or a name) but cannot quite pull it out of memory.

tolerance The need to take increasing amounts of a drug to get the same effect.

top-down processing The operation in sensation and perception, launched by cognitive processing at the brain's higher levels, that allows the organism to sense what is happening and to apply that framework to information from the world.

training Teaching a new employee the essential requirements to do the job well.

trait theories Theoretical views stressing that personality consists of broad, enduring dispositions (traits) that tend to lead to characteristic responses.

tranquilizers Depressant drugs, such as Valium and Xanax, that reduce anxiety and induce relaxation.

transactional leader An individual in a leadership capacity who emphasizes the exchange relationship between the worker and the leader and who applies the principle that a good job should be rewarded.

transference A client's relating to the psychoanalyst in ways that reproduce or relive important relationships in the individual's life.

transformational leader An individual in a leadership capacity who is dynamic and who brings charisma, passion, and vision to the position.

transgender Experiencing one's psychological gender as different from one's physical sex, as in the cases of biological males who identify as female and biological females who identify as male.

triarchic theory of intelligence Sternberg's theory that intelligence comes in three forms: analytical, creative, and practical.

trichromatic theory Theory stating that color perception is produced by three types of cone receptors in the retina that are particularly sensitive to different, but overlapping, ranges of wavelengths.

two-factor theory of emotion Schachter and Singer's theory that emotion is determined by two factors: physiological arousal and cognitive labeling.

Type A behavior pattern A cluster of characteristics—including being excessively competitive, hard-driven, impatient, and hostile—related to a higher incidence of heart disease.

Type B behavior pattern A cluster of characteristics—including being relaxed and easygoing—related to a lower incidence of heart disease.

Type D behavior pattern A cluster of characteristics—including being generally distressed, having negative emotions, and being socially inhibited—related to adverse cardiovascular outcomes.

unconditional positive regard Rogers's construct referring to the individual's need to be accepted, valued, and treated positively regardless of the person's behavior.

unconditioned response (UR) An unlearned reaction that is automatically elicited by the unconditioned stimulus.

unconditioned stimulus (US) A stimulus that produces a response without prior learning.

unconscious thought According to Freud, a reservoir of unacceptable wishes, feelings, and thoughts that are beyond conscious awareness.

validity The extent to which a test measures what it is intended to measure.

variable Anything that can change.

vestibular sense Sense that provides information about balance and movement.

volley principle Modification of frequency theory stating that a cluster of nerve cells can fire neural impulses in rapid succession, producing a volley of impulses.

vulnerability-stress hypothesis or diathesis-stress model Theory suggesting that preexisting conditions—such as genetic characteristics, personality dispositions, or experiences—may put a person at risk of developing a psychological disorder.

Weber's law The principle that two stimuli must differ by a constant minimum percentage (rather than a constant amount) to be perceived as different.

well-being therapy (WBT) A short-term, problem-focused, directive therapy that encourages clients to accentuate the positive.

wisdom Expert knowledge about the practical aspects of life.

working memory A combination of components, including short-term memory and attention, that allow individuals to hold information temporarily as they perform cognitive tasks; a kind of mental workbench on which the brain manipulates and assembles information to guide understanding, decision making, and problem solving.

Yerkes–Dodson law The psychological principle stating that performance is best under conditions of moderate arousal rather than either low or high arousal.

Credits